International Management

Managing in a Diverse and Dynamic Global Environment

International Management

Managing in a Diverse and Dynamic
Global Environment

Arvind V. Phatak
Temple University

Rabi S. Bhagat
University of Memphis

Roger J. Kashlak
Loyola College in Maryland

Boston   Burr Ridge, IL   Dubuque, IA   Madison, WI   New York   San Francisco   St. Louis
Bangkok   Bogotá   Caracas   Kuala Lumpur   Lisbon   London   Madrid   Mexico City
Milan   Montreal   New Delhi   Santiago   Seoul   Singapore   Sydney   Taipei   Toronto

INTERNATIONAL MANAGEMENT:
MANAGING IN A DIVERSE AND DYNAMIC GLOBAL ENVIRONMENT

Published by McGraw-Hill/Irwin, a business unit of The McGraw-Hill Companies, Inc., 1221 Avenue of the
Americas, New York, NY, 10020. Copyright © 2005 by The McGraw-Hill Companies, Inc. All rights reserved.
No part of this publication may be reproduced or distributed in any form or by any means, or stored in a
database or retrieval system, without the prior written consent of The McGraw-Hill Companies, Inc., including,
but not limited to, in any network or other electronic storage or transmission, or broadcast for distance learning.

Some ancillaries, including electronic and print components, may not be available to customers outside the
United States.

This book is printed on acid-free paper.

1 2 3 4 5 6 7 8 9 0 VNH/VNH 0 9 8 7 6 5 4

ISBN 0-07-111239-1

www.mhhe.com

Arvind V. Phatak:
- To all my students from the past and in the future
- To Temple University for giving me the opportunity to be in a profession that is spiritually uplifting and emotionally rewarding
- To Dr. Meena Phatak, my sister and best friend
- To Rhoda, Vikram, Raj, Viveca, and Anniina

Rabi S. Bhagat:
To my family, Ebha, Monika, and Priyanka, and three significant individuals who urged me to undertake a project of this magnitude and encouraged me throughout the process:
- Hashmukh Shah, thoracic surgeon at Baylor University and Medical Center, Dallas, Texas
- S. P. Krishnamurthy, global entrepreneur, Dallas, Texas
- Jyoti P. Bhatia, information technology consultant, Dallas, Texas

Roger J. Kashlak:
- To my parents, Walter and Rose
- To my sons, Adam and Jake

Brief Contents

Contents

Preface

The world of international management has changed dramatically since the early 1990s. Rapid developments in information technology, geopolitical transformations, and the rise of the creative class in all parts of the globe have had tremendous impact on the management of multinational and global corporations. They are able to market their products and services on a global scale unimaginable just a few years ago. Countries which differ in their business practices and paradigms are becoming interconnected through the rapid transfer of technology, knowledge, products, processes, and ideas regarding desirable lifestyles. Every day, $1.8 trillion is traded in response to fluctuations in currency exchange rates, changes in interest rates, and the ups and downs of securities markets worldwide. Interest rates, stock markets, and currency values in the major markets in the United States, Europe, and Japan are dynamically interdependent.

The drive toward free trade is in full swing. Falling trade barriers have opened up new markets, which once were closed, for products and services in countries of eastern Europe, southern Asia, the Pacific Basin, and in many other parts of the world. International trade has been growing at a skyrocketing pace. World exports of merchandise and services have mushroomed to several trillion dollars.

Innovations in information technology and the Internet have enabled people in different countries to collaborate on projects without leaving home. Global teams comprising members from two or more countries can develop new products and processes via videoconferencing without leaving home. Now one can communicate with friends and business associates at the other end of the world through instant messaging simply by clicking the "send" button. Distance is measured not in miles or kilometers, but in the time it takes to communicate from one end of the world to another.

People do not have to go where the jobs are. Jobs come to where the people are. Indian engineers and scientists who serve the needs of companies in Europe and America staff the software industry in India. Countries like China, India, Mexico, and South Korea, with low manufacturing costs and cheap labor, are becoming leaders in the manufacturing and information services sectors. Companies continue to shift jobs globally as long as the worldwide supply of skilled and unskilled workers is greater than the demand.

The excitement and opportunities of the new millennium are accompanied by many new opportunities, challenges, risks, and associated costs of doing business internationally. This book is about the unique opportunities and problems that confront international managers as they navigate the company through the extremely complex and ever-changing global economic, political, legal, technological, and cultural environments. Choices made by international managers—plant location, strategies for marketing of products and services, the entry mode to penetrate foreign markets, the hiring of personnel to manage foreign operations, the leadership and motivational techniques adopted in different foreign operations, and so on—must take into account limits imposed by the external environment, as well as the imperative to simultaneously adapt to local conditions while functioning efficiently on a global scale.

International Management is designed to help students gain insights into the complexities of managing across borders and cultures. Our goal is to provide a robust yet lively discussion of the various issues involved in managing operations of international, multinational, transnational, and global firms. This book describes theories of international management in the context of current and emerging realities in the global marketplace. For example, we learn that communication in the global economy, which might appear simple, is complicated by the fact that employees of a global corporation might not establish an adequate level of trust.

This book started from discussions among the authors during the Academy of International Business annual conference in Charleston, South Carolina, in 1999. We had known each other for quite some time and were aware of each other's disciplinary strengths and complementary interests in the field of international and global management. We also were unanimous in our assessment of the current books in the area of international management in terms of what they offered and what they didn't.

We have several decades of collective experience in teaching undergraduate and graduate international and comparative management courses. In addition, we have witnessed the challenges and opportunities that managers from advanced countries encounter in their attempts to globalize areas of the world which are distinctly different from their own countries. We have presented seminars and workshops for academics and practicing managers in numerous countries, collectively, from Europe to East Asia to Latin America, Africa, and Australia/New Zealand. In addition, we have been teaching students from many countries in our respective universities and have become familiar with their distinctive preferences in dealing with events and situations. We have also served on faculties and lectured at universities in Asia, Europe, South America, and New Zealand.

This book starts with a section dealing with macro perspectives in international management. To fully comprehend the various challenges that they face, international managers must understand the various facets of the environment where they will function. We discuss the characteristics of the economic, legal, political, and cultural environments that impact on the operations of international companies and on the choices they make in their international business transactions.

The second part of the book deals with strategic issues of managing corporations in the global context. Chapters 6 through 11 deal with the various anchors that international managers must wrestle with before they can successfully launch their operations abroad. In Chapter 6, we discuss the forces that drive the internationalization of firms and strategic planning process for international expansion. We also discuss in this chapter the global, multidomestic, and transnational orientations of international companies. Chapter 7 focuses on the different modes of entry for expansion of operations abroad such as licensing, franchising, and management service contracts. Equity joint ventures and nonequity collaborative ventures, also known as strategic alliances, have become increasingly popular among international companies. We discuss such collaborative ventures in Chapter 8. Chapter 9 explores the role of strategy on the choice of organization structure by international companies. Various models of organizing international operations are covered in this chapter. In Chapter 10, we describe the main elements in the managerial control process, such as output control, behavior control, and input control, concluding by discussing problems of control characteristic of international companies. The concept of technology and technology transfer, and the relevance of appropriate technology transfer for international management, is discussed in Chapter 11. In this section, we have also been sensitive to issues of global corporations that invest widely in the United States.

In Section 3 we discuss the micro issues of managing employees within the context of global corporations and their subsidiaries and in the various networks of global corporations. Gone are the days when traditional concepts of management discussed in textbooks written in the 1960s and 1970s can be applied in today's interrelated world. A clash of civilizations and cultures is imminent, and global corporations face challenges in adapting to the habits and preferences of global customers. Starting with Chapter 12, dealing with communication across borders and cultures, we discuss the challenges of managing negotiation and decision making, work motivation, and leadership processes. We end this section with a chapter on international human resource management. In an era where knowledge-based resources inherent in various segments of the global workforce are the primary key for sustaining competitiveness in the global economy, it is crucial that we teach our students various strategies and methods associated with managing human resources in global corporations.

We end the book in Section 4, with a chapter on ethical and social responsibilities that global corporations face today. These challenges, which are critical to sustaining the health and vitality of global corporations, confront the pivotal balance between the abstract concepts of fair play and equity on the one hand and practical concepts of growth and return on capital on the other. We believe that such an intricate topic is presented best after the students have grasped the major issues underlying the fundamentals of international management rather than during the initial stages of learning.

Examples from the business press are embedded throughout the text. Also included are practical insights captured from the business press that illustrate the application of theoretical concepts in the functioning of global companies and in today's business environment.

Teachers often look for small cases to end a classroom session. We have inserted one minicase after each chapter. The minicases are aimed at fostering discussion and bring to life concepts covered in the chapter. This book is organized into four discrete sections. A comprehensive case is included after each section. Each case has been widely used in classrooms throughout the world, and has been proven as an effective vehicle to capture the broad concepts covered in the section chapters.

To help instructors teach international management, this text is accompanied by an Instructor's Resource Manual, Test Bank, and PowerPoint presentation slides for each chapter by Ram Subramanian of Grand Valley State University. These supplements, as well as chapter quizzes and other content specifically for students, are also available on the book's Web site, www.mhhe.com/phatakle.

Acknowledgments

In working on a project of this magnitude, we are grateful to have received guidance, encouragement, and assistance from many individuals. We thank John Biernat, our editorial director, for his recognition of a project of this kind during our initial discussions with him at the Phoenix meeting of the Academy of International Business in 2000. Our initial editor, Marianne Rutter, provided useful guidance and led the initial stages of development. When Marianne moved on to other projects, we were blessed to have an editor of the caliber of Ryan Blankenship, a charming young man who understood the intricacies of what a book of this scope would require and how we could make the complex ideas more accessible. Lindsay Harmon, the editorial coordinator, worked diligently and understood some of the pressures that we worked under, given our geographical separation.

The reviewers of the book during the various phases of the review process were very helpful. We thank Preet Aulakh, York University; Bonita Barger, Tennessee Tech University; Constance Bates, Florida International University; Scott Boyar, University of South Alabama; Carl Broadhurst, Campbell University; Farok Contractor, Rutgers University; Karen Eastwood, Florida Gulf Coast University; Balasubramanian Elango, Illinois State University; Paul Fadil, Valdosta State University; Michele Gee, University of Wisconsin–Parkside; Yedzi Godiwalla, University of Wisconsin–Whitewater; Fred Hughes, Faulkner University; Stephen Jenner, California State University–Dominguez Hills; Mathew Joseph, Georgia College and State University; Jianwen Liao, Northeastern Illinois University; Marvin Loper, Oregon State University; Marina Onken, Loyola University New Orleans; Jere Ramsey, California Polytechnic State University; Clint Relyea, Arkansas State University; David Ricks, University of Missouri–St. Louis; Hugh Sherman, Ohio University; Steven Si, Bloomsburg University of Pennsylvania; Richard Steers, University of Oregon; Kevin Whattam, Washington State University; Vicki Whiting, Westminster College; Yong Zhang, Hofstra University.

Arvind: I have been teaching international management and business strategy for more than 35 years. I am fortunate to be in a profession that is both extremely challenging and exciting. By the most conservative estimate I must have met more than 2,500 students in my classes. I have thoroughly enjoyed my role as their teacher. I would also like to express my gratitude to Temple University and the Fox School of Business and Management for giving me this opportunity.

Rabi: First and foremost, I could not have undertaken a project of this magnitude without a significant sacrifice of time and commitments by my family. Many times I could not attend social and school events that my family wanted me to attend, but they understood the pressures. Therefore, I dedicate this book to them. The completion of this book would have been impossible without the persistent efforts and continuous encouragement Karen South Moustafa, PhD, my research assistant at the University of Memphis. One of the reasons for working with Karen on this project is her uncanny insights into the functioning of various cultures. She has traveled widely, and I felt free to be challenged by her insights and her assistance in developing various case-related materials and in other aspects of manuscript preparation. Perhaps most important is her ability to keep me on track. In the academic world where I live, I am requested by various journals, editors, students, and coauthors to work on various projects and reviews that would take more than 24 hours a day. It was Karen who kept reminding me of my desire to complete a book of this kind, helpful to the students and instructors, that made its completion possible. I also appreciate the encouragement I received on numerous occasions from S. Prakash Sethi, University Distinguished Professor at Zicklin School of Business, Baruch College, City University of New York and president of International Center for Corporate Accountability, Inc., and D. P. S Bhawuk of the University of Hawaii at Manoa. I wish to express my appreciation for numerous MBA and BBA students who shared their experiences, struggles, and joy in learning the various issues in international management for the past 25 years.

Roger: I express my sincere thanks to my PhD and MBA professors, my coauthor Arvind V. Phatak, and Rajan Chandran, Vice Dean at Temple University's Fox School, for stimulating a combined research and teaching enthusiasm in me. Also, the Sellinger School of Business and Management at Loyola College in Maryland and, in particular, Ray Jones, the chair of the Management and International Business Department, have supported my many global initiatives that have helped to give me both the theoretical and practical backgrounds needed to coauthor this text. I also thank Michael Kitsis, Richard McMonigle, as well as my sisters, Jane and Rosemary, and their families, for their continued support and encouragement in many aspects of my life, including this text.

About the Authors

Arvind V. Phatak

Arvind V. Phatak is Laura H. Carnell Professor of Management and International Business at Temple University's School of Business and Management. Currently he is the executive director, Institute of Global Management Studies, and the Temple University CIBER at the Fox School of Business. Dr. Phatak was the founding director of the international business program at Temple University. He has served as chairman of the General and Strategic Management Department from 1978 to 1981 and from 1987 to 1990.

Dr. Phatak has taught international management, strategic management, and general management courses at Temple University and at several colleges and universities abroad. He is the recipient of several awards, including the Great Teacher Award of Temple University (Pioneer Recipient), the Distinguished Faculty Award, the MBA Professor of the Year Award (Pioneer Recipient), and the Musser Award for Excellence in Service.

He is the author of four books and coauthor of two others in the field of strategic and international management. Currently he is the consulting editor of the *Journal of International Management.* He has also published several articles in reputable management journals. Dr. Phatak was the recipient of the Fulbright Senior Research Fellowship in 1986 for research on joint ventures in India.

Dr. Phatak has lectured on various international management topics for the U.S. State Department throughout Asia, as well as at numerous professional groups. He has presented several seminars on international and corporate business strategy in corporate settings in the United States and abroad. His corporate clients include the U.S. State Department, Arthur Andersen, John Hancock Company, Dominion Textile (Canada), Federal Reserve Bank of Philadelphia, Hiro Honda (India), CIGNA, and New York Life. Dr. Phatak has an MSW from M.S. University, Baroda India; MBA from Temple University; and PhD in management from U.C.L.A.

Rabi S. Bhagat

Rabi S. Bhagat is professor of organizational behavior and international management at the Fogelman College of Business and Economics of the University of Memphis. He was awarded the Suzanne Downs Professorship for Research (2003–2004) by the University of Memphis.

Dr. Bhagat was professor at the University of Texas at Dallas (1976–1990). He was visiting professor at the University of Illinois at Urbana–Champaign, the University of Hawaii at Manoa, and Louisiana State University. He received his PhD and MA from the University of Illinois at Urbana–Champaign and his BS from the Indian Institute of Technology in Kharagpur, India.

His teaching and research interests are in organizational behavior and international management. His research focus is in the area of megatrends in world cultures and their implications for organizational behavior and international management. He is directing a major international study on the significance of time orientation and organizational stress. He is also a collaborator in the GLOBE Project on Leadership

Effectiveness, directed by Professor Robert J. House of the Wharton School at the University of Pennsylvania.

Dr. Bhagat has published more than 50 articles and chapters in leading academic journals and research volumes. He is currently serving or has been on the editorial boards of nine journals, including *Journal of International Business Studies, Journal of International Management, Journal of Cross-Cultural Management, Applied Psychology: An International Review, Academy of Management Review, Journal of Cross-Cultural Psychology, Journal of Management, Global Focus,* and *Journal of Occupational Health Psychology.* In addition, he serves as a reviewer or as an editorial consultant for many leading journals.

Previous books include the *Handbook of Intercultural Training* (with D. Landis, Sage Publications, 1996), *Human Stress and Cognition in Work Organizations: An Integrated Perspective* (with T. A. Beehr, Wiley-Interscience, 1985), and *Work Stress: Health Care Systems in the Work Place* (with J. C. Quick, J. D. Quick, and J. Dalton, Praeger, 1987). His interest in the development of the global mindset is reflected in two books, *On Becoming a Global Manager* (with B. L. Kedia and K. S. Moustafa, Sage Publications, 2004) and *Work Stress and Coping in an Era of Globalization* (LEA Publications, forthcoming 2005).

Dr. Bhagat is a member of seven international, regional, and professional associations and has presented over 60 papers in their annual meetings in the United States and other countries. He is a fellow of the American Psychological Association, the American Psychological Society, the Society for Industrial and Organizational Psychologists, and the International Academy for Intercultural Research. He was awarded the James McKeen Cattell Award from the Society for Industrial and Organizational Psychologists, a division of the American Psychological Association. He was also awarded the University of Memphis Alumni Distinguished Research Award in Social Sciences and Business for 2004, and he was awarded the Suzanne Downs Palmer Professorship for Research for 2003–2004.

He has been a consultant for Bell Laboratories (AT&T Corporation), General Electric, Hilton Corporation, the U.S. Army, Franklin University (Ohio), and other organizations. National Public Radio, the *Commercial Appeal* (Memphis, TN), the *Dallas Morning News,* the *Richardson Morning News,* and NBC and ABC news affiliates, as well as *Psychology Today* and *APA Monitor* (American Psychological Association), have reported results of his research.

Roger J. Kashlak

Roger J. Kashlak is professor of international business and management at the Sellinger School of Business and Management at Loyola College in Maryland. He has been with Loyola College since 1993. He received a BS in economics from the Wharton School of the University of Pennsylvania, an MBA in international business from Temple University, and a PhD in international business and strategy from Temple University.

Dr. Kashlak was a member of the International Business Department at the University of Auckland (2000–2001) and continues to serve as visiting professor of international business there. He is a research fellow at the Voinovich Center for Leadership and Public Affairs at Ohio University. He has been an invited lecturer and developed courses and seminars at institutions including Thunderbird (The American Graduate School of International Management), Temple University–Japan, Manipal University (India), Katholiek University Leuven (Belgium), Institut Technologi Mara (Malaysia), and Universidad Jesuita Alberto Hurtado (Chile).

Dr. Kashlak's research has focused on topics such as international reciprocity, international negotiations, global expansion in telecom, health care, and other industries, global control and corporate governance issues, executive education pedagogies, and comparative analyses of leadership and work attitudes. His research has been published in journals such as *Journal of International Business Studies, Strategic Management Journal, Management International Review, Journal of Business Research, Group & Organization Management, Long Range Planning,* and *Journal of International Management* and presented at more than 50 national and international conferences since 1993. He serves on various editorial boards and as a reviewer for journals in the international business and management disciplines.

Dr. Kashlak's teaching focuses on international management and global strategy at undergraduate, MBA, and executive MBA levels. He has developed and conducted executive MBA courses throughout the world, including China, Vietnam, Malaysia, Thailand, South Africa, Chile, Argentina, the Netherlands, and the Czech Republic. He is the recipient of Loyola's 27th Annual Distinguished Teacher Award (1997) and other teaching honors from Beta Gamma Sigma, Loyola's Sellinger School, and Alpha Sigma Nu (the Jesuit Honor Society).

Prior to entering academia, Dr. Kashlak worked for AT&T-Communications International for six years, where he developed the initial international rate negotiation strategy and was responsible for financial negotiations with host governments and telecom entities throughout the world. Subsequent to that position, he established AT&T-Communication's Italian subsidiary. Dr. Kashlak has continued to be involved in the corporate world through executive education with firms such as AEGON (N.V.), AT&T-Hong Kong, Northrop Grumman, and Lucent Technologies.

Diverse Learning Resources

International Management: Managing in a Diverse and Dynamic Global Environment is designed to help students gain insights into the complexities of managing across borders and cultures. The authors present international management theories in the context of current and emerging realities in the global marketplace through practical examples that bring to life the opportunities, challenges, risks, and costs of doing business internationally.

Please take a moment to look through the highlighted features and better acquaint yourself with the book and its pedagogy.

An Introduction to International Management

Chapter Learning Objectives

After completing this chapter, you should be able to:

- Define the concepts of international business and international management.
- Examine the transnationality of countries and companies.
- Distinguish among the various types of international mindsets observed in international firms.
- Discuss the stages of development of an international company.
- Define and understand the strategic, marketing, and economic motives of firms seeking to expand internationally.
- Explain the strategic objectives and sources of competitive advantage for an international firm.

Chapter Learning Objectives

Each chapter begins with objectives that outline the skills that students will be able to demonstrate after reading the chapter.

Chapter Learning Objectives

After completing this chapter, you should be able to:

- Understand the concepts of culture and cultural variations in international management.
- Explain the influence of environmental factors on societal culture.
- Discuss the significance of various frameworks for understanding cultural differences around the world.
- Identify distinctive management styles that exist in different countries.

Opening Case: We Like McDonald's, but No Beef Please!!! Crisis Management in India

Within hours of the story breaking that McDonald's in the U.S. had been using oil with a beef extract for cooking its fries, the burger giant's Indian operation knew it had a crisis on its hands. The region's Hindu and vegetarian consumers were furious that they might have been eating products cooked with beef, breaking a deeply held taboo.

On May 4—a day after the story broke in the U.S.—the Indian national media had splashed the story, but also pointed out that McDonald's India fries and vegetarian products use no beef or pork flavoring. That reassurance failed to cut any ice with local activists and within a matter of hours the golden arches of the Big M were under siege. Ironically it was cosmopolitan Mumbai [Bombay] that reacted more than the sensitive northern region of India, which preferred to wait for an official explanation first. Mumbai's Thane outlet was vandalized by an angry mob of political fundamentalists, who have never been keen on the western company's presence in the market.

The McDonald's outlet near Mumbai's CST railway station was also picketed and cow dung was dropped all around the building. The western city of Pune, some three hours drive from Mumbai, was however peaceful since the fast food giant had coincidentally just a week earlier conducted media tours of its outlets, kitchens and facilities and they were happier to accept McDonald's assurances of its no-meat extract policy. But McDonald's India's crisis management machinery had already realized a strong reaction to the news was likely and had held a meeting to discuss what steps to take.

More than 80 percent of the country's one billion strong population is Hindu, and even in a cosmopolitan city like Mumbai, half of those eating at a McDonald's are vegetarian. That's no small fry since 3.5 million customers visit its India outlets each month. Revenue growth for India operations has been 80 percent every year since its first outlets opened in 1996 in Mumbai and Delhi. Fire fighting the crisis was a coordinated effort between the north and west, since McDonald's has two joint ventures in India. In Mumbai and the western region, Amit Jatia's company Hardcastle Restaurants

135

Opening Cases

Each chapter begins with a short case study, complete with discussion questions, that uses a real-life company example to introduce chapter topics.

PRACTICAL INSIGHT 4.1

"AM I NOW IN THE SHOE BUSINESS?" COUNTERFEITING IN CHINA

Counterfeiting is such a problem in China that it may drive away some foreign investors that manufacture designer-label goods, companies warn. They say that despite efforts by the authorities, they were still losing millions of dollars in revenues because of availability of counterfeit products.

Mont Blanc president Norbert Platt said: "Counterfeiting is a huge problem in China. China should understand that it's something that threatens our investment. We recently closed a shoe shop in China which sold Mont Blanc-branded shoes. And we're not even producing shoes!"

The LVMH Fashion group, the world-renowned manufacturer and retailer of fashion brands Louis Vuitton, Loewe, Celine and others, has been operating in China for 10 years. Like its business rivals, the group is hurting from the counterfeiters' operations. Despite repeated crackdowns by Chinese authorities, fake Louis Vuitton handbags can be purchased in Shenzhen shops for less than HK$100, a fraction of the HK$4,000 price for the real thing.

"The counterfeiting problem is huge, particularly in China," said Hugues Witvoet, Asia-Pacific president of LVMH Fashion. "For as long as you have strong brands, counterfeiting will always be a problem. Unscrupulous people try to copy your products and they sell them at much cheaper prices than the genuines. But they cheat their customers because the quality of their goods is not as good as the original. It's a world-wide problem which adversely affects many industries," he said.

The LVMH Fashion group's concerns are shared by Alfred Dunhill, Tim King, managing director for the firm in the Asia-

Joseph Simone, vice-chairman of Quality Brand Protection Committee (QBPC), representing 78 multinational companies including Alfred Dunhill, said seizures by US and European customs authorities had indicated that China was a big source of counterfeit goods. The number and value of seizures by US and EU customs had been increasing dramatically in the last few years, he said. QBPC believes that its member companies lose up to 15 percent of their market in China and nearby countries, which represents a potential loss of billions of US dollars a year, because of China's counterfeiters.

Guangdong is the main area for counterfeiting goods, followed by Zhejiang, Jiangsu and Fujian, Mr. Simone said. Xiao Yang, president of the Supreme People's Court, recently said the mainland judiciary had made special efforts to mark crimes that included counterfeiting.

A crackdown on counterfeit goods would focus on the involvement of gangsters who controlled the distribution of counterfeit goods, he said. Hong Kong's custom authorities have also denied assertions that Hong Kong is a large trans-shipment point of China-made counterfeits.

They admit, however, that seizures of fake goods from China, including clothes, leather goods, shoes, mobile phones and TV game accessories, reached a four-year high of HK$213.8 million last year. Seizures in the five months to May 31 amounted to HK$53.3 million.

David Fong, division commander at the intellectual property intelligence and border investigation division of Kong Customs and Excise Department, said: "It's un scribe Hong Kong as a major trans-shipment po goods made in China because the counterfeiters

Practical Insights

Practical Insight boxes in every chapter use articles from the business press to illustrate the application of theoretical concepts by global companies in today's business environment.

Summary

A major environmental context within which international companies conduct their global business is the WTO and its push toward global free trade, taking into account the progress toward integration of member countries of regional trade blocs such as NAFTA, FTAA, and the European Union. Not all trade blocs are alike; some are more developed in integrating the economies of the member countries than others. The European Union and its 15 member countries represent the most developed of the trade blocs.

Economic trade blocs can cause trade creation when new trade among member countries does not displace third-country imports. Trade creation is a positive effect of free trade. However, lowering intraregional barriers leaves relatively high barriers on nonmembers. If this leads to a substitution of efficient third-country production by inefficient production in a common market country, it may result in trade diversion. Trade blocs should create economic conditions that would not require policies leading to trade diversion.

Free trade arrangements can also have significant dynamic effects on economic growth. Market extension is one benefit of a common market. Producers have free access to the national markets of all member countries, unhindered by import restrictions. Similarly, consumers have access to products produced in all countries of the union.

GATT and its successor, the WTO, have been the driving forces to promote free trade. International companies stand to gain from the push in favor of free trade because free trade opens new markets around the world. Through its dispute settlement mechanism, the WTO provides global companies and member nations with a mechanism for resolving trade disputes.

End-of-Chapter Review

End-of-chapter summaries and discussion questions give students a chance to test their mastery of chapter objectives. Each chapter also lists key terms and concepts for review.

Minicase

Beijing Outlaws Pyramid Selling as an Evil

The Falun Gong is not the only "evil cult" raising the ire of the Chinese Govern weeks senior government officials have been using similarly loaded descriptions t nomenon that has been growing increasingly popular in China. That culminated wit last week by Vice-Premier Li Lanqing that Beijing was launching a new crackdow or the economic evil cult more commonly known as pyramid selling. Li told the c that the fresh assault on pyramid selling was at the centre of the Government's ca markets awash with fraud, counterfeit activities and tax evasion.

"The selling tactic is billed as an economic cult," Li said. "To clamp down on dinal missions in bringing the markets to order." The crackdown is not the fir adopted strong-arm tactics to control pyramid selling. In April 1998 following pyramid schemes in the mid-1990s the ruling State Council effectively banned person-to-person marketing in China for five years. The State Council described p a threat to China's social stability, similar language to that Beijing employed when Gong spiritual movement in July 1999. The Falun Gong and those pyramid schem common recruiting ground: the tens of millions of Chinese workers cast aside as efforts to reform its antiquated economy.

The Government has claimed some success from the 1998 ban, with more th mid schemes involving tens of thousands of people reportedly smashed by polic years. Several foreign companies involved in legitimate direct selling in Chin Amway and Mary Kay, were also caught up in the crackdown. Avon saw its Chi before it was able to restructure its operations from door-to-door selling to store ing. Earlier this year Beijing appeared to be relaxing its strict ban on door-to-door firms which complied with strict government tests. Some analysts suggest Chin ket, despite change as a by what Chi covered by p

More tha clever use of Security's B coming hard of the newer members to

Minicases

Short cases at the end of each chapter bring chapter concepts to life by showing how international companies have approached different management situations. Each case is followed by questions to facilitate class discussion.

Case I

Euro Disneyland

J. Stewart Black and Hal B. Gregersen

On January 18, 1993, Euro Disneyland chairperson Robert Fitzpatrick announced he would leave post on April 12 to begin his own consulting company. Quitting his position exactly one year after grand opening of Euro Disneyland, Fitzpatrick's resignation removed US management from the h of the French theme park and resort.

Fitzpatrick's position was taken by a Frenchman, Philippe Bourguignon, who had been Disneyland's senior vice president for real estate. Bourguignon, 45 years old, faced a net loss of 188 million for Euro Disneyland's fiscal year which ended September 1992. Also, between April September 1992, only 29 percent of the park's total visitors were French. Expectations were closer to half of all visitors would be French.

It was hoped that the promotion of Philippe Bourguignon would have a public relations benefi Euro Disneyland—a project that has been a publicist's nightmare from the beginning. One of the points was at a news conference prior to the park's opening when protesters pelted Michael Eis CEO of the Walt Disney Company, with rotten eggs. Within the first year of operation, Disney ha compromise its "squeaky clean" image and lift the alcohol ban at the park. Wine is now served a major restaurants.

Euro Disneyland, 49 percent owned by Walt Disney Company, Burbank, California, origin forecasted 11 million visitors in the first year of operation. In January 1993 it appeared attenda would be closer to 10 million. In response, management temporarily slashed prices at the park fo cal residents to FFr 150 ($27.27) from FFr 225 ($40.91) for adults, and to FFr 100 from FFr 150 children in order to lure more French during the slow, wet winter months. The company also red

Comprehensive Cases

Each part of the text is accompanied by a full-length case that integrates the major concepts from the preceding chapters. Every case has been widely used in classrooms throughout the world.

Supplements

Instructor's Resource CD-ROM

The Instructor's Resource CD-ROM provides professors with all of their resource material in one convenient place. It includes an Instructor's Manual, test bank (printable and computerized Diploma), PowerPoint slides, and a link to the book's Web site.

Videos

Chapter-specific videos bring international management topics to life through current footage of real companies dealing with the opportunities, challenges, risks, and costs involved with international business.

Online Learning Center

The Online Learning Center (OLC) is a Web site that follows the text chapter by chapter with digital supplementary content to accompany the book. OLCs can be delivered through the textbook Web site, through PageOut, or within a course management system (i.e., WebCT or Blackboard). The instructor's side of the OLC will contain useful resource material, including an instructor's manual, PowerPoint slides, and links to professional resources. The student's side will feature important material from each chapter of the text, including learning objectives, chapter summaries, and discussion questions.

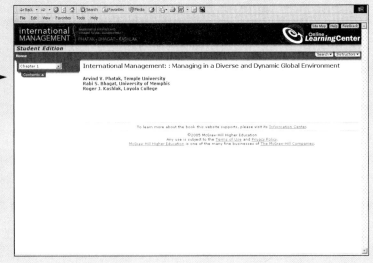

PageOut

PageOut is McGraw-Hill's unique point-and-click course Web site tool, enabling you to create a full-featured, professional quality course Web site without knowing HTML coding. With PageOut, you can post your syllabus online, assign McGraw-Hill Online Learning Center or eBook content, add links to important off-site resources, and maintain student results in the online grade book. You can send class announcements, copy your course site to share with colleagues, and upload original files. PageOut is free for every McGraw-Hill/Irwin user and, if you're short on time, we even have a team ready to help you create your site!

The International Environment

CHAPTER ONE

An Introduction to International Management

Chapter Learning Objectives

After completing this chapter, you should be able to:

- Define the concepts of international business and international management.
- Examine the transnationality of countries and companies.
- Distinguish among the various types of international mindsets observed in international firms.
- Discuss the stages of development of an international company.
- Define and understand the strategic, marketing, and economic motives of firms seeking to expand internationally.
- Explain the strategic objectives and sources of competitive advantage for an international firm.

Opening Case: Haier of China Moves Overseas . . . to South Carolina

While many American manufacturers in 2003 look to China as a place to make their products with cheap labor, an odd turnabout is taking place in this small town northeast of Columbia, South Carolina. There, one of China's best-known companies, the Haier Group, is churning out refrigerators at a factory staffed by American workers. The decision to build in South Carolina was a step toward the company's goal of making Haier a household name in America, like Whirlpool or Maytag. Haier argues that the plant saves transportation costs as well.

To the company, which had $8.5 billion in revenue during 2002, the plant is at the core of its vision to expand in the United States. The factory, completed in 2000 at a cost of $40 million, is designed to respond nimbly to American retailers, who stock little inventory but want to replenish supplies quickly when products run out, said David Parks, a senior vice president of Haier's American unit. Shipping refrigerators from Asia can take up to six weeks. "The factory makes perfect sense," Mr. Parks said. "When you ship refrigerators, you ship a lot of air, and shipping air is expensive." But the factory is about far more than saving money on refrigerators. It is an expression of nationalist pride and of the Chinese government's determination to expand overseas in markets that it considers prestigious. The government's objective is to catapult at least 50 Chinese companies onto the Fortune Global 500 list, according to its official media, up from the current 11.

Through 2003, the Haier factory has brought Zhang Ruimin, the company's chief executive, glowing coverage in the Chinese news media. Mr. Zhang has sometimes called himself the Jack Welch of China. Last year, he was admitted into the Communist Party's elite ruling club, the Central Committee. The story of his success at turning an anemic state-owned factory into an appliance giant with overseas sales has been made into a movie. Many Chinese have become more enamored with corporate executives than revolutionaries, so Mr. Zhang is something of a national hero. In that context, the opening of Haier's American factory is as much a cultural victory as a business one. To gain market share from Whirlpool and Maytag on their own turf, however, may be tough. "In this industry, people buy on the price and the name recognition," said Diane Ritchey, the editor of *Appliance,* a trade magazine. "Everybody knows Maytag or Whirlpool or Frigidaire. People are going to buy what their mothers or grandmothers used.

"Some people cannot even pronounce their name," Ms. Ritchey said of Haier. "How comfortable are you going to be to have something in your home when you cannot pronounce its brand?" The name is pronounced "higher." Haier, partially owned by the government of the northern city of Qingdao, where it is based, has made some headway in small American market niches. It had a third of the market for compact refrigerators last year, three years after it began selling them here, and it captured half the market for refrigerated wine cabinets in about a year, according to a report by McKinsey, the management consulting firm. Those products, often selling for a third less than competitive products, can be found in Target, Wal-Mart, Costco, and Best Buy stores. By 2005, Haier wants 10 percent of the United States market for standard-sized refrigerators. In 2002, it sales volume was 100,000, or 2 percent of the U.S. total. Consumers have found Haier refrigerators to be generally reliable, and cheaper than similar refrigerators selling under American brand names.

In Camden, a quiet town of 6,000, the boxlike, squeaky-clean factory among the hayfields provides 200 much-needed jobs, as several American manufacturers have shrunk or closed plants in the area. Cultural clashes are few because almost every employee at the factory is American. Inside the plant, the presence of the Chinese company is felt in dozens of slogans, written in both Chinese and English, on banners hanging from the ceilings. ("Never Say No to the Market," one says.) Managers decorate their offices with at least one award certificate issued and signed by Mr. Zhang. Haier pays its American machine operators a little more than $10 an hour, 10 times the rate in China, along with health care benefits. Donna Fortner, whose family has lived in Camden for generations, came to work for the plant three years ago. At the beginning, Ms. Fortner worked with some Chinese technicians, who all returned home a few months ago. Although she couldn't understand the accented English some of them spoke, they managed to teach her how to operate the machinery by simply showing her. When the factory was opening, Gerald Reeves, the human resources director, led a team of 10 workers to visit the headquarters in Qingdao, which is known for its sea breezes. Besides finding fermented Chinese eggs inedible, he was impressed by how disciplined Chinese workers are. "When they had their end-of-day group meetings, they stood in nice straight lines," Mr. Reeves said. "I'll never get my people to stand in lines like that." For Allan Guberski, general manager of the plant, the discovery on the trip was the "strategic business unit" approach to management, widely used at the Haier plants in Qingdao. This approach turns each worker into an independent unit, rewarded for inventing ways to save the company money and punished for wasting its resources. "I want the workers to know that their jobs each day are to contribute enough to the business to pay their own salaries," Mr. Guberski said. He is still seeking an acceptable way to put the system in place, because labor laws in the two countries are different. "Here, for example, you cannot have somebody work overtime and not pay him," he said.

The only employee from the company headquarters who has remained in Camden is Sihai Wu, 29, the factory's chief financial officer. "Finance is the most critical link," Mr. Wu said, "and the top bosses want to make sure that it is done right." Conversations between the factory and the Qingdao headquarters happen three or four times a week, Mr. Parks said. Haier designs new products mostly in Qingdao, but Camden sometimes sends ideas back to headquarters. The refrigerators the company sells in China tend to be smaller than those it offers in the United States because Chinese homes are not as big. Although Haier has widely trumpeted its overseas achievement back home, the company has refused to say how much profit it has earned in the United States.

Paul Gao, a McKinsey consultant based in Shanghai, said it is common for Chinese companies to forge ahead abroad with the domestic audience in mind. "Good news from America certainly makes the brands look stronger back at home," he said. Scholars of Chinese business say leaders of state-owned companies are often willing to try tactics that don't make economic sense for their companies but yield political benefits for themselves. The careers of top managers at companies like Haier that are entirely or partially state-owned are heavily directed by the government. "Ultimately, the managers are accountable to the political leaders," said Zhiwu Chen, from the Yale School of Management. "They are not accountable to the shareholders." Although the Chinese government does not give outright subsidies to native companies to encourage overseas expansion, it has arranged for state-run banks to offer them low-interest loans.

Other large Chinese companies eager to grab market share in the United States are not following Haier in building American factories. They know the market can be perilous. Konka, which dominates China's television market, shut its sales and promotional branch in San Diego two years ago after failing to crack the American market and hemorrhaging money for three years. At times, the government's enthusiasm makes some of the Chinese companies' American business partners cringe. Roger Zhao, who has set up a joint venture with S.V.A., a large television maker in Shanghai, to sell its products in the United States, said his objective and his partner's are "disconnected." While his aim is to maximize profit, he said, his partner's is tinged with a wish for political glory.

As for why Haier has set up an American plant, he has his own explanations. "To have it in Mexico would make more sense," he said. "But to the Chinese, expanding abroad without expanding to America doesn't feel like the real thing."

Source: From Yilu Zhao, "When Jobs Move Overseas (to South Carolina)," October 26, 2003. Copyright © 2003 The New York Times Co. Reprinted with permission.

Discussion Questions

1. What are the various strategic, market, and economic motives for Haier of China to set up manufacturing operations in the United States?
2. In your opinion, why might U.S. firms seek to invest in China?
3. What are the political and cultural factors that affect both Haier's expansion to the United States and U.S. firms' expansion into China?

The International Management Setting

The world is becoming a smaller place. Look around you. The clothes you wear, the gadgets in the kitchen, the car you drive—all may be made in China, India, or Japan. Perhaps in your refrigerator you have Mexican tacos or Indian chicken curry. Now people can communicate with friends and business associates across the world through instant messaging simply by clicking the "send" button. Distance is measured not in miles or kilometers, but in the time it takes to reach from one end of the world to another. Who is responsible for "shrinking" the world in which we live? This responsibility has been shouldered by the numerous small and large international companies, from different countries, that produce and market their wares worldwide.

Even though the world is becoming "smaller," significant political, legal, economic, and technological differences still distance us from our fellow inhabitants of Earth. In their quest to reach markets and customers in foreign countries, international companies have to navigate across the often turbulent international environment.

Consider an American company with, among other business units, sales offices in Buenos Aires, Toronto, and New York City, wholly owned manufacturing subsidiaries in Jakarta and Taipei, an equity joint venture in Shanghai, a research and development facility in Tel Aviv, and call service centers in Bangalore and Manila. In recent times, the economic collapse of Argentina, the political implosion of Indonesia, and the severe acute respiratory syndrome (SARS) scares in China, Taiwan, and Canada have exerted increased pressures, risks, and costs for that firm. Furthermore, the ongoing conflicts in the Middle East and southern Asia as well as the threat of terrorism aimed at Western targets worldwide has further increased risk and the cost of managing that risk for this company.

The excitement and opportunities of the new millennium have been accompanied by many new risks and associated costs of doing business internationally. This book is about the challenge of managing these risks of such international activities of international companies within the various international environments. Also, this book is about understanding and managing the tremendous amount of new opportunities internationally. Thus it is about the unique opportunities and problems that confront managers in international companies as they navigate through the extremely complex and ever-changing economic, political, legal, technological, and cultural environments of a world of increasingly interdependent nation-states. The choices that international managers make—plant location, products and services marketed in different countries or regions of the world, the mode used to penetrate foreign markets, the hiring of personnel to manage foreign operations, and so on—must take into account the limits imposed on such choices by the external environment, as well as the imperative to simultaneously adapt to local conditions and function efficiently on a global scale.

The need for international management arises with a firm's initial involvement in international operations by way of exports of its products, technology, or services to foreign markets. This need becomes even more critical when a company becomes involved in foreign direct investment. **Foreign direct investment (FDI)** is a long-term equity investment in a foreign affiliate or subsidiary; it gives the parent company (the investor) varying degrees of managerial control over the foreign operation, depending on the percentage of ownership by the parent company.[1] The more FDI that a company makes in a foreign affiliate, the greater the managerial control that it has over that foreign affiliate. FDI involves the establishment of facilities, buildings, plants, and equipment for the production of goods and/or services in a foreign country. And FDI is accompanied by the need to manage, market, and finance the foreign production. People manage enterprise functions like marketing, production, and finance. Managing the various enterprise functions abroad requires that managers in the parent company, as well as in every foreign affiliate, have the necessary skills and experience to manage the affairs of affiliates in countries whose political, cultural, economic, and financial environments may be very different from one another. It therefore follows that the greater a company's FDI, the greater will be its need for skilled international managers.

Figure 1.1 represents the multilevel focus of this text. We discuss international management from a variety of perspectives. In Section 1, we paint a picture of the various macro-level environments where managers must effectively manage. Section 2 elaborates on strategic management issues. That is, what are the firm-level strategic consid-

FIGURE 1.1
**Managing in the
International
Environment**

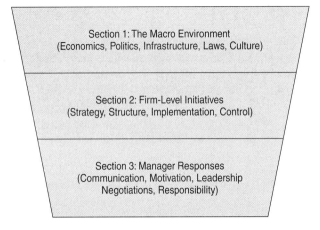

Section 1: The Macro Environment
(Economics, Politics, Infrastructure, Laws, Culture)

Section 2: Firm-Level Initiatives
(Strategy, Structure, Implementation, Control)

Section 3: Manager Responses
(Communication, Motivation, Leadership
Negotiations, Responsibility)

erations necessary to consider when expanding overseas? Finally, in Section 3, we focus on the manager level and the need to effectively communicate, motivate, lead, and negotiate in order to manage internationally.

International management activities in a firm begin either when the firm's managers initiate the establishment of a foreign affiliate from the ground up, which is called a greenfield investment, or when it acquires an existing host-country firm. Furthermore, they continue as long as the parent company owns one or more functioning foreign affiliates.

What Is International Business?

Besides foreign acquisition and greenfield investments, international companies may be simultaneously involved in several other international business activities such as export, import, countertrade, licensing, and strategic alliances. Before delving into the distinctions of these various forms of international involvement, we should first understand what international business is. Several definitions of international business have been advanced through the years. The most basic definition is "all business transactions that involve two or more countries."[2] These business transactions or relationships may be conducted by private, nonprofit, or government organizations, as well as through a combination of the various organizations. In the case of private firms the transactions are for profit. Government-sponsored activities in international business may or may not have a profit orientation, and a nonprofit firm may be competing in an industry that has firms with profit motives.

Other definitions suggest that an international business is "a business whose activities involve the crossing of national boundaries"[3] or is "any commercial, industrial or professional endeavor involving two or more nations."[4] To Charles W. L. Hill, "an international business is any firm that engages in international trade and investment . . . all the firm has to do is export or import products from other countries."[5] Kolde and Hill say that "one cannot ignore the contrasts between domestic and international business, or in a more general phrase between uninational and multinational business. The primary distinction between the two lies in the environmental framework and the organizational and behavioral responses that flow from that framework."[6]

Taking the foregoing definitions of international business into account, we define **international business** as those business activities of private or public enterprises that involve the movement of resources across national boundaries. The resources that may be involved in the cross-national transfers include raw materials, semifinished and finished goods, services, capital, people, and technology. Specific services transferred may include functions such as accounting, consulting, legal counsel, and banking activities. Technology transferred may range from simple managerial and marketing know-how to higher level managerial and technical skills to ultimately high-end technological advancements.

What Is International Management?

The noted international management theorist and scholar Jean J. Boddewyn argues that a definition of international management must include an interpretation and "elaboration of the key terms *international* and *management* as well as of their *interaction*."[7] We also agree with him that the term international means "crossing borders and [applies] to processes intersected by national borders."[8] In very general terms, international management is the management of a firm's activities on an international scale. But before we define international management in specific terms, let us define management.

Management is defined in numerous ways. We would define management as the process aimed at accomplishing organizational objectives by (1) effectively coordinating the procurement, allocation, and utilization of the human, financial, intellectual, and physical resources of the organization and (2) maintaining the organization in a state of satisfactory, dynamic equilibrium within the environment, that is, the firm's strategies and operational plans are responsive to the demands and constraints embedded in the economic, political, legal, cultural, political, and competitive environment.

This definition of management has two basic premises. First, management is needed to coordinate the human, financial, intellectual, and physical resources and to integrate them into a unified whole. Without such coordination the resources would remain unrelated and disorganized and therefore inefficiently used. The second premise in the definition is that an organization lives in a dynamic environment that constantly affects its operations. To further complicate the manager's job, the various environments have different degrees of dynamism. "The multinational setting is more dynamic than the uninational (domestic) setting. This is due partly to the different rates of speed at which the various environmental parameters are changing in the different countries and in part to the nature of the parameters themselves."[9] For instance, some of the environmental factors, such as the distinct national cultures, evolve and converge over time. Others, like the political environments, have the ability to be radically changed through elections and revolutions. Furthermore, the financial environment, especially when one considers foreign exchange rates, is continually in a state of change. Note that "for domestic businesses, the external factors are relatively constant and homogeneous. Any changes that occur are gradual and generally do not lead to any sudden differentiation among the opportunities and constraints among different industries or types of enterprises."[10] However, with expansion abroad of a firm's operation, the environmental setting can no longer be called constant. Thus one managerial task is to effectively forecast the varying environmental forces that are likely to have a significant impact on the firm in the immediate and distant future and to determine the probable impact. Also, managers must respond to the environmental forecasts by designing appropriate strategies to ensure the survival and growth of the organization as it interacts with its dynamic environment.

On the basis of the preceding meaning of the term international and definition of management, we can now define **international management** as a process of accomplishing the global objectives of a firm by (1) effectively coordinating across national boundaries the procurement, allocation, and utilization of the human, financial, intellectual, and physical resources of the firm and (2) effectively charting the path toward the desired organizational goals by navigating the firm through a global environment that is not only dynamic but often very hostile to the firm's very survival. Note that our definition is focused on the *business firm* as the primary level and unit of analysis of international management, and it excludes the management of all international organizations such as the World Trade Organization, the International Labor Organization, or the United Nations. Focusing on the international business firm as an organization allows us to define the international management domain in terms of two central themes:

1. Why, when, and how does a business firm (as an organization) decide to "go international," including the expansion and reduction of such internalization?
2. Why, when, and how is its organizational behavior—a broad term covering mission, objectives, strategies, structures, staff, and processes [particularly decision making], internal and external transactions and relations, performance, impact, etc.—altered by internationalization?[11]

International Companies and International Mindsets

International Companies

All firms, regardless of size, are affected by international competition. Specifically, any firm that has one or more foreign affiliates is involved in international management; it does not have to be a billion-dollar corporation. Even small and medium-sized firms can and do have international operations in several countries. Many international companies do not qualify for the exclusive list of the Fortune 500 or the BusinessWeek Global 1000 list of the largest international corporations. Even though they do not come close to Microsoft, Toyota, Wal-Mart, or Deutsche Bank in terms of total sales, gross profits, total assets, and similar measures of company size, they are still multinational companies. Many firms in Europe and Japan have also developed a multinational structure; and in the last 10 years or so, we have seen many government-owned enterprises that have become privatized, and subsequently multinational. The 1960s laid the foundations for the massive growth of international companies. The growth of that decade far exceeded any achieved earlier by the United States or the other industrialized countries of the world. Since then, the growth in international business activities has been exponential, culminating during the last 10 years with the significant increase in privatization and deregulation in many industries and countries.

Although international enterprises are dissimilar in many respects—size of sales and profits, markets served, and location of affiliates abroad—they all have some common features. To begin, an **international company** is an enterprise that has operations in two or more countries. If it has operations in several countries, then it may have a network of wholly or partially (jointly with one or more foreign partners) owned produc-

TABLE 1.1

Source: The BusinessWeek Global 1000, *BusinessWeek*, July 15, 2002, www.businessweek.com.

Global Rank	Company	2002 Revenues ($ millions)
1	Wal-Mart Stores	$219,812.0
2	ExxonMobil	191,581.0
3	General Motors	177,260.0
4	BP	174,218.0
5	Ford Motor	162,412.0
6	Enron	138,718.0
7	DaimlerChrysler	136,897.0
8	Royal Dutch/Shell Group	135,211.0
9	General Electric	125,913.0
10	Toyota Motor	120,814.0
11	Citigroup	112,022.0
12	Mitsubishi	105,813.0
13	Mitsui	101,205.0
14	ChevronTexaco	99,699.0
15	TotalFinaElf	94,311.0

ing and marketing foreign affiliates or subsidiaries. The foreign affiliates may be linked with the parent company and with each other by ties of common ownership and by a common global strategy to which each affiliate is responsive and committed. The parent company may control the foreign affiliates via resources that it allocates to each affiliate—capital, technology, trademarks, patents, and work force—and through the right to approve each affiliate's long- and short-range plans and budgets.[12]

As pointed out earlier, there are many small- and medium-sized multinational companies. However, generally we are talking about a large corporation whose revenues, profits, and assets typically run into hundreds of millions of dollars. For example, the most profitable international company in 2002 was ExxonMobil with profits of $15.1 billion.[13] In 2002, Wal-Mart Stores ranked number one in the world on the basis of sales, which approached $220 billion. In the same year, 13 companies accrued global revenues in excess of $100 billion. Table 1.1 lists the 15 largest international companies in terms of 2002 sales.

The top 100 international companies hold almost $3 trillion of assets outside of their home countries. The economic power of these companies is evident in the fact that they are estimated to account for more than one-third of the combined outward FDI of their home countries. Because the largest international companies control such a large pool of assets, they exercise considerable influence over the home and host countries' output, economic policies, trade and technology flows, employment, and labor practices.

In 2001 some 65,000 international companies, large and small, engaged in international production with about 850,000 foreign affiliates.[14] The foreign affiliates employed almost 54,000 people globally. The value of inward foreign direct investments worldwide in 2001 reached nearly $735 billion, of which $503 billion, or 68.4 percent, went to the developed countries in western Europe, Japan, and the United States and the balance to the developing countries in Asia, Africa, Latin America, and eastern and central Europe. This goes to show that the rich countries are getting the infusion of capital, technology, and knowledge that usually accompanies foreign direct investment, whereas the poorer countries do not enjoy such benefits from foreign direct investment. The world's gross domestic product (GDP) in 2001 amounted to almost $32 trillion, of which almost $3.5 trillion, or 11 percent, belonged to the foreign affiliates. The total world exports in 2001 amounted to $7.4 trillion, of which $2.6 trillion, or almost

TABLE 1.2 How Large Are the Top Transnational Companies (TNCs) vis-à-vis Economies in 2000? ($ billions)

Source: UNCTAD, FDI/TNC database.

Rank	Name of TNC or Economy	Value Added[a]	Rank	Name of TNC or Economy	Value Added[a]	Rank	Name of TNC or Economy	Value Added[a]
1	United States	9,810	34	Greece	113	67	Libyan Arab Jamahiriya	31
2	Japan	4,765	35	Israel	110	68	BP	30
3	Germany	1,866	36	Portugal	106	69	Wal-Mart Stores	30[c]
4	United Kingdom	1,427	37	Iran, Islamic Republic of	105	70	IBM	27[b]
5	France	1,294	38	Egypt	99	71	Volkswagen	24
6	China	1,080	39	Ireland	95	72	Cuba	24
7	Italy	1,074	40	Singapore	92	73	Hitachi	24[b]
8	Canada	701	41	Malaysia	90	74	TotalFinaElf	23
9	Brazil	595	42	Colombia	81	75	Verizon Communications	23[d]
10	Mexico	575	43	Philippines	75	76	Matsushita Electric Industrial	22[b]
11	Spain	561	44	Chile	71	77	Mitsui & Company	20[c]
12	Republic of Korea	457	45	ExxonMobil	63[b]	78	E.On	20
13	India	457	46	Pakistan	62	79	Oman	20
14	Australia	388	47	General Motors	56[b]	80	Sony	20[b]
15	Netherlands	370	48	Peru	53	81	Mitsubishi	20[c]
16	Taiwan Province of China	309	49	Algeria	53	82	Uruguay	20
17	Argentina	285	50	New Zealand	51	83	Dominican Republic	20
18	Russian Federation	251	51	Czech Republic	51	84	Tunisia	19
19	Switzerland	239	52	United Arab Emirates	48	85	Philip Morris	19[b]
20	Sweden	229	53	Bangladesh	47	86	Slovakia	19
21	Belgium	229	54	Hungary	46	87	Croatia	19
22	Turkey	200	55	Ford Motor	44	88	Guatemala	19
23	Austria	189	56	DaimlerChrysler	42	89	Luxemburg	19
24	Saudi Arabia	173	57	Nigeria	41	90	SBC Communications	19[d]
25	Denmark	163	58	General Electric	39[b]	91	Itochu	18[c]
26	Hong Kong, China	163	59	Toyota Motor	38[b]	92	Kazakhstan	18
27	Norway	162	60	Kuwait	38	93	Slovenia	18
28	Poland	158	61	Romania	37	94	Honda Motor	18[b]
29	Indonesia	153	62	Royal Dutch/Shell	36	95	Eni	18
30	South Africa	126	63	Morocco	33	96	Nissan Motor	18[b]
31	Thailand	122	64	Ukraine	32	97	Toshiba	17[b]
32	Finland	121	65	Siemens	32	98	Syrian Arab Republic	17
33	Venezuela	120	66	Vietnam	31	99	GlaxoSmithKline	17
						100	BT	17

[a] GDP for countries and value added for TNCs. Value added is defined as the sum of salaries, pretax profits, and depreciation and amortization.
[b] Value added is estimated by applying the 30 percent share of value added in the total sales, 2000, of 66 manufacturers for which the data were available.
[c] Value added is estimated by applying the 16 percent share of value added in the total sales, 2000, of 7 trading companies for which the data on value added were available.
[d] Value added is estimated by applying the 37 percent share of value added in the total sales, 2000, of 22 other tertiary companies for which the data on value added were available.

35 percent, was generated by exports of foreign affiliates. In that same year, the total sales of foreign affiliates amounted to $18.5 trillion. Therefore, sales of goods and services produced by foreign affiliates are 2.5 times greater than exports and, not counting affiliates' exports, twice as large as exports. This means that local production by foreign affiliates to serve local markets has replaced exports to those markets.[15]

International companies have been growing in size at rates exceeding those of the economies of many countries. The sales of the 500 largest firms in the world tripled between 1990 and 2001, while world GDP grew 1.5 times during this same time frame.[16] The size of the large international companies is often compared with that of countries' economies as an indicator of the power and influence of international companies in the world economy. The United Nations Conference on Trade and Development (UNCTAD) has formulated a comparison of the GDP of countries and size of transnational companies computed based on value added, depicted in Table 1.2. It shows that of 100 largest country economies and nonfinancial international companies, 29 are nonfinancial international companies. Based on the value-added measure, the world's largest international company was ExxonMobil, with an estimated $63 billion in value added in 2000. And it ranked 45th in a combined list of countries and nonfinancial companies. The size of ExxonMobil is almost equal to that of Pakistan, and it is larger than 27 other countries, including Peru, Hungary, and Nigeria. But the list of countries that are smaller than international companies includes no countries in western Europe or North America.

The foreign affiliates of international companies tend to have higher *labor productivity* (as measured by value added per employee) than domestic firms, thereby providing economic benefits to the host country. Table 1.3 illustrates this phenomenon in selected countries.

International companies have historically tended to gravitate toward certain types of business activities. The assets of large multinational companies are deployed in food and beverages, construction, petroleum, electronics and electrical equipment, electric utilities, steel and iron, trade, transportation, chemicals and pharmaceuticals, paper and pulp, financial services, and tourism and hotel industries.[17]

A large proportion of the total business activities of multinational companies is located in the developed countries of western Europe, Canada, Japan, and the United States. It is estimated that about two-thirds of the world's direct investments are targeted to developed countries. Still, because of comparatively low labor costs and increasing political and economic stability, there has been a recent trend toward investment in emerging economies. Furthermore, service industries and service firms have become more international. This is discussed later in this chapter.

TABLE 1.3

Labor Productivity of Foreign Affiliates and Domestic Firms in Manufacturing in Selected Economies

Source: *World Investment Report 2002: Transnational Corporations and Export Competitiveness* (Geneva: UNCTAD, 2002), p. 274.

Country	Foreign Affiliates	Domestic Firms	Ratio of Foreign to Domestic
U.S.	103,818	71,006	1.46
U.K.	79,402	51,885	1.53
Netherlands	105,793	69,477	1.52
Ireland	268,272	24,571	10.9
China	7,199	2,633	2.73
France	75,970	101,732	0.75
Sweden	68,845	77,417	0.89

As seen in Table 1.3, labor productivity was higher in foreign affiliates than in domestic firms, except for productivity in France and Sweden, where labor productivity of foreign affiliates was lower than in local firms.

TABLE 1.4 Data for the Transnationality Index of Host Economies, 1999

Source: UNCTAD, FDI/TNC database.

Economy	FDI Inflows as a Percentage of GDCF^a Average 1997–1999	FDI Inward Stock as a Percentage of GDP	Value Added of Foreign Affiliates as a Percentage of GDP	Employment of Foreign Affiliates as a Percentage of Total Employment	Transnationality Index
Developed economies					
Australia	7.1	30.2	17.4	12.2	16.7
Austria	6.9	11.2	10.2	10.5	9.7
Belgium/Luxemburg	90.9	105.3	43.3	24.6	66.0
Canada	16.1	26.5	15.0	12.8	17.6
Denmark	19.9	20.7	14.9	16.3	17.9
Finland	26.3	14.3	9.5	10.1	15.0
France	12.7	16.7	4.1	4.2	9.4
Germany	6.8	13.5	16.4	5.7	10.6
Greece	2.2	17.6	27.8	10.6	14.5
Ireland	47.5	45.4	40.2	9.8	35.7
Israel	9.1	17.9	8.7	10.2	11.5
Italy	2.0	9.2	3.4	3.7	4.6
Japan	0.6	1.0	0.4	0.5	0.6
Netherlands	37.9	48.4	10.1	4.3	25.2
New Zealand	14.4	59.9	22.4	15.8	28.1
Norway	12.4	20.0	19.2	2.0	13.4
Portugal	8.2	19.8	6.2	3.8	9.5
Spain	9.5	19.2	15.5	14.6	14.7
Sweden	78.9	30.5	11.5	10.9	33.0
Switzerland	17.3	30.1	5.3	4.8	14.4
United Kingdom	25.6	25.2	4.1	3.0	14.5
United States	12.8	10.5	4.9	4.5	8.2
Developing economies					
Argentina	25.3	22.0	11.2	8.0	16.6
Bahamas	26.3	29.5	9.2	1.6	16.6
Barbados	3.9	11.6	13.1	0.2	7.2
Brazil	18.3	31.0	14.6	5.0	17.2
Chile	38.0	58.0	13.9	3.7	28.4
China	12.9	30.9	4.3	9.5	14.4
Colombia	18.1	22.9	13.8	6.3	15.3
Costa Rica	19.6	30.6	8.5	8.5	16.8
Dominican Republic	21.9	24.6	19.8	2.8	17.2
Ecuador	24.1	32.7	11.6	1.9	17.5
Egypt	9.2	22.0	13.8	1.8	11.7
Guatemala	9.6	17.5	9.0	7.9	11.0
Honduras	10.6	22.2	70.7	6.3	27.5
Hong Kong, China	36.7	256.1	98.5	2.5	98.4
India	3.0	3.7	0.8	4.1	2.9
Indonesia	−0.9	46.1	23.3	0.9	17.3

Transnationality of Countries and Companies

UNCTAD has developed a **transnationality index*** to compare the transnationality of countries in which international companies operate. The transnationality index attempts to measure the transnationalization of economic activity of host countries. The

*The transnationality index is the simple average of the following four factors: (1) FDI inflows as a percentage of gross fixed capital formation; (2) FDI inward stocks as a percentage of GDP; (3) value added by foreign affiliates as a percentage of GDP; and (4) employment by foreign affiliates as a percentage of total employment.

TABLE 1.4 Data for the Transnationality Index of Host Economies, 1999—*Continued*

Economy	FDI Inflows as a Percentage of GDCF[a] Average 1997–1999	FDI Inward Stock as a Percentage of GDP	Value Added of Foreign Affiliates as a Percentage of GDP	Employment of Foreign Affiliates as a Percentage of Total Employment	Transnationality Index
Jamaica	18.6	39.7	4.4	0.6	15.8
Malaysia	17.1	62.2	26.8	16.6	30.7
Mexico	14.2	16.3	8.8	7.0	11.6
Nigeria	22.0	55.4	86.8	1.0	41.3
Panama	43.0	70.2	−0.7	0.4	28.2
Peru	15.4	17.2	7.6	2.4	10.6
Philippines	8.0	14.7	12.8	2.4	9.5
Republic of Korea	5.2	7.9	3.1	2.2	4.6
Saudi Arabia	8.1	19.5	4.1	3.2	8.7
Singapore	27.3	98.8	23.7	10.4	40.1
South Africa	8.6	39.8	22.5	23.0	23.5
Taiwan Province of China	2.7	8.0	15.0	4.1	7.4
Thailand	20.8	21.7	8.4	2.1	13.2
Trinidad and Tobago	52.3	94.7	29.4	3.8	45.1
Turkey	1.8	4.5	6.2	3.9	4.1
United Arab Emirates	−1.4	3.3	4.7	1.1	1.9
Venezuela	26.1	21.0	9.1	2.2	14.6
Countries of central and eastern Europe					
Albania	9.6	11.5	0.9	1.4	5.8
Belarus	9.6	9.5	0.6	0.3	5.0
Bosnia and Herzegovina	2.5	3.6	0.2	0.2	1.6
Bulgaria	41.1	19.4	1.7	5.4	16.9
Croatia	22.1	20.1	5.2	8.1	13.9
Czech Republic	24.0	32.1	10.2	4.2	17.6
Estonia	27.5	47.6	8.4	9.4	23.2
Hungary	18.9	40.2	24.0	27.4	27.6
Latvia	30.5	27.0	5.5	10.4	18.3
Lithuania	23.7	19.3	3.8	5.9	13.2
Macedonia, former Yugoslav Republic	9.7	6.2	0.8	2.8	4.8
Moldova, Republic	19.1	26.8	0.6	0.9	11.9
Poland	16.3	17.1	5.0	7.8	11.5
Romania	19.7	15.5	1.6	0.9	9.4
Russian Federation	7.5	8.6	0.8	1.6	4.6
Slovakia	5.9	14.3	4.4	3.6	7.1
Slovenia	5.8	13.4	3.5	8.8	7.9
Ukraine	7.8	10.3	0.5	0.7	4.8
Yugoslavia	14.2	13.2	1.1	1.7	7.5

[a]Gross Domestic Capital Formation.

transnationality of a country is the degree to which the country is linked to the world economy through FDI inflows, the amount of foreign direct investment already invested in the country, and the significance to its economy of foreign affiliates within its borders. Transnationality indexes in 1999 for countries grouped in developed, developing, and central and eastern Europe are shown in Table 1.4.

Among the developed countries, the highest three indexes belonged to Belgium/ Luxemburg (66), Ireland (35.7), and Sweden (33), and the lowest index score belonged to Japan (4.6). Hong Kong earned the top spot among the developing countries

TABLE 1.5   **The World's Top 10 TNCs in Terms of Transnationality, 2000**

Source: UNCTAD, FDI/TNC database.

Ranking in 2000		Ranking in 1999					
Foreign Assets	TNI	Foreign Assets	TNI	Corporation	Home Country	Industry	TNI[a] (%)
39	1	86	34	Rio Tinto	United Kingdom	Mining and quarrying	98.2
49	2	56	1	Thomson	Canada	Media	95.3
24	3	21	3	ABB	Switzerland	Machinery and equipment	94.9
18	4	11	2	Nestlé	Switzerland	Food and beverages	94.7
31	5	35	7	British American Tobacco	United Kingdom	Tobacco	94.4
91	6	79	4	Electrolux	Sweden	Electrical and electronic equipment	93.2
86	7	–	–	Interbrew	Belgium	Food and beverages	90.2
26	8	–	–	Anglo American	United Kingdom	Mining and quarrying	88.4
52	9	90	20	Astrazeneca	United Kingdom	Pharmaceuticals	86.9
25	10	33	35	Philips Electronics	Netherlands	Electrical and electronic equipment	85.7

[a]The transnationality index (TNI) is calculated as the average of the following three ratios: foreign assets to total assets, foreign sales to total sales, and foreign employment to total employment.

with a transnationality index of 98.4, and the United Arab Emirates had the lowest index of 1.9. Among the countries of central and eastern Europe, Hungary had the highest index of 27.6, and the lowest index of 1.6 belonged to Bosnia and Herzegovina. The transnationality index for the 74 countries was 16.9. The United States had an index of 8.2. Table 1.4 shows the numerical figures for the transnationality index of host countries.

A casual observation of the transnationality indexes indicates that the most transnationalized countries are small in size and economies. However, the transnationality index does not measure the absolute amounts of FDI inflows, FDI stock, amount of value added, or employment by international companies and their affiliates, all of which are quite large in countries like the United States, the United Kingdom, Germany, France, Finland, and China, which scored low on the transnationality index. Along the same lines, UNCTAD identified the top 10 international companies in terms of their transnationality (Table 1.5).*

Noticable is the fact that all transnationalized companies in Table 1.5 are from small domestic markets, and that 40 percent of companies in the top 10 list are from the United Kingdom. Also remarkable is the fact that several of the largest firms in the list are from countries with small domestic markets. They include ABB and Nestlé from Switzerland, Electrolux from Sweden, Interbrew of Belgium, and Philips from the Netherlands. Companies from the United States and Japan are not listed even though 11 of the 15 largest companies in the world are from these two countries (see Table 1.1). Even though companies from the United States and Japan have expanded internationally, the relative importance and large size of their domestic markets results in relatively low foreign-to-total ratios.

International Mindsets[18]

International companies and the international industries of which they are a part have certain biases, or **international mindsets.** Specific pressures affect competition in industries and firms that cross national boundaries, causing (1) a global orientation that

*The transnationality index of companies is calculated as the average of the following three ratios: (1) foreign assets to total assets, (2) foreign sales to total sales, and (3) foreign employment to total employment.

relies on coordination of worldwide activities to maximize the collective organization, and (2) a multidomestic orientation that responds to individual country opportunities and constraints.

In some industries the former strategy dominates, so that a firm's position in one competitive market is significantly affected by its competitive position in other markets. These firms have a **global orientation,** one focused on the cost benefits of scale or scope economies. The international firm with this orientation will seek to increase its efficiency through the optimum management and allocation of its global resources. Of primary importance to the firm is the need to maximize its collective organization through an efficient configuration of all of its international activities. Simply put, the international firm will have an orientation toward cost and efficiency. A global orientation would be most appropriate in the manufacturing and marketing of automobiles, electronics, tires, and farm equipment.

However, not all industries and firms which compete internationally exhibit the market interdependencies fitting the global orientation profile. Certain factors contribute to an industry's need to be more responsive to local environments. Thus the international firm will forgo an attempt at maximizing the global organization. For example, product or service requirements may substantially differ from one geographical region to another, making standardization impossible. Furthermore, the benefits from scale or scope economies derived from the sharing of costs across markets may be constrained by governments imposing protectionist policies limiting international trade opportunities. The resulting **multidomestic orientation** is an approach that manages each market individually rather than attempting to gain cost advantages from a global integration effort. To exploit potential sources of competitive advantage, firms must be able to identify and manage risk in individual foreign markets. Areas conducive to a multidomestic orientation include the fast-food industry and professions such as accounting, advertising, and consulting.

Increasingly, international companies face pressure to be both globally efficient and locally responsive.[19] These pressures derive from environmental changes such as new technologies, unanticipated competition, and the convergence of industry boundaries as is seen in information-based industries where telecommunication, Internet, entertainment, media, and cable television firms are competing in one another's core areas. Firms in these industries exhibit a **transnational orientation** to simultaneously gain efficiency and local market benefits.[20] In Chapter 6 we explore in more detail the implications of these international mindsets.

The Evolution of an International Enterprise

Foreign Market Entry Modes

A company can achieve its international business aims through different forms of foreign market entry modes, such as

- Exporting.
- Countertrade.
- Contract manufacturing.
- Licensing.
- Franchising.
- Turnkey projects.
- Nonequity strategic alliances.
- Equity-based ventures such as wholly owned subsidiaries and equity joint ventures.

We examine these entry modes in detail in Chapter 7. Also, we delve further into the strategic necessities for equity joint ventures and nonequity strategic alliances in Chapter 8.

Evolutionary Stages

A uninational or domestic company goes through several distinct but overlapping stages in its **evolution into an international enterprise.** Some companies go through these stages rapidly—in a few years—whereas others may take many years to evolve into full-fledged global firms. Companies do not all systematically proceed from one evolutionary stage to another; some in fact skip one or several of the stages. The following discussion applies mainly to manufacturing firms. The evolutionary pattern in service firms is covered later.

Stage 1: Foreign Inquiry   Stage 1 begins when a company receives an inquiry about one of its products directly from a foreign businessperson or from an independent domestic exporter and importer. The company may ignore the inquiry, in which case there is no further evolutionary development. However, if the company responds positively and has its product sold in the foreign market at a profit, then the stage is set for more sales of its products abroad, and the company executives probably become favorably disposed toward the export of their products. Other inquiries from foreign buyers are received more enthusiastically, and the company sells its products abroad through a domestic export middleperson. The middleperson could be an export merchant, an export commission house, a resident buyer (a buyer who is domiciled in the exporting company's home market and represents all types of private or governmental foreign buyers), a broker, a combination export manager (an exporter who serves as the exclusive export department of several noncompeting manufacturers), or a manufacturer's agent. (Unlike the combination export managers, who make sales in the name of each company they represent, the manufacturer's agents retain their identities by operating in their own names.)

Stage 2: Export Manager   As the company's exports continue to expand and the executives decide that the time is appropriate to take the export management into their own hands rather than rely on unsolicited inquiries from abroad, a decision is made to assume a proactive rather than a reactive posture toward exports. Hence an export manager with a small staff is appointed to actively search for foreign markets for the company's products.

Stage 3: Export Department and Direct Sales   As export sales continue their upward surge, the company has difficulty operating with only an export manager and his or her small staff. A full-fledged export department or division is established at the same level as the domestic sales department. The company then drops the domestic export middleperson and begins to sell directly to importers or buyers located in foreign markets.

Stage 4: Sales Branches and Subsidiaries   Further growth of export sales requires the establishment of sales branches abroad to handle sales and promotional work. A sales branch manager is directly responsible to the home office, and the branch sells directly to middlepersons in the foreign markets. A sales branch gradually evolves into a sales subsidiary, which is incorporated and domiciled in the foreign country, and which enjoys greater autonomy than it had as a sales branch.

Stage 5: Assembly Abroad   Assembly abroad occurs for three major reasons: cheaper shipping costs for unassembled products, lower tariffs, and cheaper labor. The company may begin assembly operation in one or more of the foreign markets if export of the disassembled product is more profitable than export of the whole product. Often tariffs and transportation costs are lower on unassembled parts and components than on the assembled, finished product. For example, the parts of an unassembled TV set can be packed in a smaller box than can a fully assembled set. Because surface freight is charged on volume, unassembled parts in a smaller box are cheaper to ship than a fully assembled set in a much larger box. Also, tariffs in the form of customs duties on imports are often lower on the unassembled product (because of the smaller amount of value added in an unassembled product) than on the finished product. A large number of Japanese TV sets are assembled in India for these reasons.

Companies often establish assembly operations abroad for a third reason—to take advantage of the foreign country's pool of cheap labor. For this purpose, many American, European, and Japanese companies have established assembly operations in countries such as China, Mexico, Singapore, Taiwan, India, Sri Lanka, Mauritius, and the Dominican Republic. Products assembled in these countries are primarily meant to serve the American and third-country markets of Europe and Japan.

Stage 6: Production Abroad   After the previous stages have been accomplished, the next step is the establishment of production abroad. At this time the company has a well-developed export program supported by country market studies, by promotion and distribution programs tailored to the needs of each country market, and by research into the identification of new foreign markets. The company's executives may now begin to experience difficulties in increasing the total sales volume and profit in foreign markets in which they currently have a foothold, or they may find it impossible to enter other potentially lucrative markets via exports. These difficulties often occur when the local governments impose high tariffs or quotas on the import of certain products. Countries also may ban the import totally if the products are being produced locally by a domestic company. In such cases the company executives decide to penetrate the foreign market by producing the product in the foreign market itself.

After establishing a manufacturing facility in a foreign market, the company now manages its total business in a foreign country. It must therefore perform many business functions abroad—purchasing, finance, human resource planning and management, manufacturing, marketing, and so on. The company is also obligated to make significant commitments of technical, management, and financial resources to the new foreign entity.

The company learns from its experience with the first foreign manufacturing venture, and this knowledge paves the way for the establishment of other foreign manufacturing plants abroad. At the same time, the company continues to export its products and to license its technology to foreign businesses and, increasingly, to its own foreign affiliates.

In maturing as an international exporter, licensor, and producer of products, the company meets the global demand for its products with exports from several of its foreign production affiliates, as well as with exports from the parent company, and with the products of the foreign licensing arrangements. As the complexity of managing the geographically far-flung operations in several countries increases, the parent company managers recognize the benefits of integrating and tightening the company's global operations and of managing the entire company as one global organizational system. The motivation to use the so-called systems approach in managing the company as one unit, with each foreign and domestic affiliate functioning as a subunit of the whole company, arises when questions such as the following emerge to confront the company:

1. Which of the several foreign affiliates should export to a third-country market?
2. Different affiliates operate in countries with differing inflation rates and corporate tax structures, so how should the financial resources of each affiliate be managed with the objective of maximizing the total global earnings of the entire company?
3. Where in the world should a product be assembled?
4. Where in the world should we conduct our research and development?

Questions such as these make the parent company management perceive the company as one global enterprise system and not merely an aggregation of several autonomous domestic and foreign affiliates. When the parent company's management begins to see the advantages of making strategic decisions in various functional areas—such as purchasing, finance, production, marketing, personnel, and research and development—from the perspective of the company as one integrated system, the stage is set for the company's evolution to a multinational enterprise.

Stage 7: Integration of Foreign Affiliates   As the parent company managers decide to integrate the various foreign[21] affiliates into one multinational enterprise system, and as the company begins to operate as in integrated network,[22] the affiliates lose considerable autonomy, as top management at the company headquarters now makes strategic decisions. The network is comprised of interpersonal ties that connect managers and subsidiaries across geographical borders.[23] Functioning as a global network facilitates exchange of ideas which promote innovation and performance of subsidiaries. The company's management begins to view the entire world as its theater of operations; it plans, organizes, staffs, and controls its international operations from a global perspective. Strategic decisions are made after a careful analysis of their worldwide implications: In what country should we build our next production facility? Throughout the world, where are our markets, and from which production center should they be served? From which sources in the world should we borrow capital to finance our current and future operations? Where should our research and development laboratories be located? From which countries should we recruit people? When the management of the company starts thinking and operating in global terms, then it has evolved into a global enterprise.

Not all companies go through each of the seven stages just described. Some companies stop short of complete integration of their domestic and foreign operations, preferring instead to manage their domestic and foreign operations in a decentralized manner, without an overall global strategy. Others may choose to coordinate the operations of affiliates in a certain region of the world, such as Europe, and keep the affiliates in other regions unattached and semiautonomous. Still other companies may decide to think globally with respect to only a few, but not all, of the enterprise functions. For instance, managers may think in worldwide terms where financial and production issues are concerned, but not for marketing, personnel, purchasing, and research and development. Thus there are different degrees of globalization of operations. Some firms may progress further along the multinational path and become totally global enterprises, whereas others may choose to end their journey along the path at various milestones along the way. Many changes in management practices and organizational structure occur as a firm evolves into a multinational company. Some of these changes involve a radical reorientation in the attitudes and values of the managers with respect to both the role of the company in the world economy and the allegiance of the company to the home country. Another significant arena for change is the managers' perceptions of people of different nationalities, cultures, and races.

The Evolution of Service Firms into Global Enterprises

In the preceding section, we examined the typical stages in the evolution of mainly manufacturing firms into global enterprises. However, we must note that not all international companies are in the manufacturing sector. In fact some of the largest global companies are in the services sector. Those that readily come to mind are firms in the banking industry such as Citicorp, Sumitomo, Sanwa, and Credit Suisse; accounting firms such as PriceWaterhouseCoopers; and consulting firms like McKinsey. Overseas expansion has also been strong during the past decade for firms in the hotel industry such as Marriott, Hilton, and Holiday Inns. Rapid expansion abroad has occurred also in firms in the fast-food industry like Pizza Hut, KFC, and McDonald's, rental car firms such as Hertz and Avis, and information-based firms such as AT&T, Time Warner, and Verizon.

During the past 15 years, the service sector has increased in importance not only as a percentage of individual countries' gross domestic product, but also in terms of world trade and overseas expansion. Unlike firms in the manufacturing sector, service firms, especially in the hotel and food sectors, do not necessarily go through the various evolutionary stages as they move from the purely domestic stage to the more mature international and global stage. After establishing franchise systems at home, service firms enter foreign markets by establishing franchises in foreign countries. Some of the foreign franchises may be wholly owned by the parent company, whereas others may be jointly owned with host country entrepreneurs, and still others may be wholly owned by host country franchisees. A franchisee does business in the host country under the franchiser's trade name and follows the policies, procedures, and operational systems established and imposed by the franchiser. In exchange, the franchisee gives fees, royalties, and other compensation to the franchiser.

Service firms that directly support international businesses have also undergone a recent increase of international expansion. These firms, including consulting, accounting, and information-based firms, have emulated manufacturing firms in that they incur the costs and risks of FDI by establishing operations overseas. They have also had many motives similar to those of manufacturing firms regarding overseas expansion.

The Emergence of the Internet as a Vehicle to Expand Overseas

In 1999, Internet-based commerce worldwide totaled $301 billion. Furthermore, estimates indicate that Internet transactions will have grown to more than $1,400 billion by 2004.[24] The global growth in e-commerce is being fueled by the development of new processes that have made consumer shopping cheaper and more entertaining and business-to-business transactions increasingly more efficient. During the last decade, the Internet has allowed firms to pursue overseas markets without the capital necessary to set up and control overseas operations. Thus it has provided the catalyst to overseas expansion by many small and privately owned firms. For example, smaller New Zealand firms specializing in goods such as indigenous arts and baby care products historically have not been able to internationalize because of the cost of marketing overseas. Since 2001, through the Internet, many of these firms have found new markets and are quickly expanding their overseas sales. Similarly, during the new millennium, the Chinese government has proactively helped many firms create Web sites to market indigenous goods internationally. Internet portals like Yahoo, eBay, AOL, and Hotmail have helped small companies to enter foreign markets. The World Wide Web has helped international companies to source their parts and components from foreign suppliers.

Continuous improvements in the Web technologies have enabled more firms to enter international markets and subsequently have put a new competitive pressure on existing international companies. Products and services are becoming more information-based and less matter-based. Furthermore, the speed of international activity, including market analyses and customer responsiveness, is increasing. Knowledge derived from the ability to access many sources of information is becoming an even more competitive weapon for international companies. The various effects of the Internet and associated technological breakthroughs and knowledge management implications are explored in Chapter 11.

Why Firms Seek to Engage in International Business

An international company may have several motivations for establishing various types of foreign operations. Some of them have been alluded to in the preceding paragraphs on the evolution of multinational enterprises. Let us examine some of the other motivations for foreign operations that are illustrated in Figure 1.2 and grouped into three categories: market-seeking motives, cost-reduction motives, and strategic motives.

Market-Seeking Motives

Historically, companies have initially looked to overseas markets when their home market became saturated. In his landmark *product life cycle theory,* Vernon theorizes that firms will search foreign markets for product that has been standardized and reached the maturity stage in its life cycle.[25] Because of social and regulatory pressures in the United States that leveled off a once growing market, the U.S. cigarette industry firms had to look to the foreign markets of eastern Europe and Asia to maintain sales volumes. Similarly, as revenue growth declined and the fast-food industry edged toward maturity in the United States, various fast-food firms like McDonald's and Pizza Hut expanded overseas to countries such as Russia, Japan, China, and India. Today, product life cycles in many industries have become very short because of next-generation technologies, so firms are seeking to penetrate overseas markets simultaneously with their respective home markets in order to recoup costs and make a profit before the next generation of technology comes to market.

Once firms have internationally expanded, many try to protect and maintain a market position abroad by establishing production facilities in foreign markets that had

FIGURE 1.2
Motives to Go International

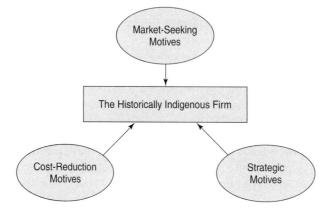

been served through exports. In this way companies bypass the threat of trade barriers such as the imposition of high tariffs or quotas. For instance, the so-called voluntary restrictions in 1980 on the export of Japanese automobiles to the United States was one factor that prompted Japanese auto companies like Toyota and Nissan to build car manufacturing plants in the United States. Toyota, Honda, and Nissan have established significant shares in the U.S. automobile market. Similarly, many U.S. and Japanese companies established plants in the 15-country European Union (EU) to circumvent potential trade barriers raised by the member countries against imports from non-EU countries. Over the years, through the efforts of the World Trade Organization (WTO), tariffs and quotas have been reduced dramatically. We elaborate on the practical and strategic implications of the EU, other trade blocs, and the WTO in Chapter 2.

The expectation of immense business opportunities in an integrated and unified market of the 15-nation European Union that includes Great Britain, Ireland, France, Germany, the Netherlands, Belgium, Luxemburg, Italy, Greece, Spain, Denmark, Portugal, Austria, Sweden, and Finland has brought an upsurge of both Japanese and American direct investment in Europe. As an example, for the past decade, Japanese banks and companies in the manufacturing sector have been continually investing, buying European companies, setting up manufacturing subsidiaries, and boosting sales forces throughout Europe. Japan's business activities in Europe intensified in 1990 when Japanese companies decided Europe was serious about market unification after 1992. The Japanese companies wanted a foothold in Europe before protectionism possibly kept them out. Japanese companies have responded by building new manufacturing plants and buying existing manufacturing capacity inside what could become a European fortress.

Historically, U.S. firms in many industries have been able to gain cost efficiencies and needed experience in their home market before venturing overseas. However, when a company's home market is not large enough to gain necessary cost efficiencies, that firm must look to international markets. The small size of the domestic market is the reason given by European companies that have developed international presences. Pharmaceuticals companies Hoffman-La Roche and Novartis (in 1996, in one of the largest corporate mergers in history, Ciba-Geigy and Sandoz merged to form Novartis), based in Switzerland—a nation whose population is less than 8 million—could not have survived in their industry had they limited their business horizons to the Swiss market. These companies, and others like them in other European countries with small populations like Holland and Belgium, were forced to seek markets abroad, which eventually led to the creation of foreign manufacturing facilities in their major markets.

Cost-Reduction Motives

Companies venture overseas to lower factor costs. Intense competitive pressures and the resulting fall in profit margins serve as a powerful inducement for affected companies to seek cost-reduction measures. Firms therefore seek countries with low wages to shift manufacturing operations.[26] The differences in hourly compensation for production workers in the United States, Japan, Europe (15 countries of the European Union, Norway and Switzerland), Canada, Mexico, newly industrialized economies (NIEs) in Asia (Hong Kong, Korea, Singapore, and Taiwan), and 28 major competitors of the United States worldwide[27] are shown in Exhibit 1.1.

Comparatively cheap labor is often the strongest incentive for companies to establish foreign operations.[28] For example, over the past two decades more than 2,000 maquiladoras have sprung up near the United States–Mexico border. These plants take advantage of cheap labor to assemble American-made components for reexport to the United States. Further inside Mexico, Japanese, German, and American

EXHIBIT 1.1   Hourly Compensation Costs in U.S. Dollars for Production Workers in Manufacturing, 1975–2000

Source: Chris Sparks, Theo Bikoi, and Lisa Moglia, "A Perspective on U.S. and Foreign Compensation Costs in Manufacturing," *Monthly Labor Review*, June 2002, p. 37.

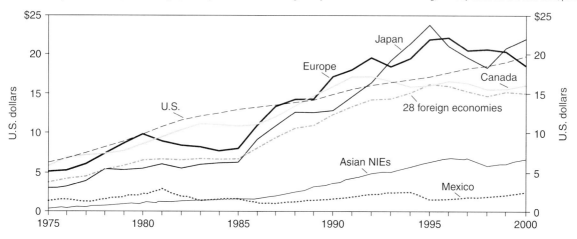

automotive firms all have assembly facilities that ship final products to the United States and global markets. The economics of assembly in Mexico are favorable because jobs that are higher priced in the United States and fully "burdened" with benefits, Social Security, and so on, can be had in Mexico for a fraction of the cost.

In the 1950s and 1960s, many American companies had established not just assembly plants, but fully integrated manufacturing plants in newly industrializing countries such as Taiwan and Singapore and the crown colony of Hong Kong. Even more foreign investment in manufacturing operations has flowed into Asia since then. Research indicates that "the high-wage differential between West Europe and Asia has been the most significant contribution to the restructuring of U.S. foreign direct investment (FDI) during 1981–2000."[29] As wages in Taiwan, Singapore, and Hong Kong rose in comparison to lesser developed Southeast Asian countries, the companies shifted their investment sights and moved to Malaysia, Thailand, and Indonesia. Most recently, even lower cost labor has been found in locales like southern China and Vietnam. During the 1990s and into the twenty-first century, Black & Decker, the U.S. power tools manufacturer, aggressively expanded production facilities for power drills throughout China, not to serve the Chinese market, but rather to export to Europe. Automobile companies have engaged in several contracts with Indian suppliers for the supply of parts and components. Practical Insight 1.1 on page 24 illustrates this phenomenon.

Another reason companies set up foreign plants is to eliminate or reduce high transportation costs, particularly if the ratio of the per-unit transportation expenditures to the per-unit selling price of the product is very high. For instance, if the product costs $10 to ship but it can be marketed for no more than $25 in the foreign market, all other things being nearly equal, the company may decide to produce it in the market to improve its competitiveness and profit margin. The trade-off for the company is giving up the economies of scale efficiencies of long production runs in one country in order to reduce transportation costs.

Costs can also be reduced for a firm through favorable host government incentives and inducements. Local production often allows the company to take advantage of incentives that the host government may be offering to foreign companies that make direct investments in the country.[30] These incentives include reduced taxes for several years, free land, low-interest loans, and a guarantee of no labor strife. This was a principal motive for Intel to establish manufacturing operations in Costa Rica, and for Mercedes, the German luxury car company, to build a manufacturing plant in Alabama.

Firms in industries with relatively high allocation of funds to research also look to overseas markets. Companies in pharmaceutical and high-technology industries that must spend large sums of money on research and development for new products and processes are compelled to look for ways to improve their sales volume in order to support their laboratories. If the domestic sales volume and exports do not raise the necessary cash flow, then strategically located manufacturing and sales affiliates are established abroad with the objective of attaining higher levels of sales volume and cash flow to support future research endeavors.

A factor that companies take into account in locating production plants is the comparative production costs in their major country markets. For example, a company that has major market positions in Japan, Germany, and the United States would be concerned about how costs are affected by the cross-exchange rates between the Japanese yen, the euro, and the U.S. dollar. If the yen were to rise significantly in value against the U.S. dollar and the euro, then exports to the United States and Germany of the company's Japanese-produced products could become relatively noncompetitive because of the rise of the yen-denominated Japanese wage rates and exports, especially if labor costs added significantly to the total product value. In such an event, the economics of production and distribution permitting, the company would gain if it could shift its production to either the United States or Germany. In fact, during the 1990s, when the yen appreciated against the U.S. dollar, Japanese auto companies used their U.S. plants to ship cars to Europe, and even back to Japan! BMW and Mercedes, two of the major luxury carmakers of Germany, decided to commence manufacture of some models in the United States because of the highly noncompetitive labor rates in Germany largely due to the high value of the German mark. Global companies invest in favor of operational flexibility and in the ability to shift the sourcing of products and components from country to country. Global companies are therefore motivated to make major investments in operations and supply sites in their major country markets.

Firms have been known to move their operations to ecologically and environmentally friendly countries in order to reduce costs of adherence, both from the operations perspective and from the political perspective. Companies have been alleged to have moved their environmentally harmful operations to countries in Africa, Asia, and Latin America whose laws for environmental protection are less strict than those in the United States and therefore are considered ecologically and environmentally friendly to businesses. But companies do not have to migrate to developing countries to avoid environmental risks. A case in point is Germany's BASF, which moved its biotechnology research laboratory focusing on cancer and immune-system research from Germany—where it faced legal and political challenges from the environmentally conscious Green movement—to Cambridge, Massachusetts, which, according to BASF's director of biotechnology research, had more or less settled any controversies involving safety, animal rights, and the environment.[31] These and other types of social responsibility issues that confront the international company are expanded upon in Chapter 17.

Strategic Motives

Firms venture overseas for many long-term strategic reasons. Strategic decisions are those that are made to maintain or enhance the competitive position of a company in an industry or market. According to Hymer, who was the first to offer an explanation of why firms start production abroad, firms use foreign production as a means of transferring and taking advantage of the host country's specialized assets, knowledge, and

PRACTICAL INSIGHT 1.1

THE ALLURE OF INDIA AS A LOW-COST, HIGH-QUALITY PRODUCTION CENTER

The scramble by the recession-wounded global automotive industry to find a source for low-cost, high-quality components has been a big boon to India's auto parts makers. Among the rash of announcements just this month was one by the Delphi Corporation, the world's largest automotive parts maker, saying that it would have $140 million worth of auto parts—forged engine parts, intricate plastic moldings and other products—made by Indian concerns, and that such orders were expected to exceed $250 million a year by 2007. The Ford Motor Company said that it expected to get more than $100 million worth of components from Indian parts makers in the next two years. Volvo said that it planned to increase its manufacturing in India to 100 million euros ($117 million) worth of parts in one year instead of three.

The demand has come even from China, a rival to India in low-cost manufacturing. And the orders are flowing throughout India's auto parts industry, to subsidiaries of Ford, General Motors, Toyota Motor and other major carmakers; to global auto parts leaders like Delphi and Visteon; and to homegrown auto parts makers, including Bhart Forge and Hi-Tech Gears. The flurry is spurring the industry to set ambitious targets.

Exports of auto parts are projected to reach $25 billion in 20 years, according to the Automotive Component Manufacturers Association of India. Already the exports, nearly two-thirds of which go to the United States and Europe, have risen to an estimated $800 million for the year ended March 31 from $578 million a year earlier—a 38 percent spurt.

While the current figure is less than a tenth of the amount India's software exports bring in, investors in India's stock markets are bidding up the prices of auto parts concerns in the belief that the industry holds as much promise. The parts makers' success thus far has come in large part from two factors that have already helped make India's software and support services industry successful: low labor costs and one of the world's largest technologically adept work forces. Additionally, locally produced raw materials like rubber and steel are inex-

pensive. "Big carmakers are under huge pressure to reduce costs," said Hans-Michael Huber, chief executive of Daimler-Chrysler India. And purchasing specialists from the unit's parent company, DaimlerChrysler A.G., are combing India for top-quality low-cost suppliers, he said.

The Toyota Motor Corporation is setting up its own auto parts unit on the outskirts of Bangalore with a $197 million investment to supply transmission systems to Toyota worldwide beginning in mid-2004. Toyota is also converting a textile machinery plant in another Bangalore suburb to produce auto parts.

Much of the outsourced business is going to a handful of the more than 400 local parts makers. For example, India's leading auto components company by revenue, Bharat Forge, says its headquarters in Pune, southeast of Bombay, is being visited two or three times a week by delegations of product and supply experts from global carmakers. Still, though India's auto parts exports are growing robustly, they account for just a minuscule portion—less than 0.1 percent—of the $1 trillion world auto parts industry. They are small even compared with those of other low-cost manufacturing centers like Mexico and Brazil.

But India's capabilities in a variety of manufacturing processes give it a competitive edge. "The level of manufacturing industry here rivals that in most of the developed countries," said Kiyomichi Ito, managing director of Toyota's new Bangalore-based unit, Toyota Kirloskar Auto Parts.

One sign of the new aggressiveness in the industry, as well as the many takers worldwide for its products, came in late May when the Automotive Component Manufacturers Association of India led a delegation of 33 domestic parts makers to the United States to meet with major manufacturers. Sundaram Clayton, Hi-Tech Gears, Shriram Pistons and Rings and Rico Auto Industries were among those represented. "On earlier visits, we got the polite brush-off," said Arvind Kapur, managing director of Rico Auto. "But this time we had more than a dozen buyers surrounding us everywhere we went. From Ford and General Motors in Detroit to Cummins in Columbus to Caterpil-

capabilities, both tangible and intangible.[32] Firms also engage in foreign operations in several countries to diversify their strategic risk.[33] Both Caves and Dunning explain foreign production by firms as a means of taking advantage of their assets, knowledge, and capabilities that are superior to firms in the foreign markets.[34] A firm can accrue many distinct strategic advantages by producing a product in a foreign market. These include the ability to meet the demand for the product quickly, good public relations with customers and the host government, and improved service.

A firm may simply follow its major customers abroad. When the Japanese automakers Honda, Toyota, Nissan, Mazda, Subaru, and Isuzu established car manufacturing plants in the United States, their Japanese suppliers followed and set up their

lar in Peoria, we sensed a desperation to source from emerging markets." Rico Auto, based in Gurgaon, outside Delhi, sold $120 million worth of aluminum and ferrous engine and braking parts to G.M., Ford and other foreign customers last year.

When India opened its doors to foreign carmakers in the mid-1990's, nearly all the global car companies entered the market through joint ventures with local companies. They set up vigorous quality processes and brought in global quality certifications. "The local industry got tuned in to international needs, quality and logistics," Mr. Huber of DaimlerChrysler said. Gradually, the bigger homegrown parts companies geared up to compete with the world's best, alongside Indian subsidiaries of international parts leaders like Delphi and Visteon. Vinay Piparsania, director of sales operations at Ford's Indian unit, said, "India's small auto parts manufacturers are as much a success story as the country's software industry."

But as local manufacturers acknowledge, it has been a slow path to maturity, and some Indian companies are only beginning to emerge as reliable suppliers. "We relentlessly pursued Ford and General Motors to source from our company," Mr. Kapur of Rico Auto said. "In the case of General Motors, we had a breakthrough after seven years."

With India's credentials now more established, automakers like DaimlerChrysler are benefiting from the cost differential. "Indian firms offer 20 to 25 percent cost reduction, and this gets automakers excited," said Deep Kapuria, chairman of Hi-Tech Gears, also based in Gurgaon. Customers for his company's transmission gears and shafts include Cummins, the diesel engine maker, and Honda Motor. Exports from India to DaimlerChrysler reached 63 million euros ($73.8 million) in 2002, up from 45 million euros in 2001. "Granted, this is only 1 to 2 percent of my company's total purchases worldwide, but the doors are now open and the most difficult part is over," Mr. Huber said. DaimlerChrysler now buys forgings in Pune in western India, wiring harnesses in Gurgaon in north India and automotive software and electronics in Bangalore in the south. "Auto parts exports to DaimlerChrysler should touch 100 million euros by 2005, conservatively speaking," Mr. Huber said.

Still, the going may not be as easy as some parts makers believe. Mr. Ito of Toyota said that the Indian legal system was not set up to uphold international business contracts, and that might hinder growth. Then there is the fact that most of the 400-odd Indian auto parts firms are family-owned. While some have technology transfer relationships with Japanese and European automakers, many others have been slow to adapt to global business standards—some are still learning, for instance, that failing to honor their commitments can incur heavy penalties.

Competition from other southeast Asian countries like Thailand, Indonesia, Vietnam and Malaysia is growing, and as in nearly every sphere of Indian exports, China is also an aggressive player. As inexpensive car batteries from China flooded the Indian market a couple of years ago, nervous Indian car parts makers scurried to China to study the competition. But the Indians breathed easier when they found that while China had an edge in the lowest-cost work, it did not necessarily have an advantage further up the quality scale.

Some Indian parts makers even sniffed opportunity there, led by Bharat Forge. Forged and machined crankshafts shipped to China now account for one-quarter of the company's $60 million in annual exports, up from nothing a year ago. "In metal-intensive components where software-oriented design and engineering is involved and where technically skilled manpower is required for manufacturing, Bharat Forge offers an advantage in terms of both price and quality," said Baba Kalyani, the company's chairman.

P. Balendran, a vice president for General Motors India, said that quality was central to India's appeal. "Qualitywise, India is better than Mexico, China, Taiwan or for that matter, Korea," he said, referring to South Korea. "In terms of price, India is 15 percent cheaper than Mexico, 10 percent cheaper than Korea and at par with China and Taiwan."

own plants in the United States. There are today approximately 270 Japanese-owned parts suppliers in the United States, representing an investment of $5.5 billion and employing more than 30,000 workers. Most of these supplier-firms provide glass, brake systems, seats, air conditioners, heaters, filters, fuel pumps, and other components directly to the production plants. This pattern has been seen in the service industries as well. As major American corporations were expanding worldwide, they demanded better and more reliable services, including telecommunications services. Consequently, AT&T began the international expansion initiative of its communications line of business in the latter half of the 1980s, setting up overseas operations in five countries. AT&T now has major subsidiary locations in more than 50 countries.

The hardware line of business of AT&T, which was eventually spun off into a separate entity named Lucent, also made a big push overseas, mainly to satisfy the telecommunications needs of its large global customers, which had made their own push into overseas markets. Fearing that its major customers—the global companies—would turn to rival companies such as France's Alcatel, Italy's Italtel, IBM, and Japan's NEC if it did not operate advanced voice and data networks around the world, the company formed several joint ventures and strategic alliances around the globe.[35] Combined employment abroad for AT&T and Lucent jumped from a mere 50 people in 1983 to more than 50,000 today. Like AT&T, Federal Express followed the lead of its customers who increasingly wanted packages sent to Asia and Europe. Accordingly, with the aim of "keeping it purple"—the color of FedEx's planes and vans—the company set out to duplicate its business abroad.

Besides following their important customers, firms exhibit a *bandwagon effect,* venturing abroad to follow their major competitors.[36] This is especially true in an industry that is characterized by an oligopolistic rivalry. A competitor's inroads in certain foreign markets may translate to losing business in other markets. Years ago, fearing that they would eventually lose some of their U.S. business with Ford and General Motors if European tire manufacturers were able to sell to those auto manufacturers in Europe, U.S. tire manufacturers followed each and established plants in Europe to better service their major accounts. Similarly, Japanese tire manufacturers like Bridgestone have established manufacturing plants in the United States to serve Japanese carmakers. More recently, from the telecommunications service perspective, MCI followed AT&T to many overseas markets.

The competitive perspective is another strategically based motive for international expansion. If a company's competitor can make unencumbered profits in a specific host country, that competitor can use a portion of those profits to attack the firm in the firm's major markets. This is called *cross-subsidization,* that is, using profits generated in one market to compete in another market. Firms strategically look overseas to gain cross-subsidization possibilities as well as to block competitors from that advantage.[37]

Rapid expansion of a foreign market for the company's product, along with the desire to obtain a large market share in it before a major competitor can get in, are other strong driving forces for companies to engage in foreign production. By being first into a new market, a firm may be able to obtain favorable deals with customers and suppliers. Furthermore, the firms may be able to secure the most efficient distribution channels and set both the strategic and technological agendas for the industry in that host country. This is an important reason for American and European companies wanting to enter the market in China.

The need for vertical integration is another strategic reason often responsible for the international expansion of operations. Companies are pushed into making direct investment abroad so that they can capture a source of supply or new markets for their products. For example, a company in the oil exploration and drilling business may integrate "downstream" by acquiring or building an oil refinery in a foreign country that has a market for its refined products. Conversely, a company that has strong distribution channels (e.g., gas stations) in a country but needs a steady source of supply of gasoline at predictable prices may integrate "upstream" and acquire an oil producer and refiner in another country.

Numerous companies have established operations abroad to exploit the strong brand name of their products. Realizing that they could not fully exploit their advantage by way of exports, they have set up plants in their major foreign markets. Examples of companies that have used this strategy are Coca-Cola, Pepsi-Cola, Budweiser, and

PRACTICAL INSIGHT 1.2

MILLER BEER IS AIMING TO BE A EUROPEAN ICON

Genuine Draft Brand to Be Billed as Sophisticated Premium Brew

SABMiller PLC plans to launch the Miller brand across Europe as part of an effort to turn a struggling U.S. icon into an upmarket global beer.

The world's second-largest brewer, after Anheuser-Busch Cos. of St. Louis, said it planned to introduce Miller Genuine Draft as a sophisticated international premium brew in Hungary, Slovakia, Romania, the Czech Republic, Poland and Italy. It said the aim is to promote Miller as the liquid symbol of America, in order to attract a new generation of European beer drinkers.

Alan Clark, managing director of SABMiller's European operations, said the company wanted to tap into Europeans' love affair with American brands such as Marlboro cigarettes and Levi's jeans. "We want to emphasize the youthful exuberance of the Miller brand and its sense of freedom," he said . . . .

SABMiller said it is optimistic that the European branding push would help create a global buzz around Miller Genuine Draft, which will be priced in the same range as other export beers such as Heineken and Stella Artois.

It said the brand would be targeted at hip bars in European capitals. The company plans to introduce a series of print and TV ads playing up the brand's U.S. roots and the American bald eagle emblazoned on the can.

Source: From *The Wall Street Journal, Eastern Edition* by Dan Bilefsky, June 13, 2003. Copyright © 2003 by Dow Jones & Co Inc. Reproduced with permission of Dow Jones & Co. Inc. via Copyright Clearance Center.

Heineken. Scotch whiskey is now produced in India, replacing exports from abroad. Practical Insight 1.2 discusses Miller Beer's attempt to exploit Europeans' fascination for American brands.

A global company may decide to locate its manufacturing plant in a country that is of strategic importance for the company's exports to a third country. For instance, Japanese companies have strictly observed the Arab boycott of Israel and therefore cannot export to Israel directly from Japan. However, Japanese plants in the United States can export their U.S.-made products to Israel, and this is exactly what Honda is doing. It is exporting Honda Civic sedans to Israel from its plant in Ohio. In the same vein, Northern Telecom Ltd. (Nortel), the Canadian telecommunications giant, has moved many of its manufacturing operations to the United States to gain the competitive edge that an American company can obtain in securing Japanese contracts. Nortel made this strategic move to the United States knowing that the Japanese would favor U.S. companies because of Japan's huge trade surplus with the United States.

As organizational knowledge is becoming a key competitive weapon, firms have recognized that scientific talent and brainpower are not the monopoly of any one country or group of countries. Thus international companies are establishing technological research and development centers around the world. Companies like IBM and Microsoft have established such centers in Japan and India respectively to tap into the "innovation culture" of those countries. Several global companies in a variety of knowledge-based industries such as biotechnology, pharmaceuticals, and electronics have set up such centers in the countries of the so-called Triad of Europe, the Pacific Basin (including Japan), and the United States. This strategy has paid rich dividends for Xerox, which has introduced 80 different office copier models in the United States that were engineered and built by its Japanese joint venture, Fuji-Xerox Company. Another example is Bangalore, India, which has become the global center for software development for major computer and software companies. The number one global carmaker, General Motors, plans to invest invest $60 million in a technology center in Bangalore, India's technology hub. General Motors plans to hire 260 engineers, who will collaborate with the company's American and European research center through high-speed communication links. Most planes flying between Mumbai (Bombay), the major international gateway to India, and Bangalore are filled with U.S. technology executives looking to source business in this emerging Silicon Valley.[38] Similarly, firms in Malaysia have proactively marketed themselves to North American and European companies as the appropriate places to outsource their technology needs.

Paralleling financial planning thinking, firms have strategically ventured overseas to diversify their operations and, in effect, to hedge against the many environmental risks of doing business in one country. This strategy ranges from simply distribution and sales in multiple countries to rationalization of production across key countries. Regarding distribution and sales, firms relying solely on the Japanese market have been hurt due to the long-lasting recession in Japan. Firms with a portfolio of country businesses have somewhat hedged against such a recession. Likewise, firms try to balance the efficiencies of long production runs with the flexibility of being able to switch production should trouble arise in a certain country. For instance, auto parts are produced in many countries, including the United States, Japan, Argentina, Mexico, India, and Indonesia. Although the comparative costs in Argentina, Mexico, India, and Indonesia are lower than in the United States and Japan, the former countries are less stable than the latter. Mexico had a financial problem in the mid-1990s. From the late 1990s until today, Indonesia saw a combination of financial and political upheaval that put many foreign investments at risk. And most recently, Argentina's financial problems have bubbled over into increased instability of the market and workforce. Thus producing all of a firm's components in any one of these countries would have proved catastrophic to a firm.

In this section, we have introduced some of the many reasons why a firm may choose to "go international." However, it is important to remember that each company's decision should be based on a careful assessment of its own distinctive strengths (and weaknesses) and the potential for it to strengthen its overall competitive position by making the international move. In the next section, we look at one proposed framework for assessing such potential benefits.

Strategic Objectives and Sources of Competitive Advantage

Sumantra Ghoshal, in his seminal article "Global Strategy: An Organizing Framework"[39] offered an excellent framework that explains the broad categories of objectives of a global firm and the sources for developing an international/global firm's competitive advantage. The framework is presented in Exhibit 1.2.

As seen in Exhibit 1.2, in its **global strategy,** a global firm pursues three categories of objectives: (1) achieving efficiency, (2) managing risks, and (3) innovating, learning, and adapting. The key is to create a firm's competitive advantage by developing and implementing strategies that optimize the firm's achievement of these three categories of objectives. This may require trade-offs to be made between the objectives because on occasion they may conflict. For example, the objective of achieving efficiency through economies of scale in production may conflict with the objective of minimizing risks emanating from economic or political conditions in a country where the plant is located.

Ghoshal identifies three sources through which a global firm may derive its competitive advantage: (1) national differences, (2) scale economies, and (3) scope economies. According to Ghoshal, the strategic task of managing globally is to use all three sources of competitive advantage to optimize efficiency, risk, and learning simultaneously in a worldwide business. The key to a successful global strategy is to manage the interactions between these different goals and means.[40]

EXHIBIT 1.2   **Global Strategy: An Organizing Framework**

Source: From Sumantra Ghoshal, "Global Strategy: An Organizing Framework," *Strategic Management Journal,* Vol. 8. Copyright © 1987 John Wiley & Sons Limited. Reproduced with permission.

Strategic Objectives	Sources of Competitive Advantage		
	National Differences	**Scale Economies**	**Scope Economies**
Achieving efficiency in current operations	Benefiting from differences in factor costs (wages and cost of capital)	Expanding and exploiting potential scale economies in each activity	Sharing investments and costs across products, markets, and businesses
Managing risks	Managing different kinds of risks arising from market- or policy-induced changes in comparative advantage of different countries	Balancing scale with strategic and operational flexibility	Portfolio diversification of risks and creation of options and side-bets
Innovation, learning, and adapting	Learning from societal differences in organizational and managerial processes and systems	Benefiting from experience, cost reduction, and innovation	Sharing learning across organizational components in different products, markets, or businesses

Achieving Efficiency

If a firm is viewed as an input–output system, its overall efficiency is defined as a ratio of the value of all its outputs to the costs of all its inputs. A firm obtains the surplus resources needed to grow and prosper by maximizing this ratio. It may enhance the value of its products or services (outputs) by making them of higher quality than those of its competitors, and at the same time it may lower the costs of inputs by obtaining low-cost factors of production such as labor and raw materials.[41] Different business functions—production, research and development, marketing, and so on—have different factor intensities. A firm could exploit *national differences* by locating a function in a country that has a comparative advantage in providing the factors required to perform it. Thus it could locate labor-intensive production in low-wage countries like Malaysia or Mexico and locate R & D activities in countries that have capable scientists who can do the work but who do not have to be paid high salaries. As an example, many American companies—Microsoft, Oracle, Hewlett-Packard, Novell, Motorola, and Texas Instruments—established centers for software development work in India, where qualified personnel to write innovative software are plentiful and can be employed for as little as $300 a month. Similarly, many U.S.-based companies have established service centers outside of America in order to gain added cost efficiencies. For instance, when talking with a Compaq computer service representative, a customer is actually talking with a technical advisor in Ottawa, Canada. Service centers for various firms have been established in countries like Ireland, India, and the Philippines as well during the first part of the twenty-first century. Practical Insight 1.3 illustrates these strategies.

A firm could enjoy the benefits of *scale economies* like lower costs and higher quality resulting from specialization by designating one plant to serve as the sole producer of a component for use in the final assembly of a product. For example, a plant in the Philippines may make transmissions, another in Malaysia the steering mechanisms, and one in Thailand the engines. Each country would then do the final assembly of the complete automobile. Toyota Motor Company is rapidly moving in this direction. Practical Insight 1.4 on page 32 illustrates steps taken by Dell Computer to take advantage of scale economies and proximity to key markets to reduce transportation costs.

The concept of scope economies is based on the notion that savings and cost reductions will accrue when two or more products can share the same asset, such as a

PRACTICAL INSIGHT 1.3

ACHIEVING COMPETITIVE ADVANTAGE THROUGH INDIA'S COMPARATIVE ADVANTAGE

After slowing in the wake of the Sept. 11 terrorist attacks, outsourcing by American companies to Indian concerns or to their own Indian units has begun to pick up. The new contracts span the technology-related spectrum, going well beyond the software code writing of the last decade to include chip design, product development, call centers, consulting and other support services. They give Indian companies the opportunity to expand their repertory with work that holds much promise for future growth. And they account for a significant chunk of business in India, especially here in Bangalore and the country's other high-technology cities.

In just the last few months, dozens of Indian concerns have garnered contracts from big American companies to take over pieces of their operations. A unit of the Bangalore-based Wipro, India's third-largest software and services exporter, will be handling some of the worldwide reservation services for Delta Air Lines, a move that Delta expects will save $12 million to $15 million annually.

India's top software company, Tata Consultancy Services, or T.C.S., part of India's Tata conglomerate, has signed up Lehman Brothers—in a $70 million-a-year deal shared with Wipro—as well as J. P. Morgan Chase, Fidelity Investments and GE Medical Systems. The local unit of Cognizant Technology Solutions, a custom software developer and services provider in Teaneck, N.J., has contracts for projects from MetLife, to upgrade its human resources administration system and streamline some computer applications, and from the UnitedHealth Group and Sallie Mae, the student loan provider.

For the American companies, which account for more than two-thirds of the work coming to India, the country has several advantages. Though wages in India have been rising, they still tend to be much lower than in the United States. That is particularly attractive in the current global economy, cost-sensitive executives say, as they follow the outsourcing path set in the early 1990's by technology companies from Silicon Valley seeking cheaper software coding operations. India also has a large, well-educated, English-speaking work force with one of the world's largest clusters of engineers and programmers.

Even Bill Gates, the Microsoft chairman who is widely revered here, has given his imprimatur. "A couple of years ago, the biggest American corporations would have considered it risky to outsource mission-critical work to India, but it is now becoming a common-sense proposition," Mr. Gates said on a visit to Bangalore last month. Microsoft is expanding its development center in the high-tech city of Hyderabad and is outsourcing some back-office work to Wipro.

The software and back-office services outsourcing is one of India's fastest-growing businesses. In the year ended March 31, it accounted for nearly 3 percent of India's gross domestic product, up from 0.3 percent three years earlier, and is expected to increase to 7 percent in 2008. It has also contributed substantially to the country's healthy state of foreign exchange reserves in recent years.

According to Gartner Inc., a research firm based in Stamford, Conn., India is leading the world in offshore outsourcing services, with annual revenue of $8 billion, and outsourced projects from American companies to Indian concerns will become increasingly common. Gartner has, however, warned that American companies that rush into outsourcing deals with Indian companies solely to cut costs are usually soon in trouble and that India's competitive edge over places like China could vanish if India does not continue to upgrade the infrastructure and stay on top of quality control.

India's three top software exporters—Wipro, T.C.S. and Infosys Technologies—said that with the post-Sept. 11 lull ended, they are busy fending off Irish, Philippine and other

production plant, distribution channel, brand name, or staff services (legal, public relations, etc.). A global company like Coca-Cola enjoys a competitive advantage because it is in a position to produce two or more products in one plant rather than two separate plants, market its products through common distribution channels, and share its world-famous brand name across a wide range of products.

Managing Risks

A global company faces a number of different types of risk including economic, political, cultural, legal, and competitive. The nature and severity of such risks are not the same for all countries. A global company is in a position to manage such risks effectively by planning and implementing effective strategies aimed at diffusing risk.[42] For example, in a country that has high levels of unemployment, a global company could

competitors. But they think they have the global edge. "No country is able to offer the cost-to-quality advantage and scaling up opportunities that India does," said N. G. Subramaniam, T.C.S.'s vice president. Companies that start with a few dozen people in a pilot project could increase to thousands in a matter of months, he said.

Many also have been working toward becoming one-stop shops. "Early Indian services companies typically gained backdoor entry as code cutters but moved up the value chain to take on strategic parts of the client's business," said Vivek Paul, vice chairman of Wipro. For instance, he said, his company's first task for Home Depot was to maintain applications, but Wipro moved up by writing software to run computerized tasks and maintaining it in all Home Depot outlets.

As the scope of work farmed out to India has broadened, so has the spectrum of American companies doing the outsourcing. Companies in the credit card, insurance and financial services industries were among the first, in the early 1990's, but new converts include even some older, highly regulated industries like utilities. Back-office and information technology service operations, like processing employee payrolls or fielding phone calls from customers, are now moving to India at an even brisker pace than outsourced software projects. Acknowledging the influx, the National Association of Software and Services Companies, the industry trade group known as Nasscom, has raised its projections for the country's back-office services industry to $21 billion, from $17 billion, by 2008.

Software companies like Wipro and Satyam Computer Services, meanwhile, are taking on the big consulting firms for large-scale consulting deals. The mostly back-office and services jobs have been flooding across India, beyond the high-tech hot spots and into big cities like Delhi and Bombay, even as American companies continue to announce layoffs. That has spurred some criticism in the United States. Recently,

when New Jersey state senator Shirley K. Turner discovered that a welfare and food stamp contractor had moved its customer service center to Bombay from Wisconsin, she sponsored a bill to require that workers on state contracts be American citizens, or legal aliens, or have some specialty for which such workers cannot be found. The bill was approved this month and forwarded to the state Assembly.

Back in India, outsourcing companies have been busy recruiting. One, ICICI oneSource, a Bangalore-based back-office concern owned by the Indian financial services giant ICICI Group, has attracted thousands of young "customer jockey" hopefuls for its call center with ads in the local newspapers saying "The C.J. Hunt is on!"

Such jobs are changing the lives of the thousands of young, urban men and women who fill the positions, toiling largely at night, synchronizing their work schedules with Americans halfway across the globe. Saranya Sukumaran, 21, who is just out of college and three months into her first job, takes home 10,000 rupees, or just over $200, a month from her job on the help desk at the local unit of an American Internet service provider in a country where nearly half the population survives on less than $1 a day. From 10:30 P.M. to 7:30 A.M. five days a week, and calling herself Sharon "no last name," she responds to calls that have been routed to Bangalore. The money enables her to help her father, a junior official with the state-owned phone company who earns 15,000 rupees a month, support the household. It also allows her to grab a $1 coffee at the hip cafes dotting Bangalore and splurge on luxuries like Levi's jeans and a Nokia cellphone. "As a teenager I wished for so many things," she said. "Now I'm my own Santa Claus."

Source: From Saritha Rai, "India is Regaining Contracts with U.S.," December 25, 2002. Copyright © 2003 The New York Times Co. Reprinted with permission.

deflect restrictive and unfriendly governmental policies by sourcing products for world markets in that country, thus increasing much-needed employment opportunities for the local populace. An example of such a strategy is the transfer of significant amounts of car production to the United States by Japanese automakers like Toyota, Honda, and Nissan. One of the principal motivations behind this strategy was to minimize the growing anti-Japanese sentiment in the United States due to the alleged job losses caused by Japanese imports.

The benefits of scale economies must be weighed against their risks. A plant located in a country because of its low wages could lose its locational advantage if the wage rates in the country rise significantly because of economic development or appreciation of the country's currency. Global companies manage such risks by distributing production in more than one country even at the expense of benefits derived from lower scale economies. Japanese car companies have managed currency and wage-rate

PRACTICAL INSIGHT 1.4

DELL COMPUTER'S SUPPLY CHAIN EXTENDS INTO CHINA

Dell Computer's competitive advantage lies in its manufacturing acumen, an upstream activity in the value chain. Dell has dispersed its manufacturing operations to large manufacturing plants strategically located in various parts of the globe primarily to take advantage of scale economies and proximity to key markets to reduce transportation costs. Now, Dell is making a big push to lower costs and prices across the board—especially in the two largest markets, Japan and China. In the past, most of the Dell computers that ended up in Japan were built at the company's giant facility in Malaysia. Now, Dell is making PCs for the Japanese market at a factory in the southeastern Chinese city of Xiamen. The switch means Dell saves a third off its manufacturing and shipping costs, says Amelio—savings Dell can pass on to customers. Dell's market share in Japan jumped from 3.8% in 2000 to 5.8% in 2001, according to Gartner Group Inc. consultants, a surge that Dell execs attribute to better management and lower prices.

Source: Reprinted from Bruce Einhorn, Andrew Park and Irene M. Kunii, "Will Dell Click in Asia? The PC Marker is Going All Out to Win a Bigger Piece of the Pie," April 22, 2002 issue of *BusinessWeek* by special permission. Copyright © 2002 by The McGraw-Hill Companies, Inc.

risks caused by rising wage rates in Japan and the much stronger Japanese yen compared to the U.S. dollar by exporting cars made in U.S.-based plants back to Japan. The flexibility afforded to Japanese car companies by having plants both in the United States and Japan was responsible for their effective management of risk. Chapters 3 and 4 further delineate the various political, legal, economic, and cultural environments and associated risks.

Innovation and Learning

A global company has a distinct advantage over its purely domestic competitor because of the multiple environments in which the global company operates. A company that has operations in many countries is exposed to a diversity of experiences and stimuli. Being in many countries allows it to develop a variety of capabilities.[43] A global company has opportunities to learn skills and acquire knowledge of a country, which can be transferred and applied in many other countries where it has operations.[44] For example, a company that has operations in Japan can learn about the very best aspects of the Japanese management system and adapt and use those that are most useful in its American or European operations. General Electric is marketing in India an ultrasound unit designed by Indian engineers, using technology developed in GE's Japanese operations.

Hewlett-Packard has continued pouring resources into the Asian region, opening a laboratory in Japan and new manufacturing facilities in Japan and Malaysia, while simultaneously beefing up its engineering, project management, and design capacity in Singapore. Such investments provide not only increased sales in the region but also skills and expertise in how to improve the production process, something that it lacks in the United States. Hewlett-Packard has learned process improvement techniques from its Asian operations and transferred the knowledge not only to its U.S. operations but also to operations worldwide.

Eli Lilly & Company, a global pharmaceutical corporation, and Ranbaxy Laboratories Limited, India's largest pharmaceutical company, have formed a path-breaking alliance to set up joint ventures in India and the United States. In the first phase, a state-of-the art research, development, and manufacturing facility is being set up in India to

FIGURE 1.3
The International
Environment

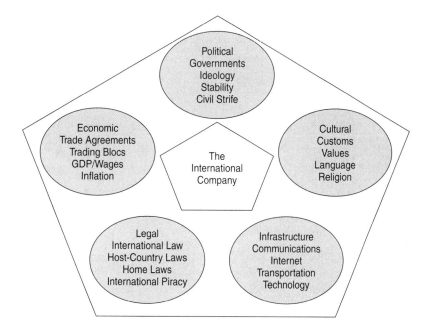

develop products for the U.S. market by undertaking chemical, pharmaceutical, and analytical research. Lilly's strategy apparently is to tap into the research capabilities of Indian scientists, and thereby to learn and develop innovative new products and processes. Moreover, the development of a new patented pharmaceutical product costs $800 million or more in the United States, but it may cost as little as $200 million in India.[45]

The framework we have discussed in this chapter is very useful in identifying possible sources of competitive advantage for an international company. However, the suggested strategies must be translated into operating decisions that can realize the broader goals. We explore this topic in depth in Chapter 6 and illustrate how an international firm establishes the optimum mix of functional and geographic integration to achieve its strategic objectives. But before we take up the issue of strategy, we turn in the next section to a discussion of the environmental context within which the international firm must operate. In the next chapter, we set the stage with an overview of the current global economic environment, highlighting some trends that are important for international managers.

The Environment of International Management

A manager in an international company performs her or his managerial functions in an environment that is far more complex than that of her or his counterpart in a domestic company (see Figure 1.3). The international environment is the total world environment. However, it is also the sum total of the environments of every nation in which the company has its foreign affiliates. The environment within each nation consists of five dimensions: economic, political, legal, cultural, and technological. Exhibit 1.3 lists the factors typically found in each of these environments. We examine the new economic infrastructure that includes trade agreements and regional economic integration initiatives in Chapter 2, the political dimension in Chapter 3, the legal dimension in Chapter 4, and the cultural dimension in Chapter 5.

EXHIBIT 1.3
The International
Environment

Economic Environment

Economic system
Level of economic development
Population
Gross national product
Per capita income
Literacy level
Social infrastructure
Natural resources
Climate
Membership in regional economic blocs
(EU, NAFTA, LAFTA)
Monetary and fiscal policies
Wage and salary levels
Nature of competition
Foreign exchange rates
Currency convertibility
Inflation
Taxation system
Interest rates

Political Environment

Form of government
Political ideology
Stability of government
Strength of opposition parties and groups
Social unrest
Political strife and insurgency
Governmental attitude toward foreign firms
Foreign policy

Legal Environment

Legal tradition
Effectiveness of legal system
Treaties with foreign nations
Patent trademark laws
Laws affecting business firms

Cultural Environment

Customs, norms, values, beliefs
Language
Attitudes
Motivations
Social institutions
Status symbols
Religious beliefs

Technological Environment

Inventions
New-product development
New-process innovations
Internet capabilities

Summary

This chapter provides an introduction to international management and to the world of the so-called international company. The nature of international business was explained first, and we saw that the need for international management and managers arises for many strategic and market reasons.

Although there are scores of small international companies, generally when one speaks about them, the reference is to the large multinationals. Increasingly, people are referring to these giant companies with operations throughout the world as international, multinational, and global companies. Because the other connotations are used more specifically in later chapters, we use the term international companies to define the entities with overseas sales and/or operations. International management and international companies are more or less like conjoined twins or the two sides of a coin. The growth of international companies has resulted from the astute management of these enterprises by international managers. And the management of these corporations epitomizes what international management is all about.

We saw something of the dimensions and drastic growth of multinational companies since the 1960s. We surveyed not only the different international business activities of international companies, but also the various international mindsets including the global, multidomestic, and transnational orientations. We also examined the typical stages in the evolution of international companies as well as the market-based, cost-

FIGURE 1.4   International Management: A Model of International Management

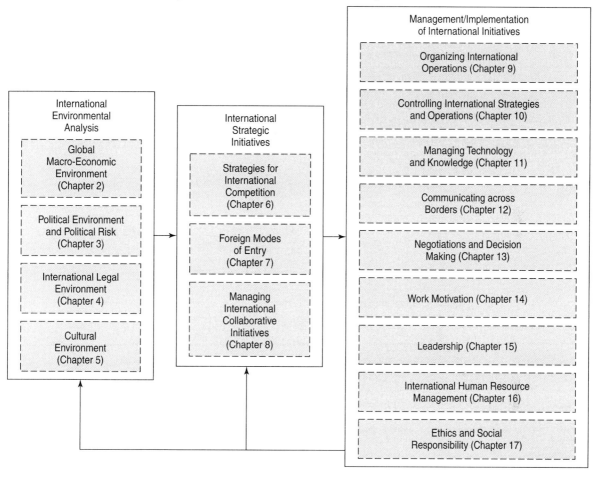

based, and strategic motives a firm has to expand internationally. After this, we studied how global companies exploit economies of scale, economies of scope, and national differences to achieve their three generic objectives: (1) efficiency in current operations, (2) managing risks, and (3) innovation, learning, and adaptation. We concluded by introducing the nature and complexity of the international environment of international companies. Figure 1.4 illustrates the roadmap for the remainder of the book.

Key Terms and Concepts

cost reduction motives for international expansion, *21*
evolution into an international enterprise, *16*
foreign direct investment (FDI), *5*
global orientation, *15*

global strategy, *28*
international business, *7*
international company, *8*
international management, *8*
international mindsets, *14*
market-seeking motives for international expansion, *20*

multidomestic orientation, *15*
strategic motives for international expansion, *23*
transnational orientation, *15*
transnationality index, *12*

Discussion Questions

1. What is international business? How does it differ from international management?
2. Discuss the characteristics of multinational companies. What forces have contributed to their development and growth?
3. How does a domestic company typically evolve into one that is multinational? How and why does change occur in the relationship between the parent company and foreign affiliates as the company becomes multinational?
4. Distinguish among the global, multidomestic, and transnational orientations exhibited by international companies.
5. What are strategic, cost-based, and marketing-based company motives to expand overseas?
6. Identify and explain the three categories of broad objectives of global companies. What strategic actions can a global company take in order to develop competitive advantage against its competitors?
7. Discuss the key differences between economies of scale and economies of scope.
8. Discuss how national differences can serve as a source of competitive advantage for a global company.

Minicase

Want to Be More Efficient, Spread Risk, and Learn and Innovate at the Same Time? Try Building a "World Car"

Japanese car companies like Toyota and the Honda Motor Company are pioneering the auto industry's truly global manufacturing system. The companies' aim is to perfect a car's design and production in one place and then churn out thousands of "world" cars each year that can be made in one place and sold worldwide. In an industry where the cost of tailoring car models to different markets can run into billions of dollars, the "world car" approach of Toyota and Honda—and which Ford is hoping to emulate—is targeted at sharply curtailing development costs, maximizing the use of assembly plants, and preserving the assembly line efficiencies that are a hallmark of the Japanese "lean" production system.

As for Honda, the goal is to create a "global base of complementary supply," says Roger Lambert, Honda's manager of corporate communications. "Japan can supply North America and Europe, North America can supply Japan and Europe, and Europe can supply Japan and the United States. So far, the first two are true. This means that you can more profitably utilize your production bases and talents."

The strategy of shipping components and fully assembled products from the U.S. to Europe and Japan couldn't have come at a more opportune time for the Japanese car companies, especially when political pressures are intense to reduce the Japanese trade surplus with the United States. The task was made easier due to the strength of the Japanese yen, which has risen about 50 percent against the U.S. dollar. That has made production of cars in the United States cheaper, by some estimates, by $2,500 to $3,000 per car. That saving more than compensates for the transportation costs for a car overseas. For the first time, Toyota is creating a system that will give it the capability to manage the car production levels in Japan and the United States. It is moving toward a global manufacturing system that will enable it to enhance manufacturing efficiency by fine-tuning global production levels on a quarterly basis in response to economic conditions in different markets.

Source: Adapted from Paul Ingrassia, "Ford to Export Parts to Europe for a New Car," *The Wall Street Journal,* September, 29, 1992, p. A5; Jane Perlez, "Toyota and Honda Create Global Production System," *The New York Times,* March 26, 1993, pp. A1, D2.

DISCUSSION QUESTIONS

1. Discuss the strategies implemented by Toyota and Honda to achieve greater efficiency in car production.

2. How do the automobile companies plan to simultaneously manage risk and gain efficiencies?

3. Discuss how the car companies use national differences to gain a strategic advantage in the global car industry.

Notes

1. Richard E. Caves, "International Corporations: The Industrial Economics of Foreign Direct Investment," *Economica* 38, no. 141 (1971), pp. 1–27.

2. John D. Daniels and Lee H. Radebaugh, *International Business: Environment and Operations,* 6th ed. (Reading, MA: Addison-Wesley, 1992), p. 8.

3. Donald A. Ball and Wendell H. McCulloch Jr., *International Business: Introduction and Essentials,* 4th ed. (Homewood, IL: BPI/Irwin, 1990), p. 17.

4. Betty Jane Punett and David A. Ricks, *International Business* (Boston: PWS/Kent, 1992), p. 7.

5. Charles W. L. Hill, *International Business,* 4th ed. (New York: McGraw-Hill /Irwin, 2003), p. 29.

6. Endel J. Kolde and Richard E. Hill, "Conceptual and Normative Aspects of International Management," *Academy of Management Journal,* June 2001, p. 120.

7. Jean J. Boddewyn, "The Domain of International Management," *Journal of International Management* 5, no. 1 (Spring 1999), p. 5.

8. Ibid.

9. Ibid., p. 121.

10. Kolde and Hill, "Conceptual and Normative Aspects of International Management."

11. Boddewyn, "The Domain of International Management," p. 9.

12. Arvind V. Phatak, *International Management: Concepts and Cases* (Cincinnati: South-Western College Publishing, 1997), p. 3.

13. The Business Week Global 1000, *Business Week,* July 15, 2002, www.businessweek.com.

14. All statistics in this paragraph are from United Nations Conference on Trade and Development, *World Investment Report 2002* (Geneva: UNCTAD, 2002), Chapter 1.

15. Ibid., Chapter 1, Table 1, p. 4.

16. Ibid., Patterns of Export Competitiveness, Chapter 6: Largest Transnational Corporations, p. 90.

17. United Nations Conference on Trade and Development, *World Investment Report 2000: Cross Border Mergers and Acquisitions and Development* (New York: United Nations, 2000), p. 87.

18. Howard V. Perlmutter, "The Tortuous Evolution of the Multinational Corporation," *Columbia Journal of World Business* 4, no. 1 (1969), pp. 9–18.

19. Sumantra Ghoshal and Nitin Nohira, "Internal Differentiation within Multinational Corporations," *Strategic Management Journal* 10, no. 4 (1989), p. 323–338.

20. Christopher Bartlett and Sumantra Ghoshal, "Managing across Borders: New Strategic Requirements," *Sloan Management Review* 28, no. 4 (1987), pp. 7–18.

21. Wenpin Ysai and Sumantra Ghoshal, "Social Capital and Value Creation: The Role of Interfirm Networks," *Academy of Management Journal* 41 (1998), pp. 464–478.

22. Nitin Nohira and Sumantra Ghoshal, *The Differentiated Network: Organizing MNCs for Value Creation* (San Francisco: Jossey-Bass, 1997).

23. Ivan M. Manev and William B. Stevenson, "Nationality, Cultural Distance, and Expatriate Status: Effects on a Managerial Network in a Multinational Enterprise," *Journal of International Business Studies* 32, no. 2 (2001), p. 285.

24. Center for Research in Electronic Commerce, University of Texas, 1999 Report.

25. R. Vernon, "International Investment and International Trade in the Product Life Cycle," *Quarterly Journal of Economics* 80 (1965), pp. 190–207.

26. D. Sethi, S. E. Guisinger, S. E. Phelan, and D. M. Berg, "Trends in Foreign Direct Investment Flows: A Theoretical and Empirical Analysis," *Journal of International Business Studies* 34, no. 4 (2003), pp. 315–326.

27. Chris Sparks, Theo Bikoi, and Lisa Moglia, "A Perspective on U.S. and Foreign Compensation Costs in Manufacturing," *Monthly Labor Review,* June 2002, pp. 5–15.

28. Peter J. Buckley and Mark Casson, *The Economic Theory of the Multinational Enterprise* (London: St. Martin's Press, 1985).

29. Sethi, Guisinger, Phelan, and Berg, "Trends in Foreign Direct Investment Flows," p. 325.

30. Ibid., p. 319.

31. Ibid., p. 100.

32. S. H. Hymer, *The International Operations of National Firms: A Study of Direct Investment* (Cambridge, MA: MIT Press, 1960).

33. A. M. Rugman, *International Diversification and the Multinational Enterprise* (Lexington, MA: Lexington Books, 1979).

34. R. E. Caves, "Industrial Corporations: The Industrial Economics of Foreign Direct Investment," *Economica* 38 (1971), pp. 1–27; J. H. Dunning, "Toward an Eclectic Theory of International Production: Some Empirical Tests," *Journal of International Business Studies* 11, no. 1 (1980), pp. 9–31.

35. Roger Kashlak, former director for Italy for AT&T International, personal communication.

36. F. T. Knickerbocker, *Oligopolistic Reaction and the Multinational Enterprise* (Cambridge, MA: Harvard University Press, 1973).

37. Gary Hamel and C. K. Prahalad, "Do You Really Have a Global Strategy?" *Harvard Business Review* 63, no. 4 (1985), pp. 139–149.

38. Saritha Rai, "World Business Briefing, Asia: India: G. M. to Invest in Technology Center," *New York Times,* June 26, 2003, p. W1.

39. Sumantra Ghoshal, "Global Strategy: An Organizing Framework," *Strategic Management Journal* 8 (1987), pp. 425–440.

40. Ibid., p. 427.

41. Alan M. Rugman, *Inside the Multinationals: The Economics of International Markets* (New York: Columbia University Press, 1981).

42. Kent D. Miller, "A Framework for Integrated Risk Management in International Business," *Journal of International Business Studies* 23, no. 2 (1992), pp. 311–334.

43. Bruce Kogut and Sea-Jin Chang, "Technological Capabilities and Japanese Foreign Direct Investment in the United States," *Review of Economics and Statistics* 73 (1991), pp. 401–413.

44. John J. Dunning, "Multinational Enterprises and the Globalization of Innovative Capacity," *Research Policy* 23 (1994), pp. 67–68.

45. Comments made by G. P. Garnier to Arvind V. Phatak at the Greater Philadelphia Global Award of which Mr. Garnier was the awardee, June 12, 2003.

CHAPTER TWO

The Global Macroeconomic Environment

Chapter Learning Objectives

After completing this chapter, you should be able to:

- Discuss potential effects of the growth of regional trade blocs on global free trade.
- Explain the differences between and similarities of a free trade area, a customs union, a common market, an economic union, and a political union.
- Describe the static and dynamic benefits of regional economic integration as well as the supply-side-led benefits that will accrue to member countries.
- Describe the key features of the Uruguay Round of the General Agreement on Tariffs and Trade and the World Trade Organization and their implications for the conduct of business between member countries.
- Discuss the significance of the World Trade Organization to international trade.
- Describe the important characteristics of the North American Free Trade Agreement and the European Union.
- Discuss the ways in which the major regional economic agreements can be expected to improve business opportunities and problems associated with their implementation.
- Examine the phenomenon of globalization and its meaning.
- Evaluate the significance of country-specific economic features and competitiveness rankings to international companies.

Opening Case: High-Tech Transnationals Take "Stateless" to the Next Level

When the first reports surfaced at 12:17 P.M. Pacific Time on Aug. 11, 2003, that the Blaster computer virus was on the loose, researchers at antivirus-software company Trend Micro Inc. scrambled to come up with a fix. Meanwhile, the company's five global alert commanders began sizing up Blaster via cell-phone calls and e-mails. At 1:55 P.M., Hammud Saway, the commander based in Japan, declared a global alert, signaling that this virus was nasty enough to require all the company's resources. Just 51 minutes later, a cure was ready. The company routinely is among the first responders to viruses, often delivering 30 minutes before market leader Symantec Corp., according to GEGA IT-Solutions in Germany, a response tester.

Trend Micro is able to respond so quickly partly because it's not organized like most companies. It has spread its top executives, engineers, and support staff around the world to improve its response to new virus threats—which can start anywhere and spread like wildfire. The main virus response center is in the Philippines, where 250 engineers are willing to work the evening and midnight shifts necessary to keep ever-vigilant. Then there are six other labs scattered from Munich to Tokyo. "With the Internet, viruses became global. To fight them, we had to become a global company," says Chairman Steve Chang, a Taiwanese who started the company in 1988.

Trend Micro is among a new breed of high-tech companies that defy conventional wisdom about how corporations ought to operate. While most large companies have extensive worldwide operations, these companies go much further—aiming to transcend nationality altogether. C. K. Prahalad, a professor at the University of Michigan Business School, calls this the fourth stage of globalization. In the first stage, companies operate in one country and sell into others. Second-stage multinationals set up foreign subsidiaries to handle one country's sales. And the third stage involves operating an entire line of business in another country.

What's different about these outfits—call them transnationals—is that even the executive suite is virtual. They place their top executives and core corporate functions in different countries to gain a competitive edge through the availability of talent or capital, low costs, or proximity to their most important customers. Trend Micro's financial headquarters is in Tokyo, where it went public; product development is in PhD-rich Taiwan; and sales is in Silicon Valley—inside the giant American market. When companies fragment this way, they are no longer limited to the strengths, or hobbled by the weaknesses, of their native lands. "This is very new, and it's important," says Prahalad. "There's a fundamental rethinking about what is a multinational company," he says. "Does it have a home country? What does headquarters mean? Can you fragment your corporate functions globally?"

There has long been talk of the stateless corporation—*BusinessWeek* even ran a cover story on it in 1990. Yet the dispersal of key corporate functions takes the idea one step further, and it's made possible by advances in technology, especially the Internet. Harvard Business School Professor Christopher A. Bartlett says improved communication is allowing an evolution toward "an integrated global network of operations." To deal with the gaps between time zones and cultures, these tech transnationals operate like virtual computer networks. Thanks to the Internet, they can communicate in real time via e-mail, instant messenger, or Web videoconferencing. Over time, these scattered experiments could coalesce into a powerful new model for business. Bartlett and other management experts say the strategy of truly globalizing core corporate functions is applicable for all kinds and sizes of companies.

Tech's transnationals are popping up all around the world. They range from business-intelligence-software maker Business Objects (BOBJ) with headquarters in France and San Jose, Calif., to Wipro (WIT), a tech-services supplier with headquarters in India and Santa Clara, Calif., to computer-peripherals maker Logitech International (LOGI) with headquarters in Switzerland and Fremont, Calif. While no one tracks the numbers, *BusinessWeek* interviewed executives at a dozen such companies, and new ones keep popping up. For instance, 24/7 Customer, a business-services provider with headquarters in Los Gatos, Calif., and Bangalore, India, just raised $22 million from Silicon Valley venture capitalists.

Running a transnational company is a tough management challenge, though. Executives are separated by oceans and time zones, making it difficult to maintain basic communications and routines that old-style companies take for granted. Then there are the cultural chasms. "The curse is that national cultures can be very different," says Trend Micro's Chang. "We have to figure out how to convert everybody to one business culture—no matter where they're from." That's why Chang is visiting the company's 20-plus sites and laying out a set of common values. Chang, who learned to do magic tricks when he performed at his parents' bowling alley in Taiwan during his youth, breaks the ice by performing sleight-of-hand with cards or coins.

In spite of the complexities of spanning the globe and a sluggish economic environment, most of these tech transnationals have been delivering outstanding financial results. Of the dozen companies

BusinessWeek studied, the average revenue increase last year was 25.4%, vs. a 4% decline for the overall tech industry, says market researcher IDC.

These companies use geo-diversity to great advantage. Logitech, for instance, has placed its manufacturing headquarters in Taiwan to capitalize on low-cost Asian manufacturing. Meanwhile, its business-development headquarters in Europe has lined up strategic partnerships that have kept the company at the cutting edge of peripherals design, particularly for optical pens and mice. That has helped Logitech hold its own against mighty Microsoft in worldwide markets for peripherals.

For Wipro Ltd., there are clear pluses to locating sales in the U.S. and engineering in India. Wipro's vice-chairman, Vivek Paul, is based in Silicon Valley to be close to the mammoth U.S. market. At the same time, the company can underprice Western rivals because 17,000 of its 20,000 software engineers and consultants are in India, where the annual cost per employee is less than one-fifth that of Silicon Valley. There are even some unintended benefits from operating transnationally. To collaborate smoothly in spite of the geographic barriers, all of the Wipro managers file electronic activity reports with their superiors on Monday, who in turn pass them along, via e-mail, until summaries reach Paul, who travels nearly constantly. Not only does Paul stay plugged in wherever he is, but the report process "steps up the pace of the organization," he says.

This next big step in globalization won't be steady—or fast. Expect startups to experiment with new ways of operating, and a few innovative established companies to tinker with their geographic organizations. But being transnational requires fundamental and difficult shifts for the giants that might not be worth the trouble. Often, the transformation requires a unique leader—and extremely flexible business unit managers. Still, given the necessity to exploit new markets and to operate ever more efficiently, the pressure won't let up to create something approaching a corporation without a country.

Source: Reprinted from Steve Hamm, "Borders Are So 20th Century: High-Tech Transnationals Take `Stateless' to the Next Level," September 22, 2003 issue of *BusinessWeek* by special permission. Copyright © 2003 by The McGraw-Hill Companies, Inc.

Discussion Questions

1. Explain the effects of technology on globalization.
2. What are the effects of globalization on firms like Trend Micro and Wipro?
3. In your opinion, why has globalization occurred? What are your concerns regarding globalization?

A New Global Economy

During the past 15 years, many of the world's nations have increasingly tried to erase barriers to free trade that had been erected over time. Efforts to bring about freer trade among nations were begun with the General Agreement on Tariffs and Trade (GATT) negotiations as early as 1948 and with the Treaty of Rome in 1957, which created the European Economic Community. The real impetus to freer trade, however, was given by the recognition by nation-states that, in the long-run, the economic benefits of free trade would spread to the peoples of all countries. The success of the original European Economic Community and its evolution into the modern-day European Union (EU) promoted freer trade and investment flows among its member countries and raised the living standards of people in the union, demonstrating the power of the free market. Moreover, the fall of Communist regimes during the past 15 years has demonstrated the economic power of the free market over state regulation of economic activity. These developments played a major role in the global push favoring freer world trade.

Major developments favoring free trade include (1) the emergence of the World Trade Organization (WTO) and (2) the emergence of regional trade blocs, such as the

North American Free Trade Agreement (NAFTA), the expanded EU, and other regional trade arrangements like MERCOSUR in South America. In this chapter we review the movement toward global free trade, starting with the General Agreement on Tariffs and Trade and its successor, the World Trade Organization.

The General Agreement on Tariffs and Trade and the World Trade Organization

The **General Agreement on Tariffs and Trade (GATT)** was created in 1947, with 23 industrialized countries as the founding members, to set fair and common rules for the way each country must conduct its trade with others.[1] GATT was created after World War II for the principal purpose of reducing tariffs and removing nontariff barriers to international trade.* The single most important principle at the heart of GATT was that discrimination poisons trade. In keeping with this principle, GATT strove to ensure that every country in GATT open its markets equally to every other. And GATT upheld the principle of "national treatment," which requires countries to treat foreign business-people and foreign companies as they do locals.

Eight rounds of GATT-sponsored multilateral trade negotiations spawned significant reductions in tariff and nontariff barriers. From the 23 countries that took part in the first round in Geneva in 1947, the number of member countries in the eighth Uruguay Round had grown to 117. (Each round is identified by the name of the place where it took place.) The Uruguay Round was concluded in Geneva on December 15, 1993, after seven years of strenuous negotiations, and the biggest ever world trade treaty was signed in Marrakesh, Morocco, on April 15, 1994, amid hopes of a more equitable and cooperative world economic order.

What GATT Left Undone

The intent of GATT was to remove nontariff barriers altogether, and its new rules were designed to discourage their proliferation. However, countries inevitably continued to impose nontariff barriers against foreign competitors. These barriers included government procurement procedures that favor domestic suppliers; weak enforcement of antitrust laws designed to foster competition; restrictions on inward direct foreign investment; and arbitrary application of food safety regulations to block imports.

The issue of a uniform code for cross-border investments was not addressed by the Uruguay Round. Thus countries were left with no restrictions on under-the-table subsidies to attract foreign investments. Although the U.S. movie industry won eventual copyright protection worldwide for its movies, U.S. negotiators failed to break a European quota system that limited foreign programming and other domestic film subsidies. Also, much was left undone in the area of free trade and investment in services. U.S. negotiators were unable to secure agreement from Asian and developing countries to permit broader entry of U.S. financial services firms into their markets.

GATT has contributed significantly to a more harmonious world trade regime. However, new issues like trade and the environment, competition and antitrust policies,

*A tariff (or customs duty) is a tax imposed by a government on physical goods as they move in and out of a country. Examples of nontariff barriers are import and export quotas; subsidies to domestic producers or exporters; dumping of products (selling a product in one national market at a cheaper price than in another market); regulations to imports with respect to safety, health, marketing, labeling, packaging, and technical standards; and local content requirements.

and regionalism in trade (e.g., NAFTA, which is discussed later in this chapter) are coming to the fore as the world economy evolves.

The World Trade Organization

The Uruguay Round of GATT created the **World Trade Organization (WTO)** to enforce the GATT agreement.[2] In 1995 the WTO replaced GATT. GATT had always been considered a partial agreement among member nations, which allowed them to effectively ignore any GATT rulings they did not like. The WTO, by contrast, is an institution, not an agreement, which has the authority to set and enforce rules governing trade between more than 140 member countries. Thus GATT, which was set up in 1947 as a temporary entity, was transformed into a permanent trade body.

The WTO, with an elaborate institutional mechanism of councils and committees, oversees the implementation of the GATT agreement by member countries. All members of the WTO, large and small alike, have equal representation in the WTO's Ministerial Conference. The conference meets at least once every two years to vote for a director general, who appoints other officials.

Settlement of Disputes by the WTO

The **WTO dispute settlement procedure** calls for the establishment of a panel of trade experts who would be called upon to resolve disputes. The WTO selects the panel from a list of trade experts provided by member countries. If the two countries involved in the dispute are unable to agree on the members of the panel, the WTO director general selects the panel. The WTO must rule on member complaints within one year, which is quite an improvement over the five or more years it took under the GATT procedures. The panel hears from both sides and makes its decision in secret.

Decisions by the trade panels are binding unless overturned by consensus of the WTO membership. As was mentioned earlier, this is quite a departure from the GATT procedures that, absurdly, allowed countries found in violation of fair trade rules to unilaterally block unfavorable panel decisions by merely ignoring them. Under the WTO process, countries that win a case they filed before the WTO receive an automatic green light to undertake retaliatory measures against the offending country if that country does not change its practices. The country that is found guilty of violating fair-trade rules has two choices: (1) change its law or (2) face sanctions, most likely in the form of tariffs slapped on its exports by the complaining country.

Critics, especially in the United States, have expressed fears that the WTO could become a foreign-dominated Supreme Court that would result in a loss of national sovereignty of member countries. These critics are afraid that the WTO could make rulings that would put the U.S. environmental, health, and safety laws at risk by labeling them nontariff barriers, thus requiring the United States to repeal them. In reality, the WTO does not have the legal power to change U.S. laws—only the U.S. Congress can do that. This is equally true for every country in the WTO. No outside body can force a country to do anything it does not want to. However, the fears of the critics are valid to the extent that in choosing not to abide by the WTO rulings, the United States, or any other country, is subjecting itself to sanctions imposed by the complaining country or countries. International business experts believe that because of its economic strength and market size, the United States has little to fear from retaliation. Experts reason that even countries that win cases before the WTO would hesitate before retaliating and are more likely to negotiate with each other to arrive at a reasonable compromise.

Country-Level Economic Integration

Continental trade blocs are emerging in many parts of the world almost in tandem. This current wave of regionalism has three important features. First, almost every country belongs to at least one trade bloc. Second, most trade blocs have been formed among neighboring countries, many along continental lines. Third, regional arrangements are put forward or accelerated in various parts of the world. For example, in the Western Hemisphere, efforts are under way to expand NAFTA to include most countries of the Americas. In South America, countries have joined together to create the Free Trade Area of the Americas (FTAA). Also in western Europe, the European Union is continuing to add more countries that once belonged to the now-defunct Soviet bloc. In Asia and the Pacific, the ASEAN bloc is expanding to include more countries in East Asia.[3] NAFTA, FTAA, the European Union, and ASEAN will be covered later in this chapter.

Regional economic integration through trade blocs, such as the North American Free Trade Agreement (NAFTA), which includes Canada, the United States, and Mexico, and the European Union have served as primary catalysts in promoting the elimination of trade barriers and trade liberalization among bloc members. One or more of the following reasons may explain why regional groupings of countries in trade blocs are formed:

- Geographical proximity and often the sharing of common borders, as in the European Union and NAFTA.
- Common economic and political interests, as in the European Union and the ASEAN.
- Similar ethnic and cultural backgrounds, as in the Free Trade Area of the Americas.
- Similar levels of economic development, as in the European Union.
- Similar views on the mutual benefits of free trade, as in NAFTA.
- Regional political needs and considerations, as in the ASEAN.

Figure 2.1 illustrates the various levels that countries may economically integrate. There are five major types of trade blocs:

1. **Free trade area (FTA).** The loosest form of economic integration is the free trade area. Many of today's stronger agreements began as simple free trade areas. In a free trade area, bloc member countries eliminate trade barriers on trade among member countries but retain the right to impose their own separate trade barriers on trade with countries outside of the trade bloc. According to this definition, NAFTA is a free trade area.

2. **Customs union.** This agreement among member countries eliminates the duties and also establishes common external positions regarding trade with non–bloc members. For instance, a tariff on bicycles being imported from China would be the same for all countries participating in a customs union.

3. **Common market.** A common market is a customs union that also allows factor mobility, that is, the free movement of resources such as labor and capital. The European Union from the 1970s through the early 1990s is an example of a common market. Citizens of its member countries could move freely throughout the other countries. AT&T's first subsidiary in Italy in the 1980s hired a support staff from Ireland, England, and Germany as well as from Italy.

4. **Economic union.** An economic union is a common market wherein the national economic policies of member countries are also harmonized. That is, the member

FIGURE 2.1
A Hierarchy of
Regional Economic
Integration Initiatives

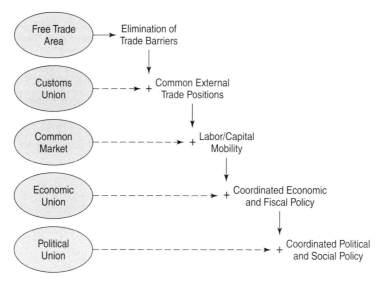

TABLE 2.1   Types of Trade Blocs

Source: Adapted from Franklin R. Root, *International Trade and Investment* (Cincinnati, OH: South-Western Publishing Company, 1992), p. 254.

Level of Integration	No Tariffs and Quotas	Common Tariffs and Quotas	No Restrictions on Factor Movements	Harmonized and Unified Economic Policies and Institutions	Unified Economic and Political Policies and Institutions
Free trade area	Yes	No	No	No	No
Customs union	Yes	Yes	No	No	No
Common market	Yes	Yes	Yes	No	No
Economic union	Yes	Yes	Yes	Yes	No
Political union	Yes	Yes	Yes	Yes	Yes

countries harmonize monetary and fiscal policies, environmental regulations, health and safety measures, agricultural policy, and technical standards. As opposed to a free trade area, a customs union, and a common market, which are created mainly by the removal of trade restrictions, an economic union demands the transfer of considerable economic sovereignty to supranational institutions. The European Union has moved to this status and has now implemented a common currency, called the *euro,* as ultimate evidence of economic integration.

5. **Political union.** A political union is the ultimate step in regional integration. Beyond the ties delineated as part of an economic union, the member countries of a political union will coordinate government and social policy as well. The former Soviet Union is an example of a political union, one that was forced upon its members. The Civil War in the United States between the North and the South was fought by the northern states to restore a political union called the Unites States of America after the South had seceded.

The essential features of each type of trade bloc are illustrate in Table 2.1.

The Effects of Economic Integration

Two main categories of effects result from **economic integration:** *static* and *dynamic.* We next examine how these effects emerge in a **common market** that provides common external tariffs and quotas against third countries and free movement of people, capital, and goods and services among member countries. Except for an economic union, a common market is the most advanced form of economic integration among countries.

Static Effects of Economic Integration

Common external trade barriers and free trade among member countries have both positive and negative effects on trade patterns. In his study of economic integration, particularly that of a customs union, Jacob Viner[4] formalized their economic benefits and costs, which may be called trade creation and trade diversion, respectively. The positive trade effect occurs when free trade among member countries leads to the substitution of inefficient domestic production in a common market country for efficient production in another country also in the common market. As an example, in the European Union, German consumers would be better off, after the lowering of tariffs, by importing products produced by a lower cost producer in Spain rather than a high-cost producer inside Germany. Trade is created between Germany and Spain, which did not exist before because tariffs on imports made the Spanish products noncompetitive against the German-made products. This is good, as it manifests comparative advantage at work. When such new trade is created among member countries without displacing third-country imports, the process is called *trade creation.*

Trade creation is a positive effect of free trade. However, lowering intraregional barriers leaves relatively high barriers on nonmembers. If this leads to a substitution of efficient third-country production by inefficient production in a common market country, *trade diversion* may result. Trade diversion occurs when consumers within a common market find that goods produced inefficiently in a member country are cheaper than efficiently produced goods in a country outside the common market, primarily because of the high tariffs imposed on imports from non–common market countries. As an example, suppose that the unit production cost of a car is $6,000 in Germany and $4,500 in South Korea. If the European Union imposes a 50 percent import tariff on imports of South Korean automobiles, the cost of Korean cars in Germany and in other European countries would be pushed above $6,000. Consumers in the European Union would therefore be more inclined to buy German cars, as opposed to Korean cars, resulting in a diversion of trade. This is bad: Comparative advantage is denied. Why? Because before the free trade was established, exporters of German and Korean cars faced the same tariff, so the importing country chose its suppliers on price and quality alone. With free trade within the common market, the importer switched to the less efficient supplier in Germany.

Under what circumstances would a common market lead to trade creation as opposed to trade diversion? Trade creation can generally be high when the economies of the member countries are very competitive and not specialized in the production of certain industries or products, that is, production is overlapping and diffused among member countries. Such conditions provide opportunities for specialization and intra–common market trade. On the other hand, if the economies of the countries prior to the formation of the common market were complementary, then opportunities for *new* trade are limited, because the economies are already specialized with respect to each other. Trade creation is expected to be high also when (1) the member countries in the common market are at similar levels of economic development; (2) the preunion tariffs of member countries were high, inducing trade creation in products that were once protected from imports; (3) transport costs are low; and (4) the size of the common market is large, because the larger the size, the greater the probability that producers would be able to lower costs through the scale effect. Trade diversion is more likely to occur in a common market of small economic size, because member countries would be inclined to protect their own relatively less efficient companies (due to higher unit costs because of the absence of the scale effect) against more efficient outsiders by raising the tariff barriers against imports.

The net effect of a common market depends on the size of trade creation relative to trade diversion. Trade creation improves the world's economic efficiency, and thus its potential welfare, by substituting lower cost production for higher cost production. Potential world welfare is lowered when trade diversion causes the substitution of higher cost production within the common market for lower cost production outside the union.

The best solution to ensure trade creation in a free trade area is to insist that "(a) members of a free-trade area set a common external tariff (and thus form a customs union) and (b) that the common tariff for any item should be set equal to the lowest tariff applied to that good by any member of the free-trade area before the union was formed."[5]

The ultimate solution to avoid trade diversion would be to eliminate all import tariffs. However, given the internal political realities of member countries, this solution may not be possible. The next best alternative would be to keep external tariffs at a bare minimum that would allow exporters in nonmember countries to compete against member country producers on factors such as quality, service, and design, but not necessarily on price.

Dynamic Effects of Economic Integration

Free trade arrangements can also have significant dynamic effects on economic growth. *Market extension* is one benefit of a common market. Producers have free access to the national markets of all member countries, unhindered by import restrictions. Similarly, consumers have access to products produced in all countries of the union. The enlarged market serves as a catalyst for many forces. It promotes *economies of scale,* not only in production, but also in marketing, research and development, and purchasing, as the large market size is able to support larger scale in these functions. Higher capital investment also boosts the returns to skilled labor by improving *productivity,* which in turn increases the accumulation of human capital, thus raising growth further. In common markets, labor mobility also increases productivity and growth as firms are able to hire skilled workers and professionals who are able to move freely in search of jobs where their abilities are most in demand. A larger market size also promotes entry of new competitors and intensifies *competition,* forcing producers to improve product and service quality, and to search for ways to lower costs by improving efficiency in all business functions. Intensified competition fosters the growth of efficient firms and the demise of inefficient ones. Growth of firms, either by internal growth, acquisition of smaller firms, or merger, results in increases in *firm size.* And large firms generally have much greater capacity to fund research and development and to compete by marketing innovative products.

Supply-Side Economics Effects

Figure 2.2 illustrates two streams of benefits of regional economic integration agreements. The first stream is derived from the lowering of per-unit costs as demand increases—assuming normal price elasticities—due to the initial lowering of price based on the removal of trade and investment restrictions. The second stream of benefits is

FIGURE 2.2
Regional Economic Integration Benefits

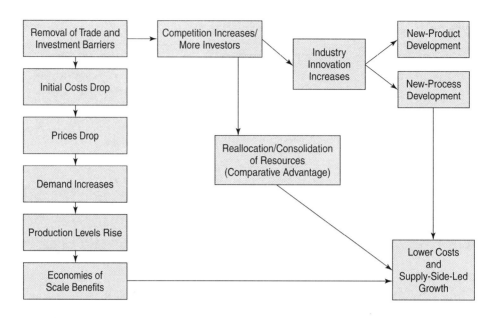

based on the increase of competition due to the emergence of a new mass market. The risk of investing is lowered and the purchasing power of the cooperative increases, thereby stimulating more investment. Increased competition will lead to new technological breakthroughs in systems and processes, which in turn lower cost. Furthermore, because of the dropoff of trade restrictions, companies can now consolidate operations in countries that have the comparative advantage within the integration agreement.

Regional economic agreements thus are supply-side-led initiatives. The producers are given the initial cost break, which is passed on to primary consumers and eventually trickles down to the entire economy.

Major Regional Economic Agreement Initiatives

The two most prominent regional trade blocs formed to promote regional economic integration are the North American Free Trade Agreement and the European Union. After we discuss these two agreement we consider other significant trade blocs throughout the world.

The North American Free Trade Agreement

The **North American Free Trade Agreement (NAFTA)** is a *free trade agreement.* It was ratified by the Congress of the United States in November 1993, and the agreement went into effect on January 1, 1994. NAFTA links the United States, Canada, and Mexico in a free trade area of 364 million consumers, 25 percent larger than the European Union,[6] and over $6.5 trillion of annual output. NAFTA unites the United States with its largest (Canada) and third-largest (Mexico) trading partners.

Building on the earlier United States–Canada Free Trade Agreement, NAFTA is expected to contribute to productive efficiency, enhance the ability of North American producers to compete globally, and raise the standard of living of all three countries. By improving the investment climate in North America, and by providing innovative companies with a larger market, NAFTA is expected to also increase economic growth. Mexico should benefit from more open and secure access to its largest market, the

FIGURE 2.3
Map of NAFTA

United States, increased confidence on the part of foreign firms to invest in Mexico, a more stable economic environment, and the return from abroad of Mexican-owned capital into the Mexican economy. Imports from Mexico to the United States from 1996 to 2000 increased by 42 percent, whereas exports from the United States to Mexico went up by 31 percent during the same period.[7] The importance of NAFTA is evident in the fact that 90 percent of all trade of Canada and Mexico occurs within the NAFTA countries, and for the United States, its trade with NAFTA countries accounts for about one-third of its total merchandise trade.[8] The clearest proof of NAFTA's success is that total trade among the three members more than doubled from 1993 (the year before NAFTA's implementation) to 2001, from $297 billion to $622 billion.[9]

Notwithstanding the long-term benefits of NAFTA to all three member countries, there has been grumbling from those industries that are affected by NAFTA's free trade initiatives. Loud complaints can be heard of job exports to Mexico by American companies to take advantage of Mexico's cheap labor. For example,

> We were promised as many as 2 million new jobs would be created in the U.S., but we've lost 750,000 manufacturing jobs that have been shifted to Mexico. While this is small in proportion to the U.S. total of 135 million jobs, it has lowered wage levels. That's because many of the workers who lost manufacturing jobs have had to take lower-paying jobs in U.S. service industries, such as health care and retail. In addition, U.S. manufacturers have used the threat of moving factories to Mexico as a weapon to bargain down wages.[10]

Similar complaints have been voiced by industries that have suffered lost markets to industries located north of the border. Practical Insight 2.1 illustrates one such complaint lodged by Mexican farmers.

In addition to dismantling trade barriers in industrial goods, NAFTA includes agreements on services, investment, intellectual property rights, agriculture, and strengthening of trade rules. There are also side agreements on labor adjustment provisions, protection of the environment, and import surges. The side agreement on labor adjustment was in response to American workers' concerns that jobs in the United States would be exported to Mexico because of the latter's lower labor wages and weak child labor laws and other conditions that afford Mexican labor an economic advantage over

PRACTICAL INSIGHT 2.1

IS THIS NAFTA'S FAULT?

On January 1, 2003, as the North American Free-Trade Agreement (NAFTA) enters its tenth year, a new phase of tariff reductions on farm produce will take place. The United States will eliminate tariffs completely on several Mexican items, including limes and winter vegetables. Mexico will eliminate them on a range of produce, including wheat, barley, rice, apples, potatoes and pork. This moves the two countries a step closer to the point, in 2008, when the last few tariffs on agricultural produce are due to be scrapped.

The Americans may be cheering, but Mexicans are not. These tariff reductions have occasioned the gloomiest predictions about the decline and fall of the entire agriculture sector, the end of the Mexican countryside, even the demise of the tortilla, the staff of Mexican life. In 2001, Mexico ratcheted up a deficit of more than $2 billion in farm trade with America. Once tariffs go, the country will surely be flooded by cheap American imports. Opposition politicians have been calling for the tariff reductions to be postponed, and even for NAFTA to be renegotiated.

Slim chance of that. But any Mexican government has to listen seriously to farmers, who make up a huge political constituency. About 8m people—22% of Mexico's active labor force—work in the countryside, although they generate only 4.4% of GDP. Yet rather than taking any difficult, strategic decisions, the government of President Vicente Fox has spent the past few months producing a tranche of subsidies, price supports and anti-dumping measures (such as a tariff of 46.5% on Yanqui Golden Delicious apples) to appease the farming lobby.

On November 18th, the government announced a $10-billion programme to "armour-plate" farmers against the supposed effects of the January tariff reductions, including higher price supports for certain grains.

Unfortunately, these measures have appeased nobody in Mexico, while escalating what is, in effect, a trade war with the United States. Farmers' groups in Mexico are unimpressed with the armour-plating, arguing that the $10 billion is in fact a re-formulation of existing funds. On the other hand, the only items that now seem to be freely traded between Mexico and the United States are recriminations over each country's subsidies. This week the under-secretary at the Department of Agriculture in Washington, J. B. Penn, argued that Mexico's subsidies "question the efficacy of agreements like NAFTA."

Sheer hypocrisy, the Mexicans reply. They are merely responding to President George Bush's farm bill, which will lavish about $180 billion on American farmers over the next ten years. Farmers north of the Rio Bravo are much more heavily subsidised than Mexicans; but they argue, in turn, that their subsidies are piffling compared with those enjoyed by farmers in Europe and Japan.

A subsidy war with America is one the Mexican government can never win in terms of hard cash. Neither will it help Mexico's farmers in anything but the shortest term, since subsidies merely entrench the manifest inefficiencies in the system. One government official in the rural state of Sinaloa, in the north-west, estimates that about 15% of subsidies, siphoned off by corrupt bureaucrats, never reach the farmers and producers in any case. More thoughtful Mexican farmers, such as

its American counterpart. The side agreement is an attempt to manage the terms of the potential change in labor markets brought about by the NAFTA accord. The agreement involves such issues as restrictions on child labor, health and safety standards, and minimum wages. In addition to signing the labor side agreement, the Mexican government has pledged to link increases in the Mexican minimum wage to productivity increases.

The side agreement on environmental cooperation explicitly ensures the rights of the United States to safeguard the environment. NAFTA maintains all existing U.S. health, safety, and environmental standards. It allows states and cities to enact even tougher standards, while providing mechanisms to encourage all parties to harmonize their standards upwards.

The side agreement on import surges creates an early warning mechanism to identify those sectors where explosive trade growth may do significant harm to domestic industry. It also establishes that, in the future, a working group can provide for revisions in the treaty text based on the experience with the existing safeguard mechanisms. During the transition period, safeguard relief is available in the form of a temporary snapback to pre-NAFTA duties if an import surge threatens serious injury to a domestic industry. These three side agreements were obviously negotiated to alleviate the fears of U.S. labor and industry groups that felt threatened by the immediate ad-

Eduardo Palau in Sinaloa, would rather see steadily liberalising trade than subsidies.

The 2003 tariff eliminations will, in fact, make almost no material difference. These tariffs have been gradually reduced since 1994; most of them will come down from only 1.5% or 2% to zero on January 1st. The real problem is not NAFTA and American subsidies, but Mexico's failure to adapt to trade liberalisation in general since the mid-1980s, when it first acceded to the General Agreement on Tariffs and Trade (GATT). Since gaining access to all those shiny new markets in America and the European Union, Mexican agricultural production has either declined, collapsed or grown only slightly. For all types of beans, for instance, production fell on average by 0.7% a year between 1980 and 2001. Wheat production has fallen by 57% since 1980, and soyabean production by about one-sixth. NAFTA merely accelerated all this. Mexicans, and world markets, have preferred cheaper alternatives.

It is the high cost of Mexican farming that makes it so uncompetitive. Mexican governments failed to take advantage of the ten-year transition period, while the tariffs were being phased out, to invest in infrastructure improvements such as irrigation. It is the high cost of Mexican farming that makes it so uncompetitive. Mr. Palau argues that farming in the state of Sinaloa has become almost as efficient as in the United States, with yields per hectare increasing from 2.9 tons in 1981 to 8.5 tons in 2001. But local farmers are still going out of business because their costs—from diesel to electricity to credit—are about a third higher than those north of the border. Poor transport makes a crucial difference: it costs about three times as much to deliver corn by rail from Sinaloa to Mexico City as it does to ship it there from New Orleans to Veracruz.

These are what the Americans this week politely, and correctly, called Mexico's "structural" challenges. While the country's farmers are being exposed to the full force of world competition, they are saddled with artificially high costs because much of the rest of the economy consists of public or private monopolies sheltering behind legal and constitutional barriers to competition.

The worst moment will come in 2008, when tariffs are eliminated on American corn. Because corn is so central to Mexican agriculture—using about 55% of cultivated land—it was afforded special protection under NAFTA in 1994, with a tariff of 206% on imports over 2.6m tons a year and a 15-year phase-out to zero. But so feebly have Mexican farmers risen to the challenge of feeding their own protected market that, since 1994, Mexican governments have regularly imported much more than the import quotas. Furthermore, they have not collected the revenue from the tariffs, arguing that they need cheap corn to keep the poor supplied with tortillas.

There are about 3m corn-growers in Mexico, with an average of five dependants each. Mexico's government has squandered the first ten years of NAFTA's transition period. It now has five years left to make its farms competitive. Don't hold your breath.

verse impact on their members. NAFTA is supposed to be the first step in the creation of a unified megamarket stretching from Alaska to Argentina in South America. This concept is supported by all Latin American countries, which are moving away from their protectionist economic policies toward privatization of state-owned enterprises and free enterprise. Still, because of political and economic concerns among countries in the region, NAFTA has been slower to expand than anticipated.

Free Trade Area of the Americas

The United States is committed to expand NAFTA to include all countries in the Western Hemisphere except Cuba. The effort to unite the economies of the Western Hemisphere into a single free trade agreement began at the Summit of the Americas, which was held in December 1994 in Miami. The region accounts for 37 percent of all U.S. trade and some $155 billion in American investment, 800 million people, and a $13 trillion economy. Negotiations among the Hemisphere countries began in June 1995 in Denver, with the last meeting in November 2002 in Quito, Equador. The participating countries are committed to conclude negotiations no later than January 2005, and to make the Free Trade Area of the Americas (FTAA) a reality no later than December 2005.[11]

The heads of state and governments of the 34 democracies in the region aim to construct an FTAA in which barriers to trade and investment will be progressively eliminated. The participating countries are Antigua and Barbuda, Argentina, Bahamas, Barbados, Belize, Bolivia, Brazil, Canada, Chile, Colombia, Costa Rica, Dominica, Dominican Republic, Ecuador, El Salvador, Grenada, Guatemala, Guyana, Haiti, Honduras, Jamaica, Mexico, Nicaragua, Panama, Paraguay, Peru, St. Vincent and the Grenadines, St. Lucia, St. Kitts and Nevis, Suriname, Trinidad and Tobago, Uruguay, the United States of America, and Venezuela. These countries expect that increased trade flows, trade liberalization, and investment in the Western Hemisphere will contribute to economic growth, job creation, higher standards of living, greater opportunities, and poverty reduction throughout the region.

Association of Southeast Asian Nations

The **Association of Southeast Asian Nations (ASEAN)** was established on August 8, 1967, in Bangkok by the five original member countries, Indonesia, Malaysia, Philippines, Singapore, and Thailand.[12] Brunei Darussalam joined in January 1984, Vietnam in July 1995, Laos and Myanmar in July 1997, and Cambodia in April 1999. The ASEAN region has a population of about 500 million, a total area of 4.5 million square kilometers, a combined gross domestic product of $737 billion, and a total trade of $720 billion.

The objectives of ASEAN are no different from those of any other trade bloc: (1) to accelerate the economic growth, social progress, and cultural development in the region, (2) to strengthen the foundation for a prosperous and peaceful community of Southeast Asian nations, and (3) to promote regional peace and stability. When ASEAN was established, trade among the member countries was insignificant. Estimates between 1967 and the early 1970s showed that the share of intra-ASEAN trade from the total trade of the member countries was between 12 and 15 percent. Thus some of the earliest economic cooperation schemes of ASEAN were aimed at addressing this situation. One of these was the Preferential Trading Arrangement (PTA) of 1977, which accorded tariff preferences for trade among ASEAN economies. Ten years later, an Enhanced PTA Program was adopted at the Third ASEAN Summit in Manila, further increasing intra-ASEAN trade.

The Framework Agreement on Enhancing Economic Cooperation was adopted at the Fourth ASEAN Summit in Singapore in 1992, which included the launching of a scheme toward an ASEAN Free Trade Area, or AFTA. The strategic objective of AFTA is to increase the ASEAN region's competitive advantage as a single production unit. The elimination of tariff and nontariff barriers among the member countries is expected to promote greater economic efficiency, productivity, and competitiveness. The Fifth ASEAN Summit held in Bangkok in 1995 adopted the Agenda for Greater Economic Integration, which included the acceleration of the timetable for the realization of AFTA from the original 15-year time frame to 10 years.

In 1997, the ASEAN leaders adopted the ASEAN Vision 2020, aimed at forging closer economic integration within the region. The vision statement also resolved to create a stable, prosperous, and highly competitive ASEAN Economic Region, in which there is a free flow of goods, services, investments, capital, and equitable economic development and reduced poverty and socioeconomic disparities. The Hanoi Plan of Action, adopted in 1998, serves as the first in a series of plans of action leading up to the realization of the ASEAN vision.

ASEAN cooperation has resulted in greater regional integration. Within three years from the launching of AFTA, exports among ASEAN countries grew from $43.26 bil-

FIGURE 2.4
Map of ASEAN
Members, 2000

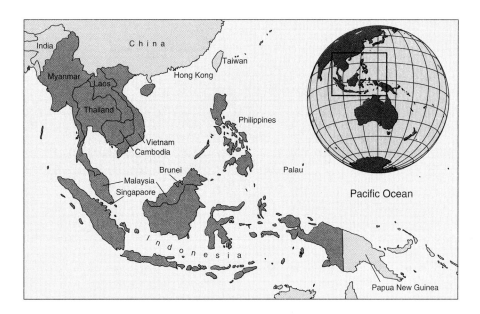

lion in 1993 to almost $80 billion in 1996, an average yearly growth rate of 28.3 percent. In the process, the share of intraregional trade from ASEAN's total trade rose from 20 percent to almost 25 percent. Tourists from ASEAN countries represent an increasingly important share of tourism in the region. In 1996, of the 28.6 million tourist arrivals in ASEAN, 11.2 million, or almost 40 percent, came from within ASEAN itself.

The expansion of ASEAN into a formidable trade bloc is quite possible given that cooperation with other East Asian countries has accelerated with the holding of an annual dialogue among the leaders of ASEAN, China, India, Japan, and the Republic of Korea.

MERCOSUR

By far the most promising free trade agreement is the MERCOSUR, comprising Argentina, Brazil, Paraguay, and Uruguay. The MERCOSUR (Mercado Común del Sur, the Common Market of the South) treaty was signed in March 1991. It committed the member nations to cut tariffs every six months, aiming to eliminate tariff barriers altogether and to create a full customs union behind a common external tariff by December 31, 1994. To meet the demands of the treaty, governments must continue to deregulate their economies. The aim is to link the four member countries in a market of nearly 200 million people covering an area of about 12.5 million square miles with a combined gross regional product in excess of $800 billion, creating Latin America's largest industrial base.[13] Other aims include increasing the negotiating power of the member nations in world trade negotiations, and competing more efficiently in international markets.

In August 1994, the presidents of the four countries formally agreed to form a customs union on January 1, 1995. This deadline was met, and both a free trade zone and a customs union have been in operation from that date. The customs union has common external tariffs in the modest range of zero to 20 percent on 85 percent of the products, with a projected common tariff for all MERCOSUR countries by 2006. Tariffs between the four countries were eliminated, although a short list of products still remain protected by each member nation. The MERCOSUR nations reached their

FIGURE 2.5
Map of MERCOSUR

agreement only after agreeing to disagree on areas where a lot of trade takes place. Capital goods, advanced electronics, and petrochemicals, which together comprise 15 percent of the trade, are treated differently from the rest.

MERCOSUR's founders envisioned not only free trade in goods, but also free movement of capital, labor, and services. Thus far, free trade in goods is almost in place, and steps have been taken to promote free movement of capital. However, no agreement for free trade in services or free mobility of labor appears likely in the near future. Nevertheless, experts in the area suggest that MERCOSUR is on the right track. The reason for such optimism is that technocrats in charge of all four countries are committed to free trade. Chile, the continent's most liberal economy, and Bolivia have become associate members since 1996.

MERCOSUR and the European Union are engaged in ambitious trade negotiations aimed at creating a free trade area between both regions covering goods, services, investment, and public procurement, as well as rules and disciplines for all sectors. This agreement aims at cutting tariffs for substantially all trade between both parties, thus providing for significant trade opportunities. Building on the proposal presented to MERCOSUR in July 2001, the EU offer foresees eliminating tariffs on 91 percent of imports from MERCOSUR into the EU. At the same time, the EU stands to gain from the tariff cuts proposed by MERCOSUR, since EU exporters currently face tariffs up to 35 percent on their exports to MERCOSUR.[14]

The European Union

The **European Union (EU)**—historically known as the Common Market—is an institutional framework for the construction of a unified Europe.[15] It was created after World War II to unite the nations of Europe through peaceful means and to create conditions for the economic recovery and growth of Europe after the devastation caused by the war. Fifteen countries are now members of the EU, and more than 320 million people share the common institutions and policies that have brought an unprecedented era of peace and prosperity to western Europe.

There are many similarities between the European Union and the United States. EU member countries have agreed to pool some of their sovereign powers for the

FIGURE 2.6
Map of the EU

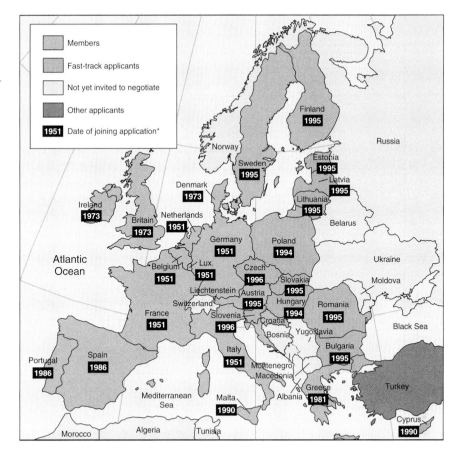

sake of unity, just as the American states did to create a federal republic. In fields where such delegation of national sovereignty has occurred—for example, in trade and agriculture—the EU acts as a full-fledged country, and it negotiates directly with the United States and other countries. EU member states retain their full sovereign powers in such fields as security and defense. The search for political unity is inspired by the U.S. federative model; however, Europeans realize that Europe will have to construct its own model for unification, one that takes full account of the rich historical, cultural, and linguistic diversity of the European nations.

The European Community Origins   On May 9, 1950, Robert Schuman, the French foreign minister, presented the so-called Schuman Declaration, a bold plan for lifting Europe out of the rubble of World War II. He proposed the pooling of European coal and steel industries as a first step toward a united Europe. Schuman's proposal called for the placement of coal and steel production of France and Germany under a common authority within an organization open to other European countries. The long-term objective of the Schuman Declaration was to lay the foundation for the economic integration of Europe, starting with coal and steel. Belgium, the Federal Republic of Germany, Italy, Luxemburg, and the Netherlands (Holland) accepted the French proposal. The six countries signed the European Coal and Steel Community (ECSC) Treaty in Paris on April 18, 1951. The six countries created the ECSC High Authority, to which each country transferred some of its sovereign power.

The Treaty of Rome On March 25, 1957, in Rome, the six nations signed two treaties, creating the European Economic Community (EEC) and the European Atomic Energy Community (EAEC). Both treaties were ratified by the parliaments of the six member countries before the end of the year. The EEC was created to merge the separate national markets of the six into a large single market, within which there would be free movement of goods, people, capital, and services. Common economic policies were also a goal of the EEC. The EAEC, or Euratom, was created to promote the use of nuclear energy for peaceful purposes.

The European Community (EC) is in fact three separate entities governed by separate treaties: the European Coal and Steel Community, the European Atomic Energy Community, and the European Economic Community. However, the name "European Community" has been in common use to refer to the three communities, since together they form a single political whole.

EC in 1992: Moving from a Common Market to an Economic Union Squabbles over the common agricultural policy coupled with the persistence of some old barriers and the creation of new ones during the 1970s—a period of "stagflation" (high inflation together with low economic growth) for most developed countries—compelled the EC to admit in the mid-1980s that its goal of a real common market was still far from reach. The main source of the EC's poor performance was attributed to the absence of an integrated Europe-wide market, which prevented European businesses from launching and implementing competitively efficient strategies. The answer was the 1985 White Paper by the EC Commission, which put forth a road map for the completion of an integrated internal market by the end of 1992. The 1985 White Paper listed almost 300 legislative measures needed to eliminate all physical, technical, and financial barriers to trade and commerce among the member countries. Specifically it called for a wide variety of reforms, including:

- An end to intra-EC customs checks and border controls.
- An EC-wide market for services, such as banking, insurance, securities, and other financial transactions.
- The mutual recognition of professional diplomas.
- The harmonization or mutual recognition of technical standards.
- The approximation of national rates and assessment criteria for EC's indirect taxes.

The EC member states signed the Single European Act (SEA) in February 1986. It became effective on July 1, 1987, after ratification by the 12 national parliaments (including the 6 original members and 6 additional countries that had joined the union). The SEA contains amendments to the EC treaties necessary to ensure the timely achievement of the 1992 program. The SEA not only aims at the completion of the integrated internal EC market, but it also calls for significant developments in economic and monetary policy, social policy, industrial relations, research and technology, and the environment. It also formalized procedures for cooperation in the sphere of foreign policy. Finally, the SEA renewed the commitment to transform relations among the member states into a European union.

At the end of 1992, the internal market became a reality. All frontiers between member countries were removed, as far as goods, services, and capital were concerned. There are no longer any customs controls on the EC's internal borders (between member states). Citizens of non-EC countries must show their passport and entry visas only at the first point of entry into any EC country, after which they can freely move anywhere within the EC member countries. Travelers may buy as many goods as they wish in any EC country for their own or their family's use, provided that they pay the appropriate tax on the goods in the country of purchase. Community citizens may take up residence in a member state other than their own as long as they wish. Professional qualifications are mutually recognized in all member states.

The EU and the Maastricht Treaty   The success of the Europe 1992 program and the changed political framework prompted the EC members to take a new step along the path of integration, creating the European Union. In Maastricht, the Netherlands, in December 1991, the heads of states of the EC member countries agreed on a Treaty on European Union. It was signed in February 1992, and after ratification by the parliaments of the EC member countries it came into force in November 1993. The Maastricht Treaty on European Union was just one more step on the road to a European constitution. Built on the structures that have been handed down, it forms an overall framework for various stages of integration.

The Maastricht Treaty on European Union had several new provisions, principally the following:

- Introduction of a common European currency by 1999.
- Eligibility for every European in the European Community to obtain a European passport, granting the person the right to move freely from one EC country to another.
- Cooperation in the fields of justice and home affairs, particularly in reference to police and judicial authorities.
- New powers allowing the EC to play a more active role in areas such as visa policy, trans-European transport, environmental protection, and consumer protection.
- Special rules on social policy and industrial relations. (These became necessary because one member state, the United Kingdom, opposed giving the EC additional responsibilities in this field or even stepping up cooperation.)
- Increased powers to the European Parliament to enact legislation.

Since Maastricht, economic integration has progressed rapidly in Europe. Trade statistics show that most of the trade of the European Union countries is with each other. With the introduction of the common currency, the euro, in 2001, the union of 15 member countries has matured into a unified market like the unified market of the United States.

Significant differences still remain between the nations. The costs of doing business vary considerably from country to country as wage rates, fringe benefits, and social security systems differ from country to country. For example, the former East Germany, the Mezzogiorno region of southern Italy, Portugal, and Greece all have lower labor costs than the rest of the member countries. And the level playing field that was supposed to come with a unified market has not completely materialized, as some governments continue to give generous subsidies to failing companies.

Future EU Expansion   During the past 45 years, the EC has enlarged its membership from 6 to 15 countries. Denmark, Ireland, and the United Kingdom joined in 1973. Greece joined in 1981, and Spain and Portugal became the 11th and 12th member states in 1986. In 1990, the former German Democratic Republic (East Germany) entered as part of a united Germany. On May 4, 1994, the EC members voted in favor of admitting Norway, Finland, Sweden, and Austria, and Finland, Sweden, and Austria joined. Norway, however, after a public referendum, refused the EC's invitation.

After successfully growing from 6 to 15 members, the European Union is now preparing for its biggest enlargement ever in terms of scope and diversity. Thirteen countries have applied to become new members. Ten of these countries—Cyprus, the Czech Republic, Estonia, Hungary, Latvia, Lithuania, Malta, Poland, the Slovak Republic, and Slovenia—are set to join on May 1, 2004. They are currently know by the term "acceding countries." Bulgaria and Romania hope to join by 2007, while Turkey is not currently negotiating its membership. To join the EU, they need to fulfill the economic and political conditions known as the "Copenhagen criteria," according to which a prospective member must:

- Be a stable democracy, respecting human rights, the rule of law, and the protection of minorities.
- Have a functioning market economy.
- Adopt the common rules, standards, and policies that make up the body of EU law.

The EU will assist these countries in taking on EU laws and will provide a range of financial assistance to improve their respective infrastructures and economies. But while the deal forged in Copenhagen paves the way for the largest expansion in the history of the EU, the candidate countries still face referendums at home on whether their people do in fact want to join. This may prove a troublesome task in many of the nations, especially Poland.

Will Regional Trade Blocs Promote Global Free Trade?

Will the existing trade blocs such as NAFTA, the EU, ASEAN, and MERCOSUR serve as catalysts for worldwide free trade? Trade among members of regional trade agreements is estimated at 43 percent of world merchandise trade.[16] Table 2.2 shows the dramatic increases in intrabloc exports during the 1990s. MERCOSUR's trade shows a drop in 1999 largely because of the economic and currency crisis faced by Argentina and Brazil during that period.

Will the trade blocs be able to achieve the vision of global free trade enshrined in the GATT and WTO charters discussed earlier? On one side, those who believe that trade blocs will not lead to global free trade base their opinion on events in the EU and NAFTA. In the EU, quotas were imposed on imports of Japanese automobiles to protect the European carmakers. In NAFTA, quotas restrict imports of some types of steel and textile products. The fear is that companies protected by common external tariff walls against competing imports will become complacent and inefficient, and they will ultimately demand ever-increasing protectionist measures for their own survival against foreign competition. Jagdish Bhagwati, one of the world's top trade theorists and adviser to the director-general of GATT (the precursor to the WTO), believes that "it is all too likely that regional trade blocs will advance the frontiers of liberal trade more slowly than the GATT, because governments will find it harder to resist the argument, put by protectionist lobbies, that 'our market is already large enough.' "[17]

On the other side are those who believe that trade blocs will expand their membership and add more countries. For instance, NAFTA has already made overtures to Chile, and there is speculation that NAFTA may eventually evolve into a large trade bloc—FTAA—that will include 34 countries in the Western Hemisphere. Similarly, the European Union, with 15 current members, is expected to expand to include all countries of western and eastern Europe during the first decade of this century. The enlarged EU will have a larger population than the United States; nevertheless, the gross domestic product of the United States is expected to be larger than that of the larger EU.

TABLE 2.2
Exports within Trade Blocs

Source: IMF, *Direction of Trade and Statistics Yearbook;* IMF, *Directory of Trade and Statistics Quarterly;* UNCTAD, *Handbook of International Trade and Development Statistics*

	1990	1995	1996	1997	1998	1999
NAFTA	$226,273	$394,472	$437,804	$496,423	$521,649	$581,162
EU	981,260	1,259,699	437,804	496,424	1,226,988	1,376,314
ASEAN	28,648	81,911	86,923	88,770	71,669	81,929
MERCOSUR	4,127	14,199	17,075	20,772	20,352	15,313

Finding that they are being discriminated against by the trade bloc countries, those countries that are left out of the trade blocs may seek to form their own trade blocs or, alternatively, seek special free trade agreements with existing trade blocs. Bhagwati offers such advice to countries like India. He believes that, in response to NAFTA and the EU, an Asian bloc may be formed, possibly centered on Japan, and countries like India that are marginalized on the outside should seek special free trade agreements with it. He believes that the Asian bloc, if it does materialize, would be inclined to seriously consider India's request because of its huge internal market and its potential as a sourcing country for foreign firms.[18] Thus, hypothetically, the number of trade blocs will multiply because each new trade bloc will serve as a stimulant for countries left on the periphery to form their own trade blocs.

Proponents of the theory that trade blocs will eventually lead to global free trade also suggest that free trade negotiations between and among trade blocs may lead to their becoming merged with one another. For instance, NAFTA and the EU may initially negotiate free trade in automobiles, which may be extended to other industries, and which in turn may eventually lead to a merger of the two blocs to form one mega–trade bloc that comprises all of the Americas and Europe. However distant the realization of this scenario may be, the thrust of the argument that free trade blocs would lead to global free trade seems valid.

Regardless of their ultimate effect on global free trade, the increasing importance of regional trade blocs will be a major consideration for international managers in the years to come, shaping the environment in which the international company does business. A significant phenomenon that was partly an outcome of the drive toward free trade is what is commonly known as *globalization*, a process that has resulted in increasing interconnectedness and interdependence among the nations of the world. Globalization has changed the landscape on which competitive battles are fought among companies in global industries. Globalization has opened up new markets that were once closed to foreign companies. Globalization has also brought into the forefront new opportunities and new challenges for international companies. The economic, political, legal, and cultural landscape has been altered by the forces that are driving the globalization engine faster and faster. We look at this phenomenon in the following pages.

Globalization

A dominant context that has had the greatest influence on the strategies and operations of international companies is the phenomenon of globalization. Much has been written about how the forces of globalization—the unremitting expansion of market forces, the breakneck speed with which capital moves around the globe, and the constant search for greater economic efficiencies—influence everything from indigenous cultures and environmental regulations to labor standards and patterns of productivity. The general catalysts of globalization were reviewed in Chapter 1. Now, we add to those general trends.

Globalization is a phenomenon that has remade the economy of virtually every nation, reshaped almost every industry and touched billions of lives, often in surprising and ambiguous ways. Definitions of globalization abound. For example,

"Globalization is a process fueled by, and resulting in, increasing cross-border flows of goods, services, money, people, information and culture."[19]

"The increasing interdependence of national economies in trade, finance, and macroeconomic policy."[20]

We define **globalization** as the growing economic interdependence of countries worldwide and the increasing integration of economic life across political boundaries, through the increasing volume and variety of cross-border transactions in goods, services, capital flows, and rapid and widespread diffusion of technology. Globalization is meant to signify integration and unity—yet it has proved, in its way, to be no less polarizing than the cold war divisions it has supplanted. The lines between globalization's supporters and its critics run not only between countries but also through them, as people struggle to come to terms with the defining economic force shaping the planet today. The debate over globalization's true nature has divided people in third-world countries since the phenomenon arose. It is now an issue in the United States as well, and many Americans—those who neither make the deals inside World Trade Organization meetings nor man the barricades outside—are perplexed.

The two sides in the discussion describe what seem to be two completely different forces. The issues debated by the proponents and opponents of globalization revolve around the role of international companies in the world economies. Questions such as the following are subject of intense debate:

> Is the world embedded in a global network of companies like Citicorp, CNN, Unilever, Microsoft, and IBM that will lead to the betterment of the quality of life of all mankind? Or is the welfare of mankind subservient to the domination and whims of greedy and corrupt global companies?

In all probability, this debate will not end in the foreseeable future. Managers in global companies would be challenged to implement corporate strategies that would induce the opponents to lower their criticism of the globalization phenomenon. To manage effectively in a globalized world, students of international management should understand the globalization phenomenon. So at the onset, let us review the forces that have served as the principal drivers of globalization.

Specific Drivers of Globalization

Tremendous Growth in International Trade and Commerce If shop windows everywhere seem to be filled with imports, there is a reason. International trade has been growing at a skyrocketing pace. World exports of merchandise and services amounted to $7.5 trillion in 2001, with merchandise exports accounting for $6 trillion. While the global economy has been expanding at a little over 3 percent a year, and countries in North America and western Europe at a rate of 3.1 and 2.3 percent, respectively,[21] the volume of world trade from 1990 to 2000 increased at the rate about twice that.[22] The increasing economic interdependence among countries of the world is evident in the fact that in the year 2001 alone, about $6 trillion of goods were sent from one country to another, up from $2 trillion a decade earlier.

Foreign products play a more important role in almost every country in the world. Just look at what you and I purchase and consume: To go to work, we drive cars made by Honda, Toyota, and Volkswagen in countries such as Brazil and Mexico in addition to the United States and Japan. To listen to music, we use a Korean-made CD player by Sanyo or Samsung, or one made by Sony from Japan. We wear Levi jeans made in Bangladesh. We drink Colombian-made coffee and Heineken beer from Holland. Parts of our Dell, Sony, and Compaq computers are sourced from dozens of countries. Similar consumption patterns exist in almost every country in the world. What is behind this dramatic growth in world trade? Some reasons follow.

Innovations in Information Technology and Transportation   The world has shrunk because of new developments in information technology, geopolitical changes, rapid growth in the speed at which people can travel around the world, and the push toward free and open trade. The countries in this world are connected by the rapid flows of knowledge and information carried by people, satellites, computers, and television.

A telephone call from the United States to India cost $5 per minute in 1960, and it took several hours to book the call through an international operator.[23] The transmission was very poor, and calls were disconnected without notice. Today it costs as little as 35 cents a minute for the same call, and all it takes to make the call is to dial the numbers on a land line or cellular telephone. In most countries cellular telephones have become as ubiquitous as toasters. One can now successfully place international telephone calls from anywhere to anywhere in the world.

Years ago, mail sent from India took two weeks to reach the United States. Now we can communicate via e-mail and chat on the Internet via Yahoo.com, Rediff.com, and AOL.com. Travel from India to the United States took four days by plane. Now, we can take off from Philadelphia and reach New Delhi 18 hours later.

Two decades ago there was no television in most of the developing countries in Asia, Africa, and Latin America. Now CNN, BBC, and Star TV blanket the television screens worldwide from transmissions originating in the United States, England, and Hong Kong, respectively. Satellite dishes on rooftops almost everywhere in the world allow villagers in the remotest parts of a country to see TV broadcasts emanating from all over the world.

Innovations in technology and transportation have promoted the interconnectedness of nations through the rapid dispersal and transfer of knowledge of products, processes, and lifestyles worldwide. Companies can now market their products worldwide via television commercials and banners on commercial Web sites. People can travel from one nation to another for in-person meetings and return home within days. Global teams comprising members from two or more countries can develop new products and processes via videoconferencing without leaving home.

Porous Borders between Countries   Before the 1970s, most countries placed strict limitations on the immigration of foreigners. Western European countries, the United States, and Australia have now opened the door to immigrants from other parts of the world. The Indian and Chinese diaspora has footprints worldwide, creating links between the adopted and mother countries of these two ethnic groups. Chinese expatriates have been transferring more than $60 billion annually to mainland China.[24] Indian expatriates have done the same to the tune of more than $10 billion annually.[25] A similar phenomenon is being played out in the case of Turkish immigrants to Europe and Koreans and Filipinos to the United States and East Asia. Furthermore, citizens of countries that belong to the European Union can travel freely, without passports or visas, throughout western Europe. They can work in any country in the EU without work permits.

Globalization and interconnectedness of countries have been enhanced by the lowering of barriers to immigration. We have witnessed an increase in the transfer of wealth, often accompanied by knowledge and technology from country to country, thereby contributing to the economic links between the adopted and mother countries. Multinational companies have been the beneficiaries of this trend as well. People with skills and expertise, from any country, can now be employed where they are most needed, anywhere in the world.

The Globalization of Financial Markets   What happens in the United States has an impact on Europe and the rest of the world. Interest rates, stock markets, currency values are all interconnected. Every day, $1.8 trillion in currencies are traded.[26] The currency and stock markets never sleep. Portfolio managers "hand off" portfolios from one market to another.

Today, the ability of a country to compete in world markets is often dictated by events in distant parts of the world. When coffee prices drop in Brazil because of a bumper crop in that country, prices of coffee drop in other parts of the world because coffee prices are set by the world commodity market. This would not have happened had there not been free trade among countries.

A recent implication of the global financial markets is the Asian crisis of the late 1990s. Chinese devaluation and a prolonged Japanese recession put downward pressures on the yuan and yen, respectively, as compared to currencies from Southeast Asia. The financial meltdown was helped as well as perpetuated because the Thai baht was linked with the U.S. dollar. As the U.S. dollar became stronger, the baht's value rose as well. Thai products and foreign investment opportunities became noncompetitive compared to countries like China.

The Creation of a Global Labor Force   People do not have to go where the jobs are. Jobs come to where the people are. The software industry in India is manned by Indian engineers and scientists who serve the needs of companies in Europe and America. Countries like China that can produce the cheapest and best quality products are dictating the world prices of consumer products. India is dictating the global prices of software development. We are fast approaching a global wage rate for skilled and unskilled workers. The global workforce determines the global prices of goods and services. This phenomenon is illustrated in Practical Insight 2.2

Rapidly Falling Freight Costs   One force that has gone unnoticed in promoting international trade is rapidly falling freight costs, that is, the costs of getting goods to market. High freight costs as a percentage of the sales price, or delays in shipments because of slow shipment of goods, can make trade impractical or impossible. Freight costs can have a huge impact both on the overall volume of trade and on individual countries' trade patterns. Trade costs today are less formidable than they used to be. This reflects three notable economic trends:

1. The world economy has become far less transport-intensive than it once was. At the turn of the twentieth century, international commerce was dominated by raw materials, such as wheat, wood, and iron, or processed commodities, such as meat and steel. These products are heavy and bulky. The cost of transporting them is relatively high compared to the value of the goods themselves, so transport costs had much to do with the volume of international trade, and countries tended to trade with their geographic neighbors. Today, finished manufactured goods, not raw commodities, dominate the flow of trade. And these are high-value goods such as computers, disk drives, and laser printers. The relative cost of transportation as a percentage of the

PRACTICAL INSIGHT 2.2

BACK-ROOM OPERATIONS IN INDIA

Thanks to the Internet and satellites, India has been able to connect its millions of educated, English-speaking, low-wage, tech-savvy young people to the world's largest corporations. They live in India, but they design and run the software and systems that now support the world's biggest companies, earning India an unprecedented $60 billion in foreign reserves—which doubled in just the last three years. But this has made the world more dependent on India, and India on the world, than ever before.

If you lose your luggage on British Airways, the techies who track it down are here in India. If your Dell computer has a problem, the techie who walks you through it is in Bangalore, India's Silicon Valley. Ernst & Young may be doing your company's tax returns here with Indian accountants. Indian software giants in Bangalore, like Wipro, Infosys and MindTree,

now manage back-room operations—accounting, inventory management, billing, accounts receivable, payrolls, credit card approvals—for global firms like Nortel Networks, Reebok, Sony, American Express, HSBC and GE Capital.

You go to the Bangalore campuses of these Indian companies and they point out: "That's G.E.'s back room over here. That's American Express's back office over there." G.E.'s biggest research center outside the U.S. is in Bangalore, with 1,700 Indian engineers and scientists. The brain chip for every Nokia cellphone is designed in Bangalore. Renting a car from Avis online? It's managed here.

Source: Reprinted from Thomas Friedman, "India, Pakistan and GE," August 11, 2002 issue of *BusinessWeek* by special permission. Copyright © 2002 by The McGraw-Hill Companies, Inc.

value of goods shipped even for heavy goods like cars and refrigerators has fallen precipitously because lightweight composites have replaced steel and light microprocessors do the job of huge control panels. And computer software can be "exported" without ever loading it on a cargo plane simply by transmitting it over telephone lines or satellites from one country to another.

2. The transportation industry has changed in remarkable ways, making it far cheaper and easier to ship goods around the world. "Containerization" and "intermodal transportation" have led to steep drops in the cost of cargo handling—and in the process, have lowered one of the biggest obstacles to trade.

3. The deregulation of the airlines and telecommunications has brought about a huge drop in the cost of air transport and data transfer. The cost of a three-minute telephone call has fallen from $300 (in 1996 dollars) in 1930 to $1 today.

The protests against globalization at the World Trade Organization's meetings in the United States, Europe, and the Middle East have brought to the forefront arguments both for and against the trend toward the increasing interdependence of nations. We now examine these differing views regarding globalization.

The Two Sides of Globalization

The growth of globalization has triggered a heated debate between constituencies supporting this phenomenon and those dramatically opposing it. We now present the arguments offered by scholars and practitioners who are in favor of globalization, followed by those of its opponents.

Arguments that Favor Globalization

The architects of globalization argue that international economic integration is not only good for the poor, it is essential. To embrace self-sufficiency or to deride growth, as some protesters do, is to glamorize poverty. The London-based Center for Economic Policy Research (CEPR) recently released a study on the positive aspects of globalization. The authors of the study noted that economic growth benefits the poor, and trade is good for growth. Closer economic ties between countries, lower tariff rates, and greater investment flows have had a large impact in reducing the poverty levels of low-income countries. Poverty levels can be further reduced as well if a low-income country accepts globalization policies and increases foreign investment opportunities. No nation has ever developed over the long term without trade. East Asia is the most recent example. Since the mid-1970s, Japan, South Korea, Taiwan, China, and their neighbors have lifted 300 million people out of poverty, chiefly through trade.

Proponents of globalization claim that it has improved the lot of hundreds of millions of poor people around the world. Poverty can be reduced even when inequality increases. And in some cases inequality can even decrease. The economic gap between South Korea and industrialized countries, for example, has diminished in part because of global markets. No poor country, meanwhile, has ever become rich by isolating itself from global markets; indeed, North Korea and Myanmar have impoverished themselves by doing so. Economic globalization, in short, may be a necessary, though not sufficient, condition for combating poverty. Markets have unequal effects, and the inequality they produce can have powerful political consequences. But the cliche that markets always make the rich richer and the poor poorer is simply not true.

As Hernando de Soto wrote in his book, *The Mystery of Capital,* "Globalization is occurring because developing and former communist nations are opening up their once protected economies, stabilizing their currencies and drafting regulatory frameworks to enhance international trade and private investment."[27] De Soto says that globalization will allow low-income countries to sell more exports, increase the wages of workers, entice new foreign capital, and become successful participants in the global marketplace. A salary of $5 a day is regarded as "shockingly poor" to antiglobalization protesters living in wealthy countries. Yet this salary level of a worker in a low-income country is five times higher than what a worker would have earned by remaining in an agricultural society. In other words, the switch to globalization policies has gradually improved workers' salaries in low-income countries. It is therefore up to wealthy countries to help integrate low-income countries in the free market economy by reducing tariffs and subsidies on agricultural products and textiles.

Globalization critics claim that corporations find the cheapest places to do business, which forces wealthy countries to purge their social safety nets and environmental standards. If this were true, say the proponents of globalization, then more investment would have flowed to the poorest countries in Africa, rather than predominantly to a small number of middle-income countries in Asia and Latin America. All things being equal, corporations shift production to those countries where labor is most productive, not cheapest. Cheap labor is not always the most productive. This critique is further discounted when figures show that 65 percent of employment of U.S. multinational corporations (MNCs) was in relatively high-wage countries, like those in western Europe, and the balance in relatively low-wage countries.[28] The notion that U.S. MNCs establish foreign operations in low-wage countries to produce for the U.S. market is also unfounded, as only 17 percent of sales of foreign subsidiaries were to U.S. customers.[29] Moreover, MNCs establish foreign operations not just to take advantage of cheap labor, but also for strategic reasons, such as exploiting a potentially large market, tapping into technology and knowledge, taking advantage of competitive forces, following major customers abroad, using locational advantage (e.g., advantage derived from being in the EU or in Hong Kong for entry into Chinese market).

Lately, technology has been the main driver of globalization. The advances achieved in computing and telecommunications in the West offer enormous, indeed unprecedented, scope for raising living standards in the third world. New technologies promise not just big improvements in local efficiency, but also the further and potentially bigger gains that flow from an infinitely denser network of connections, electronic and otherwise, with the developed world.

What has growth-through-integration meant for all the developing countries that have achieved it so far? Proponents of globalization claim that in terms of improving living standards of the common citizen, globalization is the difference between South Korea and North Korea, between Malaysia and Myanmar, between Europe and Africa.

If there is a showcase for globalization in Latin America, it lies on the outskirts of Puebla, Mexico, at Volkswagen Mexico. Every new VW Beetle in the world is made here, 440 a day, in a sparkling clean factory with the most sophisticated technology. The Volkswagen factory is the biggest single industrial plant in Mexico, employing 11,000 people in assembly-line jobs, 4,000 more in the rest of the factory—with 11,000 more jobs in the industrial park of VW suppliers across the street making parts, seats, dashboards, and other components. The average monthly wage in the plant is $760, among the highest in the country's industrial sector. The factory is the equal of any in Germany, the product of a billion-dollar investment in 1995, when VW chose Puebla as the exclusive site for the new Beetle. It is estimated that more than 50,000 people work in other companies around Mexico that supply VW.[30]

Arguments against Globalization

Having discussed the arguments in favor of globalization, let us not ignore contrary points of view. In the 1980s, the so-called Washington Consensus—highly influenced by the Reagan and Thatcher administrations in the United States and United Kingdom, respectively—held that government was in the way. The administrations pushed for privatization, deregulation, fiscal austerity, and financial liberalization in countries' economies.

Opponents of globalization argue that globalization and deregulation of the economy do not work if the institutions required to make them work are absent. A case in point is Russia, where open markets and globalization have not worked as well as anticipated due to the absence of institutions such as a reliable banking system, an effective legal system, and a culture that understands the market economy and how it should function.

To revisit the VW Mexico "showcase" example above, the value Mexico adds to the Beetles it exports is mainly labor. Technology transfer is limited in part because most foreign trade today is intracompany trade, which is particularly impenetrable to outsiders. Although Volkswagen buys 60 percent of its parts in Mexico, the "local" suppliers are virtually all foreign-owned and import most of the materials they use. Although the country has gone from assembling clothing to assembling high-tech goods, nearly 40 years later 97 percent of the components used in Mexican "maquiladoras" are still imported, and the value that Mexico adds to its exports has actually declined sharply since the mid-1970s.[31] Without technology transfer, work in maquiladoras is marked for extinction. As transport costs become less important, Mexico is increasingly competing with China and Bangladesh—where labor goes for as little as 9 cents an hour. This is one reason that real wages for the lowest paid workers in Mexico dropped by 50 percent from 1985 to 2000. Businesses, in fact, are already leaving to go to China.

Joseph Stiglitz suggests that "the gap between the poor and the rich has been growing, and even the number in absolute poverty—living on less than one dollar a day—has increased." He also suggests that "the developed world needs to do its part to reform the international institutions that govern globalization."[32]

Arguments that favor or oppose globalization can affect the operations of multinational companies. There have been instances of firebombing of the offices of multinational companies in various parts of the world. Hostility toward globalization could inhibit the flow of capital, technology, and people to parts of the world that are inhospitable and dangerous to the safety of human life and property. The same forces that have contributed to globalization of companies have done the same for Osama bin Laden. His terror network could not exist without the infrastructure that is now available to him to carry out his terrorist activities. The significance of hitting the World Trade Center's twin towers in Manhattan cannot be ignored. It was a direct hit at the global financial system of the world led by the United States and the Western world.

Many of the things that have left sophisticated Western societies vulnerable to terrorist attacks are the very efficiencies that have come as a consequence of persons', companies', and countries' relentless search for efficiency and maximum productivity. Curbside check-in, e-tickets, streamlined procedures for border crossings, freer immigration policies in industrialized societies, and just-in-time delivery of international packages and shipping were all introduced to help improve productivity and advance competitiveness.

Several of these efficiencies have been either temporarily discontinued or curtailed in the name of improving security. The fundamental question is whether all, or just some, of these globalization-era improvements will be among the early casualties of the war on terrorism, sacrificed in order to reduce societal vulnerabilities and to restore domestic tranquility. This remains to be seen.

Country-Specific Economic Environments and Country Competitiveness

The macroeconomic environment has been the focus of the chapter thus far. The macroeconomic environment is the global canopy under which international business is conducted. As they create the global strategies for their companies, managers must also examine the country-specific economic environments to look for particular opportunities or challenges that each country environment has to offer.

Table 2.3 provides the demographic data for five countries: the United States, Japan, Germany, India, and China. We chose these countries for our analysis because of their great importance to international companies. India and China have very large populations. More than a third of the populations in all five countries are 65 years and older, and more than 400 million people in India and China are in this age group. Which industries would stand to gain from marketing their products in these two countries? Probably those industries that serve the older citizens with services and products such as nursing homes, geriatric pharmaceuticals, and wheelchairs.

How products are marketed depends on the literacy rate. Printed advertisements and product-user manuals would not be effective in countries like India, with a large incidence (48 percent) of illiteracy. Companies in India have resorted to use of pictures and symbols to convey marketing messages. For example, to promote the benefits of a small family, billboards in India show a picture of a couple with two healthy children, and another picture next to it depicting a couple with five skinny children. The message on this billboard is "two are better than five."

Table 2.4 displays statistics on the economic conditions in the five countries. Although the average gross domestic product per capita is low in India and China, 34 and 30 percent of the populations in India and China, respectively, have the highest incomes in the land. Various sources have estimated that almost 100 million to 200 million Indians have purchasing power equal to that of the middle class in the United States, which has a total population of approximately 280 million. This means that the

TABLE 2.3   Demographic Data

Source: UNESCO Institute for Statistics, 2003.

	United States	Japan	Germany	India	China
Area (sq km)	9,158,960	374,744	349,223	2,973,190	9,326,410
Population (2002 est.)	280,562,489	126,974,628	83,251,851	1,045,845,226	1,284,303,705
Age 15–64 (%)	66.40	67.50	67.60	62.60	68.40
Literacy (% 1979)	97.00	99.00	99.00	52.00	81.50

TABLE 2.4   Economic Data

Source: UNESCO Institute for Statistics, 2003.

	United States	Japan	Germany	India	China
GDP ($0000, 2001 est.)					
Exchange rate basis	8.978	5.606	2.703	0.043	1.159
PPP[a] basis	10.082	3.55	2.184	2.66	6
GDP/capita ($) (OECD[b])	$35,200	$32,600	$22,500	$41	$889
GDP/capita (PPP basis) (OECD)	$35,200	$26,400	$26,300	$2,540	$4,600
GDP by sector					
Industry (%)	18	31	31	25	18
Agriculture (%)	2	1	1	25	49
Services (%)	80	68	68	50	33
Income					
Highest 10% (%)	31	22	25	34	30
Lowest 10% (%)	2	5	4	4	2
Poverty (%)	13	0	0	25	10
Inflation (CPI[c] % 2001)	2.80	−0.90	1.30	5.40	−0.80
Productivity output/capita (1989)	18,282	15,336	13,752	1,093	2,538

[a]PPP: Purchasing Power Parity
[b]OECD: Organization for Economic Cooperation and Development
[c]CPI: Consumer Price Index

market in India for products that the typical middle-class population can afford to buy is at least one-third the total population of the United States and more than three times larger than the total population of Canada, which is almost 32 million. Companies should not therefore merely look at the very low per capita income in India and conclude that the Indian market is negligible at best. Rather, companies would be prudent to look more deeply at the total number of people in the country who have the purchasing power to buy the products sold by the company.

Data on the communications infrastructure are shown in Table 2.5. All three developed countries—the United States, Japan, and Germany—have a much larger density of telephone and cellular phone use than India and China. People in the United States and Europe take for granted the ease of use of telephones and cell phones for domestic and long-distance calls. Communications within a company and with customers and suppliers is not that easy in India and China, although in large metropolitan areas in these countries the availability and use of telephones and cell phones are extensive. It is next to impossible to conduct telephone surveys for market research in India and China. In contrast, citizens in the United States are constantly bombarded by telemarketers.

The density per square mile of radio and television stations is far lower in India and China than in the United States, Japan, or Germany. Similarly, there is a very low density per capita of ownership of radios and televisions in India and China. Only 6 and 31 percent of the Indian and Chinese populations own a television set, whereas 78 percent of

TABLE 2.5 **Communications Infrastructure**

Source: UNESCO Institute for Statistics, 2003.

	United States	Japan	Germany	India	China
Telephone lines in use (1997)	194,000,000	60,381,000	50,900,000	27,700,000	135,000,000
Per capita	0.69	0.48	0.61	0.03	0.11
Cellular phones (1998)	69,209,000	63,880,000	55,300,000	2,930,000	65,000,000
Per capita	0.247	0.503	0.664	0.003	0.051
AM radio stations (1998 est.)	4,762	585	51	153	369
Per million sq/km	520	1,561	146	51	40
FM radio stations (1998 est.)	5,542	574	787	91	259
Per million sq/km	605	1,532	2,254	31	28
Radios (1997)	575,000,000	120,500,000	77,800,000	116,000,000	417,000,000
Per capita	2.05	0.95	0.93	0.11	0.32
TV stations (1997)	1,500	211	373	82	209
Per million sq/km	164	563	1,068	28	22
TVs (1997)	219,000,000	86,500,000	51,400,000	63,000,000	400,000,000
Per capita	.781	.681	.617	.060	.311
Internet service providers	7,000 (2002 est.)	73 (2000)	200 (2001)	43 (2000)	3 (2000)
Internet users (2002)	165,750,000	56,000,000	32,100,000	7,000,000	45,800,000
Per population	.591	.441	.382	.007	.036

Americans have at least one set. The use of radio and television for advertisements is pervasive in developed countries like the United States, Japan, Germany, and most wealthy countries in Europe. Millions of U.S. dollars are spent on 30-second advertisements on the major television networks. Companies spend such huge sums because of the high density per capita of television set ownership. This is not the case in India and China. Although both countries now can get several domestic television stations and all major international networks, the penetration of the marketing message is quite shallow because of the low television set ownership in these countries.

International companies are obliged to use other methods, in addition to radio and television, to advertise their products in India and China. Advertising on billboards, buses, trains, and taxis is the preferred method of communicating with customers. Multinational companies must therefore do the following before deciding on the foreign entry mode:

1. Determine the key success factors for the business, that is, the conditions that must be present in the foreign market in order to succeed in achieving the objectives of the market entry.
2. Study whether these conditions exist in the target market.
3. Determine changes in implementation strategies that would be required in order to succeed in the target market.

In general, the international firm must understand the economic environments, infrastructure development relative to other nations, and effects of membership in a regional economic integration agreements for various countries. This understanding will subsequently lead to a deeper understanding of relative country competitiveness. As has been implied throughout this chapter, countries compete in global trade markets as well as for foreign direct investment inflows. Thus international firms must be aware of each country's relative competitiveness before deciding where to expand. Table 2.6 lists the World Economic Forum's 2003 competitive ranking regarding growth opportunities for the top 30 countries, as well as for China and India. The five countries spotlighted in the earlier tables are highlighted.

TABLE 2.6
Competitive Ranking of Countries, 2003

Source: World Economic Forum: "Global Competitiveness Report."

Country	Competitiveness Ranking	Country	Competitiveness Ranking
United States	**1**	Hong Kong	17
Finland	2	Austria	18
Taiwan	3	Israel	19
Singapore	4	Chile	20
Sweden	5	South Korea	21
Switzerland	6	Spain	22
Australia	7	Portugal	23
Canada	8	Ireland	24
Norway	9	Belgium	25
Denmark	10	Estonia	26
United Kingdom	11	Malaysia	27
Iceland	12	Slovenia	28
Japan	**13**	Hungary	29
Germany	**14**	France	30
Netherlands	15	**China**	**33**
New Zealand	16	**India**	**48**

In the next few chapters, we turn to an examination of additional macro-level dimensions of that environment seen in Figure 1.3 in Chapter 1: the political, legal, and cultural dimensions of international business. Our discussion generally assumes the standpoint of individual country differences. However, to the extent that countries are united into trade blocs, the blocs themselves may also be a useful focus for addressing these environmental dimensions.

Summary

A major environmental context within which international companies conduct their global business is the WTO and its push toward global free trade, taking into account the progress toward integration of member countries of regional trade blocs such as NAFTA, FTAA, and the European Union. Not all trade blocs are alike; some are more developed in integrating the economies of the member countries than others. The European Union and its 15 member countries represent the most developed of the trade blocs.

Economic trade blocs can cause trade creation when new trade among member countries does not displace third-country imports. Trade creation is a positive effect of free trade. However, lowering intraregional barriers leaves relatively high barriers on nonmembers. If this leads to a substitution of efficient third-country production by inefficient production in a common market country, it may result in trade diversion. Trade blocs should create economic conditions that would not require policies leading to trade diversion.

Free trade arrangements can also have significant dynamic effects on economic growth. Market extension is one benefit of a common market. Producers have free access to the national markets of all member countries, unhindered by import restrictions. Similarly, consumers have access to products produced in all countries of the union.

GATT and its successor, the WTO, have been the driving forces to promote free trade. International companies stand to gain from the push in favor of free trade because free trade opens new markets around the world. Through its dispute settlement mechanism, the WTO provides global companies and member nations with a mechanism for resolving trade disputes.

The phenomenon called globalization is the driving force that is pushing the depth and breadth of international business and international companies in the world economy. Globalization is the cause of, as well as the result of, the growing interdependence of nation-states throughout the world. Several forces are the drivers of globalization. These drivers will, in all probability, intensify the speed of globalization in the years ahead. Globalization has ardent supporters as well as vehement opponents. Only time will tell which viewpoint prevails.

Key Terms and Concepts

Association of Southeast Asian Nations (ASEAN), *52*
common market, *46*
customs union, *44*
economic integration, *46*
economic union, *44*
European Union (EU), *54*

free trade area (FTA), *44*
General Agreement on Tariffs and Trade (GATT), *42*
globalization, *60*
North American Free Trade Agreement (NAFTA), *48*

political union, *45*
World Trade Organization (WTO), *43*
WTO dispute settlement procedure, *43*

Discussion Questions

1. Will NAFTA evolve into an economic union like the European Union in the future?
2. Are you in favor of free trade, even if it causes unemployment in some domestic industries?
3. Does the WTO impinge on the sovereignty of nation-states?
4. Is globalization inevitable in the world today? Can the drivers of globalization be controlled by nation-states?

Minicase

A Global European Consumer?

In 1983 Leif Johansson was a manager at Electrolux, a Swedish appliance maker. Electrolux was ready for expansion beyond the small Swedish market. Johansson was swayed by studies that showed Europe was becoming more homogeneous. In particular the study showed that unexpected parts of Europe had increased pasta consumption. It was assumed that all types of European markets would begin to show the same type of homogeneity. Johansson envisioned being able to sell the same appliance models across all of Europe, as is done in America. He persuaded his superiors to purchase Zanussi, an Italian appliance manufacturer, to increase Electrolux's European market share.

A decade later, Johansson, now Electrolux's president, has found that lifestyles in Europe are not quite as homogeneous in the appliance market as they are in the pasta market. The different parts of Europe show drastic differences in preferences when it comes to refrigerators. These preferences are mostly derived from cultural differences. In northern Europe, customers prefer larger refrigerators because they shop weekly in supermarkets. They also prefer to have the freezer on the bottom. In southern Europe, customers prefer smaller refrigerators because they shop almost daily at outdoor markets. They prefer the freezer on top. In Britain customers prefer mostly freezer, about 60 percent, as they eat lots of frozen foods. Because of such strong preferences, Johansson found that he was unable to pursue his corporate vision of selling the same models of appliances to all of Europe.

To compete in Europe, Electrolux has found that it must have 120 basic designs with 1,500 variants. The company has come to realize that its strategic vision for Electrolux in Europe was wrong. The idea of only a few brands did not work due to the cultural differences. Johansson had to review his strategic vision and alter it to fit the European market. He found he had to alter his products for each country. His new goal is "to be a good Frenchman in France and a good Italian in Italy. My strategy is to go global only when I can and stay local when I must."

Johansson is still trying to expand the market of Electrolux. He still feels a global strategy is important for Electrolux, only he has learned that culture must be taken into account in each new market. Electrolux is growing. The company has entered the American market and is looking to enter the former Soviet Union and Asia.

Source: Adapted from William Echikson, "Electrolux: The Trick to Selling in Europe," *Fortune,* September 20, 1993, p. 82.

DISCUSSION QUESTIONS

1. How is the European environment different from that of the United States? What factors are responsible for the fragmentation of the European home appliance market?
2. Are there any circumstances under which there will be a single homogeneous market for home appliances in Europe?
3. Can you identify products for which there is, or could be, a homogeneous market in all of Europe?
4. Identify and explain the functional strategies (e.g., distribution channels, advertising, purchasing) that a company like Electrolux could use to take advantage of the European Union's common market?

Notes

1. For information on the WTO refer to http://www.ciesin.org/TG/PI/TRADE/gatt.html.
2. For information on GATT refer to www.wto.org.
3. Jeffrey Frankel and Shan-Jin Wei, "Open Regionalism in a World of Continental Trade Blocs," IMF Working Paper (Washington, DC: International Monetary Fund, 1998).
4. Jacob Viner, *The Customs Union Issue* (New York: Carnegie Endowment for International Peace, 1950).
5. "The Trouble with Regionalism," *The Economist,* June 27, 1992, p. 79.
6. See *The Likely Impact on the United States of a Free Trade Agreement with Mexico* (Washington, DC: United States International Trade Commission, 1991).
7. United States Trade by Commodity with Mexico, International Trade Administration, U.S. Department of Commerce, 2002.
8. World Trade Organization, *International Trade Statistics 2002* (Geneva: WTO, 2002), p. 8.
9. Peter L. Leach, "NAFTA Nears 10: The Much-Debated Agreement May Form the Framework for the Proposed Free Trade Area of the Americas," *Journal of Commerce,* July 21, 2003, Special Reports 2, p. 36.
10. Robert Scott, director of International Economics and codirector of research at the Economic Policy Institute, quoted in Leach, "NAFTA Nears 10," p. 36.
11. For information on the FTAA refers to its Web page at http://www.ftaa-alca.org/alca_e.asp.
12. Information on the ASEAN was obtained from *official site of Association of South-East Asian Nations,* http://www.aseansec.org/.
13. Deloitte and Touche, "MERCOSUR: Executive Summary" (Buenos Aires: Deloitte and Touche, February 2003).
14. Commission of the European Communities, March 5, 2003, http://europa.eu.int/comm/external-relations/mercosur/intro/index.htm.
15. Information on the European Union was obtained from various public sources and from *Europa: The European Union On-Line,* http://europa.eu.int/index_en.htm.
16. World Trade Organization, World Trade Developments in 2001 and Prospects for 2002, International Trade Statistics (Geneva: WTO, 2001), p. 8.
17. "The Trouble with Regionalism," *The Economist,* July 27, 1994, p. 79.
18. Jagdish Bhagwati, "Negotiating Trade Blocs," *India Today,* July 15, 1993, p. 65.
19. D. Held, A. McGrew, D. Goldblatt, and J. Perraton, *Global Transformations* (Stanford, CA: Stanford University Press, 1999), p. 16.

20. R. Gilpin, *The Political Economy of International Relations* (Princeton, NJ: Princeton University Press, 1987), p. 389.

21. Global Insight, Inc., *World Economic Outlook,* Vol. 1 (Lexington, MA, Third Quarter 2002), and Energy Information Administration, Annual Energy Outlook 2003, DOE/EIA-0383(2003)(Washington, DC, January 2003), Table A20.

22. WTO, *International Trade Statistics 2002,* p. 3.

23. Experience of Arvind V. Phatak, who immigrated to the United States in 1960.

24. Steven R. Weisman, "The China Connection," *New York Times,* March 16, 1997.

25. Deepshikha Ghosh, India Abroad, in IndiaInfo.com, December 20, 2000.

26. Heinz Stecher with contributions from Michael Bailey, in "Time for Tobin Tax? Some Practical and Political Arguments," Discussion Paper for Oxfam GB, Oxfam, May 1999. www.oxfam .org.uk/policy/papers.

27. Hernando De Soto, *The Mystery of Capital* (New York: Basic Books, 2000).

28. Raymond J. Matoloni Jr., "U.S. Multinational Companies' Operations in 1998," *Survey of Current Business,* July 2000, Table 12.1, p. 40.

29. Ibid., Table 2, p. 4.

30. Tina Rosenberg, "Globalization," *New York Times,* August 18, 2002, Section 6, p. 28.

31. Ibid.

32. Joseph E. Stiglitz, *Globalization and Its Discontents* (New York: Norton, 2003).

CHAPTER THREE

The Political Environment and Political Risk

Chapter Learning Objectives

After completing this chapter, you should be able to:

- Describe the components, relationships, and interactions involved in the political systems model and explain how the one-nation model can be extended into a global business context.
- Explain the reciprocal nature of the dynamics between political and economic systems, policies, and relations.
- Define and differentiate among the various types of political risk and discuss their implications for the multinational firm.
- Discuss comprehensive frameworks for assessing political risk, from a global as well as a single-country perspective.
- Understand alternative methods used to hedge against risk from political and politically imposed economic changes in a host country.
- Understand practical implications of political risk for the manager working overseas.

Opening Case: Overseas Political Risk for U.S. Firms Rises After 9/11

U.S. companies with operations in Islamic countries face greater security risks after the September 11 attacks, and may have to pull back or face risking the security of their staff and assets, security consultants said. Since the attacks on the World Trade Center and the Pentagon U.S. firms operating in Islamic nations have been reviewing crisis management plans and beefing up security to prepare for bombing or other violence against U.S. targets. However, some companies may have to chose between the rewards of investing in a growth market with the risks of operating in politically unstable countries such as Pakistan or Indonesia, the world's largest predominantly Muslim nations. Though both countries have sided with the United States in its war against terrorism, large Islamic groups have staged anti-U.S. protests and threatened revenge because of the United States attacks on Afghanistan in 2001 and Iraq in 2003.

"Companies will increasingly have to decide between brand awareness and security. That's a question businesses are going to have to face, on the assumption that this war against terrorism will be a long and drawn out affair," said Jake Stratton, head of research at Control Risks Group, a business risk consulting firm in London, in 2001. "It has been discussed and I don't know of any companies poised to put their plans into practice. But it's a dilemma they're beginning to face when they look at their long-term strategies in places with a large or significant Muslim population," he added.

The stakes for U.S. companies can be high, as Muslims account for almost one-fifth of the world's population. U.S. heavyweights such as Procter & Gamble, Motorola, General Electric, and Halliburton Co. have stores or offices in Pakistan, a reluctant ally in the fight against the Taliban in neighboring Afghanistan. McDonald's Corp. has 11 restaurants in Pakistan, while Citigroup's Citibank has five full-service branches in the country, according to their Web sites. Since the Sept. 11 attacks, U.S. companies with operations in the Mideast and parts of Asia have been on continued heightened alert, the consultants said. Firms are rushing to update contingency and evacuation plans or implement them if none existed before, causing a surge in demand at corporate security firms.

Oil companies such as Chevron Corp. and Conoco Inc., which have operations in Muslim parts of Asia and the Mideast, have increased security at their offices and facilities in those regions, said spokesmen at both firms. Heavy machinery maker Caterpillar Inc., which has a manufacturing plant in Jakarta, Indonesia, and sales offices in the Mideast, said it has banned travel to those regions and is closely monitoring State Department advisories. And mining company Freeport-McMoRan Copper & Gold Inc., which operates the world's biggest copper and gold mine in Indonesia, said it has increased security at its Jakarta office and mining facilities. "All Western companies operating in Muslim countries are very concerned at the moment. There's concern about spillover into central Asia as well," said Martin Stone, head of country and political risk advisory services for Deloitte & Touche. "I think it's an overreaction, but for understandable reasons."

U.S. companies' international subsidiaries with prominent storefronts or brands, such as restaurants and consumer products makers, are more likely to be targets of violence, analysts said. Such businesses are seen as U.S. symbols, though they are often controlled by local companies through a joint venture or the purchase of a franchise from the U.S. parent. Should the U.S. anti-terrorism campaign continue for several years, American companies may need to reevaluate their marketing and advertising campaigns in Muslim countries, where anti-U.S. sentiment can be high. "We haven't counseled any companies about downgrading their marketing because the situation is so uncertain. But my view is that it will take many years and have long-term effects on the way Western companies do business in the Muslim world, and that will include marketing," said Stone.

As of 2002, most companies say they are taking a wait-and-see approach toward their marketing plans. Procter & Gamble, which owns plants in both Pakistan and Indonesia and has representative offices in heavily Islamic Uzbekistan and Turkmenistan, which border Afghanistan, said it has not changed its business strategy in those regions. The consumer products giant, which recently sponsored a "Miss Uzbekistan 2001" beauty contest and health education campaigns, has not yet changed its marketing plans, said a spokeswoman.

Dunkin' Donuts, which has six stores in Pakistan and 223 stores in Indonesia, leaves marketing and advertising decisions up to the local franchisees, said Bob Kendzior, vice president of international marketing. "I don't know what their marketing plans are, and I suspect there's very little going on now. But our thinking is for the short-term and to respond to the security situation as it changes," Kendzior said. Some consultants are cautioning clients against making any long-term business decisions, even as the White House prepares the United States for even a longer war against terrorism.

Source: From "Firms' Security Risks Rise in Muslim Areas," Meat Industry Internet News Service, October 13, 2001. Reprinted with permission.

Discussion Questions

1. How has political risk faced by firms investing overseas changed since September 11, 2001?
2. What are different types of political risk faced by various consumer and industrial industries?
3. In your opinion, what are the differences between short-term and long-term politically imposed risk?
4. How can firms protect themselves against the specific risks of terrorism referred to in the case?

Macro-Level Environments and Uncertainties

In the previous chapter, we discussed in detail several important dimensions of the global business environment—elements that shape the context within which international business must be conducted. We continue this macro-environmental discussion in the next two chapters by considering the governance infrastructure of host countries, which includes the political and legal institutions of those countries.[1] Many of the cross-nation differences referred to in Chapter 2 regarding economic environment and associated growth and productivity levels have been related to differences in the political and legal environments of countries.[2]

In this chapter, we start the discussion of host-country governance infrastructure by considering the political environment facing the international business manager and the problems they can pose for international operations in the form of politically imposed risk. Furthermore, we link other general environmental factors and uncertainties to a host nation's political environment. Based on Kent Miller's work, Table 3.1 illustrates various uncertainties that may arise in a host country for a manager of an international firm, and all are linked to a nation's political environment.[3]

International business has consistently emphasized the need both to understand the political dimension regarding the management of overseas activities and to include intercountry differences and changes in political environments[4] when researching strategic initiatives and expansion activities of international firms.[5]

Politics and political interests are powerful forces in every country throughout the world, and their ability to support or disrupt business operations is of major interest to the global manager. For instance, although China represents both a major production center and a significant market for many industries, the international manager can never forget that the current government of China may interfere with business plans in that country. Direct marketing companies like Mary Kay Cosmetics, Avon Products, and Tupperware were suddenly forbidden to use their business model in China. Furthermore, this policy was reversed by the Chinese government only after negotiations and diplomatic pressure by the United States government. Similarly, in the United States, where there is business-friendly Republican controlled government, a shift in Congress or the the presidency to the Democratic Party could exert new pressures on businesses operating there. Thus international managers must think not only about political risks in the turbulent Middle East and southern Asia and the effects of the conflicts in Iraq and Afghanistan; they must also think about the effect on their respective firms of the changes in their home country's government.

TABLE 3.1
Macro-Environmental Uncertainties

Political Uncertainties	Macroeconomic Uncertainties
War	Inflation
Revolution	Changes in relative prices
Coup d'état	Foreign exchange rates
Democratic changes in government	Interest rates
	Terms of trade
Government Policy Uncertainties	
	Social Uncertainties
Fiscal and monetary reforms	
Price controls	Changing social concerns
Trade restrictions	Social unrest
Nationalization	Riots
Government regulation	Demonstrations
Barriers to earnings repatriation	Small-scale terrorist movements
Inadequate provision to public service	

Only through an understanding of the fundamental elements and dynamics of political systems can one adequately appreciate their effect on the multiple operating environments facing the global firm and properly assess the degree of politically imposed risk involved in commencing or continuing operations in each. Policymakers and managers must have the tools to assess the extent of political and regulatory risk faced by a given investment project in a given country.[6]

Because of the dynamic changes taking place in various parts of the world, political forecasting is now big business. Several firms provide forecasts on the overall political conditions in various countries. Large U.S. companies like General Electric and AT&T buy such forecasts from several different consulting firms.

Why would international companies pay huge sums of money to obtain such forecasts? Firms prefer to avoid all uncertainty in the external environment that would affect the preferred outcomes of their strategies. The greater is the uncertainty, the greater is the perceived risk of operating in a particular country. Ignorance and misperceptions of facts often cause uncertainty. Therefore, firms attempt to minimize uncertainty and risk in a country through forecasts about the country's future business environment and prospects.

A clear understanding of political risk allows companies to decide how attractive a country is for exports, licensing, or direct investment in a manufacturing operation. Each of these modes of entry requires varying amounts of financial investment. The greater is the investment required to penetrate a foreign market, the greater is the risk involved in doing so. Companies therefore engage in assessing the amount of investment that they would be willing to make in the country, based on their assessment of the risks involved with each entry mode and the corresponding financial and other tangible and intangible benefits.

Political Risk Services is a firm that provides political risk analysis of several countries. This firm recently released a report on the political situation in Costa Rica, reproduced in Practical Insight 3.1.

How would a firm benefit from this report from Political Risk Services? International companies would find several useful pieces of information in this report. Of concern to companies with operations in Costa Rica would be the probability of civil strife arising from the resistance of the unions to the government's plans to privatize state-owned enterprises. There is also the danger that their interest groups would press the government to meet their demands, which could further destabilize the government. Civil strife could lead to unexpected changes in the policies of the government toward foreign businesses, or to a change in the government. (The impact of civil strife on political risk is discussed later in this chapter.)

Economic and political uncertainty are likely to increase because of the high probability of a divided government in the near and long-term future. What would a divided government's policies be towards foreign enterprises? Such uncertainty would concern foreign companies wishing to establish new operations in Costa Rica or to expand those already in place. Greater uncertainty would also confront domestic and foreign companies that were planning to enter Costa Rica by acquiring government-owned companies. The business opportunities inherent in a free trade agreement with the United States would evaporate were Costa Rica not to enter into a free trade agreement with the United States. (We discussed the many advantages of free trade in Chapter 2.)

The fear of inflationary pressures and devaluation of the currency would make domestic goods cheaper, thereby boosting exports; however, imports of products by domestic companies would become more expensive. Such prospects would discourage exports to Costa Rica and exports from domestic companies could prosper. The prospects of slow economic growth and a rapid increase in the debt burden would ne-

PRACTICAL INSIGHT 3.1

COSTA RICA'S 2003 POLITICAL FORECAST: PACHECO ON SLIPPERY SLOPE OF UNREST

President Pacheco faces a sustained and damaging bout of unrest following his government's capitulation to striking workers from the state-owned telephone and electricity monopoly demanding a $100 million bond issue to finance the company's projects. Employees of ICE [the Costa Rican Electricity Institute] have accused the government of intentionally undermining the company's efficiency in order to justify the sale of the firm to private investors.

This is the second time the government has buckled under pressure from the ICE unions since the beginning of the year. Other interest groups have surely taken notice, and will no doubt seek to exploit the vulnerability of Pacheco's minority administration to press their own demands . . . More broadly, President Pacheco's high approval ratings have taken a significant hit since the passage of controversial emergency tax measures and the introduction of an austere budget in late 2002.

Given the minority status of Pacheco's PUSC [Social Christian Unity Party] in the legislature, his administration is unlikely to pursue further measures that hold the potential to generate a popular backlash . . . Official reluctance to pursue privatization poses a threat to the country's hopes for a free-trade agreement with the US, which has pressured the government to open its utilities to competition and private investment . . . The lack of progress on privatization will also limit the opportunities for foreign investors, reinforcing wariness arising from the government's shaky financial position . . . The government's austere budget, combined with a tightening of credit availability, will create a drag on economic activity in 2003, slowing real GDP growth to 2% . . . Failure to significantly

trim the unsustainable debt burden will limit the potential for growth and hamper efforts to contain inflation. Real GDP growth will average just 3.3% annually through 2008.

Speculation that the government will pursue an accelerated devaluation of the currency to boost sagging exports will weaken the currency, pushing inflation back into double digits in 2003 . . . Over the longer term, the government's inability to contain the mounting debt burden will put persistent pressure on the currency, contributing to average annual price increases of 9% through the forecast period . . . High debt-service obligations will keep the current account deficit high, averaging $800 million annually through 2008 . . . Assistance from international financial organizations will be vital to help steady external finances, especially in light of the decline in US foreign aid.

However, a lack of commitment to economic liberalization may undercut the enthusiasm of members of the international financial community and damage relations with bilateral foreign donors, the IMF, the World Bank, and the IDB.

Forecasts of Risk to International Business

Turmoil	18-Month Low	Five-Year Low
Financial transfer	B-	B (B-)
Direct investment	B	B (B-)
Export market	B	B

	Probabilities	
Divided government	60%	65%

Source: Adapted from Political Risk Services, *Costa Rica, Forecast Highlights*, June 29, 2003; http://www.prsonline.com/.

cessitate financial help from international financial institutions. In light of the worsening relations with such institutions, however, such help may not be forthcoming. The risk of a financial crisis in Costa Rica would concern both domestic and foreign countries with operations in Costa Rica. The knowledge and information derived from this report would give a foreign company a general picture of the overall conditions and business prospects in Costa Rica.

Country-specific political risk estimates are useful to the extent that they inform the decision makers of the comparative political risks in different countries; for example, the political risk in Venezuela is triple that in Mexico. Relying solely on such overall estimates may prevent companies in certain industries from taking advantage of opportunities in countries that are ranked as highly risky. As we shall see later in this chapter, political risk in a country may not be equal for all industries. For example, it is generally well-known that the United States has poor political relations with Iran; nevertheless, several companies in the oil and natural gas and construction industries have been conducting profitable business operations in that country. During the worst of relations between the United States and Libya, American oil companies were welcomed and protected.

In addition to the country risk forecasts from consulting firms, prudent international companies conduct their own assessments of country risks for their specific industry. How to approach this task is the basis of the remainder of this chapter. Political risk is caused by the political forces in a country, as well as by the country's interactions with the political systems of other countries singly and collectively. We therefore start by examining the nature and functioning of a country's political system and of the global political system.

The political systems of individual countries are parts of a global political system, in which countries of the world interact with each other. The global political system is in turn influenced by the global economic system, and vice versa. Later in the chapter we study the functioning of the interdependent and interactive global political and global economic systems.

The Political System

When a firm crosses international boundaries, new and different political environments force that firm into various modes of adaptation.[7] Thus, because a firm must first understand the nature of the international political system and how it works, it should initially understand just what a political system is as well as its specific characteristics. Furthermore, we need to first separate the political and economic systems before integrating them into a more comprehensive framework. In this section we examine a generic model of political and economic systems, as presented in Figure 3.1.

The Players in the Political System

The **political system** consists of a set of "players," each with their own unique set of aspirations and goals, which are often in conflict with those of the other "players" in the system. The *government* is only one of many players in this system, although a key one, as it alone has the legitimacy to make authoritative decisions and to enforce those decisions by force. The other key players in the system are the various significant *groups* that exist in a society. Examples of societal groups are labor unions, environmental activist organizations, special interest groups, and religious organizations. Some of these groups, such as political parties, armed forces, labor unions, and religious organizations, are significant institutions of society; others, such as the National Rifle Associ-

FIGURE 3.1
The Political System

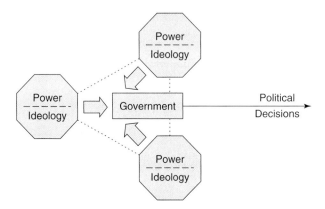

ation, Mothers against Drunk Driving, and Amnesty International, are primarily lobby groups. Finally, groups, including various terrorist organizations, exist that conduct illegal activities.

Each of these groups has a certain amount of power it can exert to control and influence the behavior of other groups and of various host governments. The amount of power in the hands of each group is not equally distributed. Some groups may be more powerful than others. The power of each group is derived from the total number of people who are firmly committed to the group's ideals and goals and from the group's stockpile of key financial, technical, and human resources.

Each societal group also has its unique political ideology. Ideology has been defined as "a set of closely related beliefs, or ideas, or even attitudes, characteristic of a group or community."[8] Similarly, a "political ideology is a set of ideas or beliefs that people hold about their political regime and its institutions and about their position and role in it."[9] The ideology of a group is the set of values and beliefs pertaining to the way in which society should be organized—politically, economically, morally—that are shared by its members. For example, in the United States the ideology of the National Rifle Association is grounded in the belief that every person has the right to bear arms, whereas on the opposite side is Hand Gun Control, Inc., which is committed to restricting the possession of handguns by lay members of society. The labor unions have as their primary objective the protection of workers from unfair treatment by the employer. The Democratic Party in the United States and the Labor Party in the United Kingdom have been historically committed to worker welfare, whereas the Republican Party in the United States and the Tory Party in the United Kingdom have been generally committed to the development and growth of business firms with little or no interference by the government.

Various groups within a society

> at given times and under given conditions, challenge the prevailing ideology. Interests, classes, and various political and religious associations may develop a "counter ideology" that questions the status quo and attempts to modify it. They advocate change rather than order; they criticize or reject the political regime and the existing social and economic arrangements; they advance schemes for the restructuring and reordering of the society; and they spawn political movements in order to gain enough power to bring about the changes they advocate. In this sense, a political ideology moves people into action. It motivates them to demand changes in their way of life and to modify the existing political, economic, and social relations, or it mobilizes them on how to preserve what they value.[10]

Thus the two important features that characterize all ideologies are a given set of beliefs that rationalizes the status quo and a competing mindset that challenges it.

Institutions and groups that appear to be alike may perform different functions in different countries. For example, in the United Kingdom, labor unions have a leftist ideology and are politically affiliated with the Labor Party, whereas in the United States the labor unions are basically "business unions" with an ideological bias in favor of private enterprise and a capitalist society. In the United States, Republican Party members believe that the Democratic Party is politically left of center, whereas in some countries outside of the United States, the Democratic Party is seen as a right-of-center party. It should be noted that the United States never had politically viable socialist or communist parties. This is not the case in many countries, including Italy, India, Sweden, and Greece. The role played by the church also varies from country to country. For instance, the Catholic Church played a crucial role in the liberation of Poland from Soviet domination and in the overthrow of the Marcos dictatorship in the Philippines, whereas the Catholic Church in India is politically neutral.

The Concepts of Legitimacy and Consensus[11]

Every group in the political system has its own objectives and aspirations, and they all attempt to influence the government and thereby translate their particular interests into authoritative political decisions. A key prerequisite for the efficient functioning of any political system is the presence of a high level of "consensus." *Consensus* is the widespread acceptance of the decision-making process in the political system by the individuals and groups in the system. Consensus is the instrument by which a government itself becomes legitimized. *Legitimacy* is the use of the power of the state by officials in accordance with prearranged and agreed-upon rules. A legitimate act is also legal, but a lawful command is not always legitimate. For example, the commands issued by the Nazi government in Germany were legal, but they were not legitimate because they violated a code of civilized behavior and morality that brought into question their legitimacy.

Legitimacy and consensus are key indicators of the effectiveness and performance of the political system. Conversely, the absence of legitimacy and consensus can cause an undermining instability of the system. A government that has no legitimacy has no right to issue authoritative directives and thus is likely to create political instability, unless it is backed up by massive coercive force to keep it in power. Examples include the now deposed brutal Taliban regime in Afghanistan, in power through coercive means until recently, and the ongoing dictatorship in North Korea.

The Political Process

The political process is composed of different groups representing different interests bargaining over different preferred outcomes. The outcomes of the political process include the myriad political decisions made by the government in response to the pressures applied by the different interest groups. Group conflict is common in an effective political system, and the strength of the political system is its ability, through the agency of the government, to resolve the intergroup conflicts peacefully. Group conflict occurs, for example, between groups that favor free trade and lower tariff barriers and those that advocate protectionism. The role of the government is to engage in the constructive management of conflict among the various interest groups.

The Global Political System

The international political system, like the political system of a nation, consists of numerous players, each of whom has its own particular interests, goals, and aspirations. The various countries of the world, the various regional trade blocs discussed in the previous chapter, and the different international organizations, including the United Nations, the World Bank, the International Monetary Fund (IMF), and the World Trade Organization (WTO), are the major participants in the international political system. "In domestic politics, goal-seeking behavior is regulated by government, which has the authority to make decisions for a society and the power to enforce those decisions. The characteristic that distinguishes international politics from internal politics is the absence of government. In the international system, no legitimate body has the authority to manage conflict or achieve common goals by making and enforcing decisions for the system; instead, decision-making authority is dispersed among many governmental, intergovernmental, and non-governmental groups."[12]

As seen in the preceding chapter, the WTO is approaching a world-type government for international trade. In 1994 the WTO was empowered by an international treaty signed by more than 100 countries to regulate world trade and investments in accordance with the rules of the treaty provisions. The WTO has the power to adjudicate in trade disputes between countries and to impose punitive measures against those that are found to be guilty of violating the treaty provisions. Similarly, international law, characterized by treaties such as the treaty for the protection of intellectual property (discussed in Chapter 4), is designed to manage conflict and cooperation in the area of intellectual property rights.

Because of the absence of a legitimate "world government" with the capability to make and enforce authoritative decisions, the various nations and international groups have had to create the appropriate rules, institutions, and procedures that manage international conflict and cooperation. Within this framework, conflict occurs within agreed-upon limits, and cooperation among nations is enhanced. However, when there are no effective rules, procedures, and institutions to manage conflict and cooperation, international conflict may rise to undesirable levels, and it may even escalate into war.

The Interaction between International Politics and International Economics

In today's world the international economic system and the international political system do not function independently of each other. The international economic relations between nation-states are determined to a large extent by their political and diplomatic relations, while the reverse holds true as well. Figure 3.2 illustrates the extreme political and economic systems. As depicted on the horizontal axis, politically, a country may range from far right totalitarianism, or fascism, to far left totalitarianism, or communism. At both extremes, there is government oppression. In the former, it is in the name of a select group in the population such as the military. In the latter, the government represents the entire people. In the depiction seen in Figure 3.2, democracy as it is represented by the United States lies in the middle. From the managerial perspective, it is interesting to realize that the United States lies within a small band relative to the world. For example, the most liberal politicians in Washington are still seen as very moderate by the extreme left throughout the world. Similarly, the most conservative Washington politicians are seen as moderates by extreme right-wingers throughout the world.

Extreme economic systems are depicted on the vertical axis in Figure 3.2. At one extreme lies a market economy. In this economic environment, market forces without

FIGURE 3.2
Political and Economic Systems

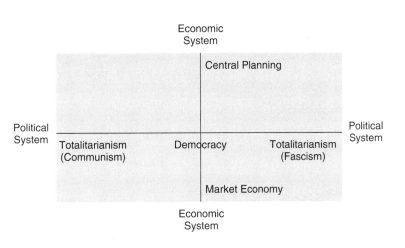

government intervention set price and quantity levels in all industries. Supply and demand principles rule and the private sector owns the factors of production. At the other extreme, a centrally planned economy, the government owns the factors of production and establishes the price and quantity levels. Subsequently, the government tries to harmonize economic plans across all industry sectors. Both extreme economic systems are theoretical, with most countries falling along the continuum where the government has some role. In these mixed economies, the government can interfere in the economic process in distinct ways. For instance, it can actually own industries or pieces of industries. Also, governments that do not have equity stakes in industries may provide financial incentives as well as strategic direction for the firms and industries in its countries.

A manager cannot assume a country that has tendencies toward a market economy is democratic. For instance, the government of Singapore has historically promoted capitalism while being less than a fully functioning democracy. South Korea and various South American countries during the 1980s had military-based governments that promoted capitalism. From another perspective, many governments that have historically been democratically driven have had both government ownership and influence of industries. India provides a good example here. Also, Japan has historically choreographed the strategic initiatives of industries deemed to be critical to the country's economic future. Moreover, democracies appear in many versions throughout the world. Malaysia and Mexico have claimed the democracy label, yet the same party held national office for decades in both countries. Indeed, the Mexican elections held in July 2000 marked the first time since the 1910 Mexican Revolution that the opposition defeated the party in government, the Institutional Revolutionary Party (PRI). Vicente Fox of the National Action Party (PAN) was sworn in on December 1, 2000, as the first chief executive elected in free and fair elections.

Where a country falls economically and politically relative to other countries is an important starting point in the political analysis of a country. Beyond that, the international manager must understand political and economic changes that have occurred in the recent past as well as those changes expected to occur in the future. Figure 3.3 presents a tool for managers to use in analyzing political and economic shifts of countries deemed important to their respective firms and industries.

FIGURE 3.3
Political and Economic Change, 1982–2002

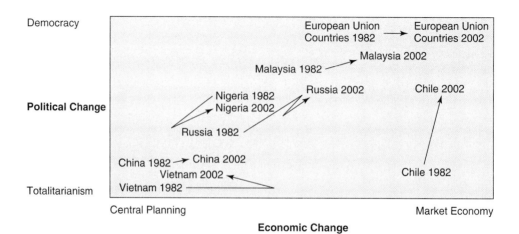

The early 1980s marked the start of a significant shift toward democracy and market economies. In some countries, including China, even though the political tone has remained totalitarian, more and more pockets of capitalism have been introduced into the historically planned economy. From another perspective, Chile represents a country that has always tended toward capitalism and, since the removal of General Augusto Pinochet as leader in the mid-1990s, has moved strongly toward democracy. Other countries have been more volatile in their political and economic movements. Nigeria has seen various military rulers as well as attempts at free elections since the 1980s. Only in the last decade has it succeeded in holding a free election, leading to the election of President Olusegun Obasanjo. Vietnam, although politically unwavering, has economically experimented since the general embargo was lifted by the United States in the mid-1990s. In that country, pockets of capitalism were introduced, then pulled back, to be followed by a slower movement toward free market postures. In general, there has been a worldwide trend toward democracy during the past two decades. Government privatization and deregulation activities, as well as the fall of major planned economies around the world, have led to a shift toward market economies.

Political factors affect economic outcomes in three ways:

1. The political system shapes the economic system, because the structure and operation of the economic system is, to a great extent, determined by the structure and operation of the international political system.
2. Political concerns often shape economic policy, because economic policies are frequently dictated by overriding political interests.
3. International economic relations themselves are political relations, because international economic interaction, like international political interaction, is a process by which state and nonstate actors manage, or fail to manage, their conflicts and by which they cooperate, or fail to cooperate, to achieve common goals.[13]

What follows is a look in some detail at these three political dimensions of international economics.

The Influence of the International Political System on the International Economic System

The influence of the international political system on the international economic system is apparent when we review the political developments during three distinct periods in history. The first is the period of nineteenth-century imperialism, the second is the post–World War II era of cold war between the Soviet Union and the Western free world led by the United States, and the third is the post–Berlin Wall demolition and the demise of the Soviet Empire era.

Nineteenth-Century Imperialism and the International Economic System

Nineteenth-century imperialism and mercantilism were driven by two major political factors: (1) powerful nation-states in Europe—the United Kingdom, France, Germany, and Holland—of nearly equal military power and (2) rampant nationalism practiced by these powerful nation-states, which drove each nation to engage in practices designed to enhance national pride, national identity, self-sufficiency, wealth, and economic power. National independence, rather than collective or cooperative relations among nation-states, was in vogue. These two conditions led to the pursuit of "empire building," characterized by the policy of colonialism under which each European power engaged in colonizing countries in Asia, Africa, and Latin America. The objective of the colonial powers was to obtain raw materials and minerals from the colonies, to process them into finished products at home, and to market the products in the captive markets of the colonies. The overriding objectives of the colonial powers were to accumulate wealth and power and to provide full employment to their citizens, at the expense of the colonized countries whose markets and production capabilities were totally controlled by the imperial powers.

The European colonial powers divided the world into parts that each controlled. Thus Britain controlled most of western and southern Asia and parts of Africa. The French controlled southeast Asia and northwest Africa. The Dutch controlled Indonesia and parts of Central and South America, and the Germans took control of parts of Western Africa. Wars erupted between the colonial powers as each attempted to increase their power by colonizing more countries. Thus the British and the French fought for control of India, and the British and the Dutch fought for parts of Africa. European imperialism determined the patterns of trade and investments—each colonial power concentrated on trade and investments within its colonial empire. Thus the international economic system of the colonial era was determined by a political system characterized by colonialism and empire.

The Cold War Era and the International Economic System

The imperialist system and the residual domination of the United Kingdom in the West ended following the end of World War II. Two major superpowers emerged in the post–World War II period, the United States and the Soviet Union. A new political and economic system emerged based on the rivalry between these two superpowers for world political and economic domination. Politically, the new system was bipolar and hierarchical. The United States was the leader of the West and a weakened Japan, as well as the dominant military power; the Soviet Union was the dominant military power and leader of the so-called Soviet bloc in the East, which comprised countries behind the "iron curtain." The developing countries of the third world, most of which had gained their freedom from the old imperial powers, remained politically subordinate to their once colonial "mother" countries. On the global arena, the United States and its allies confronted the Soviet Union and its allies in a cold war. This was the political system that determined the post–World War II international economic system.

For political reasons, the West and East were isolated in two disparate economic systems. The United States and its allies in the West adhered to the capitalist system, which championed the free enterprise and free market economic system. In the East, the Soviet Union and its allies in the Communist bloc adhered to the so-called Socialist/Marxist economic model, which called for centralized control of the economy by the government and the absence of private property. In the West, the United States was the dominant economic power, and its free market vision shaped the economic order; trade, commerce, and capital flows occurred predominantly among the free market economies. In the East, the Soviet Union forced the Eastern bloc countries to adhere to the socialist model for their economies, making them economically dependent on the Soviet Union and economically isolated from the West for political reasons. Thus politics shaped economics in the post–World War II period.

The Demise of the Soviet Union and Its Impact on the International Economic System

As before, the changing political scene in the late 1980s and the 1990s caused the breakdown of the post–World War II international economic system. The birth of democracy in Poland and Hungary, the demolition of the Berlin Wall, which resulted in the union of East and West Germany into one nation, and the subsequent breakup of the Soviet Union caused a sea change in the international economic system. Countries that once loathed capitalism and a free enterprise economy acknowledged their superiority over the socialist model, gradually adopting the salient features of both. Russia became a democracy, and China, Vietnam, and India opened their respective markets to foreign investments and trade.

Political Concerns and Economic Policy

In addition to influencing the international economic system, political concerns influence a nation's economic policies as well. Internal political processes play a role in determining a national economic policy. Economic policy is the outcome of the political bargaining process that is responsible for resolving the conflict over the outcomes preferred by different groups, each representing distinct and often conflicting interests. The outcome of the political conflict is determined by the relative power of each group vis-à-vis other groups. For instance, conflict occurs between labor unions that want to protect domestic employment and are therefore opposed to free trade and business organizations that favor free trade, with the group that has more power exerting stronger influence on determining the international economic policy.

The overriding political and strategic interests of a nation very often determine its international economic policy. In effect, international economic policy becomes a tool to fulfill a nation's strategic and foreign policy objectives. For example, embargo has been used as a tool of political warfare throughout history, as when the United States placed an embargo on trade with Cuba after Fidel Castro came to power in that country. Similarly, the United Nations placed an embargo on all trade and investments in South Africa in the 1980s as a means of dismantling the apartheid system in that country.

International economic policy, driven by political considerations, can sometimes be beneficial to international companies. For example, because of larger political and strategic interests such as maintaining a correct political balance of power among countries, nations overlook human rights violations committed by repressive governments or the abrogation of democratic freedoms by military coups, continuing to promote trade, commerce, and investments with such nations. An example of this strategy is the huge investments by Western nations and Japan in the People's Republic of China, which by all accounts has an overtly repressive regime.

International Economic and Political Relations

Earlier in this chapter, we discussed the nature of the international political system as being characterized by the absence of a legitimate body like a "world government" to manage conflict or achieve cooperation among and between the various members in the system (e.g., nation-states, global companies, and various financial and nonfinancial institutions such as the World Bank, the OPEC oil cartel, and Amnesty International). In the absence of a world government with the requisite authority and legitimacy to make and enforce decisions for the political system, decision-making authority to manage conflict and cooperation among the various members of the political system is dispersed among the members of the system.

International economic relations may be viewed as the outcome of the political process involving the management of conflict and cooperation over the acquisition of scarce resources among the various members of the political system in the absence of a centralized world government. As with all international political interaction, economic interaction ranges from pure conflict to pure cooperation. The conflict among the members of the political system is often rooted in a struggle for greater power and national sovereignty. National sovereignty is associated with national wealth. A country that is not independently wealthy becomes dependent on others and hence loses some of its national sovereignty. Therefore, the pursuit of wealth is the goal of most members in the political system, and the pursuit of this goal in the presence of scarce resources frequently leads to conflict among the system members.

Does the international political system influence the international economic system or does the international economic system influence the international political system? The debate will continue unabated, but when one accepts the notion that nations interacting with each other are the dominant players in both economic and political systems, then unquestionably the political interests embodied in national power and national sovereignty will be the primary determinants of their political as well as economic relations with other nations in the world community of nations.

Political Risk and the International Firm

Since Kobrin's work on political risk in the late 1970s,[14] this important macro-level topic has received much attention by business research scholars. Political risk has been linked to all aspects of international business and international management behavior. Some links include foreign investment flows,[15] foreign entry mode,[16] reciprocity among international alliance partners,[17] and international control systems.[18] As suggested earlier in this chapter, the change in political and economic positions causes risk for the international firm. Much of the risk stems from a change in the national laws discussed in the preceding section. Political risk in this sense has been operationalized in two distinct ways. The first is grassroots instability arising from demonstrations, riots, strikes, and political assassinations. The second is government instability arising from irregular power transfers and the imposition of political restrictions.[19]

In general, political risk is the likelihood that political forces will cause unexpected and drastic changes in a country's environment that significantly affect the opportunities and operations of a business enterprise. This definition of political risk puts emphasis on political forces as being the primary determinants of political risk in a country's environment. **Political forces** are the different participant groups in the political system. Earlier in this chapter we examined the characteristics of a political system, and the role played by the major political groups in a society in influencing the authoritative decisions of the government in power. Political risk is the degree of uncertainty associated with the pattern of decisions made by the government. There is no political risk when there is certainty about the future decisions made by the government. The higher the degree of uncertainty regarding the policy decisions made by the government, the higher is the political risk perceived by those most affected by governmental decisions.

The likelihood of political change is referred to as *political hazard.*[20] When the political institutions in a host country constrain the freedom to change policy, there is less uncertainty. Lack of constraints creates greater uncertainty, and political hazard is said to be high. International business researchers have developed measures of political hazards from the perspective of industry-level foreign investment[21] and country-level foreign investment.[22]

Countries whose governments show little or no consistency in the pattern of their decision making are more likely to be perceived as having higher political hazard and therefore greater risk than those in which the government's decisions show a pattern of consistency. Two major emerging economies—India and China—are cases in point. Since 1990 the Indian government has embarked on a slow but steady program of opening the huge Indian market to foreign competition and investments. Billions of dollars of foreign investments, mostly from the United States, have entered the Indian market. Although in the opinion of many observers, the rate at which the Indian government is opening up the market is rather slow, the (adverse) political risk that is perceived by firms doing business in India is moderate to low. In contrast, China, which also has a huge market potential for many business firms, has made much bigger strides in opening the market to foreign firms. However, the perception of the degree of political risk is much higher in China than is the case with India. This is because China as yet has neither an effective legal system nor a reliable commercial code to establish the rules of commercial interactions and obligations, and decisions made by one agency of the government are often negated by decisions of some other agency. The following story from _The Wall Street Journal_ illustrates the nature of political risk faced by McDonald's in China:

> In a move that may chill the confidence of foreign investors, Beijing ordered McDonald's to pull down the golden arches on the city's choicest corner. The city reneged on its promise to give McDonald's 20 years at the site after giving a Hong Kong developer the same prime location—the busy corner of Wangfujing Street and the Avenue of Eternal Peace. The Wangfujing outlet, just two blocks from Tiananmen Square, was one of the most lucrative of the 22 McDonald's in China.
>
> Now the 1.2 million-square-foot site surrounding the restaurant is destined to become the Oriental Plaza, a commercial, office and residential complex planned by developer Li Ka-shing, the richest man in Hong Kong. An official in Beijing's Foreign Liaison office who requested anonymity said McDonald's would have a site within the new complex once it is completed in about three years. Details of its location and of the compensation to be paid are to be negotiated between the land developer and McDonald's, he said.
>
> McDonald's representatives in Beijing and Hong Kong said they had not been officially notified of the city's decision. McDonald's officials had said earlier that they had no intention of vacating the site, and that they believed they had a legal right to stay in the building they had built.
>
> The city's decision to break the land-use agreement raises doubts about other such contracts. To encourage investment while retaining public ownership of land, Communist China usually grants investors the right to use land and build on it for several decades, sometimes longer. But a construction boom has made prime property of all central Beijing as well as other cities, tempting governments to break those pledges for the sake of higher profits. Beijing officials granted McDonald's the right to use the Wangfujing site after the army crackdown on pro-democracy protests on Tienanmen Square in 1989. Then, most foreigners were suspending or backing away from their Beijing investments. When McDonald's said it wanted that corner, the city was glad to oblige.[23]
>
> **Source:** From _The Wall Street Journal, Eastern Edition_ by Elaine Kurtenbach. Copyright © 1994 by Dow Jones & Co Inc. Reproduced with permission of Dow Jones & Co. Inc. via Copyright Clearance Center.

The experience of McDonald's in China exemplifies the devastating impact that an unanticipated decision by government officials can have on the operations of an enterprise. This potential for government officials to unexpectedly change their economic and legal policies and procedures is the very essence of political risk.

The Nature of Political Risk

Political risk may have positive consequences, too. Political risk is positive in nature when the unexpected changes in governmental policies result in favorable conditions for business. An example of positive political risk is the Indian government's policy change that now allows foreign investments in almost all industries in India. The Indian government is allowing equity participation in industries that were forbidden to foreign companies such as banking, insurance, airports, oil and gas, pharmaceuticals, fast foods, and some defense-related industries. Not many years ago, few observers would have predicted such an opening of the Indian economy to foreign trade and investments. This newly opened Indian market has provided companies worldwide with new business opportunities, and it illustrates the potentially favorable impact of political risk. The same can be said about the changes that have occurred in Russia, which has embraced capitalism and the free enterprise system following the demise of what once was the Soviet Union. Hence political risk can be positive as well as negative, depending on how it affects company operations.

The political ideology of the government and the nature of risk incurred have no established relationship. Regardless of the government's ideology, it is the behavior of the government that determines the degree of risk prevalent in a country. A government with a capitalist ideology that abruptly changes its policies may pose more risk to businesses than a socialist government with a record of maintaining consistent policies over extended periods of time.

The form of government is also not necessarily associated with the amount of risk generated in a country. Dictatorships may pose the same amount of risk as democracies. Once again it is the behavior of the government that determines the amount of risk present in a particular country.

Political risk can be country-, company-, or project-specific. *Country-specific political risk* is manifested in the mutual hostility between Israel and Syria. One would expect that Israeli companies would find little support in Syria, and the same would apply for Syrian companies in Israel. *Company-specific risk* invokes either a favorable or unfavorable response aimed at a particular company. For example, companies that are known for their technological superiority such as Motorola and Hewlett-Packard may receive favorable treatment in some countries through special incentives such as inducements to form joint ventures or to establish wholly owned subsidiaries. On the other hand, large companies may be unwelcome in a country that is afraid that they may destroy local firms. *Project-specific risk* involves special treatment bestowed on a certain type of project. For example, countries like Libya and Iran, which are very unfriendly to foreign investments from the United States, are nonetheless eager to collaborate with U.S. oil companies in oil exploration and drilling but reject business with companies in other industries.

Types of Political Risk

The impact of political decisions can be felt in three different ways: through transfer risk, operational risk, and ownership risk.

Transfer risk is the change in the degree of ease or difficulty experienced in making transfers of capital, goods, technology, and people in and out of a country. Capital controls include restrictions placed on the remittance of money to or from a country through foreign exchange controls. Similarly, governments may impose controls over the flow of goods into a country through quotas and high tariffs. The tariffs imposed on imported steel by President George W. Bush in 2003 are examples of transfer risk incurred by steel-importing companies like the automobile makers. Technology transfer may be constrained by government policy. For instance, the United States government has forbidden the exports of technology to China and India that could be used to develop products with military applications such as missiles and nuclear weapons. Similarly, most countries require work visas for foreigners, while some place limits on the number of foreign nationals who can be employed in a company, thereby limiting the free flow of human resources among the subsidiaries of international companies. American high-tech and software companies are hurting from the severe restrictions on visas granted to foreign engineers and scientists after the tragic bombing of the World Trade Center.

Operational risk is the impact on the operations of a firm caused by changes in the government's policies. For example, the enforcement of strict new environmental protection legislation may cause a firm to shift its production site from one location to another within a country, or to another country altogether. Similarly, a change in minimum-wage laws may induce a company to farm out some production work to contractors in countries with more competitive wage rates.

Ownership risk involves a change in the proportion of equity owned by a company in a foreign subsidiary. Until the late 1960s and early 1970s, the nature of the ownership risk experienced by international companies was predominantly negative. The nationalistic ideology of most developing countries—countries that had become independent from the bondage of colonialism—called for economic independence and self-sufficiency. This ideology fomented a wave of nationalization, expropriation, or forced divestment of equity of foreign companies in such countries as India, Egypt, Zimbabwe, Zambia, and Indonesia. Since the 1980s and 1990s, however, the wave of sentiment in favor of foreign enterprise has grown. The thirst for foreign technology and access to foreign markets, both of which international companies are in a good position to provide, has motivated governments in countries that once abhorred foreign companies to now offer them a welcome mat. Foreign companies that were once asked to divest their share of the equity in foreign subsidiaries are now being asked to increase their share to a majority or wholly owned status. In India and China, for example, the governments are actively seeking foreign investments in industries that were once government-owned, like banking and insurance. In these cases, ownership risk has now shifted from negative to positive. For all practical purposes, ownership risk has disappeared globally, except in countries like Zimbabwe, where President Robert Mugabe has embarked on a policy of expropriating property owned by the country's white citizenry.

The Scope of Political Risk

The scope of transfer, operational, and ownership risk may range from macro to micro,[24] two ends of a continuum. There are degrees of macro and micro risk. **Macro risks** affect the full spectrum of firms and businesses operating in a host country.[25] One macro risk is the possibility that all private enterprise is confiscated or nationalized, as was the case when Cuba became a communist country. A lesser macro risk is the possibility that only foreign companies or only certain industries are nationalized as was the case when Saudi Arabia nationalized the oil industry in that country, which removed American, British, and French oil companies' operations in that country.

At the other extreme are **micro risks,** which may entail a specific action against a specific company by a group or government. Micro risks may also affect specific business activities exclusively.[26] The bombing of the offices of El Al Airlines by the PLO and of the World Trade Center by al Qaeda terrorists, or the pressure put on Coca Cola by the Indian government in 1977 to reveal its secret syrup formula (which forced Coke to abandon the Indian market for some time), arc examples of micro risk.

The matrix in Figure 3.4 shows the relationships among the three types of risk—transfer, operational, and ownership—and the scope of such risks—micro and macro. The matrix shows that Country XYZ faces six different categories of political risk: transfer, operational, and ownership, with each of these types of risk falling anywhere along the macro–micro risk continuum. For instance, Company A in country XYZ is experiencing a medium level of micro/transfer risk, a low level of micro/operational risk, and a high level of macro/ownership risk.

FIGURE 3.4
Classification of
Types of Risk for
Company A in
Country XYZ

Risk Type \ Risk Scope	Macro Risk	Micro Risk
Transfer Risk		**
Operational Risk		*
Ownership Risk	****	

Legend: ***** = high; * = low.

Assessing Host-Country Political Risk

Doing business internationally requires that the business risks caused by the political climate be assessed in every host country in which the international firm conducts business. A valid and reliable evaluation of host-country political risk provides managers with a realistic view of the probability of being able to achieve the proposed venture's objectives. Armed with this information, managers are in a position to determine the minimum expectations for the venture in areas such as the rate of return (discounted for the level of risk), market share, and profits. They can then employ this knowledge in the ensuing negotiations with either the foreign government officials or potential business associates.

Assessing the political risk in a host country should begin with an exhaustive study of the political system and the corresponding political process in the country. As stated earlier in this chapter, the political process constitutes bargaining among different groups in the political system, representing different interests, over different preferred outcomes. Assuming that the government in power has the legitimacy to govern, the outcomes of the political process are the various political decisions made by the government. The government's decisions are in response to the lobbying efforts by the various interest groups in favor of their respective viewpoints.

An exhaustive study of the political process would entail the following steps.[27]

1. Study the Relative Power of the Dominant Groups in the Society and Become Familiar with their Ideologies Groups that are more powerful are more likely to influence politicians in the government than those with less power. Look for any dominant coalitions among one or more groups whose political aspirations may be overlapping. Coalitions among groups may help less powerful groups gain more influence in the political process than would be possible if each of the relatively less powerful groups were to operate on its own.

2. Study the Decision-Making Process in the Government Which political parties are represented in the legislative branch of the government? For example, members of the British Parliament have party affiliations that include Tory, Labor, Liberal, and Communist. The United States Senate and House of Representatives include members who are Democrats, Republican, and Independents. Understand the ideologies of the political parties in the legislative branch and the dominant groups in society whom they represent. For instance, the British Tory Party and the Republican Party in the United States both represent the interests of the various business associations within their respective business communities.

3. Evaluate the Relative Strength and Bargaining Power of the Political Parties in the Legislative Branch

Assess the relative bargaining power of the various dominant coalitions in the legislative branch. The political party or parties and dominant coalitions that have greater bargaining power are more likely to have their ideologies implemented through legislation that is enacted by the legislative body.

In a parliamentary democracy there is no separation between the legislative branch and the executive branch of government as the prime minister (the chief executive) is chosen by the majority party in the parliament. However, in the presidential system the legislative branch is separate from the executive and therefore, as has often been the case in the United States, the party in power in the legislature may not be the same as the party to which the president belongs. Therefore, in a presidential system, one must evaluate the balance of power between the president, who represents the executive branch of government, and the dominant political party in the legislative branch, because the political decisions made by the government are outcomes of the bargaining and negotiations between the legislative and the executive branches of government.

4. Identify the Key Decision Makers in both the Legislative and Executive Branches of Government

The key decision makers are those who have the most influence on the policy choices of the government. The key person may be the chairperson of a subcommittee of the parliament or congress or a senior civil servant in a governmental agency. Occasionally the most influential person may not be in the government at all. For example, Senior Minister Lee Kwan Yew (the former prime minister) is supposedly the person who is most influential in developing the policies of the Singapore government, although he is not officially in the government itself. Identifying the key decision makers may provide valuable clues on the future policy initiatives of the government.

5. Study the Economic, Social, and Foreign Policies of the Government in Power Over the Past Several Years

This information in conjunction with the information accumulated in the preceding three steps may be used to make informed judgments as to the future policy initiatives of the government.

6. Evaluate the Impacts on the Industry and Your Company of the Anticipated Political Decisions of the Government

The political risk facing the industry and company in the host country is critical. Assess the nature of the political risk—transfer, operational, ownership? Will the risk be macro or micro? What is the probability of the political risk and what is the time frame within which it is likely to materialize?

Diligently following the steps outlined above should provide international managers with a fairly good picture of the probability, intensity, and nature of the political risk that their companies are likely to face in the target country. Furthermore, assessing major changes and influences within a host country's political structure will supplement this step analysis.

Changes in Governments

When a host country government changes, political uncertainty will heighten. For example, the election in February 1999 in Venezuela of President Hugo Chavez Frias had brought a government with leftist leanings. There is now considerable uncertainty in Venezuela cause by ongoing civil strife. For most of the first half of the twentieth century, Venezuela was ruled by generally benevolent military strongmen, who promoted the oil industry and allowed for some social reforms. Democratically elected governments have held sway since 1959. Current concerns include an embattled president who is losing his once solid support among Venezuelans, a divided military, drug-related conflicts along the Colombian border, increasing internal drug consumption, overdependence on the petroleum industry with its price fluctuations, and irresponsible mining operations that are endangering the rain forest and indigenous peoples.

Though not as dramatic, political risk can arise in countries like the United States and the United Kingdom when governments change. If Congress and Parliament become more liberal if the Democratic and Labor parties respectively gain power from the Republicans and Tories, businesses in those countries may face tax and trade implications.

Changes in Party Leaders

Even if a government remains in power in a host country, a change in leadership can trigger political and economic change and subsequent risk to businesses in that country. When the Russian presidency was transferred from Boris Yeltsin to Vladimir Putin, there were concerns that Russia could move backward both economically and in political openness. Subsequent events have proven that such concerns were unfounded. India has had considerable political stability since achieving its independence from the British in 1947. Still, the economic policies of the government have varied widely and frequently under different leaders, creating considerable political risk for businesses over the years.

Religious Influences on Government

The more a host country does not separate political matters from religious influences, the higher the political risk. Pakistan, Iran, and Afghanistan are examples of countries in which strong religious overtures in society have not only influenced government actions but have controlled the political process. The more fundamentalist a country's religion, and the more that religion becomes intertwined in political matters, the more political risk will increase for a firm doing business in that country. Islamic law (as we shall see in Chapter 4) prohibits business practices that are taken for granted in most countries of a different persuasion. Banks may not be allowed to charge interest on money loaned to borrowers.

Civil Strife in the Host Country

Civil strife of any kind must have as a precondition **perceived relative deprivation,** that is, the citizens' perceptions of discrepancy between the goods and conditions of the life to which they believe they are justifiably entitled and the amounts of those goods and conditions that they think they are able to get and keep.[28] The citizens' response to perceived deprivation is discontent and anger, which may ultimately find an outlet through aggressive acts. The more intense and widespread deprivation is among the people of a country, the greater is the potential for civil strife. Four variables mediate the effects of discontent and anger, so they may not necessarily result in civil strife.[29] These variables are:

1. **Coercive potential:** The government could apply high levels of coercion, which could limit the extent of strife. Also, the more loyal the coercive forces are to the

government, the more effective they are in deterring strife. The brutal regime of Saddam Hussein in Iraq is an example of this dimension.

2. **Institutionalization:** This is "the extent to which societal structures beyond the primary level are broad in scope, command substantial resources and/or personnel, and are stable and persisting." Societal structures such as labor unions and political parties serve two purposes. First, they provide alternative means by which the citizens may attain satisfaction. Second, they provide citizens with outlets to channel their dissatisfactions and anger in a nonviolent manner. Therefore, the greater the institutionalization, the lower the magnitude of strife is likely to be. The post–Saddam Hussein chaotic conditions in Iraq exemplify the outcomes caused by the destruction of societal institutions.

3. **Facilitation:** Social and structural conditions in a country might promote the outbreak and persistence of strife. Examples of such conditions are (a) the belief held by the population, partly based on the historical experience of chronic civil strife, that violence is justified as a means of overcoming deprivation; (b) the transportation network and terrain of a country; (c) the presence of organized groups that facilitate social strife; and (d) the extent of foreign assistance to the initiators of strife. The greater the levels of past strife, and of social and structural facilitation, the greater is the magnitude of strife. Vietnam is often cited as a country that personified all of these characteristics, which led to the civil strife and the eventual unification of North and South Vietnam into a unified country.

4. **Regime legitimacy:** This variable refers to the popularity of the regime. The greater is regime legitimacy at a given level of deprivation, the smaller the magnitude of consequent strife. Opinions diverge on whether Fidel Castro has been in power for so long because he has earned legitimacy in the eyes of the Cuban people or because of his coercive tactics.

The greater is the level of civil strife, the higher is the probability that there will be a change in the government or significant changes in the government's policies. The political risk inherent in either of these two possible outcomes is that it could lead to the enactment of policies that are detrimental to the company's operations. This framework for assessing political risk derived from civil strife is displayed in Figure 3.5.

Thus, in assessing the magnitude of civil strife it is necessary, not only to establish the level of perceived deprivation but also to evaluate the *cumulative* impact of the aforementioned four mediating variables. Staff groups in multinational companies specializing in political risk forecasting could devise ways of composing indexes to measure the level of deprivation, coercive potential, institutionalization, facilitation, and

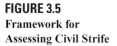

FIGURE 3.5
Framework for Assessing Civil Strife

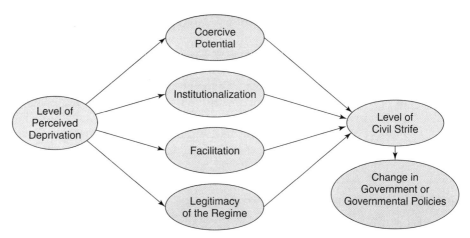

PRACTICAL INSIGHT 3.2

AMONG EXECUTIVES, FEAR OF KIDNAPPING RISES
For most of the 10 years that Michael Schwartz has been roaming Europe and Asia for a Canadian plastics company, he has not worried much about kidnapping. But these days, with bombings and kidnappings and terrorist threats being reported almost every day, he is not dismissing any possibility. He knows that the greatest chances of being kidnapped are in Colombia, Venezuela, Mexico and other Latin American countries. But he also knows that kidnappings in the Philippines have been in the news lately and that Daniel Pearl, a *Wall Street Journal* reporter, was murdered by kidnappers in Pakistan. "You definitely can't ignore it," said Mr. Schwartz, who is in charge of most international operations for Nova Chemicals in Calgary, Alberta.

Kidnapping is on the minds of lots of corporate executives these days. Two big insurers, the American International Group and the Chubb Group, say that sales have jumped sharply for insurance policies that provide negotiators to deal with kidnappers and to make ransom payments. "There is so much uncertainty in the world, people don't know what's going to hit them next," said Diane E. Borden, who is in charge of kidnapping insurance at A.I.G. "There's a general fear factor driving people."

Kidnapping insurance covers more than just abductions; it also extends to hijacking and extortion and, in some policies, terrorist attacks.

It is the unholy mixture of rising Third World criminality and widening worldwide terrorism that has fueled the surge in demand for kidnapping insurance, experts say. Since Sept. 11, big companies that already had coverage are increasing it and companies that did not have it because their international presence was limited are buying it, according to Barry K. Man-

sour, who is in charge of the coverage at Chubb. Ms. Borden of A.I.G. said there had also been a jump in inquiries about insurance that pays corporate expenses to evacuate employees from troubled countries. Most recently, A.I.G. had to pay on such policies for companies that were rushing to get their people out of Pakistan and India as the two countries moved to the brink of war.

While there is no doubt that globe-trotting corporate travelers are more worried than ever about being kidnapped, Mike Ackerman, whose Ackerman Group in Miami specializes in ransom negotiations with kidnappers, said the most likely place to be snatched was still Latin America. And, he said, most victims are wealthy local residents, since it takes time to pick out a lucrative target and plan an assault.

But business travelers are picked off from time to time, and they are prime targets of so-called express kidnappings in Mexico, Brazil and Argentina. In these assaults, the victims are grabbed as they amble out of a restaurant late at night, hustled into a car, taken to an automated teller machine and forced to make the maximum withdrawal. They continue to be held until after midnight, when a new A.T.M. withdrawal limit takes effect, and then are forced for a second time to take the money out. At that point, the kidnappers "strip the guy of his wallet and watch and cut him loose," said Brian Jenkins, an expert on kidnapping and terrorism at the Rand Corporation in Santa Monica, California.

But Latin America's pre-eminence in kidnapping notwithstanding, the radical shift in the security landscape since Sept. 11 has security experts urging business travelers to be extra vigilant in all countries. Mr. Schwartz has taken the message to heart. Even in the relatively calm countries of Europe and Asia, he says, he never hails an airport taxi to

legitimacy of the regime in a country. These indexes could then be used together to obtain the magnitude of civil strife in the country. Indexes based on uniform parameters could be constructed for various countries, which would in turn facilitate the comparison of potential political risk in two or more countries.

The country of Iran is a good example of how civil strife led to a change of the regime in power—the Shah of Iran was replaced by the Ayatollah Khomeini—which eventually resulted in unacceptable risks and the withdrawal of American firms from that country. Other countries in which civil strife has resulted in a change of government include the former republics of the Soviet Union, which have now emerged as independent countries, and South Africa. Civil strife was also one of the factors that led to the breakup of Yugoslavia into several smaller countries.

The Risk of Kidnapping

Increasingly a new type of risk has emerged, particularly in developing countries and countries of the former Communist bloc, particularly Russia. There are examples galore of kidnappings for ransom of senior executives of foreign multinationals. For exget to his hotel. Instead, he is met by a previously designated driver, taken to a hotel where security has been vetted and escorted to his room by a hotel employee to make sure nobody pounces on him along the way. He travels from the hotel only in approved limousines or with business associates, and he never goes out to restaurants alone. To avoid calling attention to himself, he dresses in modest suits. He leaves his $1,000 Omega wristwatch home and puts on something from Swatch. "You don't have to be in the hottest spot for something to happen," Mr. Schwartz said. For many executives, even a hired limousine from a familiar company is not caution enough. Emerson Fullwood, who travels the world for Xerox, says that lately he has been asking local executives to meet him at the airport in places like São Paulo and Cairo. "I take fewer chances on not knowing who's really picking me up," he said. Mr. Fullwood, who lives in Rochester, said he was also less tempted to try out-of-the-way restaurants these days. "Today," he said, "you would think twice about that."

Nova's security department sends e-mail bulletins to its business travelers to warn of new threats. Most of the companies that sell kidnapping insurance also provide travel advisories through Web sites. Kroll Associates, a corporate security firm in New York, offers a service with iJET of Annapolis, Md., that provides a security briefing, tracks travelers' itineraries and automatically e-mails pertinent alerts for $25 a trip. As an alternative, for $8 a day, iJET ships customers a satellite phone to receive the information, call anywhere in the world and instantly contact iJET's crisis center. Many security companies hold classes for business executives on how to elude kidnappers; generally, the instruction includes an analysis of home and office security and reminders to vary travel routes and times and to make sure, before setting out, that no unfamiliar people are lurking down the street.

Some insurers offer such training free to executives covered by their kidnapping policies. A.I.G. found in a study in Mexico City that people who took the course were much less likely to be victimized than those who did not. Even so, Ms. Borden of A.I.G. says, most people never get around to taking the half-day of instruction. A.I.G. requires people in Mexico City who buy its kidnapping insurance to take these classes within 60 days or lose the coverage.

Earlier this year, a wealthy Mexican who had bought the insurance was kidnapped just a few days short of the deadline. He was ambushed a few blocks from his home as he drove to work alone one morning, when most kidnappings take place, and was held hostage for a month. Had he taken the course, he might have been spared that fate. Ms. Borden says that no Mexican customers who have received the training have been kidnapped.

Mr. Schwartz, 54, knows his wife worries about him when he travels, and to ease her fears he phones her as soon as he arrives in another country and again when he checks into a hotel to give her his room number. He also keeps his office informed of his whereabouts, a precaution that he knows might get help to him faster if he ever disappears.

But if frequent travelers to high-risk nations know the dangers they face, they try not to dwell on them. "If I thought there was a high probability of being kidnapped," said Mr. Fullwood, the Xerox executive, "I probably would be talking about a different assignment."

Source: From Joseph B. Treaster, "Among Executives, Fear of Kidnapping Rises," July 2, 2002. Copyright © 2002 The New York Times Co. Reprinted with permission.

ample, on September 13, 2002, a top executive of Russia's largest oil company, Lukoil, was abducted on his way to the office. The executive, Sergei P. Kukura, 48, first vice president for finance at Lukoil, was riding in a Mercedes from his country home in Vnukova, southwest of Moscow, when masked men carrying Kalashnikov submachine guns stopped the car at a railroad crossing at about 8 A.M., a Lukoil spokesman said. The gunmen handcuffed the driver of the car and Mr. Kukura's bodyguard, and both men were then "injected with a sleep-inducing substance," Lukoil said. The driver and bodyguard awoke in a wooded area outside Moscow late in the afternoon.[30]

Executive of multinational companies routinely ride in bulletproof cars with armed guards, take different routes to work and back, hire armed guards to protect homes and family members, and have huge insurance policies purchased by companies to cover the risk of millions of dollars in ransom payments. Unquestionably, the risk of kidnappings is a risk that companies must manage. How companies and executives are coping with this risk to one's life and safety is illustrated in Practical Insight 3.2.

As evidenced by the above insight on kidnapping, the individual manager must understand personal risks that arise because of politics, political opinion, and political

EXHIBIT 3.1
**Staying Safe while
Working Overseas**

Source: Adapted from:
"Post 9–11: The View from
Abroad," *Computerworld*,
April 29, 2002.

Always remain aware of your surroundings and avoid unusual circumstances.
Walk with authority and purpose when in public areas.
Call ahead to notify others of your travel plans or appointments.
Alternate your routes to work on a regular basis.
Alternate your timing to and from your work location.
Avoid wearing American or British flag pins or other insignia in public.
Speak in the native language where you're working.

change. In the past few years, with increased terrorism aimed at Western and industrialized nation targets throughout the world, the managers of these entities in various countries are advised to rethink their behaviors in the host country. Exhibit 3.1 lists some of these behaviors for U.S. and British workers abroad, especially in the Middle East, South Asia, and Africa.

The Risk of Pirates on the High Seas

Strange as it may seem, the threat of harm from pirates and pirate ships is still prevalent in many parts of the world. In Practical Insight 3.3, Llewellyn D. Howell describes this threat.*

The impact of pirates and piracy on insurance costs is inevitable. Any operation of any size ship that goes through dangerous and uncontrolled seas now has the added cost of insurance. So it's clearly an issue and a big problem.[31]

A Global Framework for Assessing Political Risk

Up to this point we have focused on the process of evaluating political risk in a particular country. The proposed frameworks for making such an evaluation have assumed that the host country was insulated from forces and events outside the country's political boundaries. However, in the real world of interdependent nation-states this is not the case, since the political risk faced by a company is caused not only by the events and environmental changes occurring in the host country, but also by those occurring in the home country and in the international political system. Figure 3.6 depicts a framework with four basic environments: host country, home country, international environment, and international events. This framework can help the international manager identify the key actors and developments affecting an analysis of political risk.[32]

As has been the case in this chapter, one always first considers the *host country.* Analysis of political risk in the host country may follow the frameworks offered earlier in this chapter, and forecasts of the anticipated probability, degree, and nature of risk faced by the enterprise in the target country can be made by international managers.

However, political risk can originate in environments beyond the host country. For instance, there are many ways in which the *home country* can also be the source of political risk to a company's operations in the host country. Policy decisions by the home country government directed at a particular foreign country can have a serious impact on the operations of companies that have business dealings and operations in that country. As an example, the home-country government can place restrictions on technology transfers to the target country, or it may impose economic sanctions on goods exported

*Llewellyn D. Howell is senior research fellow at the Pacific Asia Management Institute, College of Business Administration, University of Hawaii at Manoa.

PRACTICAL INSIGHT 3.3

RISKS FROM PIRATES AND PIRATE SHIPS

Southeast Asia is one of three problem areas for piracy. "There are tons of thousands of pirates and pirate ships in the South China Sea and around through the Straight of Malacca and out into the Indian Ocean."

The other two areas are the east coast of Somalia and the coast of Brazil.

Often, the men aboard pirated ships are killed, the women raped. But the pirates, if they are caught, are likely to get a free pass home. In one case . . . the oil tanker *Petro Ranger* was pirated and taken to the port off the coast of China. The pirates off-loaded the oil into smaller tankers and were refitting the ship to disguise it when they were discovered by port police.

"The Chinese eventually sent the pirates back to Indonesia because they didn't know what to do with them, and they never suffered any consequences."

What does this do to the cost of insurance? "It drives it up. Any operation of any ship size that goes through these areas now has this added cost of insurance. So it's clearly an issue and it's a big problem."

Source: From L. D. Howell, "Business Strategy and Political Risks," *Global Executive Forum,* Institute of International Business, November 2002. Reprinted with permission of Llewellyn D. Howell, Professor of International Management, Thunderbird-The American Graduate School of International Management, Glendale, Arizona, USA.

FIGURE 3.6
The Environments of Political Risk

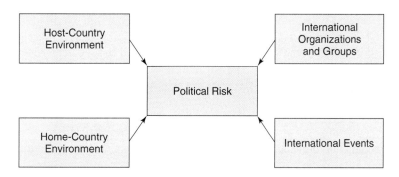

to and imported from the target country. Companies that do business in the targeted country would be affected by such home-country actions. Thus the political risk can be sourced not just in the host country, but in certain cases the home country can also become a major source of political risk for an international company. In recent years, the U.S. government has pressured various countries, such as China before its accession to the WTO, because of alleged human rights violations. If the U.S. government imposes trade restrictions on these countries, then U.S. firms that went to those countries to produce at low cost and export products back to America would be penalized.

Political risk can also arise through the impact of *international organizations and groups.* This environmental dimension consists of third parties beyond the host and home countries. These groups include Amnesty International, the various Islamic fundamentalist groups that have branches in numerous countries, the Irish Republican Army and its branches worldwide, the WTO, the International Monetary Fund, the United Nations and its various agencies. International organizations and groups can create political risk for an international company through the influence that they can exert on the political decisions of nation-states. For instance, the United Nations sanctions on trade and investments in South Africa, aimed at bringing down the minority white government in that country, forced countries to pass laws which prohibited trade and investments in that country. Polaroid, IBM, and many other large and small companies worldwide had to withdraw from South Africa.

Political risk may originate in major *international events* as well. In this environment, the effects of political risk can transcend the political boundaries of any one country or region. Political risk implications will therefore affect a firm wherever it is in the world. American interests in Kuwait were put at risk in the early 1990s when Iraq invaded Kuwait. Both the first and second Gulf Wars caused major disruptions in global economic conditions. The price of oil and energy skyrocketed. As a result, manufacturing operations worldwide were hurt by higher fuel costs. The global airline industry suffered from higher operating costs. The threat of global terrorist groups like al Qaeda, Hamas, and others based in the Philippines, Pakistan, and elsewhere, is another example of a third entity that can cause political risk for a home country's investment in a particular host country. American companies and properties have been attacked in Kenya, Somalia, Pakistan, and Saudi Arabia. Financial crises such as the financial and currency-related crisis that hit countries in Southeast Asia, Russia, and Brazil in the late 1990s had repercussions felt not only in the United States but also throughout the world. Similarly, the Argentine financial crisis of 2002 affected debt and borrowing for firms worldwide.

From the foregoing discussion, the need for conducting a realistic and thorough assessment of the political risk facing a firm should be obvious. The potential loss to a company from unanticipated political forces or actions can be substantial, even to the point of expropriation of its capital assets. The frameworks explored in this chapter can be of value in risk assessment. Their use, along with a proper categorization or classification of the specific type(s) of anticipated risks, can provide international managers with the information they need to make smart decisions that best manage the political risk inherent in a given scenario. These "tools" will be most effective for the manager who has a solid understanding of the fundamental elements and dynamics of political systems, and the ways in which they interact with economic systems and policies in forming the political environment of the international firm. As with the other environmental dimensions that we discuss in this text, the presence and potentially aversive nature of the political environment of international business presents a distinctive challenge for the global manager.

Risk Forecasting Models Used by Companies

Political risk assessment is big business. Several companies such as the Political Risk Services (PRS) Group, Business Environment Risk Intelligence (BERI), Economist Intelligence Unit (EIU), and International Consulting Resources Group (ICRG) provide an overall index of political risk for each country examined. The total risk index is derived from a sum total of scores received on several factors. Included are factors such as government stability, civil strife, health of the economy, level of political freedom, reliability of the legal environment, probability of governmental default on foreign loans, stability of currency, foreign exchange risk, inflation, and reliability of contracts. The total average of all factors represents the level of political risk in the country.

Table 3.2 is a hypothetical application of this method of political risk assessment using a few of the factors just mentioned. A significant shortcoming of this assessment method, which was pointed out earlier in this chapter, is that the total political risk index measures the overall risk of a country. It does not provide a breakdown of the level of political risk for a country, industry, or project. For instance, the level of overall political risk may be high for American companies in Libya, yet the Libyan government may protect American companies in the oil industry, as it has, even during the worst of times for American–Libyan relations. One could therefore develop indexes of political risk by measuring the most relevant determining factors of such risk for different industries or different projects in various countries.

TABLE 3.2
Political Risk
Assessment

Factor	United States	China	Brazil
Government stability	1	7	9
Probability of civil strife	1	5	8
Enforcement of contracts	1	5	5
Foreign exchange risk	4	4	10
Total risk index	7	21	32

Key: 10 = high, 1 = low.

FIGURE 3.7
Managing Political,
Legal, and Economic
Risk

	Direct	Indirect
Reactive	1. Host Operations Dependent on Home Control 2. Makeup of Management 3. Diversification	1. Risk Insurance 2. Contingency Planning 3. Home-Country Government Pressure on Host-Country Government
Proactive	1. Joint Ventures 2. Licensing Agreements 3. Others Host Partners 4. Promote Host Goals	1. Lobbying Home and Host Governments 2. Corporate Citizenship in Host Country

Managing International Political Risk

International firms cannot avoid politically risky regions because investments in these markets may provide returns that outweigh the risks.[33] An international manager cannot completely eliminate the risk that arises from changes in the political, economic, and legal environments. However, the manager and firm can employ various hedges to help mitigate this type of risk. Figure 3.7 illustrates a framework to help understand different postures international managers can take. On one hand, the international firm and manager can proactively hedge against the implications of politically imposed risk through various collaborative and strategic initiatives. The firm can also take a more defensive posture by seeking to protect itself from an expected loss. In each of these postures, the international firm can be directly or indirectly involved, as illustrated in Figure 3.7.

Proactive Hedges

Firms attempt to control political risk through various strategic and operational actions, or **proactive hedges.** A basic way that international firms shield themselves from politically imposed risks is through the appropriate mode of entry. Equity joint ventures with a host country firm will help spread risks because the firm will not be responsible for 100 percent of the investment in a given host country. Additionally, a local partner may have closer connections to the key political players and thus the venture may be politically shielded. Also, when partnering with a host country organization, an international firm may be further shielded from government interference because the government would, in effect, also be interfering with its own firm or entity. Still, downsides for the firm include some loss of control as well as the sharing of potential economic returns.

Licensing activities, where the international firm contracts a local firm (rather than investing with it), also help hedge against political risk. However, the firm loses much more control with this entry mode into the host country. Joint ventures, licensing activities, and other modes of entry are considered in detail in Chapter 7.

The international firm can form other collaborative relationships in the host country. For instance, linking with a local bank has proven to help protect against political risks. Also, the international firm can proactively promote a host country's goals, including employment, technology transfer, managerial and management skill development, and the establishment of exports and export channels. Bringing both new technology and export channels to the host country will increase the likelihood of technology exports and, subsequently, increased hard currency. During the 1990s, the Malaysia government looked favorably on Nokia's investment there because the Finnish firm brought new technology and the "export promise" to the joint venture.

Indirect proactive actions by the international firm include lobbying activities. In recent years, firms have understood that effective lobbying of both the home and host governments will help to deflect political risk. This can even be done at local levels, as has been seen in the United States. Toyota, Nissan, and Honda have all located in midwestern states and have effectively used those states as lobbying springboards to the U.S. government in Washington. Lobbying in international service industries has also been helpful in avoiding political risk. Since 1982, firms from the U.S. telecom industry have continually lobbied both the United States and host governments to gain better completion rates for international calling in order to shield themselves from radical political changes in the host countries while also lowering the cost to customers. Thus, even in countries that have undergone political upheaval, including the Philippines, Indonesia, and many African nations, the business of international calling has not been disrupted.

International firms have also realized that being good citizens of the country helps to deflect political interference. This goes beyond the proactive reinforcement of the country's economic goals and includes the integration of the firm into the local communities. For example, McDonald's (India) has transferred its entire supply chain for lettuce, potatoes, hamburger buns, cheese, and tomatoes to India, as well as transferring knowledge and technology for food processing and horticulture to Indian suppliers. A strong public relations campaign usually reinforces the social and socially responsible role of the firm as it applies in each host country. Each country will have a different perspective on what indeed is social responsibility and socially responsible behavior at both the organization and individual manager levels. Chapter 17 elaborates on corporate social responsibility.

Reactive Hedges

Firms also respond to political risk through actions, known as **reactive hedges,** that raise costs but limit exposure. From a defensive position, firms hedge against political risk through diversification. That is, they establish operations and sales expectations in many countries rather than relying on one country or region. International business scholars have suggested that diversification among politically risky countries reduces overall political risk.[34] For example, if there is a political/economic problem in one country, operations can be shifted to another country. Also, if the political/economic problem is expected to affect future revenues, the appropriately diversified international firm can shift its focus to other markets. International firms also try to control the makeup of management teams by hiring more locals who understand and have connections with key political players. An extreme defensive political hedge is the use of the host country, home country, and international legal systems to protect the firm's interests.

Indirectly, a firm can hedge against political risk through insurance. State agencies like the **Overseas Private Investment Corporation (OPIC)** and the Multilateral Investment Guarantee Agency of the World Bank (MIGA) offer U.S. firms low interest rate funding as well as insurance for operations in many emerging and lesser developed countries. OPIC has the power of the United States behind it, while MIGA's strength is derived from the World Bank. Both OPIC and MIGA provide political risk insurance up to $200 million, equity protection shields that protect the foreign operations of U.S. companies against currency inconvertibility, expropriation, and political violence for investments and returns with tailored insurance policies. It includes various forms of investments, such as capital, in-kind contributions, and loan guarantees. MIGA provides additional insurance against breach of contract should a corporation's profits be hurt due to changes in the contract imposed unilaterally by the host government. According to OPIC,

> The risks investors face in today's world are not always the same. OPIC recognizes this and is committed to customizing its Political Risk Insurance coverage to meet every client's unique project-specific risks. From large corporate investments valued in millions to those of the U.S. small business entrepreneur and everything in-between, OPIC political risk insurance can be tailored to each individual investor, providing maximum security on their investments.[35]

Exhibit 3.2 details OPIC premiums for the industries and initiatives most vulnerable to political risk. As an example, the oil and gas industry function of exploration has higher premiums for loss from political violence than for expropriation, inconvertibility, or interference with operations. However, for the industry function of development/production, the highest premiums relate to expropriation. Thus political risk is not just country specific. It is also industry-specific within a country as well as function-specific within an industry. The following are examples provided by OPIC of the type of political risks that were protected by OPIC's insurance:[36]

Political Violence

In 1988, a U.S. company made an investment in a Liberian subsidiary in order to operate a rubber plantation. Due to the Liberian civil war, the subsidiary's property was seized by rebels and then damaged and destroyed by the general military activities. OPIC found the claim to be valid and compensated the investor.

Expropriation

A U.S. investor established a fishing venture in Somalia. After a military coup occurred, the new government began a series of repeated and continuous acts of harassment and interference against the U.S. investor's personnel and operations. For example, the U.S. investor's personnel were repeatedly threatened by military and police officials, arrested and, in one instance, deported from the country. In addition, the government interfered with the company's operation of its aircraft, which was used to transport the fish, and ordered the company to permit a military observer to accompany all flights. This extra passenger displaced several hundred pounds of seafood products and added substantially to the cost of the company's operations. Viewing these and other government actions together, OPIC found that the Somalian government had expropriated the investor's project and compensated the investor.

Currency Inconvertibility

A U.S. company made an equity investment in a subsidiary in the Philippines in order to process coconuts. Sixteen years later, the subsidiary declared a dividend of over 9 million Philippine pesos payable to the U.S. parent company. The Central Bank of the Philippines had adopted restrictions on foreign currency so that the subsidiary was unable to pay the dividend in dollars. The U.S. parent company filed an inconvertibility claim with OPIC and was compensated, since the Central Bank restrictions were not in effect when the U.S. parent company originally obtained its insurance.

EXHIBIT 3.2
OPIC Political Risk
Insurance Premiums,
Annual Base Rates
per $100 of Coverage

Source: OPIC Insurance
Department, http://www.opic
.gov/Insurance/.

Manufacturing and Services

Coverage	Rate
Inconvertibility	$0.25–0.45
Expropriation	0.50–0.70
Political violence	
Business income	0.30–0.50
Assets	0.40–0.60

Institutional Loans and Leases

Coverage[a]	Covered Amount	Undisbursed Principal
Inconvertibility	$0.35–0.55	$0.20
Expropriation	0.40–0.75	0.20
Enhanced inconvertibility	0.55	0.20
Political violence	0.35–0.65	0.20

Oil and Gas

Coverage	Seismic/Exploration	Development/Production
Inconvertibility	$0.20–0.40	$0.20–0.40
Expropriation	0.35–0.50	1.35–1.65
Political violence	0.65–0.85	0.65–0.85
Interference with operations	0.35–0.55	0.35–0.55

Contractors and Exporters

Coverage	Rate
Assets	
Inconvertibility	$0.25–0.45
Expropriation	0.50–0.70
Political violence	0.40–0.60
Bid bonds	
Performance, advance payment, and other	0.40–0.60
Guaranties	0.50–0.65
Disputes	0.60–0.80

[a]The covered amount is the amount of disbursed principal plus accrued interest, less principal repaid to date.

To complement the insurance against politically imposed risk, international firms have increasingly put into action strategic contingency plans to exit countries that become too politically and economically unstable and set up similar operations in other countries. Many U.S. and European oil and gas companies had these plans in place during the late 1990s, before Indonesia experienced the political upheaval that it did. Their operations and expatriates were relocated to other Asian nations, to Latin America, and even consolidated back in their respective home countries. Contingency plans are not seen as being as proactive as a strategy of diversification. Nevertheless, these plans rest on a diversification mentality that is ready to spring to action.

Finally, from a defensive position, the international firm can use its home-country government to put pressure on a host government in a country where there is potential political risk. For instance, the U.S. government reportedly pressured the Indian government to refrain from attacking Pakistan in 2002. This action was initiated by the U.S. government in response to the lobbying by companies like IBM, HP, and Microsoft, which have significant operations in India.

The economic (Chapter 2), political, and legal dimensions (Chapter 4) of the international business environment are similar to each other in that the specific nature of each facing an international firm can generally be ascertained rather directly by researching a nation's economic statistics, legal code, and various sources regarding the nature of the political system. The cultural dimension, which we address in Chapter 5, is somewhat different, in that many of the key variables—such as attitudes and values—are invisible. The problem facing the manager is one of recognizing these underlying cultural factors and not being concerned solely with the more obvious behavioral traits they cause. This last aspect of the international environment that we discuss in this book in some ways poses the greatest managerial challenge.

Summary

A political system comprises a set of players, each with a unique ideology and some degree of power, which it uses to control and influence the behavior of other groups. One group, government, has an additional attribute—legitimacy—which it uses along with its generally greater influence to make and enforce authoritarian decisions. It does so by means of the political process, the bargaining process by which the conflicting interests and relative power of different groups are constructively managed in attaining political decisions. Today's international economic and political systems and processes are highly interdependent. Economic relations between countries are shaped to a large extent by their political relations, and vice versa. As a result of this complex interaction, political considerations can generate actions by nation-states in the economic sphere that may be detrimental to the interests of private enterprise.

The likelihood that such political forces will unexpectedly and drastically affect a firm's operations is embodied in the concept of political risk. High levels of political risk are generally associated with low levels of stability and consistency in the political system of a nation-state. Political risk may derive from transfer risk, operational risk, and ownership risk. Each of these three types of risk can be further classified as macro or micro in nature, depending on the particular circumstances. Valid and reliable assessment of a host country's political risk is an essential element of doing business internationally. A structured analytical framework involving thorough evaluation of the individual groups, ideologies, relative power relationships, and decision-making processes of the host country's political system can facilitate such an assessment.

Key determinants of political risk in many countries include a change in a country's government, a change in a country's leadership within the same party, religious influences on government, and the likelihood of civil strife leading to a mass uprising that would destabilize the incumbent political system. Although political risk is generally discussed in the context of one particular country at a time, today's global firms are exposed to such risk on a much broader front. The complex nature of the dynamics between political and economic relations requires that the modern firm extend its risk assessment framework to include not only the forces within the host- and home-country environments, but also the role played by international groups and international events.

International firms must take appropriate precautions regarding the risks that arise from international politics, economics, and law. Firms can proactively hedge these risks through vehicles such as joint ventures, promoting a host country's goals and lobbying efforts. Firms can also defensively deflect risk through diversification initiatives and the purchase of insurance.

Key Terms and Concepts

civil strife, *92*
coercive potential, *92*
facilitation, *93*
institutionalization, *93*
macro risk, *89*

micro risk, *89*
Overseas Private Insurance
Corporation (OPIC), *101*
perceived relative
deprivation, *92*

political forces, *86*
political system, *78*
proactive hedge, *99*
reactive hedge, *100*
regime legitimacy, *103*

Discussion Questions

1. What are the components of the political systems model? Apply the political systems model to your country of choice.

2. Discuss how the global political system affects the global economic system. To what extent does the global economic system influence the global political system? List some examples of how economic necessities of a nation can influence its political relations with some other countries.

3. Discuss the concept of political risk. When can political risk be favorable for international firms? Give examples of countries where such risk has been favorable to international business.

4. Apply the comprehensive framework for assessing political risk to companies doing business in the Middle East or to a country or region of your choosing.

5. Select a target country for establishing a foreign subsidiary, then (a) develop a political risk index for the target country, and (b) choose an industry in your home country and develop a political risk index for this industry in the target country.

6. How effective can the different hedging strategies be in protecting against political risk?

Minicase

The Long March Back to China

The foreign policy of the United States is to prevent the worldwide proliferation of nuclear weapons and the means to deliver them, such as intercontinental ballistic missiles. The American government did not look kindly upon the decision of China to sell such missiles to countries in the Middle East. Consequently, to punish China, the American government banned satellite exports to Beijing. China happens to be the largest market for communications satellites, in which American companies have a particularly strong position in the global market. The Chinese market (including Hong Kong) required several satellites to cope with the mushrooming amount of data traffic, telephone calls, and television broadcasts. After numerous long and drawn-out negotiations between the American and Chinese governments, China signed a binding agreement not to sell its M-9 and M-11 missiles to Arab countries. The American government responded by allowing American aerospace firms to sell satellites to China. The result? American companies could bid on up to $2 billion worth of satellite orders that the Chinese were on the brink of handing to Germany.

GM Hughes Electronics, a Los Angeles-based subsidiary of General Motors, was close to signing a deal to supplying at least 10 of the satellites. By all estimates, the trade sanctions imposed against China by the American government cost Hughes and other American satellite builders several hundred million dollars a year in lost business.

A year later, the Chinese government gave the go-ahead for China Aero-Space Corporation (CASC) to form a 50–50 partnership with Deutsche Aerospace (DASA), which is part of Germany's giant Daimler-Benz conglomerate. The joint venture planned to develop a series of telecom and Earth-observation satellites in much the same class as Hughes's big HS 601 spacecraft. The management of Hughes believes that it was not given the chance to form a joint venture with China Aero-Space for political reasons—and that DASA won the contract for the first three satellites by default.

Source: Written by Arvind V. Phatak, Carnell Professor of Management and International Business, Temple University, 2003.

DISCUSSION QUESTIONS

1. Discuss how the foreign policy of the United States played a role in its posture toward China.

2. Apply the global risk assessment framework to demonstrate how both home and host country environments can create political risks for international companies.

Notes

1. Stephen Globerman and Daniel Shapiro, "Governance Infrastructure and US Foreign Investment," *Journal of International Business* 33, no. 1 (2003), pp. 61–74.

2. R. Hall and C. I. Jones, "Why Do Some Countries Produce So Much More Output per Worker than Others?" *Quarterly Journal of Economics* 114, no. 1 (1999), pp. 83–86. Also D. Kaufmann, A. Kraay, and P. Zoido-Lobaton, *Governance Matters,* Working Paper 2196 (Washington, DC: World Bank, 1999).

3. Kent Miller, "A Framework for Integrated Risk Management in International Business," *Journal of International Business Studies* 23, no. 2 (1992), pp. 311–331.

4. G. V. Stevens, "Politics, Economics and Investment: Explaining Plants and Equipment Spending by US Direct Investors in Argentina, Brazil and Mexico," *Journal of International Money Finance* 19, no. 2 (2000), pp. 115–135.

5. C. Altomonte, "Economic Determinants and Institutional Frameworks: FDI in Economies in Transition," *Transnational Corporations* 9, no. 2 (2000), pp. 75–106.

6. Witold Henisz, *Politics and International Investment* (Cheltenham, England: Elgar Publishing, 2002).

7. J. Boddewyn and T. Brewer, "International Business Political Behavior: New Theoretical Directions," *Academy of Management Review,* January 1994, pp. 119–143.

8. John Plamenatz, *Ideology* (New York: Praeger, 1970), p. 15.

9. Roy C. Macridis, *Contemporary Political Ideologies, 5th ed.* (New York: HarperCollins, 1992), p. 2.

10. Plamenatz, *Ideology,* p. 2.

11. For more on the concepts of consensus and legitimacy, see Roy C. Macridis and Bernard E. Brown, eds., *Comparative Politics: Notes and Readings, 3rd. ed.* (Homewood, IL: Dorsey Press, 1968), pp. 107–114.

12. Joan Edelman Spero, *The Politics of International Economics Relations,* 4th ed. (New York: St. Martin's Press, 1990), p. 9.

13. Ibid., p. 4.

14. S. Kobrin, "Political Risk: A Review and Reconsideration," *Journal of International Business Studies* 10, no. 1 (1979), pp. 67–80.

15. D. Sethi, S. Guisinger, S. Phelan, and D. Berg, "Trends in Foreign Direct Investment Flows: A Theoretical and Empirical Analysis," *Journal of International Business Studies* 34, no. 4 (2003), pp. 315–326.

16. K. Brouthers, "Institutional, Cultural and Transaction Cost Influences on Entry Mode Choice and Performance," *Journal of International Business Studies* 33, no. 2 (2002), pp. 203–221.

17. R. Kashlak, R. Chandran, and A. DiBenedetto, "Reciprocity in International Business: A Study of Telecommunications Contracts and Alliances," *Journal of International Business Studies* 29, no. 2 (1998), pp. 281–304.

18. R. Hamilton and R. Kashlak, "National Influences on Multinational Control System Selection," *Management International Review* 39, no. 2 (1999), pp. 167–189.

19. K. Fatehi, "Capital Flight from Latin America as a Barometer of Political Instability," *Journal of Business Research* 30 (1994), pp. 165–173.

20. W. Henisz, "The Institutional Environment for Multinational Investment," *Journal of Law, Economics and Organization* 16 (2000), pp. 334–364.

21. W. Henisz and B. Zellner, "The Institutional Environment for Telecommunications Investment," *Journal of Economics and Management Strategy* 10 (2001), pp. 123–147.

22. W. Henisz and A. Delios, "Uncertainty, Imitation and Plant Location: Japanese MNCs, 1990-1996," *Administrative Science Quarterly* 46 (2001), pp. 443–475; A. Delios and W. Henisz, "Policy Uncertainty and the Sequence of Entry by Japanese Firms, 1980–1998," *Journal of International Business Studies* 34, no. 2 (2003), pp. 227–241.

23. Elaine Kurtenbach, "Beijing Cuts McDonald's Deal Short," *The Wall Street Journal,* November 27, 1994, p. A1.

24. Stefan A. Robock, "Political Risk: Identification and Assessment," *Columbia Journal of World Business,* pp. 9–10.

25. S. Kobrin, *Managing Political Risk Assessment* (Berkeley: University of California Press, 1982).

26. K. Miller, "Industry and Country Effects on Managers' Perceptions of Environmental Influences," *Journal of International Business Studies* 24, no. 4 (1993), pp. 693–713.

27. Based on Robock, "Political Risk," p. 16.

28. Ted Gurr, "A Causal Model of Civil Strife: A Comparative Model Using New Analysis," *American Political Science Review* 62, no. 4 (1968), p. 1104.

29. Gurr, "A Causal Model of Civil Strife," pp. 1105–1106.

30. *The New York Times,* September 13, 2002, Page W1.

31. Llewellyn D. Howell, "Business, Strategy and Political Risk," *Global Executive Forum,* Institute for International Business, University of Colorado at Denver, November 2002, p. 13.

32. J. Simon, "A Theoretical Perspective on Political Risk," *Journal of International Business Studies,* Winter 1984, pp. 123–142.

33. V. Errunza and E. Losq, "How Risky Are Emerging Markets?" *Journal of Portfolio Management,* Fall/Winter 1987, pp. 83–99.

34. J. Cosset and J. Suret, "Political Risk and the Benefits of International Portfolio Diversification," *Journal of International Business Studies* 27, no. 3 (1996), pp. 301–318.

35. OPIC Insurance Department, http://www.opic.gov/Insurance/.

36. Ibid.

CHAPTER FOUR

The International Legal Environment of Business

Chapter Learning Objectives

After completing this chapter, you should be able to:

- Integrate the legal environment into the political and economic frameworks developed in previous chapters.
- Identify the three levels of law that comprise the international legal system for business.
- Discuss the sources and characteristics of international, regional, and national law and the implications of each for the multinational firm.
- Describe the implications of various international treaties concerning intellectual property rights.
- Understand the Foreign Corrupt Practices Act and its implications for a firm's global operations.

Opening Case: Doing Business with Huawei Technologies

Huawei Technologies Company is one of the largest telecommunications equipment makers in China. The company employs 16,000 people and revenue for 2002 was 22 billion yuan ($2.7 billion). The company was established in 1988, during the peak of China's economic reform and technological advancement. Since its inception, Huawei has spent heavily in developing new products, including switching, access, transmission, and mobile communications, and it has risen to be one of the most competitive companies in the domestic market. The company has consistently allocated 10 percent of revenue to new-product development. Huawei has six research centers in major cities across China, including Beijing, Shanghai, and Nanjing, as well as operations in the United States, Russia, India, and Sweden. Huawei is one of the fastest growing telecom manufacturers in China and the largest private telecom company.

In 2002, the company began to feel the pressure of maintaining financial health dragged by heavy investment in R&D for a broad range of products and high cost of sales, while growth for its flagship products sputtered as operators cut back capital expenditures substantially. With a weak home market, Huawei shifted its attention to the international market, especially in Southeast Asia and eastern Europe, to boost sales. Huawei has developed an extensive sales network in China and 30 overseas offices for its broad product offerings. Huawei's broadband products are being used in 150 cities across China, Asia, and South America. It has sold more than 100 million parts of data equipment in Asia-Pacific and also holds 12 percent in the global optical transmission market. Huawei has sales in 40 countries, including Russia, Thailand, and Brazil. Overseas sales rose $550 million in 2002, up

25 percent from 2001, with GSM (Global System for Mobile Communication) equipment accounting for $170 million, nearly double the number in 2001.

Huawei is the shimmering jewel of China's high-tech industry. With its milewide campus bordered with palms, Huawei Technologies in the city of Shenzhen is China's answer to Silicon Valley's Cisco Systems. Its 10,000-plus engineers represent the country's best and brightest—and they work for salaries only 20 percent as high as their counterparts in California. What's more, its state-of-the-art factories, equipped with mammoth robotic parts-picking systems, fill orders for its networking gear with world-class efficiency.

Huawei appears positioned to become a power in the world's networking industry—except for one very large problem. In 2003, after an eight-month investigation, Cisco Systems launched a sweeping lawsuit against Huawei, alleging a host of intellectual property violations, and pushed for an injunction to remove certain Huawei products from the market. Huawei responded that the injunction Cisco seeks is unwarranted, and that it has already addressed Cisco's concerns. Still, the suit has derailed Huawei's expansion into the U.S. market. And it may have led Huawei to seek an alliance to bolster its presence and credibility in networking.

A month after the suit, Huawei announced a global joint venture with Cisco's longtime rival, 3Com Corporation.[1] 3Com, a leading supplier of modems, bundles QUALCOMM's popular Eudora e-mail program on CDs with its U.S. Robotics brand modems worldwide. 3Com has gained increased visibility for U.S. Robotics through cobranding in the Eudora e-mail user interface. In July 2003, Huawei announced a strategic partnership with QUALCOMM to develop CDMA (code division multiple access) services, network solutions, systems, and terminal chipsets. In August, Huawei and Siemens announced a plan to invest $100 million in a joint venture for TD-SCDMA (time division synchronous code division multiple access) production, sales, and service.

Discussion Questions

1. What are the risks of technology firms doing business in China?
2. Based on Cisco System's actions, what advice would you give to QUALCOMM and Siemens as they partner with Huawei?

Understanding Laws in the International Context

The Huawei case provides a beginning discussion point that links the international, home-country, and host-country legal environments. It also illustrates a strategic firm-level action that is a result of international law. The legal environment is intricately tied to the various political environments discussed in the preceding chapter. As suggested there, a host country's legal environment and associated legal institutions are a critical part of the governance infrastructure that an international firm must confront when expanding overseas.[2] Whereas stable legal environments may lead to greater economic growth within a country,[3] the instability of the same environment will increase pressure on a manager of an international firm and affect firm-level strategic choices and performance.[4]

An international company is obligated to operate within the boundaries of the international legal environment, and specifically within those legal precepts that pertain to international business activities. One could conceptualize the legal environment of international business as consisting of three concentric circles as seen in Figure 4.1 on page 110. The outermost circle includes international treaties and conventions which have been and continue to be the most important sources of international legal rules.[5] The middle circle represents the legal constraints and requirements imposed and incorporated in the laws of nation-states by the overarching laws of the regional trade blocs such as the European Union, North American Free Trade Agreement, and MER-COSUR. The innermost circle depicts the laws of nation-states designed to govern the behavior of the nations' citizens and business firms.

To understand the degree to which international law meets the requirements of an effective legal system we examine first, the concept of law; second, the requirements of an effective legal system; third, the functions of law; and finally, the degree to which international law meets the requirements of an effective legal system.

The Concept of Law

Law has three basic characteristics in a civilized society. First, law is a norm that prescribes what is assumed to be a proper mode of behavior. It attempts to regulate the behavior of the subjects according to certain standards set by the society or by those who control the society. Second, law not only prescribes a certain pattern of behavior but also requires that the prescribed mode be followed. We are bound to obey the law because it is the official desire of the society in which we live. Third, law includes a process approved by society for applying coercive sanctions against those who do not obey and therefore perform illegal acts.

The Requirements of an Effective Legal System

Several factors determine the effectiveness of a legal system. First, the people in the society must clearly understand and have knowledge of what the society prescribes as legal behavior. Without this knowledge one could not expect the law to be obeyed. Second, the members of society, the subjects of the legal system, must have agreed that the laws deserve to be obeyed, that is, they must regard the laws as being fair and just. Finally, an effective system for punishing illegal behavior must be in place. A number of writers have taken the position that an effective system of sanctions is all that is needed to make a legal system effective, and whether the members of society believe that the law is worthy of obedience is immaterial. The position taken in this book is that both prerequisites must be met before a legal system is deemed effective: the belief and sentiment that the law ought to be obeyed as well as a system for sanctioning illegal behavior.

In a democratic society, the government, which is duly elected by the people, provides the machinery for an effective legal system. The legislative branch of the government makes the laws, and the judicial and executive branches together perform the task of identifying illegal behavior and sanctioning the lawbreaker. A legal system functions effectively when there is a centralized process, like the government, to make and enforce the laws. The more effective that law enforcement is through the government, the less there is the danger that an individual or group might gain enough strength to disturb the stability of a society. At the same time the chances of a government remaining popular and in power are slim if an effective legal system does not exist.[6]

Functions of Law

The principal function of the legal system in a democratic society is to promote law and order with justice. Four functions of law promote this principal precept:

1. Law communicates to individuals in a society their rights and duties in their daily interactions with other people in the society. The definitions of rights and duties of individuals help prevent frequent conflicts among members of the society and also provide a basis for the settlement of disputes among them as they occur.

2. Law helps in controlling and preventing behavior that the society considers undesirable.

3. Governments use law to promote the social and economic welfare of society in the areas of child labor, social security, workmen's compensation, minimum wage, health care, food and drugs, and so on. Such laws promote order indirectly and in the long run, insofar as they help lay a solid foundation for an orderly society in the future.

4. Laws of a society reflect the norms, values, aims, and general beliefs of a society. To the extent that laws serve this function, they enhance the motivation of the members of a society to obey its laws.

International Law

Figure 4.1 illustrates the various levels of law that an international firm must be aware of. The outermost circle illustrated is **international law.** Since the seventeenth century observers of international relations have been plagued with this question: Is international law really law? If international law does exist, does it meet the requirements of an effective legal system? This question has persisted because international law, if it exists, exists in a social system that has no government. International law is true law if (1) there is a general agreement among the nations of the world (and by implications among the people in the world) regarding the nature and types of behaviors by nations and their citizens that are acceptable and those that are not; (2) nations feel obliged to obey the laws; and (3) there is a mechanism for applying sanctions against nations and their citizens if they behave in a manner deemed to be unacceptable according to generally recognized international standards.

The real underlying issue is whether an effective legal system—national or international—can exist without a centralized system, such as a government, that has the legitimacy and power conferred on it by the subjects to enact and enforce laws that conform with the values and beliefs of the members of the society who are the subjects of the law.

The Nature of International Law

Nation-states generally accept what is considered "illegal conduct" in international law. International law consists of a set of norms prescribing patterns of behavior, including illegal conduct, although those patterns are often vaguely defined. For example, ex-

FIGURE 4.1
The Legal Environment of International Business

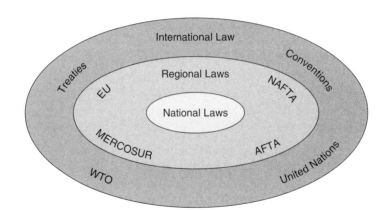

propriating the property of a foreign company without just and fair compensation for the property seized is generally considered to be unacceptable by the world community. Similarly, invasion by one country of another country merely to expand its national boundaries is viewed as illegal aggression under international law.

Moreover, in the past, as well as today, certain norms and reasons have obliged states to obey the law. The reasons are usually generated internally rather than from a central source, but they nonetheless exist in a subtle and often unarticulated form.

Finally, a system of sanctions within international law contributes to the coercive enforcement of the law. For instance, the invasion by Iraq of Kuwait led to the Gulf War in which a United Nations multinational force was involved in ousting the Iraqis from Kuwaiti soil. The United Nations enforced the international law enshrined in the principle that it is illegal for a nation to invade and seize the land and property of another sovereign nation. However, the United Nations is far from being a world government. The United Nations is in a position to take positive actions against "lawbreaker" states only if all countries that are the permanent members of the Security Council agree to not cast a veto against it. Since there is no world government in the true sense of the term, the system of sanctions in international law is not controlled by a centralized force, but is primarily administered according to the principle of self-help.

Therefore, at least in terms of the criteria employed in discussing law in democratic societies, international law can be defined as law. However, in the absence of a single formal supranational institution with the authority delegated to it by the various countries to enact laws and to force compliance to the laws by the countries and their citizens through enforceable sanctions, international law remains a decentralized or unsophisticated system of law.

The Role of the World Court and the WTO

The International Court of Justice (World Court) in the Hague, Holland, the principal judicial organ of the United Nations, is often mistakenly presumed to have the authority to adjudicate commercial disputes between companies and citizens of different countries and the power to enforce their decrees. Commercial disputes may arise: (1) between two countries; (2) between a country and a company; and (3) between two companies. The International Court of Justice can adjudicate disputes between two countries only when *both* governments involved agree to submit to the authority of the International Court of Justice. This limits the scope of this world judicial body. Disputes between a country and a company, or between two companies, can be settled in the courts of one of the parties to the dispute or through arbitration.

The WTO has a dispute settlement system. When there is a dispute between two countries or trade blocs, the director general of the WTO appoints a panel of experts to examine the dispute and then to make its decisions, which are binding unless overturned by consensus of the WTO membership. Under the WTO process, the country or trade bloc that wins a case before the WTO receives an automatic approval to undertake retaliatory measures against the offending country if that country does not change its practices. The country that is found guilty of violating fair-trade rules has two choices: It could change its law or face sanctions, most likely in the form of tariffs slapped on its exports by the complaining country. Thus even in this case, the winner of the case must take punitive actions by itself against the offending country or trade bloc. If the offending country is an economically powerful country like the United States or Japan, and hence could absorb the punitive actions imposed on it without much harm to its economy, then the aggrieved party can do little about it. Thus international managers must realize that no centralized judicial body exists to resolve commercial disputes between citizens and companies of different countries.

We next examine how international law is created and the role that custom and treaties play in this process.

International Law and the Risk of Intellectual Property Theft

International Law Creation

International law derives from four acknowledged sources that are recognized in the statutes of the International Court of Justice and taught in every international law course.[7] These sources, depicted in Figure 4.2, are:

- International treaties and conventions, whether general or particular, establishing rules expressly recognized by the contesting states.
- International customs, as evidence of a general practice accepted as law.
- General principles of law recognized by civilized nations.
- Judicial decisions and the teachings of the most highly qualified publicists of the various nations.

Today, these four main sources—treaty, custom, general principles of law, and judicial decisions and teachings—do not stand in isolation.[8] While the two preeminent sources, treaty and custom, certainly are the clearest and most frequently used, often the four work as an interrelated system to develop international law.[9]

International Custom

Historically, when international interactions were sporadic and less complex, custom was the primary source of international law. Thus **international custom** entails habitual patterns of behavior that evolve over a number of years to reach the level of obligatory rules—that is, international law—which govern how nations and their subjects interacted with one another. Customary international law must meet two requirements: habituality and a feeling of legal obligation. A rule of customary international law comes into existence when almost all states behave almost exactly the same way for a long time and feel a legal obligation to do so. Thus the essential elements of international custom include:

1. Concordant practice by a number of states regarding the type of situation falling within the domain of international relations.
2. Continuation and repetition of the practice over a considerable period of time.
3. The conception that the practice is consistent with prevailing international law.
4. General acquiescence in the practice by other states.[10]

FIGURE 4.2
Sources of International Law

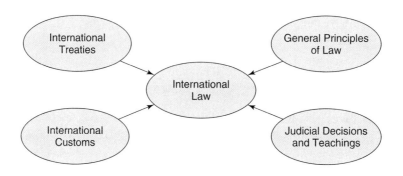

Even though it is important to understand that individual countries control the creation and legitimization of international customary law, custom in the form of unwritten but clearly understood norms has diminished as a source of international law because of the increasing interdependence and complexity of the modern world and the expansion of the international legal system beyond the confines of the "Western world." Thus we focus instead on international treaties and conventions.

International Treaties and Conventions

The working definition of an international treaty was provided in the 1969 Vienna Convention on the Law of Treaties: The **international treaty** is an international agreement concluded between states in written form and governed by international law.[11] A treaty is an agreement entered into by two or more states under general international law. If only two states are the contracting parties, it is called a *bilateral* treaty. A *multilateral* treaty is one in which more than two states are contracting parties. Sometimes a treaty is called an international *convention,* an *agreement,* a *protocol,* or a *declaration.* In most cases the title is not important. However, in the United States a distinction is made between a "treaty" and an "agreement." The U.S. Constitution stipulates that treaties are international agreements made by the president of the United States "by and with the advice of the Senate." "Executive agreements" are treaties entered into by the president, or with his authorization by someone else, without consultation with the Senate.

A treaty, like a contract, is a legal transaction by which the contracting parties intend to establish mutual obligations and rights. Countries that have signed the treaty are legally obliged and correspondingly entitled to behave as they have declared that they will behave. Therefore, if they do not behave in conformity with the contract or treaty means, they are exposed to sanctions and punishment. A treaty becomes incorporated into the laws of a nation when the nation's legislative body ratifies it. For example, in the United States, a two-thirds majority in the Senate must ratify a treaty.

Even though treaties are considered the major source of international law, this statement should not be taken literally. The thousands of treaties concluded among nations do not create one single general rule of international law. For instance, a commercial treaty between the United States and China, or a treaty to prevent double taxation between France and Morocco, does not create any rule of conduct for the family of nations. However, so-called *lawmaking treaties,* which are concluded among a number of countries in their joint interest, are intended to create a new rule. When a treaty is ratified by many nations, it creates general norms that regulate the mutual conduct among the signatory countries. A lawmaking treaty, then, is a means by which a substantial number of countries reach an agreement about a particular rule of law. It may promote new general rules for the future conduct of the member countries. A lawmaking treaty may also cause an existing customary or conventional rule of law to be modified, abolished, or codified. It may as well lead to the creation of a new international agency. The International Labor Organization is an example of an international agency that was created by a multilateral treaty signed by almost all nations to protect the health, safety, and working hours of workers and to prevent the abuse of child labor. This is the kind of treaty through which conventional international law is created.

Examples of Commercial Treaties

Treaties of Friendship, Commerce, and Navigation

Many different types of treaties are in force to govern the behavior of nations and, in turn, their citizens—for example, the Law of the Sea, military alliances like NATO, and treaties that govern global aviation and navigation. Certain treaties are of particular significance to business enterprises. For instance, the various treaties regarding friendship, commerce, and navigation (FCN) apply to an international company doing business in another country. This is seen not as a right, but as a privilege. Subsequently, this privilege and its conditions are negotiated between the host-country government and the home-country government. The United States has treaties with several dozen nations that formulate the conditions of the privilege under which American firms may do business in these nations, and vice versa. They usually include, among other things, reciprocal pledges by each of the signatory countries to honor the property of the other country's companies located within their respective national borders, and to give the other country's companies *national treatment,* meaning treatment that is no less favorable than that which is given to business firms that are its own citizens. Also included are guarantees that property will not be seized illegally and without proper compensation. Most treaties include in them the *most-favored-nation* (MFN) treatment clause. The MFN clause obligates the country to give to the imports of goods from the other country, with which it has signed a treaty, tariff treatment that is no less favorable than that given to imports from third countries.

FCN laws continue to be a current international business issue. For example, as Japanese firms have increasingly expanded into the United States during the past two decades, problems have developed between U.S. employees and Japanese employees in the United States. Because many Japanese companies limited senior management positions to Japanese expatriates, many discrimination claims were filed. Under the United States–Japan Treaty of Friendship, Commerce, and Navigation (JFCN), Article VIII provides that U.S. companies in Japan and Japanese companies in the United States can fill certain positions without restriction. In effect, Article VIII appears to exempt certain companies from complying with antidiscrimination laws in certain employment circumstances. Thus a central issue of conflict lies between the JFCN Treaty and antidiscrimination laws of the United States.[12] Furthermore, the placing of expatriates of choice by foreign companies in host countries has been found to have national security implications for the hosts,[13] an implication that reverberates loudly since September 11, 2001.

Treaties for the Protection of Intellectual Property Rights

Of particular significance today for an international company is the protection of its **intellectual property rights**—that is, proprietary property or intellectual capital. While many countries have officially signed the various treaties governing the protection of intellectual property, enforcing the treaty provisions remains a serious problem. The theft of intellectual property—ideas and innovations protected by copyright, patents, and trademarks—is a serious problem facing American industry and therefore America itself in the absence of effective domestic legislation in other countries for the protection of intellectual property.

When blockbuster movies such as *Star Wars: Attack of the Clones* and *Spiderman* were released in 2002 to theaters in the United States, they had already been available on DVD in Shanghai and Bangkok at the price of U.S. $1. Similarly, a new Tom Clancy novel may be obtained in paperback in Bombay, Hong Kong, and even Singapore before its U.S. hardback release. Many "entrepreneurs" throughout the world copy or even create Bruce Springsteen and U2 CDs. Ongoing efforts to protect these and other performers' international rights have been unsuccessful. For example,

> In December 2000, efforts to sign a global treaty for the protection of performers' rights in audiovisual works failed because of a disagreement between the United States and the European Union over the issue of transferring rights from performers to producers. Now, (WIPO) [World Intellectual Property Organization] is trying again. WIPO hopes to restart negotiations and has announced that it will schedule an informal conference for early 2003.

In 2000, WIPO members reached an agreement on 19 of the draft treaty's 20 articles, recognizing for the first time audiovisual performers' moral rights against any distribution and/or modification of their work that would somehow prejudice their reputations.

The EU has long advocated for language that would require the permission of the authors or performers themselves before allowing a transfer of rights to producers. This is already the law in several EU nations.

The United States, however, takes a different view. US officials insisted on the recognition of existing contractual arrangements that allow for the automatic transfer of rights from performers to producers. As a result, they wanted a performer's "entitlement" to exclusive rights based on consent to be governed by the law of the country most closely related to the parties or the agreement. Thus, if US law applied, consent would not be necessary. The European Union refused, claiming that such a provision would effectively impose US law on other countries. How this issue will be resolved remains to be seen.[14]

Beyond the obvious concerns for the music, cinema, and publishing industries, the concern of protecting intellectual property has reached new heights regarding software and high technology. International companies with new technologies have found increasingly that they must (1) develop mechanisms to protect against illegal pirating of their intellectual property and (2) develop patent programs to protect their inventions throughout the international market. In fact, companies that remain ignorant of foreign patent procedures and apply for patents in the traditional, one-nation manner can inadvertently destroy their opportunities to obtain foreign patents.

U.S. patents give rights only within the United States. The same rule applies to patents granted in foreign countries. To protect its foreign patent rights, a company's patent strategy and business practices must accommodate foreign rules and deadlines, making sophisticated use of complex national, regional, and global patent application strategies. To obtain patent protection in a foreign country or region, companies must ultimately obtain a patent from the appropriate foreign patent office, and the patent must be enforced in that country's or region's courts. By following proper procedures, international companies can achieve these goals.

In the United States, utility patents (patents for "any new and useful process, machine, manufacture, or composition of matter") are distinguished from design patents. Within different industries, these patents have different practical lives depending on the ease with which the patent can be extended. As an example, in 2002, extending patents in the U.S. pharmaceutical industry was made more difficult, thus allowing generic drugs easier entry into the market. A further complicating factor is the difference in the life of various types of patents from country to country. Also, countries vary in using a patent system based on a *first-to-invent* standard and one based on a *first-to-file* standard. When two or more independent inventors file overlapping patent applications, a rule must be applied to determine who will be granted the patent. Under the first-to-invent rule, an inventor who can prove that she was the first to invent a device and diligently pursue its development will obtain the patent rights. In countries using the first-to-file rule, the first party to file a patent application in a given jurisdiction is awarded the patent.

International patent protection has steadily increased for international firms. There have been ongoing efforts to secure a new global patent system for firms operating internationally.[15] Major changes finally occurred in 2002, as exemplified in the following passage:

WIPO members agreed to procedural changes to the Patent Cooperation Treaty (PCT) at the annual meeting of the WIPO General Assemblies held September 23 to October 21, 2002. The changes are intended to streamline and simplify the system for filing patents under the PCT. Included among the changes is a single flat fee for applications. Additionally, WIPO adopted changes relating to the language in which applications must be filed, the restatement of rights after failing to comply with filing requirements, and the availability of priority documents from digital libraries. These additional changes were made in order to bring the PCT into compliance with the Patent Law Treaty that was finalized in 2002.

Another change decreased the filing fees for electronic filings under the PCT by 200 Swiss francs (approximately $135). Filing fees are reduced by 75 percent for applications that originate from developing countries. The new discount took effect on October 17, 2002, and reflected the sixth consecutive year that fees have decreased.

The General Assemblies also instituted changes in regard to preliminary reports used by applicants to determine whether to proceed in seeking patent protection. Under current rules, the international phase begins with Chapter I proceedings, in which a report is prepared by an International Searching Authority (ISA) as to the patentability of the claimed invention. Then, in a separate procedure, an applicant may choose a preliminary examination report under Chapter II of the process, which involves a more extensive preliminary and non-binding opinion as to the patentability of the invention. These reports are used by the applicant to determine whether to continue to seek patent protection at the national level.

Under new procedures promulgated by WIPO, the ISA will now be responsible for drafting a report on whether an invention appears to be novel, involves an inventive step, and appears to be industrially applicable. According to WIPO, this change allows for the combination of "the international search and international preliminary examination procedures to a much greater extent than is the case at present." These changes were instituted because many applicants are forced to proceed without the benefit of a Chapter II report because of the 30-month time limit to begin the national phase.

The changes take effect on different dates. Changes relating to the international application on the restatement of rights will take effect on January 1, 2003. The changes relating to the international search system and preliminary examination, as well as the availability of priority documents from digital libraries, will not become effective until January 1, 2004.[16]

Other types of intellectual property include trademarks, copyrights, and processes. Combined losses for companies resulting from the piracy of these propri-etary properties have skyrocketed to billions of dollars. The potential piracy of a trademark, copyright, or manufacturing process represents a significant risk for the international company as well as a potential loss of worldwide competitive position-ing. Historically, many treaties have attempted to limit piracy of proprietary property. For instance, the Trademark Law Revision Act of 1988 gave federal registrations of trademarks and service marks in the United States a renewable term of 10 years (for-merly 20 years), provided that the mark is in use in interstate commerce and a spec-imen proving use is provided to the Patent and Trademark Office. Also, the Paris Convention for the Protection of Industrial Property was established as an interna-tional convention to protect trademarks. The Berne Convention for the Protection of Literary and Artistic Works was multilaterally instituted to protect copyright in-fringement around the world. Still, the piracy of a company's intellectual property continues to grow exponentially.

One of the newest intellectual property treaties is the **Madrid Protocol.** In November 2002, President George W. Bush signed into law this treaty that provides an interna-tional system for registering trademarks. It is administered by the World Intellectual Property Organization (WIPO). Firms should bear in mind that the Madrid Protocol does not replace any one country's trademark registration system. Instead, it allows a trademark owner to file a single application in his home country, called a basic regis-tration, and then designate extension of the application or registration to some or all of the member countries at a reduced fee.[17] As a result of the United States joining this treaty, its businesses will have the means to accomplish the closest thing to interna-

TABLE 4.1
The 2002 Madrid
Protocol:
Implications for U.S.
Firms Registering
International
Trademarks

Advantages to U.S. Firms	Disadvantages to U.S. Firms
Less expensive	Fewer international rights
Simpler	Linked to valid U.S. registration
Less need for foreign counsel	Trademark must be used in U.S.
Quicker	Broader foreign definitions

tional trademark registration. This is a key element to success in today's evolving global marketplace. That is, businesses must be able to protect their identities throughout the world in order to maintain sustainable competitive advantages.[18] The Madrid Protocol offers distinct benefits to international firms. Still, there are a few drawbacks, as depicted in Table 4.1, which highlights the implications for U.S. firms.

The Madrid Protocol is a simple and inexpensive option to secure international trademark protection. The trademark applicant may forgo the hiring of foreign attorneys in each country where trademark protection is sought. Furthermore, international firms are not required to file national applications, to deal with translations from and into foreign languages, and to administer a trademark portfolio on a country-by-country basis. Also, because international applications must be acted on within 12 to 18 months, the application is now a quicker process in countries where examination had taken three or four years (e.g., India). Still, there are potential drawbacks. The Madrid Protocol may offer fewer rights to U.S. companies. For instance, because the international registration depends on the original U.S. application, international protection will be canceled if the mark is not registered in the United States, even if it is able to be registered overseas. The entire application will fail if the U.S. firm has not used the mark at home within three years of allowance. Another potential drawback regards U.S. and foreign-based definitions. U.S. law requires a narrowly defined specification of goods and services. Many foreign laws allow much broader definitions. Under the Madrid Protocol, the U.S. applicant's international registration would be limited to the narrow U.S. description. While the Madrid Protocol will make it easier for U.S. applicants to achieve registrations abroad, it also will make it easier for foreign applicants to obtain rights in the United States, making the U.S. register even more crowded and increasing the risk that a U.S. firm will be forced to contend with conflicting trademarks owned by foreign entities.[19]

From counterfeit Rolex watches on Canal Street in Manhattan, to modern software factories in Asia, international companies stand to lose from piracy of intellectual property in a number of ways:

1. The international company loses sales in the copycat country itself as it is forced to compete against pirated products.
2. It loses sales in third countries where it has to compete against exported pirated products.
3. Its reputation as a producer of quality products and service suffers because pirated products of inferior quality are often sold under the company's brand name (e.g., Polo, Ralph Lauren, Rolex, Gucci, T.G.I. Friday's, Microsoft, Zantac).
4. It may be prevented entry in a foreign market because a company in the foreign market may have established a dominant market share using the international company's pirated technology or trademark.

Practical Insights 4.1 and 4.2 further illustrate this problem.

PRACTICAL INSIGHT 4.1

"AM I NOW IN THE SHOE BUSINESS?" COUNTERFEITING IN CHINA

Counterfeiting is such a problem in China that it may drive away some foreign investors that manufacture designer-label goods, companies warn. They say that despite efforts by the authorities, they were still losing millions of dollars in revenues because of availability of counterfeit products.

Mont Blanc president Norbert Platt said: "Counterfeiting is a huge problem in China. China should understand that it's something that threatens our investment. We recently closed a shoe shop in China which sold Mont Blanc-branded shoes. And we're not even producing shoes!"

The LVMH Fashion group, the world-renowned manufacturer and retailer of fashion brands Louis Vuitton, Loewe, Celine and others, has been operating in China for 10 years. Like its business rivals, the group is hurting from the counterfeiters' operations. Despite repeated crackdowns by Chinese authorities, fake Louis Vuitton handbags can be purchased in Shenzhen shops for less than HK$100, a fraction of the HK$4,000 price for the real thing.

"The counterfeiting problem is huge, particularly in China," said Hugues Witvoet, Asia-Pacific president of LVMH Fashion. "For as long as you have strong brands, counterfeiting will always be a problem. Unscrupulous people try to copy your products and they sell them at much cheaper prices than the genuines. But they cheat their customers because the quality of their goods is not as good as the original. It's a world-wide problem which adversely affects many industries," he said.

The LVMH Fashion group's concerns are shared by Alfred Dunhill. Tim King, managing director for the firm in the Asia-Pacific region, said: "It [counterfeiting] is absolutely a major challenge for major retailers in China. That is why we spend quite a lot of money on anti-counterfeiting measures . . . We check stores and work closely with the authorities to try to locate the sources of the fakes in China . . . We have been locating factories producing the counterfeit products. But the key point is how to stop the big ones, instead of merely catching the small guys who are selling them."

Globally, legitimate product manufacturers lose an estimated US$300 billion to the counterfeiters a year, or about 5 to 8 percent of world trade, estimates Peter Lowe, assistant director at the London-based Counterfeiting Intelligence Bureau (CIB). He said counterfeiting was one of the fastest growing economic crimes in the world, threatening businesses and jobs, undermining trade relationships, scaring off vital new investments and endangering public health and safety.

Joseph Simone, vice-chairman of Quality Brand Protection Committee (QBPC), representing 78 multinational companies including Alfred Dunhill, said seizures by US and European customs authorities had indicated that China was a big source of counterfeit goods. The number and value of seizures by US and EU customs had been increasing dramatically in the last few years, he said. QBPC believes that its member companies lose up to 15 percent of their market in China and nearby countries, which represents a potential loss of billions of US dollars a year, because of China's counterfeiters.

Guangdong is the main area for counterfeiting goods, followed by Zhejiang, Jiangsu and Fujian, Mr. Simone said. Xiao Yang, president of the Supreme People's Court, recently said the mainland judiciary had made special efforts to mark crimes that included counterfeiting.

A crackdown on counterfeit goods would focus on the involvement of gangsters who controlled the distribution of counterfeit goods, he said. Hong Kong's custom authorities have also denied assertions that Hong Kong is a large trans-shipment point of China-made counterfeits.

They admit, however, that seizures of fake goods from China, including clothes, leather goods, shoes, mobile phones and TV game accessories, reached a four-year high of HK$213.8 million last year. Seizures in the five months to May 31 amounted to HK$53.3 million.

David Fong, division commander at the intellectual property intelligence and border investigation division of the Hong Kong Customs and Excise Department, said: "It's unfair to describe Hong Kong as a major trans-shipment point of fake goods made in China because the counterfeiters are using many other routes." He said the Chinese counterfeiters were frequently using ports in different provinces including Huangpu, Ningbo, Fuzhou and Xiamen, to directly export their counterfeit products to different parts of the world.

They could also ship out their goods to Singapore via Shekou and Shantou, to Korea and Russia through Shenyang, Changchun and Harbin and to Pakistan from Lanzhou and Urumqi, he said. Kenn Ross, Shanghai-based senior manager at Pinkerton (China), said the problem with counterfeits had eased in the past four years, reflecting the Chinese leaders' concern with the protection of intellectual property rights as a key ingredient to the health and growth of the country's economy. The company operates 14 offices all over Asia but its largest operations are in China.

Source: From Sandy Li, "Designer Concern Over Mainland Fakes Threatens Future Investment," *South China Morning Post,* July 21, 2002. Reprinted with permission of South China Morning Post Publishers Ltd.

PRACTICAL INSIGHT 4.2

THAILAND'S STRUGGLE WITH GOODS PIRACY

Thailand is a shopper's paradise. There are cheap copies of almost every designer product ever made. The street markets do a roaring trade selling items ranging from watches, clothes and dress accessories to music CDs, digital movies and computer software. The market for pirate software is growing rapidly. DVDs and computer games are on sale on street stalls and in major shopping complexes. The more notorious of these are Pantip Plaza, Fortune Towers and Seacon Square, where authorized computer dealers and the pirates compete for customers. Digital films and videos sell for around 60% of the official price, computer games and software for about 50%. The greatest discrepancy is on Microsoft software which sells for less than 10% of the retail price. These massive savings attract a very large market.

In Bangkok it is not just foreign tourists who are buying the pirate products on sale in the major computer centers. "Only one customer in 10 is a foreigner," said Suchai, a pirate DVD stall holder in Pantip Plaza. The customers are aged from the very young to the over 70. "Even monks come here for their software needs," said Noi, a saleswoman on another stall of pirate computer games.

Registered distributors in Bangkok selling computer software and DVDs estimate that pirate sales cost them more than 50% of their potential profit. More than $53m of potential revenue was lost last year from pirated versions of business software applications alone, according the Business Software Alliance in Bangkok. And this does not cover computer games. Pirate CDs, videos, digital movies and computer software are costing manufacturers billions of dollars each year. But neither government officials, producers nor consumer groups can put a more precise value on it. "We've got no idea," said a government official in the commerce ministry who did not want to be identified. Computer businesses also say they cannot estimate the losses for the whole of the industry—or even for one title.

Government officials say that DVDs and computer games must be treated as luxury goods, especially in Thailand where the average income is low. "If these products were only available at the official retail price, then there would only be very limited extra sales," said a Thai official. This may be one reason that the Thai law enforcement agents do not seem to be very active in trying to stamp out the trade in pirate products.

"The police periodically seize fake goods that are on sale in the market places," said a local stall holder. "But these are more likely to be designer clothes and leather bags," she said.

Publicly, the Thai Government is taking a hard line on the sale of pirated goods. In July the Prime Minister, Thaksin Shinawatra, went to one of Bangkok's many night markets, One Night Bazaar, and told the stall holders that the selling of pirate films and videos must stop. This halted sales in the area for a while, but only temporarily—a week later the pirated videos and DVDs reappeared.

"The government is doing as much as possible," said a senior government official in the department for intellectual property rights in Thailand. "But we can never eliminate it completely. The best we can do is to find an accessible level of violation."

Privately many businessmen are convinced that the government is not really committed to stamping out pirate production and sales. But government officials argue that the only way to really eliminate piracy is to attack it at the source. And most of the pirate versions of CDs, videos, DVDs and computer games are not produced in Thailand. Most of them are brought across the border from Malaysia, Burma, Cambodia and Laos, according to Thai officials. China and Taiwan are the other major sources of pirated goods. "Malaysia is the main source of pirated DVDs, videos and computer games," a senior government official, who did not want to be identified, told the BBC.

Analysts in South East Asia feel that manufacturers themselves must also take action to help stop piracy by introducing more sensible pricing policies. This is something the makers and distributors of computer games in Thailand have realised. In the past few months, as a result in the growth in the sales of pirated versions, they have begun to reduce their retail prices. Many computer games are now selling at half the original price, making them now only marginally more expensive than the pirated versions.

The sales of genuine copies of computer games, which come complete with operating manuals, after-sales support and attractive packaging, have begun to rise substantially.

Source: From Larry Jagan of the BBC, "Counterfeit Rolex Watches in Thailand Software and DVDs Have Joined Watches in the Markets," BBC News Online, December 13, 2001. Reprinted with permission of BBC News Online.

Laws of Regional Trade Blocs

As alluded to in Chapter 2, the various regional economic agreements have laws that pertain to doing business in each of those pacts, whether or not the firm originates from one of the countries in the cooperative. For instance, new standards for different industries apply to all locations within the European Union. These laws entail many categories. Some of the more prominent include laws regarding:

- Agriculture
- Competition
- Consumer protection
- Education and training
- Environmental protection
- Food safety
- Fraud
- Internet marketing
- Public health
- Research and innovation
- Taxation

As an example, environmental laws within the EU apply to every firm operating in the member countries and state:

Damage to the environment has been growing steadily worse in recent decades. Every year, some 2 billion tons of waste are produced in the Member States and this figure is rising by 10% annually, while CO_2 emissions from our homes and vehicles are increasing, as is our consumption of "dirty" energy. The quality of life for people living in Europe, especially in urban areas, has declined considerably because of pollution, noise and vandalism.

Protection of the environment is therefore one of the major challenges facing Europe. The European Community has been strongly criticized for putting trade and economic development before environmental considerations. It is now recognized that the European model of development cannot be based on the depletion of natural resources and the deterioration of our environment.

Environmental action by the Community began in 1972 with four successive action programs, based on a vertical and sectoral approach to ecological problems. During this period, the Community adopted some 200 pieces of legislation, chiefly concerned with limiting pollution by introducing minimum standards, notably for waste management, water pollution and air pollution.

The introduction of this legislative framework, however, could not of itself prevent deterioration of the environment, and with the growth in public awareness of the risks posed by global environmental problems it has become clear that concerted action at European and international levels is absolutely essential.

Community action developed over the years until the Treaty on European Union conferred on it the status of a policy. A further step was taken with the *Treaty of Amsterdam,* which enshrines the principle of sustainable development as one of the European Community's aims and makes a high degree of environmental protection one of its absolute priorities.

To set about achieving this as effectively as possible, the *Fifth Community Action Programme on the Environment* "Towards Sustainability" established the principles of a European strategy of voluntary action for the period 1992–2000 and marked the beginning of a "horizontal" Community approach which would take account of all the causes of pollution (industry, energy, tourism, transport, agriculture, etc.).

This across-the-board approach to environmental policy was confirmed by the Commission in the wake of its 1998 Communication on *integrating the environment into European Union policies* and by the Vienna European Council (11 and 12 December 1998). The Community institutions are now obliged to take account of environmental considerations in all their other policies. Since then, this obligation has been taken into account in various Community acts, particularly in the fields of employment, energy, agriculture, development cooperation, single market, industry, fisheries, economic policy and transport.

A communication on the *European strategy for sustainable development* was approved in May 2001. It sets out the long-term objectives for sustainable development and essentially concerns climate change, transport, health and natural resources. The need for Community action on liability for damage caused to the environment and on making good such damage has been gaining ground since the adoption of the White Paper on *environmental liability* in February 2000.

The *sixth action program for the environment,* which is currently being adopted, sets out the priorities for the European Community up to 2010. Four areas are highlighted: climate change, nature and biodiversity, environment and health and the management of natural resources and waste. Measures to achieve these priorities are outlined: improving the application of environmental legislation, working together with the market and citizens and ensuring that other Community policies take greater account of environmental considerations. An innovation which is worth mentioning is the integrated product policy. This aims to develop a more ecological product market by making products more environmentally sustainable throughout their life cycle.[20]

Laws of Nation-States

Now, we move to the innermost concentric circle in Figure 4.1—the laws of nation-states, or country laws. In conjunction with international law (created through treaties and conventions) and regional trade bloc laws, country laws shape the legal environment of international business with which international firms must comply. We live in a world of sovereign states.

Scholars have historically classified numerous countries according to the origin of their commercial or corporate legal codes. These classifications include:

- English common law.
- Civil law of French, German, or Scandinavian origin.
- Socialist law, based on Communist principles.[21]

A disadvantage of this measure is that it classifies all formerly Communist countries in the last category, and so possibly combines the role of legal systems with other factors. Still, these classifications may be initially used to clarify the distinctions in the legal systems of various host countries.[22] It also fails to explicitly recognize Islamic law. We explore the implications of Islamic law later.

Sovereignty grants each independent nation the supreme authority to legislate laws meant to govern those within its jurisdiction. Although a country is obligated to obey the provisions and code of conduct of any international treaty or agreement to which it is party, it still retains the right to make its own laws. The international legal framework as it exists today consists of an umbrella of international law embracing various treaties and regional trade bloc law, under which are the separate national laws of independent nations.

An international company has to live within this global legal framework. It must comprehend international law, national laws of countries in which it has subsidiaries, and how international law and national laws affect its different subsidiaries individually as well as collectively. This can be quite a problem because not only are the legal systems of countries continuously evolving and changing, but the laws of two or more countries may well be in conflict. Additionally, international companies must be aware not only of the treaties that the home country has with other countries, but also of treaties that the host country has with third countries. This is because the foreign subsidiaries must obey the national laws and treaty obligations of both the home and host countries.

Common Law and Civil Law

The legal systems of different countries can be grouped into two main categories—common law and civil law. **Common law** is a set of legal principles originating in the feudal law of medieval England. **Civil law,** often referred to as "code law" or "Roman law," has its roots in the legal system of the Roman Empire. Civil law was compiled initially by Napoleon Bonaparte. The legal systems of English-speaking countries like England, Canada, the United States, and Australia and of former British colonies such as India, Pakistan, Nigeria, Kenya, and Jamaica are based on common law. Nations of continental Europe like France, Spain, and Italy and their former colonies base their legal systems on civil law.

What are the major differences between common law and civil law? Common law is based on tradition and legal precedents formulated by past court rulings, statutes, and government decrees. Included in common law, therefore, are sets of legal precepts that have gradually evolved over a number of years. The bases for common law then are past practices and precedents. Under civil law, one finds a comprehensive set of written codes or rules of law, which have been stated in general terms. These codes are then applied to specific cases as they arise because civil law recognizes that business problems are often unique and consequently need special status under the law. Therefore, civil law provides a separate code to handle commercial problems. Common law has no such commercial code specially designed for business, although it includes one set of codes that is applied to either civil or commercial disputes. International companies must understand the differences in the natures of these two systems because the due process of law may differ considerably between civil-law and common-law countries.

Islamic Law

As major Islamic countries such as Indonesia, Saudi Arabia, and Malaysia have become more prominent in international business, legal issues unique to the Islamic world arise. The *Koran,* the holiest of all holy books in Islam, is the basis for the legal system and the nature of laws in most countries that have a majority of the population belonging to the Islamic faith. **Islamic law** (*Shari'ah*) is the interpretation of the Koran. The word "Islam" means submission (i.e., to the will of God), and the word "Muslim" means one who submits.[23] The extent to which Islamic precepts govern the laws of the various predominantly Muslim countries differs. For example, by far the strictest Islamic country that western firms do business with is Saudia Arabia, which has the holy Koran as its constitution. This means that all laws in Saudia Arabia, whether civil or criminal, must reflect the principles enunciated in the Koran. Pakistan is another country that has declared itself an Islamic republic and which therefore professes to legislate according to Islamic precepts.

At the core of Islamic thinking is the right of every man or woman, Muslim or non-Muslim, to own property. Similarly, the importance of business and trade is recognized.

The prophet Mohammad was himself a businessman.[24] Islam forbids "excessive" profit, which is considered to be a form of exploitation. Islam preaches moderation and a sharing of wealth with others less fortunate, so individuals are held accountable for the well-being of the community. The concept of sharing of wealth is manifested in the *zakat,* which is annual individual tax used for the benefit of the community. Islam forbids the charging of usury or interest. The Islamic law of contracts requires that any transaction must be free of *riba,* defined as unlawful advantage by way of excess of deferment (i.e., usury or interest). To Western economists an interest rate should reflect, among other things, "pure time preference"—that is, the notion that consumption today is worth more than consumption tomorrow. The interest that is charged by the lender is meant to be a reward for forgone consumption. However, Islamic scholars argue that this justification for charging interest implies that mere hoarding of cash in a safe deposit box at home also deserves an economic reward because it too reflects forgone consumption. Moreover, an economic reward becomes available for distribution only if consumption forgone is translated into investment that yields a real economic return, that is, the investment creates wealth. Islamic scholars would agree with Western economists that lenders are entitled to have their fair share (in the form of interest) of any such return, but only to the extent that the lenders help to create wealth. This means that lenders must accept a share of the risk. Islamic contract law is very strict in its application of the concept that risks should be shared. It insists that wherever there is uncertainty, contracts that assure one party a fixed return (interest), even though no wealth was created, are not permitted.[25]

Banks in fundamentalist Islamic nations have banking systems that follow, at least in part, Islamic principles. Some circumvent the prohibition against making interest-bearing loans by buying some of the borrower's stock and selling it back to the company at a higher price. The size of the markup is determined by the riskiness of the venture, and the amount and maturity period of the loan. This loan-granting tactic is no different from the traditional criteria used in determining interest rates.[26] This practice is not approved of by strict fundamentalists. Alternatively, banks may buy equity in the venture being financed and share profits as well as losses in the joint ventures.

A variety of partnership agreements allows lending without interest. Schemes such as *mudarabha* and *musharaka* have been designed to allow banks to receive a contractual share of the profits generated by the borrowing firms. Under the mudarabha arrangement the bank supplies capital to a client and in return the bank gets a percentage of the client's net profits every year until the loan is repaid. The bank's share of the profits serves to repay the principal and a profit for the bank, which is passed on to its depositors. If the client does not make a profit, the bank, its depositors, and the borrower jointly absorb the loss, thereby putting into practice the Islamic principle that both lenders and borrowers should share in the risks and rewards of an investment. A musharaka contract is similar to the Western concept of a limited partnership. The bank and the client both share the equity capital, and sometimes even the managerial and technical expertise, of the investment project. Both the bank and the client share the profits or losses of the project according to a previously negotiated ratio. Such practices for making loans in the face of the Islamic prohibition of interest-bearing loans are examples of how the strict principles of Islamic law can be harmonized with the laws of non-Islamic legal systems.[27] Practical Insight 4.3 explores Islamic law.

The acceptance of Islamic banking has been mixed. People have the choice to opt for Islamic or traditional banking. Because international companies mostly conduct business with international banks that do not follow practices based on Islamic banking precepts, banks in Islamic countries have two options on introduction of Islamic

PRACTICAL INSIGHT 4.3

PROFIT AND THE PROPHET: INDONESIAN BANK OFFERS NO-INTEREST SERVICES

Bank Muamalat Indonesia (BMI), Indonesia's first Islamic bank, met with a mixed reaction when it opened its doors for business on 1 May. While many Islamic groups welcomed the new institution, saying it would draw new funds into the banking system, bankers criticized it as being too risky, and political analysts labeled it a thinly veiled attempt by the government to woo Muslim support. The financial sector in Indonesia, home to the world's largest Muslim community, has risen sharply in the past five years, with funds in the system increasing by more than 200% in 1987–91. Supporters believe BMI will attract business from those Muslims who object to placing their money in banks that violate the Islamic proscription on charging interest on loans.

The principle of Islamic banking is founded on a verse in the Koran in which the Prophet Mohammad forbids the practice of usury. "Usury and interest are synonymous in Islamic terminology," Seyed Ali Asghar Hedayati, a faculty member at the Iran Institute of Banking, said at a Jakarta symposium in October. While a more moderate interpretation defines usury as excessively high rates of interest, BMI subscribes to the stricter view. The issue is sensitive in Indonesia because the existence of one Islamic bank suggests that conventional banks are violating Muslim teachings. "BMI is an alternative for Muslims," says the bank's managing director, Maman Natapermadi. "If they switch to us, then Allah will forgive them (for banking at conventional banks). If they don't switch, they run the risk of (Allah's) punishment."

An Islamic bank works on a profit-sharing principle. Depositors, treated as investors, are allocated a return based on how profitably the bank invests their money. On the asset side, an Islamic bank acts like a venture-capital investor, injecting funds into companies instead of loans. Islamic banks also par-ticipate in a kind of trade financing in which they buy goods and sell them, at a mark-up, to customers.

BMI divides its assets into three kinds: trade finance, venture capital-type investments and "benevolent lending," in which the bank lends to customers who must repay the principal, but with no interest or additional charges. Trade finance is the simplest to compute. Instead of lending money to customers for purchases of raw materials or capital goods, BMI acquires the items on its own behalf and re-sells to the customer at a higher price. The mark-up usually will be equivalent to the rate customers would pay elsewhere for conventional financing. For its venture-capital investments, BMI will provide start-up capital, and the client will manage the business. "Together, we share the risks and rewards," says Natapermadi. To depositors, BMI offers products that are similar to demand and savings deposits. In an Islamic bank, the latter are called profit-sharing deposits and are distinguished by the absence of a predetermined reward.

Theoretically, the return that depositors receive depends on how well the bank "invests" its available funds. The bank and the depositor agree to a "revenue-sharing ratio" which stipulates how much of the bank's profits are kept and how much are to be paid out to the depositor. In practice, BMI's depositors will receive a return close to that offered by conventional banks. "We don't want our depositors to make less than they would make elsewhere," says Natapermadi. Periodically, BMI will adjust the revenue-sharing ratio so that the portion of profits allocated to depositors will be close to the rate of interest offered by other banks.

banking. They can establish a full-fledged subsidiary for Islamic banking or open special windows for Islamic banking at their branches. Nowhere in the Islamic world is the Islamic banking system enforced in totality. Partial Islamic banking is used in 75 countries, including Pakistan, Saudi Arabia, Iran, Kuwait, Malaysia, and Indonesia, but the total volume of deposits governed by the system is not more than $200 billion, which is far less than the conventional banking. International companies generally do not use Islamic banks when conducting business with customers in Islamic countries. However, international banks could take the opportunity afforded by Islamic banking through subsidiaries or divisions that function on Islamic banking principles. HSBC, Chase Manhattan, Citcorp, ABN Amro, Standard Chartered Grindlays Bank, Kleinwont Benson, Union Bank, and Australian Girozentrale Bank have introduced Islamic banking alongside their extant, much larger, traditional banking systems.[28]

Host-Country-Specific Laws

Different nations have their own peculiar laws, which in one way or another affect the international operations of multinational companies. In the following paragraphs we take a brief look at a few such laws. The examples given in this section are by no means all-inclusive. There are certainly many more interesting differences in the legal requirements of various countries, but our purpose here is merely to acquaint the reader with situations that may be legal in one country but not in another. Multinational companies need to give particular attention to the impact of national laws on such crucial areas as advertising, patent protection, ownership of subsidiaries, finance, and personnel.

Many countries place restrictions on the use of premiums in the promotional efforts of companies. Specific restrictions are placed on what can be advertised in some countries. For instance, advertisements for tobacco and alcoholic products lie on a continuum of country restrictions ranging from highly lenient to highly stringent. The United States is comparatively stringent relative to many other countries in this regard. The use of comparisons is among other restrictions on how a firm can advertise. In the United States, direct comparisons (e.g., Burger King vs. McDonald's; Avis vs. Hertz; Sprint vs. AT&T) are allowed. In other countries, the firms must change their approach as direct comparisons are prohibited.

The international company must understand other host-country-specific laws, beyond those that apply to marketing. For instance, some countries have unique employment laws. This is seen in severe restrictions placed on the employment of foreigners. It is also seen when the host government dictates rules regarding salary, benefits, and dismissal of local hires.

Vacation days vary among countries. A sampling of vacation and leave policies and practices from around the world provides an interesting base of comparison (see Table 4.2). Recently, a U.S. manager setting up a new subsidiary in Italy was surprised to find that the first person he hired as his secretary was entitled to—and took—six weeks vacation during her first six months on the job, leaving him to perform many of the office tasks during the start-up.

Other host-country-specific laws deal with the problem of environmental pollution. Subsidiaries operating in industrialized countries where air pollution has become a major problem must comply with the local air pollution standards or face stiff penalties.

TABLE 4.2
Vacation Policies around the Globe

Source: V. Frazee, "Vacation Policies around the World," *Personnel Journal* 75, no. 10 (1997), p. 9.

France: 2½ days of paid holiday per full month of service during the year.
Germany: 18 working days per year after 6 months of service.
Hong Kong: 7 days annual paid leave on completion of 12 months of continuous service with the same employer.
Saudi Arabia: 15 days of annual leave on completion of 12 months of continuous service with the same employer.
Japan: 10 days paid for a year of continuous service provided that the employee has been at work 80% of this time.
Italy: Varies according to length of service but usually between 4 and 6 weeks.
Indonesia: 12 days of annual paid leave for 12 months of full service.
Malaysia: Varies according to length of service but usually between 8 and 16 days.
United States: Varies according to length of service and job function but usually between 5 and 15 days.
United Kingdom: No statutory requirement. Most members of salaried staff receive approximately 5 weeks paid annual leave.
Singapore: 7 days of paid annual leave for 12 months of continuous employment.
Philippines: 5 days annual paid leave.
Mexico: 6 days annually.

Whether air pollution curbs in the United States are any stricter than those in many European countries is debatable. Still, the laws of emerging and developing countries are often more lax than industrialized country standards. One major problem concerning environmental laws is the various definitions and meanings in different host countries. It is therefore difficult to extend and enforce laws in specific host countries.[29]

Many emerging countries do not allow private ownership of certain industries, probably to prevent industries vital to the economic welfare and safety of the country from falling into foreign hands. As seen previously, there is a worldwide trend toward greater privatization of many industries, thus mitigating the control that many countries once had over vital industries.

Another locally sensitive area of law deals with manufacturing. A company could have serious problems with a subsidiary located in a country that requires that a certain percentage of the components and subassemblies used in the production of a product be sourced from local suppliers. Such laws are in effect in India, the United States, Chile, Spain, and several other countries. Problems also arise when local suppliers are not in a position to meet the quality standards of the subsidiary and/or supply the inputs at competitive world prices.

The Foreign Corrupt Practices Act and Antibribery Provisions

A United States law that applies to U.S. firms and their respective subsidiaries throughout the world is the **Foreign Corrupt Practices Act (FCPA),** which was established in 1977. The FCPA specifically permits certain types of payments, called facilitating payments, whereas it prohibits other types of payments that could be categorized as bribes. At this point in our discussion of law, it is important to examine the antibribery provisions of the FCPA in some detail, since an understanding of this legislation is crucial for international companies in order to avoid making illegal payments.[30]

U.S. firms seeking to do business in foreign markets must be familiar with the FCPA. In general, the FCPA prohibits American companies from making corrupt payments to foreign officials for the purpose of obtaining or keeping business. The Department of Justice is the chief enforcement agency, with a coordinating role played by the Securities and Exchange Commission (SEC).

Background

Investigations by the SEC in the mid-1970s revealed that more than 400 U.S. companies admitted making questionable or illegal payments in excess of $300 million to foreign government officials, politicians, and political parties. The abuses ran the gamut from bribery of high foreign officials in order to secure some type of favorable action by a foreign government, to so-called facilitating payments that allegedly were made to ensure that government functionaries discharged certain ministerial or clerical duties. Congress enacted the FCPA to bring a halt to the bribery of foreign officials and to restore public confidence in the integrity of the American business system. The antibribery provisions of the FCPA make it unlawful for a U.S. person to make a corrupt payment to a foreign official for the purpose of obtaining or retaining business for or with, or directing business to, any person.

The FCPA also requires issuers of securities to meet its accounting standards. These accounting standards, which were designed to operate in tandem with the antibribery provisions of the FCPA, require corporations covered by the provisions to maintain books and records that accurately and fairly reflect the transactions of the corporation and to design an adequate system of internal accounting controls.

Basic Provisions Prohibiting Foreign Corrupt Payments

The FCPA prohibits bribery of foreign government officials to obtain or retain business. The antibribery provisions apply to certain issuers of registered securities and issuers required to file periodic reports with the SEC and to domestic concerns. A "domestic concern" is defined to mean any individual who is a citizen, national, or resident of the United States, or any corporation, partnership, association, joint-stock company, business trust, unincorporated organization, or sole proprietorship which has its principal place of business in the United States, or which is organized under the laws of a state of the United States, or a territory, possession, or commonwealth of the United States.

The FCPA's antibribery provisions extend to two types of behavior. The basic prohibition is against making bribes directly; a second prohibition covers the responsibility of a domestic concern and its officials for bribes paid by intermediaries. The FCPA's basic antibribery prohibition makes it unlawful for a firm (as well as any officer, director, employee, or agent of a firm or any stockholder acting on behalf of the firm) to offer, pay, promise to pay (or even to authorize the payment of money, or anything of value, or to authorize any such promise) to any foreign official for the purpose of obtaining or retaining business for or with, or directing business to, any person. (A similar prohibition applies with respect to payments to a foreign political party or official of a political party or candidate for foreign political office.)

Payment by Intermediaries

It is also unlawful to make a payment to any person, while knowing that all or a portion of the payment will be offered, given, or promised, directly or indirectly, to any foreign official (or foreign political party, candidate, or official) for the purposes of assisting the firm in obtaining or retaining business. "Knowing" includes the concepts of "conscious disregard" or "willful blindness."

Enforcement

The Department of Justice is responsible for all criminal enforcement and for civil enforcement of the antibribery provisions with respect to domestic concerns. The SEC is responsible for civil enforcement of the antibribery provisions with respect to issuers.

Antibribery Provisions—Elements of an Offense

With respect to the basic prohibition of the FCPA, the following five elements must be met to constitute a violation of the act.

1. Who   The FCPA applies to any individual firm, officer, director, employee, or agent of the firm and any stockholder acting on behalf of the firm. Individuals and firms may also be penalized if they order, authorize, or assist someone else to violate the antibribery provisions or if they conspire to violate those provisions. A foreign-incorporated subsidiary of a U.S. firm will not be subject to the FCPA, but its U.S. parent may be liable if it authorizes, directs, or participates in the activity in question. Individuals employed by or acting on behalf of such foreign-incorporated subsidiaries may, however, be subject to the antibribery provisions if they are persons within the definition of "domestic concern." In addition, U.S. nationals employed by foreign-incorporated subsidiaries are subject to the antibribery provisions of the FCPA.

2. Corrupt Intent   The person making or authorizing the payment must have a corrupt intent, and the payment must be intended to induce the recipient to misuse his official position in order to wrongfully direct business to the payer. The FCPA does not require that a corrupt act succeed in its purpose. The offer or promise of a corrupt payment can constitute a violation of the statute. The FCPA prohibits the corrupt use of the mails or of interstate commerce in furtherance of a payment to influence any act or decision of a foreign official in his or her official capacity or to induce the official to do or omit to do any act in violation of his or her lawful duty, or to induce a foreign official to use his or her influence improperly to affect or influence any act or decision.

3. Payment   The FCPA prohibits paying, offering, promising to pay (or authorizing to pay or offer) money or anything of value.

4. Recipient   The prohibition extends only to corrupt payments to a foreign official, a foreign political party or party official, or any candidate for foreign political office. A "foreign official" means any officer or employee of a foreign government or any department or agency, or any person acting in an official capacity. The Department of Justice's Foreign Corrupt Practices Act Opinion Procedure can answer particular questions as to the definition of a foreign official, such as whether a member of a royal family, a member of a legislative body, or an official of a state-owned business enterprise would be considered a foreign official. Prior to the amendment of the FCPA in 1988, employees of a foreign government or agency whose duties were essentially ministerial or clerical were not considered to be foreign officials. Determining whether a given employee's duties were essentially ministerial or clerical was a source of ambiguity, and it was not clear whether the act prohibited certain "grease" payments, such as those for expediting shipments through customs or placing a transatlantic telephone call, securing required permits, or obtaining adequate police protection. Accordingly, recent changes in the FCPA focus on the purpose of the payment instead of the particular duties of the official receiving the payment, offer, or promise of payment, and there are exceptions to the antibribery provision for "facilitating payments for routine governmental action" (see below).

5. Business Purpose Test   The FCPA prohibits payment made to assist the firm in obtaining, or retaining business for or with, or directing business to, any person. It should be noted that the business to be obtained or retained does not need to be with a foreign government or foreign government instrumentality.

Third-Party Payments

Generally, the FCPA prohibits corrupt payments through intermediaries. Corrupt use of the mails or of interstate commerce in furtherance of a payment to a third party, while knowing that all or a portion of the payment will go directly or indirectly to a foreign official, is unlawful. The term "knowing" includes conscious disregard and deliberate ignorance. The elements of an offense are essentially the same as described above, except that in this case the recipient is the intermediary who is making the payment to the requisite foreign official.

Permissible Payments and Affirmative Defenses

As amended in 1988, the FCPA now provides an explicit exception to the bribery prohibition for facilitating payments for routine governmental action and provides affirmative defenses which can be used to defend against alleged violations of the FCPA.

Exception for Facilitating Payments for Routine Governmental Actions   There is an exception to the antibribery prohibition for facilitating or expediting performance of "routine governmental action." The statute lists the following examples: obtaining permits, licenses, or other official documents; processing governmental papers, such as visas and work orders; providing police protection and mail pick-up and delivery; providing phone service and power and water supply; loading and unloading cargo; protecting perishable products; and scheduling inspections associated with contract performance or transit of goods across country. Routine governmental action does not include any decision by a foreign official to award new business or to continue business with a particular party.

Affirmative Defenses   A person charged with a violation of the FCPA's antibribery provisions may assert as a defense that the payment was lawful under the written laws of a foreign country or that the money was spent as part of demonstrating a product or performing a contractual obligation. Whether a payment was lawful under the written laws of a foreign country may be difficult to determine. Moreover, because these defenses are "affirmative defenses," the defendant would be required to show in the first instance that the payment met these requirements. The prosecution would not bear the burden of demonstrating in the first instance that the payments did not constitute this type of payment.

Sanctions against Bribery

The following criminal penalties may be imposed for violations of the FCPA's antibribery provisions: Firms are subject to a fine of up to $2 million; officers, directors, and stockholders are subject to a fine of up to $100,000 and imprisonment for up to five years; employees and agents are subject to a fine of up to $100,000 and imprisonment for up to five years. Fines imposed on individuals may not be paid by the firm.

There can be civil penalties as well. The attorney general or the SEC, as appropriate, may bring a civil action for a fine of up to $10,000 against any firm as well as any officer, director, employee, or agent of a firm, or stockholder acting on behalf of the firm, who violates the antibribery provisions. Moreover, in an SEC enforcement action, the court may impose an additional fine. The specified dollar amount depends on the egregiousness of the violation, ranging from $5,000 to $50,000 for a person and from $100,000 to $500,000 for a firm.

Critics of the FCPA argue that the law exports the values of the culture of one country—the United States—to countries that do not share these values. They claim that bribery is a perfectly acceptable practice in most countries and, they say, "When in Rome, do as the Romans do." However, the fact remains that probably every country has laws that prohibit domestic bribery. Hence companies that bribe local officials in foreign countries would be breaking local laws against giving bribes to corrupt officials and bureaucrats. But local laws against giving or accepting bribes are not strictly enforced, which leaves open the opportunities for companies to engage in behavior that corrupts local officials in host countries.

The Convention on Combating Bribery

The U.S. government began to receive numerous complaints from U.S. companies that the FCPA had placed them at a competitive disadvantage in obtaining foreign contracts against their competitors from other nations that did not have any prohibitions against the bribing of foreign officials. For instance, Germany permitted resident corporations to deduct foreign bribes, known as *Sonderspesen,* or special expenses, from corporate taxes. After considerable pressure from the government of the United States, a Convention on Combating Bribery of Foreign Public Officials in International Business

TABLE 4.3
Signatories to the OECD Convention

Argentina	Chile	Hungary	Mexico	Slovenia
Australia	Czech Republic	Iceland	Netherlands	Spain
Austria	Denmark	Ireland	New Zealand	Sweden
Belgium	Finland	Italy	Norway	Switzerland
Brazil	France	Japan	Poland	Turkey
Bulgaria	Germany	Korea	Portugal	U.K.
Canada	Greece	Luxemburg	Slovakia	U.S.

Transactions was adopted by the Organization for Economic Cooperation and Development (OECD) on November 21, 1997. Argentina, Brazil, Bulgaria, Chile, and the Slovak Republic also adopted this convention.

This is the first legally binding international instrument that aims to curb the behavior of corrupt MNCs operating overseas. The convention is a historic achievement in the fight against bribery. Countries that have signed the convention were required to put in place legislation that criminalizes the act of bribing a foreign public official. All member countries have now ratified this convention, thereby incorporating the treaty's provisions into their respective legal systems. Although the text does not specifically cover political parties, the negotiators agreed that the convention would cover business-related bribes to foreign public officials made through political parties and party officials.

Africa is the only continent with no states belonging to the convention, and very few African countries have national laws attempting to fill the gap.[31] How effective will the OECD convention on combating bribery be? This is a big question mark. Countries that have enacted legislation incorporating the provisions of the OECD convention must show that they are serious about enforcing those laws in their respective domestic courts.

Summary

The international legal environment can be viewed as comprising three concentric levels around the company: the laws of the nation-states within which the firm operates, laws of the regional trade blocs to which those nation-states belong, and international law. To be effective, a legal system must (1) be understood by the people subject to it, (2) be accepted as fair and just by those same people, and (3) have an enforceable system for punishing illegal behavior. The lack of the third element sets international law apart from national legal systems—international law is implemented by the mutual agreement of nation-states, not through the power of a central enforcement authority.

International law, the outermost level of the legal environment, may be based on custom—the historical practice of generally accepted patterns of behavior—or on treaties and conventions—signed agreements governing activity between sovereign states. Treaties may be bilateral or multilateral, depending on the number of signatory countries. We discussed two types of treaties of particular importance to international companies: treaties of friendship, commerce, and navigation (FCN) and treaties for the protection of intellectual property rights.

Protection of intellectual property—patents, trademarks, and copyrights—is a primary concern of international companies. Laws governing what can and cannot be protected, and how long protection will last, vary widely among nations. While many countries are party to the Paris Convention, which standardizes and simplifies intellectual property protection, practical problems of enforcement are still widespread. Historically, GATT and, more recently, the WTO attempt to improve intellectual property protection. The Madrid Protocol, signed in 2002, offers international filers of trademarks simplicity, ease, and cost-efficiency while promoting protection of trademarks globally. Ineffective enforcement of provisions for intellectual property protection opens the door to piracy—the unauthorized and illegal use of the intellectual property of another company. Piracy is a serious problem, particularly in many developing countries. Companies may also be damaged by copying activities, which have the same effect as piracy but are technically not illegal due to differences among the protection laws of different nations.

The second level of the international legal environment of business is the regional laws that have developed along with the various regional trade blocs in recent years. These laws, particularly well developed in the European Union, standardize activity and requirements among the member nations and are designed to facilitate intraregional trade. The third level of the international legal environment is represented by the specific laws of nation-states. National legal systems, generally based on common law, civil law, or Islamic law, reflect the social, cultural, and religious norms of the people. Accordingly, the laws of different nations have many significant differences and peculiarities. Activity or behavior that is perfectly acceptable in one country may be patently illegal in others. Managers in international companies must research and be aware of these differences as they affect foreign investment and operations.

The international manager of a U.S. firm must understand the basic provisions of the Foreign Corrupt Practices Act as well as what constitutes an offense under the law. Furthermore, the FCPA applies to foreign subsidiaries of U.S corporations, including majority and minority ownership in foreign companies and participation in strategic alliances.

The legal climate for multinational operations varies widely from country to country. Even for a given country, laws affecting investment policies and operating decisions can change markedly and quickly as different political regimes and changing economic circumstances alter a nation's goals and priorities. Supranational influences, such as the WTO worldwide, NAFTA for Mexico, Canada, and the United States, or the EU in Europe, also may result in significant changes in trade-related laws. Failure to keep abreast of changes in the various legal environments in which the multinational firm operates can subject the firm and its assets—financial, plant, and intellectual property—to unnecessary risk, or even to loss. Equally unacceptable is a failure to take full advantage of the substantial investment incentives offered by many developing countries, when the investment being encouraged is in line with the firm's strategic objectives.

Key Terms and Concepts

civil law, *122*	intellectual property rights, *114*	international treaty, *113*
common law, *122*	international customs, *112*	Islamic law, *122*
Foreign Corrupt Practices Act (FCPA), *126*	international law, *110*	Madrid Protocol, *116*

Discussion Questions

1. Does international law measure up to the requirements of an effective legal system? Will there ever be an effective international legal system?
2. What role do treaties play in creating an international legal framework?
3. Discuss the different ways in which Islamic law can impact upon the operations of international companies in Islamic countries.
4. Discuss the risks an international firm incurs overseas regarding intellectual property rights and subsequent control of its proprietary technology and knowledge.
5. How has the Madrid Protocol changed the rules for filing international trademarks? What are the benefits of this new international treaty?
6. Explain the legal and operational implications of the Foreign Corrupt Practices Act as it applies to U.S. firms and their respective subsidiaries throughout the world. Do you agree with the law?

Beijing Outlaws Pyramid Selling as an Evil Cult

The Falun Gong is not the only "evil cult" raising the ire of the Chinese Government. Over recent weeks senior government officials have been using similarly loaded descriptions to label another phenomenon that has been growing increasingly popular in China. That culminated with an announcement last week by Vice-Premier Li Lanqing that Beijing was launching a new crackdown on *jingji xie jiao,* or the economic evil cult more commonly known as pyramid selling. Li told the official *China Daily* that the fresh assault on pyramid selling was at the centre of the Government's campaign to clean up markets awash with fraud, counterfeit activities and tax evasion.

"The selling tactic is billed as an economic cult," Li said. "To clamp down on it is one of the cardinal missions in bringing the markets to order." The crackdown is not the first time Beijing has adopted strong-arm tactics to control pyramid selling. In April 1998 following a massive surge in pyramid schemes in the mid-1990s the ruling State Council effectively banned all direct selling or person-to-person marketing in China for five years. The State Council described pyramid schemes as a threat to China's social stability, similar language to that Beijing employed when it banned the Falun Gong spiritual movement in July 1999. The Falun Gong and those pyramid schemes certainly have a common recruiting ground: the tens of millions of Chinese workers cast aside as a result of Beijing's efforts to reform its antiquated economy.

The Government has claimed some success from the 1998 ban, with more than 500 illegal pyramid schemes involving tens of thousands of people reportedly smashed by police over the past two years. Several foreign companies involved in legitimate direct selling in China, including Avon, Amway and Mary Kay, were also caught up in the crackdown. Avon saw its Chinese sales collapse before it was able to restructure its operations from door-to-door selling to store-based merchandising. Earlier this year Beijing appeared to be relaxing its strict ban on door-to-door selling for foreign firms which complied with strict government tests. Some analysts suggest China's direct-sales market, despite the government ban, could now be worth as much as U.S. $5 billion. Yet that could all change as a result of the Government's new crackdown. The new move appears to have been sparked by what China's state-run media have called the biggest pyramid selling scheme to have been uncovered by police.

More than 200,000 people were reportedly duped in the Guangdong-based scam, which also made clever use of the Internet to draw in new recruits. Gao Feng, vice-director of the Ministry of Public Security's Bureau of Economic Crime Investigation, told the *People's Daily* last week that it was becoming harder to uncover some of the newer pyramid selling schemes now operating in China. "Some of the newer schemes have similar characteristics to the criminal underworld," Gao said. "They lure members to their illegal activities from other cities and then make them live together so they are easier to manage. These members are effectively separated from the outside world."

The members are made to shout slogans and their spirits are controlled with fetishistic thoughts which make them infatuated with pyramid schemes and illegal activities. But it appears some foreign firms involved in direct selling may also be the target of the new Government crackdown. The giant Amway earlier this year froze the recruitment of new distributors and began an internal review of its China operations after admitting that some employees were involved in pyramid schemes. The community meetings Amway uses in China to promote its products were also temporarily suspended. Amway is by far the biggest foreign direct seller in China, with turnover in the fiscal year ending August 2000 amounting to about U.S.$225 million. The company, which recently built an expensive new factory in Guangdong province, expects its China business to grow from 5 percent of its global turnover to 10 percent over the next three years.

Eva Cheng, president of Amway's operations in China, told *Business Weekly* newspaper earlier this year that the company had sacked a large number of employees for alleged involvement in pyramid selling. This was despite changes introduced by the company to comply with the April 1998 State Council ban. "With the passing of time, some Amway employees forgot why the company changed its sales mode in China and were involved in illegal activities," Cheng said. Amway acknowledges that its new round of restructuring including significantly upgraded training for recruits is likely to result in a 25 percent drop in business volumes. But that's probably preferable to being branded by the Chinese Government as an evil cult.

Source: From *Australian Financial Review,* November 6, 2001, John Fairfax Holdings Limited. Reprinted with permission of the publisher.

DISCUSSION QUESTIONS

1. Using China as an example, how can host-country laws, and the changes in those laws, affect international firms' strategies?

2. Explain the relationship of the Falun Gong movement in China to the laws against so-called pyramid schemes.

3. What options regarding China would you recommend to firms whose core business is done through direct selling?

Notes

1. P. Burrows and B. Einhorn, "Cisco: In Hot Pursuit of a Chinese Rival, the U.S. Giant Is Suing Huawei for Theft," *Business Week,* May 19, 2003, p. 62.

2. Stephen Globerman and Daniel Shapiro, "Governance Infrastructure and US Foreign Investment," *Journal of International Business Studies* 33, no. 1 (2003), pp. 61–74.

3. O. Havrylyshyn and R. van Rooden, "Institutions Matter in Transition, but So Do Policies," *Comparative Economic Studies* 45 (2003), pp. 2–24.

4. K. Brouthers, "Institutional, Cultural and Transaction Cost Influences on Entry Mode Choice and Performance," *Journal of International Business Studies* 33, no. 2 (2002), pp. 203–221.

5. W. Coplin, *The Functions of International Law* (Chicago: Rand McNally, 1966), pp. 8–9.

6. Ibid., pp. 3–4.

7. J. Gamble and C. Lu, "International Law—New Actors and New Technologies: Center Stage for NGOs?" *Law and Policy in International Business* 31, no. 2 (2000), pp. 221–263.

8. Statute of the International Court of Justice, Article 38(I).

9. O. Schachter and C. Joyned, *United Nations Legal Order 2,* (New York: United Nations, 1995).

10. Gamble and Lu, "International Law."

11. Vienna Convention on the Law Treaties, May 23, 1969, Article 2.1(a).

12. Y. Hamabe, "The JFCN Treaty Preemption of U.S. Anti-discrimination Laws in Executive Positions: Analysis in International Context," *Law and Policy in International Business* 27, no. 1 (1995), pp. 67–136.

13. C. Saban and E. Fealy, "Making the Most of the 'FCN Treaty' and Related National Origin Defenses," *Employee Relations Law Journal* 21, no. 3 (1996), pp. 149–161.

14. K. Josephberg, J. Pollack, J. Victoriano, and O. Gitig, "WIPO Conference on Performers' Rights to Be Held in 2003," *Intellectual Property & Technology Law Journal* 15, no. 1 (2003), p. 22.

15. R. Fishman, K. Josephberg, J. J. Linn, and J. Pollack, "US to Work toward Global Patent Treaty," *Intellectual Property & Technology Law Journal* 14, no. 7 (2002), pp. 30–32; J. Boyarski, R. Fishman, K. Josephberg and J. Linn, "WIPO Members Extend Patent Cooperation Treaty Time Limit," *Intellectual Property & Technology Law Journal* 14, no. 1 (2003), pp. 26–28.

16. K. Josephberg, J. Pollack, J. Victoriano, and O. Gitig, "WIPO Agrees to Changes in Patent Application Process," *Intellectual Property & Technology Law Journal* 15, no. 1 (2003), p. 23.

17. M. Retsky, "New Law Protects Marks Worldwide," *Marketing News* 37, no. 8 (2003), p. 10.

18. L. Perez, "Protecting Brand Names Overseas," *World Trade* 16, no. 3 (2003), p. 50.

19. I. Haleen, and A. Scoville, "United States Ratifies the Madrid Protocol: Pros and Cons for Trademark Owners," *Intellectual Property & Technology Law Journal* 15, no. 4 (2003), pp. 1–4.

20. *Activities of the European Union,* November 12, 2001. *Summaries of Legislation,* "Environment: An Introduction" (Brussels: Europa, EU).

21. R. La Porta, F. Lopez-de-Silanes, A. Shleifer, and R. Vishny, *The Quality of Government* (Cambridge, MA: National Bureau of Economic Research, 1998).

22. S. Kalemli-Ozcan, B. Sorensen, and O. Yosha, "Risk Sharing and Industrial Specialization: Regional and International Evidence," *American Economic Review* 93, no. 3 (2003), pp. 903–930.

23. Jessica M. Bailey and James Sood, "The Effect of Religious Affiliation on Consumer Behavior: A Preliminary Investigation," *Journal of Managerial Issues* 5, no. 3 (1993), p. 333.

24. Mushtaq Luqmani, Zahir A. Quaraeshi, and Linda Delene, "Marketing in Islamic Countries: A Viewpoint," *MSU Business Topics,* Summer 1980.

25. "Banking behind the Veil," *The Economist,* April 4, 1992, p. 76.

26. Luiz Moutinho and M. Hisham Jabr, "Perspective on the Role of Marketing in Islamic Banking," *Journal of International Consumer Marketing* 2, no. 3 (1990), pp. 29–47; Geraldine Brooks, "Riddle of Riyadj: Islamic Law Thrives amid Modernity," *Wall Street Journal,* November 9, 1989, p. A1.

27. "Islamic Banking Rules Spell More Paperwork but the Same Result," *Business Asia,* March 11, 1991, p. 81.

28. The Pakistan Newswire, March 25, 2003.

29. D. French, "Environmental Damage in International and Comparative Law: Problems of Definition and Valuation," *Journal of Environmental Law* 15, no. 2 (2003), p. 266.

30. The material in this section was obtained from a government document, "Foreign Corrupt Practices Act Antibribery Provisions" (Washington, DC: U.S. Department of Commerce, Office of the Chief Counsel for International Commerce, 2001). It is presented in its entirety except for minor deletions and changes.

31. P. Schroth and P. Sharma, "Transnational Law and Technology as Potential Forces against Corruption in Africa," *Management Decision* 41, no. 3 (2003), p. 296.

The Cultural Environment

Chapter Learning Objectives

After completing this chapter, you should be able to:

- Understand the concepts of culture and cultural variations in international management.
- Explain the influence of environmental factors on societal culture.
- Discuss the significance of various frameworks for understanding cultural differences around the world.
- Identify distinctive management styles that exist in different countries.

Opening Case: We Like McDonald's, but No Beef Please!!! Crisis Management in India

Within hours of the story breaking that McDonald's in the U.S. had been using oil with a beef extract for cooking its fries, the burger giant's Indian operation knew it had a crisis on its hands. The region's Hindu and vegetarian consumers were furious that they might have been eating products cooked with beef, breaking a deeply held taboo.

On May 4—a day after the story broke in the U.S.—the Indian national media had splashed the story, but also pointed out that McDonald's India fries and vegetarian products use no beef or pork flavoring. That reassurance failed to cut any ice with local activists and within a matter of hours the golden arches of the Big M were under siege. Ironically it was cosmopolitan Mumbai [Bombay] that reacted more than the sensitive northern region of India, which preferred to wait for an official explanation first. Mumbai's Thane outlet was vandalized by an angry mob of political fundamentalists, who have never been keen on the western company's presence in the market.

The McDonald's outlet near Mumbai's CST railway station was also picketed and cow dung was dropped all around the building. The western city of Pune, some three hours drive from Mumbai, was however peaceful since the fast food giant had coincidentally just a week earlier conducted media tours of its outlets, kitchens, and facilities and they were happier to accept McDonald's assurances of its no–meat extract policy. But McDonald's India's crisis management machinery had already realized a strong reaction to the news was likely and had held a meeting to discuss what steps to take.

More than 80 percent of the country's one billion strong population is Hindu, and even in a cosmopolitan city like Mumbai, half of those eating at a McDonald's are vegetarian. That's no small fry since 3.5 million customers visit its India outlets each month. Revenue growth for India operations has been 80 percent every year since its first outlets opened in 1996 in Mumbai and Delhi. Fire fighting the crisis was a coordinated effort between the north and west, since McDonald's has two joint ventures in India. In Mumbai and the western region, Amit Jatia's company Hardcastle Restaurants owns and manages Big M restaurants in a 50:50 equity partnership between his family and McDonald's India. The north comes under the Delhi-based Connaught Plaza Restaurants in a 50:50 equity partnership between McDonald's India and owner Vikram Bakshi.

Back to May 4: Amit Jatia and his staff huddled together with PR specialists from Corporate Voice Shandwick, ad men from Mudra DDB, corporate affairs and legal experts. Police security for all outlets was first red alerted. Then, posters were made from office printers with the headline: "100 percent Vegetarian French Fries in McDonald's India." Below this were various bullets of information such as: "No flavors with animal products/extracts are used for preparing any vegetarian products in India." The posters were plastered over all the Big M outlets.

"We had done nothing wrong so we could afford to be bold. We could have been arrogant and said that we don't use beef flavoring in our fries, so why should we be attacked? Instead we kept all lines of communications open and supplied all proof and samples," says Jatia. They also met with key press, politicians and associations and supplied them with product samples and information.

The main imperative was to supply proof. On the day the story broke in India, McDonald's submitted samples of the fries to leading laboratories in Pune and Mumbai, such as the Council of Fair Business Practices, as well as Delhi's Central Food and Technical Research Institute. Tests were quickly done by the BMC (Bombay Municipal Corporation) and FDA (Food & Drug Administration) and local political parties. It took a week but the results were clear—no beef or meat in the oil or products—which were rapidly passed to the press. The results were also posted in the various outlets and put as inserts in the daily papers in sensitive areas like Bombay's Vile Parle, Charni Road and Thane district.

On May 5, a packed press conference was held in Mumbai and Delhi. Lamb Weston and McCain Foods, its fries suppliers, were present and supplied copies of clearance certificates once again showing there was no chemical or ingredient used with animal fats. On May 6 six press ads from Mudra DDB, on similar lines as the poster, were run across mainstream dailies of the *Times of India* (for Mumbai); *Hindustan Times* (for Delhi); *Gujarat Samachar* and *Loksatta* in English, Gujarati and Marathi languages respectively.

Meanwhile it's been "business as usual" for all Big M outlets everywhere. Even the company's worse-hit Thane office was re-opened within 24 hours and its ambitious expansion plans are on line. By 2003, there will be 80 Big M outlets in the north and west of India. Hardcastle already has 11 outlets across Mumbai and Pune and soon Gujarat will be opened. Bangalore will also launch but under the franchisee route since the investments would be too high, adds Jatia. About 17 outlets dot the northern markets of Delhi, Mathura and Jaipur. Interestingly, since the fries fracas, the product mix in sales has remained unchanged. The vegetarian contribution remains at 55 percent and non-vegetarian at 45 percent, says Jatia. And for french fries, the average units per store sold actually increased by 15 percent over the previous year.

In the wake of the U.S. fries episode, McDonald's will be stressing the vegetarian-friendly nature of its menu and manufacturing more than ever, says Jatia. More media tours are on line to bring all these consumer friendly efforts to the public eye. But for now McDonald's India management's rapid response and openness about the issue seems to have averted serious damage to brand and business.

Source: From Sarika Gupte, "McDonald's Averts a Crisis: Crisis Management Teams Reverse Damages to the Fast Food Giant in India." Reprinted with permission from the July 1, 2001 issue of *Advertising Age Global*. Copyright, Crain Communications, Inc., 2001.

Discussion Questions

1. What are the various cultural issues that McDonald's must consider when expanding internationally?
2. How can McDonald's analyze various cultural environments? What factors would you suggest distinguish cultures from each other?
3. In your opinion, are the various world cultures coming closer together? Why or why not?

What Is Culture?

Culture is a concept that has been used in several social science disciplines to explain variations in human thought processes in different parts of the world. Culture is to a society what memory is to an individual.[1] Anthropologists believe that cultures provide solutions to problems of human adaptation to the environment. Humans have evolved over the past four million years from apes to highly sophisticated beings and control most of the ecological environment of the world. In the course of this development, their adaptation has been enhanced by the development of culture.

Culture is the human-made part of environment.[2] It has both subjective and objective components. **Objective culture** components are such things as infrastructure of roads, architecture, patterns of music, food, and dress habits. **Subjective culture** components include the ways that people categorize experience, associations, beliefs, attitudes, self-definitions, role definitions, norms, and values. Subjective culture helps people survive the various demands that are present in an ecological setting since they do not have to reinvent adaptive behaviors but can imitate them or learn from previous generations. Triandis[3] suggested these two components of culture, and these distinctions provide a helpful way of understanding cultural differences. Subjective culture–related differences and the way they influence attitudes and values of people in different parts of the world are the focus of this chapter.

When you come across a man wearing an Arabic headdress or a woman in burka, you immediately think that these people have a different culture from your own. Countries also have distinctive architectural preferences—buildings in Cairo often look different from those in New York or Frankfort, Germany. When you go to Moscow, the golden domes on the churches tell you that you are in a country whose culture is different from your own. Similarly, when you listen to the distinctive rhythms of Japanese music, you realize that it is a different culture. All of these are examples of objective culture, and they are easily seen and experienced. However, the man wearing an Arabic headdress may be fluent in English and educated in the West, and he may understand how Westerners think and behave. He can therefore be said to have a very good grasp of the subjective culture found in the West. Subjective culture differences are not easily visible to the eye, and they must be interpreted in terms of differences in rituals, customs, and other practices.

In this chapter and throughout this book we are concerned with subjective culture, and we use the concept of culture to reflect subjective culture of groups of people in a given geographical location. Two countries may show differences in objective parts of their culture but be quite similar in terms of their underlying subjective cultures, such as the United Kingdom and the United States. Although the castles and royal palaces found in the United Kingdom are strikingly different from most of the houses of the rich and famous in the United States, the underlying subjective cultures are very similar. However, two countries may have similar objective cultures and considerably different subjective cultures, such as Sweden and the United Kingdom. Although both countries have similar patterns of buildings and roads and dress habits (objective culture), their subjective cultures are very different; societal norms and values of the English differ considerably from those of the Swedes.

Practical Insight 5.1 shows the importance of cultural awareness and some of the difficulties in bridging the culture gap.

Difference between Learning a New Language and a New Culture

In many ways, the language of a country influences the evolution of cultural patterns. Leading researchers find sharp similarities and contrasts in learning a new language and a new culture.[4] Table 5.1 presents the parallel principles of learning a new language and

PRACTICAL INSIGHT 5.1

BRIDGING THE CULTURE GAP

In the U.S. and abroad, cultural awareness is more important than ever for salespeople

Before heading to an important series of business meetings in Indonesia recently, Aric Peters did his homework. He read up on some of the cultural norms of the Southeast Asian nation, and he and his team arrived prepared. But what he saw at his client lunch surprised him: His hosts used left and right hands while eating. "I had read this was taboo," says Peters, who is manager of aviation safety products for Butler National Corporation, based in Olathe, Kansas. "So I just asked, 'What's the deal with this?' And they said, 'Oh, that's a very old tradition. It's not something anyone worries about anymore.'"

Live and learn. The nature of cultural differences is forever evolving. Many companies, even those that do business solely in the United States, must be prepared to deal with cultural differences that may arise in a client relationship. They can be as minor as social niceties, or as vast as differing views on U.S. involvement in Iraq. And as Peters' Indonesian lunch demonstrates, just when you think you have the cultural road map read, the rules may have already changed. "This is an important issue for business, with or without the backdrop of war," says Sanjeev Agarwal, professor of international business and marketing at Iowa State University. But potential dividers grow more dangerous when geopolitical tensions loom, he says.

That's led many firms to develop ongoing strategies to manage cross-cultural issues. The Telvista Company is headquartered in Dallas, but as a provider of call center and help desk solutions, it has functions based in Mexico. While the offices aren't far apart in terms of mileage, there are times the Mexican and American business cultures will clash on anything from workday hours to business attire. In addition to teaching the surface elements of social exchange, Telvista has gone one step further, requiring managers in both countries to take ongoing lessons in English and Spanish. This is more than a day-long training session in cultural sensitivity, says Paulo Silva, president of Latin American client engagements for Telvista. "This will help us achieve more comfort in doing business with each other," he says.

Andy Weissberg also believes in cultural training, even though many of his clients will never venture outside the U.S. Weissberg's firm, CPRi Communications, based in Teterboro, New Jersey, trains pharmaceutical reps, because cultural issues crop up regularly between reps and their physician customers. And sometimes those issues extend between those customers and their patients. "We have to talk about how different racial and ethnic populations may respond to pharmaceuticals," he says. "There have been lots of studies that show that reaction can be very different and call for different behavior on the part of the sales rep." A key tactic: CPRi has developed online training that allows salespeople to role play through potential culture clashes, and then follow up with questions or comments via online messaging with trainers. "Culture issues aren't just international issues," Weissberg says. "They're in our neighborhoods, too."

Source: From *Sales & Marketing Management* "Bridging the Culture Gap," by Ellen Neuborne, June 2003. Copyright © 2003 by VNU BUS PUBNS USA. Reproduced with permission of VNU BUS PUBNS USA via Copyright Clearance Center.

a new culture. Just as the first language greatly influences the way we learn both content and verbal intonation patterns of the second language, values of one's native culture continue to influence and sometimes even distort the learning of a new culture. When an individual is in a new cultural setting, whether in the role of a manager of a subsidiary or in a joint venture, people treat him or her differently and expect conformity to the norms and mores of the host culture. These expectations make it necessary for the manager to quickly learn new patterns of thinking, valuing, and behaving. The longer it takes to learn the values of new culture, the more difficult it becomes for the manager to function successfully.

Culture and Its Effects on Organizations

As stated previously, culture is to a society what memory is to an individual. It consists of standard operating procedures and unstated assumptions, ways of perceiving, evaluating, and acting, for a group of people who live in the same historical period, in the same geographical region of the world. The shared outlook results in common codes of conduct and expectations that influence and control a large majority of beliefs, norms, and values. Individuals are born into a given culture and they gradually experience the

TABLE 5.1

Similarities and Contrasts in Learning a New Language and a New Culture

Source: Adapted from G. M. Guthrie, "A Behavioral Analysis of Culture Learning." In R. W. Brislin, S. Bochner, and W. J. Lonner, eds., *Cross-Cultural Perspectives on Learning* (New York: Sage, 1975), pp. 95–116.

Learning Language	Learning Culture
Learned in early childhood, generally by age five. New languages can be learned somewhat easily by children.	Learned in early childhood, generally by age five. New culture can be learned somewhat more easily by children than by adults.
One's native language largely determines one's style of thinking.	One's native culture largely determines one's values.
One's native language largely influences the mistakes made in learning a second language.	One's native culture introduces errors of judgment in interpreting the new culture.
One must learn a new set of pitch levels and intonation patterns in learning a second language.	One's native culture has some unique gestures and body language which are always correctly interpreted by members of that culture.
An accent remains, which reveals the nature of the native language.	Values of the native culture often introduce "noise" when learning the values of the second culture.
In dealing with significant difficulties and stressful experiences, one is usually more comfortable thinking in the native language.	In dealing with significant difficulties and stressful experiences, one is usually more comfortable with coping styles learned in childhood.
One's most affectionate feelings are best expressed in one's native language.	One's behavior is best understood in terms of one's long-standing, deeply rooted values. It is easier for us to learn to appreciate a different cuisine than to learn a new way of expressing affection or love.
One tends to think in one's native language when reflecting on personal values or problems.	One's native culture determines how one views and values an event, either favorably or unfavorably. Profound emotions are generally determined by one's native culture.

subtle internalizing effects of their culture through various social institutions, such as family, school systems, and work organizations.

Over time, cultures evolve as societies adapt to transitions in their internal and external environments. Internal environments consist of the political system, customs, and traditions that are found in a given locale, whereas external environments consist of the ecological setting where the members of a society reside and other events (such as war with another nation) that are not controlled directly by the group. Cultures of traditional societies, such as Greece, India, China, Japan, and Egypt, have gone through changes due to internal and external adaptations through their experiences during the colonial era, independence movement, and globalization in the later part of the last century. As depicted in Exhibit 5.1, several layers of environmental variables affect the functions of the international manager, and the cultural layer is very important. Cultural variables determine basic attitudes toward time, work, materialism, and norms concerning how relationships are maintained and sustained over time.

It is clear that cultural variables—shared beliefs, values, and attitudes—affect how managers in global corporations develop their policies and execute various tasks. One example of how culture affects organizational processes is reflected in the frequent resistance in some countries to technological improvements that might otherwise lead to improvements in quality of life. Clashes between culture and technology can often be unpleasant, and we (from a Western point of view) might wonder why certain nations are not willing to absorb technology in the way we do. Some have argued that the effects of culture are much clearer at the individual level than at the organizational level.[5]

Convergence of cultures around the world is taking place continuously, but at a relatively slow pace. A group of scholars in the 1960s published a study, called *Industrialism and the Industrial Man,*[6] in which they argued that as colonial influences decline around the world, the governing elites of many of these countries would like to see their cultures **converge,** that is, come together, with those of the developed countries. While this has taken place, **divergence,** that is, the refusal to accept foreign cultural values,

EXHIBIT 5.1

Environment
Influences on
International
Management
Functions

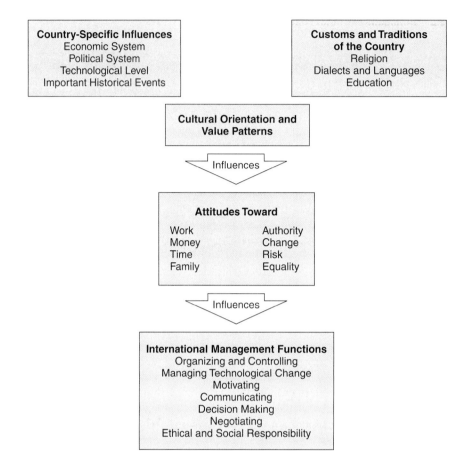

Country-Specific Influences
Economic System
Political System
Technological Level
Important Historical Events

**Customs and Traditions
of the Country**
Religion
Dialects and Languages
Education

**Cultural Orientation and
Value Patterns**

Influences

Attitudes Toward

Work   Authority
Money   Change
Time   Risk
Family   Equality

Influences

International Management Functions
Organizing and Controlling
Managing Technological Change
Motivating
Communicating
Decision Making
Negotiating
Ethical and Social Responsibility

has also been persistent. Many parts of the world, such as the Middle East, Africa, and Latin America, do not necessarily like to change their dominant value orientations. It is important to realize that convergence and divergence are parallel processes and are taking place all the time.

The effect of culture on a specific management activity becomes evident when the manager of a global corporation attempts to impose his or her values and systems on the workers of another society that is culturally dissimilar from the manager's. Exhibit 5.2 depicts values that are prevalent in the United States and alternative value patterns that are found in other parts of the world. This exhibit also shows the various management functions that are affected when these alternative value profiles contrast sharply with the U.S. pattern.

A first step toward increasing adaptation of a subsidiary of a global corporation in a new country is to encourage expatriate managers to develop cultural sensitivity. **Cultural sensitivity** may be defined as a state of heightened awareness for the values and frames of reference of the host culture.[7] Managers with higher levels of cultural sensitivity tend to be less parochial in their thinking and are often willing to examine the way management practices might be implemented in dissimilar cultures.

- **Parochialism** is the belief that there is no way of doing things other than that found within one's own culture, that is, that there is no better alternative. This notion is very common, and this tendency is found in all cultures of the world. An American

EXHIBIT 5.2   Dominant U.S. Values and Possible Alternative Scenarios

Source: Adapted from P. R. Harris and R. T. Moran, *Managing Cultural Differences,* 4th ed. (Houston: Gulf, 1996), p. 51.

U.S. Cultural Value	Alternative Cultural Value	Managerial Function Affected
The future can be changed by the individual: "Where there's a will, there's a way."	The future is ordained by God, and humans cannot change it.	Planning
The environment can be changed and improved.	People should adjust to the environment.	Organizational climate, morale, and productivity
Hard work will allow us to achieve our objectives.	Wisdom, luck, time, and hard work will allow us to achieve our objectives.	Motivation and distribution of rewards
Individuals should be realistic in aspirations.	One should pursue aspirations regardless of how realistic they seem to others.	Goal setting and career development
People should do what they say they are going to do—commitments are to be honored.	Conflicting requests may prevent people from fulfilling their commitments, or an agreement may indicate intention only, not actual performance.	Negotiation and conflict management
"Time is money."	Time is not a resource that can be spent or saved or wasted—it is renewable.	Planning and scheduling
Positions should go to the best qualified individual.	Considerations besides qualifications, such as family and friendship connections, are important.	Selection, recruitment, development, and distribution of rewards

manager who assumes that people in non-U.S. cultures will take a very short time for bereavement leave and fails to consider the custom in other countries is being parochial.

- **Ethnocentrism** is similar to parochialism and tends to reflect a sense of superiority. Ethnocentric individuals believe that their ways of doing things are the best, no matter which cultures are involved.
- **Geocentrism** is very different from both parochialism and ethnocentrism. It reflects a belief that being responsive to local cultures and markets is necessary. Companies exhibiting geocentrism usually use both local and international managers. Executives in the headquarters can come from any region of the world.

Improvements in cultural sensitivity will occur only after managers examine the deep-seated values of their own culture. Examples of the organizational problems that result from being insensitive are numerous. A few examples are striking:[8]

> Procter and Gamble blundered in Japan when trying to sell Camay soap. It seems that it aired a popular European television advertisement showing a woman bathing. In the ad, her husband enters the bathroom and touches her approvingly. The Japanese, however, considered this behavior to be inappropriate and in poor taste for television.
>
> Saudi Arabia nearly restricted an airline from initiating flights when the company authorized "normal" newspaper advertisements. The ads featured attractive hostesses serving champagne to the happy airline passengers. Because in Saudi Arabia alcohol is illegal and unveiled women are not permitted to mix with men, the photo was viewed as an attempt to alter religious customs.
>
> Green, for instance, is often associated with disease in countries that have dense, green jungles, but is associated with cosmetics by the French, Dutch, and Swedes. Various colors represent death. Black signifies death to Americans and many Europeans, while in Japan and many other Asian countries white represents death. Latin Americans generally associate purple with death, but dark red is the appropriate mourning color along the Ivory Coast. And even though white is the color representing death to some; it expresses joy to those living in Ghana.

PRACTICAL INSIGHT 5.2

COPING WITH CULTURE SHOCK

From business cards to handshakes and working hours—working in a different country is littered with hidden traps. One faux pas could scupper the deal—and your credibility.

Living in a new culture gives you time to observe, learn and adapt. The business traveler does not have that luxury.

Japanese woman Hisako Imura spent ten years in New York after graduating in her hometown of Tokyo.

"For me as a Japanese woman, a foreign country gave me a much better opportunity than maybe I would have had in Japan. Now it's changing but it's still a very much male-dominated society," Imura said.

She moved to Sydney this year, but found the change hard.

"I noticed the Japanese way of doing business, also the relationship with other people, was quite different from in New York or in Sydney.

"In Japan as a business person your life revolves around your business. Your colleagues are like part of your family.

"In Australia they maybe work shorter hours, but work very hard, then they leave the office and spend as much time with their family as possible."

Chris Brewster, a professor of human resources at London's South Bank University, says Imura has begun to understand some of the cultural differences between Japan and Australia.

"These differences are much more than the handing out of business cards. These are about deep-seated cultural values,

ideas of what's good and bad, right and wrong, and these spill over into business.

"It's the way that you have to deal with those when you're in business that creates the problem because often you have very little time to learn."

One option when entering a different culture is to explain that it is a new experience for you, Brewster advises.

"You can say to people: 'I respect your culture, but I don't understand it. I'm going to make mistakes, it's bound to happen but I'm really trying to do the best I can.'"

He also advises being modest when it comes to selling a product. "There's a lot of process involved in reaching deals, in coming to agreement. And if people don't understand that, however good their product or their service is, they're not going to be successful in the deal. They've got to be modest, they've got to realise that it's not just about their product, it's also about the process."

From her own experience, Imura suggests learning about the culture before you visit, and talk to friends and colleagues who have been where you are going.

"Then when you arrive you should really abandon your preconception about other people. You just open up yourself first. And don't be afraid of rejection."

Source: From "Coping with Culture Shock," November 27, 2002. Copyright © 2002 Cable News Network LP, LLLP.

Managers of international and global corporations should be aware of the flux of cultural variables that they might be submerged in and realize their effects on workplace behaviors. Appreciation of cultural diversity and the ability to develop effective relationships across cultures should be important goals of managers in this increasingly global marketplace.

The Dimensions of Culture

Countries differ in terms of their underlying cultures. Just to say that the culture of Japan is different from that of the United States is not enough. It is correct, but it does not give us enough insight in terms of how the Japanese workers might react to certain managerial practices, compared to American workers. It would be more useful to say further that the Japanese worker places a great deal of emphasis on the hierarchical arrangements within the company. This attitude prevails because in a Japanese company, a superior has more access to certain important resources than an American in the same position. Cultural differences result from the variations given to different values. Conflicts and misunderstandings occur when members of a group take the view that their values are correct and best.

Cultural dimensions are basic concepts that help us understand how two or more cultures might be different or similar along each dimension. Various frameworks have

EXHIBIT 5.3
Cultural Emphases on Important Dimensions

Source: Adapted from F. Kluckhohn and F. L. Strodtbeck, *Variations in Value Orientations* (Evanston, IL: Row, Peterson, 1961).

Dimensions	Emphasis in Culture		
Relation to nature	Subjugation	Harmony	Mastery
Basic human nature	Evil	Mixed	Good
Time orientation	Past	Present	Future
Space orientation	Private	Mixed	Public
Activity orientation	Being	Thinking	Doing
Relationships among people	Hierarchical	Group-based	Individualistic

been developed, and we will discuss a few of these frameworks as a guide to understanding the various cultures of the world. These frameworks have been developed at different times using different approaches. However, they have resulted in very similar descriptions of the various issues or dimensions that different countries and cultures of the world emphasize. We will describe the very first framework developed by Kluckhohn and Strodtbeck and end with the framework described by Triandis, dealing with the notions of vertical and horizontal types of cultures.

These frameworks represent average tendencies or norms of the major value systems that define a culture. They are meant neither to describe exactly how a culture evolves and functions nor to stereotype how a particular person may behave. Not everyone in a particular culture or country behaves in the same way. By defining the United States in terms of its ranking on different dimensions of a framework, we are not saying that all Americans behave the same way. These cultural dimensions represent general tendencies found in a particular region of the world.

Kluckhohn and Strodtbeck's Framework

Kluckhohn and Stodtbeck developed a framework to describe the emphasis a culture places on various dimensions.[9] These are called *dimensions of value orientation,* and they are described in Exhibit 5.3.

The dimension of *relation to nature* is concerned with the extent that a culture copes with its relation to nature most of the time by subjugating to it, being in harmony with it, or attempting to master it. Polynesians from islands in the South Pacific have a *subjugation orientation.* They believe that what happens to them is their luck or destiny, and they are not able to change it by their behavior. A culture that emphasizes *harmony,* like the Japanese, emphasizes the value of coexisting with nature, rather than changing it. For example, Japanese planned areas of parks within cities before this became a popular aspect of city planning in the United States. Cultures with a *mastery orientation,* like the United States and most of the Western world, believe that some of nature's forces can be controlled. Continuous emphasis of technology, such as air-conditioning systems and flood control, reflects this tendency to seek mastery over nature to the greatest extent possible.

The dimension of *basic human nature* reflects how cultures socialize individuals to develop beliefs about the inherent character of human beings: as evil, good, or mixed. Cultural values greatly determine whether people believe that the fundamental nature of humans is changeable. In Japan, for example, executives have historically trusted each other enough so that verbal agreements are used for major business deals. In a culture that believes that people are basically evil, there is a lack of trust in business deals, and explicit contracts are needed. The *Wall Street Journal* reported that American workers are among the most carefully watched workers in the world, due to electronic monitoring devices.[10] The primary reason for careful monitoring initially was to check on the rate of production and theft and industrial espionage. We might speculate that the tendency to monitor people increased a great deal in the United States after suicide bombers struck the Pentagon and demolished the World Trade Center's twin towers on September 11, 2001. The notion that human beings can be easily trusted has been completely discarded in favor of tight monitoring at the airports and in many office buildings. A society with a mixed orientation views people as basically good and trustworthy but recognizes that they are capable of committing serious acts, violating society norms, in some situations. Norway reflects this orientation in that there is a general atmosphere of goodwill and trust among its citizens, but very strict laws governing the use of alcohol.

The dimension of *time orientation* reflects a society's emphasis on the past, present, or future. A *past orientation* emphasizes customary, tradition-bound, and time-honored approaches. Asian Indians, Middle Easterners, and those from Mediterranean countries such as Greece, Italy, and Turkey have a profound tendency to emphasize past precedents in resolving important issues. The relevance of past approaches is not the point. Rather, the way a similar issue was resolved in the past and the extent to which deviating from the past pattern might be considered inappropriate in that culture are the overriding factors. A *present-oriented* culture generally focuses on short-term approaches. Americans are particularly present-oriented in terms of time, and managers are socialized to look at quarterly financial reports and daily returns on stock market performance. A *future-oriented* society emphasizes long-term approaches. Many Japanese and Korean global companies have plans for improving their performance in the long term, which may range from 5 to 10 years. East Asians often engage in activities that are designed to benefit future generations rather than providing immediate gratification for themselves.

The dimension of *space orientation* indicates how people define the concept of space in relation to other people: Is it public, or private, or mixed? In a society that emphasizes a *public orientation,* space belongs to not just one person but to everyone. It is not uncommon in Japanese companies to arrange office space in the form of an open layout. In societies that value *privacy,* such as Germany, the United Kingdom, and the United States, employees consider it important to have their own space. Senior managers and other high-status employees are often provided large private office spaces. In societies reflecting a *mixed orientation,* the tendency is to combine both public and private emphases on space. In India, for example, whereas lower level employees may share a common area of work, senior managers have private offices that are not easily accessible.

The *activity orientation* of a culture focuses on doing, being, or thinking. In a culture emphasizing *doing,* such as the United States, people are always moving from one activity to another, and their days are heavily scheduled or organized to accomplish a series of things from morning to evening. Continuous focus on getting tasks done is the primary orientation of these cultures, and it contrasts with those cultures where a *being orientation* is emphasized. Rural areas of Mexico, India, and Latin America are examples of being-oriented cultures where spontaneous reactions to feelings are expected, decisions and rewards are based on emotions, and performance criteria are broad and variable. A *thinking orientation* is also known as a controlling and containing orientation. Individuals are socialized to take time off from work, enjoy each other's company, exchange greetings, and achieve a balance in their work and nonwork life. The French, the Spanish, and those from Mediterranean countries adopt this mode of functioning.

The dimension of *relationships among people* reflects the extent to which a culture emphasizes individualistic, group-oriented, or hierarchy-focused ways of relating to one another. Cultures emphasizing *individualistic orientation* tend to focus on people relating to each other in terms of their personal characteristics and achievements. In the United States, Canada, and most parts of the Western world, employees receive rewards for their own achievements, work on their own personal agenda, and relate to each other one on one. In a *group-oriented society,* people relate to each other in terms of focusing on the needs of the group to which they belong. Emphasis is on harmony, equality, unity, and loyalty to group objectives. The Japanese make decisions by referring to group consensus and working from lower levels and moving upward. *Hierarchical societies,* while valuing group relationships, emphasize awareness of the status of the individual that one is talking to or relating with. Venezuela, Colombia, Mexico, the Philippines, and India reflect this orientation.

Hofstede's Framework

Geert Hofstede, a Dutch researcher, used five dimensions of culture to explain differences in behaviors from one culture to another.[11] His work is based on questionnaires completed by IBM employees from 70 countries, one of the largest studies in international management ever conducted. Although Hofstede's work has been criticized because his data reflected a single company, he believed that using employees from the same company would clearly show national cultural differences because the IBM employees were matched in other respects, such as their type of work and educational levels for similar occupations. Hofstede's five dimensions are (1) individualism and collectivism, (2) power distance, (3) uncertainty avoidance, (4) masculinity and femininity, and (5) time orientation.

Individualism and Collectivism Hofstede identified **individualism versus collectivism**[12] as an important dimension of culture. A number of other scholars have argued that this dimension of cultural variation is the major distinguishing characteristic in the way that people in various societies of the world analyze social behavior and process information.[13] Individualism and collectivism are social patterns that define cultural syndromes.[14] *Cultural syndromes* are shared patterns of beliefs, attitudes, norms, values, and so on, organized as one theme. Some countries are more individualistic than others. *Individualism* may be defined as a social pattern that consists of loosely linked individuals who view themselves as independent of groups and who are motivated by their own preferences, needs, rights, and contracts. *Collectivism,* on the other hand, may be defined as a social pattern that consists of closely linked individuals who see themselves as belonging to one or more groups (e.g., family, co-workers, in-groups, organizations, tribes) and who are motivated by norms, duties, and obligations identified by these groups. People give priority to the goals of these groups over their own personal goals. People of a given culture emphasize and sample different segments of information from a given body of knowledge, but they believe that their ways of thinking about themselves and their groups are obviously correct and do not question their validity. Exhibit 5.4 summarizes key differences between individualistic and collectivist societies.

Included in Hofstede's work is the idea that countries with higher per capita gross national product (GNP) exhibit more individualism. In other words, countries that are more individualistic are also wealthier, more urbanized, and more industrialized.[15] Hofstede also found that countries with moderate and cold climates tend to show more individualistic tendencies, and he speculated that this finding was a result of the personal initiative required for survival in these climates.[16] Exhibit 5.5 compares individualism with GNP per capita in selected countries.

EXHIBIT 5.4
Key Differences between Individualistic and Collectivist Societies

Source: From Geert Hofstede, *Culture's Consequences: International Differences in Work-Related Values*, 2nd edition, Sage Publications, 2001. Reprinted with permission of the author.

Collectivist	Individualist
People are born into extended families or other in-groups which continue to protect them in exchange for loyalty.	Everyone grows up to look after himself or herself and his or her immediate (nuclear) family only.
Identity is based in the social network to which one belongs.	Identity is based in the individual.
Children learn to think in terms of "we."	Children learn to think in terms of "I."
Harmony should always be maintained and direct confrontations avoided.	Speaking one's mind is a characteristic of an honest person.
The purpose of education is learning how to *do*.	The purpose of education is learning how to *learn*.
The employer–employee relationship is perceived in moral terms, like a family link.	The employer–employee relationship is a contract based on mutual advantage.
Hiring and promotion decisions take into account the employee's in-group.	Hiring and promotion decisions are based on skills and rules only.
Management is management of groups.	Management is management of individuals.
Relationship prevails over task.	Task prevails over relationship.

EXHIBIT 5.5 1970 Individualism Scores versus 1990 GNP per Capita for 50 Countries (for country name abbreviations see Exhibit 5.8)

Source: From Geert Hofstede, *Cultures and Organizations: Software of the Mind*, McGraw-Hill/UK, 1991, p. 75. Reprinted with permission of the author.

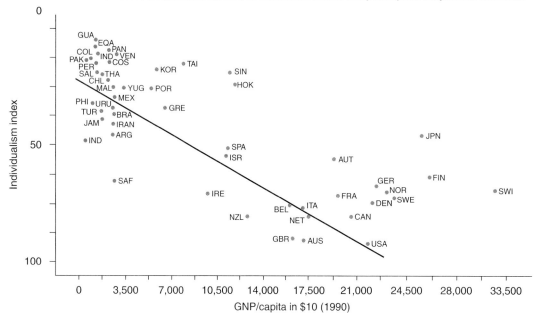

Power Distance Another cultural dimension to consider is **power distance,** "the extent to which the less powerful members of institutions and organizations within a country expect and accept that power is distributed unequally."[17] Power distance scores

inform us about dependence relationships in a country. In small power distance countries there is limited dependence of subordinates on bosses, and a preference for consultation, that is, interdependence between bosses and subordinate. In large power distance countries there is considerable dependence of subordinates on bosses.[18]

In high power distance societies, a centralized authority generally designates the procedures for employees to follow, and inequalities in rewards are easily accepted. On the other hand, centralized authority and severe inequalities in rewards are difficult to maintain in low power distance societies.

EXHIBIT 5.6
Key Differences between Low and High Power Distance Societies

From Geert Hofstede, *Cultures and Organizations: Software of the Mind,* McGraw-Hill/UK, 1991, p. 37. Reprinted with permission of the author.

Low Power Distance	**High Power Distance**
Inequalities among people should be minimized.	Inequalities among people are both expected and desired.
Teachers are experts who transfer impersonal truths.	Teachers are gurus who transfer personal wisdom.
Hierarchy in organization means an inequality of roles, established for convenience.	Hierarchy in organization means there are inequalities between superiors and subordinates.
Decentralization is popular.	Centralization is popular.
The salary range between the top and bottom of the organization is narrow.	The salary range between the top and bottom of the organization is wide.
Subordinates expect to be consulted.	Subordinates expect to be told what to do.
The ideal boss is a resourceful democrat.	The ideal boss is a benevolent autocrat, or good father.
Privileges and status symbols are frowned upon.	Privileges and status symbols for managers are both expected and popular.

EXHIBIT 5.7
The Position of 50 Countries and Three Regions on the Power Distance and Individualism–Collectivism Dimensions (for country name abbreviations see Exhibit 5.8)

From Geert Hofstede, *Cultures and Organizations: Software of the Mind,* McGraw-Hill/UK, 1991, p. 54. Reprinted with permission of the author.

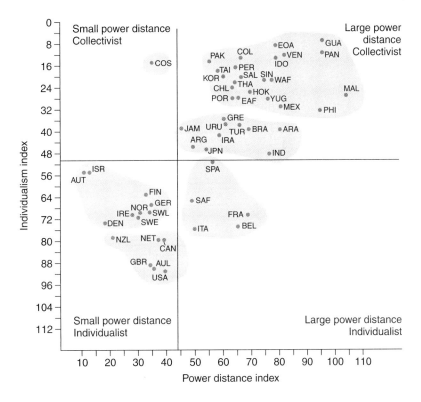

Lower level employees in low power distance societies follow procedures outlined by their superiors, unless they disagree or feel that the directions are wrong. In high power distance countries, strict obedience to superiors is expected even when their judgments are considered to be wrong. Power distance is reflected in the way that companies are organized. In high power distance societies, centralized organizations are the norm, whereas decentralized decision making is more common in low power distance societies. Exhibit 5.6 summarizes differences between low and high power distance societies.

Individualism and Collectivism versus Power Distance   Hofstede compared societies that scored high on individualism or collectivism with their scores on power distance. The result is the graph seen in Exhibit 5.7.

EXHIBIT 5.8 **Abbreviations for the Countries and Regions Studied**

Source: From Geert Hofstede, *Cultures and Organizations: Software of the Mind,* McGraw-Hill/UK, 1991, p. 55. Reprinted with permission of the author.

Abbreviation	Country or Region	Abbreviation	Country or Region
ARA	Arab-speaking countries (Egypt, Iraq, Kuwait, Lebanon, Libya, Saudi Arabia, United Arab Emirates)	JAM	Jamaica
		JPN	Japan
		KOR	South Korea
ARG	Argentina	MAL	Malaysia
AUL	Australia	MEX	Mexico
AUT	Austria	NET	Netherlands
BEL	Belgium	NOR	Norway
BRA	Brazil	NZL	New Zealand
CAN	Canada	PAK	Pakistan
CHL	Chile	PAN	Panama
COL	Colombia	PER	Peru
COS	Costa Rica	PHI	Philippines
DEN	Denmark	POR	Portugal
EAF	East Africa (Ethiopia, Kenya, Tanzania, Zambia)	SAF	South Africa
EQA	Equador	SAL	Salvador
FIN	Finland	SIN	Singapore
FRA	France	SPA	Spain
GBR	Great Britain	SWE	Sweden
GER	Germany F.R.	SWI	Switzerland
GRE	Greece	TAI	Taiwan
GUA	Guatemala	THA	Thailand
HOK	Hong Kong	TUR	Turkey
IDO	Indonesia	URU	Uruguay
IND	India	USA	United States
IRA	Iran	VEN	Venezuela
IRE	Ireland (Republic of)	WAF	West Africa (Ghana, Nigeria, Sierra Leone)
ISR	Israel		
ITA	Italy	YUG	Yugoslavia

Cultures that are relatively individualistic generally have lower power distance, whereas those that are relatively collectivistic generally have higher power distance. There are exceptions. Costa Rica is a strongly collectivistic country with small power distance. Other countries rank toward the middle on both dimensions, such as Spain and India.

Uncertainty Avoidance   The degree to which individuals avoid uncertainty in their environments and the resulting anxiety varies from society to society. Hofstede found this dimension as a derivative of power distance and coined the term **uncertainty avoidance** to define the "extent to which the members of a culture feel threatened by uncertain or unknown situations"[19] or by ambiguity in a situation. Cultures that are high in uncertainty avoidance tend to be more expressive, that is, they use body language to release their anxiety and to ensure their message is conveyed. Weak and strong uncertainty avoidance societies are contrasted in Exhibit 5.9.

Masculinity and Femininity   The use of **masculinity versus femininity** as a measure has been controversial, but Hofstede indicates that he developed these dimensions from male and female stereotypical gender roles:

> *Masculinity* pertains to societies in which social gender roles are clearly distinct (i.e., men are supposed to be assertive, tough, and focused on material success whereas women are supposed to be more modest, tender, and concerned with the quality of life); *femininity* pertains to societies in which social gender roles overlap, i.e., both men and women are supposed to be modest, tender, and concerned with the quality of life.[20]

EXHIBIT 5.9
Key Differences between Weak and Strong Uncertainty Avoidance Societies

Source: From Geert Hofstede, *Cultures and Organizations: Software of the Mind,* McGraw-Hill/UK, 1991, p. 125. Reprinted with permission of the author.

Weak Uncertainty Avoidance	**Strong Uncertainty Avoidance**
Uncertainty is a normal feature of life and each day is accepted as it comes.	The uncertainty inherent in life is felt as a continuous threat that must be fought.
Low stress; subjective feeling of well-being.	High stress; subjective feeling of anxiety.
Aggression and emotions should not be shown.	Aggression and emotions may be ventilated at appropriate times and places.
Ambiguous situations and unfamiliar risks cause no discomfort.	Familiar risks are accepted; ambiguous situations and unfamiliar risks raise fears.
What is different is curious.	What is different is dangerous.
Rules should be limited to those that are strictly necessary.	There is an emotional need for rules, even if they will never work.
Comfortable feeling when lazy; hard work only when needed.	Emotional need to be busy; inner urge to work hard.
Tolerance of deviant and innovative ideas and behavior.	Suppression of deviant ideas and behavior; resistance to innovation.
Motivation by achievement and esteem or belongingness.	Motivation by security and esteem or belongingness.

EXHIBIT 5.10   **Masculinity Index Values for 50 Countries and 3 Regions**

Source: From Geert Hofstede, *Cultures and Organizations: Software of the Mind,* McGraw-Hill/UK, 1991, p. 84. Reprinted with permission of the author.

Score Rank	Country or Region	MAS Score	Score Rank	Country or Region	MAS Score
1	Japan	95	28	Singapore	48
2	Austria	79	29	Israel	47
3	Venezuela	73	30/31	Indonesia	46
4/5	Italy	70	30/31	West Africa	46
4/5	Switzerland	70	32/33	Turkey	45
6	Mexico	69	32/33	Taiwan	45
7/8	Ireland (Republic of)	68	34	Panama	44
7/8	Jamaica	68	35/36	Iran	43
9/10	Great Britain	66	35/36	France	43
9/10	Germany FR	66	37/38	Spain	42
11/12	Philippines	64	37/38	Peru	42
11/12	Colombia	64	39	East Africa	41
13/14	South Africa	63	40	Salvador	40
13/14	Equador	63	41	South Korea	39
15	USA	62	42	Uruguay	38
16	Australia	61	43	Guatemala	37
17	New Zealand	58	44	Thailand	34
18/19	Greece	57	45	Portugal	31
18/19	Hong Kong	57	46	Chile	28
20/21	Argentina	56	47	Finland	26
20/21	India	56	48/49	Yugoslavia	21
22	Belgium	54	48/49	Costa Rica	21
23	Arab countries	53	50	Denmark	16
24	Canada	52	51	Netherlands	14
25/26	Malaysia	50	52	Norway	8
25/26	Pakistan	50	53	Sweden	5
27	Brazil	49			

In masculine societies, success and money are dominant values; in feminine societies, the quality of life is the dominant value. For example, in masculine societies such as Japan, the workplace is generally high in job stress and supervisor oversight. However, in more feminine societies such as Scandinavia, cooperation and security are emphasized. Female managers are more common in organizations in feminine societies than in masculine societies. Exhibits 5.10 and 5.11 summarize this dimension.

EXHIBIT 5.11

Key Differences between Feminine and Masculine Societies

Source: From Geert Hofstede, *Cultures and Organizations: Software of the Mind*, McGraw-Hill/UK, 1991, p. 96. Reprinted with permission of the author.

Feminine	**Masculine**
Dominant values in society are caring for others and quality of life.	Dominant values in society are material success and progress.
People and warm relationships are important.	Money and things are important.
Everyone is supposed to be modest.	Men are supposed to be assertive, ambitious, and tough.
Both men and women are allowed to be tender and concerned with relationships.	Women are supposed to be tender and take care of relationships.
Sympathy for the weak.	Sympathy for the strong.
Work in order to live.	Live in order to work.
Managers use intuition and strive for consensus.	Managers should be decisive and assertive.
Stress on equality, solidarity, and quality of work life.	Stress on equity, competition, and performance.
Conflicts are resolved through compromise and negotiation.	Conflicts are resolved by fighting them out.

EXHIBIT 5.12

The Position of 50 Countries and 3 Regions on the Masculinity–Femininity and Uncertainty Avoidance Dimensions (for country name abbreviations see Exhibit 5.8)

Source: From Geert Hofstede, *Cultures and Organizations: Software of the Mind*, McGraw-Hill/UK, 1991, p. 87. Reprinted with permission of the author.

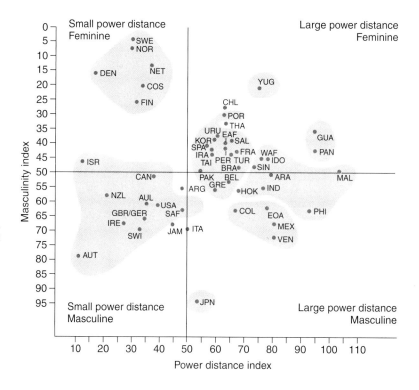

Power Distance versus Masculinity and Femininity This comparison is not as distinct as the comparison between individualism and collectivism versus power distance. Exhibit 5.12 displays the position of 50 countries and 3 regions on the masculinity–femininity and uncertainty avoidance dimensions (for country name abbreviations see Exhibit 5.8).[21] Exhibit 5.13 shows country scores on all dimensions.

Time Orientation Societies place different emphasis on time. In some cultures, efficient use of time is emphasized. In the United States, the common phrase "time is money" denotes the fact that time has value. Western Europeans and Canadians are also very time-conscious. However, in other countries, time is considered to be not limited and valuable but an inexhaustible resource. This attitude makes individuals in

EXHIBIT 5.13
Scores for Countries Using Hofstede's Dimensions and Data

Source: From Geert Hofstede, *Cultures and Organizations: Software of the Mind,* McGraw-Hill/UK, 1991. Reprinted with permission of the author.

Country	Power Distance	Individualism	Masculinity	Uncertainty Avoidance
Argentina	49	46	56	86
Australia	36	90	61	51
Austria	11	55	79	70
Belgium	65	75	54	94
Brazil	69	38	49	76
Canada	39	80	52	48
Chile	63	23	28	86
Colombia	67	13	64	80
Costa Rica	35	15	21	86
Denmark	18	74	16	23
Equador	78	8	63	67
Finland	33	63	26	59
France	68	71	43	86
German FR	35	67	66	65
Great Britain	35	89	66	35
Greece	60	35	57	112
Guatemala	95	6	37	101
Hong Kong	68	25	57	29
India	77	48	56	40
Indonesia	76	14	46	48
Iran	58	41	43	59
Ireland	28	70	68	35
Israel	13	54	47	81
Italy	50	76	70	75
Jamaica	45	39	68	13
Japan	54	46	95	92
Malaysia	104	26	50	36
Mexico	81	30	69	82
Netherlands	38	80	14	53
New Zealand	22	79	58	49
Norway	31	69	8	50
Pakistan	55	14	50	70
Panama	95	11	44	86
Peru	64	16	42	87
Philippines	94	32	64	44
Portugal	63	27	31	104
Salvador	66	19	40	94
Singapore	74	20	48	8
South Africa	49	65	63	49
South Korea	60	187	39	85
Spain	57	51	42	86
Sweden	31	71	5	29
Switzerland	34	68	70	58
Taiwan	58	17	45	69
Thailand	64	20	34	64
Turkey	66	37	45	85
United States	40	91	62	46
Uruguay	61	36	38	100
Venezuela	81	12	73	76
Yugoslavia	76	27	21	88
Regions				
East Africa	64	27	41	52
West Africa	77	20	46	54
Arab countries	80	38	53	68

these cultures very casual about such things as keeping appointments and deadlines. The differences in **time orientation** can cause anxiety and frustration on the part of individuals from both types of culture.

In the United States, the time spent waiting for a person beyond the appointed time is a measure of the importance of the person kept waiting. The longer the waiting time, the less important the person kept waiting is deemed to be. This is why Americans consider having to wait to be an affront. In other areas, such as the Middle East, there is no such interpretation of waiting time. A visitor may wait for a long time, but once the visitor is seen, the interview will last as long as necessary to complete the business between the individuals. However, the next visitor may be kept waiting a long time as a result of this practice. This happens at all levels of society. The following incident during Secretary of State Warren Christopher's visit to Saudi Arabia illustrates this point:

> Secretary of State Warren Christopher was on a visit to Saudi Arabia to discuss critical Middle East issues with King Fahd. The King kept his guest waiting for more than six hours beyond the expected meeting time and met him shortly before 10 P.M. Mr. Christopher used the free time to tour the old section of Jedda, rest, and have dinner. The King apologized for the delay but offered no explanation. The whole incident was written off by the U.S. State Department saying that it was nothing personal and that such things happen all the time in that part of the world.[22]

If the individuals involved had both been from countries where "time is money," the incident would have caused a furor.

When two individuals engaged in a business transaction have different time orientations, problems are likely to develop. For example, in most Middle Eastern cultures, deadlines are considered an affront in the same way that Americans would be offended if someone backed them into a corner in a threatening manner. Americans set deadlines to get things done. Middle Easterners use a different method, which Americans consider rude: needling. An Arab businessman explained how he gets his car repaired in a timely manner:

> First, I go to the garage and tell the mechanic what is wrong with my car. I wouldn't want to give him the idea that I didn't know. After that, I leave the car and walk around the block. When I come back to the garage, I ask him if he has started to work yet. On my way home for lunch, I stop in and ask him how things are going. When I go back to the office, I stop by again. In the evening, I return and peer over his shoulder for a while. If I didn't keep this up, he'd be off working on someone else's car.[23]

FedEx first entered the European market with a final pickup time set for 5 P.M., although the Spanish, for example, work as late as 8 P.M. FedEx had assumed that work schedules and times were the same in Europe as in the United States.[24]

Trompenaars's Framework

Another European researcher, Fons Trompenaars, conducted research with 15,000 managers from 28 countries, representing 47 national cultures.[25] He describes cultural differences using seven dimensions. Five dimensions are concerned with how people relate to each other: (1) universalism versus particularism, (2) individualism versus collectivism, (3) neutral versus affective relationships, (4) specific versus diffuse relationships, and (5) achievement versus ascription. The sixth dimension deals with time—whether the culture emphasizes the past, present, or future and whether the time is sequential or synchronic. The final and seventh dimension is the relation to nature, focusing on internal or external orientation.

Universalism versus Particularism   In cultures emphasizing a *universalistic orientation,* people believe in the definition of goodness or truth as being applicable to all situations. Judgments are likely to be made without regard to situational considerations. On the other hand, people in *particularistic societies* take the notion of situational forces more seriously, and judgments take into account contingencies that affect most circumstances. In universalistic cultures, such as the United States, the United Kingdom, and Germany, there is a tendency to rely on legal contracts defining a business relationship. These legal contracts are considered to reflect what the parties should do and are referred to in times of disputes and conflicts. In particularistic cultures, such as China and parts of Latin America, legal contracts do not carry much significance. The contract may reflect an initial agreement, but how the parties relate to each other depends on many factors in the situation.

Individualism versus Collectivism   This dimension is almost identical to the Hofstede's dimension. In *individualistic societies,* an individual pursues his or her own personal goals, and the focus tends to be on continuous improvement of one's self-worth. Laws and regulations make the rights of individuals of paramount importance. Most Western cultures share this value orientation. *Collectivistic societies* emphasize group well-being and an individual learns to subordinate his or her personal goals in favor of group goals. Cultures in most parts of east and south Asia, as well as Latin America, the Middle East, and Africa, are collectivistic in their orientation. About 70 percent of the world's cultures are collectivistic.[26]

Neutral versus Affective Relationships   In this dimension, Trompenaars focuses on the appropriateness of expressing emotions in different cultures. In *neutral cultures,* the tendency is to control one's emotion so that it does not interfere with judgment. In contrast, *affective cultures* encourage expression of emotions as one relates to others. In a business situation, members of affective cultures, such as Brazil, Mexico, and Italy, may express emotions such as anger, joy, or frustration more freely compared to members of neutral cultures, such as the United Kingdom, Singapore, and Japan.

Specific versus Diffuse Relationships   This dimension of culture focuses on how a culture emphasizes notions of privacy and access to privacy. In *specific cultures,* individuals have large public spaces and relatively small private spaces. The distinction between public and private spaces is clear, and the private space retains its private character with limited access to people except those in one's inner circle. The United States is a good example of a specific culture, but the United Kingdom is even more specific. One often must go through several levels of receptionist, secretary, and personal assistant to reach the manager, even for a specified appointment. On the other hand, members of *diffuse cultures,* such as those found in parts of Latin America and southern Europe, draw no clear distinction between public and private spaces. In diffuse cultures, a business executive's office and home are not divided as clearly as they are in specific cultures, and work relationships often extend into personal relationships.

Achievement versus Ascription   This dimension describes the methods used to achieve power and status. Achievement cultures, such as the United States and the United Kingdom, are those emphasizing competence (special skills, knowledge, and talent) in attaining position status and power. Ascription cultures, such as Saudi Arabia and China, are those where position status and power come from membership in groups—those in power have been born into influence.

Relationship to Time The first aspect of Trompenaars's time dimension is similar to Hofstede's; there are different emphases on the past, present, and future. The second, sequential versus synchronic, is quite different. In *sequential cultures,* time is viewed as being linear and divided into segments that can then be divided and scheduled. In sequential cultures, such as the United States and the United Kingdom, schedules rule the business and private lives of individuals and are generally more important than relationships. On the other hand, in *synchronic cultures,* time is viewed as circular and indivisible, and relationships are more important than schedules. In synchronic cultures such as Portugal and Egypt, activities are not scheduled with definite starting or ending times, and individuals move from event to event, rather than from deadline to deadline.

Relationship to Nature This dimension is similar to Kluckhohn and Strodtbeck's dimension. In *internal-oriented cultures,* individuals control situations. In the United States, for example, if one is late to an appointment, it is his or her fault. In *external-oriented cultures,* individuals do not control situations. In Argentina, for example, if one is late for an appointment, the fault is not considered to be his or hers, but that of the situation that prevented a prompt arrival.

Ronen and Shenkar's Framework

In this framework, shown in Exhibit 5.14, countries of the world are clustered based on attitudinal dimensions that Ronen and Shenkar found by conducting a smallest-space analysis of their data.[27] This framework provides another interesting way of clustering countries and naming them in a fashion to be somewhat consistent with the regions of the world from where they come. Nine clusters were found based on employee attitudes toward importance of work roles, need fulfillment, job satisfaction, managerial

EXHIBIT 5.14

Ronen and Shenkar's Framework

Source: From *Academy of Management Review,* September 1985, by S. Ronen and O. Shenkar. Copyright © 1985 by Academy of Management. Reproduced with permission of Academy of Management via Copyright Clearance Center.

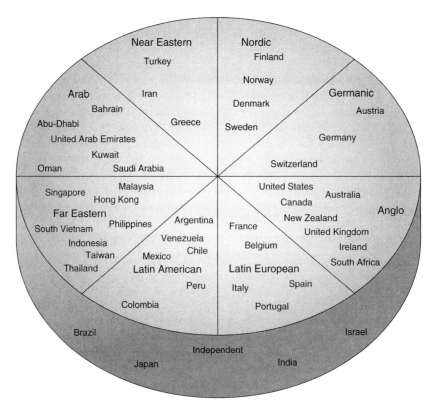

and organizational variables, and interpersonal orientation. In addition to the country clusters resulting from smallest-space analysis, per capita gross national product was used to determine the relative placements in the circle. It seems as though most highly developed countries are on the right side of the circle. While this may indicate some consistency between a country's level of economic development and generally endorsed patterns of values and work attitudes, no firm conclusions can be drawn.

Schwartz's Framework

Another important framework is based on the work of Shalom Schwartz, an Israeli cross-cultural researcher, and his collaborators from different parts of the world.[28] They were interested in identifying the content and organization of human values based on their similarities and differences. Schwartz proposed that fundamental issues facing mankind need to be identified before one can meaningfully sample all of the important value differences. Three fundamental needs were regarded as the basis for this value study: social coordination needs, biological needs, and survival and welfare needs. Working from this foundation, Schwartz identified 56 values and constructed a method in which respondents from more than 50 countries in all regions of the world indicated the extent to which each value was a guiding principle in his or her life. The human values were grouped into three dimensions, based on the fundamental needs Schwartz identified. Schwartz's dimensions are significant because they show that the values have the same meanings and are important concepts in all cultures. The value dimensions are seen in Exhibit 5.15.

EXHIBIT 5.15
Schwartz's Value Dimensions

Source: From S.H. Schwartz, "Beyond Individualism/ Collectivism: New Dimensions of Values." In U. Kim, et al., *Individualism and Collectivism: Theory, Application, and Methods.* Copyright © 1994 by Sage Publications, Inc. Reprinted by permission of Sage Publications, Inc.

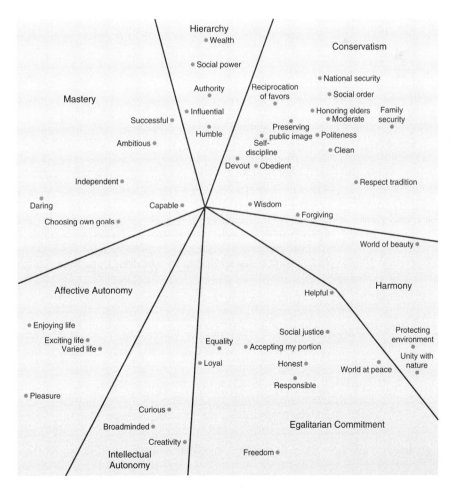

Conservatism versus Autonomy In countries where *conservatism* is emphasized, maintenance of the status quo and restraint of personal actions that disrupt solidarity, cohesiveness, and traditional order are valued. Examples of such values include obedience, respect of tradition, family security, social order, and reciprocation of favors. *Intellectual autonomy,* in contrast, emphasizes independence of ideas and the rights of an individual to pursue his or her own intellectual goals. Examples include values of curiosity, broad-mindness, and creativity. *Affective autonomy,* which is also opposite to conservatism, focuses on individuals' right to have pleasurable experiences, such as enjoying life, having an exciting life, having a varied life, and pursuit of pleasure. Countries that emphasize conservatism include China, India, and Greece as well as the Middle East. Emphasis on intellectual autonomy is found in countries which are also high on Hofstede's dimension of individualism, such as the United States, United Kingdom, Australia, and Germany. Affective autonomy is especially emphasized in the United States and other individualist countries, such as Australia and the United Kingdom.

Hierarchy versus Egalitarianism In countries that emphasize the value of *hierarchy,* individuals are socialized to respect the obligations and rules attached to social roles. Sanctions are imposed if they deviate from these expectations. This value type accepts the unequal distribution of power, wealth, authority, and influence. On the other hand, countries emphasizing the value of *egalitarianism* reinforce the need for individuals to cooperate voluntarily and feel a sense of genuine concern for everyone's welfare. This value type deemphasizes personal interests in favor of equality, responsibility, and freedom. Hierarchy is particularly found in countries that are also high in Hofstede's dimension of power distance, such as Latin American countries, Middle Eastern countries, and some eastern and southern Asian countries. Egalitarianism is found in countries that are low in power distance and high in femininity, such as the Scandinavian countries of Denmark, Sweden, and Norway.

Mastery versus Harmony In countries that emphasize *mastery,* people are socialized to control and change the natural and social world, to exert some degree of control, and to exploit it. This value type stresses the importance of getting ahead through assertiveness. Ambition, success, independence, and individual capability are highly valued in these countries. *Harmony,* on the other hand, advances the preservation of the ecological and social worlds as they are. This value type emphasizes protection of the environment and unity of nature. The value of mastery is found in the United States and some western European countries, whereas the value of harmony is found in east Asian countries, particularly in Japan. However, the ecological movement is becoming very strong in the United States and western European countries, and time will show whether the values of mastery retain their hold on these countries.

Hall's Framework

Edward T. Hall, an American anthropologist, used the concept of context to explain cultural differences between countries.[29] *Context* refers to cues and other information present in a given situation. In *high-context cultures,* such as Japan, Spain, and the Middle Eastern countries, information is embedded in the social situation and is implicitly understood by those involved in the situation. Use of body language and tone of voice in conveying sentiments and messages is common. In *low-context cultures,* such as Switzerland, Germany, and the United States, information tends to be explicitly stated. Use of words to convey meaning is emphasized, and little information is left that is not explicitly stated. For example, Swiss and Germans are relatively direct in their style of communication, whereas Japanese and Chinese expect that implicit messages that are in the context will be easily understood.

Triandis's Framework

Harry C. Triandis, a prominent cross-cultural researcher, developed a framework around the concept of subjective culture.[30] He advanced the notion that to analyze culture systematically, one needs to understand the significance of the *cultural syndrome,* which is composed of (1) cultural complexity, (2) tightness versus looseness, and (3) two aspects of individualism versus collectivism.

Cultural complexity is largely determined by the ecology and history of the society. Societies where people are hunters and gatherers of food tend to be simple. Agricultural societies are a little more complex, and industrial societies tend to be still more complex. Societies where large volumes of information are continuously being exchanged tend to be most complex. According to this scheme, the culture of the Eskimos is relatively simple, whereas the culture of cities like metropolitan New York is one of the most complex. Most international business occurs in more complex societies that have established infrastructure.

The second aspect of the syndrome, *tightness versus looseness,* is concerned with the degree of enforcement of social norms in the society. In the United States, where culture is loose, deviation from social norms is tolerated more easily than in tight cultures, such as those found in most east Asian (e.g., Japan and China), Mediterranean (Greece and Egypt), and Middle Eastern (e.g. Egypt and Jordan) countries. Impulsive behaviors and those that lead to self-gratification appear more frequently in U.S. and Western television programs than in those of countries that are tighter in the enforcement of norms. Tight cultures do not tolerate deviation from norms and expected role behaviors, and severe sanctions are imposed on those who violate expectations. Triandis noted that self-control and control of impulsive behavior are learned more easily in cultures that are tight.[31] The significance of this aspect of the cultural syndrome is discussed in the chapter on leadership (Chapter 15) as well as the chapter on negotiation and decision making (Chapter 13).

The third aspect of this syndrome is concerned with cultural patterns of individualism versus collectivism coupled with the notion of *verticalness versus horizontalness.* Triandis and his colleagues suggest that there are two kinds of collectivism and two kinds of individualism.[32]

The first kind of collectivism, *horizontal collectivism,* emphasizes interdependence of action and equality with others. The second type of collectivism, *vertical collectivism,* emphasizes interdependence of action but the concept of being different from others. Horizontal collectivism is found in Israeli *kibbutim.* This particular cultural pattern is not widely observed. Vertical collectivism cultures are traditional China, India, most of Latin America, and many of the Mediterranean and African countries.

The first kind of individualism, *horizontal individualism,* emphasizes independence of action and equality with others. Australia, Sweden, and Denmark are good examples of countries that are high on horizontal individualism. The second type of individualism, *vertical individualism,* emphasizes independence of action and the need to stand out from others. This is a characteristic of most wealthy Western countries, and is particularly prevalent in the United States, United Kingdom, and France.

Triandis's framework is important because the preference for management style differs, in part due to these cultural syndromes. The significance of the framework will also be seen in the chapter on managing technology and knowledge (Chapter 11). Table 5.2

TABLE 5.2
A Synthesis of the
Basic Cultural
Dimensions

Areas	Dimensions	Authors
Relation to nature	Mastery, harmony, subjugation	Kluckhohn and Strodtbeck
	Internal versus external	Trompenaars
	Mastery versus harmony	Schwartz
Basic human nature	Good, mixed, evil	Kluckhohn and Strodtbeck
Time orientation	Past, present, future	Kluckhohn and Strodtbeck
	Long-term versus short-term	Hofstede
	Sequential versus synchronic	Trompenaars
Space orientation	Public, mixed, private	Kluckhohn and Strodtbeck
	Specific versus diffuse	Trompenaars
Activity orientation	Doing, being, thinking	Kluckhohn and Strodtbeck
Relationship orientation	Individualistic versus group	Kluckhohn and Strodtbeck
	Individualism versus collectivism	Hofstede
	Power distance	Hofstede
	Uncertainty avoidance	Hofstede
	Masculinity versus femininity	Hofstede
	Universalism versus particularism	Trompenaars
	Individualism versus collectivism	Trompenaars
	Neutral versus affective	Trompenaars
	Conservatism versus intellectual autonomy	Schwartz
	Hierarchy versus egalitarianism	Schwartz
	High versus low context	Hall
	Cultural complexity	Triandis
	Tightness versus looseness	Triandis
	Verticalness versus horizontalness	Triandis

outlines the basic cultural dimensions. Practical Insight 5.3 on page 160 illustrates some of the intricate details that international managers must know about the cultures they want to do business with.

Language Barriers

Language is another problem for international managers. In English-speaking countries alone, the variety can cause difficulties. In England, India, New Zealand, and Australia, the word "trousers" is used to connote a two-legged garment worn by both men and women; the word "pants" denotes undergarments worn under the trousers. Many Americans have made this error in polite conversation. In the same way, the U.S. auto body shop becomes a panelbeater's shop, the wrench becomes a spanner, the trunk of a car becomes its boot, and granulated sugar becomes caster sugar. And this is just in English. Imagine the difficulties in other, less familiar languages.

American brand names can take on unexpected meanings when they are translated. Companies have become more careful recently, but there are some interesting examples. The famous Pepsi-Cola slogan "Come alive with Pepsi" became "Come out of the grave" in Germany and "Bring your ancestors back from the dead" in Taiwan. More examples are shown in Practical Insight 5.4 on page 162.

Culture and Management Styles in Selected Countries

Management practices based on cultural differences vary. For example, in high power distance cultures such as those found in Asia, an effective leader is one who is a benevolent autocrat. In low power distance countries such as the United States, the effective leader is the one who is people-oriented and practices participative decision making. In collectivistic societies such as those in Latin America, the most appropriate reward to individuals is based on the performance of their group. However, in individualistic countries such as those in western Europe, the most appropriate reward system would be to reward individuals for their own performance, as opposed to group performance.

In countries with masculine cultures, such as Japan, women are expected to play certain roles, such as staying home and taking care of the children, or working as nurses or secretaries. In Japan, women may be fired when they get married, and they are not expected to assume managerial positions at any time. In cultures with a more feminine perspective, such as the Scandinavian countries, women have equal status with men, reflected in the societal expectation that women should work. Businesses are required to make this easier by providing both paternity and maternity leave so that parents can take care of newborn children. In high uncertainty avoidance cultures, such as Japan and Italy, organizations generally have rules and procedures to reduce uncertainty about behaviors in particular circumstances. This creates stability and certainty, and individuals are less likely to change jobs readily. Low uncertainty avoidance countries, such as the United States and Great Britain, favor organizations that provide managers with freedom to take prudent risks. These countries are also known for very high rates of job mobility.

Now we examine the cultural patterns of four countries. These countries were chosen because of their importance in international trade with the largest economic power of the world, the United States.

Cultural Patterns of Japan

About 140 million Japanese live on four main islands in the Pacific that are shaped like a crescent. These islands are largely mountainous and the population is crowded in a small part of the total surface of the land near coastal areas. Japan's industrial growth over the past 50 years has been astounding, especially in light of its defeat in World War II. There are huge urban areas about 300 miles long running northeast from the enormous industrial city of Tokyo through Osaka and Kobe. It is the second largest economic power in the world, after the United States, with a gross GDP of more than $3 trillion.

The Japanese are a homogeneous people, and they have lived relatively independently for thousands of years. The royal family claims ancestry back over 2,000 years. The people practice a unique combination of Shintoism and Buddhism. The Japanese were known to reject foreign influences, often feeling that they had little to learn from the *gaijins* (foreigners), until their self-imposed isolation ended in the 1700s.

Japanese culture is based on the principle of *wa* (peace and harmony). Wa is connected to the value of *amae* (spiritual harmony). Amae, in its turn, leads to *shinyo* (mutual interdependence, faith and honor), which is necessary to execute business relationships. Although Japan is a country that is high in pragmatism, as well as masculinity, power distance, and uncertainty avoidance (three of Hofstede's value dimensions), much significance is given to the values of loyalty, interpersonal empathy, and continuous guidance and development of subordinates. This results in a curious mix of authoritarianism and humanistic values, and the company is often seen as a reflection of one's family.

In competing with Japan, one often encounters the phrase "competing with Japan, Inc." In several visits to Japan, the authors of this book noted a remarkable sense of affinity that the Japanese have with their community, company, and their country. They take great pride in their country's achievement.

PRACTICAL INSIGHT 5.3

HOW TO DO BUSINESS IN ISLAMIC COUNTRIES

The business scene in the Islamic world may be as complex as its 1.3 billion people, but one rule is nevertheless quite straight-forward for Westerners who want to do deals.

"One thing you do not bring up is the Palestinian–Israeli situation," advised Samuel L. Hayes III,* an expert on Islamic finance and an emeritus professor of investment banking at Harvard Business School.

Hayes, who continues to travel regularly to Islamic countries for research and consulting, offered advice to HBS students on January 23 as part of the school's post–September 11 speaker series, "Rising to the Challenge." He was joined by a specialist in Islamic law, Harvard Law School professor Frank E. Vogel,[†] for the series' discussion on doing business in the Islamic world. Vogel and Hayes are also co-authors of the book *Islamic Law and Finance: Religion, Risk and Return* (Kluwer Law International, 1998).

According to Hayes and Vogel, business people, particularly Westerners who work in the Persian Gulf and other Islamic regions such as Asia and North Africa, need to appreciate the extent to which religion and Islamic law are intertwined and permeate all levels of society, including commerce, to greater and lesser degrees depending on the country. "This law is seen as deriving from direct, divine command," said Vogel. "This is important to grasp."

Executives who understand the basic tenets of the Islamic religion as it relates to commerce will have an easier time abroad, they said. According to Hayes, the following principles of comportment are expected among businesspeople:

- Contracts should be fair to all parties. Partnership is preferred over hierarchical claims.
- Speculation is prohibited. "They don't like gambling," said Hayes. "For instance, if you invested in an Islamic mutual fund, among those industries which would be barred from representation as funds would be the gambling industry. But gambling also relates to futures; it relates to currency hedging; so it's a major situation that you have to be aware of."
- Interest is prohibited. "This is probably the thing that is most often identified with Islamic finance. Back in the time of the prophet Mohammed, some of the most rapacious individuals were the moneylenders; and so as a response to the things that these moneylenders did which were so reprehensible, part of the religious belief is that you do not charge interest or accept interest. Now, of course, that isn't always practiced, but it is the theory."
- Compassion is required when a business is in trouble. "In any country that has Islamic influences in its legal structure, if somebody is in bankruptcy or if somebody is experiencing financial reversals, you can't put pressure on them, because that is not an appropriate thing to do when somebody is down. You don't kick them when they're down," said Hayes.

Like religious people everywhere, Vogel said, not all Muslims follow the faith in every respect. Some do deal in futures, for instance. "What Frank and I found after working with religious mullahs for most of the 1990s—and Frank a lot longer than that—is that it's a process of education," Hayes told the group. "When they get to understand what's involved in an international transaction, they are more willing to interpret an option, for instance, as not being speculative.

"There are very few who are doing that yet," he added. "As a result, truly few Muslims who are international businesspeople are exposed to the vagaries of currency exchanges." There are religiously acceptable options for commodities, but they're very cumbersome, he said.

Cultural Patterns of Germany

Germany is the largest country located in central Europe, with more than 90 million people. Despite its current status as the third largest economic power in the world, it has had one of the most turbulent political histories of any western European country in the last two centuries. After World War II, Germany was completely devastated, and the United States developed the Marshall Plan for the economic recovery of Europe, which led to the reconstruction of West Germany. West Germany's economic performance after 1945 has been no less than remarkable. It reflects the tremendous resilience of Germans to rebuild the economic backbone, which was one of the strongest in western Europe throughout the last two centuries. The reunification of Germany after 1990 led to considerable economic difficulties, particularly because the economic infrastructure of East Germany had been much weaker than that of West Germany. De-

More Tips

On a practical basis, names are very important for doing deals in Islamic countries, as in most of the world, the professors said. Who you know is key. Similarly, relationships and family connections are vital in business. "Relationships that have gone on over time inspire confidence, and of course that's no different than in [the U.S.]," said Hayes.

Personal staff can be very influential and should not be underestimated, he continued. The man who meets you at the airport or who chats you up in a company's waiting room may turn out to be a relative or confidant of the person you're there to do business with.

While it's good for Westerners to be able to speak Arabic socially in the Gulf region, Hayes said, many people would be insulted if you try to speak Arabic about something as important as a deal: "That would be like suggesting that they don't speak English well enough." Those at the business level have usually gone to college in the U.S., Britain, or Australia. Speaking English is a status symbol.

Perhaps surprisingly, Western women sometimes have an advantage doing business in some Islamic countries, Hayes pointed out. They're seen as special and different, almost a "third sex," since most companies send men on the assumption that men will be more acceptable. "Women seem to be able to get to people quicker than the men can," he observed.

Forward and Back

Membership in the World Trade Organization should loosen up the Middle East and particularly the Gulf economically, said Vogel, yet only countries around the periphery of the Arabian peninsula have joined so far. "The big elephant," he said, is Saudi Arabia. It is nowhere near being able to join the WTO, according to Vogel, in part because it is unwilling to enforce foreign arbitration awards.

"It's very important to watch how fast Saudi Arabia moves toward WTO membership. It will have a great deal to do with the political stability of the country, its dealing with the challenges of the future—very serious ones like a demographic bubble that is terribly frightening, affecting, particularly, young males otherwise prone to all sorts of radical beliefs—and a lot of other things, such as the status of women.

"Adaptation and liberalization can happen quickly if the government is in the mood," said Vogel. "It hasn't got there. So far there's too much freight Saudi Arabia is holding back."

Asked if they see a lessening of dependence on Gulf oil since the September 11 terrorist attacks, Vogel said Central Asia should be tapped to counterbalance dependence on Gulf countries and OPEC, while Hayes offered a realist perspective. The U.S. political system is very short sighted, Hayes said. American politicians, who only look two years down the road to the next election, try to "placate the electorate" with short-term benefits at the expense of long-term solutions.

"I think President Carter was right when he tried to initiate a number of long-term energy projects which would have given us greater independence from the Gulf area," said Hayes. "But of course they were completely chucked as soon as he left office.

"So I'm not optimistic about this, and I therefore think we will find ourselves continuing to be vulnerable to that part of the world."

*Samuel L. Hayes III holds the Jacob H. Schiff Chair in Investment Banking at the Harvard Business School, Emeritus.

†Frank E. Vogel is the Custodian of the Two Holy Mosques Adjunct Professor of Islamic Legal Studies and director of the Islamic Legal Studies Program at Harvard Law School.

Source: From "How to Do Business in Islamic Countries," by Martha Lagace, *HBS Working Knowledge,* February 4, 2002. Reprinted with permission of HBS Working Knowledge.

spite the economic difficulties that accompanied unification, Germany has emerged as the economic leader of the European Union (see Chapter 2).

One of the most important aspects of German culture is the continuous emphasis on planning and orderliness to manage uncertainty. The German emphasis on low power distance is expressed in the formal structures of corporations—a practice somewhat uncommon in the United Kingdom and the United States. This approach to managing business leads to a structural rather than liberal view of management.[33] Long-term thinking in all aspects of organizational planning is valued, and high product quality is important. Management qualifications focus more on highly technical knowledge than on work experience, in contrast to other countries. Adherence to procedures is strongly encouraged, and the decision-making style tends to be based on appropriate risk calculations and tends to be slow.

PRACTICAL INSIGHT 5.4

SIGNS IN ENGLISH ALL OVER THE WORLD

Here are some signs and notices written in English that were discovered throughout the world.

- **In a Tokyo hotel:** Is forbidden to steal hotel towels please. If you are not a person to do such a thing is please not to read notis.
- **In a Bucharest hotel lobby:** The lift is being fixed for the next day. During that time we regret that you will be unbearable.
- **In a Leipzig elevator:** Do not enter lift backwards, and only when lit up.
- **In a Belgrade hotel elevator:** To move the cabin, push button wishing floor. If the cabin should enter more persons, each one should press a number of wishing floor. Driving is then going alphabetically by national order.
- **In a Paris hotel elevator:** Please leave your values at the front desk.
- **In a hotel in Athens:** Visitors are expected to complain at the office between the hours of 9 and 11 A.M. daily.
- **In a Yugoslavian hotel:** The flattening of underwear with pleasure is the job of the chambermaid.
- **In a Japanese hotel:** You are invited to take advantage of the chambermaid.
- **In the lobby of a Moscow hotel across from a Russian Orthodox monastery:** You are welcome to visit the cemetery where famous Russian and Soviet composers, artists and writers are buried daily except Thursday.
- **In an Austrian ski lodge:** Not to perambulate the corridors during the hours of repose in the boots of ascension.
- **On the menu of a Swiss restaurant:** Our wines leave you nothing to hope for.
- **On the menu of a Polish hotel:** Salad a firms' own make; limpid red beet soup with cheesy dumplings in the form of a finger; roasted duck let loose; beef rashers beaten up in the country people's fashion.
- **Outside a Hong Kong tailor shop:** Ladies may have a fit upstairs.
- **In a Bangkok dry cleaners:** Drop your trousers here for best results.
- **Outside a Paris dress shop:** Dresses for street walking.
- **In a Rhodes tailor shop:** Order your summer suit. Because is big rush we will execute customers in strict rotation.
- **From the *Soviet Weekly:*** There will be a Moscow Exhibition of Arts by 150,000 Soviet Republic painters and sculptors. These were executed over the past two years.
- **A sign posted in Germany's Black Forest:** It is strictly forbidden on our black forest camping site that people of different sex, for instance, men and women, live together in one tent unless they are married with each other for that purpose.
- **In a Zurich hotel:** Because of the impropriety of entertaining guests of the opposite sex in the bedroom, it is suggested that the lobby be used for this purpose.
- **In an advertisement by a Hong Kong dentist:** Teeth extracted by the latest Methodists.
- **In a Rome laundry:** Ladies, leave your clothes here and spend the afternoon having a good time.
- **In a Czech tourist agency:** Take one of our horse-driven city tours—we guarantee no miscarriages.
- **Advertisement for donkey rides in Thailand:** Would you like to ride on your own ass?
- **In a Swiss mountain inn:** Special today—no ice cream.
- **In a Bangkok temple:** It is forbidden to enter a woman even a foreigner if dressed as a man.
- **In a Tokyo bar:** Special cocktails for the ladies with nuts.
- **In a Copenhagen airline ticket office:** We take your bags and send them in all directions.
- **On the door of a Moscow hotel room:** If this is your first visit to the USSR, you are welcome to it.
- **In a Norwegian cocktail lounge:** Ladies are requested not have children in the bar.
- **In the Budapest zoo:** Please do not feed the animals. If you have any suitable food, give it to the guard on duty.
- **In the office of a Roman doctor:** Specialist in women and other diseases.
- **In an Acapulco hotel:** The manager has personally passed away all the water served here.
- **In a Tokyo shop:** Our nylons cost more than common, but you'll find they are best in the long run.
- **From a Japanese information booklet about using a hotel air conditioner:** Cooles and Heates: If you want just condition of warm in your room, please control yourself.
- **From a brochure of a car rental firm in Tokyo:** When passenger of foot heave in sight, tootle the horn. Trumpet him melodiously at first, but if he still obstacles your passage then tootle him with vigor.
- **Two signs from a Majorcan shop entrance:** English well speaking . . . and . . . Here speeching American.

Source: *Air France Bulletin*, December 1, 1989.

Cultural Patterns of China

About 1.1 billion people live in the world's largest communist state, the People's Republic of China. The population density of mainland China tends to be high in coastal regions and in the fertile plains along the Yangtze River. Even though Mandarin is spoken by all of the Chinese, different dialects are found throughout China. In 1979, Deng Xiaoping opened the economy to foreign investment. The annual increases in foreign direct investment averaged more than 40 percent during the 1990s, reaching a high point in 1993 at 175 percent. In the world's economic history, increases of this magnitude over such a short time have not been seen. After the political integration of Hong Kong with mainland China in 1997, the interest of international and global companies to invest in China increased again.

How people in society should relate to each other and behave is strongly influenced by Confucian thought, and has been for many centuries. To understand the cultural pattern of China and its emergence as a leading economic power in the twenty-first century, we must understand the role of Confucian Dynamism, which values thrift and persistence, as well as concern for future generations. In the Chinese culture, the influence of current actions on future generations is a significant concern. Investments in work organizations, both in human and monetary terms, are regarded as long term. Michael Bond's research shows the importance of four cultural characteristics: persistence (or perseverance), respect for relationships according to status and family connections, thrift, and a sense of shame.[34] The Chinese Culture Connection Study of 1987 showed that Asian nations do not all hold the same exact values,[35] but they do generally hold these four basic cultural values in common.

Cultural Patterns of Mexico

Mexico borders the United States on the south. It has a population of 103 million, living in an area slightly less than three times the area of Texas. The population is mixed with mestizo (Amerindian-Spanish) at 60 percent, Amerindian (Native American) at 30 percent, and white at 9 percent. Spanish is the predominant language. Mexico's economy is a free market economy mixing old and new industry and agriculture, with the private sector becoming increasingly dominant. Income is not consistently distributed, and 40 percent of households fall below the poverty level. Currently, Hispanics, and especially people of Mexican origin, are the largest ethnic minority in the United States.[36] Since NAFTA was implemented in 1994, trade with the United States and Canada has tripled. Because of the importance of Mexico for the NAFTA community, an understanding of some of the dominant cultural patterns of Mexico is necessary.

The cultural pattern of Mexico is highly collectivistic, high in power distance, and high in uncertainty avoidance. Using Triandis's framework, discussed earlier, Mexico is a good example of a vertical collectivistic country. Mexicans do not value time and the concept of punctuality in the same way they are valued in the United States and would not find a half hour to an hour wait for a business meeting unusual. Mexicans value formality and should be addressed by their title and family name. Triandis noted that the concept of *sympatia* (understanding another's feelings as one's own) is crucial to understanding the way that Mexicans expect colleagues to behave.[37] The importance of family should never be underestimated in doing business with Mexico. The cultural significance of work and business is not the same in Mexico as in the United States and Canada. The negotiation process can be long and filled with interruptions, and one must exercise patience.

The Internet and the Evolution of Newer Cultural Groups

With the advent of the Internet, new cultural forms are emerging in work groups. Effects of the Internet and computer-mediated communication on the evolution of new cultural norms has not been widely researched, but some interesting patterns are useful for international managers to think about. Clearly, the Internet has changed the way individuals work together throughout the world and, like television, telecommunication, and other inventions, will make the world smaller.

Computer-mediated communication, which allows subsidiaries to be more closely linked with their headquarters and with each other, is creating shifts in the cultural patterns of the various countries where the subsidiaries are located. Similar occupational groups in various subsidiaries of a multinational or global corporation tend to develop similar cultural norms and patterns of work habits. The electronic age, which is the creation of the rapid flow of information and ideas over the Internet, is shifting the national cultures of the countries in ways that are not fully understood yet. But one thing can be said with confidence: As countries become more affluent, they tend to become more individualistic. In the earlier section, we talked about the role of individualism and power distance. These concepts might need to be revised in light of the rapidly expanding flow of communication and increasing affluence.

Summary

The cultural environment of international business is the focus of this chapter. Culture is to a society what memory is to an individual. Many problems facing managers who live abroad arise from conflicts between the value orientations of different cultures.

Many frameworks can be used to analyze cultural differences. Hofstede's framework, for example, includes (1) individualism and collectivism, (2) power distance, (3) uncertainty avoidance, (4) masculinity and femininity, and (5) time orientation. These frameworks help us understand the differences in cultures. Hall's work on context of cultures helps managers understand such things as communication and use of space in cultures. Language difficulties, along with cultural differences, make it difficult for subsidiaries around the world to function effectively, even as they are brought closer together by the Internet.

In this chapter, we discuss management styles around the world. International managers must learn the intricacies of cultural differences that are present and should develop cultural sensitivity as they expand global operations.

Key Terms and Concepts

convergence of cultures, *139*
cultural sensitivity, *139*
culture, *137*
divergence of cultures, *139*
ethnocentrism, *141*
geocentrism, *141*

individualism versus collectivism, *145*
masculinity versus femininity, *148*
objective culture, *137*

parochialism, *140*
power distance, *146*
subjective culture, *137*
time orientation, *152*
uncertainty avoidance, *148*

Discussion Questions

1. Define the concept of culture and some of its consequences for international management. Why should managers of multinational and global corporations be concerned with cultural issues in different countries?

2. Discuss the differences between learning a new language and learning a new culture.

3. What is cultural sensitivity? What steps should international companies take to improve cultural sensitivity of managers?

4. Discuss the significance of Kluckhohn and Strodtbeck's values framework.

5. Describe Hofstede's framework for understanding cultural differences. Explain the significance of each of the dimensions.

6. What are the differences between Trompenaars's framework and Hofstede's framework? Provide a few examples along the dimensions in which there are differences.

7. What is a cultural syndrome as proposed in Triandis's framework? Distinguish between the concepts of vertical individualism and horizontal collectivism. Give examples.

Minicase

The Controversy over the Islamic Head Scarf: Women's Rights and Cultural Sensibilities

Taraneh Assadipour walked briskly through the international arrival terminal of the Orly Airport in Paris. Her flight from Tehran had landed a few minutes earlier and Taraneh, accompanied by her 13-year-old daughter Shireen, was back in the city she had known as an undergraduate student, more than 20 years ago. She felt exhausted: it had been only a six-hour flight from Tehran, but a long and arduous journey for the 44-year-old woman. Taraneh was leaving behind the constraints and rigors of life under the strict Islamic code enforced in her homeland, to start a new life abroad.

She had not left Iran for 15 years, and the sight of bare-headed, smartly dressed Parisian women was startling. Taraneh loosened her scarf and let her neatly combed black hair free. Her daughter looked on disapprovingly; the slightly built teenager, her round face enveloped by a tightly knotted white scarf, had been reluctant to leave the only country that she had ever known. In contrast to her mother, she wholeheartedly embraced the Islamic code of behavior and vehemently rejected any suggestion that they restricted women's basic rights.

Shireen had been raised in an environment where gender segregation had become the norm. Women were separated from men in all public places, in schools as well as on city buses, at cultural and sporting events, even on the beaches. Shireen maintained, with all the conviction of her 13 years, that the constraints imposed on women, such as the mandatory use of head scarves and loose fitting garments in public, actually enhanced the status of women. Toeing the arguments put forth by the fundamentalists rulers of Iran, the young girl denounced Western attire as demeaning to women: fashionable clothing made them physically attractive to men, she said, thus reducing them to mere objects of desire. Modesty, on the other hand, underscored the Muslim woman's dignity.

Taraneh, a professional woman who had fought to preserve women's rights in her country, and had suffered subsequently the consequences of their loss, had resigned herself to her daughter's intransigence. She felt confident that once Shireen was exposed to a different environment, her views would moderate. One day, maybe, they could understand each other better. For now, however, mother and daughter were walking silently side by side.

A sensation of freedom seized Taraneh: she felt eager to rush forward and embrace a new life full of promise as well as uncertainties. Memories, however, kept racing through her mind. She remembered the heady days of 1979, when like so many other young Iranians, she had left a lucrative job abroad to come home and help build the new postrevolutionary Iran.

"How enthusiastic and naive we were!" she thought to herself. Like many other members of the secular middle class, she had been slow to acknowledge the ominous signs of a new dictatorship taking shape: anticlerical publications were shut down, peaceful demonstrations were repeatedly and violently disrupted by young toughs—the self-described members of a shadowy and nebulous "Party of God"—and increasingly stringent demands were raised for the so-called Islamization of public life.

As the noose of the newly established theocracy tightened, fear fast replaced the enthusiasm of yore. Taraneh vividly recalled how the newly consolidated regime required all women to wear the "hijab," either a full-length cloth covering from head to toe, or, at the very minimum, a head scarf concealing the hair.

To protest these new restrictions on clothing, a group of educated urban women, braving the rising tide of intimidation, had called for a demonstration on the International Woman's Day, March 8, 1980. Taraneh could never forget that day: as demonstrators gathered to march, they were quickly surrounded by young toughs, some carrying clubs or chains, who mercilessly threatened and taunted them, before actually assaulting many. Taraneh remembered the fear that gripped her as the bearded young men lunged at her, chanting "Yah roossaree, yah toossaree!" ("either scarf on the head or blows to the head!"), and the stream of insults, especially the cries of "Prostitute! Prostitute!" leveled at female demonstrators. Soon, panic set in, and the demonstrators, some wounded or badly beaten, dispersed.

That night, Taraneh watched in dismay as the state television news broadcast reported, "The outraged citizens of our Islamic country spontaneously stopped a group of provocateurs, remnants of the ousted imperial regime and other counterrevolutionaries, from defiling the dignity of the Muslim woman."

The short-lived transition period between the fall of the imperial tyranny and the consolidation of the new dictatorship, which had witnessed the blossoming of freedoms and the rise of great expectations, had drawn to an end.

Most people withdrew from the public sphere and took refuge in their private lives. Many women were forced to resign from their jobs in public and private institutions as the expropriations and policy uncertainties contributed to deepen an economic downturn. Then came the Iraqi attack and a protracted and bloody war that was to last eight years. It was a time of extreme hardship with scant hope for better days. It was also then that Taraneh met Behrooz.

Like Taraneh, Behrooz had pursued graduate studies in the United States. It was difficult and risky to meet and virtually impossible to go out together, given the extraordinary circumstances of war and the newly enacted rules banning intermingling and socialization between the sexes as being tantamount to debauchery and perversity. As a result, the two married before they could get to know each other well. It was an unhappy marriage. The only fleeting moment of joy came when Shireen was born. After several years of strained relations, Taraneh sought a divorce. She then discovered, much to her dismay, that profound changes had taken place in the country's judicial system: the civil laws had been replaced by an Islamic code in various legal areas, from business practices to laws governing family matters. The rights of women, in particular, had been severely curtailed. Taraneh could not get a divorce unless her estranged husband consented to it. Further, the courts gave custody of children to fathers, in most cases.

For four long years, Taraneh tried to obtain a divorce and leave the country to join her brother Khosrow in France or her sister Afsaneh, a resident of the United States. Finally, shortly after Behrooz met and married another woman, he consented to the divorce and gave his first wife the custody of their daughter. It took Taraneh another year to sell off her belongings and secure the necessary documents to travel. She had eagerly awaited the day when she could start a new life abroad and that day had finally arrived.

Taraneh quickened her pace, tugging Shireen along. After undergoing extensive questioning by stern and suspicious immigration officials, the mother and daughter emerged into the crowded arrival hall. Khosrow was waiting there, beaming. The brother and sister embraced. Khosrow then turned to the niece he had never met. Shireen gingerly stepped back and extended her arm. They shook hands.

It took several months for Taraneh to adjust to the new environment. France had much changed from the days when Taraneh haunted the hallways of its venerable universities. The number of immigrants from Third World countries had risen and so had resentment against them. This hostility extended to the French-born children of immigrants, especially those of North African origin. Known as "Beurs," these young French citizens of Arab origin were mostly the offspring of unskilled workers who had settled in France during the 1960s and 1970s to work in the factories or to take menial jobs that the French-born increasingly shunned. They grew in the sprawling housing developments that ringed the major cities. As economic conditions deteriorated in the 1980s and 1990s, unskilled immigrants were the first to lose their jobs and many became dependent on public assistance. The younger generation of people of North African ancestry was also besieged by a high incidence of unemployment. Some of its members had turned to petty larceny or other illegal activities. Most felt alienated from their parents' culture, and at the same time, rejected by French society.

Indeed, populist and outright xenophobic political parties were successfully exploiting the resentment and fears of the populace. The National Front, in particular, had grown from a marginal and insignificant organization of the extreme right in the 1970s, into a major political party of the 1990s, capturing 15 percent of the popular vote in the 1995 presidential elections. Its leader, the charismatic Jean-Marie Le Pen, repeatedly demanded that France be for the French, denouncing the loss of national character, rising crime rates, unemployment and empty public coffers, all allegedly resulting from the presence of immigrants and their offspring.

A National Front mayoral candidate darkly warned of a future where a mayor could be named Mohammed, while others raised questions about the influence of Islamic fundamentalists among the several million Muslims living in France. The specter of a rising Islamic tide lapping at the borders of the secular French republic and threatening its very foundations had become a popular and entrenched image. Muslim residents, especially observant or pious individuals, were facing deep suspicion. Although many among them rejected religious intolerance, they were widely viewed as the Trojan horses of fundamentalism.

Taraneh was anxious. She was especially concerned about her daughter Shireen, who steadfastly refused to take off her head scarf in public. Shireen had made great strides in learning French and had started to attend the local public school. Her attire, however, had given rise to strong objections from the school administrators.

The principal and her associates were well prepared to manage the situation. As early as 1989, indeed, in the Paris suburb of Creil, a schoolgirl's insistence on covering her hair with a scarf had caused a nationally publicized confrontation. School authorities considered that wearing the scarf was tantamount to religious proselytism, and thus incompatible with the secular nature of the French republic and its institutions. The public school system was always considered a pillar of secularism and a conduit through which children of immigrants could be inculcated with ideas and beliefs that would facilitate their insertion in the French society. Thus the defiance of Muslim schoolgirls, first in Creil and later in a number of other localities, was considered a serious threat that had to be thwarted. The tug-of-war between school administrators and a majority of instructors, on the one hand, and devout Muslim girls and their parents on the other resulted in several expulsions of students and a call for national guidelines. In the fall of 1994, Francois Bayrou, then minister of education, issued a decree, formally prohibiting the use of any "ostentatious religious signs" in public schools and mandating punishments, starting from initial warnings to eventual expulsions, for those who did not obey the new regulations. As a result, scores of Muslim high school students were forced to stop attending the public school system.

Taraneh had tried to coax her daughter into removing her scarf during school hours, but to no avail. The school had already issued several warnings to Shireen, and Taraneh knew that ultimately, she may have to leave for a country where her daughter's beliefs, as well as her own, could be accommodated. In fact, Taraneh had decided to move to the United States, should the pressure on her daughter become unbearable. She had already contacted the Houston, Texas, company where she had worked in the late 1970s, and knew that she could be rehired.

One day Shireen came home in tears. "I am not allowed to go to school anymore," she announced. Taraneh took her daughter into her arms, and while consoling her, tried one last time to persuade her to submit to the school regulations. "Never!" cried out the adolescent girl. "It is not my head scarf that they hate, it is me!"

Three months later, Taraneh was sitting in the personnel manager's office of the Houston company, listening intently. "Things have changed a lot since you were last here, Terry—I can call you Terry, right?" The lanky Texan continued without waiting for an answer. "Our company has grown tremendously, but we have maintained our employee-friendly orientation: indeed, we are very much aware of the diverse backgrounds of our staff and try to be very responsive to their special needs. In particular, we are committed to create an environment where cultural diversity can thrive. As you have noticed, you will be working with people of many different ethnic backgrounds. Our company has been a leader in promoting multiculturalism in the workplace."

Source: Written by Farid Sadrieh, Ph.D. student in International Business, Temple University. Copyright © 1997 by Arvind V. Phatak.

DISCUSSION QUESTIONS

1. It is said that a person's freedom ends where it encroaches on another person's rights. Give your interpretation of this idea using examples. Do freedom and individual rights have a universal meaning or should they be defined differently in different countries?

2. Consider the head scarf controversy as a symbol of the broader debate on the status of women. Develop a cultural relativist approach and take sides in the events depicted in the case accordingly. What can you say about the mandatory use of head scarves in Iran? About their mandatory removal in French public schools?

3. In the controversy over head scarves in French schools, many liberals and intellectuals have found themselves siding with extreme rightists and nationalist groups denouncing the use of head scarves. What are the likely motivations of the first group and what probably incites the nationalist groups to oppose head scarves?

4. What may explain American society's greater tolerance for publicly expressed differences in religious or cultural behavior? Does the emphasis on multiculturalism reduce the possibility for minority groups to fully participate in mainstream society? How could it strengthen or weaken the national unity and sense of purpose of a country?

5. What factors affect the status of women in a society beside the cultural tradition? How are attitudes toward women in conservative Muslim countries reminiscent of those prevailing in America at an earlier time?

6. Imagine that you are the manager of a French subsidiary of an American multinational company. How would you handle the problem of several of your French managers objecting to the Islamic dress code observed by immigrant women secretaries?

Notes

1. H. C. Triandis, "Greek Identity: Implications for Individual Development in English Speaking Countries," paper presented at the Fifth International Conference on Greeks in English Speaking Countries, Speros Basil Vryonis Center for the Study of Hellenism, Sacramento, California, 2000; H. C. Triandis, *Individualism and Collectivism* (Boulder, CO: Westview Press, 1995); H. C. Triandis, *Culture and Social Behavior* (New York: McGraw-Hill, 1994).

2. M. J. Herskovits, *Cultural Anthropology* (New York: Knopf, 1955).

3. H. C. Triandis, *The Analysis of Subjective Culture* (New York: Wiley, 1972).

4. G. M. Guthrie, "A Behavioral Analysis of Culture Learning." In R. W. Brislin, S. Bochner, and W. J. Lonner, eds., *Cross-Cultural Perspectives on Learning* (New York: Sage, 1975), pp. 95–116.

5. J. Child, "Culture, Contingency, and Capitalism in the Cross-National Study of Organizations." In B. Staw and L. L. Cummings, eds., *Research in Organizational Behavior* (Greenwich, CT: JAI Press, 1981); J. Veiga, M. Lubatkin, R. Calori, and P. Very, "Measuring Organizational Culture Clashes: A Two-Nation Post-hoc Analysis of a Cultural Compatibility Index," *Human Relations* 53, no. 4 (2000), pp. 539–557.

6. C. Kerr, J. L. Dunlop, M. Harbison, and J. Meyer, *Industrialism and the Industrial Man* (New York: Oxford University Press, 1964).

7. K. Cushner and D. Landis. The Intercultural Sensitizer." In D. Landis and R. S. Bhagat, eds., *Handbook of Intercultural Training,* 2nd ed. (Thousand Oaks, CA: Sage, 1996), pp. 185–202.

8. D. A. Ricks, *Blunders in International Business,* 3rd ed. (Malden, MA: Blackwell, 1999). Examples from pp. 50, 67, and 32, respectively.

9. F. Kluckhohn and F. L. Strodtbeck, *Variations in Value Orientations* (Evanston, IL: Row, Peterson, 1961).

10. A. Q. Nomani, "Labor Letter: A Special News Report on People and Their Jobs in Offices, Fields, and Factories," *Wall Street Journal,* August 2, 1994, p. A1.

11. G. Hofstede. *Culture's Consequences: International Differences in Work-Related Values,* 2nd ed. (Thousand Oaks, CA: Sage, 2001); G. Hofstede, *Cultures and Organizations: Software of the Mind* (New York: McGraw-Hill, 1991); G. Hofstede, *Culture's Consequences: International Differences in Work-Related Values* (Beverly Hills, CA: Sage, 1980).

12. Ibid.

13. P. C. Earley and C. B. Gibson, "Taking Stock in Our Progress on Individualism–Collectivism: 100 Years of Solidarity and Community," *Journal of Management* 24 (1998), pp. 265–304; M. Erez and P. C. Earley, *Culture, Self-Identity, and Work* (New York: Oxford University Press, 1993); H. C. Triandis, "Vertical and Horizontal Individualism and Collectivism: Theory and Research Implications for International Comparative Management." In J. L. Cheng and R. B. Peterson, eds., *Advances in International Comparative Management,* vol. 12 (Greenwich, CT: JAI

Press, 1998), pp. 7–35; Triandis, *Individualism and Collectivism;* Triandis, *Culture and Social Behavior;* H. C. Triandis, "Cross-Cultural Studies of Individualism and Collectivism." In J. J. Berman, ed., *Nebraska Symposium on Motivation,* Vol. 37 (Lincoln: University of Nebraska Press, 1990), pp. 41–133; H. C. Triandis, "The Self and Social Behavior in Differing Cultural Contexts," *Psychological Review* 96 (1989), pp. 269–289.

14. Earley and Gibson, "Taking Stock in Our Progress on Individualism–Collectivism"; Hofstede, *Culture's Consequences,* 2nd ed.; Hofstede, *Cultures and Organizations;* Triandis, "Vertical and Horizontal Individualism and Collectivism"; Triandis, *Individualism and Collectivism;* Triandis, *Culture and Social Behavior.*

15. Hofstede, *Cultures and Organizations,* p. 75.

16. Ibid., p. 76.

17. Ibid., p. 28.

18. Ibid., p. 25.

19. Ibid., p. 113.

20. Ibid., pp. 82–83.

21. Ibid., p. 87.

22. Adapted from E. Sciolino, "Christopher Confers with Saudi King on Aid and Arms," *The New York Times,* March 13, 1995, p. A7.

23. E. T. Hall and W. F. Whyte, "Intercultural Communication: A Guide to Men of Action," *Human Organization* 19, no. 1 (1960), p. 9.

24. D. Pearl, "Federal Express Finds Its Pioneering Formula Falls Flat Overseas," *The Wall Street Journal,* April 15, 1991, p. A1.

25. F. Trompenaars, *Riding the Waves of Culture: Understanding Diversity in Global Business* (London: Economist Books, 1993).

26. Triandis, *Culture and Social Behavior.*

27. S. Ronen and O. Shenkar, "Clustering Cultures on Attitudinal Dimensions: A Review and Synthesis," *Academy of Management Review* 10, no. 3 (1985), pp. 435–454.

28. L. Sagiv and S. H. Schwartz, "Value Priorities and Readiness for Outgroup Social Contact," *Journal of Personality and Social Psychology* 69 (1995), pp. 245–272; S. H. Schwartz, "Universals in the Content and Structure of Values: Theoretical Advances and Empirical Tests in 20 Countries." In M. P. Zanna, ed., *Advances in Experimental Social Psychology* (San Diego: Academic Press, 1992), pp. 1–65; S. H. Schwartz, "Beyond Individualism/Collectivism: New Dimensions of Values." In U. Kim, H. C. Triandis, C. Kagitcibasi, S. C. Choi, and G. Yoon, eds., *Individualism and Collectivism: Theory, Application, and Methods* (Newbury Park, CA: Sage, 1994); S. H. Schwartz and W. Bilsky, "Toward a Universal Psychological Structure of Human Values," *Journal of Personality and Social Psychology* 53 (1990), pp. 550–562.

29. E. T. Hall, *Beyond Culture* (New York: Anchor/Doubleday, 1976).

30. Triandis, *Culture and Social Behavior.*

31. Ibid., p. 160.

32. H. C. Triandis, D-K. Chan, D. P. S. Bhawuk, S. Iwao, and J. B. P. Sinha, "Multimethod Probes of Allocentrism and Ideocentrism," *International Journal of Psychology* 30 (1995), pp. 461–480; H. C. Triandis and M. Gelfand, "Converging Measurement of Horizontal and Vertical Individualism and Collectivism," *Journal of Personality and Social Psychology* 74 (1998), pp. 118–128.

33. D. J. Hickson and D. S. Pugh, *Management Worldwide: The Impact of Societal Culture on Organizations around the Globe* (London: Penguin, 1995).

34. M. H. Bond, ed., *The Handbook of Chinese Psychology* (Hong Kong: Oxford University Press, 1996).

35. Chinese Culture Connection, "Chinese Values and the Search for Culture-Free Dimensions of Culture," *Journal of Cross-Cultural Psychology* 18 (1987), pp. 143–164.

36. *USA Today,* June 19, 2003.

37. Triandis, *Culture and Social Behavior.*

Case I

Euro Disneyland

J. Stewart Black and Hal B. Gregersen

On January 18, 1993, Euro Disneyland chairperson Robert Fitzpatrick announced he would leave that post on April 12 to begin his own consulting company. Quitting his position exactly one year after the grand opening of Euro Disneyland, Fitzpatrick's resignation removed U.S. management from the helm of the French theme park and resort.

Fitzpatrick's position was taken by a Frenchman, Philippe Bourguignon, who had been Euro Disneyland's senior vice president for real estate. Bourguignon, 45 years old, faced a net loss of FFr 188 million for Euro Disneyland's fiscal year which ended September 1992. Also, between April and September 1992, only 29 percent of the park's total visitors were French. Expectations were that closer to half of all visitors would be French.

It was hoped that the promotion of Philippe Bourguignon would have a public relations benefit for Euro Disneyland—a project that has been a publicist's nightmare from the beginning. One of the low points was at a news conference prior to the park's opening when protesters pelted Michael Eisner, CEO of the Walt Disney Company, with rotten eggs. Within the first year of operation, Disney had to compromise its "squeaky clean" image and lift the alcohol ban at the park. Wine is now served at all major restaurants.

Euro Disneyland, 49 percent owned by Walt Disney Company, Burbank, California, originally forecasted 11 million visitors in the first year of operation. In January 1993 it appeared attendance would be closer to 10 million. In response, management temporarily slashed prices at the park for local residents to FFr 150 ($27.27) from FFr 225 ($40.91) for adults, and to FFr 100 from FFr 150 for children in order to lure more French during the slow, wet winter months. The company also reduced prices at its restaurants and hotels, which registered occupancy rates of just 37 percent.

Bourguignon also faced other problems, such as the second phase of development at Euro Disneyland, which was expected to start in September 1993. It was unclear how the company planned to finance its FFr 8–10 billion cost. The company had steadily drained its cash reserves (FFr 1.9 billion in May 1993) while piling up debt (FFr 21 billion in May 1993). Euro Disneyland admitted that it and the Walt Disney Company were "exploring potential sources of financing for Euro Disneyland." The company was also talking to banks about restructuring its debts.

Despite the frustrations, Eisner was tirelessly upbeat about the project. "Instant hits are things that go away quickly, and things that grow slowly and are part of the culture are what we look for," he said. "What we created in France is the biggest private investment in a foreign country by an American company ever. And it's gonna pay off."

IN THE BEGINNING

Disney's story is the classic American rags-to-riches story which started in a small Kansas City advertising office, where Mickey was a real mouse prowling the unknown Walt Disney floor. Originally, Mickey was named Mortimer, until a dissenting Mrs. Disney stepped in. How close Mickey was to Walt Disney is evidenced by the fact that when filming, Disney himself dubbed the mouse's voice. Only in later films did Mickey get a different voice. Disney made many sacrifices to promote his hero-mascot, including selling his first car, a beloved Moon Cabriolet, and humiliating himself in front of Louis B. Mayer. "Get that mouse off the screen!" was the movie mogul's reported response to the cartoon character. Then, in 1955, Disney had the brainstorm of sending his movie characters out into the "real" world to mix with their fans and he battled skeptics to build the very first Disneyland in Anaheim, California.

When Disney died in 1966, the company went into virtual suspended animation. Their last big hit of that era was 1969's *The Love Bug,* about a Volkswagen named Herbie. Today, Disney executives trace the problem to a tyrannical CEO named E. Cardon Walker who ruled the company from 1976 to 1983, and to his successor, Ronald W. Miller. Walker was quick to ridicule underlings in public and impervious to any point of view but his own. He made decisions according to what he thought Walt would have done. Executives clinched arguments by quoting Walt like the Scriptures or Marx, and the company eventually supplied a little book of the founder's sayings. Making the wholesome family movies Walt would have wanted formed a key article of Walker's creed. For example, a poster advertising the unremarkable *Condorman* featured actress Barbara Carrera in a slit skirt. Walker had the slit painted over. With this as the context, studio producers ground out a thin stream of tired, formulaic movies that fewer and fewer customers would pay to see. In mid-1983, a similar low-horsepower approach to television production led to CBS's cancellation of the hour-long program *Walt Disney,* leaving the company without a regular network show for the first time in 29 years. Like a reclusive hermit, the company lost touch with the contemporary world.

Ron Miller's brief reign was by contrast a model of decentralization and delegation. Many attributed Miller's ascent to his marrying the boss's daughter rather than to any special gift. To shore Miller up, the board installed Raymond L. Watson, former head of the Irvine Co., as part-time Chairperson. He quickly became full time.

Miller sensed the studio needed rejuvenation and he managed to produce the hit film *Splash,* featuring an apparently (but not actually) bare-breasted mermaid, under the newly devised Touchstone label. However, the reluctance of freelance Hollywood talent to accommodate Disney's narrow range and stingy compensation often kept his sound instincts from bearing fruit. "Card [Cardon Walker] would listen but not hear," said a former executive. "Ron [Ron Miller] would listen but not act."

Too many box office bombs contributed to a steady erosion of profit. Profits of $135 million on revenues of $915 million in 1980 dwindled to $93 million on revenues of $1.3 billion in 1983. More alarmingly, revenues from the company's theme parks, about three quarters of the company's total revenues, were showing signs of leveling off. Disney's stock slid from $84.375 a share to $48.75 between April 1983 and February 1984.

Through these years, Roy Disney, Jr. simmered while he watched the downfall of the national institution that his uncle, Walt, and his father, Roy Disney, Sr., had built. He had long argued that the company's constituent parts all work together to enhance each other. If movie and television production weren't revitalized, not only would that source of revenue disappear but the company and its activities would also grow dim in the public eye. At the same time the stream of new ideas and characters that kept people pouring into the parks and buying toys, books, and records would dry up. Now his dire predictions were coming true. His own personal shareholding had already dropped from $96 million to $54 million. Walker's treatment of Ron Miller as the shining heir apparent and Roy Disney as the idiot nephew helped drive Roy to quit as Disney vice president in 1977, and to set up Shamrock Holdings, a broadcasting and investment company.

In 1984, Roy teamed up with Stanley Gold, a tough-talking lawyer and a brilliant strategist. Gold saw that the falling stock price was bound to flush out a raider and afford Roy Disney a chance to restore the company's fortunes. They asked Frank Wells, vice chairperson of Warner Bros., if he would take a top job in the company in the event they offered it. Wells, a lawyer and a Rhodes scholar, said yes. With that, Roy knew that what he would hear in Disney's boardroom would limit his freedom to trade in its stock, so he quit the board on March 9, 1984. "I knew that would hang a 'For Sale' sign over the company," said Gold.

By resigning, Roy pushed over the first of a train of dominoes that ultimately led to the result he most desired. The company was raided, almost dismantled, greenmailed, raided again, and sued left and right. But it miraculously emerged with a skilled new top management with big plans for a bright future. Roy Disney proposed Michael Eisner as the CEO but the board came close to rejecting Eisner in favor of an older, more buttoned-down candidate. Gold stepped in and made an impassioned speech to the directors. "You see guys like Eisner as a little crazy . . . but every studio in this country has been run by crazies. What do you think Walt Disney was? The guy was off the god-damned wall. This is a creative institution. It needs to be run by crazies again."[1]

Meanwhile Eisner and Wells staged an all-out lobbying campaign, calling on every board member except two, who were abroad, to explain their views about the company's future. "What was most important," said Eisner, "was that they saw I did not come in a tutu, and that I was a serious person, and I understood a P&L, and I knew the investment analysts, and I read *Fortune.*"

[1]Stephen Koepp, "Do You Believe in Magic?" *Time,* April 25, 1988, pp. 66–73.

EXHIBIT 1
How the Theme
Parks Grew

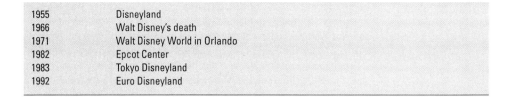

1955	Disneyland
1966	Walt Disney's death
1971	Walt Disney World in Orlando
1982	Epcot Center
1983	Tokyo Disneyland
1992	Euro Disneyland

In September 1984, Michael Eisner was appointed CEO and Frank Wells became president. Jeffrey Katzenberg, the 33-year old, maniacal production chief followed Eisner from Paramount Pictures. He took over Disney's movie and television studios. "The key," said Eisner, "is to start off with a great idea."

DISNEYLAND IN ANAHEIM, CALIFORNIA

For a long time, Walt Disney had been concerned about the lack of family-type entertainment available for his two daughters. The amusement parks he saw around him were mostly filthy traveling carnivals. They were often unsafe and allowed unruly conduct on the premises. Disney envisioned a place where people from all over the world would be able to go for clean and safe fun. His dream came true on July 17, 1955, when the gates first opened at Disneyland in Anaheim, California.

Disneyland strives to generate the perfect fantasy. But magic does not simply happen. The place is a marvel of modern technology. Literally dozens of computers, huge banks of tape machines, film projectors, and electronic controls lie behind the walls, beneath the floors, and above the ceilings of dozens of rides and attractions. The philosophy is that "Disneyland is the world's biggest stage, and the audience is right here on the stage," said Dick Hollinger, chief industrial engineer at Disneyland. "It takes a tremendous amount of work to keep the stage clean and working properly."

Cleanliness is a primary concern. Before the park opens at 8 A.M., the cleaning crew will have mopped and hosed and dried every sidewalk, every street and every floor and counter. More than 350 of the park's 7,400 employees come on duty at 1 A.M. to begin the daily cleanup routine. The thousands of feet that walk through the park each day and chewing gum do not mix, and gum has always presented major clean up problems. The park's janitors found long ago that fire hoses with 90 pounds of water pressure would not do the job. Now they use steam machines, razor scrapers, and mops towed by Cushman scooters to literally scour the streets and sidewalks daily.

It takes one person working a full eight-hour shift to polish the brass on the Fantasyland merry-go-round. The scrupulously manicured plantings throughout the park are treated with growth retarding hormones to keep the trees and bushes from spreading beyond their assigned spaces and destroying the carefully maintained five-eighths scale modeling that is utilized in the park. The maintenance supervisor of the Matterhorn bobsled ride personally walks every foot of track and inspects every link of tow chain every night, thus trusting his or her own eyes more than the $2 million in safety equipment that is built into the ride.

Eisner himself pays obsessive attention to detail. Walking through Disneyland one Sunday afternoon, he peered at the plastic leaves on the Swiss Family Robinson tree house noting that they periodically wear out and need to be replaced leaf by leaf at a cost of $500,000. As his family strolled through the park, he and his eldest son Breck stooped to pick up the rare piece of litter that the cleanup crew had somehow missed. This old-fashioned dedication has paid off. Since opening day in 1955, Disneyland has been a consistent money-maker.

DISNEY WORLD IN ORLANDO, FLORIDA

By the time Eisner arrived, Disney World in Orlando was already on its way to becoming what it is today—the most popular vacation destination in the US. But the company had neglected a rich niche in its business: hotels. Disney's three existing hotels, probably the most profitable in the US, registered unheard-of occupancy rates of 92 percent to 96 percent versus 66 percent for the industry. Eisner promptly embarked on an ambitious $1 billion hotel expansion plan. Two major hotels, Disney's Grand Floridian Beach Resort and Disney's Caribbean Beach Resort, were opened during 1987–9. Disney's Yacht Club and Beach Resort along with the Dolphin and Swan Hotels, owned and operated by Tishman Realty & Construction, Metropolitan Life Insurance, and Aoki Corporation opened dur-

EXHIBIT 2
Investor's Snapshot:
The Walt Disney
Company (December
1989)

Source: *Fortune,* December 4,
1989.

Sales	
(latest four quarters)	$4.6 billion
Change from year earlier	Up 33.6%
Net profit	$703.3 million
Change	Up 34.7%
Return on common stockholders' equity	23.4%
Five year average	20.3%
Stock price average	
(last 12 months)	$60.50–$136.25
Recent share price	$122.75
Price/Earnings Multiple	27
Total return to investors	
(12 months to 11/3/89)	90.6%

ing 1989–90. Adding 3,400 hotel rooms and 250,000 square feet of convention space, this made it the largest convention center east of the Mississippi.

In October 1982, Disney made a new addition to the theme park—the Experimental Prototype Community of Tomorrow or EPCOT Centre. E. Cardon Walker, then president of the company, announced that EPCOT would be a "permanent showcase, industrial park, and experimental housing center." This new park consists of two large complexes: Future World, a series of pavilions designed to show the technological advances of the next 25 years, and World Showcase, a collection of foreign "villages."

TOKYO DISNEYLAND

It was Tokyo's nastiest winter day in four years. Arctic winds and eight inches of snow lashed the city. Roads were clogged and trains slowed down. But the bad weather didn't keep 13,200 hardy souls from Tokyo Disneyland. Mikki Mausu, better known outside Japan as Mickey Mouse, had taken the country by storm.

Located on a fringe of reclaimed shoreline in Urayasu City on the outskirts of Tokyo, the park opened to the public on April 15, 1983. In less than one year, over ten million people had passed through its gates, an attendance figure that has been bettered every single year. On August 13, 1983, 93,000 people helped set a one day attendance record that easily eclipsed the old records established at the two parent US parks. Four years later, records again toppled as the turnstiles clicked. The total this time: 111,500. By 1988, approximately 50 million people, or nearly half of Japan's population, had visited Tokyo Disneyland since its opening. The steady cash flow pushed revenues for fiscal year 1989 to $768 million, up 17 percent from 1988.

The 204 acre Tokyo Disneyland is owned and operated by Oriental Land under license from the Walt Disney Co. The 45 year contract gives Disney 10 percent of admissions and 5 percent of food and merchandise sales, plus licensing fees. Disney opted to take no equity in the project and put no money down for construction.

"I never had the slightest doubt about the success of Disneyland in Japan," said Masatomo Takahashi, president of Oriental Land Company. Oriental Land was so confident of the success of Disney in Japan that it financed the park entirely with debt, borrowing ¥180 billion ($1.5 billion at February 1988 exchange rates). Takahashi added, "The debt means nothing to me," and with good reason. According to Fusahao Awata, who co-authored a book on Tokyo Disneyland: "The Japanese yearn for [American culture]."

Soon after Tokyo Disneyland opened in April 1983, five Shinto priests held a solemn dedication ceremony near Cinderella's castle. It is the only overtly Japanese ritual seen so far in this sprawling theme park. What visitors see is pure Americana. All signs are in English, with only small *katakana* (a phonetic Japanese alphabet) translations. Most of the food is American-style, and the attractions are cloned from Disney's US parks. Disney also held firm on two fundamentals that strike the Japanese as strange—no alcohol is allowed and no food may be brought in from outside the park.

However, in Disney's enthusiasm to make Tokyo a brick-by-brick copy of Anaheim's Magic Kingdom, there were a few glitches. On opening day, the Tokyo park discovered that almost 100 public telephones were placed too high for Japanese guests to reach them comfortably. And many hungry customers found countertops above their reach at the park's snack stands.

"Everything we imported that worked in the US works here," said Ronald D. Pogue, managing director of Walt Disney Attractions Japan Ltd. "American things like McDonald's hamburgers and Kentucky Fried Chicken are popular here with young people. We also wanted visitors from Japan and Southeast Asia to feel they were getting the real thing," said Toshiharu Akiba, a staff member of the Oriental Land publicity department.

Still, local sensibilities dictated a few changes. A Japanese restaurant was added to please older patrons. The Nautilus submarine is missing. More areas are covered to protect against rain and snow. Lines for attractions had to be redesigned so that people walking through the park did not cross in front of patrons waiting to ride an attraction. "It's very discourteous in Japan to have people cross in front of somebody else," explained James B. Cora, managing director of operations for the Tokyo project. The biggest differences between Japan and America have come in slogans and ad copy. Although English is often used, it's "Japanized" English—the sort that would have native speakers shaking their heads while the Japanese nod happily in recognition. "Let's Spring" was the motto for one of their highly successful ad campaigns.

Pogue, visiting frequently from his base in California, supervised seven resident American Disney managers who work side by side with Japanese counterparts from Oriental Land Co. to keep the park in tune with the Disney doctrine. American it may be, but Tokyo Disneyland appeals to such deep-seated Japanese passions as cleanliness, order, outstanding service, and technological wizardry. Japanese executives are impressed by Disney's detailed training manuals, which teach employees how to make visitors feel like VIPs. Most worth emulating, say the Japanese, is Disney's ability to make even the lowliest job seem glamorous. "They have changed the image of dirty work," said Hakuhodo Institute's Sekizawa.

Disney Company did encounter a few unique cultural problems when developing Tokyo Disneyland:

The problem: how to dispose of some 250 tons of trash that would be generated weekly by Tokyo Disneyland visitors?

The standard Disney solution: trash compactors.

The Japanese proposal: pigs to eat the trash and be slaughtered and sold at a profit.

James B. Cora and his team of some 150 operations experts did a little calculating and pointed out that it would take 100,000 pigs to do the job. And then there would be the smell . . .

The Japanese relented.

The Japanese were also uneasy about a rustic-looking Westernland, Tokyo's version of Frontierland. "The Japanese like everything fresh and new when they put it in," said Cora. "They kept painting the wood and we kept saying. 'No, it's got to look old.' " Finally the Disney crew took the Japanese to Anaheim to give them a first hand look at the Old West.

Tokyo Disneyland opened just as the yen escalated in value against the dollar and the income level of the Japanese registered a phenomenal improvement. During this era of affluence, Tokyo Disneyland triggered an interest in leisure. Its great success spurred the construction of "leisurelands" throughout the country. This created an increase in the Japanese people's orientation towards leisure. But demographics are the real key to Tokyo Disneyland's success. Thirty million Japanese live within 30 miles of the park. That is three times more people in the same proximity to Anaheim's Disneyland. With the park proven such an unqualified hit and nearing capacity, Oriental Land and Disney mapped out plans for a version of the Disney-MGM studio tour next door. This time, Disney talked about taking a 50 percent stake in the project.

BUILDING EURO DISNEYLAND

On March 24, 1987, Michael Eisner and Jacques Chirac, the French Prime Minister, signed a contract for the building of a Disney theme park at Marne-la-Vallee. Talks between Disney and the French government had dragged on for more than a year. At the signing, Robert Fitzpatrick, fluent in French, married to the former Sylvie Blondet and the recipient of two awards from the French government, was introduced as the president of Euro Disneyland. He was expected to be a key player in wooing support from the French establishment for the theme park. As one analyst put it, Disney selected him to set up the park because he is "more French than the French."

Disney had been courted extensively by Spain and France. The Prime Ministers of both countries ordered their governments to lend Disney a hand in its quest for a site. France set up a five-person team headed by Special Advisor to Foreign Trade & Tourism Minister Edith Cresson, and Spain's negotiators included Ignacio Vasallo, Director-General for the Promotion of Tourism. Disney pummeled both governments with requests for detailed information. "The only thing they haven't asked us for is the color of the tourists' eyes," moaned Vasallo.

The governments tried other enticements, too. Spain offered tax and labor incentives and possibly as much as 20,000 acres of land. The French package, although less generous, included spending of $53 million to improve highway access to the proposed site and perhaps speeding up a $75 million subway project. For a long time, all that smiling Disney officials would say was that Spain had better weather while France had a better population base.

Officials explained that they picked France over Spain because Marne-la-Vallee is advantageously close to one of the world's tourism capitals, while also being situated within a day's drive or train ride of some 30 million people in France, Belgium, England, and Germany. Another advantage mentioned was the availability of good transportation. A train line that serves as part of the Paris Metro subway system ran to Torcy, in the center of Marne-la-Vallee, and the French government promised to extend the line to the actual site of the park. The park would also be served by A-4, a modern highway that runs from Paris to the German border, as well as a freeway that runs to Charles de Gaulle airport.

Once a letter of intent had been signed, sensing that the French government was keen to not let the plan fail, Disney held out for one concession after another. For example, Disney negotiated for VAT (value added tax) on ticket sales to be cut from a normal 18.6 percent to 7 percent. A quarter of the investment in building the park would come from subsidized loans. Additionally, any disputes arising from the contract would be settled not in French courts but by a special international panel of arbitrators. But Disney did have to agree to a clause in the contract which would require it to respect and utilize French culture in its themes.

The park was built on 4,460 acres of farmland in Marne-la-Vallee, a rural corner of France 20 miles east of Paris known mostly for sugar beets and Brie cheese. Opening was planned for early 1992 and planners hoped to attract some 10 million visitors a year. Approximately $2.5 billion was needed to build the park making it the largest single foreign investment ever in France. A French "pivot" company was formed to build the park with starting capital of FFr 3 billion, split 60 percent French and 40 percent foreign, with Disney taking 16.67 percent. Euro Disneyland was expected to bring $600 million in foreign investment into France each year.

As soon as the contract had been signed, individuals and businesses began scurrying to somehow plug into the Mickey Mouse money machine—all were hoping to benefit from the America dream without leaving France. In fact, one Paris daily, *Liberation,* actually sprouted mouse ears over its front page flag.

The $1.5 to $2 billion first phase investment would involve an amusement complex including hotels and restaurants, golf courses, and an aquatic park in addition to a European version of the Magic Kingdom. The second phase, scheduled to start after the gates opened in 1992, called for the construction of a community around the park, including a sports complex, technology park, conference center, theater, shopping mall, university campus, villas, and condominiums. No price tag had been put on the second phase, although it was expected to rival, if not surpass, the first phase investment. In November 1989, Fitzpatrick announced that the Disney-MGM Studios, Europe would also open at Euro Disneyland in 1996, resembling the enormously successful Disney-MGM Studios theme park at Disney World in Orlando. The new studios would greatly enhance the Walt Disney Company's strategy of increasing its production of live action and animated filmed entertainment in Europe for both the European and world markets.

"The phone's been ringing here ever since the announcement," said Marc Berthod of EpaMarne, the government body that oversees the Marne-la-Vallee region. "We've gotten calls from big companies as well as small—everything from hotel chains to language interpreters—all asking for details on Euro Disneyland. And the individual mayors of the villages around here have been swamped with calls from people looking for jobs," he added.

EXHIBIT 3
Chronology of the
Euro Disneyland
Deal

Source: From Geraldine E.
Willigan, "The Value-Adding
CFO: An Interview with
Disney's Gary Wilson,"
Harvard Business Review,
January–February 1990,
pp. 58–93.

1984–85	Disney negotiates with Spain and France to create a European theme park
	Chooses France as the site
1987	Disney signs letter of intent with the French government
1988	Selects lead commercial bank lenders for the senior portion of the project
	Forms the Societe en Nom Collectif (SNC)
	Begins planning for the equity offering of 51% of Euro
	Disneyland as required in the letter of intent
1989	European press and stock analysts visit Walt Disney World in Orlando
	Begin extensive news and television campaign
	Stock starts trading at 20–25 percent premium from the issue price

Euro Disneyland was expected to generate up to 28,000 jobs, providing a measure of relief for an area that had suffered a 10 percent plus unemployment rate for the previous year. It was also expected to light a fire under France's construction industry which had been particularly hard hit by France's economic problems over the previous year. Moreover, Euro Disneyland was expected to attract many other investors to the depressed outskirts of Paris. International Business Machines (IBM) and *Banque National de Paris* were among those already building in the area. In addition, one of the new buildings going up was a factory that would employ 400 outside workers to wash the 50 tons of laundry expected to be generated per day by Euro Disneyland's 14,000 employees.

The impact of Euro Disneyland was also felt in the real estate market. "Everyone who owns land around here is holding on to it for the time being, at least until they know what's going to happen," said Danny Theveno, a spokesman for the town of Villiers on the western edge of Marne-la-Vallee.

Disney expected 11 million visitors in the first year. The break-even point was estimated to be between seven and eight million. One worry was that Euro Disneyland would cannibalize the flow of European visitors to Walt Disney World in Florida, but European travel agents said that their customers were still eagerly signing up for Florida, lured by the cheap dollar and the promise of sunshine.

PROTESTS OF CULTURAL IMPERIALISM

Disney faced French communists and intellectuals who protested the building of Euro Disneyland. Ariane Mnouchkine, a theater director, described it as a "cultural Chernobyl." "I wish with all my heart that the rebels would set fire to Disneyland," thundered a French intellectual in the newspaper *La Figaro*. "Mickey Mouse," sniffed another, "is stifling individualism and transforming children into consumers." The theme park was damned as an example of American "neoprovincialism."

Farmers in the Marne-la-Vallee region posted protest signs along the roadside featuring a mean-looking Mickey Mouse and touting sentiments such as "Disney go home," "Stop the massacre," and "Don't gnaw away our national wealth." Farmers were upset partly because, under the terms of the contract, the French government would expropriate the necessary land and sell it without profit to Euro Disneyland development company.

While local officials were sympathetic to the farmer's position, they were unwilling to let their predicament interfere with what some called "the deal of the century." "For many years these farmers have had the fortune to cultivate what is considered some of the richest land in France," said Berthod. "Now they'll have to find another occupation."

Also less than enchanted about the prospect of a magic kingdom rising among their midst was the communist-dominated labor federation, the *Confédération Générale du Travail* (CGT). Despite the job-creating potential of Euro Disney, the CGT doubted its members would benefit. The union had been fighting hard to stop the passage of a bill which would give managers the right to establish flexible hours for their workers. Flexible hours were believed to be a prerequisite to the profitable operation of Euro Disneyland, especially considering seasonal variations.

However, Disney proved to be relatively immune to the anti-US virus. In early 1985, one of the three state-owned television networks signed a contract to broadcast two hours of dubbed Disney programming every Saturday evening. Soon after, *Disney Channel* became one of the top-rated programs in France.

In 1987, the company launched an aggressive community relations program to calm the fears of politicians, farmers, villagers, and even bankers that the project would bring traffic congestion, noise, pollution, and other problems to their countryside. Such a public relations program was a rarity in France, where businesses make little effort to establish good relations with local residents. Disney invited 400 local children to a birthday party for Mickey Mouse, sent Mickey to area hospitals, and hosted free trips to Disney World in Florida for dozens of local officials and children.

"They're experts at seduction, and they don't hide the fact that they're trying to seduce you," said Vincent Guardiola, an official with *Banque Indosuez,* one of the 17 banks wined and dined at Orlando and, subsequently one of the venture's financial participants. "The French aren't used to this kind of public relations—it was unbelievable." Observers said that the goodwill efforts helped dissipate initial objections to the project.

FINANCIAL STRUCTURING AT EURO DISNEYLAND

Eisner was so keen on Euro Disneyland that Disney kept a 49 percent stake in the project, while the remaining 51 percent of stock was distributed through the London, Paris, and Brussels stock exchanges. Half the stock under the offer was going to the French, 25 percent to the English, and the remainder distributed in the rest of the European community. The initial offer price of FFr 72 was considerably higher than the pathfinder prospectus estimate because the capacity of the park had been slightly extended. Scarcity of stock was likely to push up the price, which was expected to reach FFr 166 by opening day in 1992. This would give a compound return of 21 percent.

Walt Disney maintained management control of the company. The US company put up $160 million of its own capital to fund the project, an investment which soared in value to $2.4 billion after the popular stock offering in Europe. French national and local authorities, by comparison, were providing about $800 million in low interest loans and poured at least that much again into infrastructure.

Other sources of funding were the park's 12 corporate sponsors, and Disney would pay them back in kind. The "autopolis" ride, where kids ride cars, features coupes emblazoned with the "Hot Wheels" logo. Mattel Inc., sponsor of the ride, is grateful for the boost to one of its biggest toy lines.

The real payoff would begin once the park opened. The Walt Disney Company would receive 10 percent of admission fees and 5 percent of food and merchandise revenue, the same arrangement as in Japan. But in France, it would also receive management fees, incentive fees, and 49 percent of the profits.

A Saloman Brothers analyst estimated that the park would pull in three to four million more visitors than the 11 million the company expected in the first year. Other Wall Street analysts cautioned that stock prices of both Walt Disney Company and Euro Disney already contained all the Euro optimism they could absorb. "Europeans visit Disneyworld in Florida as part of an 'American experience,' " said Patrick P. Roper, marketing director of Alton Towers, a successful British theme park near Manchester. He doubted they would seek the suburbs of Paris as eagerly as America and predicted attendance would trail Disney projections.

THE LAYOUT OF EURO DISNEYLAND

Euro Disneyland is determinedly American in its theme. There was an alcohol ban in the park despite the attitude among the French that wine with a meal is a God-given right. Designers presented a plan for a Main Street USA based on scenes of America in the 1920s, because research indicated that Europeans loved the Prohibition era. Eisner decreed that images of gangsters and speak-easies were too negative. Though made more ornate and Victorian than Walt Disney's idealized Midwestern small town, Main Street remained Main Street. Steamships leave from Main Street through the Grand Canyon Diorama en route to Frontierland.

The familiar Disney Tomorrowland, with its dated images of the space age, was jettisoned entirely. It was replaced by a gleaming brass and wood complex called Discoverland, which was based on themes of Jules Verne and Leonardo da Vinci. Eisner ordered $8 for $10 million in extras to the "Visionarium" exhibit, a 360-degree movie about French culture which was required by the French in their original contract. French and English are the official languages at the park and multilingual guides are available to help Dutch, German, Spanish, and Italian visitors.

EXHIBIT 4
The Euro Disneyland Resort

Source: Roger Cohen, "Threat of Strikes in Euro Disney Debut," *The New York Times,* April 10, 1992, p. 20.

5000	Acres in size
30	Attractions
12,000	Employees
6	Hotels (with 5,184 rooms)
10	Theme restaurants
414	Cabins
181	Camping sites

EXHIBIT 5
What Price Mickey?

Source: *BusinessWeek,* March 30, 1992.

	Euro Disneyland	Disney World, Orlando
Peak season hotel rates		
4-Person Room	$97 to $345	$104–$455
Campground space		
	$48	$30–$49
One-day pass		
Children	$26	$26
Adults	$40	$33

With the American Wild West being so frequently captured on film, Europeans have their own idea of what life was like back then. Frontierland reinforces those images. A runway mine train takes guests through the canyons and mines of Gold Rush country. There is a paddle wheel steamboat reminiscent of Mark Twain, Indian explorer canoes, and a phantom manor from the Gold Rush days.

In Fantasyland, designers strived to avoid competing with the nearby European reality of actual medieval towns, cathedrals, and chateaux. While Disneyland's castle is based on Germany's Neuschwanstein and Disney World's is based on a Loire Valley chateau, Euro Disney's *Le Château de la Belle au Bois Dormant,* as the French insisted Sleeping Beauty be called, is more cartoon-like with stained glass windows built by English craftsmakers and depicting Disney characters. Fanciful trees grow inside as well as a beanstalk.

The park is criss-crossed with covered walkways. Eisner personally ordered the installation of 35 fireplaces in hotels and restaurants. "People walk around Disney World in Florida with humidity and temperatures in the 90s and they walk into an air-conditioned ride and say, 'This is the greatest,'" said Eisner. "When it's raining and miserable, I hope they will walk into one of these lobbies with the fireplace going and say the same thing."

Children all over Europe were primed to consume. Even one of the intellectuals who contributed to *Le Figaro*'s Disney-bashing broadsheet was forced to admit with resignation that his ten-year-old son "swears by Michael Jackson." At Euro Disneyland, under the name "Captain EO," Disney just so happened to have a Michael Jackson attraction awaiting him.

FOOD SERVICE AND ACCOMMODATIONS AT EURO DISNEYLAND

Disney expected to serve 15,000 to 17,000 meals per hour, excluding snacks. Menus and service systems were developed so that they varied both in style and price. There is a 400-seat buffeteria, six table service restaurants, 12 counter service units, ten snack bars, one Discovery food court seating 850, nine popcorn wagons, 15 ice-cream carts, 14 specialty food carts, and two employee cafeterias. Restaurants were, in fact, to be a showcase for American foods. The only exception to this is Fantasyland which recreates European fables. Here, food service will reflect the fable's country of origin: Pinocchio's facility having German food: Cinderella's, French; Bella Notte's, Italian; and so on.

Of course recipes were adapted for European tastes. Since many Europeans don't care much for very spicy food, Tex-Mex recipes were toned down. A special coffee blend had to be developed which would have universal appeal. Hot dog carts would reflect the regionalism of American tastes. There would be a ball park hot dog (mild, steamed, a mixture of beef and pork), a New York hot dog (all beef, and spicy), and a Chicago hot dog (Vienna-style, similar to bratwurst).

Euro Disneyland has six theme hotels which would offer nearly 5,200 rooms on opening day, a campground (444 rental trailers and 181 camping sites), and single family homes on the periphery of the 27-hole golf course.

DISNEY'S STRICT APPEARANCE CODE

Antoine Guervil stood at his post in front of the 1,000-room Cheyenne Hotel at Euro Disneyland, practicing his "Howdy!" When Guervil, a political refugee from Haiti, said the word, it sounded more like "Audi." Native French speakers have trouble with the aspirated "h" sound in words like "*hay*" and "*Hank*" and "Howdy." Guervil had been given the job of wearing a cowboy costume and booming a happy, welcoming Howdy to guests as they entered The Cheyenne, styled after a Western movie set.

"Audi," said Guervil, the strain of linguistic effort showing on his face. This was clearly a struggle. Unless things got better, it was not hard to imagine objections from Renault, the French car company that was one of the corporate sponsors of the park. Picture the rage of a French auto executive arriving with his or her family at the Renault-sponsored Euro Disneyland, only to hear the doorman of a Disney hotel advertising a German car.

Such were the problems Disney faced while hiring some 12,000 people to maintain and populate its Euro Disneyland theme park. A handbook of detailed rules on acceptable clothing, hairstyles, and jewelry, among other things, embroiled the company in a legal and cultural dispute. Critics asked how the brash Americans could be so insensitive to French culture, individualism, and privacy. Disney officials insisted that a ruling that barred them from imposing a squeaky-clean employment standard could threaten the image and long-term success of the park.

"For us, the appearance code has a great effect from a product identification standpoint," said Thor Degelmann, vice president for human resources for Euro Disneyland. "Without it we wouldn't be presenting the Disney product that people would be expecting."

The rules, spelled out in a video presentation and detailed in a guide handbook, went beyond height and weight standards. They required men's hair to be cut above the collar and ears with no beards or mustaches. Any tattoos must be covered. Women must keep their hair in one "natural color" with no frosting or streaking and they may make only limited use of make-up like mascara. False eyelashes, eyeliners, and eye pencil were completely off limits. Fingernails can't pass the end of the fingers. As for jewelry, women can wear only one earring in each ear, with the earring's diameter no more than three-quarters of an inch. Neither men nor women can wear more than one ring on each hand. Further, women were required to wear appropriate undergarments and only transparent pantyhose, not black or anything with fancy designs. Though a daily bath was not specified in the rules, the applicant's video depicted a shower scene and informed applicant's that they were expected to show up for work "fresh and clean each day." Similar rules are in force at Disney's three other theme parks in the US and Japan.

In the US, some labor unions representing Disney employees have occasionally protested the company's strict appearance code, but with little success. French labor unions began protesting when Disneyland opened its "casting center" and invited applicants to "play the role of [their lives]" and to take a "unique opportunity to marry work and magic." The CGT handed out leaflets in front of the center to warn applicants of the appearance code which they believed represented "an attack on individual liberty." A more mainstream union, the *Confédération Française Démocratique du Travail* (CFDT), appealed to the Labor Ministry to halt Disney's violation of "human dignity." French law prohibits employers from restricting individual and collective liberties unless the restrictions can be justified by the nature of the task to be accomplished and are proportional to that end.

Degelmann, however, said that the company was "well aware of the cultural differences" between the United States and France and as a result had "toned down" the wording in the original American version of the guidebook. He pointed out that many companies, particularly airlines, maintained appearance codes just as strict. "We happened to put ours in writing," he added. In any case, he said that he knew of no one who had refused to take the job because of the rules and that no more than 5 percent of the people showing up for interviews had decided not to proceed after watching the video which also detailed transportation and salary.

Fitzpatrick also defended the dress code, although he conceded that Disney might have been a little naive in presenting things so directly. He added, "Only in France is there still a communist party. There is not even one in Russia any more. The ironic thing is that I could fill the park with CGT requests for tickets."

Another big challenge lay in getting the mostly French "cast members," as Disney calls its employees, to break their ancient cultural aversions to smiling and being consistently polite to park guests. The individualistic French had to be molded into the squeaky-clean Disney image. Rival theme parks in the area, loosely modeled on the Disney system, had already encountered trouble keeping smiles on the faces of the staff, who sometimes took on the demeanor of subway ticket clerks.

The delicate matter of hiring French citizens as opposed to other nationals was examined in the more than two-year-long pre-agreement negotiations between the French government and Disney. The final agreement called for Disney to make a maximum effort to tap into the local labor market. At the same time, it was understood that for Euro Disneyland to work, its staff must mirror the multicountry make-up of its guests. "Casting centers" were set up in Paris, London, Amsterdam, and Frankfurt. "We are concentrating on the local labor market, but we are also looking for workers who are German, English, Italian, Spanish, or other nationalities and who have good communication skills, are outgoing, speak two European languages—French plus one other—and like being around people," said Degelmann.

Stephane Baudet, a 28-year-old trumpet player from Paris, refused to audition for a job in a Disney brass band when he learned he would have to cut his ponytail. "Some people will turn themselves into a pumpkin to work at Euro Disneyland," he said. "But not me."

THE OPENING DAY AT EURO DISNEYLAND

A few days before the grand opening of Euro Disneyland, hundreds of French visitors were invited to a pre-opening party. They gazed perplexed at what was placed before them. It was a heaping plate of spare ribs. The visitors were at the Buffalo Bill Wild West Show, a cavernous theater featuring a panoply of "Le Far West," including 20 imported buffaloes. And Disney deliberately didn't provide silverware. "There was a moment of consternation," recalls Fitzpatrick. "Then they just kind of said, 'The hell with it,' and dug in." There was one problem. The guests couldn't master the art of gnawing ribs and applauding at the same time. So Disney planned to provide more napkins and teach visitors to stamp with their feet.

On April 12, 1992, the opening day of Euro Disneyland, *France-Soir* enthusiastically predicted Disney dementia. "Mickey! It's madness," read its front page headline, warning of chaos on the roads and suggesting that people may have to be turned away. A French government survey indicated that half a million might turn up with 90,000 cars trying to get in. French radio warned traffic to avoid the area.

By lunch time on opening day, the Euro Disneyland car park was less than half full, suggesting an attendance of below 25,000, less than half the park's capacity and way below expectations. Many people may have heeded the advice to stay home or, more likely, were deterred by a one-day strike that cut the direct rail link to Euro Disneyland from the center of Paris. Queues for the main rides such as Pirates of the Caribbean and Big Thunder Mountain railroad were averaging around 15 minutes less than on an ordinary day at Disney World, Florida.

Disney executives put on a brave face, claiming that attendance was better than at first days for other Disney theme parks in Florida, California, and Japan. However, there was no disguising the fact that after spending thousands of dollars on the pre-opening celebrations, Euro Disney would have appreciated some impressively long traffic jams on the auto route.

OTHER OPERATING PROBLEMS

When the French government changed hands in 1986, work ground to a halt, as the negotiator appointed by the Conservative government threw out much of the ground work prepared by his Socialist predecessor. The legalistic approach taken by the Americans also bogged down talks, as it meant planning ahead for every conceivable contingency. At the same time, right-wing groups who saw the park as an invasion of "chewing-gum jobs" and US pop-culture also fought hard for a greater "local cultural context."

On opening day, English visitors found the French reluctant to play the game of queuing. "The French seem to think that if God had meant them to queue, He wouldn't have given them elbows," an American noted. Different cultures have different definitions of personal space, and Disney guests faced problems of people getting too close or pressing around those who left too much space between themselves and the person in front.

Disney placed its first ads for work bids in English, leaving smaller and medium-sized French firms feeling like foreigners in their own land. Eventually, Disney set up a data bank with information on over 20,000 French and European firms looking for work, and the local Chamber of Commerce developed a video text information bank with Disney that small- and medium-sized companies through France and Europe would be able to tap into. "The work will come, but many local companies have got to learn that they don't simply have the right to a chunk of work without competing," said a Chamber official.

Efforts were made to ensure that sooner, rather than later, European nationals take over the day-to-day running of the park. Although there were only 23 US expatriates amongst the employees, they controlled the show and held most of the top jobs. Each senior manager had the task of choosing his or her European successor.

Disney was also forced to bail out 40 subcontractors, who were working for the Gabot-Eremco construction contracting group which had been unable to honor all of its commitments. Some of the subcontractors said they faced bankruptcy if they were not paid for their work on Euro Disneyland. A Disney spokesperson said that the payments would be less than $20.3 million and the company had already paid Gabot-Eremco for work on the park. Gabot-Eremco and 15 other main contractors demanded $157 million in additional fees from Disney for work that they said was added to the project after the initial contracts were signed. Disney rejected the claim and sought government intervention. Disney said that under no circumstances would they pay Gabot-Eremco and accused its officers of incompetence.

As Bourguignon thought about these and other problems, the previous year's losses and the prospect of losses again in the current year, with their negative impact on the company's stock price, weighed heavily on his mind.

This case was prepared by Research Assistant Sonali Krishna under the direction of Professors J. Stewart Black and Hal B. Gregersen as the basis for class discussion. Reprinted by permission of the authors.

Managing International Strategic Planning and Implementation

Strategies for International Competition

Chapter Learning Objectives

After completing this chapter, you should be able to:

- Discuss the roots of international strategy, including ethnocentric, polycentric, and geocentric organizations.
- Explain the facilitators of international expansion for firms.
- Employ various analytical and portfolio thinking to understand how firms decide which countries to expand to.
- Distinguish among the global, multidomestic, and transnational mindsets of firms and industries.
- Describe the fit of various value chain activities into a firm's total international strategy.
- Explain the levels of strategic integration, including stand-alone, simple integration, and complex integration.
- Integrate the specific firm-level initiatives of core competency leveraging, counterattack, and glocalization to a firm's international strategy.

Opening Case: Maytag—Three Countries, One Dishwasher

Maytag dishwashers have Chinese motors, Mexican wiring, and are put together in a sprawling American factory in Tennessee. Some refer to this three-tiered approach to manufacturing as a triad strategy. Maytag calls it trying to keep ahead of imports. For a long time, bulky appliances like washing machines and refrigerators largely were insulated from competition with cheap imports because of their cavernous size. "Big boxes of air are expensive to ship across the ocean," says Maytag Corp.'s Jim Starkweather.

Over time, though, sharply lower labor and production costs in Asia have offset high freight costs, enabling some imported appliances to be sold in the U.S. at lower prices. China's Haier and South Korea's LG Electronics started out small with microwaves and minirefrigerators, but are moving to bigger appliances. At the same time, Maytag's U.S. competitors, General Electric and Whirlpool, have already turned Mexico into a prime location for making appliances for the U.S. market. GE owns 48% of Mexico's largest appliance maker and Whirlpool recently acquired full control of the second-largest. Both are exporting Mexican-made appliances to the U.S. by the truckload, which means Maytag's biggest import threat is, ironically, its domestic rivals. Now Asian appliance makers, including LG, are opening plants in Mexico to save on shipping.

With the arrival of low-priced imports, Maytag had to radically rethink how and where it builds refrigerators, washing machines and dishwashers; it found the triad strategy works best for now. "It's a logical progression for us," says Art Learmonth, senior vice president of supply chain, noting that Maytag wants to avoid a wholesale shift of production out of the U.S. The company says it wants to stay as close as possible to its end market and avoid shedding American jobs whenever possible. In the case of dishwashers, Maytag buys motors in China, from a plant owned by GE, because the design is standardized and stable and China offers the lowest price. Maytag makes wire harnesses for dishwashers in Mexico because those harnesses tend to be different in each dishwasher model, so sudden shifts in demand could make it difficult to supply from farther away.

European companies are also using a version of the triad approach, increasingly buying components in the Far East and setting up production in Eastern Europe to augment what they do at home, says Anand Sharma, president of TBM Consulting Group Inc., which specializes in "lean manufacturing" techniques.

For Maytag, the strategy involves dissecting appliances to determine the cost of every component. Whenever a competitor introduces a new dishwasher, for example, Maytag buys one and brings it here to Jackson to dismantle it. In a makeshift workshop known as "the aquarium" because blue plastic sheeting conceals work on new models, engineers examine rival appliances' every O-ring and steel tube and estimate what it costs to make the appliance in the United States and compare that to what it would cost to make it in Mexico. Competitors aren't making dishwashers in Mexico yet, but Maytag thinks it's only a matter of time. "Everything we do is aimed at staying competitive once product starts coming from Mexico," says Mr. Learmonth.

Maytag's new approach to production began three years ago, when other companies had already established footholds in Mexico. Rather than build a plant there, Mr. Learmonth leased a small factory in the Mexican border town of Reynosa and ordered every division to determine what portions of their subassembly work could be sent there. Subassembly work tends to be labor intensive, but not very skill intensive. The moves lowered Maytag's costs because Mexican workers are paid less than U.S. workers. Since then, the company has bought another factory in Reynosa for subassembly work. Sometimes, work that leaves the U.S. returns. Subassembly work for dishwashers, essentially putting pumps and motors together in one piece with cables and connectors, was done in Reynosa, and shipped to Tennessee. But eventually it grew more cost-effective to do the work in Tennessee: A simpler design was introduced, reducing labor, and it used less-expensive motors from China rather than Mexico.

Still, Maytag says it wouldn't build certain items in China. Maytag teamed with a German supplier to develop a "turbidity sensor" that scans water coming out of a dishwasher to determine how clean the dishes are. As long as it detects the tiniest bits of macaroni or mashed potatoes, the dishes are deemed dirty and the machine keeps churning. Mr. Learmonth says the company wouldn't try to have the sensors built in China, because the Chinese "aren't as protective of new technology" and so such proprietary technology is at greater risk of being stolen.

Maytag does the same cost analysis with its other appliances. It took apart one of GE's Mexican-made side-by-side refrigerators and decided it couldn't match GE prices without building its side-by-sides in Mexico, too. So Maytag is building a plant in Reynosa dedicated to making those models. It is set to open next year.

In some cases, after a careful review, Maytag decides it simply can't compete with imports. Profit margins on refrigerators with the freezer on top, rather than alongside or on the bottom, were so measly due to cheap imports that Maytag decided to quit making them. Instead, next year it will pay Daewoo Electronics Corp. in Korea to produce those models and ship them to the U.S. to be sold under the Maytag name. That decision was linked to the anticipated closing of a sprawling two-million-square-foot refrigerator factory in Galesburg, Ill., where those models are made. That plant, shutting down in stages, is expected to close its doors for good late next year.

Discussion Questions

1. How does international diversification of operations fit into Maytag's strategy?
2. In your opinion, what factors should Maytag consider when deciding where to produce its appliances? Where to sell them?
3. What are the overall pressures for firms competing in the global appliance industry?

The Roots of International Strategy

A pioneer in the field of international business, Howard V. Perlmutter, identified three states of mind or attitudes that can be inferred from examining the managerial practices of international firms.[1] He called them "ethnocentric," "polycentric," and "geocentric." It is from these foundations that a discussion on international strategies may be approached.

As represented in Figure 6.1, **ethnocentrism** represents an extreme orientation. An ethnocentric attitude looks upon everything that originates from an organization's home country as the best in the world. Thus the international firm's headquarters controls all that goes on in the world for that firm, including managerial personnel, management techniques and practices, products, marketing techniques, and overall strategy. The approach of ethnocentric companies is one of centralization. The firm's primary purpose is to extend to foreign subsidiaries that which has proved to be effective for it in its home country. Standardization of both products and processes is emphasized.

Polycentrism represents that opposite extreme. A polycentric attitude is an orientation that assumes that countries have vast differences in their economic, political, and legal systems deriving from culture, language, and race. Because of the great differences in these aspects, home-country nationals would be unable to really understand the foreign environments. Hence management in the parent company should give foreign subsidiaries as much freedom as is possible to manage their own affairs. This creates a highly decentralized organization where headquarters control is not emphasized. The subsidiaries may therefore have different operations and human resource processes. Furthermore, the product offered throughout the world may be adapted to each individual country.

Geocentrism is a world-oriented attitude, with no predisposition regarding degree of control or centralization. Rather, interdependence among headquarters and all foreign subsidiaries is emphasized. Communications and shared perspectives are key. Subsequently, managers at the parent company and in the foreign subsidiaries are in close

FIGURE 6.1 **International Orientations**

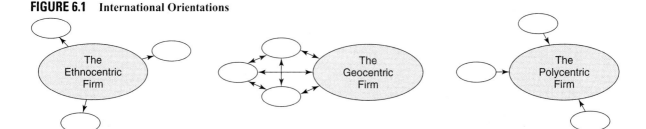

communication with one another and are aware of the objectives of the entire enterprise. Decisions are made at the parent-company level as well as in subsidiaries only after a thorough analysis of worldwide opportunities and threats. The geocentric attitude is characterized by an absence of parochial thinking within the parent and subsidiaries. This does not mean that the host country's needs are ignored. On the contrary, a geocentric firm wants to be a good citizen of the host country and makes its global plans after taking into account the aspirations of host countries. The incentive system is designed to motivate each subsidiary manager to attain not only the objectives of the subsidiary but also those of the entire international company. Unlike in a polycentric firm, managers of foreign subsidiaries in a geocentric firm have the opportunity to move into parent-company management. This is in response to the philosophy of a geocentric firm to place in each job the person who can do it best, regardless of nationality or other considerations like race or religion—provided that mobility across national borders is permitted by immigration laws of sovereign states.

Strategically Expanding Overseas

Facilitators of International Expansion

During the past decade, international business researchers have suggested various rationales for firms to expand overseas. Chapter 1 presented factors specifically oriented to the firm's strategy. Macro-environmental forces, discussed in Chapter 2, are higher level facilitators of internationalization. Combining these factors, we find that global strategy is initially determined by the external industry globalization drivers related to market, cost, government, and competitive factors[2] and, most recently, the emergence of technological factors. The cost, market, and competitive factors were evidenced in this chapter's opening case regarding Maytag.

Internationalization has been facilitated through various factors as seen in Figure 6.2. From the mid-1980s through today, *government and political forces* have gone through dramatic upheavals worldwide. These changes have been key catalysts in internationalization. A significant example is the shift of many countries from communism and planned economies toward democracy and markets unencumbered by significant government intervention. Many industries worldwide have been privatized. In 1998, for instance, 69 countries agreed to a schedule of privatization of their respective telecom industries. This opened the door for many foreign firms in that industry to expand internationally. Complementing the privatization initiatives, many governments of the world have proactively instigated increasing deregulation to many of their respective industries.

FIGURE 6.2
Macro-Environmental Facilitators of Internationalization

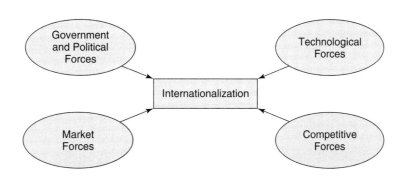

A second facilitator of internationalization has been *technological forces.* Initially, technology gave the firm the simple ability to communicate more efficiently with overseas subsidiaries and partners, including agents and export intermediaries. This ability led to a higher level of control not previously afforded the firm. Technology also leads to increased efficiencies in transportation. For instance, because of improvements in transportation technology of wine, many nations, including Chile, Argentina, and Slovenia, now have the ability to compete in lower and middle-end wine markets in the United States. Most important, technological advances dealing with the Internet have opened up international markets to many smaller and medium-size firms that do not possess the cost efficiencies or global resources to expand internationally. Today, a small firm in Bombay, Beijing, or Barcelona may market its goods worldwide without the costs and resources once associated with this initiative. For example, a small start-up in Ambler, Pennsylvania, Lucidsecurity, has a Web page for its Internet intrusion prevention product called *ip*Angel that has elicited inquiries and brought in customers from countries such as Brazil, Taiwan, India, and Hungary. Practical Insight 6.1 depicts global Internet initiatives of firms and industries in New Zealand and India.

A third facilitator of internationalization has been *market forces.* Because of increased travel, 24-hour global news, and ease of communication and associated knowledge transfer, once-distinct cultures now are overlapping. Demand for American fast food and soft drinks cuts across all cultures. Similarly, demand for new Japanese electronics technology developed by Sony is not bound by national borders. The French hotel firm Accor offers its Sofitel and Novatel hotels from New Zealand to the Ivory Coast. That same Paris-based firm has a discount hotel strategy as well, including Red Roof Inn and Motel 6 in the United States. Complementing the overlap of cultures is the increase of disposable income in many countries. Thus a higher percentage of people can now afford the luxury of goods imported from another country or a differentiated good made in its own country.

Beyond these forces, *competitive forces* within industries have facilitated internationalization. As we will discuss in Chapter 8, international joint ventures and international strategic alliances have proliferated during the past 15 years. Firms that wanted to internationalize have increased options besides going at it alone. Also, many industries have had tremendous cost pressures. Subsequently, we have seen a significant rise in international mergers and acquisitions. For example, in the global pharmaceutical industry, the cost of research and development—even for a blockbuster drug—has become prohibitive for many companies. Thus, besides various joint venture initiatives, full mergers and buyouts have increased in the past 15 years. Likewise, in technology-based industries, where the life cycle of a generation of technology is sometimes too short to recoup costs of investment in traditional ways, cross-national mergers have allowed companies to pool resources in order to compete. Consumer nondurables are affected as well. For example, the Chinese beer industry has seen activity during 2003 where South African Breweries (SAB), the world's second largest brewer, purchased a 29.6 percent stake of China's fourth biggest brewer, Harbin Brewery Company, at a cost of $86.6 million. This gives SAB stakes in 31 Chinese brewers and makes it the biggest foreign brewer in China.

Where to Expand Internationally

How do firms decide where to expand overseas? This question was posed in the opening case of this chapter. Maytag needed to examine various alternatives before deciding on the triad approach to manufacturing its dishwashers.

PRACTICAL INSIGHT 6.1

LOCAL PRODUCTS GO GLOBAL

New Zealand Baby and Child Products Are Now Global

Historically, New Zealand has had a well-developed baby and child products industry nationally. Since 2000, many firms in the industry have begun to leverage their competitive advantages in design and relative costs through exports to other Anglo nations. For instance, approximately 20 brands of New Zealand baby and child products were exported and sold in the United Kingdom in 2001. Many of the industry firms, small in size relative to firms from other Western countries, have banded together to promote the industry through the Internet.

An example of these firms is Baby Shade Limited, a designer and supplier of woolen liners and shades for baby carriages, strollers, and car seats. Women from a coffee circle, who simply wanted to have fun and make extra money, formed the company in the late 1990s. The products that the firm sells have a distinct New Zealand design and are manufactured to be able to fit any baby apparatus worldwide. Thus there is a global standardized approach of this industry, as exhibited by Baby Shade's worldwide consistent marketing message and production of goods. From 2000 to 2003, Baby Shade began a proactive promotion of its products to Australia and the United Kingdom through the Internet. Today, the Internet reach has expanded to the United States and is poised to market to most of continental Europe.

Surat Diamond Jewelry's International Expansion

In 1997, a small mail-order jewelry manufacturer in India, Surat Diamond Jewelry (SDJ), began to target overseas customers exclusively through the Internet. During the first year that SDJ began to market on the Internet, the company received more orders from Americans who had no family or cultural connections to India as compared to Indians residing in the United States. There was a similar pattern in the other regions. Eventually, SDJ began offering products adapted to the cultural tastes of each region, while keeping the traditional product line for the Indians living both in India and worldwide.

Because of the ease and efficiency of using the Internet, SDJ was able to better investigate specific customer needs in different countries. They found that, in the jewelry industry, the tastes and preferences across cultures were differentiated. Furthermore, the Internet allowed the company to efficiently yet selectively serve targeted customer needs, while keeping the assets centralized in Mumbai, India. Today, SDJ has regular clients in 15 different countries and is investigating further country expansion. Thus the Internet provided the pathway for a small, indigenous firm to compete internationally in a locally responsive, multidomestic fashion, without the capital resources historically deemed necessary.

Source: Written by Mahesh Joshi, Hugh Sherman, and Roger Kashlak, 2003.

In general, a number of tools are available to each firm. For instance, country attractiveness ratings will rate countries on a variety of aspects, including the following dimensions:

- Political risk
- Cultural distance
- Geographic distance
- Economic environment
- Foreign exchange volatility
- Market size
- Market growth
- Regulatory environment

These various ratings will then be combined to yield an overall attractiveness rating relative to other countries. Firms may then derive (1) a measure of *country risk* from these ratings and (2) a measure of *expected return.* Subsequently, each country may be comparatively viewed from this risk–return perspective.

Firms also use the *analytical hierarchy process*[3] for making internationalization decisions. In this approach, the firm develops a list of important variables to consider (e.g., political instability, market growth). Then the firm uses these variables to rate

EXHIBIT 6.1
An Analytical
Hierarchy Approach
to International
Expansion, 2003

Factor	Weighting	Chile	Brazil	Ecuador	Venezuela
Political stability	.1	10	6	3	2
Market size	.4	2	10	3	5
Cultural nearness	.1	8	6	5	9
Regulatory leniency	.2	10	6	5	6
Repatriation of profits	.2	9	8	4	6
Total score		39	36	20	28
Total weighted score		6.4	8.0	3.8	5.5

each country under consideration for expansion. Complementing this rating is the firm's determination of relative weights given to each variable. For instance, if market size as determined by level of disposable income is deemed most critical, the weighting given to that factor would be higher than other factors. Using this approach, firms will develop the type of grid illustrated in Exhibit 6.1, which depicts an international expansion analysis for BellSouth, the American telecom firm, into Latin America. As seen in this exhibit, five factors enter into the decision: political stability, market size, cultural nearness, regulatory leniency, and the ability to repatriate profits. Each of the four countries in Latin America has relative strengths when compared to the others. Before the effect of weighting the variables, Chile appears to be the best candidate for expansion. However, when market size is weighted as the most critical factors for the firm, Brazil emerges as the best opportunity for expansion.

Strategic Planning for Foreign Market Entry

In today's global environment, many businesses have a set of strategic goals in addition to the traditional financial goals.[4] Any company that wants to assume global leadership in its industry must be adept at discovering new market opportunities, establishing a presence in those markets, and subsequently securing a sustainable competitive advantage.[5] There are more than 200 countries in the world, and obviously not all would be of interest to an international company. Many countries are eager to get foreign direct investments for a variety of reasons, including the importation of new technology and products that the foreign companies would bring, the creation of new jobs, and the building of much-needed infrastructure.

The process of planning for foreign market entry consists of seven discrete steps that are explained in the following paragraphs. Note that the entire process is iterative.

1. Identify the Company's Objective in Its Foreign Market Entry

At the outset, management must clearly identify the reasons for its foreign market entry. In Chapter 1 we discussed the different motives for entering foreign markets. They include, but are not limited to, motives such as exploiting a large and virgin market, obtaining a competitive advantage over a competitor, securing essential raw materials, or cutting costs by employing a relatively inexpensive skilled and unskilled labor force in the production of components or product assembly. There may be many more, and different, foreign market entry objectives driving a company's foray into foreign markets.

Establishing the objectives for foreign market entry is important because those countries that, at first glance, meet the foreign market entry objectives are included in the group of countries subjected to further analysis, and those that do not are dropped for further consideration.

2. Preliminary Country Screening

As a start, a comparative analysis of different countries may yield a select few that meet the needs of the "investment screen." The investment screen is based on the company's predetermined market entry objectives. It allows countries to go through the preliminary approval process only if they meet certain minimum predetermined criteria. As one would expect, the nature of the investment screen and the embedded criteria would be different for different industries and companies. For example, the investment screen of a large pharmaceuticals company with innovative products may include criteria such as guaranteed patent protection and a big enough pool of host-country chemists and scientists. On the other hand, countries like Germany, France, and the United States would not seep through the investment screen of an automobile parts company that is searching for countries with low labor costs; however, India, China, and Sri Lanka would pass this screening test.

A country with a small population of 25 million would be eliminated in favor of that with a population of 900 million by a breakfast cereal company like Kellogg or General Mills, provided that the population in the latter country has the purchasing power to afford its products. However, lack of patent protection would be of no concern. Large insurance companies like the U.S.-based AIG search for countries with large populations, in which a significant percentage is uninsured. This criterion has induced AIG to enter the huge markets of China and India because both countries pass the test of this investment screen.

The country screening process generates a select group of countries in which a market entry is contemplated. The countries in this group are subjected to an intensive, detailed investigation from which emerges a selected few that are the most attractive investment opportunities. For instance, the preliminary investment screen might produce 10 countries that meet the investment criteria. From this small group of companies a smaller number of countries—probably only two or three—are chosen for market entry by the company.

3. What Are the Opportunities and Constraints in the Target Market?

In Chapters 2 to 5, we examined the characteristics of the global, regional, and country-specific economic, legal, political, and cultural environments. Each of these environmental sets would influence the types of opportunities and constraints imposed on a foreign company. For instance, opportunities may exist for a product that has a huge potential market. However, the country may be a developing economy and therefore have poor infrastructure such as roads and a transportation network.

The legal system of the target country may be extremely sophisticated in its protection of a company's patents and trademarks. Such countries offer opportunities for companies that market patented products, and those that leverage their trademarks and brand names like Coca-Cola, Mercedes, and Sony. However, the lack of such protections has been the principal constraint for companies selling patented pharmaceutical products and branded men's and women's clothing.

4. What Capabilities, Resources, and Skills Are Needed to Succeed in the Foreign Market?

The analysis and determination of the various opportunities and constraints leads to a set of factors, called *key success factors,* in which the company must excel in order to succeed in the targeted foreign market. For example, a franchiser like McDonald's, which is required to maintain a consistent image worldwide, must excel in the following key success factors in every country in which it operates its restaurants: (1) consistent product quality, (2) consistency in taste, (3) standardized production process (e.g., how long its french fries must be fried), (4) cleanliness in the seating areas and in the toilet areas, (5) identical service standards and procedures, and (6) standardized menu in all restaurants worldwide.

One of the authors of this book visited the chief executive officer (CEO) of McDonald's India, who related his experiences in opening a McDonald's restaurant in Mumbai (Bombay):

- Potatoes did not contain the required moisture. The CEO had to teach local suppliers how to grow potatoes that met the required moisture standard.
- Tomato farmers were taught to grow tomatoes that met the quality standards.
- The staff was not used to serving customers with the courtesy and speed that signified McDonald's standards.
- The restaurant was vandalized because of the rumor that its french fries were fried in animal fat.
- McDonald's India was the only franchisee that sold lamburgers because religious beliefs prohibited the consumption of beef. The restaurant subsequently temporarily dropped meat from its hamburgers because customers suspected that beef was added to the ingredients.

This example illustrates the key success factors for all McDonald's restaurants worldwide, and the resources and capabilities that the CEO of McDonald's India had to deploy to make the franchise succeed in India.

It is well known that the success of Wal-Mart stores is based on superior logistical capabilities. The company is able to maintain a very small inventory of goods in stores and warehouses because of its effective and efficient system of transporting goods by trucks from the supplier to the stores. Wal-Mart also has a system to detect the sales volume and stock of each product sold in every store, so that it knows which store needs which product and when. This information is used to replenish the inventory needed in every store. This system has allowed Wal-Mart to obtain goods at the lowest prices from suppliers and pass the low prices to its customers. Wal-Mart has scored high on the key success factors of speed of delivery, reliability of service, and low prices. Other companies like Kmart have tried to emulate Wal-Mart's business practices, but they have not succeeded. Wal-Mart has now opened stores in several countries. The success of Wal-Mart in foreign markets will depend on its ability to score high on the aforementioned key success factors.

Other industries may include key success factors such as channels of distribution, a constant stream of innovative products, and product design. The U.S.-based company Procter & Gamble has had considerable trouble in gaining market share for its soap and laundry products in the huge market of one billion people in India. The constraint facing Procter & Gamble was the country's poor infrastructure, which prevented the products from reaching markets in distant small towns and villages. On the other hand, its main competitor, Lever Brothers, has been extremely successful. Over several decades, ever since it entered the country when it was a colony of Great Britain, it has developed a distribution network that extends deep into the hundreds and thousands of villages through trucks, rickshaws, bicycle, and by foot. In this example, the size and quality of the distribution network in India was quite different from that which Procter & Gamble had in it home market—the United States—or in advanced countries in Europe. In these countries a huge network of supermarkets and chain stores was there to be exploited.

Other key success factors include the ability to withstand substantial financial loss in the market development stage, the ability to develop good relationships with governmental bureaucrats, and high tolerance by expatriate staff of cultural differences.

5. Does the Company Have the Core Capabilities and Resources to Score High on the Key Success Factors? What Are Our Strengths and Weakness on the Key Success Factors?

This is the extension of the previous step. Comparing the country market's key success factors to the core capabilities and resources of the company results in the evaluation and determination of the company's strengths and limitations for success.

6. Should the Company Enter the Target Market, and How?

Now the management is ready to decide whether to enter the target market. If the answer is in the affirmative, then a further examination of the areas in which the company has strengths and weaknesses leads to an evaluation and decision on the most appropriate mode of entry. Should it enter the foreign market via exports, or through contractual agreements like licensing, franchising, contract manufacturing, or management contracts. Or is the best mode of entry through a foreign direct investment in a joint venture or in a wholly owned subsidiary?

7. Compare and Rank the Targeted Countries

The process discussed in Steps 1 to 7 is carried out in each target foreign market under consideration. A ranking of the attractiveness of each foreign market is made based on the company's assessment of its own propensity to take risk and the expected level of achievement of the objectives (Step 1) for seeking the particular market entry. An executive decision is then made on which foreign markets to enter and in which sequence, as well as the most desirable mode of entry in each market.

Managing a Portfolio of Country Subsidiaries

Beyond the decision on where to expand next, most firms also need to understand the various strategies and linkages that may be associated with each of their respective overseas subsidiaries. In this section, two portfolio approaches are presented. The first approach is based on the intersection of host-country attractiveness and the firm's competitive strength within that host country. The second approach enhances the portfolio analysis perspective by integrating the risk–expected return perspective borrowed from financial management thinking.

Host-Country Attractiveness versus Competitive-Strength Matrix

As illustrated in Figure 6.3, the firm may have a portfolio of international subsidiaries. These overseas positions may be in a variety of host countries. The relative attractiveness of these countries may be determined through the political, economic, cultural, and market factors delineated above. The firm's competitive strength in a given host country may be measured through many different factors. These factors, which are compared to the firm's competition in each host country, include:

- Relative market share
- Relative market support
- Technology fit with the host country
- Relative contribution margin
- Brand recognition

In Figure 6.3, one can see that when a host country has a high attractiveness and the firm has relatively strong competitive strength in that country, the firm should leverage its competitive advantages and pursue *growth strategies*. This strategic initiative will

FIGURE 6.3
Managing a Portfolio of International Subsidiaries

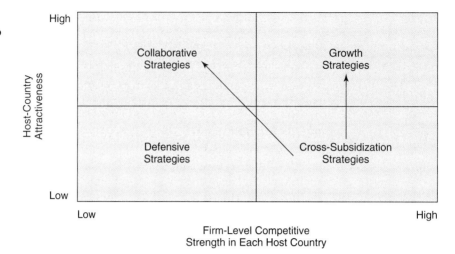

correlate to a strong capital commitment by the firm. Depending on the industry, this commitment may be geared toward increased production, increased research and development, or increased marketing and promotion efforts. From 1995 to 2003, U.S firms like Black & Decker and Wal-Mart aggressively expanded into Latin America and Asia, attractive regions in which each firm showed competitive strength.

When the host country is attractive but the firm does not possess relative competitive strength in that country, the firm faces a difficult decision. Because of its attractiveness, the country will demand more investment. However, because of its competitive weakness in that country, the firm will not be able to fully fund the necessary strategic initiatives. Because the country represents a long-term opportunity, the firm cannot look to divest away from it. Subsequently, the firm should consider a *collaborative strategy* such as an international joint venture or strategic alliance. Here the firm will give up some control and future profits to a partner, but in return it will receive the ability to maintain a presence in this attractive country. Various types of collaborative efforts and the specific implications of these strategic endeavors are developed in Chapter 8.

When the host country is not attractive and the firm has relatively little competitive strength in that country, a *defensive* (or *reactive*) *strategy* must be undertaken. The firm can divest its holdings in that country. By doing this, the firm acknowledges the unattractiveness of doing business in that country, although it still may have strategic reasons to maintain a presence there. The country could be a source of low-cost inputs into other country subsidiaries. The country may also be a piece of an international marketing message. For instance, the ability to use a service or buy a product "anywhere in the world" may be an important part of a company's international brand positioning. Thus many firms may consider nonequity arrangements to stay in the country. When the country is unattractive and the company has little strength there, a significant number of licensing initiatives may keep a firm interested. Types of licensing arrangements are further elaborated on in the next chapter. During the 1990s through the early part of the twenty-first century, U.S. health care providers divested many of their overseas holdings because of a combination of strict host-country regulations and lack of competitive advantage compared to host-country health care providers.

Finally, when the host country is unattractive but the firm has substantial competitive strength in that country, a recommended strategy is one of *cross-subsidization.* Be-

FIGURE 6.4
International
Risk–Return
Portfolio

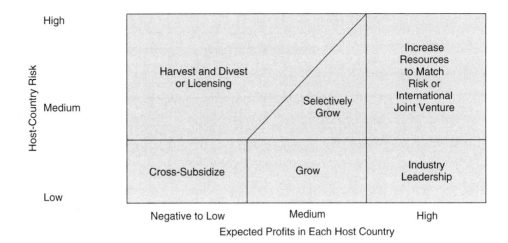

cause the country is unattractive, it does not demand the investment and associated resources necessary for future growth. Still, because the firm has some strength, it is accumulating more profits relative to its competitors. These profits may subsequently be sent to fight other strategic battles in more highly attractive countries. Another way to effect cross-subsidization would be to share resources (marketing, manufacturing, etc.) from the subsidiary in this country with those countries that are looking for future growth. During the past decade, many U.S. and Japanese firms have seen their respective home markets mature and thus become less attractive for added investment. They then use home-country-generated profits to help facilitate international expansion. An example of this is the U.S. cigarette industry, where firms like Philip Morris have fueled expansion into eastern Europe and Asia through a highly competitive position in the United States, which represents a declining market for cigarettes due to social and legal environmental changes.

The International Risk versus Return Portfolio

In the host-country attractiveness versus competitive-strength matrix, the underlying perspective is one of profitability. It implicitly suggests where profits are going (the high-attractive countries) and where profits are coming from (the high-strength countries). By collapsing this matrix into one dimension, we begin to form a basis for the next portfolio matrix to consider. The horizontal axis of Figure 6.4 illustrates this perspective: expected future profits in a specific host country. It is the intersection of a country's attractiveness and the firm's competitive position in that country. The vertical axis represents risk, or uncertainty. From a statistical perspective, risk represents variance about an expectation. Thus this axis measures how uncertain an outcome is in a particular host country. A high level of uncertainty will have different strategic implications for the firm than a country with relatively low risk.

The underlying premise in this matrix is that a firm, to manage risk or uncertainty, must expend more resources. Thus when a relatively high level of risk (usually associated with developing or emerging countries) is combined with minimal or negative expected return, a firm usually looks to exit that country. However, if there is a strategic imperative to stay there, the various licensing options will deflect much of the associated risk. With the same level of expected return coupled with a low level of risk (as seen in many developed countries), a firm may truly understand the future and opt to stay in that country to pursue a cross-subsidization initiative as described above. In countries where there is a medium level of expected profits, a firm will look to pursue growth. This growth will be more aggressive as risk drops and more selective as risk increases. Finally, when the expected profits from the host country are high, the firm must take advantage of its strongly competitive position in a highly attractive country. If risk is low, it may look beyond growth and pursue industry leadership in that country. This initiative may include setting both the strategic and technological standards for the industry in that host country. As risk increases, the firm must dedicate more and more resources to manage and deflect that uncertainty. If the resource commitment becomes too great, the firm will consider an equity-based joint venture, where it will cede some control in return for assets and resources that complement its current position.

Modern International Strategic Orientations

At the beginning of this chapter, the roots of international strategic thinking were introduced. That thinking has evolved into broader international orientations and mindsets. These mindsets, although grounded from a strategic perspective, will also be used as we discuss various organizational behavior and human resource issues in later chapters. Many scholars and observers have chosen to classify companies with international operations into four categories: international, multinational, global, and transnational. These orientations and associated pressures leading to each are illustrated in Figure 6.5.

Both global integration pressures and local responsiveness pressures will affect competition in industries and firms crossing national boundaries.[6] When an industry or firm has no overriding pressures to be globally integrated, cost efficient, or locally responsive, an **international orientation** is observed. An international company is defined by some as one in which top management focuses on domestic operations, and the international operations are treated as accessories whose main purpose is to support the domestic operations by providing critical raw materials or components or incremental sales of the domestic product lines. Besides the international orientation, three orientations—global, multidomestic, and transnational—form a basis for much of international management behavior. We discuss these orientations next.

FIGURE 6.5

Strategic Orientations of International Firms and Industries

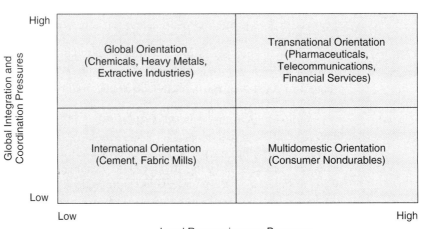

Global versus Multidomestic Strategic Orientations

Roth, Schweiger, and Morrison linked organizational design by international firms to two strategies: (1) a global orientation that relies on coordination of worldwide activities to maximize the collective organization, and (2) a multidomestic orientation that responds to individual country opportunities and constraints.[7]

Global Orientations In some industries, the former strategy dominates, so that a firm's position in one competitive market is significantly affected by its competitive position in other markets.[8] These firms follow a **global orientation,** deriving the cost benefits of scale or scope economies. This strategic orientation matches the integration approach where the international firm seeks to increase efficiency through the optimum allocation of global resources.[9] Of primary importance to the international firm is the strategic need to maximize its collective organization through an efficient configuration of all of its global activities. Simply put, the international firm will have an orientation toward cost and efficiency.[10] Subsequently, there will be a relatively high level of centralization and control, similar to the ethnocentric perspective. Thus a company with a global orientation is described as one that searches for commonality among countries in aspects such as consumer tastes and preferences, market segments, and lifestyles. As such, global companies attempt to standardize products and marketing approaches that are sold globally, and they also find ways to squeeze efficiency from the production function by manufacturing the products on a global scale in a few very efficient plants strategically located in different parts of the world. Such companies require a considerable degree of coordination among the various worldwide operations, and generally it is provided by various product or business managers with worldwide responsibility. Strategic decisions are made at the parent-company level and foreign subsidiary managers are expected to play the role mainly of implementers of centrally designed strategies. Some aspects of the simple and complex integration strategies that are discussed later in this chapter are present in the functioning of a global company.

Companies with global strategies aim to have standardized products with strong brand names that have global recognition. Adaptations to local or regional conditions and tastes are kept to a minimum. Marketing strategies are designed to be implemented uniformly worldwide, except for minor modifications to suit local and regional differences in cultural attributes and legal requirements. Competitive moves in any particular country market are undertaken only after forethought of their impacts on other country markets.

An integrated network of interdependent value chain activities supports the global strategy. The value chain illustrated previously is broken up and activities are strategically placed in different parts of the world to take advantage simultaneously of locational advantages, risk reduction, and counterattack capability against a competitor. These issues are elaborated upon later in this chapter.

Multidomestic Orientations Not all industries and firms which compete internationally exhibit the market interdependencies fitting the global orientation profile. Doz and Prahalad suggested that certain factors will contribute to an industry's need to be more responsive to local environments. These factors include different local tastes, different cultures, different regulatory requirements, and different laws. Thus the international firm will forgo an attempt at maximizing the global organization.[11] For example, product or service requirements may substantially differ from one geographical region to another, making standardization impossible. Furthermore, the benefits from scale or scope economies derived from the sharing of costs across markets may be constrained by governments imposing protectionist policies limiting international trade opportunities.

Roth and Morrison found that these local responsiveness pressures are industry forces necessitating local context-sensitive strategic decisions. The resulting multidomestic strategy is an approach that attacks each market individually rather than attempting to gain cost advantages from a global integration effort.[12] To exploit potential sources of competitive advantage, firms must be able to identify and manage risk in individual foreign markets.[13] Sources of systematic risk of particular importance to multidomestic firms include a host government's regulatory, monetary, and fiscal policies as well as market risk derived from various levels of cultural differences between the home and host countries.[14]

A company with a **multidomestic orientation** is defined as a company whose top management appreciates the importance of foreign operations to its overall profitability and competitive strength. Companies in this category adopt products, strategies, and management practices country by country. Their worldwide strategy is an amalgam of the multiple, country-based approaches of its foreign subsidiaries. A multidomestic strategy requires that each foreign affiliate serve primarily the host-country market. Products and services are customized to the needs of each country market. Marketing strategies are fully tailored for each country. All or most of the value chain is reproduced in every country. Few efforts are made by the parent-company to integrate the operations in host countries with parent-company operations or with operations in other host countries, although some functions in the value chain may be integrated across countries. Competitive moves are made without consideration of their impact on other countries. Multidomestic strategies allow for differentiated strategic approaches across country locations. The strategy of each affiliate is driven by local conditions. Affiliates have considerable autonomy to respond effectively to local conditions. Standalone and simple integration strategies, which are discussed below, are most commonly found in multidomestic strategies.[15]

The Transnational Orientation Imperative

Companies with a **transnational orientation** attempt to balance the need to be responsive to host-country markets through adaptation of the product, marketing strategies, and management practices to suit local conditions with the need to obtain global efficiencies by linking and coordinating the dispersed operations. The resources and activities are distributed to specialized foreign operations, and they are integrated into an interdependent network of worldwide operations.[16] Complex integration strategies discussed below are representative of the functioning of a transnational company.

Firms in industries like pharmaceuticals and telecommunications are examples of companies that must strive toward global efficiency. Because of the high cost of research and development, pharmaceutical firms must closely integrate and coordinate worldwide efforts. Similarly, as international calling and peripheral services have tended toward commoditylike status, telecom firms must have highly efficient global networks and close coordination of all activities. Firms in these industries must also strive to respond to local markets. In pharmaceuticals, both government regulation and social norms dictate the demand for specific drugs. In telecom, patterns of phone usage as well as various technological protocols are locally determined.[17]

The Value Chain Configuration and Strategic Orientations of Firms

One approach to understanding global versus multidomestic industries is by examining the concept of a firm's "value chain." The famous management scholar Michael Porter introduced the **value chain** concept: "The value chain groups a firm's activities

FIGURE 6.6   **Upstream, Support, and Downstream Activities and Competitive Advantage**

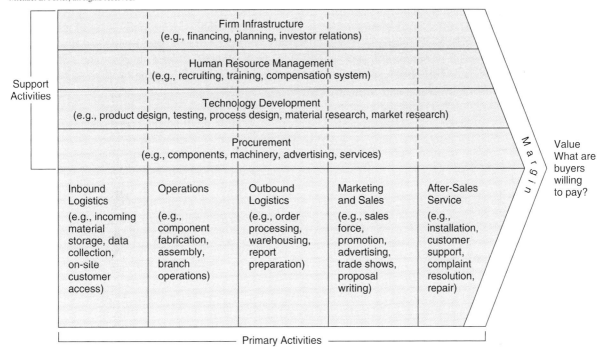

into several categories, distinguishing between those directly involved in producing, marketing, delivering, and supporting a product or service; those that create, source, and improve inputs and technology; and those performing overarching functions such as raising capital, or overall decision making."[18]

Figure 6.6 illustrates a typical value chain of a firm. The value chain consists of two distinct types of activities. *Primary activities* are those activities that are directly involved in producing and marketing goods or services of a firm. *Support activities* are those that facilitate and enhance the effectiveness and efficiency of the various links in the primary activities chain. Furthermore, the primary value chain activities could be labeled as either *upstream* (inbound logistics, operations) or *downstream* activities (outbound logistics, marketing and sales, after-sales service).

Downstream activities are generally closely associated with the customer, and therefore are performed in close proximity to the customer. For instance, the sales force, advertising in newspapers, channels of distribution like stores, shops, and supermarkets, and service centers are situated where the customer lives and works. On the other hand, *upstream* and support functions, like purchasing and shipping raw materials to the production plants, manufacturing operations, and plant maintenance can at least conceptually be uncoupled from where the buyer is located.

The distinction between upstream and downstream activities has strategic implications for how companies compete in an industry. Competitive advantage in upstream and support activities often grows more out of the *entire system of countries* in which a firm competes than from its position in any one country. Downstream activities create competitive advantages that are largely *country-specific,* such as product or service brand name and distribution network in a country.[19]

In industries where upstream and support activities are vital to competitive advantage, companies tend to have global strategic orientations. Companies in such industries emphasize the gaining of efficiencies in current operations through economies of scale and scope in upstream activities in the value chain—for example, operating large manufacturing plants in a few countries rather than many small plants in many countries; bulk purchases of raw materials to be used in strategically located plants worldwide as opposed to buying locally; centralized research and development of new products and processes to be used globally; sharing of huge warehouse spaces; and sharing of advertisements in many countries. Companies in industries where downstream activities connected to buyer satisfaction are key to competitive advantage—such as a superior brand image, service satisfaction, adaptation of products and services to suit local tastes and culture—are more multidomestic in orientation.[20]

Gupta and Govindarajan argue that in the twenty-first century, international firms need to redesign their value chains because of the turbulent environment that exists in many global industries. Three principles should guide the firm's redesign of its value chain: (1) redesigning the set of activities as well as the interfaces across activities, such as supplier and customer linkages; (2) redesigning in order to accrue significant gains in the firm's cost structure, asset investment, and/or speed of responsiveness to external environmental changes; and (3) redesigning to ensure rapid growth in market share and economies of scope expansion into other related products and services.[21]

Worldwide Dispersal and Reintegration of Value Chain Activities

Complementing its direction of international expansion and overall international orientation, the international firm must integrate its various functions into the larger worldwide mosaic. Thus international firms have rapidly moved to put in place integrated systems of international production and distribution capable of most effectively achieving the three objectives discussed in Chapter 1: efficiency in current operations, risk management, and global learning and innovation. Such a system incorporates (1) the dispersal of the company's various activities and functions in the value chain, and their location in different parts of the world to take advantage of national differences, and (2) a reintegration of the dispersed activities and functions to benefit from scale and scope economies. In this section we examine the characteristics of this system.

First we study the functional scope of the value chain dispersal and reintegration strategies, to be followed by a description of the geographic scope of such strategies.

The Functional Scope of Value Chain Dispersal and Integration Strategies

In the initial stages of internationalization, products are exported by the company to foreign markets from the home country. As the company expands its markets abroad to include several countries, it may choose to perform one or more activities in the value chain in foreign locations with the principal purpose of taking advantage of national differences, scale economies, and scope economies.

The foreign location of a particular activity may, or may not, be in a country where the company's products or services are currently marketed. Factors such as the following induce companies to disperse the different activities in the value chain to various locations throughout the world:

- Comparative advantage of the country (competitive input costs, low levels of political risk, market size, proximity to major markets or supply sources, availability of knowledge and skills in the population, etc.).

- Efficiency gains from economies of scale and scope derived from an increased internal functional specialization and international division of labor.

- Competitive pressures from domestic and foreign-based companies and the necessity to compete in competitors' home and third-country markets.

- The benefits of flexibility and risk reduction derived from multiple sourcing points and destination points for components, products, and capital.

- The opportunities to innovate and learn from diverse cultures and economic systems.

- The dispersal of human, capital, material, and knowledge-based resources throughout the world, not in any one country or region; and tariff and nontariff barriers that prevent market penetration via exports.

Having dispersed the value chain activities in different parts of the world, international companies implement plans to reintegrate those activities in response to a global strategy designed to enable the company to achieve its objectives most efficiently and effectively, under an umbrella of an acceptable level of risk.

The level of integration, which varies from company to company, can be categorized as (1) stand-alone, (2) simple integration, and (3) complex integration. The value chain of a firm describes how it organizes and performs the many discrete activities that add value to the goods and services the firm produces and markets. Some of these activities are vertically and sequentially linked, and others are linked horizontally and cut across the various vertical links in the value chain. The vertically linked activities are in-bound logistics, components production, assembly, distribution, marketing, and after-sales service. The horizontally linked activities include research and development, human resource management, procurement, finance, accounting, and other management functions like planning, organizing, and controlling. The horizontally linked activities are performed in all links of the value chain; for example, human resource management—which includes salary administration and staffing—is carried out in each and every operation in the horizontally linked value chain. The same can be said of the other horizontally linked activities. How effective and efficient a firm is in managing the most critical links in the value chain is what ultimately determines how competitive it will be in the industry.

Stand-Alone Strategies

Highly differentiated national tastes and habits or trade barriers such as high tariffs, import quotas, and local content requirements are some factors that have motivated companies to establish stand-alone affiliates in some countries. Under a **stand-alone strategy**, each foreign affiliate is responsible for the performance of almost all of the required activities in the value chain in the host country. The output produced by an affiliate is marketed primarily in the host country, although some of the output may be "exported" to other affiliates and to the parent company. The foreign affiliate may also "import" the output produced by other affiliates for sale in the host-country market. For instance, an affiliate in France may produce camcorders, another in Germany may produce VCRs, and the parent company may produce television sets. Each unit may export its respective outputs to the other two and each would then have three products to sell in each country market.

Except possibly for the export and import of outputs, there is no integration of value chain activities among the affiliates themselves or between the parent and affiliates. The principal linkage between the parent and an affiliate is through ownership, supply of long-term capital, and transfer of technology. The parent does not interfere in the activities of an affiliate as long as the affiliate is profitable and does not deviate from the company's mission and business portfolio.

Factors such as trade barriers (tariffs and quotas), high transportation costs, and communications barriers may cause a company to establish a stand-alone affiliate abroad. Stand-alone strategies are particularly prevalent in service industries. Services like fast-food restaurants, advertising agencies, computer services, management consulting, banking, insurance, and engineering and construction are not tradable, and hence affiliates in these industries are established as self-contained units, mirroring the "production" organization of their parents.

Simple Integration

A **simple integration strategy** calls for the integration of a few activities in the value chain among some or all affiliates of an international company. The integration might be unidirectional or multidirectional. In unidirectional, or one-way, integration, an affiliate might be responsible for producing components for use in another affiliate. For instance, an affiliate in China may have the sole responsibility for the efficient production of an engine which is then used in a tractor assembled in Taiwan, Australia, and Brazil. Or an affiliate in Switzerland or Singapore might be responsible for raising funds from local banks and financial institutions for use in other affiliates. These affiliates may also serve as a cash cow for investments in other functions such as research and development or advertising expenditures to gain a bigger market share in a key country market.

In multidirectional integration, there is *interdependence* among the affiliates and between the affiliates and the parent. For example, an English affiliate may manufacture and export an engine to an Italian affiliate and in return it may import a transmission manufactured by the Italian affiliate. Or the parent might import and assemble different components produced in different affiliates, and subsequently export the assembled products to the affiliates for marketing through their respective distribution channels.

The practice of *outsourcing* by some international companies represents simple integration in its most popular form. Outsourcing is performing some activities in the value chain in foreign countries and linking them to work done elsewhere, mainly in the home country. International outsourcing is the farming out of some value chain activities to countries other than the home country and the major market countries of the product or service. The unit producing the outsourced product may be controlled by the international parent either through equity control or through nonequity contractual arrangements with nonaffiliated foreign contractors. Outsourcing enables an international company to focus on certain activities in the value chain and to delegate other activities in the chain to subcontractors who can specialize in those activities. Contractors who have associated with an international company for many years, in effect, become part of the value chain of the international company. In such cases, contractors not only produce a component but also design it for the international company. Nike and Adidas (basketball shoes), Levi Strauss & Company (jeans), and Wal-Mart and Marks and Spencer (clothing) have significant outsourcing operations in countries like Bangladesh, Turkey, and China. Many software developers use foreign affiliates or subcontractors in India and Ireland to process data or write software. Advances in telecommunications have made possible the transfer of computer programs by communications satellites. India, for example, has the second largest information technology base in Asia after Japan, and it has emerged as the primary development center for sophisticated software and hardware for international companies like IBM, Motorola, and Hewlett-Packard.

PRACTICAL INSIGHT 6.2

DISPERSAL OF THE VALUE CHAIN ACROSS CONTINENTS: INDIA AS A CENTER FOR BACKROOM OPERATIONS

Thanks to the Internet and satellites, India has been able to connect its millions of educated, English-speaking, low-wage, tech-savvy young people to the world's largest corporations. They live in India, but they design and run the software and systems that now support the world's biggest companies, earning India an unprecedented $60 billion in foreign reserves—which doubled in just the last three years. But this has made the world more dependent on India, and India on the world, than ever before.

If you lose your luggage on British Airways, the techies who track it down are here in India. If your Dell computer has a problem, the techie who walks you through it is in Bangalore, India's Silicon Valley. Ernst & Young may be doing your company's tax returns here with Indian accountants. Indian software giants in Bangalore, like Wipro, Infosys and MindTree, now manage back-room operations—accounting, inventory management, billing, accounts receivable, payrolls, credit card approvals—for global firms like Nortel Networks, Reebok, Sony, American Express, HSBC and GE Capital.

You go to the Bangalore campuses of these Indian companies and they point out: "That's G.E.'s back room over here. That's American Express's back office over there." G.E.'s biggest research center outside the U.S. is in Bangalore, with 1,600 Indian engineers and scientists. The brain chip for every Nokia cellphone is designed in Bangalore. Renting a car from Avis online? It's managed here.

Source: From Thomas L. Friedman, "India, Pakistan and GE," August 11, 2002. Copyright © 2002 The New York Times Co. Reprinted with permission.

Practical Insight 6.2 illustrates the dominant role that India now plays in performing so-called backroom operations. Companies like General Electric, Dell, British Airways, Nortel Networks, Reebok, Sony, American Express, HSBC, and GE Capital have established operations in India to perform various skilled functions like accounting, inventory management, billing, accounts receivable, payrolls, credit card approvals, technical support, and answering service calls.

To a large extent, outsourcing is cost-driven as companies search for locales that offer cheap production inputs like labor, raw materials, and energy. However, companies also source abroad in more than one locale, through affiliates or subcontractors, as a hedge against economic, political, and currency risks. Having more than one source country allows an international company to reduce the risk of overdependence on only one source of supply. Thus, all other things being equal, a company that has operations in Japan as well as in Italy could easily shift its supply source from Japan to Italy in response to an exorbitant rise in the value of the Japanese yen or in the Japanese wage rates that make imports from Japan expensive and economically nonviable. Also, firms that play the role of subcontractors need to be functionally integrated into the parent company's value chain through the establishment of functional linkages. For instance, a subcontractor in Taiwan that manufactures desktop computers for an American company would have its research and development, manufacturing, and purchasing functions integrated with that of the American company. Thus integration of some functions of the parent company with those of the subcontractor may be necessary. In a similar vein, affiliates in various parts of the world which serve as suppliers of parts or subassembly modules, or perform some other value chain activities, also must be functionally integrated with the parent.

Complex Integration

The ability of international companies to transfer goods, services, components, capital, technology, and information among the parent and affiliate companies has been facilitated by major changes in the world economy including diminishing market barriers in developed and developing countries; the liberalization of international trade; the emergence of trade blocs like the European Union, NAFTA, and MERCOSUR; advances in global telecommunications and computer networks; and the spread of information technology. This business-friendly environment has precipitated the entry of new firms from developed and developing countries, which has led to intensified global competition in most industries.

Convergence of consumer tastes for some products (refrigerators, automobiles, television sets, personal computers, VCRs, camcorders, etc.) has reinforced the standardization of products across national boundaries. Standardization of products provides companies with the opportunity to reduce unit production costs through economies of scale. There is still the simultaneous need to engage in product adaptation to make some products suitable to local and regional tastes. For example, refrigerators in Europe are half the size of those in the United States; and washing machines in Europe are side-loaded with a horizontal rotating drum, whereas those in the United States are top-loaded with an agitator action. Shortened product life cycles and the corresponding imperative to develop new and innovative products have propelled companies to search for new ideas and human capital throughout the world.

This process has led international companies to redesign the pattern by which they manage and organize their physical, financial, technological, and human assets worldwide. Through **complex integration strategies**, international companies are transforming their geographically dispersed affiliates and fragmented production, financial, and marketing systems into functionally integrated regional or global networks of affiliates.

Complex integration strategies are characterized by a dispersal of the value chain into discrete functions—component production, assembly, finance, research and development, distribution, and so on—and their location in the place where they can be best carried out in response to the overall goals and strategy of the firm as a whole. A foreign affiliate may be selected by the parent to perform functions for the international company as a whole (either by itself or in close interaction with other affiliates or the parent company) on the basis of a sophisticated intrafirm division of labor. For example, an affiliate in England may be responsible for research and development for the whole company, an affiliate in Switzerland for finance, and those in the United States and Belgium for marketing of products in North America and Europe respectively. Similarly, the production chain for the manufacture of an electric fan might be dispersed as follows: purchasing done by a central purchasing office in France; manufacturing of components in Mexico (frame), Germany (motor), and India (blades) for final assembly in Singapore (electric fan); and marketing in North America and Europe by affiliates in the United States and Belgium respectively.

Complex integration strategies create a network of linkages among the various affiliates including the parent. The linkages among the various units represent substantial unidirectional and multidirectional flows of technology, people, products, services, components, capital, and information. The distinction between the parent and affiliates becomes blurred in the corporate network as an increasing number of affiliates assume primary responsibilities for functions that are supposed to serve as inputs to other functions performed elsewhere in the network.

Complex integration represents the most advanced level of globalization of a company. Firms that have a complex integration strategy in place are not just a collection of discrete affiliates at home and abroad, but rather a system of interdependent affiliates in which each affiliate's functions are designed and carried out in response to a unified strategy for the company as a whole.

TABLE 6.1 **Integration Strategies and Antecedent Factors**

Integration Strategy	Type of Intrafirm Linkage	Degree of Integration	Environment

Stand-alone strategy
    Multidomestic orientation
    Polycentric firm
	Ownership, technology, intracompany trade in goods and services	Weak, self-contained affiliates	Host-country barriers; market entry allowed via direct investment

Simple integration strategy
    Early global orientation
    Ethnocentric firm
	Financial, technology, components, uni- or multidirectional	Strong at some links in the value chain, frequent outsourcing to independent contractors	Moderate financial, political, currency risks; significant differences in comparative advantages of countries; free trade

Complex integration strategy
    Later global and transnational orientations
    Geocentric firm
	All functions, multidirectional network	Strong linkages and interdependencies throughout value chain links	Free trade, trade blocs, convergence of consumer tastes, intense competition from global competitor

Merging Strategic Orientations and Functional Integration Strategies

Our discussion of (1) the global-multidomestic-transnational orientations and (2) the functional integration strategies discloses a clear overlap. To conclude our brief look at the different types of global strategies that a firm may employ in its international activities, Table 6.1 summarizes international orientations and integration strategies. It also integrates the roots of international strategy discussed at the beginning of this chapter. Finally, it illustrates the intrafirm linkages, degree of integration, and environmental characteristics most associated with each functional integration strategy.

Firm-Level Strategies for International Competitiveness

The global-multidomestic-transnational distinction is indeed at the heart of international strategic thinking. Thus these orientations connect throughout the remainder of this book. We have also identified the overlap and consistency with various integration strategies. A final piece of the international strategic discussion now focuses on three specific firm-level initiatives that must be identified: core competency leveraging, counterattack, and glocalization.

Core Competency Leveraging

Core competency leveraging is a strategy being used by companies that are gaining prominence in a variety of businesses. It is a strategy that is not readily apparent to their less perceptive competitors. The thrust here is to gain superiority by building on one or more core competencies. Fundamental to the concept of core competence is the recognition of the distinction among core competence, core product, and end products.

Core competence may be defined as the distinctive ability to excel in a key area, upon which a company can build a variety of businesses and develop new generations of products, some of which customers may need but have not yet imagined.[22] *Core products* are the intermediate linkages between core competencies and end products. They are the subassemblies or components that actually make significant additions to the value of the end products. To be in a position of world leadership, a company must be in a position of strength at all three levels: core competencies, core products, and end products. For example, Honda has developed core competence in engines and power-train technology that was physically embodied in its core product (the engine), which it skillfully incorporated in a variety of end products such as lawn mowers, generators, marine engines, motorcycles, and cars. At the core competence level, the goal is to attain state-of-the-art, world-class leadership in a key field. For example, Sony developed the capacity to miniaturize, and Canon's competencies are in 3-D technologies, optics, imaging, and microprocessor controls, which are used in computers, digital cameras, document scanners, and video camcorders.

At the core products level, the goal is to maximize world manufacturing share. This goal is achieved by manufacturing a core product for sale to both internal and external customers. For example, Briggs and Stratton focuses on the manufacture of engines that are used in lawnmowers, power washers, chainsaws, and generators by many other companies. Korean companies such as Goldstar and Samsung began by manufacturing VCRs for American and European consumer electronics companies. The objective of such supply relationships was to build core product leadership in key components such as diverse displays and semiconductors. Another strategic objective of these Korean companies is to prevent their potential American and European customer competitors from making manufacturing investments in the Korean companies' core products, and thus displacing them from value-creating activities.

Serving as a manufacturing base for other companies gives core product manufacturers an opportunity to build manufacturing share without the risk and expense of building downstream brand share. Product feedback received from buyer companies provides free and invaluable market research data on customer preferences and market needs. Such information is used by a core product manufacturer to improve the core product. Furthermore, this kind of information serves as a lever to develop the end product by itself and to enter the end product market independently. This strategy was used quite effectively by Japanese television makers such as Sony and Hitachi in their quest to enter the U.S. market. They first served as original equipment manufacturers (OEMs) of private-label, black-and-white television sets for American department stores. Subsequently, they used the experience and knowledge gained in the process to upgrade their presence in the United States from OEMs to independent marketers of color TV sets under their own brand names. More important, in doing so the Japanese companies managed to displace American TV manufacturers like RCA, GE, and Sylvania.

A dominant world manufacturing share in a core product may not necessarily mean an equally strong position in the market for end products. For example, Canon supposedly has a dominating world manufacturing share in desktop laser printer engines; however, its brand share in the laser printer business is actually quite small. Similarly, Matsushita has a huge market share worldwide in compressors, its core product. Its brand share in the air conditioner and refrigerator businesses, however, is negligible. Clearly, the strategic objective for obtaining the maximum possible manufacturing market share for core products is to generate revenue and customer feedback, which in turn can be used to improve and extend core competencies. The focus is on enhancing and replenishing a company's core competencies and leveraging them to later develop and market a variety of end products, with core products serving as their backbone.

Examples of companies that have effectively leveraged their core competencies are Casio, 3M, and Canon. Casio drew on its expertise in semiconductors and digital displays by producing calculators, small-screen television sets, musical instruments, and watches. The 3M Company combined competencies in substrates, coatings, and adhesives to produce Post-it Notes, magnetic tape, photographic film, pressure-sensitive tapes, and coated abrasives—quite a diversified product portfolio driven by only a few shared core competencies. Canon has leveraged its competencies in optics, imaging, and microprocessor controls to produce copiers, laser printers, cameras, and image scanners. Core competence is important because, in the short run, the quality of a company's product and its performance determine its competitiveness. In the long run, however, the global competitiveness of a company depends more on its ability to grow through internal development, licensing deals, or strategic alliances. Its core competencies, however, are what give birth to new generations of products, and at a rate faster than the competition.

Thus far, we have focused on technological core competence. However, companies can develop core competencies in a variety of functional areas. For example, the Maine-based catalogue sales retailer L.L. Bean's core competence is in logistics and distribution, and Philip Morris (Altria Group) is unbeatable in its ability to identify emerging market segments for consumer products, which it has leveraged in businesses other than cigarettes, like soft drinks, beer, and fast foods. Core competency may also be developed in other functions like purchasing, service after sales, product design, and advertising. For instance, the Italian company Benneton, retailer of sportswear and casual clothing, has a celebrated expertise in developing extremely successful and relatively inexpensive, albeit often controversial, advertising campaigns.

Counterattack

The typical response of U.S. companies to foreign competition in the home market was to assume that foreign companies, especially those from Japan and the Pacific Basin countries, were able to effectively compete in the U.S. market because of lower costs derived from cheap labor rates in their own countries. In response, U.S. companies **counterattacked** by establishing offshore assembly and manufacturing sites in Asia to lower their own production costs.[23] American companies also observed that the Japanese were taking advantage of lower costs from scale economies derived from production in large world-scale plants. In response, American companies followed suit and also established world-scale plants. However, such strategies did not prevent a market share decline in the U.S. market of American companies as Japanese companies continued to take over the market share. What the American companies did not recognize was that a strategy based on low labor costs was vulnerable to fluctuating exchange rates and rising labor costs. This phenomenon is exactly what has taken place in Japan. Wage rates there have risen significantly in the last three decades and are now high enough to be noncompetitive in comparison to wage rates in other Asian countries such as China, Malaysia, Thailand, and Sri Lanka. Moreover, the strategy of lowering production costs through scale advantages derived from large-scale plants also proved to be vulnerable to technological improvements in the production process brought about by such factors as robotics and computer-aided, flexible manufacturing.

With the increasing globalization of industries, international companies have come to realize that a competitive attack against a home market can be launched by foreign companies that, at the time of the attack, may have a relatively small presence in it. Today, global competition is characterized by a series of competitive attacks and counterattacks by global companies in each other's home and third-country markets. Companies that cannot engage in such battles are doomed to lose market share, both at home and abroad. For example, an American company that is attacked by a Japanese company cannot spend all its resources only on defending its home market, while the Japanese company faces no such threat in its own home market. The American company must be capable of attacking the Japanese company in the Japanese market or in a third-country market where the Japanese company is vulnerable. The Japanese aggressor, when attacked by the American defender on its (Japanese) home ground, is forced to divert resources to defend its home market and is thus averted from attacking the foreign American market. In actual military combat, a defender must be able to attack the enemy in the enemy's home territory in order to repel the enemy's attack. The same holds true in business warfare. To launch a counterattack, however, one must have the required "firepower," which, in business terms, is the cash flow to launch an attack.

Cash flows are needed to develop the various capabilities required to make an effective attack or counterattack. The types of capabilities needed are (1) channels of distribution through which to direct an attack, (2) investment in key core competencies, and (3) a wide range of products that can benefit from the same distribution channels. With these capabilities in place in major world markets, companies can engage in cross-subsidizing across countries and markets.

Cross-subsidization, identified in the matrices illustrated earlier in this chapter, involves the deployment of resources generated in one area or country for use in another location. For instance, using cash flows generated in Japan or elsewhere, a Japanese company can launch an attack on an American company in the U.S. market or in a third-country market in which the American company is weak. Such an attack might involve lowering the Japanese company's prices in the U.S. market just enough to squeeze the profit margins of the U.S. company. The objective here is to reduce the cash flows of the American company, and drain them away from activities such as marketing and research and development. Without channels of distribution in the foreign company's home market, the American company is in no position to cross-subsidize and counterattack. The American company is thus weakened and unable to make necessary improvements in its products or to launch expensive advertising and marketing campaigns. Consequently, the American company loses market share and the Japanese company then proceeds to raise its prices and increase its margins, which are, in turn, used to continue such attacks in other countries and markets.

Cash flows are also required to develop effective channels of distribution in major markets of the world. To be a global player in a global industry, a company must have an effective presence in three areas of the world—the United States, Europe, and Asia. Developing channels of distribution is an expensive endeavor for which enormous amounts of cash are needed. Cash flows are also vitally needed to develop core technologies and core competencies, which, as just discussed, are key requisites of a global company's competitive advantage. Companies that can generate such competencies can leverage them in the ways that were discussed earlier. Cash flows are also needed to develop a large enough portfolio of contiguous products that can be funneled through the existing distribution channels to utilize the channels to their maximum capacity. Examples of contiguous products are cereals, soups, and frozen foods, which can be marketed through a company-owned distribution channel in a region.

Each of the above activities, carried out on a global scale, requires cash flows. These activities, in turn, generate necessary cash flows, and the cycle of cross-subsidization, attack, and counterattack continues on a global scale. Companies that do not perceive the strategic intent of global companies playing the game of cross-subsidization are paving the path to their own extinction. The strategic intent of global competitors is to wage battles worldwide. They want not only to capture world volume but also to generate the cash flow necessary to support the creation of new core technologies; enhance core competencies; establish strong distribution channels; acquire or build world-class, efficient plants; and achieve global brand recognition through massive advertising and marketing campaigns. A historical example of an effective counterattack strategy is the invasion by Eastman Kodak of the home market of Japan's Fuji Photo Film.[24] Kodak launched the attack against Fuji in response to Fuji's attack on Kodak's lucrative markets in America and Europe, where for decades Kodak had maintained a dominant market share in the color film business. Fuji's attack shrank Kodak's margins and forced it to cut prices. Realizing that it faced a global challenge from Fuji that would only grow stronger, Kodak struck back and invaded its rival's home market. The results were dramatically favorable for Kodak, whose sales jumped sixfold within a few years. It put Fuji on the defensive; Fuji's domestic margins were squeezed, and some of Fuji's best executives were recalled to Tokyo. In Kodak's estimation, its invasion of the Japanese market forced Fuji to divert its resources from overseas in order to defend its home market, where it had enjoyed a commanding 60 percent share of the market in color film.

The implementation of a counterattack strategy has several critical implications for the management of a global company. For instance, to assist a parent company in a global counterattack, the foreign affiliates in the company have to relinquish much of their autonomy to the parent company or to divisional management. The relationship between and among the affiliates and the parent company has to be one of resource interdependence rather than independence. The strategies and implementation plans of each affiliate have to be coordinated with those of the parent company and the other affiliates. This coordination is necessary so that resources required for launching offensive or preemptive cross-subsidization strikes against competitors can be marshaled from the most appropriate sources within the global network of the company. The managerial philosophy underlying a counterattack strategy is that in a global industry, competition in an affiliate country does not always emanate from other local companies; rather, it can come from affiliates of foreign companies that are members of powerful networks of global companies having worldwide access to resources. Therefore, a foreign affiliate left to fend for itself with only its own country-based resources would be no match for an aggressive global company's attack without help from sister affiliates or the parent company. Collaboration among the affiliates and the parent company in the sharing of resources through cross-subsidization is the only way to deflect an attack by a global company against a weak affiliate.

At the parent-company level, divisional management and strategic business units (SBUs) have to abandon a "my division" or "my business unit" attitude and think more in terms of interdivisional and cross-SBU relationships. Like foreign affiliates, they, too, have to collaborate and share resources among themselves and seek to agree on, and implement, strategies that add value and strength to the company as a global whole.

Investments abroad in manufacturing, research and development, marketing, and other functional areas have to be made for strategic reasons, such as establishing a beachhead in major markets of the world or in the home market of a foreign competitor. Such investments are based primarily on their strategic importance to any future offensive or defensive counterattack strategies, and not necessarily on financial considerations, such as return on investment or profitability.

Glocalization

In core competency leveraging and counterattack, the parent company clearly plays a central role in coordinating its network of globally dispersed affiliates. The parent company makes the network operate as one integrated, collective global unit. Global companies, however, must be careful that, in their zealous pursuit of an effective global strategy, they do not neglect managerial initiative at lower levels in the organizational hierarchy, especially at the regional and subsidiary levels. Phatak coined the word **glocalization** to represent a firm-level strategic response that parallels the industry-level, total firm transnational orientation. Glocalization is simply thinking globally but acting locally. It includes an optimal mix of parental control where it counts, and local initiative at regional and subsidiary levels. This structural balance has proved to be most fruitful for well-managed global companies.[25] More recently, the following thoughts have been offered to further delineate Phatak's glocalization:

> The introduction of the terms "glocal strategy" and "glocalization" may be a compromise to improve the present usage of the term global strategy. The glocal strategy approach reflects the aspirations of a global strategy approach, while the necessity for local adaptations and tailoring of business activities is simultaneously acknowledged. The "glocal strategy" concept comprises local, international, multinational, and global strategy approaches.[26]

A successful strategy incorporates the glocalization of the following interrelated elements: management, foreign affiliates, exports, products, and production.[27]

Glocalization of Management   Adopting a global strategy that does not stifle local initiative requires a delicate balancing act. It often means giving regional and subsidiary managers the freedom to develop their own implementation plans for products, marketing, financing, and production that are consistent with local political, economic, legal, and cultural demands. For example, Levi Strauss & Company, the jeans maker, maintains tight headquarters control where it matters most. As a company that cherishes brand identity and quality, Levi's has organized several foreign manufacturing subsidiaries rather than relying on a patchwork of licensees that are hard to control. It has also exported its pioneering use of computers to track sales and manufacturing and, in so doing, keep a step ahead of fashion trends. Levi's also allows local managers to make decisions about adapting products to suit local tastes. In Brazil, Levi's local managers make decisions regarding distribution. For example, local initiative and knowledge of the market enabled Levi's to establish a chain of over 400 *Levi's Only* stores, some of them in tiny, rural towns in Brazil's fragmented market. Levi's approach represents a slogan that is symbolic of what glocalization stands for: "Be global, act local."

In the Sony Corporation, apart from the long-term strategy handed down from Tokyo, regional managers make all their own investment and product decisions on the spot. Top managers from Sony's subsidiaries around the world meet twice a year to hammer out the basic details of the company's operations.[28] Insiders say that this international-top-meeting arrangement is the main reason for Sony's ability to respond to market changes and launch new products so swiftly.

A glocalization of management philosophy is also evident in Toshiba and Matsushita Electric Industrial Company, which have delegated decision-making authority to regional headquarters. Toshiba has a tripolar regional management structure for Asia, Europe, and the United States. Each area manager has decision-making authority for manufacturing, sales, and some research and development. At Matsushita Electric, which has regional headquarters for Asia, Europe, and the United States based in Singapore, London, and New Jersey, respectively, most local decisions are now made locally, and the three top regional heads are all members of Matsushita Electric's board of directors. Again, each region has manufacturing, marketing, and product-related research and development capability, and Matsushita plans to develop some regional basic research facilities as well.[29]

Glocalization of Foreign Affiliates   Strong presence in a foreign market requires the physical presence of manufacturing facilities in the market itself. Governments are making market entry easier for companies, provided that company management agrees to base production of the product in the foreign country as soon as possible. Companies are also realizing that, as good corporate citizens, they ought to make a significant contribution to the economic development and social welfare of their host countries. Transferring production technology to the host country and increasing the ratio of locally produced items in the production process or the final product are two ways to contribute to a host country's economic well-being. Training and developing local suppliers of components and subassemblies enhances the technological base of a nation. Such a transfer of technology could be brought about by entering into technical collaboration agreements with local partners, forming joint ventures with local capital, or establishing a wholly owned subsidiary that is owned by the parent company.

The economic and political conditions in a country or region, as well as market size and the capabilities of the local partner, often dictate the mode of collaboration. For example, Japanese manufacturers have chosen to enter European markets mainly through joint ventures because of a preference, in Europe, for such collaborations and the hostility toward wholly owned Japanese plants exhibited by European governments. In the United States, Japanese companies have shown a preference for wholly owned plants, although they have also established several joint ventures with American companies.

Glocalization of Exports   Using foreign production plants as export bases to third-country markets is yet another way to become a "local" company in a foreign country. The Japanese have been exporting U.S.-made Japanese automobiles back to Japan and to European markets. Similar strategies have been adopted by global companies which export from developing countries in Asia and other parts of the world. Glocalization of exports is the outcome of a deliberate strategy of helping host countries earn foreign exchange from exports of products and becoming a good citizen of the host country. The benefits accrued from goodwill may far outweigh the added costs of exports from a country that may not be the most suitable from a purely economic measure.

Glocalization of Products   Should a company standardize its product or service throughout the world by selling the same product without making variations to suit differences in local taste and use? Or should the product or service be tailored and customized to comply with local taste and use? This issue has been debated ad infinitum, and the answer to the question is that, to the extent that standardization is possible, a company should attempt it. Some products and services can be standardized globally, such as fax machines and telephones. On the other side of the scale, however, are products such as coffee and soups, which must be modified to make them more palatable to the tastes of people in various countries and cultures.

Companies are resolving this dilemma by realizing that some products have certain core technologies, subassemblies, or components that can be standardized on a worldwide basis, while other parts or configurations of the same product require adaptation to local conditions. For example, Whirlpool Corporation saw a growing market in India for washing machine sales to the growing number of middle-class, two-income families in that country. The washing machines sold in Europe and America, however, were not suited to wash the traditional, five-yard-long saris worn by Indian women. Whirlpool formed a joint venture with an Indian partner to produce and market a Western-style automatic washing machine that is compact enough to fit into Indian homes and which incorporates specially designed agitators that will not tangle saris. Variations of the same machine, internally dubbed the "World Washer," are also built and sold in Brazil and Mexico. In the aftermath of the glocalization-of-exports strategy discussed above, Whirlpool exports these machines from factories in those countries to other Asian and Latin American markets. Except for minor variations in controls, the three barebones washers are nearly identical; they all handle only 11 pounds of wash, which is about half the capacity of the typical U.S. model.[30] Whirlpool illustrates the slogan of product glocalization, which is: Standardize worldwide what you can, and adapt what you cannot.

PRACTICAL INSIGHT 6.3

CHEESE KATSU BURGER ANYONE?

For Toshihiro Imagawa, a recent breakfast under the Golden Arches consisted of two rice balls and a cup of what you might call McMiso soup.

"So finally, it's come this far," says the 23-year-old fast-food fan, sampling items from McDonald's newest breakfast offerings here. Squirting concentrated miso paste into a cup of hot water, he wonders: "Do Americans know about this stuff?"

Perhaps not, but rising competition on Japan's fast-food front is forcing McDonald's Corp. to stretch its imagination beyond the Egg McMuffin. Local rivals are bombarding the market with increasingly exotic menus, such as rice burgers (which sandwich shredded beef between grilled rice in the shape of a bun) and seaweed soup. In particular, the Mos Burger chain is putting McDonald's—Japan's biggest fast-food company—on the defensive.

"Consumers are now looking for the homemade touch, the Japanese taste," says Toshio Hayashi, a McDonald's spokesman. So the company is fighting back by launching more new items than any other chain, including such localized fare as steamed Chinese dumplings, curry with rice and roast pork-cutlet burgers oozing with melted cheese.

Last year, McDonald's added fried rice to its menu, four years after Mos Burger introduced its Rice Burgers in 1986.

Also last year, McDonald's came up with a Cheese Katsu Burger, which encloses cheese in the traditional Japanese roast pork cutlet, drenched in the traditional katsu sauce and topped with shredded cabbage. But that was patterned after Mos Burger's Mos Roast Katsu Burger, which hit the menu in 1988. KFC, meanwhile, deep-fried the chicken cutlet, topped it with cabbage and splashed it with teriyaki sauce.

In the meantime, fast-food chains are trying new ways to increase profits. KFC, which bought Pizza Hut's Japanese operation, will soon start delivery of Japanese-style box lunches as well. McDonald's hopes to set the scene for big outlets—seating 250, compared with 100 in most standard outlets—by building them next to Toys 'R' Us and Blockbuster video-rental stores, both of which the company or an affiliate has a stake in.

Japan's fast-food chains say they are also continuing their experiments in the kitchen. But they will take a while longer to win over the likes of 22-year-old Kento Yamada, who would rather stick to the good old Big Mac.

Source: From *The Wall Street Journal, Online,* May 29, 1992, by Yumiko Ono. Copyright © 1992 by Dow Jones & Co Inc. Reproduced with permission of Dow Jones & Co. Inc. via Copyright Clearance Center.

Fast-food chains have given up on the strict code of offering the same menu globally. In response to local cultural demands, McDonald's has vastly modified its menu in its restaurants in India. It does not offer its traditional beef hamburger because the majority Hindu population will not eat beef. For some time, McDonald's India offered instead the lamburger, which was made from lamb meat, but that item was temporarily dropped because of the customers' suspicion that it could contain beef. The company now offers such offbeat menu items as the Chicken Maharaja Mac; Paneer Salsa Wrap made from ricotta cheese; McVeggie, a vegetable burrito; and the McAllo, a potato patty burger. McDonald's has made similar glocalization moves in other countries, including Japan, described in Practical Insight 6.3.

Glocalization of Production   Companies are splitting the production process and farming out parts of it to different countries. They are doing so in order to exploit the advantages of lower costs derived from scale economies, international specialization (where some countries are better at doing certain things than others), and locational advantages such as proximity to markets, cheap labor, freedom from significant political risk, and local incentives such as tax holidays and government subsidies. Japanese automobile companies have targeted Asian countries for the expansion of their production activities because of the long-term growth potential of markets there. For example, one result of the Japanese expansion is the beginning of a parts-supply network that spans Southeast Asia. To achieve economies of scale, Japan's carmakers produce different parts in different countries. Nissan, for example, wants to concentrate on production of diesel engines in Thailand, mechanical parts in Indonesia, wire harnesses in the Philippines, and clutches and electrical parts in Malaysia. Toyota has also invested in facilities to support a similar parts production program.

The farming out of production to different countries also extends to finished products. For instance, a company that produces a variety of models of the same product might assign a subsidiary in one country to specialize in the production of one model and a subsidiary in yet another country to specialize in a second model. The two subsidiaries then export to each other the models they produce. In this way, both subsidiaries have two models to market in their respective regions, but each is responsible for the production of only one of them. This strategy is common in the global automobile industry, and General Motors and Ford already practice it in Europe.[31]

Summary

This chapter begins Section 2 of the book, our discussion of the strategic initiatives international firms use in response to the changing environments we discussed in Section 1. We presented Perlmutter's ethnocentric, polycentric, and geocentric attitudes, which the international firm may exhibit, and offered a three-dimensional framework for classifying international firms on the basis of those three attitudinal orientations and the functional and geographical orientations to integration strategies described in the chapter.

We identified various decision processes, including the analytical hierarchy process, that firms may use when they look to overseas markets and international locations for production. We then introduced the portfolio-analysis framework to help the firm manage its various international subsidiaries. Subsequently, the implications of global-multidomestic-transnational mindsets were linked into the discussion.

We also used the concept of the value chain to illustrate the functional and geographic scope of integration strategies available to the international firm in responding to different environmental contexts. Stand-alone strategies, based on a high degree of autonomy for operating units, require the least amount of centralized coordination. Simple and complex integration strategies offer more opportunity to capitalize on global economies of scale and scope, but they require greater degrees of coordination and control among the different subunits.

The chapter concluded with specific strategic initiatives that international firms must undertake to sustain their respective competitive advantages. These include core competency leveraging, counterattack, and glocalization.

Key Terms and Concepts

complex integration strategy, *204*
core competency leveraging, *205*
counterattack, *207*
ethnocentrism, *186*

geocentrism, *186*
global orientation, *197*
glocalization, *209*
international orientation, *196*
internationalization, *187*
multidomestic orientation, *198*

polycentrism, *186*
simple integration strategy, *202*
stand-alone strategy, *201*
transnational orientation, *198*
value chain, *198*

Discussion Questions

1. Pick an industry and develop a list of factors that you believe are critical to consider when deciding to expand overseas.
2. Why will implementation of the transnational approach require more of a firm's resources?
3. Why is the value chain important to understand in relation to a firm's international strategic approach?
4. Link the levels of integration strategies to (a) ethnocentrism, polycentrism, and geocentrism and (b) the global, multidomestic, and transnational approaches.
5. Give examples of the various ways a firm can glocalize.

Minicase

CIENA's Globalization

CIENA'S CORE COMPETENCY AND GROWTH

In the early nineties, CIENA began to capitalize on the changes in U.S. rules relating to telecom carriers. The firm introduced equipment using disruptive technology of dense wave division multiplexing (DWDM) for long-range transmission of digital data. In very simple terms, DWDM is multiplexing signals using different colors of light over a single fiber pair.

This technology increased the data transmission capacity of telecom carriers beyond imagination. It enabled transmission of 196 channels over a fiber pair with each channel carrying 10 gigabytes per second (GB/sec) (OC-192) of digital data; this is many times more than the size of a computer's hard drive and can provide millions of phone calls all on the same fiber pair. This paved the way for development of CIENA's Optical Switch. This switch has been very well received by the telecom carrier industry. It saves both millions of dollars and floor space for the carriers. Until now, due to technological limitations, carriers had been using older telecom equipment like the add drop multiplexers (ADMs).

CIENA continues to innovate not only by offering new hardware, but also by offering complete solutions for telecom carriers to enable them to upgrade their networks and offer cost-efficient solutions to their customers. In doing so, software plays a major role by efficiently utilizing the hardware and automating manual tasks.

CIENA was recently added to the Standard & Poor's 500; yet that is only a part of the story. It is the change in the size of its hardware and software R&D teams that is worth noting. As of April 2003, the senior vice president responsible for hardware had 269 engineers and managers while the senior vice president responsible for software had 480 direct reports. The reason for this increase in software team numbers is that software improves the efficiency and reliability of the deployed hardware. Software also allows the carrier to manage (monitor and control) hundreds of network elements deployed across the continental United States and Europe from a single location.

Using this ability to control from a single location, carriers can now provision and monitor circuits for their customers in a few seconds, rather than the hours and even days required in the past. These circuits can originate from a building in one city and terminate at a building in the same city or in a different state or country. The carriers love this ability; it enables them to save huge amounts of money on training and personnel expenses. Consequently, they can now pass on some of the savings to their customer, which increases revenue and allows the carriers to competitively price their offerings.

In 2002, British Telecom (BT) signed CIENA to supply equipment and solutions for its next-generation network. Before signing, they approached AT&T to observe firsthand CIENA's capabilities. AT&T uses CIENA's switches and metro transmission equipment. An AT&T executive demonstrated to his BT counterpart the efficiency and cost savings achieved because of CIENA's innovations. He took the BT executive to a nearly deserted operations center and told him that the reason for the empty chairs is that they have been replaced by CIENA's software.

DRIVERS FOR GLOBALIZATION: REVENUE AND PROFIT GROWTH

The dot-com boom of the late 1990s brought into play the need for increased data transmission. That in turn brought about the birth of many new telecom carriers, and since they were starting from scratch they bought a lot of equipment from CIENA. The traditional carrier already had networks in place and hence orders from them were limited. Also, these carriers wanted to continue to use their traditional suppliers.

The dot-com boom is history and those new carriers have either gone under or are struggling. But the traditional carriers have realized the benefits of CIENA's solutions and now buy more from CIENA. A few of CIENA's traditional telecom carrier customers are AT&T, BT, Sprint, Qwest, and Verizon. But the traditional carriers are not spending as much compared to a few years ago and the revenue from the new carriers has all dried up.

Experiences in Europe have shown that the carriers there are more resistant to change and continue to buy from traditional suppliers like Alcatel, Marconi, Ericsson, Nokia, and Nortel. Currently, there is an ongoing initiative with French Telecom and Telia but orders from them and other European carriers are expected to be limited. Additionally now there are price threats from companies like Huawei, which have started to offer products in the transmission segment. In comparison to CIENA, Huawei is based in China and has very low R&D and manufacturing costs. CIENA continues to enjoy a great lead in the switching segment. But this competitive threat pressures CIENA to look for ways to cut its cost and increase its market share.

To reduce costs and to increase its market, CIENA is considering the following:

1. Reduce costs by moving some of its software development operations to India.
2. Aggressively expand into China for revenue enhancement and also to further prevent the expansion of companies such as Huawei into the U.S. and European markets by competing with them on their home turf (similar to the Kodak and Fuji situation in Japan). And once substantial sales are realized in China, establish a manufacturing base in China.

In the following sections, India's emergence as a location of choice for software development and the benefits offered to companies by regional (state) and central governments to establish and operate from India will be analyzed. In addition to outsourcing issues, CIENA must also address how it wants to enter China and, specifically, how to ensure that its mode of entry protects its proprietary product technology. There is the specific need to explore the area of legal risk in China and discuss why creating a wholly owned subsidiary makes the most sense for CIENA.

INDIA'S EMERGENCE AS A PREFERRED LOCATION FOR SOFTWARE DEVELOPMENT

Due to the economic liberalization in the early nineties, India has continued to see an increase in multinational companies setting up software development centers within its borders. Initially this growth was presumed to be dot-com driven; however, other factors also explain the rise of software development in India. Listed below are a few internationally renowned technical companies that have expanded into India in the post-dot-com era for advanced/innovative research and development:

EDS opened a new offshore facility in 2003.

Siemens located its global applications development function in 2003.

Oracle chose India as a key overseas hub in 2002.

Ford opened an IT hub in 2001.

Since 2000, Microsoft, IBM, and Lucent all have expanded their existing Indian facilities.

The Indian laws are continuing to improve providing protection against illegal copying of intellectual property; this makes India more lucrative for businesses thinking of outsourcing work to India. Also, the policies of the U.S. government continue to favor software development in India, having few restrictions regarding movement of U.S. software initiatives into India. The Indian education system puts a lot of stress on science and technology. A 2002/2003 report on CBS's "60 Minutes" talked about the Indian Institute of Technology. It demonstrates the quality and capabilities of technical graduates from India. In the late 1990s, a great number of IT workers were needed in the United States and a large number of them came from India. Since the bust of the dot-com era, many of these workers have returned to India. Being trained in U.S. methods of operation, they are valuable assets for U.S. companies in India.

Another attraction for U.S. companies is the salary in India. For the same qualifications, Indian salaries were nearly 10 times less than U.S. salaries in 2003. Given the huge population and education system that stresses math and science in India, every year there are a significant number of technical graduates to choose from for companies setting up in India. Last, English is widely spoken and accepted in India. Not only is English the medium of instruction in technical colleges and universities, but it is the accepted language for interbusiness and business-to-government interactions. It is also used widely within subsidiaries in India and for those subsidiaries' interactions with headquarter in the United States. In general, when considering expansion to India, the pros and cons may be summarized as follows. The pros are:

1. Lower labor cost for same levels of qualifications.
2. English as a prevalent language.
3. A large pool of qualified hi-tech labor.
4. Government subsidies and tax breaks.
   a. Software Technology Parks of India (STPI) certification to provide a 10-year tax holiday on revenues if the product is marked 100 percent export from India.
   b. No import tax on factors of production such as computers and network equipment.
   c. Subsidies on floor space.
   d. Subsidies and promise of continued power.
   e. Subsidies on telephone charges.

The cons are:

1. Weak antipiracy laws.
2. Changes in government policies.
   a. In its 2002–2003 budget, the government imposed a 10 percent tax on STPI exempt exports.
   b. The costs of various factors of production (floor space, telecom charges, power charges) can increase if the government subsidies are reduced or eliminated.
3. Cost of facilities.
   a. Telecom and electricity, if not subsidized, can become very expensive.
   b. Good office locations with air-conditioned floors are expensive.
4. Hidden labor costs.
   a. 13 months salary. It is customary to pay one month's salary as bonus, which is not tied to the performance of the company.
   b. Overhead of 20 to 25 percent relating to benefits.

The Indian government is going ahead with its economic liberalization programs. It is expected that with the privatization of telecom and power companies the costs for both will become comparable to or lower than those in the United States and subsidies will not be required. The tax breaks will continue to be available to global companies, to attract them to continue to invest in India. The reason is that these investments create employment that in return creates a tax base for the government. The exports of software helps the Indian government balance the imports it needs to improve the infrastructure of the country to support the overall economic development of the country. Additionally, the benefit for business because of this is the improvement in quality of labor and factors of production. But with overall economic improvements the costs of labor will go up too. As the income levels increase, the purchasing power of people in India will increase, which will in turn make India a lucrative market for the products of these foreign firms. Increased revenue from sales will be much more than increased labor costs.

CIENA'S PROPOSED ENTRY INTO CHINA AND INTELLECTUAL PROPERTY ISSUES

A second issue is how CIENA should proceed into China. What is China's legal environment like? How are intellectual property rights (IPRs) enforced? Clearly, competitive threats exist. The aforementioned Chinese rival Huawei Technologies Company has produced products "similar" to CIENA's product line. CIENA cites patent infringements by Huawei. In January 2003, Cisco, another high-tech firm, sued Huawei, charging that the company had copied and misappropriated Cisco software, copied copyrighted Cisco manuals, and infringed Cisco patents. A U.S. federal judge temporarily blocked Huawei from distributing software and user manuals related to Cisco software or having employees familiar with that software develop similar products. Will the same thing happen when CIENA begins selling its products in China? What are the business risks?

Intellectual property refers to products of the mind, ideas (e.g., books, music, software, designs, technological know-how). Patents, copyrights, and trademarks can protect intellectual property. The patent protects the owner for a limited period, generally 20 years in this industry. The owner of a U.S. patent can stop anyone from making, selling, or offering for sale the invention in the United States. In addition, a U.S. patent owner can stop anyone from importing unauthorized copies of the invention into the United States. However, U.S. patent rights stop at the American border. An inventor cannot use a U.S. patent to stop someone from making, selling, or using the invention in another country. To do that, American inventors must acquire patent rights in that country and rely on rules of reciprocity in international treaties. Reciprocity means that when an inventor from Country A applies for a patent in Country B, the inventor will be treated in the same manner as inventors living in Country B. This reciprocal treatment extends only to inventors who live in nations that have signed the treaty.

Trade Related Aspects of Intellectual Property Rights (TRIPS) is an agreement among members of the World Trade Organization (WTO) to enforce stricter intellectual property regulations, including granting and enforcing patents lasting at least 20 years and copyrights lasting 50 years. China has committed to full compliance with the TRIPS agreement upon its year 2001 admission to the WTO. Chinese leaders have acknowledged that protection of patents, copyrights, and trademarks is needed to promote a knowledge-based economy. China has completed a revised patent law and is now reviewing and revising its trademark and copyright laws to ensure consistency with the TRIPS requirements. In spite of steady, significant progress in improving its intellectual property legal and regulatory regime, IPR protection in China remains weak. Trademark and copyright violations are blatant and widespread. While Chinese officials are increasing enforcement efforts, IPR violations, including growing exports of counterfeit products, continue to outpace enforcement. Enforcement of existing IPR laws is uneven and is sometimes impeded by local interests. The Business Software Alliance estimates that more than 90 percent of business software used in China is pirated. China's criminal sanctions against IPR violations are seldom used, in part because of restrictions on types of admissible evidence and cumbersome procedures.

Combating IPR violations in China is a long-term, multifaceted undertaking. China has established special IPR courts in all provinces and major cities. Judges in Chinese courts are charged with fact-finding and have greater discretion in the adjudication of cases than those in the United States. However, the lack of legal training of many trial court judges undermines the effectiveness of these courts. Laws and regulations in China tend to be far more general than in other countries. This vagueness allows Chinese courts and officials to apply them flexibly, which results in inconsistencies.

Source: Written by Sanjay Kumar, Dena Lorenzi, and Roger Kashlak, 2003.

QUESTIONS FOR CIENA TO CONSIDER

1. Should CIENA look to move software development operations into India?
2. Should CIENA pursue the Chinese market, establish production facilities there for export purposes, or do both?
3. How can CIENA protect its intellectual property in each country?

Notes

1. Howard W. Perlmutter, "The Tortuous Evolution of the Multinational Corporation," *Columbia Journal of World Business* 3, no.1 (1969), pp. 9–18.
2. J. Johansson, *Global Marketing: Foreign Entry, Local Marketing and Global Management* (New York: Irwin/McGraw-Hill, 2000); G. S. Yip, "Global Strategy . . . in a World of Nations?" *Sloan Management Review,* Autumn 1989, pp. 29–41.
3. T. Saaty, *The Analytical Hierarchy Process* (New York: McGraw-Hill, 1980).
4. S. T. Cavusgil and S. Zou, "Marketing Strategy–Performance Relationship: An Investigation of the Empirical Link in Export Market Ventures," *Journal of Marketing* 58, no. 1 (1994), pp. 1–21.
5. A. Gupta and V. Govindarajan; *Global Strategy and Organization* (New York: John Wiley & Sons, 2004).
6. C. Prahalad and Y. Doz, *The Multinational Mission: Balancing Local Demands and Global Vision* (New York: Free Press, 1987).
7. K. Roth, D. Schweiger, and A. Morrison, "Global Strategy Implementation at the Business Unit Level: Operational Capabilities and Administrative Mechanisms," *Journal of International Business Studies* 22, no. 3 (1991), pp. 369–402.
8. T. Hout, M. Porter, and E. Rudden, "How Global Companies Win Out," *Harvard Business Review,* September/October 1982, pp. 98–108.

9. Y. Doz and C. Prahalad, "Patterns of Strategic Control within Multinational Corporations," *Journal of International Business Studies* 15, no. 3 (1984), pp. 55–72.

10. Michael E. Porter, *Competitive Strategy: Techniques to Analyzing Industries and Competitors* (The Free Press: New York, 1980).

11. Doz and Prahalad, "Patterns of Strategic Control."

12. K. Roth and A. Morrison, "An Empirical Analysis of the Integration–Responsiveness Framework in Global Industries," *Journal of International Business Studies* 21, no. 4 (1990), pp. 541–564.

13. S. Ghoshal, "Global Strategy: An Organizing Framework," *Strategic Management Journal* 8 (1987), pp. 428–448.

14. S. Chatterjee and M. Lubatkin, "Corporate Mergers, Stockholder Diversification and Changes in Systematic Risk," *Strategic Management Journal* 11 (1990), pp. 256–280.

15. C. Bartlett and S. Ghoshal, *Managing across Borders. The Transnational Solution* (Boston: Harvard Business School Press, 1989).

16. C. Bartlett and S. Ghoshal, "Organizing for Worldwide Effectiveness: The Transnational Solution," *California Management Review,* Autumn 1988, pp. 54–74.

17. R. Kashlak, "Establishing Financial Targets for Joint Ventures in Emerging Countries: A Conceptual Model," *Journal of International Management* 4, no. 4 (1998), pp. 241–258.

18. M. Porter, *Competitive Advantage* (The Free Press: New York, 1985), p. 11.

19. M. Porter, *On Competition* (Boston: Harvard Business School Press, 1998), p. 6.

20. Michael E. Porter, "Changing Patterns of International Competition," *California Management Review* 28, no. 2 (1986), pp. 9ff.

21. Gupta and Govindarajan, *Global Strategy and Organization.*

22. C. K. Prahalad and G. Hamel, "The Core Competence of the Corporation," *Harvard Business Review,* May/June 1990, pp. 79–91.

23. G. Hamel and C. K. Prahalad, "Do You Really Have a Global Strategy," *Harvard Business Review,* July/August 1985, pp. 139–148.

24. "The Revenge of Big Yellow," *The Economist,* November 10, 1990, pp. 66–68.

25. A. Phatak, *International Management: Concept and Cases* (Cincinnati: Southwestern Publishing, 1997).

26. G. Svensson, "Glocalization of Business Activities: A Glocal Strategy Approach," *Management Decision* 39, no. 1 (2001), pp. 6–22.

27. Phatak, *International Management: Concept and Cases.*

28. Nicholas Valery, "Consumer Electronics Survey," *The Economist,* April 13, 1991, p. 16.

29. "The Goal Is Genuine Internationalism," *BusinessWeek,* July 16, 1990, p. 81.

30. David Woodruff, "A Little Machine that Won't Shred a Sari," *BusinessWeek,* June 3, 1991, p. 100.

31. Phatak, *International Management: Concept and Cases.*

CHAPTER SEVEN

Modes of Entry into Foreign Markets

Chapter Learning Objectives

After completing this chapter, you should be able to:

- Understand the different modes of entry into foreign markets.
- List the advantages, disadvantages, and risks in various entry modes.
- Explain why control of foreign operations is important for an international company.
- Distinguish between equity-based and non-equity-based control mechanisms.
- Understand the nonequity entry modes such as licensing, franchising, and management service contracts, and their differences.
- Describe the factors that influence the choice of entry modes.

Opening Case: Starbucks' Overseas Expansion Is Running into Trouble

When Starbucks Corp. opened its first Japanese cafe in Tokyo's fashionable Ginza shopping district in 1996, it was an overnight smash. Today, with 467 Starbucks stores—117 opened last year alone—Japan boasts Starbucks' biggest foray outside the U.S. And it is the centerpiece of the company's critical overseas expansion strategy. Trouble is, after just two profitable years, Starbucks is no longer making money in Japan. On May 20, Starbucks' Japanese business, a joint venture with the tea-shop and interior-goods chain Sazaby Inc., announced an annual loss of $3.9 million on revenues of $467 million.

It isn't just Japan. From Zurich to Tel Aviv, Starbucks' overseas expansion is running into trouble. Now operating in 30 countries beyond the U.S. and Canada, Starbucks cafés have encountered a host of problems, from high startup costs to stiff competition, and, in many cases, resistance to the Starbucks experience. While it has scored big in the U.S. as a hip purveyor of better coffee, it is often seen abroad, especially by European café-goers, as an overpriced imitation of the real thing. To date, Starbucks' 1,532 overseas stores, which account for 23% of its stores, yet only 9% of sales, are a net money loser.

The lukewarm overseas performance is a setback for Starbucks Chairman Howard Schultz, who had been counting on foreign expansion to keep growth percolating once the torrid pace of U.S. expansion cools down. That hasn't happened yet. For the first half of 2003, net earnings increased 31%, to $130 million, while sales jumped 23%, to $2 billion. But with a Starbucks seemingly at every other intersection in America, Schultz knows the chain will eventually run out of room in the U.S.

Yet overseas expansion has been tricky. Unlike in the United States, Starbucks faces big rivals in Europe and Asia. In Britain, where Starbucks has about 330 locations, Chief Financial Officer Michael

Casey says tough competition is the problem. Rivals often charge lower prices: In London, a Starbucks tall latte sells for $2.93, while the same drink goes for $2.12 at the rival Caffe Nero Group. In Germany, imitators have saturated Frankfurt and Berlin with Starbucks-like coffee bars. Likewise in Japan, coffee sippers are increasingly finding their caffeine fix elsewhere. Tokyo secretary Ritsuko Oomi started frequenting the Ginza Starbucks in 1996. Now, she says, "I never go to Starbucks if I can help it. The coffee tastes artificial." Her favorite brand now: Tully's Coffee Corp., a Seattle rival. She has company: Starbucks' same-store sales in Japan fell 17% last year.

Another reason Starbucks hasn't been as successful abroad as in the U.S. may be the complex series of joint ventures Schultz agreed to in order to expand quickly. While the company gets a slice of revenues and profits as well as licensing fees for supplying its coffee, it has been harder than in the U.S. to control costs. One profit killer: real estate and labor costs far higher than those in the U.S.

Can Starbucks freshen its performance overseas? It's a double tall order, but doable. Starbucks execs insist the international rollout, after making adjustments, is on track. The company bought out partners in its troubled Swiss and Austrian stores. It's closed six unprofitable Starbucks in Israel and cut international expansion by 50 stores, to 400 this year. Says CFO Casey: "We're meeting our financial targets." But some industry experts disagree. They say rethinking the joint-venture strategy is key. The company also needs to be more competitive on price. Says Mitchell J. Speiser, an analyst at Lehman Brothers: "The expansion strategy internationally is not bulletproof as it is in the U.S."

The company has time to get things right. Starbucks is nearly debt-free and has more than $300 million in annual free cash flow, part of which it can use to finance its overseas ambitions. Casey predicts Starbucks' international business will turn a profit in fiscal 2004. But there's a big difference between crawling back into the black and driving future growth. And that's a bitter brew for Starbucks to swallow.

Source: Reprinted from S. Holmes, with I. Kunii, J. Ewing and K. Capell, "For Starbucks, There's No Place Like Home: Its Overseas Expansion Is Running Into Trouble," June 9, 2003 issue of *BusinessWeek* by special permission. Copyright © 2003 by The McGraw-Hill Companies, Inc.

Discussion Questions

1. Why did Starbucks choose international joint ventures to expand overseas?
2. Starbucks may expand internationally through franchising as well as through wholly owned operations. What are the pros and cons of each of these modes of entry relative to the joint venture approach?

Environmental Influences on the Foreign Entry Mode Decision

The choice of foreign entry mode has been identified for over two decades as one of the most crucial decisions associated with a firm's international strategy. From Wind and Perlmutter in 1977[1] to contemporary researchers (e.g., Ekeledo and Sivakumar)[2] the mode of foreign entry has been an important conceptual consideration as well as the subject of many empirical studies, especially in manufacturing industries (e.g., Andersen and Agarwal and Ramaswami).[3] From a service industry perspective, research initiatives regarding both internationalization and foreign entry mode have been increasing, beginning with Erramilli and Rao in 1993[4] and continuing with Roberts in 1999[5] and Domke-Damonte in 2000.[6]

The external environmental factors that were studied in the first section of this book, including the cultural, political, legal, and economic environments, have been identified as contingency variables that affect foreign market entry choice. Ekeledo and Sivakumar generally proved this in their 1998 study. More specifically, Kogut and Singh in 1988,[7] as well as Barkema, Bell, and Pennings in 1996,[8] linked cultural distance to the mode of foreign entry. Host-country market size and market potential have also been found to affect the mode of foreign entry.[9] Furthermore, firms have entered highly competitive foreign markets that are not oligopolistic[10] and a host country's geographic proximity to the home country would affect the firm's choice of entry mode into new countries.[11]

Besides the external environmental factors, the strategic decision on choice of mode of entry into foreign markets has also been related to various internal factors of the firm. These factors include the firm's size, the firm's marketing strategy,[12] its cumulative international experience, its degree of control and resource commitments, and its overall profitability relative to its competition.[13]

An international company can avail itself of several different modes of entry into foreign markets. These include:

- Exporting
- Countertrade
- Contract manufacturing
- Licensing
- Franchising
- Management service contracts
- Turnkey projects
- Nonequity strategic alliances
- Equity-based joint ventures
- Wholly owned subsidiaries

Typically, an international company may engage in each of these foreign market entry modes in different world markets. And in any country market, a subsidiary may be engaged in one or more of these entry modes. The parent company of the international enterprise decides which foreign affiliate will be responsible for which international business activities. Pan and Tse illustrated the entry mode choices through a hierarchical framework.[14] They separated entry modes into equity and nonequity categories. They further delineated equity modes as equity joint ventures and wholly owned subsidiaries. Similarly, they separated nonequity modes into exports and contractual agreements. As Figure 7.1 illustrates, mode of foreign entry can be viewed from a cooperative perspective as well as from a wholly owned perspective. As internationalization has exponentially grown during the past two decades, increasing emphasis, as depicted in Figure 7.1, has been on equity choices. For instance, firms that once exported

FIGURE 7.1 **Foreign Mode of Entry Choices**

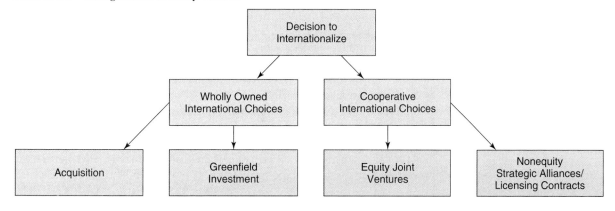

to culturally and politically distant countries like China, and eventually invested in those countries, are now seeking to "go it alone."

In this chapter, we first examine various entry modes. Exporting, countertrade, and licensing are reviewed first because of their historic and current importance in international business. These entry modes are reviewed in this chapter also because of the increasing importance of equity choices for the firm during the past 10 years, and because of the organizational complexity that comes with foreign investment and a network of subsidiaries. Subsequent chapters in this section further detail these entry choices and focus on their management as well. Now let us begin our discussion with a look at the most basic of the market entry strategies, exporting.

Exporting

The process of exporting is sending a firm's products or services to international destinations. A company seeking international markets may choose among various ways to export its products. In some instances the company does nothing more than supply the products for export. For example, the company may deal with a home-based export firm that buys on its own account, sells abroad through its own affiliates or branches, and often maintains its own logistical support systems including warehouses, shipping docks, and transportation facilities. A company could also sell through an export commission house or through an export buyer acting as a purchasing agent for various foreign buyers. For the company these processes are exporting in name only, since the sales transactions take place in the home country itself; the actual export activity is accomplished by the buyer of the company's products. There are two basic methods of export management, the indirect approach and the direct approach. It is not uncommon for a company to use both approaches simultaneously.

Indirect Exporting

Indirect exporting refers to a firm's products eventually being sent overseas without the firm's ultimate involvement. Many small and medium-sized firms do not have the cost efficiencies, scale economies, or foreign market knowledge to export directly. In contrast, a large international company would not generally resort to this method of exporting as it has the efficiencies to internalize the export function. Thus small and medium-sized firms, particularly those just getting started in export, may prefer to begin with the indirect approach by entering into a contract with a combination export manager or with a manufacturer's export agent, both of which would be based in the company's home market.

A *combination export manager (CEM)* is an independent firm that acts as the export department of the company. The CEM sells the company's products together with allied, but noncompetitive lines of other companies through its own network of foreign distributors, which conduct business in the name of the company they represent. To potential buyers abroad, the CEM is the export department of the product manufacturing firm. Contracts with buyers are negotiated in the manufacturer's name. Correspondence may be on the manufacturer's letterhead, thus affording it an opportunity to establish its brand name abroad. All quotations and orders are also subject to approval by the manufacturer. Most CEMs operate mainly on a commission basis. A CEM often takes over all risks and problems of export.

The CEM provides a manufacturer with one of the fastest routes of entering foreign markets as well as its ready-made experience—a very important factor in international marketing because of the differences between the markets in various countries in areas like culture, channels of distribution, and product liability laws. The CEM is actually a ready-made export department for the manufacturer, considering that the CEM not only researches foreign markets, but also chooses the type of distribution channel to be used and does its own advertising and sales promotion. The CEM may also give credit assistance to the manufacturer where buy-and-sell arrangements are involved. The manufacturer, therefore, must maintain close liaison with the CEM on policies concerning advertising, sales promotion, pricing, financing, and credit extension.

An alternative to hiring a CEM is engaging a manufacturer's export agent. A *manufacturer's export agent,* unlike the CEM, does not make sales in the name of each manufacturer it represents but retains its own identity by operating in its own name. This firm works on a straight commission basis. Unlike a CEM, a manufacturer's agent does not assume responsibility for advertising and financing.

Direct Exporting

Direct exporting happens when a company internalizes the export function and takes responsibility to sell its products, without an intermediary, to an importer or buyer located in a market abroad. The direct approach involves more expense and detail than the indirect method. However, over the long haul, the results can be far superior in comparison to the indirect approach.

The exporting company may create a separate export department to enable its own staff to concentrate on developing new markets abroad. An *export department* is a distinct, self-contained department that handles most of the export activities. The export department may be organized by territory, product, customer, or any combination of these. A separate export department enables exporting to be handled by specialists in the area who are committed to its success.

Companies that want to separate international marketing from its domestic counterpart may form a separate export sales subsidiary. An *export sales subsidiary* is a semi-independent corporation, that is, a separate corporation wholly owned by the parent company. Very often the export sales subsidiary is made a profit center to enable the parent company to better monitor how successful its foreign marketing efforts have been. A major advantage of an export sales subsidiary is that it can be organized as a domestic international sales corporation (DISC), a Western Hemisphere trade corporation (WHTC), or an export trade corporation—any of which, if properly utilized, could accrue substantial tax benefits to the parent company.

Companies that feel the need for closer supervision over the sales of their products in a certain market may choose to establish their own selling offices abroad functioning as foreign sales branches of the home company. *Foreign sales branches* handle all sales and promotional activities in a specified market and generally sell to wholesalers, dealers, and at times to industrial users. They are usually located only in large markets because the sales volume must justify the cost involved in establishing and operating a branch office. Usually, a foreign sales branch is established only after representatives and distributors have developed a market for the company's products.

In time, the foreign sales branch may be incorporated by the company as a *foreign sales subsidiary,* the foreign counterpart of the home-based export sales subsidiary. A foreign sales subsidiary is far more independent than a foreign sales branch because of its foreign incorporation and domicile. The staff of the subsidiary can evaluate the market, suggest product changes, and judge the effectiveness of advertising, public relations, and promotional efforts from the foreign consumer's point of view.

Countertrade

As liquidity pressures have increased in emerging, economically transitioning and lesser developed nations during the past 15 years, pressure to fund global trade and investment without using capital has increased. Subsequently, various and unique forms of countertrade have emerged. In regular business transactions, goods or services flow in one direction while the money being paid for them flows back in the other. **Countertrade** refers to arrangements whereby the flow of goods or services in both directions is an integral element of the specific terms of the business transaction. An advantage of countertrade is market penetration where a country lacks hard currency. It is also seen as a foreign exchange hedge. However, countertrade activities may lead to a company getting into an industry where it is not an efficient competitor, potentially raising costs. Costs also tend to increase when a firm, recognizing its lack of competency in a new industry, hires an agent to sell the goods from the foreign country. Of the many varieties of countertrade, we discuss four principal ones: pure barter, switch trading, counterpurchase, and buyback.

Pure Barter

In *pure barter,* each side in the business arrangement agrees to accept the other's goods as payment for the transaction. The most famous example historically is PepsiCo's agreement with Russia nearly 40 years ago to trade its syrup for Stolichnaya vodka. Russia marketed Pepsi domestically under a franchising arrangement with PepsiCo, which received an equivalent value of Stolichnaya vodka in return for the franchise rights and syrup that it sold to the Soviets. PepsiCo in turn marketed the Russian vodka in the United States.

Another countertrade example is Chrysler's (before its integration into Daimler-Benz) agreement with South Africa to exchange autos for platinum. The platinum was then used in Chrysler's manufacturing operations, especially for catalytic converters. In another interesting deal involving PepsiCo, the company agreed to sell Ukrainian-built commercial ships in the world market in exchange for the opportunity to market Pepsi and open several Pizza Hut restaurants (which PepsiCo owned at the time) in Ukraine. This arrangement between PepsiCo and the Ukrainian government and another between McDonnell Douglas and the Ugandan government are presented in Practical Insight 7.1.

Switch Trading

Switch trading is trade involving three or more countries. For instance, England agrees to trade computers worth $500,000 to Brazil in exchange for coffee that has an equivalent market value of $500,000. The English may not want the coffee and so, with the help of a switch specialist, they sell the coffee to an Italian company for $450,000. England gets the cash for the sale minus the 5 to 10 percent that may be paid to the switch trader. Because the English side knows in advance that the coffee will be sold elsewhere at a discount, it will have hiked the price of the computers upward to compensate for the discount and the commission paid to the switch trader.

Counterpurchase

In a counterpurchase deal, Country A exports to Country B, and in return promises to spend some or all of the receipts on imports from B. The details of those imports need not be specified, but they must be bought within a particular period, usually two to three years. During the late 1980s, Peru, undergoing liquidity problems under President

PRACTICAL INSIGHT 7.1

COUNTERTRADE DEALS MAKE LIFE INTERESTING FOR GLOBAL FIRMS

Pepsi for Commercial Ships

For more than 20 years, PepsiCo Inc. has been engaged in countertrade with the former Soviet Union. Under the agreement with PepsiCo, the Soviet Union obtained the right to market Pepsi in the Soviet Union and PepsiCo, in exchange, received Stolichnaya vodka, which it marketed in the U.S.A. A much more unique version of countertrade was a deal signed by PepsiCo with the Soviet Union in the early 1990s. Under this agreement, PepsiCo agreed to accept not only Russian vodka but also ships built in the Ukraine as a way to conduct commerce in Russia, which lacked convertible currency. PepsiCo sells the vodka and the commercial ships in the world market. Now, in an effort to further boost its sales in the former Soviet Union, PepsiCo has entered a joint venture with Ukraine worth $1 billion to market in the world market commercial ships built in the Ukraine. Under the agreement, Pepsi will cooperate with three Ukrainian companies to market the ships. Some of the proceeds from the ship sales will be reinvested in the shipbuilding venture, and some will be used to build five Pepsi bottling plants and to buy soft-drink equipment. The balance will be used to finance the opening of 100 Pizza Hut restaurants in the Ukraine. Pepsi also owns the Pizza Hut chain. Since the Ukraine does not have the hard currency, this type of arrangement will be very beneficial to both PepsiCo and the Ukraine.

Helicopters for Passion Fruit

Uganda wanted to buy 18 helicopters to help eradicate elephant and rhino poaching but didn't have the $25 million to pay for them. Enter McDonnell Douglas Helicopter. McDonnell Douglas set up several projects in Uganda to generate the hard currency required. It set up a plant to catch and process Nile perch and a factory which produced pineapple and passion fruit concentrate, for which McDonnell Douglas found buyers in Europe. Uganda received the badly needed 18 helicopters and McDonnell Douglas got paid in the convertible currency.

Source: Adapted from "Why Countertrade Is Getting Hot," *Fortune,* June 29, 1992, p. 25; and Michael J. McCarthy, "Pepsi Seeking to Boost Sales to Ukrainians," *The Wall Street Journal,* October 23, 1992, p. A9.

Alain Garcia, insisted that firms exporting to Peru accept most of their expected revenues in Peruvian goods. Since then, many countries have employed this type of countertrade. When the good being exported is more valued by the importing country, the counterpurchase demands become less stringent. This is especially the case with high-technology goods. For example, Northrop Grumman has received relatively lenient agreements with countries like Algeria, which are in need of the aerospace technology being supplied.

Buyback

Buyback entails licensing of patents or trademarks, selling production know-how, lending capital, or building a plant in another country and agreeing to buy part or all of its output as payment. In one case of buyback, the General Electric Company provided Poland with the technology and equipment to manufacture electrocardiogram meters, which, in turn, Poland shipped back to General Electric. In another famous deal, Fiat built an automobile factory in Russia, and the Russians paid Fiat for the factory partly in Russian-made Fiats. Levi-Strauss was compensated for building a blue jeans manufacturing facility in Hungary with guaranteed output from the plant. Finally, Occidental Petroleum was paid in output from the ammonium plant the firm built in Russia.

Contract Manufacturing

A contractual agreement between a company and a foreign producer under which the foreign producer manufactures the company's product is called **contract manufacturing.** Under this agreement the company retains responsibility for the promotion and distribution of its product. For example, an American pharmaceutical company may contract a company in India to manufacture its cough syrup. The Indian company manufactures it and does all the packaging of the product as required by the American company. Then the American company takes the packaged product and markets it in India or even globally. Nike, the athletic gear company, uses contract manufacturers throughout Asia to manufacture its footwear and sportswear. In this sense, the company limits its politically imposed and economically imposed financial risk

Licensing

An alternative route to markets abroad, one which falls somewhere between exporting and manufacturing abroad, is licensing. In a foreign **licensing** agreement the international company, or *licensor,* agrees to make available to another company abroad, the *licensee,* use of its patents and trademarks, its manufacturing processes and know-how, its trade secrets, and its managerial and technical services. In exchange, the foreign company agrees to pay the licensor a royalty or other form of payment according to a schedule agreed upon by the two parties. The licensing agreement could be between the parent company of the international enterprise and one or more of its foreign affiliates, or it could be between the international enterprise and an independent foreign, private, or government enterprise. For example, beer manufacturers have used the licensing of their brand names and trade secrets to foreign companies as an alternative to exporting. Movies and television programs have been licensed to foreign distributors and television networks mainly after they have run their course in the home market.

Foreign licensing involves more risk than straight exporting from the home country, but it does not have the risks that go with the start-up of foreign manufacturing facilities abroad. The licensor is in fact exporting its know-how instead of products. A company might have many reasons to use licensing as a means of tapping foreign markets. Figure 7.2 illustrates some of these reasons. In general, overseas licensing activities may be a source of additional immediate profit for the firm through lowering costs and/or increasing revenues. Licensing is a way to capitalize on revenues in foreign markets when the capital expenditures of foreign investment into those markets are beyond a firm's internal capabilities. Licensing is also a way to accrue additional revenues when trade barriers are blocking or raising the cost of potential export activities. Licensing gives the firm the ability to quickly enter a new market at relatively low cost. Furthermore, licensing may help a firm gain the potential low-cost ad-

FIGURE 7.2
Licensing as a Foreign Entry Choice

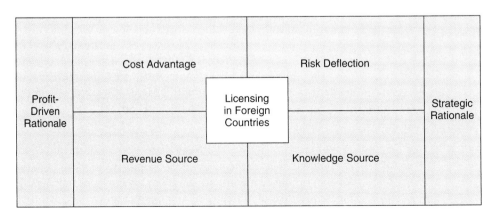

vantages of particular host countries without committing the resources abroad. This may come from comparative low-cost labor or efficient access to necessary components or raw materials.

Overseas licensing activities may have a strategic rationale as well. For instance, when an international firm allows another firm to incur the cost of sales in a foreign country, that licensee incurs the bulk of the various economic risks, whether politically or culturally imposed. Licensing is also a way for a firm to scope out and then develop a potential market for long-term investment activity. It adds to the firm's knowledge of the nuances of the overseas markets without incurring the potential associated risks. Strategically, licensing may help a firm diversify not only its scope of country operations, but its mode of entry as well. Thus the international firm may have a portfolio of both countries and types of operations within those countries. As knowledge creation and accumulation have become important pieces of international competitive advantage, licensing offers the international firm the ability to acquire reciprocal benefits from foreign know-how, research, and technical services.

License agreements are defined by the nature and content of the rights granted by the licensor to the licensee. A simple licensing agreement is limited to a patent or trademark. But more complex licensing agreements include the delivery by the licensor to the licensee of one or more of the following:

- A patented product or process
- A trademark or trade name
- Manufacturing techniques
- Proprietary rights generally referred to as company or industry know-how
- Supply by the licensor to the licensee of components or equipment
- Technical advice and services of various sorts
- Marketing advice and assistance of various sorts
- Capital and/or managerial personnel

As illustrated in Figure 7.2, licensing has several advantages. It may offer a foothold in a foreign market without requiring a large capital investment. Thus it can be less risky than starting a manufacturing operation. Licensing is most attractive to firms that are new to the international business arena. Most countries specify that patents and trademarks be used within a certain number of years of their grant and registration, respectively, or they are canceled, which makes licensing a viable option for protecting the company's patents and trademarks.

Import restrictions and tariffs that are suddenly imposed after a company has established a market for its products in the country through exports pose a difficult problem for the company: Should it abandon the proven market for its products? Should it establish a manufacturing facility in the country? Is licensing the best alternative, given the global strategic interests of the company? It may resort to licensing if it decides not to jump over the trade barriers by establishing its own manufacturing plant in the country. Licensing of the products to a local company enables the firm to retain a foothold in such markets, which would otherwise be completely lost. Some licensors consider the acquisition of patents from foreign patent holders to be one of the major benefits of foreign licensing operations. Reciprocal license grants are frequently made by the licensee as partial compensation for the rights and know-how made available by the licensor.

As illustrated in Figure 7.3, licensing also has disadvantages. The disadvantages regarding licensing as a technique for penetrating foreign markets should be recognized and clearly understood by multinational companies. Every licensee is a potential

FIGURE 7.3
Concerns of Foreign
Licensing

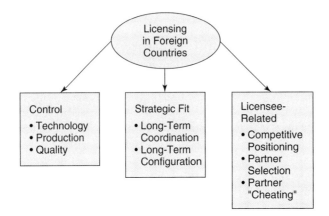

competitor of the licensor. If the original licensing agreement does not stipulate the region within which the licensee may market the licensed product, the licensee could create problems for the licensor by insisting on marketing the product in third-country markets in competition with products already served in the market by the licensor.

The licensee may develop a formidable market with the use of licensed patents, trademarks, technology, or process. It may then reap huge profits, much to the chagrin of the licensor, who did not foresee the huge markets developing and therefore is receiving a comparatively negligible royalty under the license agreement in effect at the time. The experience of many firms indicates that it is very difficult for the licensor to have completely satisfactory control over the licensee's manufacturing and marketing operations. This could result in damage to the licensor's trademark and reputation.

Also, several companies have had difficulties with licensees who refuse to pay royalties, claiming that the original product or process was altered and no longer in use. Moreover, if the licensing agreement calls for a payment of royalties in local currency, devaluation of the local currency would result in a decline of the value of royalty payments in the home-country currency.

How a licensing program fits into a company's overall long-range strategic objectives and policies is an extremely important consideration. If a company can establish its own manufacturing and sales facilities, it should do so, because developing and running its own business abroad, and reaping maximum benefits from the global markets for its products, offers clear advantages. Possible repercussions on domestic, export, and other foreign operations as well as prospective return in terms of resources and risks involved must be carefully determined prior to signing any license agreement with a foreign firm. If a company does decide to enter into a licensing agreement, it should consider the following steps. Before entering into a licensing agreement, the licensor must know the market's potential and the cost of developing it. The company must do its own research and gather its own information rather than relying solely on data provided by the licensee. The company should take care not to underestimate or overestimate the market potential. If it does the former, it might sell itself short; if it does the latter, it might make unrealistic demands of the licensee in terms of royalties and market development expectations. One company made just such arrangements in a foreign country: It oversold its franchise, demanded unrealistic results, and then expected the licensee to expend unreasonable sums of money to develop the market without hope of commensurately adequate compensation. The result was disastrous. Legal proceedings ensued with the licensor demanding compensation for loss of profits, and the licensee counterclaiming on the grounds that he had been deliberately misled on the value of the franchise.

TABLE 7.1

Foreign Licensing: Factors for Success and Failure

Factors Leading to Success	Factors Leading to Failure
Choice of reliable and competent partner	Inadequate market analysis by licensor
Inherent value of patent, trademark, or know-how licensed	Higher start-up costs than anticipated by licensee
Goal congruence with partner	Insufficient attention paid to activity by top management of licensor
Some participation in ownership	Poor timing
Close personal contact with licensee	Lack of goal congruence with partner
Appropriate level of control by licensor	Unanticipated competition from home-, host-, and third-country competitors
Reputation of licensor and licensed asset	Inadequate licensee after-sales effort
Sales assistance to licensee	Partner rigidity
Support of licensor's top management	Insufficient marketing effort by both licensor and licensee
Flexibility by both partners	Weak licensee market research
Correct timing and pacing of activity	Lack of fit with other licensor activities
Detailed spelling out of contract obligations and responsibilities	Lack of sales assistance to licensee
Effective coordination with other parts of licensor's overseas activities	
Thorough research and market knowledge	

The company must clearly state in the licensing agreement its expectations in terms of income from royalties and the effort to be expended in terms of financial and managerial resources by the licensee to develop the market. Unrealistic demands should not be made of the licensee, who should be fairly compensated for the time, effort, and money spent by him or her on the task. A successful licensing arrangement should result if both parties to the agreement feel that they are getting a fair bargain for their efforts.

The quality of the partner must be thoroughly investigated by the licensor company. The licensee need not be a big firm; however, it must have the managerial and financial strength to carry out its side of the agreement. Also, the licensee should have a good image in the host country.

Serious problems may occur if a multinational company does not retain control over the production and marketing of its products by the licensee. A company can retain control over production by providing for quality control in the agreement. For example, the licensor can permanently station a technical representative in the licensee's plant to check on the quality of the products produced or the process being used. Or the licensee may be required to submit samples of production runs to the multinational company for approval. Periodic visits by the multinational company's production and quality control personnel to the production site could also help prevent the marketing of inferior quality products.

Several studies and company experiences appearing in the popular business press reported specific success factors for company licensing programs. Others reported factors that led to failed overseas licensing attempts. Table 7.1 lists these factors.

Most troublesome of all for potential licensors is accurately gauging the size of the market, obtaining meaningful clues about the nature of the market and probable competition, and verifying such information by effective test marketing or market research. Some companies reported their failure to realize that their "new" products would not be sufficiently "new" or different to capture the overseas public's fancy.

In preparing a licensing contract, a company should ask the following questions:

- How may patents, processes, or trademarks will be used?
- How will technical assistance be rendered?
- Which products are included in the agreement, and to what extent?

- What territory is to be covered by the license?
- How should the licensee be compensated?
- What is the currency in which payments will be made to the licensor?
- What happens if compensation cannot be paid by the licensee?
- If sublicensing is permitted, how should it be carried out?
- Are there any geographical limitations on the marketing of the licensed product or service?
- What are the provisions for the duration of the agreement and its cancellation?
- What rights does the licensor have in developments by licensee?
- What visitation and inspection privileges are held by the licensor?
- Can the parent company inspect accounts?
- What provisions are there for satisfactory promotional/sales performance and adequate quality control?
- What home- and host-government approvals are required?
- What tax factors are involved?
- How will disputes be settled?

Although this list is not exhaustive, it pinpoints the key issues that should be included in a typical licensing agreement.

Franchising

In the opening case of this chapter, Starbucks had to consider the relative benefits and disadvantages of franchising compared to other entry modes. **Franchising,** a very common form of licensing, is defined as a transfer of technology, business system, brand name, trademark, and other property rights by a franchisor to an independent company or person who is the franchisee. There has been an explosion of franchising throughout the world in recent years. Almost 50 percent of all major retail businesses are franchises.[15] Franchising involves two business people or entities: the *franchisor,* who has developed the business or product and lends its name or trademark to it, and the *franchisee,* who buys the right to operate the business under the franchisor's brand name or trademark. Usually a company initially establishes a brand name for its products, service, quality, and so on, in the home market, and a standardized business system to operate the business. It then franchises the entire business system, including the trademark and brand name, to the franchisee in a foreign country. The franchisee depends on the franchisor for the business system, and the franchisor depends on the franchisee for royalties or fees. Most developed and developing countries have drafted specific legislation to attract foreign franchisors.

The franchisee operates the business under the franchisor's trademark or brand name and is contractually obligated to adhere to the procedures and methods of operation prescribed in the business system. The franchisor generally maintains the right to control the quality of the franchisee through quality control of products and service so that the franchisee cannot harm the company's image. In exchange the franchisor receives a fee based on the volume of sales. Sometimes the franchisor mandates that the franchisee buy from it the equipment and some key ingredients used in the products. For example, Burger King and McDonald's require the franchisee to buy from the company cooking equipment and other products that bear the company name. Or the franchisor requires that the franchisee obtain the ingredients from local sources, provided they maintain the franchisor's quality requirements. For example, McDonald's has helped its franchisee in India to set up a domestic supplier network for items such as potatoes and buns. It even helped the Indian franchisee to grow potatoes that contained the right amount of moisture in them. Coca-Cola and PepsiCo send the syrup—the key ingredient in the soda—to its franchisees, who bottle and market the drink. Marriott, Holiday Inn, Hilton, McDonald's, Burger King, Avis, Hertz, Coca-Cola, and Pepsi are examples that have become household names throughout the world using the franchising entry mode

The Franchise Agreement

Franchise agreements vary from franchise to franchise. Identifying every term and issue that should be considered in every situation would be impossible. However, this checklist should be a valuable tool if you're interested in buying a franchise. A franchise agreement includes five major areas:[16]

1. ***A detailed list of issues to consider regarding the cost of the franchise:*** What does the initial franchise fee purchase? What are the payment terms: amount, time of payment, lump sum or installment, financing arrangements, and so on? Are there periodic royalties? If so, how much are they and how are they determined? How and when are sales and royalties reported, and how are royalties paid? How are advertising and promotion costs divided? If royalty payments are in whole or part payment for services by the franchisor, what services will be provided? Must premises be purchased or rented, and are there further conditions on either of these (from franchisor, selected site, etc.)?

2. ***A detailed list of issues to consider regarding the location of the franchise:*** Does the franchise apply to a specific geographical area? If so, are the boundaries clearly defined? Who has the right to select the site? Will other franchisees be permitted to compete in the same area, now or later? Is the territory an exclusive one, and is it permanent or subject to reduction or modification under certain conditions? Does the franchisee have a first-refusal option as to any additional franchises in the original territory if it is not exclusive? Does the franchisee have a contractual right to the franchisor's latest products or innovations? Will the franchisee have the right to use his own property and buildings? Or will the franchisor lease his property to the franchisee?

3. ***A detailed list of issues pertaining to the buildings, equipment, and supplies terms:*** Must equipment or supplies be purchased from the franchisor or approved supplier, or is the franchisee free to make his own purchases? What controls are spelled out concerning facility appearance, equipment, fixture, and furnishings, and their maintenance or replacement? Is there any limitation on expenditures involved in any of these? When the franchisee must buy from the franchisor, are sales considered on consignment? Or will they be financed and, if so, under what terms?

4. ***A detailed list of issues pertaining to the operating practices terms:*** Must the franchisee participate personally in conducting the business? If so, to what extent and under what specific conditions? What degree of control does the franchisor have over franchise operations, particularly in maintaining franchise identity and product quality? What continuing management aid, training, and assistance will be provided by the franchisor, and are these covered by the service or royalty fee? Will advertising be local or national and what will be the cost-sharing arrangement, if any, in either case? If local advertising is left to the franchisee, does the franchisor exercise any control over such campaigns or share any costs? Are operating hours and days set forth in the franchise contract? Are there any limits as to what is or can be sold?

5. *A detailed list of issues pertaining to termination and renewal terms:* Under what conditions (illness, etc.) can the franchisee terminate the franchise? In such cases, do termination obligations differ? Is the franchisee restricted from engaging in a similar business after termination? If so, for how many years? If there is a lease, does it coincide with the franchise term? Has the franchisor, as required, provided for return of trademarks, trade names, and other identification symbols and for the removal of all signs bearing the franchisor's name and trademarks?

Advantages and Disadvantages of Franchising

The advantages and disadvantages of franchising are similar to those of licensing. Franchising is an inexpensive way of exploiting a foreign market. Little or no political risk is involved. The risks of failure and its associated costs are borne by the franchisee. And it is a fast and relatively easy avenue for leveraging globally a company's assets such as a brand name and standardized business system. Because the franchisees have made a significant financial investment in the business, they are more likely to be better motivated to maximize sales and minimize costs than hired managers. Franchisees can be significant providers of innovative ideas. For instance, KFC's franchisee in Japan was responsible for the concept of KFC kiosk restaurants. This idea has been implemented by KFC worldwide.

Franchising has disadvantages as well, however. The franchisee may spoil the franchisor's image by not upholding the standards for quality established by the franchisor. Sometimes, exercising control over the franchisee may be very difficult because the traditional management–employee relationship is absent. At times, franchisees may attempt to deviate from the policies and standards established by the franchisor. Franchisees may fight attempts by the franchisor to implement changes, such as introducing a new product line or eliminating one already in place. Even if the franchisor is able to terminate the agreement, the franchisee may still stay in business by slightly altering the company's brand name or trademark. For example, the former franchisee of TGI Friday's in Mexico City merely changed its name to TGI Freeday and continued to do business. A citywide noodle shop in Shanghai uses a logo almost identical to KFC's. Thus a franchisee may actually help to establish a competitor.

Management Service Contracts

During the British Colonial heyday British companies that specialized in the management of enterprises commonly entered into management service contracts with local companies in the British colonies like India, Kenya, and Hong Kong. The management service contracts required the local companies to delegate all managerial functions to the British management service companies while still retaining the ownership of all of the companies' assets. Top and senior managerial personnel from England, Scotland, and Ireland were sent to the colonies to manage the locally owned companies, and in exchange the British companies received a fee based on a predetermined formula. This system was known as the British Agency management system and it flourished until the demise of the British Empire.

More recent examples of management service contracts can be found in industries like hotels, hospitals, and infrastructure entities like airports, seaports, and public utilities. A **management service contract,** to Contractor and Kundu, "is a long term agreement, of up to ten years or even longer, whereby the legal owners of the property and real estate enter into a contract with the (hotel) firm to run and operate the hotel on a day to day basis, usually under the latter's internationally recognized name."[17] In such agreements, "quality control, daily management and senior staffing . . . principally rest with the international (hotel) firm and not the property owners. But the operation is run as if the property were part of the global chain. Customers cannot tell the difference."[18]

This definition of management service contracts is equally applicable to hospitals and airports. For example, the Dutch management company Schiphol Group manages Amsterdam's Schipol Airport. Schiphol also has a contract to renovate and run Terminal 4 at New York's John F. Kennedy Airport. Germany's Frankfurt Airport Group operates baggage services at Stockholm's Arlanda Airport and Newark Liberty International Airport (in New Jersey) and manages the entire airport in both Indianapolis, Indiana, and Harrisburg, Pennsylvania. And the British BAA Group runs retail and catering facilities in Pittsburgh and Newark.[19] Similarly, companies that specialize in the management of gambling casinos and holiday resorts have contracts to manage properties owned by local investors in several countries worldwide. The international firm managing the property gets a commission based on the gross revenues of the managed property as well as yearly minimum lump-sum payments.

Turnkey Projects

When an international company engages in setting up a **turnkey** operation abroad, it assumes responsibility for the design and construction of the entire operation, and, upon completion of the project, it hands over the total management to local personnel whom it has trained. In return for the completion of the project, the international company receives a fee, which can be quite substantial. Turnkey operations generally involve projects such as the construction of airports, dams, electric power stations, roads, and factory complexes such as steel mills, refineries, chemical plants, and automobile plants.

Examples of American companies that have completed turnkey projects abroad include Bechtel and Fluor, which have built many foreign plants and projects. Cogentrix, an American power company, has built electric power generation plants in several countries. An entire automobile plant was constructed in Russia by Fiat, the famous Italian company. Foreign companies have built hospitals in Saudi Arabia; and South Korean, Chinese, and Indian companies have built highways in Africa and the Middle East under turnkey contracts. AT&T's former Network Systems built the communications infrastructures for both Saudi Arabia and Iran.

Equity-Based Ventures through Foreign Direct Investment

As opposed to the modes of entry already discussed, in equity-based foreign market entry an international company has equity ownership and control of a foreign venture through foreign direct investment (FDI). The foreign venture may serve several purposes. It may be established to obtain raw materials for use by the company in production in other countries or for sale on world markets. Companies in the petroleum, aluminum, steel, and copper industries have established numerous foreign ventures for these purposes. An equity-based venture may also be established to produce components or products that are mainly exported to the home country or to third countries. A company may establish such an enterprise in a foreign country to take advantage of the availability of labor, energy, or other inputs at competitive prices. International companies, especially in the electronics industry, have established subsidiaries to source components and products in Mexico, China, and many countries in the Pacific Basin. In fact, the governments of Malaysia, India, and several other countries have established high-tech centers to facilitate foreign investment in high-technology ventures.

An equity-based foreign venture need not involve production. It may distribute the company's products or market a service such as advertising, accounting, engineering, legal, or management consulting. An international company may decide to establish an equity-based venture in a foreign country to produce and/or market a product or service mainly to serve the foreign market itself. It may export some of the production to the home market or to third-country markets; however, the host-country market is the principal target market for the products produced by the venture. For example, several Japanese multinational automobile companies, including Nissan, Honda, Toyota, Subaru, and Mazda, have set up U.S. manufacturing plants which have the latest manufacturing technology and management techniques. Their purpose is to give the Japanese companies the greatest competitive edge in serving the domestic U.S. market as well as a base for sales to Europe, which tightly limits imports from Japan but not from the United States.

An equity-based venture abroad could be a *greenfield* investment—establishing the venture from the ground up—or it may involve the *acquisition* of an existing firm. It may finance the new venture abroad from its own funds, or it may borrow the necessary funds from financial institutions and equity markets in the home-, host-, or third-country markets.

An equity-based venture could be *wholly owned* by the parent international company, or it could be a *joint venture* in which the international company shares its ownership with another company. Managing a wholly owned foreign subsidiary is less complex than managing a joint venture. Sharing of the management of the enterprise with a foreign partner is responsible for the greater complexity of managing a joint venture. The joint venture route is a popular mode for foreign market entry among international companies.

In the following sections, we outline the nature of joint ventures. Because of the exponential growth and subsequent importance of international joint ventures during the past 15 years, we dedicate Chapter 8 to a fuller discussion of both joint ventures and strategic alliances with foreign partners.

An international joint venture is a business collaboration between companies based in two or more countries which share ownership in an enterprise established jointly for the production and/or distribution of goods or services. Pure trade agreements are excluded from our concept of a joint venture. International joint ventures can take many forms, depending on the needs and circumstances of the partners and the conditions under which the collaboration agreement is consummated. Factors such as the percentage of the total equity in the joint venture held by each partner, the number of partners involved in the joint venture, and the characteristics of the partners vary among international joint ventures. An international company's ownership of a joint venture may range from a majority to an equal or minority participation in the total equity capital of the joint venture.

The number of partners involved in a joint venture may also vary. When firms or small groups of interests from two or more countries form a joint venture, only two or three partners may be involved. For example, companies from England, France, and Holland are partners in the development and production of the Airbus, which is popular in the airline industry. However, numerous partners are involved when the equity of the joint venture is dispersed in the hands of the general public through the sale of stock. Several American companies have formed such joint ventures in India. This arrangement allows the international company to maintain effective managerial control over the joint venture and at the same time satisfies the requirement of the government that a majority of the equity be in the hands of its citizens. An international company

TABLE 7.2

Type and Degree of Parent Company Control over Foreign Operations

Source: Adapted from Farok J. Contractor and Sumit Kundu, "Modal Choice in a World of Alliances," *Journal of International Business Studies* 29, no. 2 (1998). Reproduced with permission of Palgrave MacMillan.

Mode of Entry	Strong Control	Weak Control	Nonexistent Control
Contract manufacturing		A	B, C, D
Licensing	D	C	A, B
Franchising	D	C	A, B
Management service contract	D	A, C	B
Joint venture	D	A, B, C	
Wholly owned subsidiary	A, B, C, D		

Key:
A = daily management and quality control
B = control over physical assets
C = control over tacit expertise and knowledge
D = control over codified assets

could have a variety of partners in a foreign joint venture. The partner could be a local company, another international company, the host-country government, or the general public in the host country.

Now that we have examined the various modes of entry, we shall review the factors that have a significant bearing on which mode of entry is chosen by a company to enter a foreign market.

Entry Mode and Control

Each entry mode includes varying degrees of control through different control mechanisms. Contractor and Kundu classify these into four types: (1) daily operational and quality control in each foreign entry; (2) control over the physical assets or over the real estate and its attendant risks; (3) control over tacit expertise embedded in the routines of the firm; and (4) control over the codified assets such as a global reservation system or the firm's internationally recognized brand name.[20] The degree of control for each type of mechanism in each entry mode is depicted in Table 7.2.

Table 7.2 shows that a multinational company can exert control over its foreign operations through various means, and that it does not necessarily need a significant equity in the foreign operation to control it. For example, a hotel chain like Marriott can impose considerable influence over a franchisee hotel abroad because it controls the global reservation system. The franchisee hotel depends on filling its hotel rooms through customers that the global reservation system provides.

Factors Influencing the Entry Mode Choice by International Firms

The choice of the mode of entry in a foreign country by a firm is perhaps one of the most widely researched areas in the international business arena. It ranks with the most significant decisions that a firm will make as it embarks on a global strategy to penetrate foreign markets. The choice of an entry mode is critical in a firm's globalization strategy. As shown in Table 7.2, each entry mode discussed earlier in this chapter differs in the degree of control, the degree of systemic risk experienced, the degree of dissemination risk experienced, and the amount of the firm's resources committed. *Degree of control* is the authority over operational and strategic decision making that a company has over its foreign operations.[21] **Systemic risk** is the level of political, economic, and financial risks faced by the particular entry mode. **Dissemination risk** is the risk that firm-specific advantages in know-how will be expropriated by a partner in a foreign venture.[22] *Resource commitment* refers to the amount of resources invested in revenue-generating assets in a foreign venture such as plant and equipment, training

TABLE 7.3 **Characteristics of Entry Modes**

Type of Entry Mode	Degree of Control	Systemic Risk	Dissemination Risk	Resource Commitment
Export	Low	Low	Low	Low
Countertrade	Low	Low	Low	Low
Contract manufacturing	Medium	Medium	Low to medium	Low
Licensing	Low	Low	High	Low
Franchising	Low to medium	Low	Medium	Low
Management service contract	Medium	Low	Medium	Low
Turnkey	Low	Low	Low	Low
Equity-based entry: joint venture	Medium-high	Medium-high	Medium to high	Medium to high
Equity-based entry: wholly owned subsidiary	High	High	Low	High

imparted to personnel, and the costs of penetrating a foreign market, all of which cannot be redeployed to alternative uses without incurring substantial sunk costs.[23]

The degree of control of a foreign operation ranges from low for exporting, countertrade, and licensing, to high for wholly owned subsidiaries. Systemic risk varies from low for exporting, countertrade, licensing, franchising, management service contracts, and turnkey projects, to high for the wholly owned entry mode. Dissemination risk is highest for licensing, and resource commitments are highest for wholly owned ventures. Table 7.3 is a suggested representation of these concepts as they are compared across the various modes of entry.

Several theoretical perspectives, such as transaction cost economics, industrial organization, and strategic behavior, have been advanced to explain the choice of entry mode by global companies. Over the past two decades, researchers have empirically tested several existing explanations for this phenomenon, and new explanations have been offered.

Determinants of Foreign Mode of Entry

Research on entry mode strategies has yielded 25 different factors as determinants in the entry mode choice. However, the research findings do not agree on the significance of some of these factors. Some studies identify certain factors as being significant in their impact on the entry mode decision, and others negate such conclusions. We have therefore selected 17 variables that were tested and found to be statistically significant in eight empirical studies conducted between 1987 and 1992. The eight studies were built on the accumulated knowledge and findings of previous research, and therefore reflect the key findings of earlier studies as well as new developments in the area. We next present a brief review of each of these 17 variables.

1. Firm Size Firm size is one of the measures of managerial capabilities and resources of a firm, and as such could influence the choice of entry mode. Empirical evidence shows that firm size has a positive impact on foreign direct investment; that is, generally firm size would have a positive correlation with foreign market entry, and in particular with entry through wholly owned or joint venture modes.[24]

2. Multinational Experience Multinational experience reduces the uncertainty associated with assessing the true economic worth of entry into a foreign market. It follows, therefore, that firms with little or no experience with international business or multinational operations would seek to limit their risk exposure. Such firms would prefer low control/low resource, noninvestment-type entry modes like exporting or licensing.[25] In contrast, firms with significant multinational experience would prefer high control/high resources, investment-type modes like joint ventures or wholly owned affiliates.

3. Industry Growth   Industry growth in the target country is an indicator of the degree of competition and profitability that a firm would experience in that country. Industry growth is therefore expected to influence the entry mode choice. Kogut and Singh found that the entry mode preference of a firm is dependent on competitive assumptions.[26] They also found evidence (albeit weak) for the proposition that the joint venture entry mode is encouraged when the industry is growing.

4. Global Industry Concentration   Hamel and Prahalad argue that in a global industry characterized by global competition, firms that function under a global strategy umbrella respond to their competitor's competitive moves not only in their home market, but also in the competitor's home market or in third-country markets.[27] For such firms it is imperative that they have control of their foreign affiliates, without which they could not implement a global response to a competitor's onslaught.[28] Assuming that high global industry concentration is associated with a high degree of global competition, firms operating in such industry conditions would prefer high control entry modes like wholly owned subsidiaries.

5. Technical Intensity   Most studies find that failure of markets to mediate the exchange of technology and tacit knowledge leads firms in technically intense industries to prefer the wholly owned affiliate entry mode.[29] However, an entering firm that is seeking technology and tacit knowledge is more likely to enter the foreign market through a joint venture with a firm that has the needed technology.

6. Advertising Intensity   A firm in an industry that is characterized by high advertising intensity is inclined to shy away from joint ventures and be favorably inclined to seek entry modes that provide full control over the foreign venture.[30]

7. Country Risk   Firms prefer to avoid countries with high political risk (e.g., expropriation or nationalization) or economic risk (e.g., restrictions on remittances of assets) and limitations on operational and managerial choice. But if they do choose to make an entry into such countries, they would do so utilizing noninvestment (low control) entry modes.[31]

8. Cultural Distance   Firms entering culturally distant countries prefer licensing agreements or joint ventures over wholly owned affiliates.[32]

9. Market Potential   In high market potential countries, firms are inclined to pursue joint ventures or wholly owned entry modes, which provide higher profitability and market presence.[33]

10. Market Knowledge   Firms can be expected to pursue the wholly owned entry mode rather than a joint venture as firms gain experience and learn more about the local environment.[34] Firms are likely to use high control entry modes when following a client into a country market.[35] For example, firms that are suppliers of components to major automobile companies have followed them in their foreign market entries by establishing manufacturing plants that are either wholly owned or joint ventures with local partners. Therefore, prior experience with a country market and/or following a buyer is expected to be associated positively with high control entry modes.

11. *Value of Firm-Specific Assets* If the firm-specific assets, such as specific technologies that give the firm a sustainable competitive advantage, are highly valued in the venture, then firms are likely to prefer entry modes that allow full control of the venture and to avoid joint ventures with local partners, who they fear will be self-serving.* Researchers have used different variables to capture the value of firm-specific assets. Agarwal and Ramaswami use the firm's "ability to develop differentiated products."[36] Gatignon and Anderson use the "value of firm-specific know-how" to represent the value of firm-specific assets involved in a venture.[37]

12. *Contractual Risk* If the cost of making and enforcing contracts to prevent opportunism by local partners is high, then the firm will prefer entry modes that offer high control over their assets and skills.[38] Therefore, when the contractual risk is high, firms are likely to pursue high control entry modes.

13. *Tacit Nature of Know-How* If the nature of the firm-specific know-how is tacit—that is, not amenable to efficient transfer to a partner—then wholly owned operations increase the firm's ability to efficiently utilize the accumulated tacit knowledge.[39] Therefore, tacit know-how is expected to be positively associated with degree of control.

14. *Venture Size* Gatignon and Anderson argue that the size of the operation will have an impact on the extent of control sought by the entrant.[40] Empirical evidence supports the proposition that firms shy away from wholly owned entry modes in favor of joint ventures when the size of the venture is big.[41]

15. *Intent to Conduct Joint R&D* Modes of entry that do not involve an equity stake may not provide the requisite control to manage the complex judgmental tasks involved in conducting R&D.[42] Therefore, if the intent of a firm entering a foreign market is to conduct research and development work in conjunction with a partner, it will be inclined to favor a joint venture as opposed to other low-control governance structures.

16. *Global Strategic Motivation* Some researchers argue that foreign market entries are motivated by strategic factors that go beyond immediate efficiency considerations.[43] Strategic goals like establishing a strategic outpost and developing a global sourcing site, or moving into a market to deny a profit sanctuary for competitors, motivate firms to prefer wholly owned or joint venture entry modes as opposed to low control licensing agreements.[44]

17. *Global Synergies* Firms seek hierarchical control over affiliates when there is a high degree of interaction between and among the foreign affiliates and the parent company in pursuit of an integrated global strategy.[45] Therefore, when the potential synergies from global integration of companywide strategies are high, firms are likely to pursue high control entry modes like wholly or majority-owned affiliates.

Theory of Multinational Investment

In addition to the foregoing types of entry mode, scholars have proposed various theories to explain the reasons for foreign involvement by international companies and the circumstances underlying the entry modes choices. One can postulate that two

*Examples include the joint venture partner taking the technology, upgrading it, and refusing to give royalties to the international company.

main reasons motivate a firm to engage in international investment: (1) to serve a local market better, and (2) to get lower cost inputs.[46] Foreign direct investment (FDI) to serve local markets better involves "horizontal" FDI (HFDI), in which the production process is duplicated as additional plants are established to supply different locations. HFDI replaces exports with local production, and thus substitutes for trade. The motive for HFDI is either to improve the firm's competitive position in the market or to reduce the costs associated with supplying the foreign market (such as transportation costs or tariffs).

Foreign direct investment made to obtain low-cost inputs is often referred to as "vertical" FDI (VFDI). VFDI involves the splitting of the vertical chain of production (the value chain) and locating parts of the chain in a low-cost location; for example, computers may be assembled in Taiwan even though the components are manufactured in the United States and the computers are marketed there. The low-cost inputs might be unskilled labor, a cheap energy source, highly educated scientists or engineers, or even access to the knowledge embedded in an industrial cluster (such as the electronic industry clusters in Silicon Valley, California, Boston, Massachusetts, or Austin, Texas). VFDI usually increases trade, because dispersal of links in the value chain to different locations necessitates shipping between different locations. The economic rationale for this phenomenon rests on the idea that different parts of the production process have different input requirements. Furthermore, because input prices vary across countries, splitting the value chain and distributing the performance of the various links and activities to those countries where they could be performed most efficiently and effectively may enhance profits.

Although fundamental differences exist between horizontal and vertical integration, very often the distinction can be fuzzy as the strategic intent to establish a plant abroad might be based on the low costs as well as the demand for the final product in the local market.

Factors that influence the choice of entry mode in a specific market have been identified by earlier studies in the fields of international trade, international organization, and market imperfections. Normally a firm is likely to choose a foreign entry mode that offers the best return after discounting for the level of risk that is associated with it. However, researchers in the field have found that the choice of an entry mode is also influenced by two factors: (1) the resources available to the firm in the form of financial and managerial capacity needed to serve a specific foreign market, and (2) the firm's felt need for control over the strategies and operations in the foreign market in order to improve its position and maximize the returns on its assets and skills dedicated to the foreign venture.[47]

A higher level of ownership of the foreign venture results in greater operational control over it. However, it is accompanied by a greater level of risk due to the higher commitment of resources required to sustain its presence in the market.

Experience shows that the level of risk-adjusted return on investment, resource commitments, and degree of control increase as the firm's involvement in foreign operations increases from exporting to licensing/franchising to a joint venture and finally to a wholly owned subsidiary. The wholly owned subsidiary has the greatest level of risk-adjusted return on investment, high resource commitment, and high level of control, whereas the exporting mode has the smallest of each of these attributes. The choice of an entry mode is a compromise involving a trade-off between the risk, return, resource commitment, and control associated with each entry mode.

Two fundamental questions should be asked when considering the mode of entry: Under what circumstances would a firm export products abroad or choose to produce locally in the foreign market? And if a firm chooses to produce the product locally, how would it do so? This leads to a third question: Would it choose to adopt nonequity entry modes such as licensing, franchising, or management service contracts; or would it choose equity modes like joint ventures or wholly owned subsidiaries?

The O-L-I Framework and Internationalization

Dunning proposed a comprehensive framework which includes the impact of firm-specific and location-specific factors that influence a firm's choice of entry mode after taking into account the risk, return, control, and resource commitments associated with each mode.[48] Specifically, Dunning's framework proposed that an entry mode for a target market is influenced by three determining factors: **ownership advantage, location advantage** (or *disadvantage*) of the target market, and **internalization** (by which he meant the advantages that would accrue to the firm from retaining specific transactions within the firm). As Dunning puts it:

> The propensity of an enterprise to engage in international production—that financed by foreign direct investment—rests on three main determinants; first the extent to which it possesses (or can acquire, on more favorable terms) assets which its competitors (or potential competitors) do not possess; second whether it is in its interest to sell or lease these assets to other firms, or make use of—internalize—them itself; and third, how far it is profitable to exploit these assets in conjunction with the indigenous resources of foreign countries rather than of the home country. The more the *ownership-specific advantages* possessed by an enterprise, the greater the inducement to *internalize* them; and the wider *the attractions of a foreign rather than a home country production base,* the greater the likelihood that an enterprise, given the incentive to do so, will engage in international production.[49]

We discuss the principal elements of Dunning's ownership, location, and internalization framework in the following paragraphs.

Ownership Advantages Over the past three decades, international business literature has identified several reasons for international companies to enter foreign markets financed by foreign direct investment. One of the most frequently mentioned reason focuses on so-called ownership advantages. A firm's assets and skills include proprietary rights such as patents, trademarks, brand names, brand reputation, customer base, technological and marketing capability, particular raw materials essential to the production of the product, economies of large-scale production, and exclusive control over particular market outlets.[50] Firms enter foreign markets to exploit ownership advantages developed in their home- or third-country markets. In doing so they endeavor to choose an entry mode that allows a high degree of control. Ownership advantages also include tacit assets such as complex learning capabilities and organizational and operational routines which cannot be taught or learned through written or spoken words.[51]

The net ownership advantages give international firms absolute advantage over firms in almost all locations. To compete with host-country firms in their own markets, firms must possess superior and additional ownership advantages sufficient to outweigh the costs of servicing an unfamiliar or distant environment.[52] This competitive advantage of firms is explained by imperfections in markets for goods or factors of production. In a theoretical world of perfect competition, firms produce homogeneous products and have equal access to all productive factors. In the real world of imperfect competition, as explained by industrial organization theory, firms acquire competitive advantages through product differentiation, brand names, marketing expertise, and technological superiority. A foreign firm that enjoys such a competitive advantage can extract a high enough rent because of the inability, or lack of access, to the knowledge and skills owned by the foreign competitor.

Internalization An international company can choose among a variety of entry mode choices, each of which affords the company varying degrees of control. The international operations of firms can be organized "internally," within wholly owned subsidiaries, or "externally," under arm's-length contracts with independent local producers. Internationalization keeps activities and ownership of assets used in foreign operations within the firm. A pharmaceutical company that establishes a wholly owned subsidiary abroad, rather than entering into a contractual agreement with a foreign company to manufacture its patented product in the latter's home-country plant, is an example of internalization.

The main arguments for internalization extend the market imperfections approach by focusing on imperfections in intermediate-product markets such as knowledge and expertise embodied in patents rather than on final-product markets, knowledge underlying production, marketing, or other activities. As claimed by Johnson,[53] McManus,[54] and Magee,[55] knowledge is a public good,* and as such it can be transferred at zero or marginal cost from one party to another. Consequently, the firm that is responsible for its creation faces the difficulty of reaping the appropriate financial and nonfinancial benefits by itself. The optimal pricing of intermediate-product markets, particularly for types of knowledge and expertise embodied in patents and human capital, is extremely difficult under arm's-length transactions.[56] Property rights on the knowledge embodied in R&D-intensive products cannot be easily defined and enforced through contracts. It is difficult to write complete contracts between the international firm and third parties for the production of innovative products embodying breakthrough knowledge and technology. According to Kogut and Zander, the less codifiable, less teachable, and more complex the knowledge is, the more difficult it is to replicate and transfer across firms.[57] When production is carried out abroad, there is always the danger that proprietary knowledge can easily be dissipated to third parties in production because of knowledge spillover or because of their opportunistic behavior. Moreover, the characteristics of such products cannot be specified a priori without disclosing proprietary information. Such market failures lead to a preference for internalizing transactions; that is, the system of hierarchical intrafirm relations replaces market-based transactions.[58]

The fact that the public good character of knowledge makes it easily transferable and hard to protect lies at the core of the theory of internationalization. Buckley and Casson's landmark statement brings this idea to the fore:

> There is a special reason for believing that internalization of the knowledge market will generate a high degree of multinationality among firms. Because knowledge is a public good which is easily transmitted across national boundaries, its exploitation is logically an international operation; thus unless comparative advantage or other factors restrict production to a single country, internalization of knowledge will require each firm to operate a network of plants on a worldwide basis.[59]

Market failures of the type discussed in the preceding paragraph can occur also in a purely national firm and for transactions taking place in one country alone. However, the likelihood of market failures is greater when transactions occur between parties across national boundaries (e.g., an American international company conducting business transactions with a company based in India). Market failures are more frequent in

*Bruce Kogut and Udo Zander explain the concept of a public good as follows: "By public good, it is meant that one party may enjoy the use of a common good (such as the rose bush planted on the property of the other party) without diminishing its availability to the other. The issue of market failure arises out of a problem whether the owner of the rose can 'appropriate' a pecuniary payment from the neighbor." In " Knowledge of the Firm and Evolutionary Theory of the Multinational Corporation," *Journal of International Business Studies* 24, no. 4 (1993), p. 643.

TABLE 7.4
The O-L-I Theory
of FDI

	Ownership Advantage	Location Advantage	Internalization
Export	X		X
Contractual/licensing, etc.	X	X	
Wholly owned	X	X	X

foreign operations because of higher uncertainty involved (e.g., exchange rate fluctuations, political instability), insufficient information on the foreign market, problems with legal protection of property rights, and looser enforcement of contracts.

Location Advantages An international company is likely to invest in the most advantageous and attractive location. The attractiveness of a location is determined by its market potential and investment risk, investment incentives offered by the host-country government, location within, or in proximity to, a trade bloc (e.g., European Union, NAFTA), resource endowments, inexpensive unskilled or highly educated labor force (e.g., high-tech telecommunications and computer-related U.S. firms in India and China), and so on.

Several authors, including Buckley,[60] Casson,[61] and Dunning,[62] emphasize the need for evaluation of an international company's ownership or firm-specific advantages in relation to its competitors or in light of the competitive environment in host countries. This is because a specific advantage is valued in relation to the capabilities of competitors and peculiar characteristics of host countries.[63] For instance, a technologically intensive company like the U.S. company Hewlett-Packard may conceivably enjoy a greater competitive advantage over firms in a less developed country like Indonesia than over those in western Europe. Table 7.4 is a representation of the O-L-I theory of FDI.

The OLI framework proposed by Dunning has been updated and revised and so remains the standard theoretical model for explaining the development of the multinational enterprise. This is not to say that there have not been challenges and variations proposed by other scholars.

An Alternative View on the Evolution of an International Company

The notion that *all* knowledge is a public good has been challenged by Kogut and Zander. They argue that knowledge, especially that which is tacit and learned over a period of time within an organization (which they refer to as a social community), can be transferred (sold) to a third party at a price:

> The decision to transfer technology within the firm or in the market can be explained by the attributes of knowledge that constitute the ownership advantage of firms. A firm is a repository of knowledge that consists of how information is coded and action coordinated. The mode by which technology is transferred, e.g., within the firm or by licensing to other parties, is influenced by the characteristics of the advantage that motivates the growth of the firm across borders.[64]

They also challenge the notion that market failure (i.e., the hazard or cost of relying on the market) for intermediate goods leads to their internalization within the firm, which leads to the creation of international companies when such a transaction occurs across national boundaries. They write:

> The multinational corporation arises not out of failure of markets for the buying and selling of knowledge, but out of its superior efficiency as an organizational vehicle by which to transfer this knowledge across borders . . . The view we develop is that firms are social communities that serve as efficient mechanisms for the creation and transformation of

knowledge into economically rewarded products and services. The relevant benchmark for whether a firm will transfer a technology internally is its efficiency in this respect relative to other firms. Market considerations are not required.[65]

Another view on the theory of FDI is the notable behavioral-based international network theory. This theory describes a multinational company (MNC) as an internally differentiated and heterogeneous organizational system.[66] The MNC is viewed as a company that approaches global production, sales, and competition through a network of differentiated and interdependent subsidiaries that fulfill different objectives for the MNC. In addition, the MNC is viewed not as a static entity in the global marketplace but as one that is constantly changing. This description of the MNC has three central elements:

1. Strategic diversity in its organizational structure.
2. Internal relations and coordination mechanisms.
3. Internal flexibility and dynamism.

International network theory claims that the overseas subsidiaries of a multinational company can play different roles and have different responsibilities in the MNC global strategy that reflect differences in external environments and internal capabilities. Therefore, whereas the O-L-I rationale would argue that a firm engage in direct investment in a certain country, from a global strategic viewpoint international network theory may recommend licensing in that country, regardless of the resources and capabilities of the firm. The organizational structure and entry mode choices of the MNC are a function of its overall strategic goals.

Summary

We looked in this chapter at the factors affecting an international company's choice of mode for entering a foreign market. Generally, markets are entered to improve a company's competitive position, as an outgrowth of the corporate strategic process that we discussed in Chapter 6. In the next chapter, we focus on the types of strategies embraced by international companies in their search for a global competitive advantage.

A company desiring to enter foreign markets can choose from among several different modes of entry: exporting, countertrade, contract manufacturing, licensing, franchising, management service contracts, turnkey projects, and equity-based ventures. Each mode involves different levels of control over foreign operations, capital investment, risk, and potential returns.

Exporting, the selling of one's goods or services in another country, is the simplest means of entering foreign markets. This is usually the first step for a company going international. Exporting can be accomplished either indirectly, by an agent or forwarder, or directly, by an organizational subunit or subsidiary of the exporting company.

Countertrade refers to transactions involving a flow of goods or services in two or more directions. This is an important aspect of world trade, especially with developing and controlled economies. Countertrade can ease problems with inconvertible and fluctuating currencies, but it requires the ability to profitably dispose of the goods acquired through the countertrade agreement.

Licensing agreements allow a foreign company to use, in exchange for fees or royalties, another's patents and trademarks, manufacturing processes and know-how, trade secrets, or managerial and technical services. Foreign licensing involves more risk than straight exporting or countertrade, but it is less risky than direct investment in foreign production. Essentially, the firm is exporting its know-how instead of its products.

Franchising is a special type of licensing agreement. It involves a transfer of technology, business system, brand name, trademark, and other property rights by a franchisor to an independent company or person who is the franchisee. The franchisee is expected to duplicate the business model of the franchisor. The fast-food chain McDonald's has franchise restaurants all over the world.

A management service contract is an important vehicle for leveraging a firm's specialized technical know-how, tacit knowledge, and expertise in the management of specific types of enterprises in service industries such as hotels, hospitals, and airports. The international company does not own the property or physical assets of the enterprise that is under its management.

Equity-based ventures—both wholly owned and joint ventures—involve some degree of ownership and control of a foreign venture by the international company. The choice of joint venture will be influenced by company, industry, market, and country conditions. Maintaining the necessary control over a joint venture is crucial for the international company. However, control can be imposed by equity as well as nonequity mechanisms.

The chapter concluded with a discussion of the theories that try to explain different entry mode choices by a multinational company. Specifically we discussed Dunning's O-L-I theory and some dissenting viewpoints.

The choice of entry mode by an international firm is among the most significant decisions that a firm will make. It is influenced by firm capability, industry factors, location-specific factors, venture-specific factors, and strategic factors. Risk and resource requirements must be balanced in a manner appropriate to each entry mode decision.

Key Terms and Concepts

contract manufacturing, *225*
countertrade, *224*
dissemination risk, *235*
franchising, *230*
internalization, *240*

licensing, *226*
locational advantage, *240*
management service contract, *232*

ownership advantage, *240*
systemic risk, *235*
turnkey, *233*

Discussion Questions

1. What factors do international firms consider when choosing how to enter a foreign market?
2. What are the pros and cons of international licensing agreements as compared to exporting and foreign direct investment?
3. What is the O-L-I framework? Give examples of each dimension of this framework.

Minicase

Tommy Hilfiger in India

Mohan Murjani, the Hong Kong–based nonresident Indian who owns the rights for Tommy Hilfiger in India, has been instrumental in bringing about a strategic licensing agreement between the $6 billion Tommy Hilfiger Corporation and the Arvind Group of Ahmedabad. Under the licensing agreement, Arvind Brands, a wholly owned subsidiary of Arvind Mills of the Lalbhai Group, will sell Tommy Hilfiger apparel in India. Plans are afoot to market these products through exclusive Tommy Hilfiger stores and departmental chains. The approvals from the Reserve Bank of India and Foreign Investment Promotion Board are awaited.

DISCUSSION QUESTIONS

1. Evaluate the long-term implications of the decision of Tommy Hilfiger to sell the rights for Tommy Hilfiger products in India to Mr. Murjani.
2. What should Tommy Hilfiger consider in the licensing agreement with the Arvind Group?
3. Could Tommy Hilfiger have refused to sign the licensing agreement with the Arvind Group?
4. How can Tommy Hilfiger ensure its brand reputation in India?
5. Can Tommy Hilfiger control the operations of Arvind Brands?

Notes

1. Y. Wind and H. Perlmutter, "On the Identification of Frontier Issues in International Marketing," *Columbia Journal of World Business* 12 (1977), pp. 131–139.
2. I. Ekeledo and K. Sivakumar, "Foreign Market Entry Mode Choice of Service Firms," *Academy of Marketing Science Journal* 26, no. 4 (1998), pp. 274–292.
3. O. Andersen, "Internationalization and Market Entry: A Review of Theories and Conceptual Frameworks," *Management International Review* 37, no. 2 (1997), pp. 27–42; S. Agarwal and S. Ramaswami, "Choice of Foreign Market Entry Mode: Impact of Ownership, Location and Internalization Factors," *Journal of International Business Studies* 23, no. 1 (1992), pp. 1–28.
4. M. Erramilli and C. Rao, "Service Firms' International Entry Mode: A Modified Transaction–Cost Analysis Approach," *Journal of Marketing* 57, no. 3 (1993), pp. 19–38.
5. J. Roberts, "The Internationalisation of Business Service Firms: A Stages Approach," *Service Industry Journal* 19, no. 4 (1999), pp. 68–88.
6. D. Domke-Damonte, "Interactive Effects on International Strategy and Throughput Technology on Entry Mode for Service Firms," *Management International Review* 40, no. 1 (2000), pp. 41–59.
7. B. Kogut and H. Singh, "The Effect of National Culture on the Choice of Entry Mode," *Journal of International Business Studies* 19, no. 4 (1988), pp. 411–432.
8. H. Barkema, J. Bell, and J. Pennings, "Foreign Entry, Cultural Barriers and Learning," *Strategic Management Journal* 17 (1996), pp. 151–166.
9. S. Agarwal, "Socio-cultural Distance and the Choice of Joint Venture: A Contingency Perspective," *Journal of International Marketing* 2, no. 2 (1994), pp. 63–80.
10. F. Root, *Entry Strategies for International Markets* (Lexington, MA: Lexington Books, 1994).
11. V. Terpstra and C. Yu, "Determinants of Foreign Investment in U.S. Advertising Agencies," *Journal of International Business Studies* 19, no. 1 (1988), pp. 33–46.
12. K. Banerji and R. Sambharya, "Vertical Keiretsu and International Market Entry: The Case of the Japanese Automobile Ancillary Industry," *Journal of International Business Studies* 27, no. 1 (1996), pp. 89–113.
13. Y. Pan, S. Li, and D. Tse, "The Impact of Order and Mode of Entry on Profitability and Market Share," *Journal of International Business Studies* 30, no. 1 (1999), pp. 81–103.
14. Y. Pan and D. Tse, "The Hierarchical Model of Market Entry Modes," *Journal of International Business Studies* 31, no. 4 (2000), pp. 535–554.
15. A. S. Konigsberg, "Around the World with Franchise Legislation," *Franchising World,* May–June 1999, pp. 18–22.
16. CCH Business Owners Toolkit: Checklist of Basic Franchise Agreements, http://www.toolkit.cch.com/tools/franch_m.asp.
17. Farok J. Contractor and Sumit K. Kundu, "Modal Choice in a World of Alliances," *Journal of International Business Studies* 29, no. 2 (1998), pp. 325–356.
18. Ibid., p. 329.
19. William Echikson in Brussels, with Jack Ewing in Frankfurt, Heidi Dawley in London, and Carol Matlack in Paris, "Is Your Flight Late? Have a Massage (int'l edition)," *BusinessWeek Online,* June 26, 2000.

20. Contractor and Kundu, "Modal Choices in a World of Alliances," p. 329.
21. Charles W. Hill, Peter Hwang, and Chan W. Kim, "An Eclectic Theory of the Choice of International Entry Mode," *Strategic Management Journal* 11(1990), pp. 117–128.
22. Ibid.
23. Ibid.
24. S. Agarwal and S. Ramaswami, "Choice of Foreign Market Entry Mode." *Journal of International Business Studies* 23, no. 1 (1992), pp. 1–28.
25. Krishna M. Erramilli, "The Experience Factor in Foreign Market Entry Behavior of Service Firms," *Journal of International Business Studies* 22, no. 3 (1991), pp. 479–501.
26. Bruce Kogut and Harbir Singh, "Entering United States by Joint Venture: Competitive Rivalry and Industry Structure." In Farok Contractor and Peter Lorange, eds., *Cooperative Strategies in International Business* (Lexington, MA: Lexington Books, 1988).
27. Gary Hamel and C. K. Prahalad, "Do You Really Have a Global Strategy?" *Harvard Business Review,* July–August 1985.
28. Hill, Hwang, and Kim, "An Eclectic Theory of the Choice of International Entry Mode."
29. Oliver E. Williamson, *Markets and Hierarchies: An Analysis of Antitrust Implications* (New York: Free Press, 1975); David J. Teece, "The Multinational Enterprise: Market Failure and Market Power Considerations," *Sloan Management Review,* September 1981.
30. Kogut and Singh, "Entering the United States by Joint Venture."
31. Agarwal and Ramaswami, "Choice of Foreign Market Entry Mode."
32. Chan W. Kim and Peter Hwang, "Global Strategy and Multinationals' Entry Mode Choice," *Journal of International Business Studies* 23, no. 1 (1992), pp. 29–53.
33. Agarwal and Ramaswami, "Choice of Foreign Market Entry Mode."
34. Bruce Kogut and Harbir Singh, "The Effect of National Culture on the Choice of Entry Mode," *Journal of International Business Studies,* Fall 1988.
35. Krishna M. Erramilli and C. P. Rao, "Choice of Market Entry Modes by Service Firms: Role of Market Knowledge," *Management International Review* 30, no. 2 (1990).
36. Agarwal and Ramaswami, "Choice of Foreign Market Entry Mode."
37. Hubert Gatignon and Erin Anderson, "The Multinational Corporation's Degree of Control over Foreign Subsidiaries: An Empirical Test of a Transaction Cost Explanation," *Journal of Law Economics and Organization* 4, no. 2 (1988).
38. Agarwal and Ramaswami, "Choice of Foreign Market Entry Mode."
39. Kim and Hwang, "Global Strategy and Multinationals' Entry Mode Choice."
40. Gatignon and Anderson, "The Multinational Corporation's Degree of Control."
41. Gatignon and Anderson, "The Multinational Corporation's Degree of Control"; Kogut and Singh, "The Effect of National Culture on the Choice of Entry Mode."
42. Richard N. Osborn and Christopher C. Baughn, "Forms of Inter-organizational Alliances," *Academy of Management Journal* 33, no. 3 (1990), pp. 503–519.
43. Hamel and Prahalad, "Do You Really Have a Global Strategy?"
44. Kim and Hwang, "Global Strategy and Multinationals' Entry Mode Choice."
45. Ibid.
46. Georgio Barba Navaretti, Jan I. Haaland, and Anthony Venables, "Multinational Corporations and Global Production Networks: The Implications for Trade Policy." Report prepared for the European Commission Directorate General for Trade, Centre for Economic Policy Research, London, 2002.
47. Frank V. Cespedes, "Control vs. Resources in Channel Design: Distribution Differences in One Industry," *Industrial Marketing Management* 17 (1988), pp. 215–227; John M. Stopford and Louis T. Wells, *Managing the Multinational Enterprise: Organization of the Firm and Ownership of the Subsidiaries* (New York: Basic Books, 1972); Erin Anderson and Hubert Gatignon, "Modes of Foreign Entry: A Transaction Cost Analysis and Propositions," *Journal of International Business Studies* 17 (Fall 1986), pp. 1–26.

48. John H. Dunning, "Toward an Eclectic Paradigm of International Production: A Restatement and Some Possible Extensions," *Journal of International Business Studies* 19 (Spring 1988), pp. 1–31.

49. John H. Dunning, "Toward an Eclectic Theory of International Production: Some Empirical Tests," *Journal of International Business Studies* 11, no. 1 (1980), p. 9.

50. Ibid., p. 10.

51. Alan M. Rugman and Alain Verbeke, "Extending the Theory of the Multinational Enterprise: Internalization and Strategic Management Perspectives," *Journal of International Business Studies* 34, no. 2, (2003), p. 127.

52. Dunning, "Toward an Eclectic Theory of International Production," p. 9. Also Sanjeev Agarwal and Sridhar N. Ramaswami, "Choice of Foreign Market Entry Mode: Impact of Ownership, Location, and Internalization Factors," *Journal of International Business Studies,* First Quarter, 1992, p. 4.

53. J. Johnson, "The Efficiency and Welfare Implications of the Multinational Corporation." In Charles Kindelberger, ed., *The International Corporation* (Cambridge, MA: MIT Press, 1970).

54. J. McManus, "The Theory of the International Firm." In G. Paquet, ed., *The Multinational Firm and the Nation State* (Ontario: Collier Macmillan Canada, 1972).

55. Stephen Magee, "Information and the Multinational Corporation: An Appropriability Theory of Foreign Direct Investment." In Jagdish N. Bhagwati, ed., *The New International Economic Order* (Cambridge, MA: MIT Press, 1977).

56. Peter J. Buckley and Mark Casson, *The Future of the Multinational Enterprise* (New York: Holmes and Meier, 1976), p. 33.

57. Bruce Kogut and Udo Zander, "Knowledge of the Firm and the Evolutionary Theory of the Multinational Corporation," *Journal of International Business Studies* 24, no. 4 (1993), pp. 625–646.

58. Navaretti, Haaland, and Venables, "Multinational Corporations and Global Production Networks."

59. Buckley and Casson, *The Future of the Multinational Enterprise,* p. 45.

60. Peter J. Buskley, "Problems and Developments in the Core Theory of International Business," *Journal of International Business Studies* 21, no. 4 (1990), pp. 657–666.

61. Mark C. Casson, *The Firm and the Market* (Oxford: Basil Blackwell, 1987).

62. Dunning, "Toward an Eclectic Theory of International Production."

63. Sanjay Lall and S. Siddharthan, "The Monopolistic Advantages of Multinationals: Lessons from Foreign Investment in the U.S.," *Economic Journal* 92 (September 1982), p. 679.

64. Kogut and Zander, "Knowledge of the Firm and the Evolutionary Theory of the Multinational Corporation," p. 626.

65. Ibid., p. 627.

66. Christopher A. Bartlett and Sumantra Ghoshal, *Managing across Borders: the Transnational Solution* (Boston: Harvard Business School Press, 1989). Also Nitin Nohria and Sumantra Ghoshal, *The Differentiated Network: Organizing Multinational Corporations for Value Creation* (San Francisco: Jossey-Bass, 1997).

Managing International Collaborative Initiatives

Chapter Learning Objectives

After completing this chapter, you should be able to:

*   Understand various types of international collaborative agreements, including equity joint ventures and international strategic alliances.
*   Discuss the various motivations for firms to enter into international joint ventures.
*   Delineate the many advantages as well as potential pitfalls associated with international joint ventures.
*   Gain the ability to pick the right international alliance partner.

Opening Case: Strategic Alliances in the Automobile Industry

General Motors' alliance strategy and its initiatives to develop new markets are key elements in the company's approach to globalization. Alliances afford the opportunity for component and architecture sharing as well as the reduction in R&D costs that will be critical for manufacturers looking ahead to hybrid vehicle technology and, ultimately, hydrogen-based fuel-cell vehicles. By pulling together the talents and resources from its global R&D network, GM has been able to reduce redundancy, accelerate ongoing development and jump-start new development.

During the last decade, to meet the ever-growing need for advanced technology, General Motors has recruited a rich blend of international talent, with engineers and scientists from North and South America, Europe, the Middle East, China, Taiwan, India, and Korea. This melting pot of technologists has created a bubbling cauldron of exciting ideas that General Motors is applying to the development of a vast array of product, technology and business innovations. In fact, one of the biggest benefits of globalization for GM has been access to technology being developed around the world. Today, our most advanced research programs, such as our fuel cell technology development, are being conducted across several continents.

During the past few years, the auto industry has undergone major structural changes to an extent not seen since the early formation of the industry. There are now a number of major alliance groups, although there are also individual companies that will probably remain independent, such as Honda and BMW. The GM alliance network includes General Motors, Opel/Vauxhall/Holden, Saab, Fiat Auto, Isuzu, Fuji Heavy Industries (Subaru), and Suzuki.

While GM has 100-percent equity ownership of some of its key units—such as Opel and Saab—the company has used an approach that is more akin to a "loose confederation" in joining recently with other partners such as Suzuki, Fuji and Fiat Auto. GM has a minority equity stake in each of these companies. In addition, GM has major joint ventures in both China and Russia.

An important incentive for GM to form alliances with companies such as Suzuki is to more quickly develop a presence in the Asian markets. It takes a long time to start from scratch in a new market. It may take even longer to create brand equity for a new product in spite of the fact that the manufacturer might have a strong corporate brand. Many of GM's new partners have a rich portfolio of products that are smaller and lower-priced than the typical entry-level vehicles sold in the United States and, therefore, are better suited for emerging markets. The GM–Suzuki alliance is a win-win for both partners. GM has not only gained increased market presence, but also has access to Suzuki small car platforms and its low-cost manufacturing expertise. The tie-up gives Suzuki access to GM advanced technologies, particularly alternative propulsion and hybrid systems, entry to the growing Latin American market, and worldwide component sourcing.

As noted above, automotive alliances afford the opportunity for component and architecture sharing. For example, Fiat and GM have formed a joint venture to develop engines for both companies. Successful platform synergies are more complex (and more difficult to achieve). By using a well-defined "bandwidth" for architectural dimensions of the body and by imposing constraints on the chassis, it is possible to develop several models from a given platform. These models will appear different from one another in terms of styling and may well have very different features, especially in the interior of the car.

A key advantage of platform sharing is that a common body manufacturing system can be used to produce all the models. Obviously, this is easy to accomplish for body-on-frame vehicles, but it can be done even with unibody construction. As a result, two alliance partners can develop different models tailored for different markets but share many of the upfront engineering and development costs and use common manufacturing and assembly equipment. In effect, this is a way to generate larger volumes, from a single product development investment. The challenge, however, is to make the different models truly unique, so that customers do not feel their purchase is a "look-alike" with another product. All manufacturers are getting very good at this, notwithstanding some early setbacks in the U.S. when the Big Three first switched from full-frame to unibody construction to reduce the weight of their vehicles.

Another important incentive driving automotive alliances is the need for the auto companies to reduce their research and development costs. GM is working with its alliance partners on more than 50 joint technology development projects, ranging from pedestrian protection and 42-volt electrical architecture to all-wheel-drive and clean diesel engines. This has resulted in savings and cost avoidance in the millions of dollars. R&D is critical today because manufacturers are under tremendous pressure to provide more innovative products. Customers continue to raise the bar with respect to styling, quality, reliability, and safety. At the same time, manufacturers face difficult technical challenges on the energy and environmental front. They must make continual improvements in vehicle fuel economy and reductions in tailpipe emissions everywhere in the world.

While there is more improvement to be squeezed out of the conventional internal combustion engine, manufacturers are looking ahead to hybrid vehicle technology and, ultimately, to a hydrogen-based fuel-cell vehicle. The development costs and infrastructure changes necessary to take the step to fuel cell technology are staggering, so it makes sense for auto manufacturers to team up and share knowledge in order to move the industry as a whole ahead faster.

In addition to the equity alliances mentioned, GM has formed research partnerships with other manufacturers, suppliers, universities, and governmental agencies. These research alliances cover such topics as advanced internal combustion engine development, fuel cell technology, advanced chassis systems, electronics and communications systems, and many others. They are truly global, involving companies and universities in Canada, Europe, Japan, China, and the Middle East. By pulling together the talents and resources from this global R&D network, redundancy has been reduced, ongoing development accelerated, and new development jump-started. GM's electrical architecture program is an excellent example of global collaboration. Instead of more than 10 separate projects, we now have one single program with clearly defined technology roadmaps and deliverables for each partner.

Discussion Questions

1. What are various reasons for a firm to engage in an international joint venture?
2. What concerns do you have regarding GM's joint ventures in Russia and China?
3. In your opinion, what are the risks of international joint ventures?

The International Collaboration Imperative

As illustrated in Chapters 6 and 7, globalization has both prompted and been prompted by interfirm collaboration across borders to control against the various macro-level environmental risks that were discussed in the first section of this book. Managing a collaborative relationship is a relatively more complex endeavor than managing a wholly owned subsidiary.

An international collaborative relationship can take many forms. In this chapter, even though many of the benefits and risks overlap, we distinguish between the international equity joint venture and the nonequity strategic alliance. **Equity alliances,** or international joint ventures, may be generally defined as "*formal agreements between two or more business organizations to pursue a set of private and common interests through the sharing of resources in contexts involving uncertainty over outcomes.*"[1]

Management of an equity joint venture or a nonequity strategic alliance is complex because the management of the enterprise is shared with a foreign partner. The collaborative route is a popular mode for foreign market entry among international companies. These strategic initiatives take many forms.[2] For instance, they may be

- Explorative or exploitative.[3]
- Cross-border or home-country based.
- Equity- or contractual-based.
- Two or multiple partners.
- Short-term project-based or long term.[4]

Furthermore, the collaborative initiatives can be focused on various stages of the respective firms' value chains. Link alliances connect different stages of the partners' value chains and subsequently bring together different knowledge levels and skills. Scale alliances focus on similar stages of partner firms to gain increased economies of scale and cost efficiencies.[5]

Many companies shun international joint ventures and strategic alliances, insisting on wholly owned subsidiaries as a mode of foreign market entry. An increasing number of companies, however, conclude that under certain circumstances a joint venture mode of market entry can be beneficial to all parties involved in its formation. As discussed throughout this text so far, in the current environment of international business globalization is affected by various initiatives. These include governments moving more toward market economies and subsequently initiating increased privatization and deregulation activities. Also, regional economic integration, like NAFTA and the EU, promotes increasing globalization. In Chapter 6, we saw that firms are continually balancing global efficiency with national responsiveness. Overall, because of these increased pressures of globalization, an international firm must engage in many activities simultaneously and quickly. The international firm must also accumulate more and more knowledge as well as the capacity to learn in order to keep current competitive advantages and develop new ones. The international joint venture has become a strategic vehicle for firms to penetrate markets without exhausting capital, to deflect some of the risks associated with going overseas, and to increase their knowledge bases.

Equity International Joint Ventures

As exemplified by the various initiatives of General Motors depicted in the chapter opening case, an international joint venture is a business collaboration between companies based in two or more countries, which share ownership in an enterprise established jointly for the production and/or distribution of goods or services. More narrowly defined, it is the pooling of a portion of the resources of two or more firms from different nations within a common legal organization.[6] The separate entity can be a partnership or a closely held corporation and can issue corporate securities in its own right.[7] In this text, we define an **equity international joint venture (EIJV)** as a separate legal organizational entity representing the partial holdings of two or more parent firms, in which headquarters of at least one is located outside of the country of operations of the joint venture. The entity is subject to joint control of its parent firms, each of which is economically and legally independent of the other(s).[8]

An equity international joint venture is often established to jointly develop a new technology or to obtain resources that require huge amounts of capital—for example, jointly exploring for oil and natural gas. Pure trade agreements are excluded from our concept of a joint venture. Of particular interest to us in this chapter are joint ventures in which one of the partners is an international company and the other is a national of the host country.

International entry, where the firm maintains wholly owned control, has been identified as highly risky, especially in terms of expected profits and risk. Researchers like Woodcock, Beamish, and Makino suggest that the total costs of international acquisitions, including the costs of procuring additional resources and the costs of control, are higher relative to cooperative international entry modes.[9] These authors found that EIJVs outperform international acquisitions. Specifically regarding international joint ventures, this entry mode mitigates the political, cultural, and financial risks associated with foreign direct investments. Furthermore, this risk-sharing function is more critical in research-intensive industries, where high costs of technology and short product life cycles leave little time to amortize development costs.[10]

As illustrated in Figure 8.1, international equity joint ventures are a form of international cooperation where the level of interdependence between partners is the highest. As suggested in Chapter 7, the level of control is the highest as well, although the international firm does give up some control and profits, in contrast to going at it alone. In the following sections, we examine the nature of joint ventures, their advantages and disadvantages, and how they can be best utilized by international companies.

Conditions that Influence the Choice of the Joint Venture Mode

The affinity of companies for joint ventures abroad is influenced by several factors. The following are some of the most influential.

Legislation   The laws in some countries mandate that foreign firms must form joint ventures with local partners (rather than establishing wholly foreign-owned subsidiaries) in order to conduct business within their borders. Often this rule is applied

FIGURE 8.1
Cooperative
Strategies

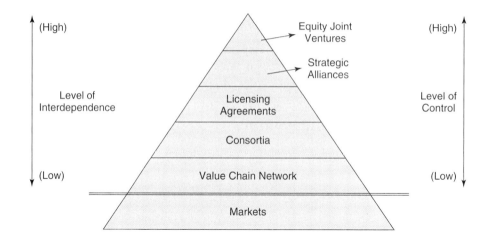

for certain industries only. Even when no such legal requirement exists, the attitude of the host government may be so heavily biased in favor of joint ventures that this seems the only practical entry mode available to a foreign company. Historically, China represented this type of environment. However, international firms are increasingly going at it alone in China. Vietnam represents an environment today where joint ventures are the primary, if not only, way of gaining a foothold in the country.

Protecting a Profitable Market Tariffs or import barriers imposed by a host-, home-, or third-party government may threaten a profitable export market developed in a country by an international company. If the local government has policies that discourage or disallow wholly owned subsidiaries, then the multinational company can choose to effect a licensing agreement with a local company. However, if the international company decides that neither licensing nor contract manufacturing is an attractive alternative to pursue, then it is left with two alternatives: (1) form a joint venture with a local partner or (2) abandon the market altogether. Only if an international company has a firm policy of its own of not forming joint ventures under any circumstances will it decide to abandon the market despite its already established position.

Technological Characteristics Companies that have products whose value is based on a unique production process, trademark, brand name, or trade secret are hesitant to form joint ventures because of the danger that the production process and trade secret may be leaked to third parties. Such companies are reluctant to form joint ventures also because of the risk of eroding the value and prestige associated with the quality of their product, brand name, or trademark, which could happen if the joint venture is unable to maintain the original quality standards.

Integrated Network of Subsidiaries Companies that have several subsidiaries abroad that are integrated globally or regionally in a network of production-assembly-distribution systems are likely to oppose joint ventures. The reason for this is that joint ventures with local partners decrease their flexibility, as well as increasing the control required to optimally integrate the different subsidiaries involved in this network. For example, local partners are more likely to be interested in the profitability of the joint venture and would therefore be inclined to oppose any plans to curtail production in the joint venture and shift it to another subsidiary or to supply third markets from another subsidiary, even though the multinational company considered such plans to be in the

FIGURE 8.2
Motives for International Joint Ventures

Source: Adapted from
P. Beamish, A. Morrison,
A. Inkpen, and P. Rosenzweig,
*International Management: Text
and Cases,* 5th ed. (New York:
McGraw-Hill/Irwin, 2003),
p. 123.

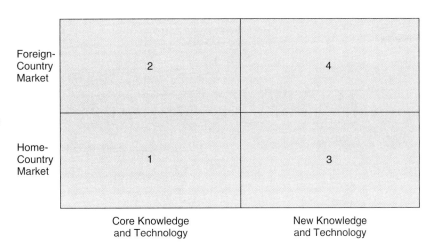

interests of its global operations. Therefore, a joint venture that has been established primarily to produce products for the national market only may be more suitable for an international company than one that may have to be integrated in a global or regional network of subsidiaries. Exceptions to this policy are invoked when the international company has an overwhelming majority equity interest in the joint venture, which gives it a veto power over the decisions made by the joint venture management.

Acquisition of Knowledge and Expertise Companies seek joint ventures when they need expertise that can be best provided by a local company, such as a well-developed marketing and service organization; well-established and proven contacts with important officials in the host government; an established name and place in the host country's industrial sector; and a competent management team and labor force.

Motives for International Joint Ventures

Figure 8.2 is a matrix that suggests four distinct reasons a firm will form an international joint venture.[11] The first rationale is seen in quadrant 1. There, a firm desires to further penetrate its current market with its existing products and technologies. Thus the firm relies on its existing products and existing market knowledge. In many cases, it is the small or medium-sized firm that basically needs more cost efficiencies to compete against the larger firms in the industry. Often, the cooperating companies limit the joint venture to a platform technology or product to gain cost efficiencies, as evidenced by the GM–Fiat venture depicted in the opening case of this chapter. Subsequently, each takes responsibility for integrating that jointly developed platform into its respective autonomous downstream activities. For example, the two American companies Merck and ProMetic BioSciences have formed a comarketing and technological cooperation alliance for monoclonal antibody purification. By pooling their respective resources and technologies, Merck and ProMetic can now offer clients an integrated solution to problems. The value of this comarketing agreement is substantial for both companies because the combined product offerings complement each one's core competencies. The partners hope that the alliance will bolster sales of their respective products and strengthen the market position of each. These types of ventures are often seen in the pharmaceutical industry, where small, limited-product firms collaborate to support research and development at an intermediate level. Figure 8.3 illustrates this type of joint venture.

FIGURE 8.3
R&D Joint Ventures

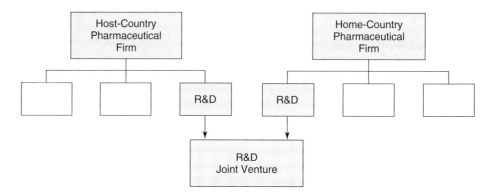

In quadrant 2 of Figure 8.2, the firm is looking to extend its product offerings to a new country. That is, it has a core technology or knowledge that is giving it a competitive advantage in its home country and now desires to extend that advantage overseas. As seen in Chapter 6, the new country may be a market that is potentially attractive, although the firm has little competitive strength. Or it can be a higher risk market where the firm wishes to hedge against that risk. Furthermore, the firm may not have the necessary capital or knowledge to expand in that market on its own. Thus it requires a local partner. During the 1990s and into the twenty-first century, various Japanese auto parts firms sought to follow their customers (Toyota, Honda, Nissan and Mitsubishi) to the United States in order to continue to provide the low-cost, innovative technology that they did in Japan. Because of capital costs and perceived new-market risks, the Japanese firms decided to expand through joint ventures.

Quadrant 3 is actually the reverse of quadrant 2. Here the firm is the foreign partner looking to collaborate with a home international firm. As was seen in the U.S. auto parts industry, U.S. firms were eager to collaborate with Japanese partners in order to learn new, low-cost industry technologies. As seen above, the Japanese firms were actually examples of firms in quadrant 2. They were seeking local market knowledge and contacts in the United States as well as deflecting some financial risks. Practical Insight 8.1 illustrates these motives for Cummins Diesel partnering with Tata in India.

Finally, firms located in quadrant 4 of Figure 8.2 are those that are looking to diversify away from current products, technologies, and markets and enter both different industries and new markets. As seen in Chapter 6, firms attempt to enter new industries and new markets simultaneously for distinct reasons, including home-market saturation, as illustrated by the U.S. cigarette industry during the past 15 years.

Figure 8.4 illustrates a typical international joint venture where partnering firms form a new, autonomous company. International joint ventures can take many forms, depending on the needs and circumstances of the partners and the conditions under which the collaboration agreement is consummated.

International joint ventures can vary depending on such factors as the percentage of the total equity in the joint venture held by each partner, the number of partners involved in the joint venture, and the characteristics of the partners. An international company could have a variety of partners in a foreign joint venture. The partner could be a local company, another international company, the host-country government, or the general public in the host country. Also, an international company's ownership of a joint venture may vary from a majority to an equal or minority participation in the total equity capital of the joint venture. Practical Insight 8.2 depicts a 50–50 international joint venture between Anheuser-Busch and Bacardi.

PRACTICAL INSIGHT 8.1

TATA CUMMINS LIMITED

Tata Cummins Limited (TCL) is a 50–50 joint venture between Tata Engineering, India's largest automobile manufacturer, and Cummins Engine Company Inc. (USA), a world leader in the manufacturing and design of diesel engines. Tata Engineering is the largest manufacturer of commercial vehicles in India, while Cummins Engine Company is the largest 200+ HP diesel engine manufacturer in the world. The joint venture was incorporated in October 1993, with commercial production commencing on January 1, 1996. Tata Cummins is located in India, in Jamshedpur, and manufactures fuel-efficient, low-emission, environment-friendly diesel engines. These engines are used in Tata Engineering's new generation medium and heavy commercial vehicles that conform to European Union standards. The primary market is the Indian commercial vehicle business, with Tata Engineering as their largest customer and "delivery partner." Cummins brought new technology, including both manufacturing and distribution, and capital to the partnership. Tata has the India market knowledge and embedded base of customers.

The mission of TCL continues to be widely acknowledged and the company is benchmarked as one of the best in the world. Its core values are care for customers, obsession for quality, deep concern for people, commitment to do what's right and not what's convenient, guaranteed leadership, responsible citizenship, and relentless improvement. End users of TCL's engines perceive the products to be more powerful and more efficient, to have higher reliability, lower life cycle cost, lower emissions, and lower maintenance costs, to be easier to recondition, and to use up to 40 percent fewer parts in comparison to competitive designs.

TCL has a goal of bringing delight to customers through excellent customer support, and making "Customers for Life." The engines reach the end users quickly through TCL's delivery partners, Tata Engineering and Cummins India. Technical training is provided various dealers as well as roadside mechanics. Expert service engineers can be reached 24 hours a day through a help line at TCL.

TCL has very strong systems and IT infrastructure that control and facilitate its operations. In June 2000, a Web-based supply chain management system was implemented to further increase efficiency. They have been awarded excellence awards by the Eastern Region and are a QS 9000 company.

While mainly poor, India is very labor-intensive and boasts top-notch intellectual capital. The human talent makes an excellent target for industrial development. Both Cummins Engine Company and Tata Engineering Company were looking for continual learning, innovation, and efficiency. Cummins's option to pursue this joint venture was fueled by highly attractive future profitability prospects in a high-risk country. It was a place where Cummins wanted to expand its core technologies, but didn't want to risk going into the country alone. Tata's existing infrastructure and cultural knowledge made it an excellent prospective partner. Also, Cummins's low competitive strength in the highly attractive country further suggested joint venturing.

The transfer of technology and knowledge between Cummins and Tata benefit both companies and their markets. Teaming up and sharing technology has put the joint venture at a competitive advantage. The two companies are well ahead of their competition and this partnership would ensure keeping them the biggest and best in the business. There is a good strategic fit between the companies, as they are in the same industry, excel in the same expertise, and target the same markets. Strong parent companies help make the transition into a joint venture a little bit easier. Strong financial backgrounds for both companies indicate a history of success and determination, which are favorable in looking for a joint venture partner.

Source: Written by Melissa deWitt and Roger Kashlak, 2002.

The number of partners involved in a joint venture may also vary. There might be more than two partners involved when firms or groups of interests from two or more countries form a joint venture. For example, the U.S. Cargo Sales joint venture, formed by Air France, Delta Air Lines, and Korean Air expanded in 2003 as Alitalia joined the alliance.

Advantages of International Joint Ventures

A joint venture may be the only possible way to set up a business in a country. This may be particularly true in the case of certain industries that are regarded as politically sensitive such as the petroleum industry, aircraft manufacture, or transportation or utility companies.

PRACTICAL INSIGHT 8.2

ANHEUSER BUSCH–BACARDI JV: A "MALTERNATIVE" BEVERAGE

In February 2002, Anheuser Busch (A-B), the largest brewery in the world, and Bacardi, maker of the world's number 1 selling rum, formed a team to produce the newest entry into the specialty alcohol market. The new malt beverage will be called Bacardi Silver to compete with Smirnoff Ice, Mike's Hard Lemonade, and SKYY Blue. The joint venture will be a 50–50 partnership. Both companies have strong brand awareness throughout the world and already have established loyal customers. The venture seems to have combined the strengths of each company to offer the best chance for success.

In the past, the market was divided into three large segments—beer, wine, and spirits—and consumers stayed loyal to their preferred segment. Today, the market still has three segments, but many more consumers are experimenting with beverages among the segments. Market growth rates have slowed because of the plethora of breweries in the market causing companies to streamline operations and look for cost efficiencies. Companies are attempting these efficiencies through joint ventures and mergers such as happened between South African Brewery (SAB) and Miller Brewing, formerly the third and seventh largest breweries in the world. Barriers to entry are relatively low for the industry, but any new entrant must have the spending power to invest enormous sums of capital to compete with the likes of Anheuser-Busch, Miller, and Coors.

The specialty alcohol market began in the early 1990s. As recently as 2001, the specialty market has seen a large influx of new products. Currently, Smirnoff Ice, a product from Diageo, commands the largest market share globally. Smirnoff Ice is followed by Mike's Hard Lemonade, Bacardi Silver, and then SKYY Blue in the "malternative" market. SKYY Blue, a product of Miller, was introduced in March 2002. The malternative beverage has seen rapid growth and a variety of products that have entered the market have grabbed market share from the other three segments of beer, wine, and spirits.

A-B offers over 15 alcoholic beverages to entertain a wide range of customers. Its products include Bud, Michelob, Busch, and O'Doul's. Its domestic partnerships include Redhook and Widmer breweries in the northwest United States. Its foreign joint ventures are located in China, Chile, and Mexico with the Wuhan Brewery (China) and the Grupo Modela Brewery (Mexico) the largest and most profitable. Its domestic strategy is to build market share by spending heavily on advertising, emphasizing quality, and copying innovations like malternative beverages. Its international strategy is to market Budweiser as a premium export and to pursue partnerships with other brewers. The company is in an industry with serious competitors that are offering multiple products to compete with Bud.

Bacardi is the world's best selling rum and owns other popular brands such as Martini & Rossi, Dewar's Scotch whiskey, Bombay gin, and DiSarano amaretto. It has production facilities

FIGURE 8.4
The Equity Joint Venture

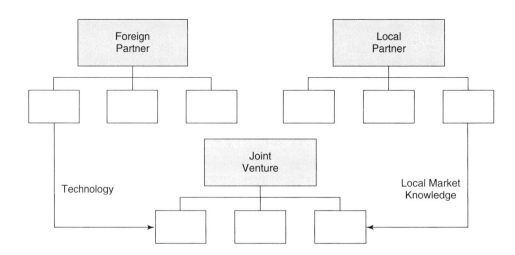

in nine countries within the Americas, the Carribean, and Europe. Bacardi's main rivals are Diageo and Pernod Ricard, which have started to enter partnerships with other companies in the beer and wine segment to complement their spirit brands.

The new malternative product is targeted at the largest growing segment in the alcohol industry, the 21- to 27-year-old segment. The aggressive marketing campaign for Bacardi Silver that A-B plans to roll out will focus on both women and men in this segment. The company does not want to market the product as a woman's drink only. The product will also be directed to an older woman population because of its smooth, appealing taste. It will promote the product's "mixability" characteristic, meaning that it can be combined with juices or other spirits to create new drinks. Bacardi Silver will be positioned primarily in bars and clubs since research has shown that most consumers will experiment with new drinks in these atmospheres.

The joint venture is a combination of each company's strengths, which is a typical precursor to a partnership. The venture will utilize A-B's strength in promotion and distribution along with Bacardi's one-of-a-kind rum flavor. Since the new product is not first to market, A-B's distribution channels will help Bacardi Silver reach the market very quickly and in a variety of locations. The brand recognition for both companies is extremely strong throughout the world, and especially in North America, its target market. Speed to market and consumer knowledge of established brands are two of the most important factors for a successful joint venture.

The joint venture will be a 50–50 partnership and receive a large commitment from both firms. A-B will contribute its modern production capabilities, distribution channels, and promotional prowess to the venture, while Bacardi will supply the rum flavor and logo of the product. The venture's 50–50 ownership does not give one firm an advantage over the other to exploit the partnership in its own opportunistic way. With the strong commitment from each company the dedication and motivation to succeed will be overwhelming. This display of compelling reciprocity is another key for joint venture success.

Both firms have been involved in multiple partnerships throughout their long histories. Experience in joint ventures gives valuable knowledge on how to handle a situation where people come from different cultures and work backgrounds. There are cultural differences between the two firms: A-B is U.S.-based and Bacardi is based primarily in the Caribbean. The geographic distance between companies is relatively short. The geographic closeness and the experience of each firm are important factors in the survival of this joint venture.

The venture could lead to future developments of malternative products. If the specialty alcohol market continues to gain market share on the remaining alcohol market, the two firms could extend the product line to include new flavors or frozen drinks. This is a strong possibility due to the saturation occurring in the market and growing consumer demand for new products.

Source: Written by Andrew Larson and Roger Kashlak, 2002.

A firm with limited resources is able to enter a greater number of markets through the joint venture route than would be possible with a policy of establishing only wholly owned subsidiaries abroad. In some developing countries in particular, where large local firms do have capital but are short of technical and managerial know-how, a multinational company can form a joint venture with a local firm, without making any capital outlays, by receiving equity in the joint venture in exchange for its patents and know-how.

In countries where the fervor of nationalism is high, a joint venture with a local firm or government agency could help in substantially lowering the governmental and societal hostility to a foreign firm.

In many instances, the local partner is able to circumvent red tape and bureaucratic harassment, which afflict multinational companies in many countries. Through well-established contacts with the right people, the local partner is often able to obtain important permits and licenses for imports, foreign exchange, plant expansion, water and electricity supply, and so on.

First-class managerial talent is difficult to find everywhere, but this is particularly evident in developing countries. The best way of obtaining high-quality managerial talent that is knowledgeable about local conditions is often through a joint venture with a successful local firm.

Another advantage of an intangible nature is the effect on the local employees of a joint venture. It was reported that in India the sale of 10 percent of the stock of a once wholly owned subsidiary to the Indian public had a significant positive impact on the morale of the Indian staff.

Government contracts are sometimes given only to domestic firms. International firms in certain industries are therefore obliged to form joint ventures with local companies in order to qualify for government contracts.

Developing countries have been insisting that joint ventures include their respective governments because of a historical distrust of foreign countries arising from their experience with colonialism. This distrust is transferred to foreign companies, which, it is feared, might exert undue political and social influence. A minority participation of the government in a joint venture would allow its representatives to sit on the board of directors, thus permitting direct scrutiny of the workings of the joint venture. However ill-founded such anxiety may be, allaying it may be a valid motive for a multinational company to form a joint venture with the government. Civil servants on the board of directors also can be helpful in obtaining favorable rulings from the government on vital matters such as price increases and import permits. As a partner in the joint venture, the host government is in a position to examine the problems and needs of the joint venture, as well as its contributions to the country's economy, from the inside.

International companies are often confronted with a peculiar problem that forces them to form joint ventures. For example, foreign companies planning to establish manufacturing facilities in a country may find that certain prominent local business firms have managed to corner permits that are no longer granted by the government, but are required to produce products that the international company wants to produce. Hence they are compelled to form joint ventures with local firms that own the required permits to produce the products.

Many companies form joint ventures with local firms that have the ability to provide the foreign partner with a steady stream of quality raw materials and/or components. A joint venture with a local firm is especially useful when imports of the required materials have been cut off by the government and when a license for their production has been given to the local firm.

Disadvantages of International Joint Ventures

Joint ventures can have several disadvantages as well. International companies therefore should carefully weigh the advantages against the disadvantages of joint ventures before deciding for or against them.

Consider a company with a planning system that attempts to mobilize and deploy its worldwide resources with the aim of achieving its global objectives effectively and efficiently. This requires that actions be taken based on decisions that are in the interests of the company as a whole, even though the interests of one or more of its subsidiaries may have to be sacrificed in the process. A multinational company can take such actions only if each subsidiary's objectives are derived from, and dovetail with, the global company objectives. Problems in achieving global objectives could arise if a foreign joint venture partner refuses to go along with decisions of the international company that may be in the best interests of its global objectives but which may not be in the best interests of the joint venture partner. For example, the local partner may resist efforts by the international company to have one of its wholly owned subsidiaries in another country, rather than the joint venture, serve third-country markets. A multinational company may propose this if it is more efficient and cheaper to serve a third-country market from a wholly owned subsidiary. For example, the Australian market may be served more efficiently from a newly established subsidiary in Indonesia than from a joint venture in Mauritius or Sri Lanka. The local partner is likely to resist such a shift even more because it may mean a loss in sales revenue, and particularly when exports are essential to keep the joint venture operating at full capacity.

Sourcing of components and raw materials could also cause problems in a joint venture. For example, manufacturing certain components in a third county and importing them for final assembly in the joint venture might be cost-efficient. However, the local partner is not likely to look favorably on this idea, especially if, as is very often the case, the joint venture partner is capable of making the components, and importing them would mean an increase in costs and a decrease in the joint venture's profits.

Problems could arise if the local partner—in the absence of any prior agreement precluding any such action—insists on exporting the products of the joint venture into world markets. A multinational company may find itself in a very grave predicament if the products of the joint venture were to compete in third markets with similar products produced by its other subsidiaries. And should the joint venture products appear in the home market of the multinational company itself, this would be worse still.

The preceding examples illustrate how a joint venture could disrupt a multinational company's plans for a regional or worldwide integration of its production-assembly-marketing operations in view of its total company objectives. Problems could also arise in other areas. The long-term success of a joint venture depends not only on how and to what extent the capabilities and contributions of each partner reinforce the other's, but also on the combination of their respective risk-versus-gain and time-versus-return attitudes. Let us see how the risk–gain and time–return attitudes of the partners could affect a joint venture's prospects.

The desire for growth and the propensity to assume corresponding risks to achieve it may differ between the partners. For example, a multinational company, because of its bigger size and stronger financial position, might be willing to assume financial risks on projects that have prospects of high returns. Such high risk–high return projects might appear as reckless behavior to the local partner, which might be relatively more conservative because of its smaller size and weaker financial position. Because of the differences in the willingness to assume risks, friction could arise between the joint venture partners on issues such as the extent to which the joint venture company is an aggressive price leader; the debt-to-equity ratio assumed; whether some budget items are capitalized or expensed; the handling of employee pension funds; the amount of resources committed to marketing capabilities to exploit new markets; and the aggressiveness of marketing policies.

The time–return attitudes of the two partners might also vary and cause problems. This is not to be confused with the conservative-versus-liberal attitude toward risks, which has to do with a company's propensity to take risks. The time-versus-return attitude of a company measures its willingness to wait in anticipation of a future return. For example, the local partner might be unwilling to commit the company's resources to research and marketing programs that promise high long-term returns but sacrifice the joint venture's short-term competitive edge and immediate profits.

Conflicts could also occur due to the different tax laws and foreign exchange considerations affecting the two partners. A U.S. international company, for example, may wish to forgo dividends in order to defer U.S. taxes on dividends repatriated to the United States. But this may conflict with the desire of the local partner for dividends and immediate cash.

An international company that has a joint venture in a country with a history of currency devaluations would prefer to keep the joint venture's current assets to a minimum to limit its losses from local currency depreciation. It would also prefer to borrow from the local capital markets to meet the joint venture's working capital needs. This again may be unacceptable to the local partner, which has no such losses to worry about and may therefore object to the idea of incurring heavy interest payments by borrowing for working capital requirements. Joint ventures could, in this way, reduce the flexibility of an international company to respond strategically to exploit profit opportunities arising from differences in tax laws and currency fluctuations.

Disagreements also could arise over staffing practices in the joint venture. In some countries top management personnel are commonly recruited from a particular social class. It is also common in some countries, like India, for owners of firms to give good jobs to family members or members of the same community. An international company, which desires to employ competent managerial personnel in the joint venture, might have a conflict over such a policy.

The Importance of Having the Right IJV Partner

New organizational structures, such as joint ventures, have a greater chance of releasing conflicts that past structures were able to contain within their hierarchies and regulations.[12] Thus conflicts that arise in front-end negotiations of IJVs may threaten the sustainability of these agreements. Lyles studied various mistakes of international joint ventures, grouping these errors into technological, human resources, negotiations, partner, and strategic goal categories. The truth is that many international joint ventures fail. That is, they are either dissolved before they were expected to be, or they do not meet the objectives that were laid out at the beginning of the collaboration. The reasons for failure include

- Lack of trust between partners.
- Different partner objectives.
- Hidden partner objectives.
- Changing partner objectives.
- Clashing partner national cultures.
- Clashing partner organizational cultures.
- No real strategic fit between partners.
- Opportunistic behavior by a partner.
- Lack of knowledge reciprocity between partners.[13]

As can be seen, selecting the right partner is critical for a firm initiating an international joint venture. Figure 8.5 illustrates that most joint ventures begin where the partners see a strategic fit but do not understand that their cultures—national, organizational, or both—do not efficiently mesh to do business. Other joint ventures begin where there is a high degree of cultural fit—for instance, the firms of two friends who went through a rigorous MBA program together—but no real strategic complementation. Without a doubt, the firm should look for a partner where high degrees of both cultural and strategic fits are likely. Practical Insight 8.3 describes two joint venture failures in Japan caused by partnering with a wrong local company.

Maintaining Control Over an International Joint Venture

Maintaining control over a joint venture is crucial for an international company with a plan to integrate it into its global production-assembly-marketing plan. However, it is also necessary to maintain control of some sort over the joint venture even if the international company has no such plans.

PRACTICAL INSIGHT 8.3

CHOOSE THE RIGHT PARTNER OR FAIL: JOINT VENTURE FAILURES IN JAPAN

British drugstore chain Boots Co. announced in July that it would close all four of its outlets here. Other retailers, including such established players as U.S. clothing and outdoor goods retailer L. L. Bean, have had to close some stores and revamp marketing strategies in response to stagnating sales. Analysts blame the withdrawals on discounting by rivals, poor selection of joint venture partners and the failure to build brands.

[Boots] fell victim to a couple of the classic blunders made by firms entering the Japanese retail market. "The most important failing was the choice of trading firm Mitsubishi Corp. as a joint venture partner," said Merrill Lynch's Suzuki. "Trading firms lack the retail expertise necessary to succeed in Japan. Boots should have tied up with a retailer instead."

She said French supermarket Carrefour could suffer a similar fate. "Japanese shoppers go to Carrefour and are disappointed because it does not have a French-enough feel and seems too much like a Japanese supermarket," she said. "To succeed, foreign retailers have to create a distinctive atmosphere." Carrefour refuses to comment on the performance of its Japanese branches.

Meanwhile, even more established retailers like L. L. Bean, which is regularly rated the No. 1 lifestyle and outdoor brand in the country, are having to revamp. L. L. Bean dissolved its joint venture with department store operator Seiyu Ltd. in March and set up a wholly owned unit instead. It now has just nine stores, down from a peak of 22 in 1997. The new subsidiary, L. L. Bean International Japan, is adopting a new "multichannel" strategy for Japan combining catalog sales, retail sales and sales via the Internet at a new Japanese-language Web site due to begin operations early next year.

Source: Adapted from Graeme Kerr, "Feeling the Pinch," Asahi News Service, August 1, 2001. Copyright 2001 Asahi News Service.

FIGURE 8.5
EIJV Partner Selection

Source: Adapted from P. Beamish, A. Morrison, A. Inkpen, and P. Rosenzweig, *International Management: Text and Cases,* 5th ed. (New York: McGraw-Hill/Irwin, 2003), p. 131.

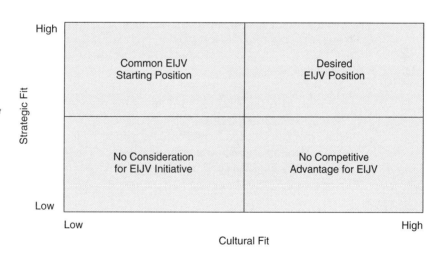

There is no control problem if the joint venture is wholly owned by a multinational company or when it owns a majority of its equity. However, how can a company minimize problems in a joint venture in which it has minority or 50–50 ownership of the equity? Here are some techniques that have been used by international companies.

An international company can negotiate a management contract with the local partner giving it the authority to manage the joint venture. This method is frequently used by international companies in developing countries. The developing countries are often willing to give up managerial control of joint ventures if they do not have the trained personnel necessary to manage them. Managerial control can be obtained in various ways. One method is to give an international company a majority representation on the board of directors. If a majority cannot be obtained, then the next alternative is to have equal representation by the two sides on the board of the joint venture but to provide in the joint venture contract that the views of the international company would be upheld in the event of a deadlock. If the local partner does not agree with this alternative, then the international company may be able to negotiate an agreement that gives it the right to veto any unacceptable policy decision.

Another method of obtaining managerial control is to negotiate the authority to appoint members to the executive committee of the joint venture. The executive committee is concerned with the day-to-day management of the enterprise, whereas the board of directors is concerned with the formulation of the major policies and plans of the enterprise. The board of directors also has the responsibility of overseeing the total management of the enterprise and appointing the key management personnel. Technically, the board of directors can overrule the decisions of the executive committee. But in the event that an international company cannot obtain control over the joint venture's board, then it may have to settle on the right to name the executive committee members. A company can also negotiate the right to select the managing director and/or the technical director of the subsidiary, which in essence gives it the authority to make strategic decisions for the joint venture.

Taking local financial institutions such as banks and/or insurance companies as majority partners in a joint venture is a device often used by multinational companies. Financial institutions quite often take little or no interest in the actual day-to-day management of the enterprise, thus enabling the multinational company to retain control over its management.

A multinational company could obtain a controlling interest in a joint venture, although it may not hold a majority interest, by taking two or more local firms as partners. For example, an international company could own a 40 percent share of a joint venture with the balance owned by two or more other partners. Although the other partners theoretically could collude and form a voting bloc against the international company, in reality the odds are against this outcome.

Selling sufficient stock on the local stock market is one variation of the above method that can be used to prevent bloc voting by local partners. The public issue of shares represents an ingenious technique of local public participation because the public is generally not interested in taking an active role in the day-to-day management of the joint venture. So, even if a multinational company holds a minority of the voting shares, it can still exercise effective control.

Actual control over a joint venture can be exercised by an international company through a license agreement. When the joint venture cannot operate effectively without the license, and the license is terminable by the international company, the significance of the license to the control of the joint venture is obvious. Similar results can be obtained through the lease of equipment and various types of technical and financial assistance agreements.

A multinational company could also negotiate a contract which gives the local partner a controlling equity interest in the joint venture with the stipulation that all output of the enterprise, or at least that which is exported, be marketed by a separate marketing company that is wholly owned by the international company. It is not, however, uncommon for the local partner to own up to 49 percent of the voting shares of the marketing company. The key is for the international firm to control the management of the marketing company. This device is used to prevent the local partner from disrupting the global marketing plans of the international company. In the absence of this type of control by the international company over the marketing of products, the local partner could start to export the products produced by the joint venture to third-country markets already served by the international company's subsidiaries in other countries.

Negotiating the International Joint Venture

In international joint ventures, as in the case of negotiations in general, the power of each prospective partner relative to each other will influence the front-end negotiations process.[14] If this, in turn, leads to contentious communications, the ultimate success of the venture may be jeopardized.[15] Thus the partner with the most relative power will have the ability to influence front-end discussions and ultimately the joint venture structure.

Weiss proposed a framework to analyze the negotiations leading to international joint ventures. Studying a proposed alliance in the international telecommunications industry, he suggested a complex web of interrelationships that must be addressed during the negotiation. External environmental conditions as well as internal conditions such as EIJV partner objectives were proposed to influence the negotiations, strategy, implementation, and eventual partner benefits of the EIJV.[16] Earlier international business researchers suggested that three distinct entities—the international firm, the local firm, and the host government—will each have its objectives directly influenced by external environmental forces that include the various cultural, economic, and political systems. Each entity will bring its desired goals to the EIJV table. In turn, these objectives, diverse in nature, will lead to varying degrees of negotiating conflicts and cooperation.[17] Comparing U.S. problem-solving negotiation methods with the cultures of the Japanese, South Koreans, and Taiwanese, researchers found that the perceived satisfaction of outcomes of negotiations were based primarily on partner attractiveness and compatibility.[18]

Incorporating a political dimension into negotiations, the international firm must realize that in many countries, the host government is a key stakeholder in the venture and thus will exert power during the negotiations.[19] Doz argued that negotiations between an international firm and a host government will center on the division of profits. Consistent with the strategic thinking identified in Chapter 6, he identified three strategies that the international firm may adopt when dealing with host governments:

- Integration, where the firm seeks to increase efficiency through the optimum allocation of global resources.
- Multifocal, where the firm permits a degree of influence over its strategies in exchange for host-government support.
- National responsiveness, where the international company positions itself as a partner to the local government.[20]

Incorporating lessons learned from the previous chapters exploring the external environment where international firms must exist, Table 8.1 illustrates the effect of these factors on the front-end negotiations of international joint ventures.[21] A perceived riskier environment clearly will influence the firm to seek higher financial guarantees during negotiations.

During international joint venture negotiations, the financial targets alluded to in Table 8.1 may include (1) cost-based criteria such as share of global research and development and share of central overhead and technology transfer costs, and (2) market-based criteria related to the net incremental revenues from the new market.[22] International negotiations, with applications formation and partner decisions, are explored further in Chapter 13.

TABLE 8.1
Host-Country Effects on EIJV Negotiations Financial Targets

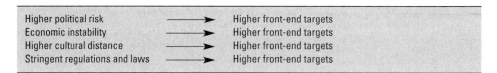

Higher political risk	⟶	Higher front-end targets
Economic instability	⟶	Higher front-end targets
Higher cultural distance	⟶	Higher front-end targets
Stringent regulations and laws	⟶	Higher front-end targets

Nonequity Strategic Alliances

Not a week goes by without an announcement in the business press of a strategic alliance between two or more companies. Almost every internationally minded company trying to become global will consider forging a strategic alliance with another company as a fast track to that goal. A strategic alliance is a collaborative arrangement that a company makes with competitors, suppliers, customers, distributors, or firms in the same or different industries in order to develop, produce, distribute, or market a product or service. Strategic alliances are also formed to obtain technology, minimize environmental risks, or gain key human and material resources. The joint venture discussed to this point in this chapter is actually an equity-based strategic alliance. In this section, we focus on **nonequity alliances**—strategic alliances as collaborative initiatives without equity.

Thus compared to the equity-based joint venture, the **international strategic alliance** is a loose association between companies. An example is the alliance begun between the Japanese company Mitsubishi and the German company Daimler-Benz (before it merged with Chrysler from the United States). The two companies worked on 11 joint projects involving cars, aerospace, and integrated circuits. Similarly, Sony, the dominant Japanese and world firm in the electronics and entertainment industries, has forged alliances with many small, high-technology companies in the United States and Europe during the past 15 years. The company shares its research staff, production facilities, and even business plans for specific products with small companies. Sony has worked with Panavision Inc. to develop a lens for high-definition television cameras now in use, with Compression Labs Inc. on a videoconferencing machine, and with Alphatronix Inc. to develop rewritable, optical-disk storage systems for computers.[23]

A specific type of nonequity strategic alliance is the non–cash partnership, where each company has a stake in the other and they trade assets. Such cash-neutral transactions may become a trend in a credit-sensitive international environment. Examples of such alliances abound in the international airline industry, where clusters of firms have forged marketing and operations alliances. Star Alliance, a consortium that includes United Airlines, Lufthansa, and Air New Zealand, among other carriers, is an alliance where the member carriers market, operationally support, and logistically offer ease of connection with each member's routes. Delta and Air France have a similar arrangement, as do British Air and Qantas.

Reasons for Creating Strategic Alliances

Beyond the apparent marketing and operations synergies just suggested, there are, of course, other reasons for strategic alliances. Many of these rationales are similar to the reasons identified earlier in this chapter regarding international joint ventures. They include

- Penetrating new foreign markets.
- Sharing marketing costs.
- Sharing research and development costs and risks.

PRACTICAL INSIGHT 8.4

STRATEGIC ALLIANCE BETWEEN MERCK KGaA (SLP PROCESSING) AND PROMETIC BIOSCIENCES FOR MONOCLONAL ANTIBODY PURIFICATION

SLP [Merck's Scientific Laboratory Products division] has entered into a strategic alliance with ProMetic BioSciences. The agreement between the two parties outlines the co-marketing and technological cooperation terms in effect. This document was prepared by Merck and ProMetic to provide additional information to the joint press release. By pooling their respective resources and technologies, Merck/SLP Processing and ProMetic can now offer clients an integrated solution including both a superior ion exchange step and a robust synthetic affinity step. This has now become a coordinated, integrated effort better suited to addressing the current and emerging bioprocess recovery needs of biotech companies.

What Merck brings to ProMetic:

- Worldwide sales force and corporate network
- Technical support for sales and marketing
- Application laboratory that will provide client services using Merck and ProMetic technologies with initial data for process development
- Access to worldwide distribution
- Proprietary technology for high performance polymeric media
- Broad range of highly accepted ion exchange bioprocessing media (Fractogel®) successfully competing with Amersham Pharmacia Biotech
- Complementary technologies and products such as advanced and specific enzymes and buffers

What ProMetic brings to Merck:

- R&D capabilities in the critical area of affinity chemistry
- Access to the ProMetic platform technology for mAb [monoclonal antibody] purification

- Combinatorial libraries of high performance ligands (non-protein/peptide, synthetic chemical compounds)
- Track record of scalability, delivering products in GMP [Good Manufacturing Practice] condition to extremely demanding clients such as Aventis Behring, Genzyme Transgenics Corp., etc.
- Complimentary technology conducive to better penetration of the mAbs market
- Technological edge to compete aggressively with Amersham Pharmacia Biotech and Millipore
- More technologically integrated solution for customers (lower cost, stronger, etc.)

The value of this co-marketing agreement is substantial for both companies because the combined product offerings complement each one's core competencies. Each company is confident that the relationship will bolster sales of its respective products and strengthen its respective market position. In the USA, ProMetic will maintain its marketing presence, which will be coordinated with Merck's marketing and sales team . . .

Even though the marketing process will constitute a "joint presentation" of an integrated process featuring both Merck and ProMetic technology, each company will sell its respective products and invoice its client independently. It is expected that the majority of clients will choose to incorporate these new recovery tools in processes for new entities, and it will be 3–5 years between the time Merck and ProMetic technology is adopted by a client and the time significant commercial sales are generated. However, this alliance will lay the foundation for an impressive pipeline of mAb projects, ensuring a solid base of growing annuity revenues for both Merck and ProMetic.

Source: From ProMetic Biosciences Ltd, www.prometic.com. Reprinted with permission.

- Launching a counterattack against competitors.
- Pooling global resources.
- Learning from partners.

Companies form strategic alliances as a cheap and more efficient way of entering either a partner's home market or a third-country market in which a partner is especially strong. During the 1990s, AT&T Network Systems (now Lucent) partnered with various European firms to effectively distribute its products throughout Europe. In return, AT&T distributed its partners' products in the United States.

Practical Insight 8.4 illustrates a nonequity strategic alliance between Merck and ProMetic BioSciences for researching and marketing monoclonal antibodies. It illustrates what each partner brings into the strategic alliance.

The Risks of Managing Strategic Alliances

Potential concerns of international strategic alliances are similar to those regarding international joint ventures. All strategic alliances are not successful. In fact, many alliances are terminated for a variety of reasons, including many risks that affect the international strategic alliance. *Relational risk,* for example, is concerned with the probability that a partner firm does not fully commit itself to the alliance and the potential consequences that ensue. This lack of commitment may affect the attainment of front-end alliance strategic objectives, based on the premise that both (or all) partners forgo opportunistic behavior.[74] As an illustration of this risk, partners who are direct competitors will incur more relational risk in their alliance, and thus the alliance is not predicted to be as successful as alliances between noncompetitors.[25]

A second risk posed is *performance risk.* This refers to external environmental factors, in the home country, the host country, or globally, that jeopardize the attainment of the alliance's strategic objectives. These factors include political changes, economic changes, and shifts in law. Whereas performance risk deals with many strategic initiatives of an international firm, relational risk focuses on the internal dynamics of international alliances in particular. Figure 8.6 illustrates the linkages between these external and internal risks and international alliance type.[26]

In light of relational or internal risks specific to international alliances, among the most common reasons for the failure of these partnerships are the following:

- *Clash of cultures:* Communications and decision-making differences because of cultural differences (discussed in Chapter 5) could lead to serious problems between the alliance partners.

- *Unrealized partner expectations:* One or both partners might conclude that the alliance is not realizing the objectives that were the predominant reasons for forming the alliance.

- *Surrender of sovereignty:* A smaller partner in an alliance may lose its independence if it becomes overly dependent on the larger partner for things like money, new technology, or market access in a key country.

- *Risk of losing core competence to a partner:* When an alliance is formed, there is generally a transfer of knowledge among the partners. For example, Company X

FIGURE 8.6
Risks in International Collaborative Initiatives

Source: From T. Das and B. Teng, "A Risk Perception Model of Alliance Structuring," *Journal of Management,* 2001. Copyright © 2001 *Journal of Management.* Reprinted with permission.

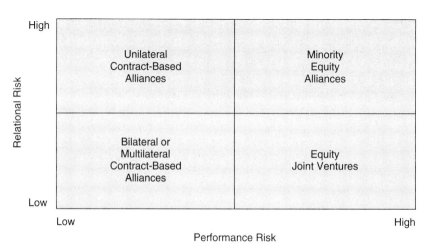

may learn how to market a product in Company Y's home market, and Company Y may learn from Company X a secret process for manufacturing a patented product. Later Company Y may enter a foreign market and compete with Company X with products using the secret process. The original alliance may fail because of this strategy implemented by Company Y.

Making International Collaborative Initiatives Work

Whether the international cooperative arrangement is equity based or nonequity based, certain aspects must be considered in order to help ensure the success of the initiative. Parkhe suggested that reciprocity, trust, and lack of opportunistic behavior between and among partner firms were critical components to success of the international partnership.[27] Steensma and Lyles studied EIJVs in economically transitioning nations and suggested that an imbalance in the management control structure of the partnership may lead to conflict and ultimate failure.[28]

Although there are no magical prescriptions to ensure the success of equity and nonequity alliances—that is, joint ventures and strategic alliances—some guidelines could enhance the chances of their survival.

Trust Is Built in Small Steps Trust among partners is critical to the success of any joint venture or strategic alliance. But trust cannot be written into a legal document in the form of a contract. It is each participant's observed behavior that builds trust in any relationship, and this fact is true in a strategic alliance as well. Partners must keep trust in mind and behave in an open manner that enhances the bonds of that trust between them. Each of the partners must attempt to find ways of working together without either one feeling that the other is trying to steal technology or take advantage in any way. Such trust takes time to develop, and relationships based on trust need to be developed in a deliberate fashion.[29]

Pick a Compatible Partner Any alliance must be important enough to have a strategic impact on the future well-being of both partners. If one of the partners considers the alliance of merely peripheral importance, the seeds of dissolution are sown. Cultural compatibility is an absolute prerequisite for the success of any partnership. Therefore, if the partners in an alliance have greatly divergent cultures, it would be advisable to have one of the partners play a dominant role in the day-to-day management of the venture once the strategic intent of the alliance has been mutually agreed upon. This arrangement is the one under which the New United Motor Manufacturing, Inc. (NUMMI), partnership between General Motors and Toyota was administered, with Toyota managing the venture on a daily basis. Figure 8.7 illustrates the following partner factors that correlate with eventual alliance success:

- ***Reciprocity:*** Both partners give and take their knowledge (market knowledge, technology, etc.) equally. Equal reciprocity, as opposed to unequal reciprocity among alliance partners, has been linked to long-term alliance profitability.[30]
- ***Trust:*** Both partners honor the commitments and duties of the final strategic alliance agreement. Interorganizational trust has been linked to improved market performance of international alliances.[31] Trust between partners helps to deter opportunistic behavior, which is discussed next.[32]
- ***Lack of opportunism:*** In the case of a changing environment and new opportunities, neither partner uses the joint venture or strategic alliance exclusively to its own benefit and to the detriment of the other partner.[33]

FIGURE 8.7
**International
Strategic Alliance:
Partner Success
Factors**

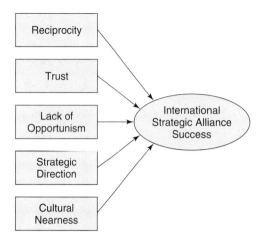

- ***Strategic direction convergence:*** Both partners have similar strategic goals from the international alliance.
- ***Cultural nearness:*** From an organizational perspective and in a national context, each organization understands the other's motives and actions.

Create and Maintain an Alliance with Equal Power An alliance in which one of the partners is more powerful than the other is in danger of collapsing, unless the more powerful partner treats the weaker partner as an equal. Power derives from one's ability to deliver something (technology, capital, information, or resources) to another, something that the other party cannot obtain in the marketplace or develop by itself at an acceptable cost. The power that a company can muster in an alliance is not necessarily associated with its relative size vis-à-vis its partner. For example, a company that has the proprietary knowledge and expertise to develop a breakthrough drug for the treatment of a fatal disease, or that can develop a better and faster computer chip, will have the power to deal on equal terms with a much larger company. The power balance in an alliance is what matters. A small company may have the technology, but a large firm could provide the required capital to develop and commercialize it. As long as the relationship maintains a power balance, the partnership should not expect trouble. However, when a power imbalance develops in an alliance, the company emerging as the more powerful should be careful to limit its use of power in order for the alliance to survive.

Understand the Control Structure of the Partnership Overlapping with the power balance is the control structure of the partnership. Two types of control exist for an EIJV. The first, *ownership control,* is the legitimate authority each partner has over specific assets.[34] This is based on relative equity each firm has in the partnership. The second, *management control,* is the decision-making power that each partner has. It may be linked to ownership control, but it may also be an offshoot of various informal practices, implementation techniques, and political processes.[35] These pieces of the overall control structure must be clearly communicated to all partners.

Be Patient   An infinite amount of patience is needed on both sides during the various stages of an alliance. During the initial negotiation phase, patience is necessary to ensure that the alliance is properly structured in terms of who is responsible for what types of decisions, including production, marketing, labor relations, and pricing. Spending extra time and effort on ironing out such issues early in the alliance helps prevent future problems. Patience is also needed when the alliance begins to function. Expecting immediate results can prove fatal. Managers on both sides must recognize that delays and unexpected technical and people-related problems will emerge in any organization, and that the chances of such problems arising increase greatly when two companies are engaged in a collaborative effort.

Joint ventures, strategic alliances, and wholly owned subsidiaries will continue to be among the three most dominant modes of entry into foreign markets. In the next chapter we discuss strategies implemented by global companies to gain a competitive advantage.

Summary

By focusing on a specific strategic initiative and mode of entry, we emphasized the importance as well as the risks of collaborating with international partners. The equity-based joint venture was discussed initially from the perspective of environmental conditions that influence this choice of entry mode. Then we looked at firm-specific motives for international joint ventures and illustrated a matrix that delineates product and geographic diversification rationales. Advantages and disadvantages of this entry mode were delineated and we further emphasized the importance of choosing the right partner to avoid the fate of many international joint ventures—failure to meet stated objectives and premature dissolution. Also, issues dealing with control over and negotiations of the international joint venture were uncovered.

The chapter then identified another form of international collaboration, the nonequity strategic alliance. The motives, advantages, and risks were shown to parallel those already discussed for international joint ventures. Furthermore, we discussed tactics for actually making both equity and nonequity alliances work, including partner selection, trust established continually yet incrementally, maintaining a balanced power structure between alliance partners, and patience by the alliance partners. We also discussed the framework for partner selection, which includes reciprocity, trust, lack of opportunism, strategic direction convergence, and cultural nearness.

Key Terms and Concepts

equity alliances, *250*
equity international joint venture (EIJV), *251*

international strategic alliance, *264*

nonequity alliances, *264*

Discussion Questions

1. Why do firms pursue international joint ventures?
2. What are the various advantages and disadvantages of international joint ventures for the international firm?
3. Create a profile of a foreign partner for your international joint venture. What characteristics are desirable? What characteristics would you wish to avoid?
4. Compare nonequity strategic alliances with equity international joint ventures.

Minicase

Can Little Fish Swim in a Big Pond? Strategic Alliance with a Big Fish

Globalization and the Internet have created unprecedented opportunities for small and medium-sized businesses in Canada—an environment where competition is fierce. To take advantage of these opportunities, while avoiding some of the competitive obstacles often faced by the little fish in the big ocean, many of these businesses are forming partnerships or, more precisely, strategic alliances.

"There are various advantages to forming strategic alliances," says Estelle Metayer, president of Montreal-based Competia Inc., a leading competitive intelligence and strategic planning company and publisher of Competia Online. "One is the ability to penetrate markets that would be too costly to develop on your own. For example, if you form an alliance with an American partner who can take on your products and distribute them through their network, you could save a lot of money on the marketing side." Another big advantage comes from joining forces with a business that can provide your enterprise with access to expensive technology you might not be able to afford otherwise.

Management-based strategic alliances are also advantageous, Ms. Metayer says. "Often, smaller companies don't have big management teams. So if they need someone who has a certain expertise, but they really can't afford to hire such a person, then they can form an alliance with a company that has that management expertise."

Forming an alliance with a larger company is sometimes the only way to have access to the type of capital and resources they need to be able to grow, says Gary Shiff, a partner at the Toronto-based law firm Blake, Cassels & Graydon LLP. "For example, we have a client, a very small company of two people, and the only way it could get its product into the marketplace was to establish an alliance with a large company, which it did. The large company will give them a large sum of money. In return, our client will give up a lot of its equity—it will only own 30% or 40%—but over time, if the product is successful, our client can repurchase some of that equity," Mr. Shiff says.

Strategic alliances also benefit the big companies. "With large corporations, one of the problems often is the inability to move quickly, because of bureaucracy and more complicated internal politics. Smaller companies are able to react more quickly to changes in the marketplace. So from both parties' perspectives, it serves their needs," he says.

Although the concept of a strategic alliance can sound so appealing to a struggling small business that they might be tempted to run out and get one, experts warn businesses should not rush into partnerships, especially if another company comes courting.

"As a small company, we get five or six requests for alliances a week from companies I don't know anything about, and suddenly they want to form an alliance. So my advice is not to rush into an alliance. You have to be proactive," Ms. Metayer warns.

The first step is to examine your business and determine what gaps need to be filled. "Say I'm a small company that is in textile products and I'm finding that to penetrate the U.S. market, I need to be very close to a furniture manufacturer, since they are the ones who will use my textiles. I might want to build an alliance with a big player in the U.S., and thus be able to penetrate the large distribution channels."

Once need is determined, the search for a partner can begin. "Alliances don't work when you don't know each other well," Ms. Metayer says. Thorough research of a potential partner is critical. Check out a potential partner's current viability, look into the company's management style to see if it is compatible with yours, contact former partners, current and past clients and suppliers. "The way a company treats its suppliers can be indicative of how they will treat their partner."

She also suggests a small business position itself as a client of a potential partner, to experience how the candidate treats its clients. Even after thorough research, do not rush into an alliance, she says. "Do a project together, for example, work together so you can really see if it works before you go on a larger scale. You also need to make sure legally you have a very tight agreement, in particular one that allows the alliance to dissolve easily. If it doesn't work, you need to make sure you've planned for that."

Besides legal advice, businesses entering into an alliance should seek out professional accounting advice, Mr. Shiff says. "A strategic alliance will have tax implications, and those tax issues need to be addressed right at the beginning."

While rushing into an alliance can court a nasty breakup, choosing a partner that is so similar it could be a competitor is courting disaster, Ms. Metayer and Mr. Shiff concur.

"Go back to the example of the textile business—if you build an alliance with someone who builds the frames for the chairs, you're never going to compete. But if you form an alliance with someone in the U.S. who also makes upholstery textile, eventually one or the other is going to say, 'hey, I can do this by myself,' " Ms. Metayer says. The last thing any company needs is a rival who has intimate knowledge of its internal operations.

Source: Alexandra Lopez-Pacheco, "You're Not Alone: Strategic Alliances Often Give Little Fish the Push They Need to Swim in the Ocean. The Key Is to Pick a Partner that Is a Good Fit," *The National Post,* September 23, 2002, Toronto Edition. Special Report: Financial Post: Enterprise, p. SR1. Material reprinted with the express permission of: "National Post Company," a CanWest Partnership.

DISCUSSION QUESTIONS

1. Why would small companies want to form alliances with much bigger companies?
2. What risks do small companies face in forming such alliances?
3. Discuss how a company should approach the opportunity to form an alliance with another company.

Notes

1. A. Arino, J. de la Torre, and P. Ring, "Learning from Failure: Towards an Evolutionary Model of Collaborative Ventures," *Organization Science* 9, no. 3 (2001), pp. 306–325.
2. A. Arino, "Measures of Strategic Alliance Performance: An Analysis of Construct Validity," *Journal of International Business Studies* 34 (2003), pp. 66–79.
3. M. Koza, and A. Lewin, "The Co-evolution of Strategic Alliances," *Organization Science* 9, no.3 (1998), pp. 255–264.
4. Arino, "Measures of Strategic Alliance Performance."
5. P. Dussuage, B. Garrette, and W. Mitchell, "Learning from Competing Partners: Outcomes and Durations of Scale and Link Alliances in Europe, North America and Asia," *Strategic Management Journal* 21, no. 2 (2000), pp. 99–126.
6. B. Kogut, "Joint Ventures: Theoretical and Empirical Perspectives," *Strategic Management Journal* 9 (1988), pp. 319–332.
7. K. Harrigan, "Joint Ventures and Competitive Strategy," *Strategic Management Journal* 9 (1988), pp. 141–158.
8. W. Newberry and Y. Zeira, "Generic Differences between Equity International Joint Ventures, International Acquisitions and International Greenfield Investments: Implications for Parent Companies," *Journal of World Business* 32, no. 2 (1997), pp. 87–102.
9. C. Woodcock, P. Beamish, and S. Makino, "Ownership-Based Entry Mode Strategies and International Performance," *Journal of International Business Studies* 25, no. 2 (1994), pp. 253–273.
10. F. Contractor, and P. Lorange, "Why Should Firms Cooperate? The Strategy and Economics Basis for Cooperative Ventures," *International Marketing Review,* Spring 1986, pp. 74–85.
11. P. Beamish, A. Morrison, A. Inkpen and P. Rosenzweig *International Management: Text and Cases,* 5th ed. (New York: McGraw-Hill/Irwin, 2003), p. 123.
12. J. Brett, D. Shapiro, and A. Lytle, "Breaking the Bonds of Reciprocity in Negotiations," *Academy of Management Journal* 41, no. 4 (1998), pp. 410–424.
13. M. Lyles, "Common Mistakes of Joint Venture Experienced Firms," *Columbia Journal of World Business,* Summer 1987, pp. 79–85.
14. A. Inkpen and P. Beamish, "Knowledge, Bargaining Power and the Instability of International Joint Ventures," *Academy of Management Review* 22, no. 1 (1997), pp. 177–202.
15. Brett, Shapiro, and Lytle, "Breaking the Bonds of Reciprocity in Negotiations."

16. S. Weiss, "Analysis of Complex Negotiations in International Business: The RBC Perspective," *Organization Science,* May 1993, pp. 269–283.

17. D. Datta, "International Joint Ventures: A Framework for Analysis," *Journal of General Management,* Winter 1988, pp. 78–91.

18. J. Graham, "The Influence of Culture on the Process of Business Negotiations," *Journal of International Business Studies,* Spring 1998, pp. 81–96.

19. K. Brouthers and G. Bamossy, "The Role of Key Stakeholders in International Joint Ventures: Case Studies from Eastern Europe," *Journal of International Business Studies* 28, no. 2 (1997), pp. 359–373.

20. Y. Doz, "Government Policies and Global Industries." In M. E. Porter, ed., *Competition in Global Industries* (Boston: Harvard Business School Press, 1986), pp. 225–266.

21. R. Kashlak, "Establishing Financial Targets for Joint Ventures in Emerging Countries: A Conceptual Model," *Journal of Management* 4 (1998), pp. 241–258.

22. F. Contractor, "Strategies for Structuring Joint Ventures: A Negotiations Planning Paradigm," *Columbia Journal of World Business,* Summer 1984, pp. 30–39.

23. U. Gupta, "Sony Adopts Strategy to Broaden Ties with Small Firms," *The Wall Street Journal,* February 28, 1991, p. B2.

24. T. Das, and B. Teng, "A Risk Perception Model of Alliance Structuring," *Journal of Management* 7 (2001), pp. 1–29.

25. S. Park and M. Russo, "When Competition Eclipses Cooperation: An Event History Analysis of Joint Venture Failure," *Management Science* 42 (1996), pp. 875–890.

26. Das and Teng, "A Risk Perception Model of Alliance Structuring."

27. A. Parkhe, "Messy Research, Methodological Predispositions and Theory Development in International Joint Ventures," *Academy of Management Review* 18 (1993), pp. 794–829.

28. H. Steensma and M. Lyles, "Explaining IJV Survival in a Transitional Economy through Social Exchange and Knowledge-Based Perspectives," *Strategic Management Journal* 21 (2000), pp. 831–851.

29. Anoop Madhok, "Revisiting Multinational Firms' Tolerance for Joint Ventures: A Trust-Based Approach," *Journal of International Business Studies,* First Quarter 1995, pp. 117–137; Paul W. Beamish and John C. Banks, "Equity Joint Ventures and the Theory of the Multinational Enterprise," *Journal of International Business Studies* 18, no. 2 (1987), pp. 1–16; Arvind Parkhe, "Interfirm Diversity, Organizational Learning, and Longevity in Global Strategic Alliances," *Journal of International Business Studies* 20 (1991), pp. 579–601.

30. R. Kashlak, R. Chandran, and A. DiBenedetto, "Reciprocity in International Business: A Study of Telecommunications Contracts and Alliances," *Journal of International Business Studies* 29 (1998), pp. 281–304.

31. P. Aulakh, M. Kotabe, and A. Shay, "Trust and Performance in Cross-Border Marketing Partnerships: A Behavioral Approach," *Journal of International Business Studies* 27, no. 5 (1996) pp. 1005–1032.

32. J. Bradach, and R. Eccles, "Price, Authority and Trust: From Ideal Types to Plural Forms," *American Review of Sociology* 15 (1989), pp. 97–118; A. Parkhe, "Strategic Alliance Restructuring: A Game Theoretic and Transaction Cost Examination of Interfirm Cooperation," *Academy of Management Journal* 36, no. 4 (1993), pp. 794–829.

33. Parkhe, "Strategic Alliance Restructuring."

34. A. Yan, "Structural Stability and Reconfiguration of International Joint Ventures," *Journal of International Business Studies* 29 (1998), pp. 773–796.

35. H. Mjoen and S. Tallman, "Control and Performance in International Joint Ventures," *Organization Science* 8 (1997), pp. 508–527.

CHAPTER NINE

Organizing International Operations

Chapter Learning Objectives

After completing this chapter, you should be able to:

- Understand the relationship between an organization's international strategies and its organizational structures.
- Describe the factors that affect an organization's choice of structure.
- Distinguish among various global structures, including product structure, geographic structure, the global matrix structure, and transnational and heterarchical structures.
- Discuss the benefits and potential problems of each distinct global-oriented structure.

Opening Case: The Americanization of a Japanese Icon

Since moving to the U.S. 15 years ago, Nicaragua-born Roberto Castillo has had a series of jobs at car dealerships—first Ford, then Pontiac, and eventually Hyundai. But two years ago, he landed the job he really wanted: selling Toyotas. "Toyotas are easier to sell than any other car," he says. "Everyone knows the reputation, so you never have to sell [people] on the benefits." Nowadays, Castillo works at Longo Toyota in the Los Angeles suburb of El Monte. Castillo isn't Longo's top salesman, but last year he piled up commissions worth more than $80,000. As he says: "You can make good money with Toyota."

Tell that to Tetsuo Kawano. He runs a Toyota dealership in a beachfront Yokohama suburb in Japan. Recently Kawano held a promotion featuring FM deejay Haruhisa Kurihara. The event drew about 75 young Japanese with bleached hair, baggy pants, and goatees. The idea was to move a few Toyota Vitz subcompacts; the crowd enjoyed the music and free doughnuts, but there wasn't much interest in the product. "I'm here because I like the deejay," said Kidokoro Katsumi, 21. And the cars? "I just bought a Honda." Says a rueful Kawano: "We're selling into a shrinking market."

Booming in the U.S., but running out of gas in Japan? That was never Toyota's global strategy. Ten years ago, Japan's foremost auto maker had a multipronged attack plan: grow steadily at home, make modest gains in the U.S., make money in Europe, and take over Southeast Asia. Well, things have changed. Japan has become the incredible shrinking market. The European conquest, though still possible, is a dream deferred. And Southeast Asia has stalled out. That leaves the U.S., the one market where sales remain robust. Toyota's American strategy, in short, has become Toyota's lifeline.

The importance of the U.S. raises questions about what kind of company Toyota will become. How far will the Japanese leadership let the Americanization of Toyota go? How will the importance of the North American market affect Toyota's international thrust? And most important, with future profits so dependent on the U.S., how easy will it be for Toyota to drive its current 10% share of the U.S. market to 15%—or even 20%?

Toyota, the world's third-largest auto maker—2001 sales hit $108 billion and operating profits $4.2 billion—will struggle with these and other questions over the next few years. Still, despite trepidation about the company's increasingly American tilt back at headquarters in Toyota City, about 100 km east of Nagoya, the way forward seems clear. Says Toyota Chief Executive Fujio Cho: "We must Americanize." The process is already well under way. Consider the following facts, including some statistics that scare the wits out of Toyota's rivals in Detroit:

- Last year, Toyota sold more vehicles in the U.S. (1.74 million) than in Japan (1.71 million). Although Toyota doesn't break out foreign-derived earnings, analysts figure that almost two-thirds of the company's operating profit comes from the United States.
- Toyota's U.S. factories and dealerships currently employ 123,000 Americans—that's more than Coca-Cola (KO), Microsoft (MSFT), and Oracle (ORCL) combined.
- Toyota's top U.S. execs are, increasingly, local hires. The recently appointed manager of the key Georgetown (Ky.) plant, which makes the Camry, is Ford Motor Co. veteran Gary Convis. "Thirty years ago, we were more dependent on Japan," says James Press, chief operating officer of Toyota Motor Sales USA Inc. in Torrance, Calif. Now, "there's not much Japanese influence on a day-to-day basis."
- Toyota's biggest hits in the U.S.—the Camry sedan, Tundra pickup, and Sequoia SUV—were all designed with the American consumer in mind with significant input from U.S. design teams. Now, Toyota is launching a much-anticipated third brand: Scion, aimed at America's youth.
- With its 10% U.S. market share, Toyota is within striking distance of DaimlerChrysler's 14.5%. Some auto executives think it's only a matter of time before Toyota steals DaimlerChrysler's place in the Big Three.

It's easy to see why Toyota has become so focused on the U.S. market. While the company has never forfeited its dominant position in Japan, its market share is slipping steadily, while profit margins per vehicle are now an estimated 5%, vs. 13% in the U.S. In recessionary Japan, Toyota failed to shift production quickly enough into minivans and cheaper subcompacts, sticking instead with pricier sedans. Its rivals, by contrast, have adapted to changing demand, putting unaccustomed pressure on Toyota. "The Japanese market has gotten much more competitive, with Nissan back on track and Honda on a roll," says Chris Richter, an analyst at HSBC Securities Inc. in Tokyo. And Toyota's move into Europe has been slower than expected. While Toyota is doing better than Honda and Nissan, it still loses money on nearly every car it sells there.

Which brings us back to the U.S. Toyota's top brass won't discuss market-share goals: The last thing the company wants to do is ruffle feathers in Washington by publicly targeting DaimlerChrysler. But top Toyota officials are emphatic about where Toyota will direct its energies. "The American market is our top priority, bar none," says Cho, who in February became the first foreign exec to be inducted into the U.S. Automotive Hall of Fame. "We'll do whatever it takes to succeed there." The company is already planning to ramp up production capacity in the U.S. to more than 1.45 million units by 2005, from 1.25 million now. And in the next two to three years, it hopes to be selling a total of 2 million vehicles a year, including imports, in the U.S. market.

Of course, deep inside Toyota, ambivalence lingers about the growing clout of the American division. Toyota traditionalists are reluctant to stray even an inch from the Toyota Way, a philosophy set forth by the company's legendary founder, Kiichiro Toyoda, a zealot for consensus-style decision-making, merciless cost-cutting, and fanatical devotion to quality and customer satisfaction. Toyoda's focus on such basics has guided Toyota's growth over the past 65 years. In fact, it has been U.S. auto makers who learned from the Japanese, not the other way around.

To ensure that Toyota doesn't lose the essence of what makes it great, the company in February opened the Toyota Institute, an internal, MBA-style program near Toyota City whose faculty will comprise Toyota execs and visiting professors from the University of Pennsylvania's Wharton School. "We don't have the bench strength to rely solely on Japanese managers anymore," says Takashi Hata, Toyota's global human-resources guru. "But we must remain faithful to the fundamentals that got us where we are today as a company."

The fact is Toyota and its U.S. subsidiaries don't always see eye to eye, especially when it comes to making design choices for the American market. Sometimes the conflicts are over small issues; one Toyota official in Japan, for example, says interior color schemes are a constant source of friction. At other times, there are clashes over crucial product-strategy decisions. "They have to be dragged kicking and screaming into bigger products," says Jim Olson, a senior vice-president at Toyota Motor North America Inc. in New York City.

In the late 1990s, Japanese product planners resisted their U.S. colleagues' idea that the company should produce a V8 pickup truck for the American market. To change their minds, U.S. execs took their Japanese counterparts to a Dallas Cowboys football game—with a pit stop in the Texas Stadium parking lot. There, the Japanese saw row upon row of full-size pickups. Finally, it dawned on them that Americans see the pickup as more than a commercial vehicle, considering it primary transportation. Result: the red-hot Tundra, which sells for about $25,000.

Now, it's harder than ever for executives in Japan to second-guess their American colleagues. "Once we started building products [in the U.S.] and we were responsible for keeping those factories running," says Donald V. Esmond, senior vice-president of the Torrance sales arm, "then the chief engineers started listening a lot closer in terms of what products we need in the market." The proof that American marketers know their business is in the numbers. March sales of the $20,000 Camry, a sedan revamped for the U.S., surged 24.1% over the same month last year. Sales of the Highlander SUV were up 28.4%.

However successfully Toyota blends the essence of the Toyota Way with a dash of American salesmanship, increasing market share in the U.S. from now on will be a bigger challenge. "Toyota [has] very complete product coverage," says George Peterson, president of AutoPacific Group Inc., a market-research company in Tustin, Calif. "There are very few holes in its lineup." More ominously, Toyota could face in the U.S. the same problem it does in Japan: smaller rivals taking daring design steps that attract new customers. Already, Nissan Motor Co.'s redesigned Altima and Infiniti G35, with their head-turning styling, are luring Americans from the Camry and Lexus line. And South Korea's traditionally no-frills Hyundai is moving inexorably upscale with such cars as the XG350, a family sedan that is thousands of dollars cheaper than the Camry.

Still, given Toyota's U.S. momentum, even stiffer competition from Honda and Nissan won't have a dramatic impact in the short term. Indeed, to increase market share, all Toyota need do is crank up U.S. production. Right now there is more demand for such models as the Lexus RX 300 and Highlander SUVs than Toyota can fill. "They could get a full share point just by bringing Highlander production to the U.S.," says a well-placed analyst. The company already plans to make the RX 300 in Canada. As a result, Toyota should have no trouble "dialing up their U.S. sales through the remainder of the decade," says one analyst.

But Toyota does have an Achilles' heel: its aging customer base. The average age of a Toyota buyer in the U.S. is 45, the highest among Japanese carmakers. Press says Toyota has already halted the aging process by revamping the Celica coupe and MR2 Spyder roadster. Yet neither sold well last year. Nor did the Echo, the first Toyota subcompact aimed at Generation Y and younger. A moderate hit in Japan, it is a flop with young drivers in the U.S., who prefer the Ford Focus or any Volkswagen.

Toyota Chairman Hiroshi Okuda jokingly said last year that his company should move its headquarters to the U.S. That is extremely unlikely. Nonetheless, this most Japanese of Japanese auto makers knows its U.S. strategy is crucial to future prosperity. The company that Kiichiro Toyoda founded still has its roots in Japan, but its destiny is all-American.

Discussion Questions

1. What type of strategic mindset (global, multidomestic, transnational) does Toyota exhibit?

2. How might the emerging importance of the U.S. market and the subsequent "Americanization of Toyota" affect the way the firm is organized internationally?

3. Are communication and knowledge flow important for Toyota? What international organization structure would you recommend for Toyota to implement?

The Strategy–Structure Linkage for the International Firm

> They say that structure should follow strategy, and indeed it should, in ideal circumstances. Structure is one of the administrative elements of a business, and it exists to make operations and strategy work better.[1]

Designing an international firm's organization structure must be thought of as a continual process[2] that answers one question: How should an international business design its organization to achieve both effectiveness and efficiency of globally integrating its business functions? Toyota, in the opening case, is facing this challenge as the American market grows in strategic importance. This is a tremendous challenge for international firms as they disperse business activities worldwide to cope with increased global pressures.[3] The strategy–structure linkage is an international business topic that is both highly discussed and highly researched.[4] Organizations have a variety of hierarchical and nonhierarchical structures[5] that are designed to effectively implement given strategic initiatives. In general, organizations are structured to link the behavior of individuals; to collect and pool information, skills, or capital; to engage in related actions to achieve a set of goals; and to monitor performance, initiate corrections, and define new goals.

In a strictly domestic enterprise, these aims can be achieved with a two-dimensional organization, that is, an organization that concerns itself with resolving the potentially conflicting demands of functional (production, finance, marketing, etc.) and product-line requirements. As exemplified in the previous chapters, the organization has various strategic choices regarding expansion. Figure 9.1 illustrates these choices as:

- *Vertical expansion,* which takes the firm into new activities either forward or backward along the value chain of its existing product line.

- *Product expansion,* which takes the firm into new product markets, whether related or unrelated to its current core businesses.

- *Geographic expansion,* which takes the firm into new overseas markets, thus creating the multinational enterprise.

Practical Insight 9.1 illustrates the general linkage between a firm's expansion and its new organization of activities.

A two-dimensional organization is not the appropriate structure for a multinational enterprise because it must be able not only to resolve functional and product-line demands, but also to deal effectively with the external environmental concerns outlined in Section 1 of this book. Thus a more appropriate organizational form for a multinational enterprise combines four dimensions:

- *Functional expertise* of the value chain activities in which the firm is involved.

- *Product and technical know-how* of the various lines of business in which the firm is involved.

PRACTICAL INSIGHT 9.1

SINGAPORE'S OCBC BANK ANNOUNCES GLOBAL RESTRUCTURE

The Oversea-Chinese Banking Corporation Ltd has announced a *global organization structure* designed to enhance customer focus and facilitate growth. With this new structure, the bank will be organized along four groupings covering customers, products, support functions and geography.

Customer, product and support functions heads will now have global responsibility with direct authority for the bank's operations in Singapore, Malaysia, China and the eleven other countries that comprise OCBC Bank's international network. Geographic heads will have stewardship responsibility within their respective areas, concentrating on franchise management, regulatory relationships and legal compliance, in addition to ensuring overall country profitability and growth.

Deputy president Ooi Sin Teik will take on a new role as Head of External Affairs, which includes stewardship responsibility for all the bank's legal vehicles in Singapore. Datuk Albert Yeoh will continue in his role as CEO of OCBC Bank (Malaysia) Berhad (OBMB), reporting directly to the OBMB Board of Directors and Mr. David Conner, Chief Executive Officer. Division Heads within the four groupings will all report directly to Mr. Conner. There will be two customer divisions: Group Business Banking and Group Consumer Financial Services. Product management will comprise Group Treasury, Group Consumer & Community Lending, Group Investment Banking, Group Asset Management and the newly created Group Transaction Banking. Support functions will comprise Group Finance, Group Operations, Group Technology, Group Risk Management, Group Human Resources, Group Corporate Communications, Group Secretariat and Group Property Management.

"The new organization structure was developed through a collaborative effort of 10 members of the Bank's senior management team representing OCBC Bank's core business and functional areas," said Mr. Conner. "The structure will enhance customer focus and product innovation by clarifying roles and responsibilities. It will also streamline reporting, eliminate duplication across our international network and ensure that we operate as one team. We intend to stay clearly focused on expanding our customer base and developing innovative, best-in-class products, while providing business units with efficient support capabilities. The new organization will provide us with an even stronger growth platform."

The Singapore based bank has branches and representative offices in 14 countries, including Malaysia, China, Hong Kong SAR, Japan, Australia, UK and USA. In Asia, it has one of the most extensive networks among regional banks.

Source: Adapted from *Asia Pulse Limited,* October 22, 2002, and *Asia Banker Journal,* October 31, 2002.

FIGURE 9.1
Firm Expansion and Organization of Activities

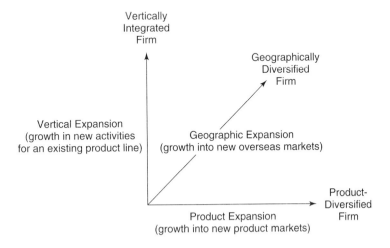

- *Knowledge of the countries and regions* where the firm has business interests.
- *Customer expertise* regarding similar market segments and major accounts that cut across various regions and countries.

The manner in which these dimensions are combined should and does differ from one international company to another. There is no one best way to organize an international

FIGURE 9.2
Linking International Strategy Formulation and Implementation

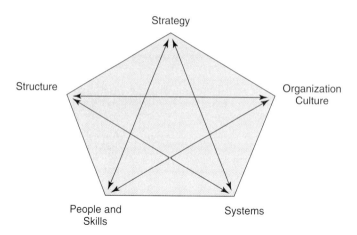

company, and each company will combine these four dimensions in an organizational structure that it tries to make consistent with its own particular strategy.

As Figure 9.2 illustrates, to implement its desired strategies, an international firm must effectively link its structure, culture, systems, and people with its stated strategy. In this chapter, we focus on the various structures that international firms use to successfully implement their respective strategies. We discuss the traditional structures as well as newer ways to organize in light of the tremendous changes occurring in the various industry and country environments.

In the early stages of international business as a discipline, the firm's international organization was identified as a response to three major strategic concerns: (1) how to encourage a predominantly domestic organization to take full advantage of growth opportunities abroad; (2) how to blend product knowledge and geographic area knowledge most efficiently in coordinating worldwide business; and (3) how to coordinate the activities of foreign units in many countries while permitting each to retain its own identity.

Responses to each of these concerns differ, depending on the firm's situation and the overall philosophy of top management. In this chapter we focus on the organizational design of international enterprises, that is, on the formal arrangement of relationships between the various domestic and foreign organizational units in the multinational network and the mechanisms provided for their coordination into a unified whole. Our treatment is limited to the level of the senior managers who report directly to the president's office. We are not concerned with the specific organizational structure of each foreign affiliate but emphasize the structure inside the parent company, whose purpose is to plan and control the multinational network, and the structure of the network itself. Our treatment of the organizational structure excludes recognition of the legal or statutory features of an enterprise. The legal structure is classified in accordance with government regulations for tax and cash-flow purposes, and it seldom reflects the actual manner in which an enterprise is managed. Because this chapter is concerned with managerial aspects of an international company, the legal structure is omitted.

In the first part of the chapter, we look at the organizational structures of international firms, including the following basic hierarchical structures: the pre–international division phase, the international division, the global product structure, and the global area structure. The benefits and concerns of these structures are identified. Furthermore, we examine newer structures that must be considered by firms operating in cer-

FIGURE 9.3
**International
Strategy versus
International
Structure**

Source: Adapted from
W. Egelhoff, "Strategy and
Structure in Multinational
Corporations: A Revision of the
Stopford and Wells Model,"
Strategic Management Journal,
Vol. 9 (1988), pp. 1–14.

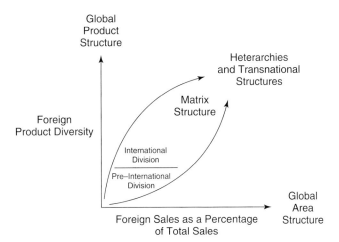

tain international industries: the matrix organization, the transnational structure, and the heterarchical structure. Figure 9.3 illustrates these various structures and provides a framework to understand how a firm may evolve its international structure. The framework is based on two critical dimensions for the international firm. The first, *foreign product diversity,* is an indicator of the number of different products and services a firm sells internationally. It represents the breadth of the firm's international activities. The second dimension is *foreign sales as a percentage of total sales,* which is an indicator of the importance to the firm of the aggregate overseas markets. This framework provides a basis for our discussion of the strategy–structure linkage as well as for changes in a firm's organizational structure.

In most cases, a multinational firm's organizational structure is neither predetermined nor permanently fixed, but rather evolves continuously to correspond with changes in the firm's strategy. As a firm's operations grow and spread to new foreign markets, its organizational structure typically becomes overburdened. As these pressures intensify and threaten the current organizational structure, the firm is compelled to experiment with and evolve to alternative organizational forms. Furthermore, the structure must fit with the firm's international environment.[6] Eventually the firm chooses a structure consistent with its new international expansion strategy and capable of handling its expanding operations. The replacement structure chosen is typically influenced by the structure that preceded it because the experience of the company with one structure provides a building block for future structures.

We stated earlier that no one organizational structure is best for multinational enterprises; this does not mean that every firm's organizational structure is unique or that a firm's structural development is arbitrary. On the contrary, firms of like strategy develop certain regular organizational patterns through which multinational firms with changing strategies evolve.

Pre–International Division Phase

A firm with a technologically advanced product in the new-product stage is well positioned to exploit foreign markets. Generally, initial exploitation occurs through exports—the first stage in the evolution of a multinational company. At this stage, the firm is relatively small by multinational enterprise standards, and its activities are generally confined to a few products and markets. Thus it has neither the diversity in

FIGURE 9.4
The Pre–International
Division Structure

the breadth of its overseas offerings nor a critical mass of overseas sales compared to its domestic sales. The firm therefore has to deal with a comparatively limited number of strategic dimensions, most of which are related to the domestic market, and which can be addressed directly by the president with input from managers who report directly to the president. Since the firm's technologically advanced product stands on its own, there is little need to develop expertise in the foreign markets in which the firm sells. Assistance in exporting is usually provided initially by an independent export management company and later by an in-house export manager. In most cases, an in-house export manager is thought of as an adjunct to marketing, whose principal communication needs are with the marketing vice president and others in the marketing group. The organizational arrangements for a firm in this stage of multinational development are rather simple; in an organization with a narrow product line the export manager reports to the chief marketing officer, and in an organization with a broad product line the export manager reports directly to the chief executive officer (see Figure 9.4).

As the firm's exports increase and its product matures, certain pressures develop that tend to threaten the firm's foreign market share. Such threats can originate from one of two sources. First, competitors at home and abroad begin to share the firm's special knowledge and special skills. Thus the threat of competition becomes more tangible. Second, as local demand and sales volume increase in a country, an importing country begins to encourage local production. The government does this by imposing restrictions such as "buy-local" policies on its own agencies and other public buyers or by enacting import restrictions such as tariffs and quotas.

Faced with increased competition from other producers and higher comparative costs resulting from freight and tariff costs, the exporting firm feels pressed to defend its foreign market position by establishing a production facility inside the foreign market. Once established, the foreign production unit supplies the foreign market as the former technologically advanced product matures or makes its way through the maturity stage and into the standardized-product stage of the product cycle. The same cycle may be repeated by the firm in the markets of other nations as the firm tries to protect its market share by establishing local production units to supply local markets. At first the management of the newly formed foreign subsidiaries remains quite polycentric and decentralized. Here, the foreign subsidiaries report directly to company presidents or other designated company officers, who carry out their respective responsibilities without assistance from a headquarters staff group. As the firm increases its investment in foreign operating units, however, and as these become more important to the firm's

FIGURE 9.5
The International
Division Structure

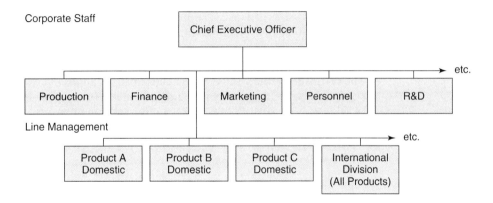

overall financial performance, greater emphasis is placed on international product coordination and operations control. This creates pressure to assemble a headquarters
staff group to assist the officer in charge and to develop a specialized international expertise. The group essentially takes control of all international activities of the firm and
evolves into a separate international division in a new and comparatively more complex organizational structure.

International Division Structure

As international activity increases, the firm faces pressure to evolve away from the
simple structure just described. Still, the relative product diversity and overseas sales
have not reached a critical stage that would require a more global structure. Thus, in the
international division form of organization, all international activities are grouped into
one separate division and assigned to a senior executive at corporate headquarters. The
senior executive is often given the title of vice-president of the international division or
director of international operations and is at the same level as the other divisional and
functional heads of the company in the organizational hierarchy (see Figure 9.5).

The head of the international division is generally given line authority over the subsidiaries abroad, and the international division is made into a profit center. The formation of the international division in effect segregates the company's overall operations
into two differentiated parts, domestic and international. As far as the top management
at headquarters is concerned, the international division is expected to manage the nondomestic operations, and therefore to be the locus of all international expertise there is
or should be in the company. Contact or interaction between the domestic and international sides is limited, and all coordination between the two segments of the company
occurs at the company's top management level.

Organizationally, the formation of an international division lessens the autonomy of
the foreign subsidiaries, because authority to make strategic decisions is pulled up into
the hands of the head of the international division. However, this change is accompanied by a far greater measure of guidance and support from the top to the foreign subsidiaries.

In general, companies that are still at the developmental stages of international business involvement are likely to adopt the international division structure. Other factors
favoring the adoption of this structure are limited product diversity; comparatively
small sales generated by foreign subsidiaries (compared to domestic and export sales);

limited geographic diversity; and few executives with international expertise. Because the international division represents a structure in which domestic sales overshadow international sales, we see this structure as an intermediate structure in countries with large domestic markets, where firms can attain cost efficiencies without leaving home. Thus firms from the United States and Japan are more likely to adopt this form than are firms from relatively small-market countries. The latter firms need to more quickly expand internationally in order to capture the economies of scale benefits of longer production runs and experience.

In the international division, executives are able to supervise the establishment and growth of one or more product lines in several foreign markets and, at the same time, develop new opportunities for expansion in others. In this structure, executives are providing the concentration of managerial expertise necessary for the effective promotion of the company's international efforts. During the period in which the company is establishing itself in international markets, international operations tend to remain, in the minds of the corporate executives of domestic operations, a sideline of minor importance. The use of an international division structure offers several advantages. The concentration of international executives within the division ensures that the special needs of emerging foreign operations are met. The presence of the head of international operations as a member of the top management planning team serves as a constant reminder to top management of the global implications of all decisions. The international group provides a unified position regarding the company's activities in different countries and regions as it makes an effort to coordinate the operations of foreign subsidiaries with respect to the functional areas of finance, marketing, purchasing, and production. For example, central coordination of international activities enables the company to make more secure and more cost-efficient decisions about where to purchase raw materials, where to locate new manufacturing, and from where to supply world customers with products. Also, when the financial function of the international division is coordinated, investment decisions can be made on a global basis and overseas development can turn to international capital markets, instead of just local ones, for funds. The international division also will not strain the capabilities of product or functional managers within the domestic divisions because these persons are not required to work with unfamiliar environments.

Because the international division structure has several drawbacks, a company will use this structure only if the benefits from its adoption as a coordination mechanism clearly outweigh the costs. One principal disadvantage of the international division structure is the separation and isolation of domestic managers from their international counterparts, which may prove to be a severe handicap as the company continues to expand abroad. If foreign operations should approach a level of equality with domestic operations in terms of size, sales, and profits, the ability of domestic managers to think and act strategically on a global scale could be critical to the success of the company. Also, an independent international division may constrain top management's effort to mobilize and allocate the resources of the company globally to achieve overall corporate objectives. Even with superb coordination at the corporate level, global planning for individual products or product lines is carried out at best awkwardly by two "semi-autonomous" organizations—the domestic portions of the company and the international division.

The potential for conflict between the domestic and international groups is another drawback of this structure. Where the domestic business represents the current success of the firm and generates the majority of the revenues, the international business represents the future of the firm and has a seemingly disproportionate budget. Anecdotally, there have been many "sour-grape" stories from domestic managers who fly coach class to unglamorous meeting locations and regular hotels in the United States only to learn of their international counterparts flying business or first class to Paris or Beijing and staying at five-star hotels.* Conflicts also occur occasionally between the domestic product divisions and the international division, particularly when the international division asks for help from the domestic divisions and gets what it considers to be inadequate technical support and second-rate staff members for special assignments abroad.

Still another problem with the international division is that the firm's research and development remains domestically oriented. Consequently, new ideas originating abroad for new products or processes are not easily transmitted to or enthusiastically tackled by the predominantly domestically oriented research and development personnel who remain, after all, in the domestic setting of the organization.

As international sales and production capacity grow, and as more markets are entered, product lines begin to diversify to serve a variety of end users. Considerations such as transfer pricing (charging a higher or lower price between divisions than is charged to an outside buyer) then come into play; the international division structure gets strained to its limits and is unable to fulfill its former role. Faced with this situation, the company may continue to use the international division structure by subdividing further as a response to diversification either by product line, if product diversification is causing the problem, or by area, if regional diversification is straining the organization.

Many firms use the following rule of thumb: When the sales of the international division exceed those of the largest domestic division, the international division structure is disaggregated and a structure more in tune with the firm's evolving global posture is established. One alternative is to take the profit responsibility from the international division and reorganize the entire company on either a product or area division basis, keeping the international division in an advisory capacity.

Studies have shown that the following factors play a major role as indicators that the international division is no longer an appropriate structure for an international company:

1. The international market is as important as the domestic market.
2. Senior officials of the corporation have both foreign and domestic experience.
3. International sales represent 25 to 35 percent of total sales.
4. The technology used in domestic divisions has far outstripped that of the international.

Other studies have shown that the pressures to reorganize on an integrated, worldwide basis by dismantling the international division mount when the division has grown large enough to be equal in size to the largest product division.[7] This is to a large extent due to the struggles that take place between the international and domestic divisions over capital budgeting and transfer pricing issues. But the structural conflict between the geographic (foreign) orientation of the international division and the product orientation of the domestic divisions is the most important factor motivating top management to reorganize the company in a fashion that merges the domestic and international sides of the business into one integrated global structure.

*Most companies have the eight-hour rule, which allows managers to fly business or first class if the duration of the flight is eight hours or more.

Global Hierarchical Structures

Up to this point we have been concentrating on the typical stages in the evolution of the organizational structure of a company as it becomes increasingly involved in international business activities. As the firm gains experience in operating internationally, the initially limited involvement in foreign direct investment gradually turns into a full-fledged commitment. Top management begins to perceive the company as a truly multinational enterprise, the company enters a new phase in its evolution, and the domestic–foreign bifurcation is abandoned in favor of an integrated, worldwide orientation. The hierarchical structure is the organization design most frequently used by international firms. This structure ranks staff members who are experts in a pyramid according to the difficulty of the problems they can solve.[8] The ranking is based on authority over the implementation and control of a firm's assets[9] and information.[10]

Strategic decisions that previously were made separately for the domestic and international parts of the company are henceforth made at the corporate headquarters for the total enterprise, without any distinctions of domestic versus foreign. Top management considers the home market to be only one of many markets, and operational and staff groups are given global responsibility. Under such an attitudinal setup at corporate headquarters, corporate decisions are made with a total company perspective, for the purpose of achieving the company's overall mission and objectives. Decisions on where to establish a new production facility, where to raise capital, what businesses and products to be in, where to obtain resources, what methods to use for tapping foreign markets, what subsidiary ownership policies to adopt, and so on, are all made from this perspective.

The shift to a global orientation in company management must be accompanied by the acquisition and allocation of company resources on the basis of global opportunities and threats. These changes require an organizational structure that is consistent with, and supportive of, this new managerial posture. The new organizational structure includes, as all structures do to varying degrees, three types of informational input: product, geography, and function. Although the structures adopted by various companies differ, the structure an international company adopts is certain to be based on one of these basic orientations: a worldwide area or a worldwide product (or, occasionally, a worldwide function).

The Global Product Structure

When the international division is discarded in favor of a **global product structure,** the domestic divisions are given worldwide responsibility for product groups. The manager in charge of a product division is given line authority and responsibility for the worldwide management of all functional activities that are related to a product or product group, such as finance, marketing, and production.[11] Within each product division, an international unit, or even a more refined subdivision based on one area, may exist (see Figure 9.6).

Each product division functions as a semiautonomous profit center. Divisional management has considerable decentralized authority to run the division because of the unique multinational environmental pressures under which it must operate. However, corporate headquarters provides an umbrella of companywide plans and corporate strategy. This umbrella provides both the protection and the constraints under which product divisions are expected to formulate divisional plans and strategy. A product division receives general functional support from staff groups at the corporate level, but at the divisional level it may also have its own functional staff, specialized to provide

FIGURE 9.6
The Global Product
Division Structure

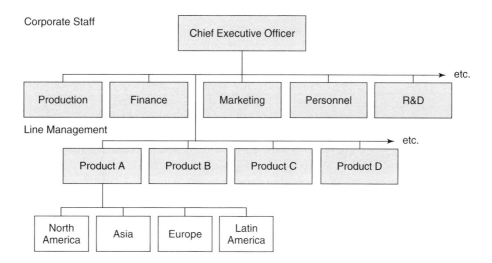

services tailored to the division's unique market situation. The product division head is given worldwide responsibility to develop and promote his or her product line.

The following conditions favor the global product structure:

1. The level of product diversity is high; that is, the firm manufactures products that require different technologies and that have dissimilar end users.

2. The product divisions seldom use common marketing tools and channels of distribution.

3. The need to globally integrate production, marketing, and research related to the product is significant.

4. Little need is found for local product knowledge and product adaptation as the firm expands into new countries.

5. The products involved need continuous technical service and inputs and a high level of technological capability, requiring close coordination between divisional staff groups and production centers abroad.

Industries such as chemicals, pharmaceuticals, and computer manufacturing would be inclined to use this structure.

Some products require close, product-oriented technological and marketing coordination between the home-market affiliates and foreign affiliates. This interdependence between the home and foreign affiliates—the latter needing help from the former in matters pertaining to the production and promotion of the growth product in a foreign market—calls for products, and not markets, as the primary organizing dimension.

To maximize the benefits of basing divisions on a global product structure, a firm must be able to produce a standardized product that requires only minor modifications for individual markets, and for which world markets can be developed. Division managers are expected to take advantage of the structure to generate global economies of scale in production, resource acquisition, and market supply. This makes the structure particularly suited to firms that use capital-intensive technology.

Benefits of the Global Product Structure   The major advantages of this form of organization are the ease and directness of flow of technology and product knowledge from the divisional level to the foreign subsidiaries and back, which tends to put all facilities, regardless of location, on a comparable technological level. Additionally, the global product form preserves product emphasis and promotes product planning on a global basis, it provides a direct line of communications from the customer to those in the organization who have product knowledge and expertise, thus enabling research and development to work on the development of products that serve the needs of the world customer, and it permits line and staff managers within the division to gain expertise in the technical and marketing aspects of products assigned to them.[12]

In addition, the global product division structure facilitates the coordination of domestic and foreign production facilities according to natural resource availability, local labor cost and skill level, tariff and tax regulations, shipping costs, and even climate, in order to produce the highest quality product possible at the lowest cost.

Drawbacks of a Global Product Structure   Several critical problems are associated with a global product structure. One is the duplication of facilities and staff groups that takes place as each division develops its own infrastructure to support its operations in various regions and countries of the world. Another is that division managers may pursue geographic areas that offer immediate growth prospects for their products and neglect other areas where the current prospects may not be bright but the long-run potential is significant. A far more serious problem is that of motivating product division managers to pursue the international market when the preponderance of their current profits comes from domestic business and most of their experience has been domestic.

Beyond these concerns lies an important inherent characteristic and subsequent concern of this structure. It represents a hierarchical organization structure, one that potentially limits communication, information flow, knowledge crossover, and, ultimately, organizational learning across divisions. It is a biased structure, where all managers are concerned with their specific niche, so that motivation to share knowledge across product boundaries does not exist. International companies have tried to alleviate these difficulties by adopting a multidimensional structure, which we discuss later in this chapter.

The Global Area Structure

Firms abandoning the international division as a structure may also choose to coordinate their global operations by using area (or geography) as the dominant organizational dimension. Looking back at Figure 9.3, we see that firms favoring the **global area structure** more than likely will have a relatively large percentage of their total sales derived from the overseas markets.

In the international division structure, the company's worldwide operations are grouped into two regions—domestic and international. Thus, in a way, the international division structure is also an area-based structure. But as we define an area-based global structure, the company's worldwide operations are grouped into several coequal geographical areas, and the head of an area division is given line authority and responsibility over all affiliates in the area.[13] There is no one fixed pattern for carving up the geographical areas; each enterprise has its own circumstances and needs that determine how countries are grouped into regions. Factors such as locations of affiliates, customers, and sources of raw materials influence the grouping of countries into manageable geographic units.

An area structure reflects a very significant change in the attitudes of top management toward international operations and the allocation of the company's resources. In the international division structure, the domestic–nondomestic bifurcation of the company's global operations reflects the point of view of top management that the domestic side of the business is as important as all the international operations together. The

FIGURE 9.7
The Global Area
Division Structure

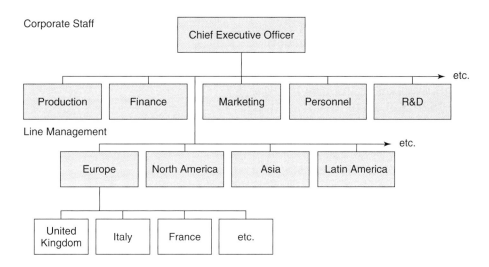

area structure embodies the attitude that the domestic market is just one of many markets in the world (see Figure 9.7).

The manager in charge of an area is responsible for the development of business in his or her region. However, the firm's area plans and strategies have to be consistent with those of the company as a whole. Area managers and their counterparts participate in the formulation of companywide plans and strategies. Such participation in total company planning gives each area manager an appreciation of how his or her area operations and results fit with total company plans and performance. Practical Insight 9.2 illustrates a software firm's reorganization to a global area structure to better develop regional markets and business linkages.

Advantages of the Global Area Structure   A global area structure is most suited to companies having these characteristics: They are businesses with narrow product lines; they have high levels of regional product differentiation; and they have the opportunity to attain high levels of economies of scale in production, marketing, and integrated resource procurement on a regional basis. Industries with these characteristics include cosmetics, food, beverage, and other consumer goods companies.

The principal advantage of an area structure is that the authority to make decisions is pushed down to the regional headquarters. This means that decisions on matters such as product adaptation, price, channels of distribution, and promotion can be made near the scene of the action. For example, a company that makes soups, coffee, and prepared frozen foods must take into account regional and even country differences. The Italians and Turks like dark, bitter coffee, whereas Americans like the lighter and less bitter variety. The English like bland soups, whereas the French prefer those with a blend of mild spices. Different countries have different taste preferences. By and large the peoples of the Middle East and Asia like their foods spiced, whereas those in Europe and America like theirs bland. Information on such differences among regions and country markets can be considered at low levels in the organizational hierarchy, which helps in the making of plans and strategies consistent with the existing regional and country conditions.

The other advantage of the area structure is that it promotes the finding of regional solutions to problems. Ideas and techniques that have worked in one country are easier to transfer to other countries in the region. And the area manager can resolve conflicts

PRACTICAL INSIGHT 9.2

ROGUE WAVE SOFTWARE ANNOUNCES NEW INTERNATIONAL STRUCTURE AND STRATEGY

Rogue Wave Software, Inc., of Boulder, Colorado, a leading global software and consulting services company, today announced an updated strategic direction for the future that positions the company as a global infrastructure supplier rather than a tools developer for the programming community. These initiatives are the first in a series of strategic moves planned by new CEO John Floisand, following his internal review of the company's operations. In support of its expanded international strategy, Rogue Wave announces the development of three new divisions and the appointment of three regional general managers to oversee operations in the Americas, Europe and Asia Pacific. All three general managers share a common background in previously helping the Borland Software Corporation transition its focus to that of an infrastructure player, as did Floisand. Their past experience is essential in assisting Rogue Wave to create both reseller and technology development partnerships.

Each manager is tasked with bringing greater sales and marketing discipline to their respective regions, as they work to develop a new customer base and reinvigorate existing relationships. While the Americas are Rogue Wave Software's largest and most stable geographic line of business, Europe and Asia Pacific represent significant growth opportunities. In particular, the Asia Pacific region has three of the largest global markets for C++ products: Japan, China and India. As the regional general managers build operations in each market, they lay the groundwork for the future sale of the company's infrastructure technologies. The named regional heads include:

John Racioppi, Vice President & General Manager of Americas

Gidi Schmidt, Managing Director of Europe

Raymond Bradbery, General Manager of Asia Pacific

"We are truly fortunate and excited to add leaders of this caliber and with their depth of experience to the Rogue Wave family," stated Floisand. "Their impact will be felt immediately. First in exploiting our core business opportunities internationally, and then longer-term, in our transformation up the value chain to become an infrastructure supplier to our customers. There is a large international market for leveraging both our core business, and future technologies and partnerships. It was crucial to commit to these three markets and reorganize our business structure to capitalize on revenue opportunities in each region. In addition, we need to ensure our customers, domestically as well as internationally, are serviced correctly. My direct experience in working with these individuals gives me great confidence we are headed in the right direction. Our initiatives will provide the framework to allow our core C++ business to grow."

Source: From "Rogue Wave Software Announces New International Structure and Strategy," PR Newswire Association, Inc., March 25, 2002. Reprinted with permission of PR Newswire.

between subsidiaries by finding solutions that optimize the operations in the region as a whole. For example, when a new country market opens up, which subsidiary in the region is in the best position to serve it through exports? Conflicts could occur if more than one subsidiary attempts to export to the new market, but with the area structure, the area manager is in a position to resolve such problems.

Drawbacks of a Global Area Structure   The main disadvantage of the area structure is the difficulty encountered in reconciling product emphasis with a geographically oriented management approach. Since a certain amount of product expertise has to be developed by the area unit, a duplication of product development and technical knowledge is often required. At the same time, functional staff responsibilities overlap with those of the worldwide headquarters. All of this adds to overhead costs and creates an additional tier of communications.

Other drawbacks reported by executives are difficulty in coordinating research and development programs, difficulty in global product planning, inconsistent efforts to apply newly developed domestic products to international markets, delays in the introduction to the domestic market of products developed overseas, and weakness of product knowledge. In many respects, the advantages of a global area structure are the disadvantages of a global product division structure, and vice versa. The answer to the product-versus-area dilemma may be in an organizational structure that incorporates in its authority, responsibility, and communications lines a blend of these two dimensions.

As was the case with the global product structure, the hierarchical area structure leads to relative inefficiencies of communication, both formal and informal, as well as information flow, knowledge crossover, and long-term organizational learning and its concomitant competitive benefits. Like the product structure, it is a biased structure, where all managers are concerned with their specific niche. For instance, the salesperson in Palermo is concerned only with that city. His boss is concerned only with Sicily. Her boss's focus is strictly Italy. As you move up the European hierarchy, concerns rest in southern Europe and finally the vice-president for Europe is focused on Europe. As there is no incentive for the Italian country manager to share information with the German or Dutch manager, there is no real incentive for the VP-Europe to share information and knowledge with regional vice-presidents in other areas of the world such as Latin America or Asia. Thus knowledge never crosses geographic boundaries.

Multidimensional Global Structures

In deciding whether to organize on a product or area basis, managers of international companies must weigh the benefits of each against the costs. The particular dimension that is chosen as the primary basis for organizing a company's operations should be that which offers the best benefits-to-costs ratio. When one of these structures is chosen as the primary organizational form, management still tries to utilize the advantages of the remaining dimension, along with a functional perspective, at lower levels in the structure. For example, a company that is organized on a product division basis may have its own functional staff at the divisional level, and each of the product divisions may be further subdivided on a geographic basis. However, many international companies have found that none of the global structures discussed previously is a totally satisfactory means of organizing because some problems remain untouchable, and therefore unsolved.

The international firm needs to change the biased nature of the hierarchical structures. It needs to influence multidimensional perspectives. Some companies have attempted to do this by establishing product committees in area-based structures and area committees in product-based structures. Membership of such committees is comprised of divisional managers and staff specialists who are assigned the collective responsibility for coordinating transactions that cut across divisional lines.

Another alternative is to create staff positions for advisers and counselors. For instance, a product division structure might have area specialists for each of the major regions served by the company. These persons are given the task of exploring new opportunities and developing new markets for the company's products in their respective regions, thus maintaining the distinct advantages of the product structure without losing sight of the unique characteristics of each regional market. Similarly, in an area-based structure, the position of product manager would have responsibility for the co-ordination of the production and development of his or her product line across geographic areas.

Other tactics used by firms include cross-functional/cross-area task forces, management rotation, and liaison assignments. In each of these instances, the firm has its managers actually coming together with other parts of the organization to influence informal communication and longer term knowledge transfer. Still, each of the preceding structural arrangements implicitly assumes that an organizational structure can have only one dominant dimension. Because the advantages of the other dimensions are lost when only one is chosen, an attempt is sometimes made to correct the situation by overlaying the dominant dimension with some aspects of the others.

The International Matrix Structure

Some international companies are rejecting the notion that authority must flow in a clear line from the top to the bottom in an organizational hierarchy—with a manager at a given level reporting to only one superior at the next highest level in the hierarchy. Companies that have adopted what is known as the **matrix structure** have cast this so-called principle of the unity of command aside. In a matrix, the organization avoids choosing one dimension over another as the basis for grouping its operations; instead it chooses two or more: "The foreign subsidiaries report simultaneously to more than one divisional headquarters; worldwide product divisions share with area divisions responsibility for the profits of the foreign subsidiaries."[14] Thus the matrix, by its nature, involves dual-authority relations.[15]

For instance, a subsidiary manager may report to an area manager as well as a product manager. In a pure product division or area structure, only the manager in charge of the dominant dimension has line authority over a foreign subsidiary in her or his unit. In a matrix structure, both product and area managers have some measure of line authority over the subsidiary. Thus the unity-of-command principle is abrogated in favor of a coordinating mechanism that considers differences in products and areas to be of equal importance. Firms using the matrix structure are attempting to integrate their operations across more than one dimension simultaneously (see Figure 9.8). Firms should consider adopting the matrix structure if conditions such as the following exist:

1. Product and area are substantially diversified.
2. Product and area demands require simultaneous responses.
3. Constraints on resources require that they be shared by two or more product, area, or functional divisions.
4. Significant problems are created and opportunities lost due to emphasis on only the product or area dimension.
5. Formulation of corporate strategy requires the simultaneous consideration of functional, product, and area concerns.

FIGURE 9.8
The International Matrix Structure

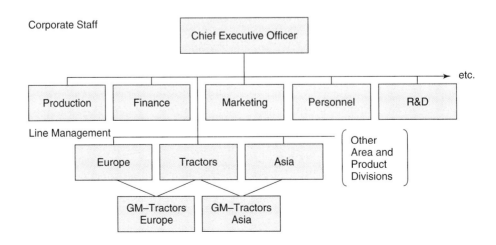

Adoption of a matrix structure requires a commitment on the part of top management, not only to the structure itself, but also to the essential preparation required for it to be successful. Executive groundwork must be laid; executives must understand how the system works, and those who report to two or more superior managers, such as the subsidiary managers, must be prepared to work through the initial confusion created by dual reporting relationships. The structure must be reinforced by systems such as dual control and evaluation systems, by leaders who operate comfortably with lateral decision making, and by a culture that can negotiate open conflict and a balance of power. The mere adoption of a matrix structure does not create a matrix organization.

Adoption must be followed by some fundamental changes in technical systems and management behavior. Managers must recognize the need to resolve issues and choices at the lowest possible level, without referring them to a higher authority. A delicate balance of power must be maintained among managers face to face. A tilt in favor of one organizational dimension or another would cause the organization to fall back to the old single-dimensional, vertical hierarchy, with a resulting loss of the benefits of a matrix structure. Absence of cooperation between facing managers, even when a perfect power balance exists, could cause so many unresolved problems and disputes to be referred up the hierarchy that top management would become overloaded with interdivisional matters.[16]

The benefits of a matrix structure flow directly from the conditions that induce enterprises to adopt it. A matrix organization can respond simultaneously to all environmental factors that are critical to its success. Decision-making authority can be decentralized to an appropriate level. Policy decisions are made in concert with people who have relevant information, and the design also facilitates a flow of information that promotes better planning and the implementation of plans.

The matrix structure does take time, effort, and commitment by executives to make it work. Although Peter Drucker says that the matrix structure "will never be a preferred form of organization; it is fiendishly difficult," he nevertheless concludes that "any manager in a multinational business will have to learn to understand it if he wants to function effectively himself."[17] Percy Barnevik, the former CEO of Asea Brown Boveri (ABB), suggested that any manager operating in the global environment must have, at the minimum, a matrix mindset. Many industries can no longer be focused on only a unitary, biased hierarchical perspective. ABB, the Swedish-Swiss diversified company that was created following the merger of Sweden's Asea and Switzerland's Brown Boveri, was one of the first examples of a global matrix structure. How the company has organized its matrix management structure is presented in Practical Insight 9.3. More recently, many firms are developing their own versions of the matrix, as illustrated by OCBC of Singapore (seen in Practical Insight 9.1 earlier in the chapter) and by AIS of Thailand in Practical Insight 9.4.

The matrix structure provides better communications, movement of information, and creation of knowledge for the international firm; moreover, it promises to open up multiple channels of formal and informal communications, to nurture more perspectives, and to give the organization more flexibility. In spite of all this, the matrix is not an easy structure to implement and has been a difficult structure to manage on a global basis. The dual reporting structure leads to more conflicts and confusion. The proliferation of channels of reporting leads to corporate logjams. Overlapping responsibilities lead to power struggles and loss of accountability. More details slip through the cracks than with a hierarchy. Furthermore, even though decisions ultimately are better due to the multiple perspectives generated, many times they take much longer to reach. When conflicts arise, the decisions are pushed up the corporate ladder—an inefficient use of

PRACTICAL INSIGHT 9.3

COMPANY PROFILE: GLOBAL HERO

When the electromechanical activities of Switzerland's BBC Brown Boveri merged with the Swedish engineering company ASEA in 1988, the newly forged giant received a mixed reception: applause for the swiftness and secrecy with which the deal was executed, skepticism over whether the instant conglomerate could work.

Four years later, the doubts have been replaced by almost universal admiration. ABB Asea Brown Boveri has 1,300 companies and 214,000 employees operating in 65 business areas in 140 countries. It is a world leader in the generation, transmission and distribution of electricity, in industrial process automation, in systems and products for environmental control and in rail transport systems. It is also a management model of a new type of conglomerate that achieves global reach through a network of deep local roots, a model from which other conglomerates, notably IBM, draw inspiration. "ABB is extremely focused," says research analyst Martin Neusome of Goldman Sachs in London. "It knows what it wants to be and goes about it very quickly."

The helmsman who has steered ABB through its great leap forward is its president and chief executive, Percy Barnevik, a lean and bearded Swede who was formerly managing director of ASEA. His strategy for ABB is based on three internal contradictions. "We want to be global and local, big and small, radically decentralized with centralized reporting and control," he says. Barnevik manages this many-tentacled operation by way of a matrix system. A 12-member executive committee, which he heads, sets strategy and reviews the performance of the whole. Each committee member manages one of eight business segments—power plants, power transmission, power distribution, transportation, industry, environmental control, financial services and a miscellaneous segment, called "various activities," which embraces robotics and telecommunications—and/or a country or region. Each reports to the group at meetings held every three weeks in a different country. At the same time a centralized reporting system, named Abacus, collects performance data on the company's 5,000 profit centres, compares them with budgets and forecasts, converts them into dollars to enable cross-border analyses, and consolidates or breaks them down by segment, country and local company.

The group is then divided vertically by business area and horizontally by country. Business area leaders set the rules on a global level, determining strategy, organization, manufacturing and product development. They also allocate export markets to specific factories. Country managers run line operations, establishing balance sheets and income statements and administering their own career ladders, while fulfilling their obligation to respect ABB's worldwide objectives—not always an easy task, Barnevik admits. "Thirty of the companies we have bought had been around for more than 100 years," he says. "We have to convince country managers that they gain more than they lose when they give up some autonomy." Answering to both business area managers and country managers are the bosses of the myriad local companies.

"The only way to structure a complex, global organization is to make it as simple and local as possible," Barnevik says. "ABB is complicated from where I sit, but on the ground, where the real work gets done, all our operations must function as closely as possible to stand-alone operations. I don't expect most of our people to have global mindsets, to do things that hurt their business but are 'good for ABB'."

The ambiguity of evolving a multi-cultural environment with a multiple management structure is a further problem, raising the possibility of conflict or confusion. "The matrix management does not dissolve centrifugal forces within a company," says Miles Saltiel, a research analyst at the Nomura Research Institute in London. To avoid such confusion, ABB has set out its values in a 40-page booklet. They include ethics, individual responsibility and initiative and, crucially, openness to foreign cultures.

Source: Romy Joyce, "Global Hero," *International Management,* September 1992, pp. 82, 85.

executive time. When the complicating factors of distance, culture, time, and language that arise with international operations are added in, an international matrix does not adequately serve many international firms. It is simply too cumbersome to manage effectively.

Still, firms need to be more efficient in communication, information flow, and knowledge creation across the various lines of business. This is especially true for firms in industries that are undergoing turbulence, where speed is of the essence and where the product life cycles have significantly shortened. Firms in these industries need a malleable, flexible structure. Thus, the next section addresses these ever-evolving structures.

PRACTICAL INSIGHT 9.4

AIS GOES "MATRIX": NEW STRUCTURE HAILED FOR ITS EFFICIENCY

Thailand's No. 1 cell-phone firm, Advanced Info Service (AIS), has decentralized its organizational structure as part of a major new change intended to enable it to move faster in capturing a larger market share. Termed the Matrix Organization, the new structure will transform AIS from a hierarchical firm to a network-oriented organization and will enable it to serve its customers four times faster, said Somprasong Boonyachai, AIS chairman and president.

In 2002, AIS—the mobile-phone flagship of Shin Corp., founded by Prime Minister Thaksin Shinawatra—targeted 6 million new subscribers to add to its existing 7 million. Therefore, it must make the change first to be ahead of its rivals. "Now AIS signs up as many as 500,000 subscribers monthly and also plans to massively expand its subscription base, so the old structure is not responsive enough to support this mission," Somprasong said.

Under the new scheme, AIS has created four new positions—chief of commercial and customer service, chief network officer, wireless corporate planning chief, and future business opportunities chief—which all are empowered with presidential authority. This allows them to manage and make crucial decisions rapidly and more flexibly without reporting to Somprasong at all times, as was the case previously. For example, if the chief of network thinks it is time for AIS to quickly invest further in networks to respond to faster growth, he can make the decision without waiting for approval from the president . . .

Somprasong claims that AIS is the first cell-phone operator adopting the Matrix structure. "We're the first to embrace this kind of management, which we've adapted from the models of several global giant companies like IBM or Nokia," he said.

Decentralization would allow Somprasong to take time off from day-to-day management to concentrate on working on AIS' future plans and maximizing benefits for shareholders. "The restructuring also reflects our policy of giving priority to training executives, to allow them to shine in their capacity," Somprasong said.

AIS has also set up three regional headquarters in the North, East and Northeast as part of its plan to aggressively penetrate the provincial market. Provincial consumers account for 60 per cent of AIS' total subscribers. "AIS will open another headquarters in the South soon to help it increase the number of provincial customers," he added.

Source: From "Cell-Phone Sector: AIS Goes 'Matrix,' " *The Nation* (Thailand), May 10, 2002. Reprinted with permission.

Heterarchical Structures and Transnational Mindsets

In Chapter 6, we distinguished among the multidomestic, global, and transnational orientations. Here we extend that thinking to see the cost and efficiency benefits of the global orientation matched to the global product structure. Similarly, the marketing and differentiation benefits associated with the multidomestic orientation overlap similar benefits discussed with the global area structure. As firms in many dynamic and turbulent industries are confronted with the dual mandate of global efficiency and national responsiveness, organizational structures must evolve to complement these newer strategic initiatives. Practical Insight 9.5 depicts a firm in the global robotics/proteomics industry restructuring around critical activities including global sales, strategic alliances, emerging markets, and global information.

Given the complexity and volatility of many industries within the global environment, a single, biased hierarchical structure will no longer fit for many firms in the future. These firms need to build strategic and operational flexibility. Thus we need to explore some of the more subtle as well as sophisticated ways of thinking about the organizational challenges facing managers in international firms. This points to the necessity to understand the transnational mentality and associated heterarchical[18] structures.

A **heterarchy** is distinguished from a hierarchical structure in various aspects. For instance, decision making is dispersed throughout the organization and not concentrated at the top levels. Also, lateral managerial relationships exist as complements to the

PRACTICAL INSIGHT 9.5

CRS ADOPTS NEW ORGANIZATION TO EXPLOIT EMERGING MARKETS

CRS Robotics Corporation of Ontario, Canada, announced changes to its organization structure in order to take advantage of the new emerging proteomic markets and to exploit opportunities with OEM's on a worldwide basis. These changes will allow CRS to continue to be a leader in Life Sciences markets including the proteomics market, which is expected to grow at a CAGR [compound annual growth rate] of 38% over the next five years according to industry reports

Dr. Hansjoerg Haas, currently Managing Director, Laboratory Automation, will become Senior Vice President Sales responsible for directing all sales activities on a global basis. CRS will now be able to deliver all of its products through one consolidated and coordinated sales channel. Mr. Paul Ritchie, formerly Managing Director, Standard Products, has been appointed Senior Vice President Operations. His key responsibilities will be managing all of CRS' manufacturing and production activities on a global basis, ensuring seamless adherence to customer commitments. Mr. Rod Rafauli P. Eng., formerly VP Operations, will assume the role of Vice President and Chief Information Officer. His key activities will be to manage CRS' global information needs.

CRS has committed itself to investing in alternative sales channels through the formation of two new positions called Business Unit Managers. These positions will be responsible for developing strategic alliances and OEM relationships through which CRS' proprietary mover and software technolo-gies can be directed. In addition, CRS will continue to develop alliances with vendors of consumables, bioinformatic and genomic/proteomic technologies in order to provide customers with an integrated product offering unmatched by any other supplier. Mr. Trevor Jones P. Eng, formerly Chief Technical Officer, will assume the position of VP & Business Unit Manager, OEM and Mr. Robert Cooper the position of VP & Business Unit Manager, End User. The product management function of CRS will report to these positions.

With this new structure CRS is better equipped to take advantage of the exceptional growth opportunities in the life sciences market. CRS is dedicated to customer excellence through its extensive quality program and ISO 9001 accredited. The consolidation of key resources will bring focus to our goal of being a leader in our chosen markets.

CRS has been acknowledged as one of the few companies on the forefront of laboratory automation technology. Core competencies of the company include integrated lab automation solutions using advanced software in biotechnology and pharmaceutical research applications marketed worldwide. In addition, CRS manufactures and supplies robotic systems for advanced manufacturing niche markets. CRS is headquartered in Burlington, Ontario, and has subsidiaries in the United States and Europe.

Source: "CRS Adopts New Organization to Exploit Emerging Markets," September 24, 2001. Reprinted with permission of Thermo Electron Corporation.

---

usual vertical relationships, and firm-level activities are coordinated across multiple dimensions including product, function, and geography.[19] Scholars have suggested that emerging organizations are more likely to be characterized by decentralization of decision making, and in order to facilitate this, they are likely to be designed as distributed organizations, such as heterarchies and transnationals.[20]

Specifically, these structures have the following characteristics compared to the more traditional product and area structures. They are:

1. Less systematic.
2. More flexibly coordinated.
3. Nimbler.
4. Less hierarchical.

Furthermore, these structures have

1. High levels of interdependency among the subsidiaries.
2. Frequent exchange of knowledge, especially informal knowledge.
3. Informal coordination processes.
4. Potentially shifting positions and relationships.

5. Lateral as well as vertical sharing of knowledge.

6. Consensual decision making.

When a firm moves to a **transnational structure,** it goes through a number of processes. For example, ABB used an internal entrepreneurial process, where even middle-level managers were given the autonomy to be entrepreneurs. Also, consistent with the autonomy given to managers is the underlying radical decentralization, where business units and in-country offices are left alone from a control aspect. Still, the price that these units and managers pay is one of high-level accountability. Thus the in-country managers have specific goals and the flexibility to reach those goals the way they consider most beneficial.[21]

The horizontal integration process that is associated with these structures includes intensive informal communications implemented primarily by middle-level managers. Additionally, continual learning and renewal processes, which shape the organizational purpose, are led by the top management teams.[22]

Bartlett proposes a management structure that balances the local, regional, and global demands placed on companies operating across the world's many borders.[23] In the volatile world of transnational corporations and heterarchical mindsets, he sees various groups of specialists including business managers, country managers, and functional managers. Furthermore, the top executives of the international firm must not only manage the complex interactions between these three manager roles, but also identify, develop, and socialize the talented personnel that the transnational requires.

Another overriding feature of these structures is the emphasis on creativity at all levels of management. Complementing this emphasis is the critical role of socialization of the organization's managers to build a strong corporate culture and shared vision of just who the organization is and where it is headed. It is this last point, regarding the managers or staff of the international firm, that leads to its success. Not all managers are able to handle the ambiguity of this structure and systems associated with it. Not all managers are able to effectively move knowledge and actually create knowledge. The front-end hiring process therefore becomes critical.

As suggested, the heterarchical structure and transnational orientation are ambiguous to say the least. What tangible form may these self-organizing structures take? A firm may start with a traditional hierarchy and relax its constraints. For instance, think of an organization built around multiple hierarchies, where a manager's position in one of the organization's hierarchies does not necessarily prevent or suggest a distinctly different position in another of the hierarchies. Suppose a firm has the following critical activities:

- Penetrating the Chinese market during the next three years.
- Building on its research and development capabilities.
- Successfully launching a newly developed standardized product in world markets during the upcoming quarter.
- Investigating various acquisitions and mergers with European firms.
- Effectively managing the 10 existing joint ventures and strategic alliances throughout the world.
- Managing major customer accounts consistently throughout the world.

Of course, these critical activities will overlap. That is, the international joint venture initiatives will affect the Chinese market as well as potential European acquisitions and marketing and R&D efforts. Here a structure that consists of multiple hierarchies might be appropriate. In this structure, the skills and knowledge necessary are brought

FIGURE 9.9
(a) Multiple Hierarchies Structure and (b) Network Effect

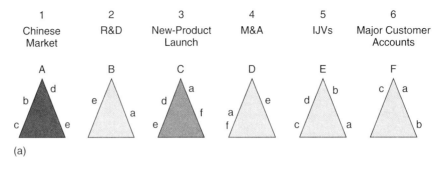

(a)

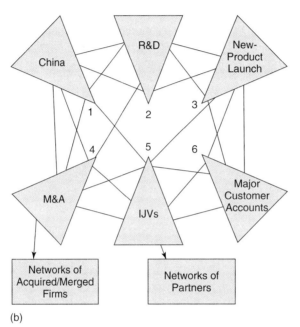

(b)

to the forefront of each hierarchy. Thus the manager who leads the Chinese initiative may be in the middle of a few of the hierarchies supporting other critical initiatives. To illustrate the effect of this orientation and shifting relationships, we have kept this simple, using only six critical activities: The Chinese Market, R&D, New-Product Launch, Mergers and Acquisition (M&A), IJVs, and Major Customer Accounts. Figure 9.9 illustrates the orientation and dynamic capabilities of this type of structure.

As seen, when the individual hierarchies are combined in Figure 9.9*b,* and when the individual managers' roles in each hierarchy are connected, we begin to form a spider-web. The ultimate effect is a networklike web structure, one that we all know will facilitate communication while efficiently and rapidly moving knowledge throughout the organization. Furthermore, when this weblike structure is connected to the skills, knowledge, and resources of joint venture/strategic alliance partners and acquisition firms, the communication and knowledge benefits can potentially grow exponentially. Network structures may be appropriate designs to cope with the complex and dynamic forces of globalization facing organizations.[24] These structures thus may help international firms thrive in an era of turbulence due to new technologies, uncertain competition, and host-government involvement.[25]

The network structure illustrated in Figure 9.9*b* is one example of a malleable, flexible structure that can quickly bring the correct perspectives to critical decisions.[26] Still, it must be understood that these structures are much less defined than the traditional product and area orientations. As organizations shift toward the transnational orientation, a significant amount of knowledge that was based on industry and firm traditions may be lost. These new models are discontinuous with the old ones and give the firm a competitive advantage in developing new knowledge and technology rather than exploiting old knowledge and technology. The new structures support radical rather than incremental change. Many firms in stable industries may be destabilized if they try to force this type of structure into their organizations. Indeed, a traditional consumer goods or industrial goods firm may be better off with an area or product structure, respectively.

However, firms in transnational industries like pharmaceuticals and telecom may need to explore these new structures. In both of those industries, we previously discussed the intense pressures to be globally and efficiently coordinated while also responding to individual market needs. These industries are also good examples of industries whose conventional boundaries have been shattered during the past 15 years. Telecom is now a part of a larger "infocom" industry, which includes media, cable television, Internet, and entertainment. The global pharmaceuticals industry has seen the once-typical focused drug firms turn into full-line global companies while also venturing into chemical and biotech businesses. Furthermore, linkages may be made to the automobile industry, as evidenced by Toyota's new critical contingencies in the United States (depicted in the opening case of this chapter) and GM's international joint venture initiatives depicted in the opening case of Chapter 8.

Still, these models ignore some of the traditional social institutions upon which the organization was based and from which it drew support and strength. These social institutions include the community, the family, specific ethnic groups, and a nationality. In contrast, the transnational firm is one whose boundaries venture beyond any one country or industry. Subsequently, the firm must have a structure which ventures beyond tradition as well.

Summary

This chapter was concerned with the typical stages in the evolution of the basic structures of international companies. Specific traditional organizational structures—the pre–international division phase; the international division structure; the global product structure; and the global area structure—were discussed. We also considered the key current issues that face organizations today: efficient communication, information sharing, and the creation and movement of knowledge throughout the entire organization.

Finding the organizational structure best suited to a company's global corporate strategy is a challenge that an international company's top management executives must meet effectively and efficiently. The imperative to coordinate the functions, products, and areas has created problems and tensions in the internal transactions and management of international companies. Companies usually modify the structures and make trade-offs among the various approaches while attempting to integrate their geographically far-flung operations. This led to the exploration of multidimensional structures as well as ways that firms enhance the traditional hierarchies. The international matrix structure was investigated and shown to offer a variety of advantages over the traditional structures as well as many distinct comparative disadvantages.

Another challenge facing international company managers is that, after finding a suitable structure for a particular global corporate strategy at a certain point in time, they must keep modifying the structure to suit evolving company strategy. This requirement for change is ever present in international enterprises. Thus we ended with an investigation of the self-organizing structures that are becoming associated with transnational firms. We illustrated the heterarchical structure by looking at an organization with multiple hierarchies and ultimately a weblike network structure.

Key Terms and Concepts

global area structure, *286*
global product structure, *284*

heterarchy, *293*
international division, *281*

matrix structure, *290*
transnational structure, *295*

Discussion Questions

1. Compare and contrast the international product division structure and the international area division structure. What are the major benefits and drawbacks of each?
2. Why is the international matrix structure used by some firms? What are the problems in trying to implement this structure globally?
3. The heterarchy is a new form of organization structure. Why has it evolved? In your opinion, within which industries does this structure fit best? Why?

Minicase

The New Organizational Structure of Sumitomo Mitsui Financial Group

Sumitomo Mitsui Banking Corporation [SMBC] announced its plan for the organization structure of Sumitomo Mitsui Financial Group (SMFG), the holding company, which will be established on December 2, 2002. It also announced its plan for the reorganization of SMBC's head office, which will become effective on December 2, 2002.

SMFG will be responsible for corporate strategy and management, resource allocation, financial accounting, investor relations, IT strategy, nomination of executives, risk management, and audit of the Group as a whole with ten departments as follows: Public Relations Department, Corporate Planning Department, Investor Relations Department, Financial Accounting Department, Subsidiaries & Affiliates Department, IT Planning Department, General Affairs Department, Human Resources Department, Corporate Risk Management Department and Audit Department. The Risk Management committee, Compensation Committee, and Nominating Committee will be established within the Board of Directors and be responsible for supervising the operations of the Group as a whole. Regarding the Organizational Revision of SMBC, the following changes will be instituted:

An Asset Restructuring Unit will be established and the following departments will be integrated into the Unit in order to focus further on reengineering and restructuring of SMBC's corporate customers' businesses. This realignment will accelerate the improvement in the SMBC's loan portfolio in advance of the implementation of the New Basel Accord:

(a) Credit Administration Department (Transferred from Corporate Service Unit)

(b) Credit Department I and II (Transferred from Middle Market Banking Unit)

(c) Credit Department II and III (Transferred from Corporate Banking Unit).

Talented staff with essential know-how for corporate revitalization, such as securization, debt-equity swaps, and DIP (Debtor in Possession) finances, and those with accounting and legal expertise from throughout SMBC will be gathered under the Planning Department of the Asset Restructuring Unit in order to strengthen SMBC's commitment to reengineering and restructuring of its corporate customers' businesses.

Regarding the Reorganization of Existing Departments, in the *Corporate Staff Unit,* the Investor Relations Department of SMBC will be abolished and the Investor Relations Department of SMFG will have a comprehensive responsibility for the Group's investor relations activities. The Portfolio Management Department, Market Risk Management Department, and Kobe General Affairs Department will be abolished and functions of these departments will be transferred and consolidated into their related departments. The Equity Portfolio Management Department will be placed under the Financial Accounting Department.

In the *Corporate Service Unit,* the Operations Planning Department will be reorganized to reflect the completion of adjustment and integration of operational processes after the merger. The International Market Operations Department and Settlement & Clearing Services Department within the Operating Planning Department will be abolished and a new department, *Operations and Administration Department,* will be responsible for managing the Group's operational subsidiaries.

The *E-Business Planning Department* will be integrated into the Electronic Commerce Banking Department along with the Investment Banking Unit's e-Business, Media and Telecom Department, and the e-Business Patent Department will be abolished and some of its functions will be transferred to the Corporate Staff Unit's Legal Department.

In the *Internal Audit Unit,* the Audit Department and Inspection Department will be merged and become *Audit Department,* and the planning function of the Group's entire Audit Department will be transferred to SMFG. The Audit Departments for the Americas and for Europe will be integrated as part of the *Internal Audit Department* and *Credit Review Department,* strengthening their functions.

In the *Consumer Banking Unit,* the Products & Marketing Department will be reorganized into the following three departments: *Financial Consulting Department* (responsible for advisory businesses for investment products such as mutual funds, foreign currencies deposit; and insurance); *Consumer Loan Department* (responsible for businesses such as housing loans); and *Consumer Finance Department* (responsible for business such as personal revolving loans, personal short-term deposits, and settlement).

In the *Middle Market Banking Unit,* the Kobe Public Institutions Banking Department will be integrated into the *Public Institutions Banking Department* in order to unify and fortify the promotion of business to the public institution market. The Credit Department I and Credit Department II, in charge of credit monitoring in the eastern region of Japan, will be merged to form a new *Credit Department I,* and the Credit Department III, in charge of the western region, will be renamed *Credit Department.* The Operations & Systems Department will be abolished and certain functions will be transferred to the *Branch Operations Department of the Consumer Banking Unit.* The Business Reengineering Department and New Business Promotion Department within the Business Promotion Department will be abolished and the *Business Promotion Department* will become directly responsible for their functions.

In the *International Banking Unit,* the Asia Pacific Department will be abolished and its planning and administrative functions concerning office operations in Asia will be transferred to the *Planning Department.* The Operations & Systems Department will be reorganized and become *Systems Department.*

In the *Investment Banking Unit,* the Syndications Department will be integrated into the *Securitization & Syndication Department.* Certain functions of the Securitization & Syndication Department will be transferred to a new department, *Structured Finance Department,* which will be established to promote business such as project finance, real estate finance, lease finance, insurance finance, and management/ leverage-buy-out finance. The Asset Management Planning Department will be abolished and its functions for defined contribution pension funds will be transferred to the *Corporate Employees Promotion Department* of the Consumer Banking Unit.

Source: From "The New Organizational Structure of Sumitomo Mitsui Financial Group," *The Asian Banker,* November 30, 2002. Reprinted with permission.

DISCUSSION QUESTIONS

1. Why is Sumitomo Mitsui Banking Corporation changing its organization structure?
2. What type of structure is Sumitomo Mitsui Banking Corporation implementing? What are the main characteristics of the design?
3. In your opinion, does the proposed structure fit with the global environment in which the company is operating? Why or why not?

Notes

1. J. Peters, "On Structures," *Management Decision* 31, no. 6 (1993), pp. 60–63.
2. R. Engdahl, R. Keating, and K. Aupperle, "Strategy of Structure: Chicken or Egg?" *Organization Development* 18, no. 4 (2000), pp. 21–34.
3. K. Kim, J. Park, and J. Prescott, "The Global Integration of Business Functions: A Study of Multinational Businesses in Integrated Global Industries," *Journal of International Business Studies* 34, no. 4 (2003), pp. 327–344.

4. A. Harzing, "An Empirical Analysis and Extension of the Bartlett-Ghoshal Typology of Multinational Corporations," *Journal of International Business Studies* 31, no. 1 (2000), pp. 101–120.

5. M. Harris and A. Raviv, "Organization Design," *Management Science* 48, no. 7 (2002), pp. 852–866.

6. S. Ghoshal and N. Nohria, "Horses for Courses: Organizational Forms for Multinational Corporations," *Sloan Management Review* 34, no. 2 (1993), pp. 23–36.

7. J. Stopford and L. Wells Jr., *Managing the Multinational Enterprise* (New York: Basic Books, 1972), p. 51.

8. L. Garicano, "Hierarchies and the Organization of Knowledge in Production," *Journal of Political Economy* 108 (2000), pp. 874–904.

9. O. Hart and J. Moore, "On the Design of Hierarchies: Coordination Versus Specialization." Working paper, Department of Economics, Harvard University, Cambridge, MA, 1999.

10. D. Vayanos, "The Decentralization of Information Processing in the Presence of Interactions." Working paper, MIT, Cambridge, MA, 2002.

11. J. Daniels, D. Pitts, and R. Tretter, "Strategy and Structure of U.S. Multinationals: An Exploratory Study," *Academy of Management Journal* 27, no. 2 (1984), pp. 292–308.

12. A. Phatak, *Managing Multinational Corporations* (New York: Praeger, 1974), p. 183.

13. Daniels, Pitts, and Tretter, "Strategy and Structure of U.S. Multinationals."

14. Stopford and Wells, *Managing the Multinational Enterprise,* p. 87.

15. P. Jennergren, "Decentralization in Organizations." In Paul C. Nystrom and William H. Starbuck, eds., *Handbook of Organizational Design* (New York: Oxford University Press, 1981).

16. C. Bartlett and S. Ghoshal, "Matrix Management: Not a Structure, a Frame of Mind," *Harvard Business Review,* July–August 1990, pp. 138–145.

17. P. Drucker, *Management: Tasks, Responsibilities, Practices* (New York: Harper & Row, 1974), p. 598.

18. G. Hedlund, "A Model of Knowledge Management and the N-Form Corporation," *Strategic Management Journal* 15 (1994), pp. 73–90.

19. J. Birkinshaw and A. Morrison, "Configurations of Strategy and Structure in Subsidiaries of Multinational Structure," *Journal of International Business Studies* 26, no. 4 (1995), pp. 729–753.

20. J. R. Galbraith, Edward E. Lawler III, and Associates, eds., *Organizing for the Future: The New Logic for Managing Complex Organzations* (San Fransisco: Jossey-Bass, 1993).

21. Hedlund, "A Model of Knowledge Management."

22. G. Hedlund, "The Hypermodern MNC—A Heterarchy," *Human Resource Management* 25, no. 1 (1986), pp. 9–25.

23. C. Bartlett, "What Is a Global Manager?" *Harvard Business Review* 81, no. 8 (2003), p. 101.

24. C. Bartlett and S. Ghoshal, *Managing across Borders: The Transnational Solution* (Boston: Harvard Business School Press, 1989); M. S. Gerstein and R. B. Shaw. In D. A. Nadler, M. S. Gerstein, R. B. Shaw, and Associates, eds., "Organizational Architecture for the Twenty-First Century," *Organizational Architecture: Designs for Changing Organizations* (San Francisco: Jossey-Bass, 1992), pp. 263–73.

25. M. Gerstein and R. B. Shaw, "Organizational Architecture for the Twenty-First Century."

26. A. Mukherti, "The Evolution of Information Systems: Their Impact on Organizations and Structures," *Management Decision,* 40 no. 5/6 (2002), pp. 497–508.

Controlling International Strategies and Operations

Chapter Learning Objectives

After completing this chapter, you should be able to:

- Describe the main elements in the managerial control process.
- Compare and contrast output control, behavior control, and input control.
- Discuss problems of control that are particular to international companies.
- Discuss the different categories of parent–subsidiary relationships and the strategic control mechanisms appropriate to each.
- Identify the effects of various host-country environments on a firm's international control system.
- Describe the key attributes of an effective international control system.
- Distinguish among a dependent, independent, and interdependent foreign subsidiary in its relationship with its headquarters organization.

Opening Case: How Well Does Wal-Mart Travel?

In the decade since Wal-Mart Stores, Inc., began its international exploits with a joint venture in Mexico, its record abroad has been full of merchandising missteps and management upheaval. Such blunders explain why German shopper Claudia Gittel grouses about the meat selection at the Wal-Mart in Esslingen and how the prices were lower when local chain Interspar ran the store. And why rival retailers from Brazil to South Korea scoff at Wal-Mart's product choices and "cookie-cutter" outlets. "We don't see Wal-Mart as a threat anymore," sniffs Hong Sun Sang, assistant manager for E-Mart, a 35-store chain in South Korea.

But with its persistence and deep pockets, it would be a mistake to underestimate the world's largest retailer. Just look at the U.S. grocery business, where Wal-Mart is a leader after early stumbles with its huge "supercenters." Likewise, the Bentonville (Ark.) chain has learned some painful lessons about consumers, regulators, and suppliers around the world. Through trial and error, the company has quietly built a powerful force outside the U.S. It's now the biggest retailer in Canada and Mexico. Its $32 billion international business equaled 17% of its $191 billion in sales last year, with more than 1,100 stores in nine countries. And its operating profit abroad rose 36% last year, to $1.1 billion, about 12% of total profits. The trend continued in the first half of this year, with international sales rising 9.6% and operating profit jumping 39%.

Wal-Mart finally started getting its international act together in 2000 after then-chief financial officer John B. Menzer took charge of the International Division. The low-key Menzer was credited with tightening financial discipline and boosting return on assets for the parent company. Now he's bringing a similar focus to Wal-Mart's sprawling operations abroad, where he's pushing more authority into the field, working to develop a corps of top managers, and spreading "best practices" from the U.S. and elsewhere around the world. And for the first time, Wal-Mart is building a global sourcing operation to use its huge sales volumes to command better deals, higher quality, and more innovation from both U.S. and foreign suppliers.

The company is backing these efforts with big bucks. It is estimated that Wal-Mart will devote 26% of its $9 billion in capital expenditures this year to operations abroad, adding about 120 stores. "As a global organization, they've become more savvy," says Ira Kalish, director of global retail intelligence at PricewaterhouseCoopers.

Wal-Mart believes that it has no choice but to expand rapidly abroad. Its culture and stock price are built on the expectation of double-digit sales and profit gains year after year. Analysts figure that the company's expanding chain of U.S. supercenters will carry the burden for at least four to eight years. But "someday the U.S. will slow down, and international will be the growth vehicle for the company," says Menzer.

Still, to get there Menzer must clear some high hurdles. The biggest one is Germany, where Wal-Mart bought the 21-store Wertkauf hypermarket chain in 1997 and then 74 unprofitable and often decrepit Interspar stores in 1998. Problems in integrating and upgrading the stores resulted in at least $200 million in losses in 2000, on roughly $3 billion in sales, estimates analyst Robert Buchanan of A. G. Edwards and Sons, Inc. Wal-Mart has stopped predicting when it might make money in Germany. Some analysts believe that it won't break even until at least 2003. "There was a steep learning curve that wasn't expected," says Jim Leach of Strong Capital Management.

Many of the wounds were self-inflicted. Wal-Mart failed to understand Germany's retail culture, the regulations that can add five years or more to the launch of a new hypermarket, and the stiff competition among some 14 hypermarket chains in a stagnant market. German managers who had been running the Wertkauf and Interspar stores for years didn't always take kindly to American "mentors" who were telling them how to do things when they didn't even speak German. Vendors balked at switching to a new supply system; when Wal-Mart tried to force them to supply its new centralized warehouses, it often found itself with empty shelves.

Subsequently, the German Cartel Office compelled Wal-Mart and some rivals to raise prices on milk, butter, and some other staples that they were found to be selling below cost. Wal-Mart denies that but admits it underestimated the difficulties it would face. "We just walked in and said, 'We're going to lower prices, we're going to add people to the stores, we're going to remodel the stores because inherently that's correct,' and it wasn't," says Wal-Mart CEO H. Lee Scott Jr. "We didn't have the infrastructure to support the kind of things we were doing."

Wal-Mart still needs a bigger presence in Germany to compete effectively, many analysts and suppliers contend. They point especially to food, where its market share is put at less than 2%. But Wal-Mart executives insist that they don't need more stores to make the German operation a success. "We have the scale; we just have to operate better," says Menzer.

To fix those operational problems, Wal-Mart recently hired a new country head, poaching him from a German tobacco-and-food supplier. Instead of the expensive renovations completed on 24 stores last year, Wal-Mart is carrying out more modest face-lifts on 35 outlets this year. And this year it will open its first two new stores since the acquisitions. Wal-Mart is also working more closely with suppliers to boost its centralized distribution effort. About 50% of the products Wal-Mart has targeted for the program now move through central warehouses. Says Menzer: "We set ourselves back a few years, and now we're rebounding."

Wal-Mart executives say the German experience helped when they bought the British chain ASDA in 1999. Wal-Mart acquired a strong chain and gave local managers the freedom to run the business. While ASDA is still No. 3 in the grocery market, its share grew from 7.4% in 1995 to 9.6% last year, according to Verdict Research. Wal-Mart gave ASDA better technology for tracking store sales and inventories. And it pulled ASDA into its global buying effort, led by a 40-person unit in Bentonville that helps negotiate prices for products that can be sold in different markets. This enabled ASDA to cut prices on fans and air conditioners, for example, by 50%, boosting sales threefold.

Perhaps most important, says ASDA President Paul Mason, "this is still essentially a British business in the way it's run day-to-day." Indeed, one of Menzer's main priorities is to push operational authority to the country chiefs and closer to customers. That has meant cutting the international staff in Bentonville from 450 to 137. Now, Menzer focuses on enforcing certain core Wal-Mart principles, such as "every day low pricing," recently rolled out in Mexico and Argentina. But country managers handle their own buying, logistics, building design, and other operational decisions. "I have the autonomy to do what I need to do to run Wal-Mart Canada," says Mario Pilozzi, president of that business. In contrast, when Wal-Mart entered Canada in 1994, its blueprint specified what to sell and where to sell it—including liquid detergent and Kathie Lee clothing that flopped there. In the past, says CEO Scott, "we could get very specific on what should be on an end cap [a store display at the end of an aisle] . . . I think we've matured."

Still, critics believe that the company retains a headquarters-knows-best mind-set. That raises the question, is Wal-Mart truly a global company, or just a U.S. company with a foreign division? Vijay Govindarajan, a professor of international business at Dartmouth's Tuck School of Business, says Wal-Mart has few top managers who aren't American and few who speak more than one language and have been posted in several spots abroad. That might be one reason why some competitors scoff at Wal-Mart's claim that it's now sensitive to local tastes. "I get the impression that Wal-Mart is insisting on the American-style layouts and business approach," says Seol Do Won, marketing director at Samsung Tesco Co. in South Korea, which runs seven Home Plus stores. "It's good to introduce global standards, but you also need to adapt to local practice," he says.

Menzer insists he's doing just that, and that the lessons are flowing back to Bentonville, too. The U.S. stores and distribution centers, for instance, are now adopting ASDA's system for replenishing fresh food more quickly and in the right quantities. And ASDA's popular line of George brand clothing is being rolled out in the women's department of all U.S. stores this Christmas season. Thomas M. Coughlin, president of the Wal-Mart Div., even removed all the chairs from the room where his managers hold their weekly meeting after he saw ASDA's "air-traffic controllers" room in Leeds. There, managers meet every morning around a high table with no chairs—to keep meetings short and to encourage action—as they pore over figures charted on the walls. As Menzer and Scott have made clear, there's no turning back in Wal-Mart's plan to conquer the world.

Source: Reprinted from W. Zellner, with K. Schmidt, M. Ihlwan, and H. Dawley, "How Well Does Wal-Mart Travel? After Early Missteps, the Retailing Giant May Finally Be Getting the Hang of Selling Overseas," September 3, 2001 issue of *BusinessWeek* by special permission. Copyright © 2001 by The McGraw-Hill Companies, Inc.

Discussion Questions

1. What control issues have surfaced for Wal-Mart regarding its foreign subsidiaries and joint ventures?

2. In your opinion, can an American "Wal-Mart formula" be easily transferred to countries like Germany, England, and South Korea?

3. What ongoing environmental factors may affect how Wal-Mart controls its overseas operations as it continues to expand internationally?

Global Strategy, Structure, and Organizational Control

An international company derives its strength from its ability to recognize and capitalize on opportunities anywhere in the world and its capacity to respond to global threats to its business operations in a timely fashion. On the basis of an evaluation of global opportunities and threats as well as a company's strengths and weaknesses, top management executives of a multinational at the parent-company level formulate corporate strategy for the whole company. The objectives of a multinational company serve as the umbrella under which the objectives of divisions and subsidiaries are developed. The parent company, divisions, and subsidiaries engage in a considerable amount of give and take before the divisional and subsidiary objectives are finally agreed to by executives at all three levels. In the opening case, Wal-Mart is discovering these issues as it intensifies its international expansion initiatives.

As discussed in the previous chapter, an international firm must link its global strategic initiatives to an appropriate organization structure in order to efficiently implement those initiatives. Similarly, controlling the network of domestic and overseas subsidiaries must be consistent with the strategies and structure of the firm. For instance, Practical Insight 10.1 illustrates Cisco's change to a new structure with an inherent centralized control process.

The objective of managerial control is to ensure that strategic, operational, and tactical plans are implemented correctly. Thus control can be defined as any process that helps align the actions of individuals with the interests of their employing firm.[1] In this chapter, the focus is on the parent company's managerial control over its foreign subsidiaries. We examine first the salient features of the managerial control process. Then, because multinational companies experience problems controlling their far-flung operations, we look at those problems and their causes. Next we review the typical characteristics of control systems used by international companies, and we conclude with the integration and effects of the external environments discussed in Section 1 of this book with control processes.

The Managerial Control Process

Managerial control is a process directed toward ensuring that operations and personnel adhere to parent-company plans. A control system is essential because the future, especially when dealing with the dynamic international environment, is uncertain. Assumptions about the internal and external environment that were at one time the basis of a forecast may prove invalid. Furthermore, strategies may not be applicable, and current budgets and programs may not be effective in the longer term. Managerial control is a process that evaluates performance and takes corrective action when performance differs significantly from the company's plans. With managerial control, any deviations from forecasts, objectives, or plans can be detected early and corrected with minimum difficulty.

Managerial control involves several management skills: planning, coordinating, communicating, processing and evaluating information, and influencing people. The managerial control process entails four main elements:

1. The setting of standards.
2. The development of methods to monitor the performance of an individual or an organizational system.
3. The comparison of actual performance measures to planned performance in order to determine if current performance is sufficiently close to what was planned.

PRACTICAL INSIGHT 10.1

CISCO SCRAPS CORPORATE STRUCTURE, CENTRALIZES ENGINEERING

Cisco Systems Inc. has turned its corporate structure upside down, scrapping its three-pronged decentralized business structure and creating a centralized engineering unit that will work in parallel with a centralized marketing organization.

The move does away with the structure Cisco put in place in 1997, on the eve of the internet and telecoms explosion, which saw the company organized around three lines of business: enterprise, commercial, and service provider. The new structure and associated centralized control system will see the company's engineering efforts focused on the following segments: access; aggregation; Cisco IOS Technologies Division; internet switching and services; Ethernet access; network management services; core routing; optical; storage; voice; and wireless. Cisco's declared aim in breaking out into 11 segments is to meet customers' demands for products addressing multiple segments under a common architecture. Nevertheless, identifying each market and its corresponding

engineering effort may also give the company a clearer view when it comes to axing technologies or projects in which it sees little future. The company says its current plan is to continue with all its existing technologies.

The company reshuffled its management at the same time as imposing the new structure, with Mario Mazzola, previously senior vice president of the company's new business ventures group, becoming chief development officer, overseeing the 11 technology groups. Internet switching and services will be the largest of the groups, and will be headed up by Michelangelo Volpi, previously chief strategy officer, who will report direct to Mazzola. The marketing organization will be headed up by former enterprise chief James Richardson. The company insisted the move was not a response to the current downturn in its core markets, saying it could have opted to make the changes at any time. In a statement, Chambers said the company is making the changes in its control structure at a time when it is seeing signs of stabilization in the market.

Source: From ComputerWire, August 24, 2001. Reprinted with permission.

4. The employment of effectuating or action devices that can be used to correct significant deviations in performance.

Managerial control and planning are closely related. Managerial control depends on the objectives set forth in tactical plans, which in turn are derived from the strategic plans of the organization. Tactical plans encompass the short-term contributions of each functional area to strategic plans, goals, and objectives.

Setting Control Standards

The first step in the control process is the setting of standards. These standards are derived from the objectives defined in the planning process. Without a definition of objectives, standards cannot be formulated. After standards are formulated, management needs to establish a hierarchy of degrees of importance. However, it would be inefficient and unrealistic to set specific standards for every organizational activity. Instead, management should continuously monitor the performance of activities in essential geographic, product, and project areas. In key areas, standards need to be as concrete and as specific as possible, while taking into consideration the fact that some key areas, such as management development, cannot be expressed in specific and concrete terms.[2]

Monitoring Performance

Once standards have been established, the next step is the development of techniques to monitor and accurately describe performance. Budgets, managerial audits, and financial statements are the main measuring devices used to assess the performance of organizational systems. A *budget* is a detailed listing of the resources or money assigned to a particular project or unit. Here, standards of performance are translated into dollar amounts for each item in the budget. However, the dynamic, changing character of a business environment necessitates some flexibility with budgets. Several methods can be used to make budgets flexible without eventually losing managerial control, such as the adoption of supplemental budgets, alternative budgets, and variable expense budgets. Supplemental budgets amend budgets that establish limits on expenditures for plant expansion, capital improvements, and so on. If a capital expenditure budget proves to be too low because of inaccurate costing in the planning stage, a supplemental budget can be prepared and added to the original budget.[3]

Alternative budgeting is another form of controlled budgeting. A budget is usually prepared on the basis of an organization's assessment of the most probable future conditions. However, if there is a real possibility that, for example, future sales may be lower (or higher), alternative budgets are also prepared based on the implications of specific lower or higher sales figures.

A third type of budgeting is the variable expense budget found mostly in manufacturing organizations. Variable expense budgets are devised to ensure proper coordination of activities as changes take place in sales of manufactured goods. These budgets are schedules of costs of production that tell managers what levels of critical activities actually should be established as changes occur in sales and output volume. All of these budgetary techniques require accurate and timely communication. Variable expense budgets, in particular, depend on accurate and prompt reports from production and sales.

Another typical control mechanism of organizational systems is financial statements, particularly the income statement, which details the sources of revenues and expenses for a given year—the profit and loss statement, balance sheets, and so on.

Comparing Performance to Plan

As has been evident throughout this text, comparative analyses are at the heart of international management. Thus the third step in the managerial control process is comparing the performance measures obtained from the different monitoring devices to the company's objectives and evaluating whether current performance is sufficiently close to the company's original plan. Management must decide how much variation between the standard and actual performance is tolerable and what "sufficiently close" means for the organization. Changes in the external environment may affect the limits of possible performance, which in turn may necessitate a change in the performance standards. Once the limits of the possible performance are altered, management must decide how the values in the standards of measurement should be altered. Naturally, when the external environment does not deviate from the forecast, the task of managerial control is simply to evaluate whether performance is within acceptable limits.

Another aspect of the evaluation phase of the control process is related to feedback and feed-forward controls. With feedback controls, the focus is on information about events that have already occurred, such as production and actual sales. This information is compared with a standard of performance so that necessary corrections for the future can be determined. For example, feedback control is typically used to monitor the productivity and performance of a factory worker against a preset production rate. Feed-forward controls are different in that the deviations from standards are anticipated or predicted before they occur. When those conditions do occur, certain actions are scheduled to take place in anticipation of the outcome of the first occurrence. For example, when sales volume reaches a predetermined level, management is automatically obliged to increase the level of inventory. This action is taken to prevent inventories from running out, a situation that would otherwise occur as the result of the first occurrence—the sales increase. Feedback control cures problems, whereas feed-forward control systems are meant to prevent problems before they occur. "An ounce of pre-vention" is clearly better than a cure here. Companies use both types of control, al-though feedback is more common because it is less complicated and requires less forecasting. From this discussion, we see that accurate communication and a perva-sive managerial information system are essential in management control. Manage-ment cannot appraise, compare, or correct performance without the proper reporting of appropriate and meaningful information.

Correcting the Deviations

The fourth step in the control process is correcting significant deviations from the standards. For this step, effectuating or action devices must be employed. The appli-cation of action devices requires many management skills—decision making, per-suading, effectively communicating, and so on. When a subsystem of an organization needs help, the corrective action might be to use different budgeting techniques or to impose control mechanisms on costs, expenses, and so on. When the deviation con-cerns organizational personnel, the action devices could be either positive (promo-tions, salary increases, increased responsibility, and special privileges) or negative (reprimands, withdrawal of privileges, demotions, salary reductions, and termination of employment).[4]

The overriding human dimension is essential to the managerial control process. The steps or elements in the control process are not automatic, but are activated by man-agement. Monitoring, comparing, and action devices depend on human intervention. The necessary communication is between people. The effectiveness of the control sys-tem depends on the acceptance of the system as necessary, legitimate, and appropriate by the members of the organization. This human dimension is most significant in the managerial process in a multinational company.

Types of Control Systems

The control process has two distinct parts, the antecedent conditions and the various forms of control. The antecedent conditions include the availability of output measures and the knowledge of the transformation process, that is, an organizational under-standing of how inputs are converted into outputs.[5]

When both **output measure availability** and the **knowledge of the transformation process** are high, an organization has the flexibility to use either output or behavior performance measurement systems. As output measures become less available, a firm must adopt more behavioral measures. Conversely, as the knowledge of the transfor-mation process declines, an output measurement orientation is preferred. Finally, as both parameters simultaneously tend toward the negative extremes, a firm will tend to adopt ritual or clan control. This control form achieves efficiency under conditions of high performance and low opportunism and takes place when goal incongruence is high and performance ambiguity is low. Under conditions of low outcome observabil-ity, even when information about an agent's behavior is incomplete, a behavior control system is possible under the assumption that information and information systems play a proactive role.[6]

The discussion of output and behavior control has excluded two other organizational mechanisms that help align the interests of the employee and the firm, the recruitment and selection of new employees and the training of individuals after they have joined the organization. Both of these mechanisms fall under another type of control system, input control. Input control complements the output/behavior choice and incorporates organizational socialization, staffing procedures, and ongoing training and development programs. Furthermore, input control is the formal bureaucratic human resource management system, such as selection and training, rather than the less observable influences, such as socialization or clan control. Input controls regulate the antecedent conditions of performance, including the knowledge, skills, abilities, values, and motives of employees. In contrast, behavior control regulates the transformation process and output control regulates the results. The U.S. foreign service corps represents an example of input control where cause-and-effect relationships for these personnel are incomplete and results are difficult to measure. Subsequently, a difficult selection process and a rigorous training process are both used to improve the organizational control.[7]

A firm's strategic context, including the extent of its product-market variation, its work flow integration, and its size, will affect the firm's ability to develop well-delineated, measurable performance standards as well as its knowledge of the cause–effect relationships. The strategic context influences administrative information, which, in turn, influences control. The various strategic control options for the international firm are delineated next.

Input Control **Input control** is a control system that emphasizes employee selection and training,[8] as well as socialization of the employees to the organization and its values, vision, and objectives.[9] This type of control can be assessed by the degree to which an employee of an international firm is provided substantial training before assuming responsibility. Also, within this system, the firm establishes the best staffing procedures available; becomes involved in the training and skill development of an employee; performs multiple evaluations before hiring an individual; provides opportunities for broadening a skill set of an employee; and takes pride in hiring the best employees possible. In turn, the employees are socialized within the organization and subsequently share the firm's overriding values and vision. Consistent with input controls are informal systems to continually integrate the managers into the organization.[10]

Behavior Control **Behavior control** is a control system that emphasizes top-down control in the form of articulated operating processes and procedures.[11] This form of control can be assessed by analyzing the following organizational attributes:

- The degree to which a firm weighs evaluations based on behavior.
- Whether an employee is held accountable regardless of the outcome.
- The degree to which procedures or methods are valued.
- The degree to which performance programs are imposed from the top down.
- The frequency at which employees receive feedback or performance information.

Output Control **Output control** is a control system that sets and measures actual targets, such as financial results[12] and productivity. This system may be implemented by an international firm along the following dimensions:

- Use of evaluations with significant weightings on results.
- Pay based on performance.
- Preestablished targets used for evaluating personnel.
- Numerical records as indexes of effectiveness.
- Performance linked to concrete results.
- Appraisals based on goal achievement.

FIGURE 10.1

A Model of MNC Control Selection

Source: From Hamilton and Kashlak, "National Influences on MNC Control System Selection," *Management International Review*, Vol. 39, No. 2, 1999. Reprinted with permission.

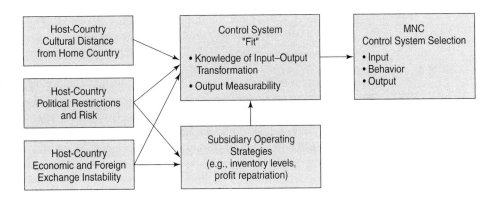

Ideally, control systems should regulate both motivation and ability. The use of behavior control ensures motivation through close supervision and, to a lesser extent, facilitates the ability of subordinates to perform well by articulating operating procedures. Output control focuses on motivation through the use of incentives, providing virtually no direction about how results should be accomplished. Finally, input control ensures that employees have the requisite ability to perform well. These issues are further elaborated upon in Chapter 14, when we discuss motivation of the international work force. Because the three types of control have overlapping effects, firms tend to use elements of input behavior and output control simultaneously. Figure 10.1 illustrates the dependence of these control system options on various host-country environmental factors. We next begin to discuss these factors and the problems and concerns that arise with them.

Problems of Control in an International Company

An international firm's control system must not only support the firm's strategy; it must produce behavior and flexibility by subsidiary managers to manage within various host-country environments.[13] Thus control systems and the problems associated with them are far more complex in a multinational company than in one that is purely domestic, because the multinational operates in more than one cultural, economic, political, and legal environment. Let us examine a few of the most important international variables having a major negative impact on the flow of information between headquarters and subsidiaries. These variables, in turn, influence the effectiveness of the international company's control system.

Despite the sophistication and speed of contemporary communication systems, the geographic distance between a parent company and a foreign affiliate continues to cause communication distortion. Differences in language between the parent company and its foreign affiliates are also responsible for distortions in communication. Language barriers caused by language differences involve both the content and the meaning of messages. Many ideas and concepts are not easily translatable from one language to another. Moreover, geographic distances prevent most face-to-face communication, so the messages of nonverbal communication are lost.

Problems are also caused by misunderstanding the communication habits of people in other cultures. Managers of different cultures may interact and yet block out important messages, because the manner in which the message is presented may mean something different in the sending and receiving cultures. For example, a manager may make a wrong judgment about a subordinate's performance because he or she is unaware of culturally different communications habits. As an illustration, consider that the aborigines in Australia exhibit attention by listening intently with their faces and bodies turned away from the speaker, and with no eye contact.[14] Looking directly at the eyes of another is considered rude in Arab cultures, whereas in Western cultures it is interpreted as an attempt to hide something or as shame. Such behavior could easily be misread by a member of a different culture—one who is accustomed to associating body posture and eye contact with attention. Cultural distance is as significant as geographic distance in creating communication distortions. Lack of understanding and acceptance of the cultural values of a group may impair a manager's ability to evaluate information accurately, to judge performance fairly, and to make valid decisions about performance. This failure could create problems in an international company in the area of employee performance appraisal.

In some cultures one does not make criticism bluntly, but discusses critical areas in an oblique fashion. In contrast, as seen with Wal-Mart in the opening case of this chapter, the American managerial style is direct in identifying responsibilities for achieving certain organizational goals by specific members in the organization. Other control mechanisms are also affected by cultural differences, again as exemplified by Wal-Mart's operations in South Korea, Germany, and even Great Britain—a country culturally similar to the United States on many of the cultural dimensions discussed in Chapter 5. The detailed reporting required by some "tight" managerial control systems is not acceptable to some cultures. Also, the degree of harmony valued in a culture may make the accurate reporting of problems difficult.[15] For example, in the Japanese culture, maintaining group cohesiveness is considered to be far more important than reporting a problem to a superior who would place blame on the group or an individual within the group. It is therefore not unusual for Japanese supervisors not to report a problem to upper management, in the hope that it can be resolved at the group level.

Communication distortion between the parent company and a foreign affiliate may occur because of the differing frames of reference of these two organizational units. The parent company may perceive each foreign affiliate as just one of many, and therefore may have a tendency to view each affiliate's problems in light of the company's entire global network of operations. However, foreign affiliate heads may view the problems of their own operations as being very important to them and their affiliates. Both the parent company and the affiliate heads may try to communicate their feelings and views to each other without much success because each could be communicating from a different frame of reference.

International Environments and Control Systems

Differences and changes in the various host-country environments will affect a firm's ability to use the different forms of control described earlier. Specifically, the alterations along three external environmental dimensions—cultural differences, political risk, and economic factors—will affect the knowledge of cause-and-effect relationships as well as the degree of crystallization of standards and, subsequently, the choice of an international firm's control systems. As an organization increases its overseas presence, the process of coordination and communication with its overseas subsidiaries becomes strained,[16] necessitating increased integration and interdependence among the affiliates as well as between the affiliates and headquarters. Thus, within the larger global structure, specific control systems must be adapted to host-country environmental influences.

Specific **host-country environmental factors** could increase market variation and must be considered when developing performance measurement and control systems. These factors include:

1. The cultural distance between the headquarters's home country and the country hosting the international firm's subsidiary.
2. The degree of host-country political risk as reflected in the host governments restrictions on the international firm's operations.
3. Economic factors such as the volatility of a host country's foreign exchange rates and host-country inflationary pressures that are linked to foreign exchange movements.[17]

The influence of these three factors on an international firm's control system is discussed in the following sections. In general, as the host country moves further away from the origin in terms of cultural distance, political risk, and economic instability, the control system will tend more toward input control.

Cultural Distance

Both national culture and the distance between national cultures are significant influences on decision making and strategies. A firm will initially expand overseas to countries most similar in culture and business culture to the home country in order to more easily implement and control its strategies. Specifically, cultural distance affects many behaviors and managerial decisions, including work values, patterns of negotiation, international joint ventures establishment and operations, overseas entry mode, and degree of partner reciprocity.

The greater the extent to which an organization's headquarters and subsidiaries are culturally distant, the more difficult effective supervision of the various units becomes. If the headquarters–subsidiary relationship is viewed from a transaction cost perspective, costs will increase relative to cultural distance. Thus a decreasing level of cultural distance will reduce the expenses of adapting a firm's control system to a host-country subsidiary.[18] More explicitly, the degree of cultural distance between home and host countries will influence the parent–subsidiary performance ambiguity and task definition. As a result, the knowledge of input–output transformation and output measurability will decline. Therefore, when cultural distance between the home and host countries is low, performance measurement in the host country will be determined by outcome measurability and the knowledge of input–output transformation. As cultural distance increases, overseas subsidiary performance evaluation through output or behavior systems becomes increasingly difficult. As a result, an input control system becomes more attractive as a control mechanism.

Political Risk and Host-Country Restrictions

Differences between home- and host-country political systems and the resulting risk and restrictions arising in the host country may affect an international firm's control system. Politically imposed country-level restrictions may be seen as opportunistic behavior by the foreign government partners seeking to redistribute gains of the multinational enterprise (MNE) within the host country.

In Chapter 3, the political environment was related to international business activities through the concept of political risk. Political differences and political risk have been identified as factors that influence strategic and tactical behavior. The political environment of a host country is a critical dimension in distinguishing among opportunities in foreign markets, and firms today view both the assessment and management of changes in the various sociopolitical environments as critical components of strategic

FIGURE 10.2 **Controlling International Political Linkages**

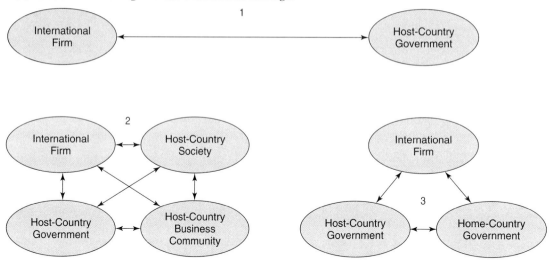

decision making. In general, when a firm crosses international boundaries, new and different political environments force that firm into various modes of adaptation. The implementation of control systems represents one critical mode of adaptation for the international firm.

Political risk may consist of government or societal actions, may originate either within or outside of the host country, and will limit an international firm's strategic flexibility in a host country. Specifically, various linkages, when politically strained, engender restrictions which affect long-term as well as day-to-day flexibility of an MNC's in-country manager. As illustrated in Figure 10.2, these linkages include (1) host government–firm; (2) host society–host business community–host government–firm; and (3) home government–host government–firm.

One operationalization of political risk that helps clarify the discussion of control systems is government instability arising from irregular power transfers and the imposition of political restrictions. These politically based restrictions include profit repatriation limits, price controls, protectionistic trade policies, host-government tax policy, monetary policy, and legal restrictions. All of these factors are indicators of political uncertainty and will affect the international business sector. Some international firms cannot avoid politically unstable regions because investments in these markets may provide returns that outweigh the risks. Other firms pursue diversification initiatives among politically risky countries to reduce the overall political risk. Thus, many international firms have an imperative to continue expansion into countries where political risk and associated host-government restrictions limit the subsidiary managers' strategic flexibility. Subsequently, as it expands, a firm must meet these varied restrictions with more flexible control systems.

As political uncertainty rises and the potential for a host government to interfere with the operations of a firm also increases, the firm must be ready to adapt its control systems. Consistent with the cultural distance discussion above, host-country politically imposed restrictions will affect a firm's knowledge of input–output transformation and output measurability. Under conditions of low or nonexistent host-government restrictions, the organization can use either output or behavior control. We make the assumption that output control, with less observation costs, will be the preferred choice.

As political risk and corresponding restrictions in a host country increase, the input form of control system is increasingly employed because of the levels of complexity and uncertainty the firm faces.[19]

Host-Country Economic Factors

The third environmental factor suggested as an influence on an international firm's control system is the level of the host-country economic stability. In many countries, foreign exchange rate fluctuations arbitrarily penalize or reward subsidiary managers after a global consolidation of financial statements. International firms have historically attempted to discount this uncontrollable element when accounting for and measuring performance. For instance:

> Losses or gains from foreign-exchange variations affect the units of a multinational enterprise just as they do any national enterprise. At times, however, in measuring the performance of a manager of the unit of an MNE (multinational enterprise), it may be necessary to consider whether the policies that generate gains or losses of this sort should be counted as part of a manager's responsibilities.[20]

Reliable financial control systems for international firms must include the complicating factors of exchange rate fluctuations, relative inflation rates, and government-imposed exchange controls. In fact, an international firm's accounting-related performance measurement process correlates directly to the host country's economic environment.[21] As a host country's economic climate becomes increasingly turbulent due to high inflation and volatile foreign exchange, a firm must move away from strict reporting measures. Thus an international firm may need to consider alternative strategic control systems. Also, as a host country's financial/monetary environment becomes increasingly unstable, performance ambiguity increases for the MNC due to the negative effects on output measurability. The ability to have accurate performance measures declines. As a result, an MNC will increasingly tend to employ an input control system as its primary control system.

A Comprehensive Framework of International Control

Hamilton and Kashlak developed a framework linking the various external environmental variables to a firm's international control system selection. Each of the identified host-country environmental factors is individually an important variable for selecting an international firm's control system. A host country may, however, be on different positions along each of these dimensions simultaneously. All three of the host-country factors may be combined into a general framework to offer additional explanatory insights in situations that have two or three different environmental variables. Figure 10.3 illustrates the synthesis of the three host-country environmental variables and allows the manager to select control systems for host countries that vary along the three different dimensions. Each of the key intersections along these three dimensions has been numbered to identify the various intersections of cultural distance, host-government restrictions, and host-country economic environment.[22]

Maximum parental subsidiary control is represented by position 1. This situation occurs when comparatively stable foreign exchange and inflation rates are combined with low host-government restrictions and close cultural proximity. A Canadian MNC with a subsidiary in the United Kingdom would exemplify this situation. In the more stable country the parent can accurately interpret outcomes and has limited performance ambiguity associated with behavior control. In short, the clarity of the situation allows for either market outcomes or behavior measures to be used, and no adjustment

FIGURE 10.3   **Host-Country External Environments and International Control Systems**

Source: From Hamilton and Kashlak, "National Influences on MNC Control System Selection," *Management International Review,* Vol. 39, No. 2, 1999. Reprinted with permission.

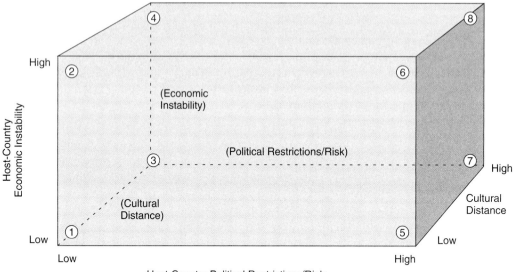

of the budgeted and actual rate of foreign exchange is required. Specifically, when host-country restrictions and cultural distance are low, the host-country manager may positively impact an overseas location's performance through the knowledge of expected fluctuations and strategies to counter the potential effects of those movements derived from the planning process. Potential operating-level strategies include repatriating profits, maintaining inventory levels at a minimum, borrowing in host-country capital markets, and matching assets and liabilities. Furthermore, when the financial environment is relatively stable, the importance of these tactics is minimized. The overall situation allows the MNC headquarters a full range of options to monitor overseas managers.[23]

Conversely, a host-country environment may be characterized by severe political constraints imposed by the host country coupled with a high degree of cultural distance and significant economic instability. This combination of conditions is identified in Figure 10.3 as position 8. As exemplified by Japanese subsidiaries in modern-day Russia, the instability and uncertainty in the environment make assessment of subsidiary performance exceptionally difficult even after using a transformational process on a subsidiary's results. In this example the linkage of an inadequate outcome measurement combined with a lack of knowledge of the input–output transformation provides the managers with the highest degree of performance ambiguity. As a result of the headquarters's extreme difficulty in understanding the relationship between host-manager activity and performance, an input control system has the highest probability of being employed.

The remaining positions in the matrix (2 through 7) are characterized by at least one of the host-country variables constraining the knowledge of the input–output transformation or output measurability. As a result, an international firm's ability to employ behavior and output control systems is correspondingly reduced. The firm must identify the form of control that maximizes the fit with the country characteristics. Table 10.1 further delineates Figure 10.3.

TABLE 10.1
Relationship of
Host-Country
Environment to
Control System

Position	Cultural Distance	Political Risk	Economic Instability	Control System
1	Low	Low	Low	Output or behavior
2	Low	Low	High	Behavior
3	High	Low	Low	Output
4	High	Low	High	Input
5	Low	High	Low	Output
6	Low	High	High	Behavior and input
7	High	High	Low	Output and input
8	High	High	High	Input

Designing an Effective International Control System

An effective control system cannot rely on reported profits and return on investment (ROI) as the dominant measures of performance of a foreign subsidiary, because the corporate headquarters of the company, rather than the subsidiary manager, makes most of the major decisions affecting the profitability of the subsidiary. To obtain a more accurate picture of a subsidiary's performance one must be certain to eliminate extraneous factors—results, positive or negative, caused by decisions made above the subsidiary level, or results due to environmental variables, such as unprecedented fluctuations in the price of raw materials (e.g., the sharp increase in the price of petroleum in 2003), or results due to government actions over which subsidiary management could not exercise any control. Thus a subsidiary manager should be held accountable only for results that were caused by actions that he or she could initiate, without external interference, and by decisions that he or she could make unilaterally. The profit-and-loss statement or the ROI of a subsidiary should be adjusted to reflect the subsidiary's actual performance, taking into account the previously mentioned factors. It is quite conceivable, under such a system, for subsidiary managers to be rated favorably in spite of their having a poor profit-and-loss statement. The opposite is also possible; a manager who shows huge profits may still be judged a poor manager if his or her performance warrants such a judgment.

In addition to financial measures, an assessment should also use nonfinancial measures of performance, such as market share, productivity, relations with the host-country government, public image, employee morale, union relations, and community involvement. Most companies do take into account some nonfinancial factors. However, formalizing the process, assigning scorecard ratings for all subsidiaries based on the same broad range of variables, might give a fuller picture. Finally, the level of performance expected from a foreign subsidiary in the following year should consider the characteristics of its environment and changes that are likely from the current year. Thus an environment that was generally favorable one year might be expected to change for the worse the following year, and the level of performance expected should be appropriately lowered as well. Not doing so could lead to unhealthy pressure on the subsidiary manager, perhaps inducing him or her to make decisions about maintenance expenditures or service to customers or the funding of process improvements that are detrimental in the long run to both the subsidiary and the company as a whole.

The control procedures and techniques to be used should be understandable and acceptable to the subsidiary heads concerned, and the subsidiary heads should actively participate in formulating them. Each subsidiary should be given realistic objectives that take into account its internal and external environment. The control system should detect and report deviations from subsidiary plans as soon as, or before, they occur. This information should then be made available to higher management and to the subsidiary head. The control system should not be allowed to stagnate, but should be revised and improved as changes in the subsidiary's environment require. Top management must tie compensation to results actually achieved, and outstanding performance must be tangibly rewarded.

Strategic Intent and Subsidiary Control

The strategic intent of the parent company in establishing a foreign subsidiary is often forgotten when the parent evaluates the performance of all subsidiaries. The evaluation process that is based on financial considerations alone does not account for the variety of strategic considerations that may have come into play in the original decision to establish a foreign subsidiary.

For example, if General Motors establishes an assembly operation in China to take advantage of that country's cheap labor, then Ford may follow suit primarily to stay even with one of its chief competitors. The risk of a rival exploiting a low-labor-cost country to gain a superior long-run competitive advantage would be too big for Ford to take. There might be other strategic considerations in establishing foreign subsidiaries. For instance, international companies may establish vertically integrated subsidiaries in key foreign markets in response to political pressures imposed by host-country governments to do so. During the 1990s, Japanese car manufacturers established operations in Europe and in North America, largely to alleviate the political fallout from the huge trade deficits that Europe and the United States have had with Japan over the last several years—although the high value of the Japanese yen, which makes exports from Japan very difficult, is also a key factor in setting up manufacturing and assembly operations outside of Japan. Subsidiaries may be established in key foreign markets to serve as bases for launching counterattacks against competitors. For instance, a company that is attacked in the United Kingdom by a Japanese competitor may launch strikes against the "aggressor" in Japan or in a third-country market like the United States, where the Japanese company may have a strategic market position to protect. Several international companies have established such "launching pads"—subsidiaries for launching retaliatory strikes—in North America, Europe, the Pacific Basin, and Japan. The subsidiaries are placed in these areas because they represent big markets with the most growth potential—markets in which most international companies have operations.

In each of the preceding examples, the financial calculations of ROI alone might not provide the justification for the establishment of a foreign subsidiary. However, strategic considerations provide the necessary motives for setting up the foreign operation. Therefore, when it comes to evaluating the performance of foreign subsidiaries, parent-company executives ought to consider the original strategic intent in establishing each subsidiary and measure its performance in terms of the extent to which it has served its strategic intent. When strategic considerations of the types discussed are involved, ROI or profitability should not be used in a subsidiary's performance evaluation.

Parent–Subsidiary Relationships and Strategic Control Mechanisms

Two issues regarding the foreign subsidiaries of an international firm are the role that the subsidiaries play for the organization and the relationships between the subsidiaries and the organization's headquarters. Regarding the **foreign subsidiary roles** of an international firm, Figure 10.4 depicts four separate roles for these entities based on the competence of the subsidiary and the strategic importance of the host country.

FIGURE 10.4

Foreign Subsidiary Roles

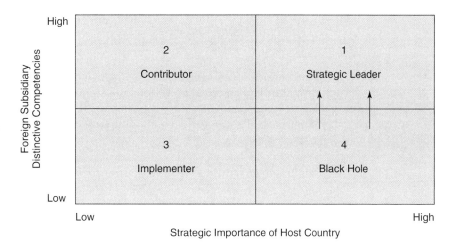

In quadrant 1, when both the core competence of the subsidiary is high and the strategic importance of the host country is high, the foreign subsidiary takes on the role of *strategic leader.* Consistent with the geocentric orientation of a firm, the subsidiary partners with headquarters in strategy formulation and implementation on a global basis. Overall, the entities in this quadrant have a subsidiary mandate, that is, strategic responsibilities beyond their national market.[24]

In quadrant 2, where the foreign subsidiary remains highly competent but the host country becomes an environment that is not strategically important, the role of the subsidiary becomes that of a *contributor.* That is, the firm must recognize and employ the distinctive competencies of the subsidiary to help the rest of the organization gain new knowledge and learning for future strategic initiatives.

Quadrant 3 represents an environment where the host country is not strategically important, and the foreign subsidiary lacks distinctive competencies. The resulting role for that subsidiary is the *implementer.* Here, the local market potential is limited. Subsequently, consistent with an ethnocentric orientation of the firm, the foreign subsidiary reacts to headquarters' demands. Finally, when the distinctive competency of the foreign subsidiary is low but the strategic importance of the host market is high, a problem exists for the international firm. Whereas the challenge in the other three segments of Figure 10.4 is to manage the situation with the appropriate role given to the foreign subsidiary, in quadrant 4 the *black hole* role represents an unacceptable position for the firm. The host country is a critical link within the greater international strategy of the firm. Thus the firm must find a way to enhance the capabilities of the subsidiary in order for it to be strategically positioned within the host country.[25]

Regarding the headquarters–subsidiary relationship, the network of subsidiaries in an international company is characterized by three types of relationships between each subsidiary and the parent company: dependent, independent, and interdependent. A *dependent subsidiary* is one that is unable to generate strategic resources—such as technology, capital, management, and access to markets—independently of the parent company and must therefore obtain such resources from the parent company or from other subsidiaries after prior approval of the parent company. At the other extreme is the *independent subsidiary,* which can generate all the required strategic resources on its own. Between the two extreme positions is the *interdependent subsidiary–parent relationship* in which the parent and the subsidiary are able to generate some, but not all, of the required strategic resources. As such, in the interdependent relationship each side is dependent on the other for some strategic resources that it cannot generate by itself. For example,

- A *dependent subsidiary* is established only to operate in the home market of a competitor and to launch strategic counterattacks locally against the competitor. The subsidiary is dependent on the parent company for the financial resources needed to stay in business. The strategic intent of the parent company in establishing the subsidiary was mainly to keep an eye on the competitor and to gather information on the competitor's strategic moves. The dependent subsidiary cannot survive for long without the strategic resources provided by the parent.

- An *independent subsidiary* is established in a country that has substantial restrictions on international trade, which prevents the subsidiary from linking its production, marketing, financial, product, or service functions with the parent and other sister subsidiaries. As such, the subsidiary is self-sufficient in the strategic resources required to implement its mission in the host country.

- With *subsidiary–parent interdependence,* the subsidiary serves as a cash cow to the parent company. In return the parent provides the subsidiary with the state-of-the-art technology to maintain the subsidiary's competitive advantage in the host country. Neither the parent nor the subsidiary can do without the strategic resource that each provides to the other.

Prahalad and Doz identified two principal methods by which a parent company could exercise *strategic control,* which they define as "the extent of influence that a head office has over a subsidiary concerning decisions that affect subsidiary strategy:"[26]

- **Substantive control,** restricting the flow of strategic resources.
- **Organizational context,** a blending of organizational structure, measurement and reward systems, career planning, and a common organizational culture, which would create the type of relationship between the parent and the subsidiary that would facilitate the continued influence of the former over the latter.[27]

Two examples of organizational contexts that would strengthen the parent's ability to exercise strategic control are (1) rewarding subsidiary managers for implementing strategies that support the global strategies of the international company and (2) making the position of subsidiary manager a "stop" on the way to higher level positions in the company.

Substantive controls can be effective in influencing the strategy of dependent subsidiaries. Subsidiaries that are independent cannot be controlled with substantive controls alone because of their self-sufficiency from the parent company. In this case, the organizational context is most effective in compensating for the erosion of the parent's capacity to exercise strategic control. As the ability to use substantive control diminishes, the dependence of the parent company on organizational context to influence strategy of subsidiaries increases.[28]

The parent company will need to balance substantive control with the effective use of organizational context to control the strategies of subsidiaries with which it is in an interdependent relationship. We shall call the joint use of both methods *combination strategic control.* Reliance solely on either substantive control or organizational context would cause loss of strategic control (see Figure 10.5). Practical Insight 10.2 depicts Nestlé's transition from a decentralized global organization to a hybrid of centralized and decentralized control, one that adapts to its strategic initiatives.

PRACTICAL INSIGHT 10.2

NESTLÉ IS STARTING TO SLIM DOWN AT LAST

An avid mountain climber, Peter Brabeck-Letmathe has scaled peaks from the Alps to the Andes. But his job as chief executive of Nestlé is more akin to moving a mountain. It's not just that $60 billion-a-year Nestlé is the world's biggest food company, with some 8,000 brands ranging from Nescafé instant coffee to Purina pet food to KitKat candy bars. While other food companies in recent years have scrambled to slash costs, Nestlé has stood pat, insisting that robust sales growth was its top priority. The result: Operating margins at Nestlé have trailed those at rivals such as Unilever, Group Danone, and Kraft Food by as much as 50%. So it's no surprise that, based on their price-earnings ratio, Nestlé shares have long underperformed those of most rivals.

Now, there are rumblings of change inside Mt. Nestlé. In the past two years, Brabeck has delivered more than $1.5 billion in cost savings by streamlining and integrating the farflung Nestlé operations, while pushing the company toward business lines that yield wider margins. First-half operating profits rose to $3.7 billion, 15% more than the same period in 2002. And operating margins reached 12.3%—still less than Unilever's 14.5%, but well above the 10.3% that Nestlé was delivering five years ago. And Brabeck is just getting started, with a further $2.5 billion in cost cuts planned over the next three years. "The company is getting fitter and fitter every day," the CEO says in an interview at his office overlooking Switzerland's Lac Leman. ***Brabeck's key challenge has been to gain control of the company's decentralized structure, in which country managers have traditionally been given wide leeway on everything from purchasing to capital investment.*** It's an arrangement that has helped Nestlé on the marketing side, since local managers can tinker with a product's flavoring, portion size, and packaging to suit local tastes. But from an efficiency standpoint, it has been a disaster. For example, internal reviews ordered by Brabeck found that in Switzerland, each candy and ice cream factory was ordering its own sugar. Moreover, different factories were using different names for the identical grade of sugar, making it almost impossible for bosses at headquarters to track costs.

To tighten things, Brabeck did away with country-by-country responsibility for many functions. For example, he established five centers worldwide to handle most coffee and cocoa purchasing. He is also overhauling the information-technology systems at Nestlé to give management the data it needs to compare the performance of units worldwide and identify those needing a tune-up. Managers' bonuses are now linked to improvements in profit margins. And Nestlé factories are making more efficient use of manpower and technology. The Nescafé instant-coffee factory at Cagayan de Oro in the Philippines has boosted efficiency 15% over the past three years by retraining maintenance teams to work faster and by increasing the amount of coffee treated in each production batch.

Source: C. Matlock, *BusinessWeek* October 27, 2003, p. 56.

FIGURE 10.5
Parent–Subsidiary Relationship and Strategic Control Mechanisms

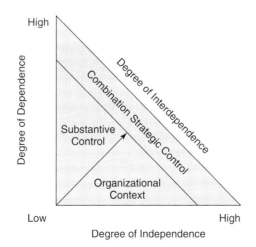

Up to this point, we have covered a variety of the key dimensions of managing in the global environment, including (1) understanding the macro-level environments of different nations and (2) understanding the various firm-level strategic initiatives and associated structures and control systems. In the final section of the book, we address topics relevant at the manager-level of management, including motivation, leadership, human resources, and communications. We also take an in-depth look at the role and influence of ethical considerations for international managers.

Summary

In this chapter we looked at the managerial control process in an international context. The focus was on the problems and characteristics of control systems adopted by multinational companies to manage their foreign subsidiaries, with emphasis on ways to improve the process.

Managerial control is the process of ensuring that actual performance is equal to planned performance. The purpose of control is to facilitate the implementation of plans by continuously monitoring the performance of the people responsible for carrying them out.

There are four principal elements in the control process: (1) establishing standards against which performance is to be measured; (2) developing devices or techniques to monitor individual or organizational performance; (3) comparing actual performance with planned performance; and (4) taking corrective action to eliminate significant deviations of performance from plans.

There are four separate types of control processes. Output control is based on specific measures of performance. Behavior control measures processes and the means–ends relationships within an organization. Input control is grounded in rigorous attention to hiring the right people and subsequently socializing them to "buy in" to the shared values and mission of the firm.

The process of control and the problems associated with it are far more complex in an international company than in its purely domestic counterpart because of the multiple cultural, economic, political, and legal environments in which its subsidiaries operate. Several divisive factors, such as geographic distance, language barriers, cultural distance, and differing frames of reference between the parent company and foreign subsidiary managers are responsible for distortion in the information that is required for control purposes.

Different host-country environmental factors limit the ability of the international firm to globally standardize its control systems. As host-country cultural distance, political risk, and economic instability increase, the firm has less and less ability to accurately hold its subsidiary managers to specific, tangible outputs or behaviors.

The choice of strategic controls on a subsidiary also depends on the role that the subsidiary plays in the host country as well as globally, and whether the subsidiary is highly dependent on the parent, highly independent from the parent, or whether there is a high degree of interdependence between the two. Substantive controls and control by means of organizational context can be balanced as appropriate to each relationship.

Key Terms and Concepts

behavior control, *308*	input control, *308*	output control, *308*
foreign subsidiary roles, *316*	knowledge of the	output measure availability, *307*
host-country environmental	transformation process, *307*	substantive control, *318*
factors, *311*	organizational context, *318*	

Discussion Questions

1. Why is the control process more difficult to implement in a multinational company than in a purely domestic company? Discuss factors that influence the effectiveness of a multinational company's control system.

2. What are output, behavior, and input controls? Give examples.

3. Explain why the reported profits of a foreign affiliate may not be a good measure of its true performance.

4. What are the essential features of a sound international control system?

5. Explain how a host country's cultural distance, economic instability, and political risk can affect a company's control system for its subsidiaries in that country.

6. Distinguish among and give examples of the dependent subsidiary, independent subsidiary, and a subsidiary that is interdependent with headquarters.

Minicase

Computerlinks, Inc.

Computerlinks is an international company with gross sales revenue of $250 million a year. Foreign sales of laptop and notebook computers, the company's main line of business, account for 55 percent of total sales and 70 percent of net profits. Foreign affiliates are located in six countries—Mexico, France, England, Spain, India, and Japan. Affiliates in England and France are wholly owned subsidiaries. Those in Mexico, India, and Japan are joint ventures with leading domestic companies in which Computerlinks, Inc., owns majority stakes in excess of 51 percent.

The affiliates in France and England were established in the early 1960s in anticipation of the unification of the markets of Western Europe into a unified common market. Most businessmen, politicians, and economists expected the European Union (EU) to flourish and to enrich all member countries. In anticipation of this prospect, companies from North America and Japan were making huge direct investments mainly in England, France, Holland, and Germany. The Japanese subsidiary was set up in 1975 primarily to keep an eye on the Japanese competitors and as a window to Japanese technology. The Spanish subsidiary was established in 1987 following Spain's entry in the EU. Labor being cheaper in Spain than in other European countries was also a reason for establishing the Spanish operation. The Mexican subsidiary was established in 1993 following the creation of NAFTA primarily to take advantage of cheap labor and secondarily to exploit the growing Mexican market. The subsidiary in India was established in 1993 to capitalize on the liberalization of the economy by the Indian government which enabled foreign companies to satisfy the huge appetite of the Indian middle-class for computer technology and products. Skilled and unskilled labor is also very cheap in India.

The English and French affiliates imported components made in the Spanish subsidiary for assembly in plants in Manchester and Montpellier respectively. The English affiliate specialized in laptops, and the French affiliate in notebooks. Laptops assembled in England and notebooks imported from the French affiliate were primarily targeted by the English affiliate to the domestic English market and to markets in Scotland, Ireland, Norway, Sweden, Finland, and Denmark. Notebooks assembled in France and laptops imported from England were marketed by the French affiliate in France, as well as in the rest of Europe. The English and French affiliates exported laptops and notebooks respectively to the Spanish affiliate, which were then sold by it in the domestic market.

Components imported from the Mexican subsidiary and some from the Spanish subsidiary were assembled in San Jose, California. Laptops and notebook computers assembled in the United States were marketed in the home market and exported to Canada, Mexico, and markets in Central and South America. The Indian subsidiary bought 40 percent of components sourced from indigenous suppliers, of which there were many, and the rest were imported from the Spanish subsidiary. Almost 80 percent of laptops and notebooks made by the Indian affiliate were sold in the Indian market, and the rest were exported to neighboring countries of Sri Lanka, Nepal, and Bangladesh. The long-term plan of Computerlinks was to make the Indian affiliate the principal source of its products for exports to South Asia and the Middle East.

The markets in Mexico and India were booming, growing at the rapid pace of 10–15 percent during the past five years; the Spanish market at a steady pace of 6 percent during the same period; and those in France, England, and Japan at the rate of 2–3 percent per annum. The European market as a whole has been growing at 4 percent per annum. The company's home market in the United States is growing at a steady clip of 7 percent a year. Growth rates are expected to remain the same in these markets in the foreseeable future.

During the past five years annual inflation was pegged at the average rate of 50 percent in Mexico, 20 percent in Spain, 8 percent in France, Japan, and India, and 5 percent in England. Annual inflation during the same period stayed at 2.5 percent in the United States. The Mexican peso and the Spanish peseta have been devaluing steadily against the U.S. dollar at an average rate of 25 percent per year for the past five years. The exchange rates of the British pound, the French franc, and the Indian rupee have been floating in world currency markets and have held their value firmly against the U.S. dollar. The Japanese yen has been appreciating rapidly in value, from a rate of $1 = 350$ yen in July 1975 to $1 = 81$ yen in June 1995.

Competition in laptops and notebooks has been intensifying in the U.S. and European markets. Every major portable computer company in the world is engaged in the European market, with no single company holding more than a 20 percent market share in the United States and 10 percent in Europe. IBM and Fujitsu hold dominant market shares of 35 percent each in the highly competitive Japanese market.

Computerlinks has a policy of setting prices of products and components in intra-affiliate trade at levels designed to maximize companywide profits after taxes. In the past it has often shifted the sourcing of components and products from one affiliate to another to take advantage of exchange rate fluctuations.

John Volkmar, president of Computerlinks, is reviewing recommendations for salary raises and bonuses for each domestic and foreign affiliate manager submitted by Devin Gabriel, his director of human resources. The reports include an assessment of the performance of each affiliate against a set of uniform financial criteria such as after-tax profits, return on assets, and return on equity. The results showed that the Spanish, U.S., and Japanese operations ranked lowest on these criteria, the English and French fell somewhere in the middle, and the Mexican and Indian affiliates showed the best results. John Volkmar is puzzled by the report. "How can I justify to the Spanish, American, and Japanese subsidiary heads that they do not deserve as big a bonus and salary increase as the others?" he asked of himself. "Surely there must be a better way of making a more valid evaluation of each of these foreign affiliates?" he asked Devin Gabriel.

Source: Copyright © 1997 by Arvind V. Phatak.

DISCUSSION QUESTIONS

1. Is there anything wrong with the approach of Devin Gabriel to evaluate the performance of Computerlinks' foreign and domestic affiliates? Explain why.

2. If you do not agree with the method used by Devin Gabriel, recommend one that you believe would give a true picture of each affiliate's performance.

Notes

1. S. Snell, "Control Theory in Strategic Human Resource Management: The Mediating Effect of Administrative Information," *Academy of Management Journal* 35, no. 2 (1992), pp. 292–318.

2. George A. Steiner, *Strategic Planning* (New York: Free Press, 1979), p. 268.

3. Ibid., p. 220.

4. Ibid., p. 157.

5. W. Ouchi, "The Relationship between Organizational Structure and Organizational Control," *Administrative Science Quarterly,* March 1977, pp. 95–113.

6. V. Govindarajan and F. Fisher, "Strategy, Control Systems and Resource Sharing: Effects on Business-Unit Performance," *Academy of Management Journal* 33 (1990), pp. 259–285.

7. Snell, "Control Theory in Strategic Human Resource Management."

8. A. Jaeger and B. Baliga, "Control Systems and Strategic Adaptation: Lessons from the Japanese Experience," *Strategic Management Journal* 6 (1985), pp. 115–134.

9. V. Govindarajan and F. Fisher, "Strategy, Control Systems and Resource Sharing."

10. B. Chakravarthy and Y. Doz, "Strategy Process Research: Focusing on Corporate Self-Renewal," *Strategic Management Journal* 13 (1992), pp. 5–14; C. Bartlett and S. Ghoshal, *Managing across Borders: The Transnational Solution* (Boston: Harvard Business School Press, 1989).

11. M. Hitt, R. Hoskisson, and R. Ireland, "Mergers and Acquisitions and Managerial Commitment to Innovation in M-Form Firms," *Strategic Management Journal* 11 (1990), pp. 29–47.

12. C. Hill and R. Hoskisson, "Strategy and Structure in Multiproduct Firms" *Academy of Management Review* 12 (1987), pp. 331–341.

13. W. Chan and R. Mauborge, "Effectively Conceiving and Executing Multinationals' Worldwide Strategies," *Journal of International Business Studies* 24, no. 3 (1993), pp. 419–448.

14. David Clutterbuck, "Breaking Through the Cultural Barriers," *International Management,* December 1980, p. 41.

15. Arvind V. Phatak, *Managing Multinational Corporations* (New York, Praeger, 1974), p. 225.

16. R. Vernon, L. Wells, and S. Rangan, *The Manager in the International Economy,* 7th ed. (Upper Saddle River, NJ: Prentice Hall), 1996.

17. R. Hamilton, V. Taylor, and R. Kashlak. "Designing a Control System for a Multinational Subsidiary," *Long Range Planning* 29, no. 6 (1996), pp. 857–868.

18. L. Gomez-Meija and L. Palich, "Cultural Diversity and the Performance of Multinational Firms," *Journal of International Business Studies* 28, no. 2 (1997), pp. 309–335; K. Roth and S. O'Donnell, "Foreign Subsidiary Compensation: An Agency Theory Perspective," *Academy of Management Journal* 39, no. 3 (1996), pp. 678–703.

19. R. Hamilton and R. Kashlak, "National Influences on MNC Control System Selection. Management," *International Review* 39, no. 2 (1999), pp. 167–189.

20. Vernon, Wells, and Rangan, *The Manager in the International Economy.*

21. D. Lessard and P. Lorange, "Currency Changes and Management Control: Resolving the Centralization–Decentralization Dilemma," *Accounting Review,* July 1977, pp. 628–637.

22. Hamilton and Kashlak, "National Influences on MNC Control System Selection."

23. Ibid.

24. J. Birkinshaw, "How Multinational Subsidiary Mandates Are Gained and Lost," *Journal of International Business Studies* 27, no. 3 (1996), pp. 467–496.

25. C. Bartlett and S. Ghoshal, "Tap Your Subsidiaries for Global Reach," *Harvard Business Review,* November–December 1986, pp. 1–11.

26. C. K. Prahalad and Yves I. Doz, "An Approach to Strategic Control in MNCs," *Sloan Management Review,* Summer 1981, pp. 5–13.

27. Ibid., p. 8.

28. Ibid.

Managing Technology and Knowledge

Chapter Learning Objectives

After completing this chapter, you should be able to:

- Understand the concept of technology and the process of technology transfer.
- Explain the relevance of appropriate technology transfer for international management.
- Define and distinguish among the concepts of data, information, and knowledge.
- Understand the relevance of these three commodities for international management.
- Explain the process of creation, transformation, and transfer of knowledge.
- Identify the processes that integrate management of technology and knowledge with strategic processes of international and global corporations.
- Understand the concept of learning organizations.

Opening Case: Transferring Knowledge in Global Corporations

Ford: Europe Has a Better Idea

Can Detroit Replicate the European Turnaround at Home?

In the annals of Ford Motor Co., 2001 will go down as its *annus horribilis*. The world's No. 2 auto maker was hit by a second Firestone tire recall, recalls of key vehicles like the Explorer, other quality glitches, and launch delays. Not to mention angry dealers, demoralized employees, and the autumn ouster of its CEO—all culminating in a $5.4 billion annual loss. Amid all this gloom and doom, though, there was one bright spot. Ford of Europe Inc., a subsidiary with almost $30 billion in sales, battled its way to breakeven after a $1.1 billion loss in 2000. This year a modest profit is likely, thanks to aggressive cost-cutting and a refreshed lineup.

Nice work. But Europe isn't just a bright spot for Ford—it's the model for the entire turnaround effort for Ford in North America. Nicholas V. Scheele, Ford president and chief operating officer, and Chairman William C. Ford Jr.'s right-hand man, engineered the rescue of Ford of Europe. Bill Ford is gambling that Scheele can replicate his lifesaving strategies in Detroit: "Ford of Europe was the biggest turnaround of any unit in Ford's history," he says. "In many ways, it's the template for what to do here." But this strategy is not without risks. If the rebound at Ford of Europe stalls, then doubts about Ford's overall strategy will quickly multiply.

For clues, investors will be watching Scheele, the 58-year-old Briton who led the turnaround of Ford of Europe after having overhauled the Ford-owned Jaguar marque. The European unit racked up $2.5 billion in losses through the 1990s. "It was a broken business," says David W. Thursfield, Scheele's former No. 2 and current Ford of Europe Chairman. Development time for new models was laughably slow: The Fiesta compact bumped along for 12 years without a major remake. And Europeans had concluded that Fords were duds to drive and embarrassing to own. From 1994 to 2000, the Ford brand's share of the European car market shrank by one-fourth, to 8.2%. Nearly one-third of Ford's European production network sat idle. Capacity utilization—a key gauge—sank to 71% in 2000, well below the break-even level.

Scheele and Thursfield embarked on an overhaul. In just two years, they shuttered three plants and slashed more than 2,000 jobs—or nearly 2% of the unit's total workforce. The pair whittled away a fourth of the Ford brand's production capacity—600,000 units. One painful move was the decision to stop assembling cars at the Dagenham (Britain) factory after 69 years.

Just as important, Scheele and Thursfield overhauled Ford's four big car-assembly plants in Europe so they could produce more than one model on the same line. Such "flex factories" can save the company hundreds of millions of dollars it otherwise would have to spend on separate assembly lines. "Ford did it right in Europe," says J. P. Morgan Securities analyst Himanshu Patel.

The duo also attacked the lackluster lineup. Luckily, Ford already had one hit on its hands, the stylish $12,200 Focus compact, launched in 1998, and another in the pipeline, the $17,500 Mondeo, which debuted two years ago. *Auto Motor und Sport* magazine rated the Mondeo best in its class in 2001, ahead of VW's popular Passat. And this year's edition of the annual TUV quality survey showed the Focus had fewer defects than any other car sold in Germany since 1999. Bolstered by the success of these two models, Ford's market share in Europe has climbed to 8.8%, ahead of Fiat Auto. "The Focus is selling very well. It's a good value for the price," says Hans-Joachim Kremer, owner of the Ford Autohaus Kremer dealership in Frankfurt.

Ford of Europe is now rolling out more new cars—and faster. A new $10,200 Fiesta was launched last year nine months ahead of schedule, and the Fusion, a compact minivan, is due out in October. The Fusion is targeted at the growing number of Europeans who want something small and fuel-efficient but more versatile than a sedan.

These are the broad outlines of the Ford turnaround. But the little moments count, too. Thursfield convened weekly meetings in a "war room" at Ford's Merkenich design studio near Cologne (no sitting allowed). At one of those encounters, executives discovered they were paying one gas-tank supplier twice as much as another for the same-quality product. By picking up on those discrepancies, Scheele saved $900 million over the past two years. Thursfield wants to wring out a further $400 million this year. Says one Ford official: "The trick is to look at everything."

That's what Scheele plans to do in Michigan, where staff already has adopted some of the European methods. Dearborn headquarters now boasts its own war room, though officials prefer to call it the "energy room." Ford is also looking across the Atlantic for lessons on how to make better use of its plants. Ford's revamped Cologne factory is capable of assembling any model in the European lineup, from the Ka minicar to the Galaxy van. Bill Ford wants that kind of versatility in North America, where the company has no flex factories. "You don't need all your plants to be flexible, but you need a portion, probably about a third," he says.

To stanch the red ink at domestic operations, Bill Ford is adopting many of the measures the company implemented in Europe even before it's clear whether they are working there. Ford models are doing well now in Europe, but it's an unusual moment in the Continent's car cycle. Market heavies Renault and Volkswagen are both in the midst of major makeovers of their lineup. That's giving Ford some needed breathing room—but it won't last forever. PSA Peugeot Citroen is on a product roll, and GM's Opel is about to embark on a restructuring. Meanwhile, luxury marques such as Mercedes-Benz and BMW are putting the squeeze on middle-market players by producing smaller, more affordable models.

And the trade-offs Ford of Europe made between savings and quality may still come back to haunt the company. The new Fiesta has gotten knocks for its plasticky, cheap-looking dashboard. And the Focus comes less richly equipped than rivals. Antilock brakes are standard on the Fiat Stilo and the Peugeot 307. On most of the Focus range, they're an option. Small details, but they add up—and sometimes they turn potential customers off. Bill Ford can learn some lessons from Europe. He just has to make sure they're the right ones.

Source: Reprinted from Christine Tierney and Kathleen Kerwin, "Ford: Europe Has a Better Idea: Can Detroit Replicate the European Turnaround at Home?" April 15, 2002 issue of *BusinessWeek* by special permission. Copyright © 2002 by The McGraw-Hill Companies, Inc.

Discussion Questions

1. How will Ford replicate European practices, that is, technological know-how, in its Detroit location?
2. What are the potential effects of ineffective transfers on global companies such as Ford?
3. What are some of the difficulties of transfers of technology and scientific know-how across borders and cultures?

Understanding Technology

Consider an international company that, among other business units, has a sales office in Argentina, a manufacturing subsidiary in China, and a research and development office at corporate headquarters in the United States. As we discussed in Chapter 1, international management is about the challenge of managing the international activities of such companies. Among the many activities of international companies, the management of technology and knowledge is crucial. An international company must answer questions such as: How does the company create new forms of technology that are needed in the manufacturing subsidiary in China? How does it successfully transfer knowledge created in Argentina about the emerging market trends to its headquarters in the United States?

Technology and knowledge transfer are not new. They have existed in the field of international business for more than a century. The complexities surrounding the process of transfer of technology and new forms of knowledge created in important subsidiaries around the world are important to understand, especially in today's highly competitive international environment. Consider the experience of the Ford Motor Company. In the past, the Ford Motor Company created new forms of innovation in the design of cars solely in the corporate headquarters located in the United States. In 1994, the company moved its design office, where new technology and knowledge is created, to one of its European subsidiaries in Germany. The company decided that moving the design office from Detroit would strengthen the technology and knowledge transfer process from the German subsidiary, which was relatively more effective in developing new designs for cars.[1]

The People's Republic of China is becoming one of the fastest growing markets for software products from companies such as Microsoft and Intel. However, vast linguistic, cultural, and legal differences characterize China and the United States, where headquarters of some of the largest software companies in the world are located. Microsoft's and other software companies' success in China depends heavily on their effectiveness in customizing the user interface of their products, something more easily planned than accomplished. Thus, given the large market, Microsoft decided to locate one of the biggest research programs in language recognition and speech input in China. Technological advances and knowledge emerging from these activities in China will assist Microsoft to increase its market share, not only in China and East Asia, but also in other parts of the world.[2] Details are discussed in Practical Insight 11.1.

Before we can understand the process and the complexities that accompany the transfer of technology across various subsidiaries of a global corporation, such as in the case of Microsoft discussed on page 328, we need a better grasp of the concept of technology. When the clock radio comes on in the morning, waking you with the news, it is also sharing $73 billion in annual advertising spending by various international corporations. Your toothpaste is a product of millions of dollars of research investment and much more in building technological facilities to create the product. On a purely cost basis, 50 percent of the price represents the cost of technological knowledge. The car you drive to work in probably has more computing power than was available for Apollo 11 scientists to put two men on the moon. Today's automobiles "know" how much fuel you have and when your tires are low, and they can give you directions and even maps. The information-infused car, with voice-activated Internet access, real-time traffic information, and the ability to diagnose problems, is a phenomenon that 1960s automobile engineers could not imagine. Information, technology, and knowledge are embedded in almost all of the products that we use in today's world, and more and more products, even those sold in developing parts of the world, contain these three commodities.

Technology and Technology Transfer

Technology comprises a systemically developed set of information, skills, and processes that are needed to create, develop, and innovate products and services. This definition suggests that new forms of technology are developed in organizations that would like to launch new products or services in order to increase their market share. **Technology transfer** is the movement of technology from one person to another, one unit to another, or from one company to another.

Technological competence is important, not only for sustaining international competitiveness, but also for emerging economies, such as India and China, and in less developed countries, such as the African states. Sophisticated technologies are transferred to these countries when prevailing economic conditions are appropriate. For example, computer use is very difficult in countries where the electric infrastructure is inconsistent—that is, where the electricity supply can go on and off without warning—and baby-food processing plants have difficulty operating in countries that do not have clean water. In addition, the transfer of technologies has to meet local objectives and priorities, such as government regulations, export requirements, and licensing agreements. One of the key factors that influences technology transfer is the extent of capital participation and payments for technology as agreed upon by the two countries. Technology transfers are relatively quicker and more efficient among subsidiaries of global corporations, because policies and programs pertaining to implementation are relatively uniform.[3]

Organizational cultures also play a role. Global corporations that emphasize technology transfer among subsidiaries routinely are generally successful. International and global companies compete fiercely to launch new technologies today. They concentrate on three types of technology: product-embodied technology, process-embodied technology, and person-embodied technology.[4]

Global companies transfer *product-embodied technologies* by transferring the physical product itself. When the Caterpillar Company, headquartered in Peoria, Illinois, or Komatsu Incorporated of Japan transfers heavy earth-tilling machinery and related products, such as bulldozers, to a country such as Kuwait or Argentina, it is engaging in the process of transferring product-embodied technology. Transferring product-embodied

PRACTICAL INSIGHT 11.1

AT CHINA'S GATES: MICROSOFT BOSS CONQUERS A KEY ASIAN MARKET

On the expressway running north from Hong Kong to the Chinese city of Guangzhou, a small convoy is creating quite a commotion. A white Mercedes-Benz, escorted by a police car with blaring sirens and flashing lights, speeds past construction ditches, shacks and bicycles, dodging container lorries on the way. The scene startles other road users—and small wonder. In a little liberty taken to avoid a detour caused by road works, the cars are racing up a southbound lane, forcing oncoming vehicles to move out of the way.

Stopping at a city pier, the Mercedes' occupant boards a boat for a river crossing to the back entrance of a hotel. Inside, more than a thousand admirers and local dignitaries, squeezed into not one but two auditoriums, eagerly await his entrance.

Who is this great man? Some icon from the communist pantheon in Beijing, a Western pop superstar?

No, this is Bill Gates: chairman of Microsoft, supplier of computer programs to the world.

There is some irony in the reception that awaited Gates's December visit. Less than two years ago, the Microsoft boss travelled practically unnoticed in China. Even to those who recognized the name, he was the American who lost a fight with President Jiang Zemin over a Chinese version of Windows (Microsoft's flagship operating system) that had been developed partly in Taiwan.

The transformation in Microsoft's profile in China since then, coupled with its increasing inroads in other parts of Asia, underlie the software giant's jump into top spot among multinationals in the REVIEW 200 survey. And it's a development that has enormous implications not only for Microsoft but also for the future of computing throughout the region.

In an interview, Gates acknowledges the importance of the huge Chinese market and the rest of Asia for his company. "It's the highest-growth region" in the world, he says, and Microsoft can expect "a lot of growth" itself. China, he adds "has a low level of sales right now, but that's okay. We're taking the long-term view."

The first step was to resolve Microsoft's problems with the Chinese government, which has now approved Windows 95 as one of several standard platforms for software development. That means program writers will have government approval to produce software that works with the Windows operating system. In turn, this will help Microsoft increase its market share. The company reckons that over half of all PCs in China already use authentic or pirated versions of Windows.

China, though, isn't the only Asian country Microsoft has mastered since it set up its first Asian office—in Japan—about a decade ago. It is now No. 1 in sales of software for desktop PCs in Japan, South Korea and Hong Kong, counting both operating systems and applications, says Charles Stevens, Microsoft's vice-president for the Far East.

Microsoft's success is putting other software developers—American and Asian alike—on edge, not to mention government officials trying to jumpstart indigenous software industries. "We don't want anyone to dominate," says Chen Chong, deputy director of the computer department at China's Ministry of Electronics. "China wants to create a fair and competitive environment."

Gates plays down the fears that Asia will become swamped with American computer software—a worry exacerbated by the increasing popularity of the Internet, the worldwide computer network, which will help American programs to reach Asia faster than ever before. "If people have such a pessimistic view, they need to be in a different business," he quips. As for the Internet, he notes, it provides a channel for a two-way flow of information, removing geographical constraints on selling all sorts of goods and services. "You have an opportunity to be in markets that you could not participate in before."

In any case, it's not that easy for even mighty Microsoft to dominate Asia. "We don't have indigenous competition in other places," Gates says, acknowledging the rise of Asian software developers, particularly in Japan. And as strong as Microsoft is in the region, he notes, "our market share in Asia is lower than anywhere else in the world."

Asian software developers, moreover, can sometimes play rough. South Korean on-line service providers, for example, recently misinformed the press that Seoul had banned Microsoft Service Network, an adjunct of Windows 95 that helps users connect to the Internet. Once it became clear that

technologies is routine. Global corporations from the Group of 7 (G-7) industrialized countries, as well as those in emerging economies such as India, Brazil, and China, transfer technologies to countries that are less developed and are able to pay for such technologies.

Developers transfer *process-embodied technology* by transferring blueprint or patent rights of the actual scientific processes and engineering details. Examples include transfer of chemical technology for the manufacture of synthetic fabrics and offshore oil exploration technology. When ExxonMobil or Texaco transfers oil-drilling technol-

wasn't the case, they threatened to follow the American Justice Department's lead and file an antitrust suit. "But they won't do anything unless the United States does," Stevens, the Microsoft vice-president, predicts.

The fiercest competition comes from copycats. Pirated versions of Windows 95, the latest version of the operating system, were available in Hong Kong as soon as the authentic version was officially released. "There are a lot of strong local competitors," says Stevens. "But the biggest competition by far is piracy."

Piracy, however, has helped Asia's PC markets grow rapidly—and with them Microsoft's market share. The easy availability of copied Microsoft software has thwarted potential local competitors by making it tougher for them to enter the business. The downside for Microsoft is that although it has a high market share, its Asian revenues are low. The region accounts for only about 10% of its worldwide sales, according to industry sources. (Microsoft declines to confirm the number.) Describing his company's prospects in the Chinese market, where piracy is rampant, Gates wryly told a Hong Kong audience: "Hopefully, as it grows, people will actually pay for the software as well."

Whatever the misgivings about Microsoft's dominance, more Asian software developers are switching to its Windows platform. Microsoft boasts of conferences attended by thousands of Chinese developers anxious to learn more about the program. Wee Liang Toon, a software analyst at International Data Corp., which watches the computer industry, concurs: "Developers are beginning to see the advantage of developing on a Windows platform."

Despite rampant piracy, Microsoft's Asian sales are doing well. IDC forecasts that as many as one million copies of Windows 95 will be sold in Japan this year—out of more than 10 million that Gates says are now in use worldwide.

Microsoft's Japanese office employs around 1,000 people and is its largest subsidiary in terms of revenues outside the United States, exceeding the company's operations in France, Britain or Germany. Microsoft has also invested in software development in Japan—as it has in China, South Korea and Taiwan.

These local labs, the only ones of their kind in Microsoft's empire outside the U.S., customize the company's products for Asian markets, enabling it to deliver local versions faster than if it was developing them in the U.S. When the company introduced Windows 3.0 in Hong Kong in 1990, it took two more years to come out with a Chinese version. This year, it released a local version of Windows 95 in Hong Kong only three months after the English one. A version based on the simplified Chinese script used in the mainland is due out in the first quarter of 1996.

In addition to customizing Microsoft's products for local users, the company's developers in Asia are also researching leading-edge programs for the future. Among other things, these may eventually enable users to speak instructions to their PCs rather than use a keyboard. Microsoft's biggest research program in language recognition and speech input is in China.

The company has also built up a sizable support network for Asian developers and customers. It claims to have more than 30 engineers in Hong Kong manning phone lines to answer questions from customers. The company has also begun to offer consultancy services. In Hong Kong, it has helped set up a telephone betting system for the Jockey Club and a database for Hongkong Telecom.

As for Microsoft's future in Asia, its executives talk of expanding its presence in software businesses ranging from traditional spreadsheet and database-management systems to consumer applications and interactive television. The one thing Microsoft says it doesn't want to do in Asia is design company-specific programs that have to conform with local accounting, inventory and tax requirements. "If we had a million people we couldn't develop that expertise," says Stevens.

In Guangzhou, Gates tells his Chinese audience he wants local help in turning his vision of an information age into reality. As for worries that Asian developers might be squelched in the process by the Microsoft juggernaut, he says: "Somebody's confused. Software is a huge industry."

Source: From *Far Eastern Economic Review* "At China's Gates: Microsoft Boss Conquers a Key Asian Market," by Emily Thornton, December/January 1996. Copyright © 1996 by Dow Jones & Co., Inc. Reproduced with permission of Dow Jones & Co., Inc. via Copyright Clearance Center.

ogy to its subsidiaries in Saudi Arabia or Nigeria, it is transferring process-embodied technology. Blueprints and working know-how of these technologies can be transferred relatively easily using the Internet or by trained technical personnel who physically carry the manuals and procedures with them.

By contrast, *person-embodied technology* is transferred through continuous dialogue between the supplier and the recipient organizations pertaining to the intrinsic nature, diffusion, and utilization of scientific details that are hard to articulate in the form of either process or product. The intrinsic nature of person-embodied technology makes transfer as a one-shot or quick process difficult. A series of exchanges may be needed for a global company, such as Bechtel, headquartered in San Francisco, to transfer its technology for creating nuclear power plants to a company located in Bombay, India, or Seoul, South Korea. Transferring person-embodied technologies is the most difficult of the three types. An advanced technological infrastructure and a trained work force at the receiving end are required before such exchanges can be successfully initiated. In addition, strong regulations govern transfers of nuclear fuel, rocket, satellite, and other advanced technology.

In recent years, almost all types of technology that have been created involve some form of product-, process-, and person-embodied technologies. Competition for creating new forms of process- and person-embodied technologies is increasingly fierce among various companies within a particular industrial sector.

Success in creating certain highly marketable technologies does not imply that a company will be successful in transferring this technology to its various subsidiaries. In international management, the common expression used is "technology transfer," not "technology sale."[5] Global companies, such as Procter & Gamble, may license a producer in a different country to manufacture its popular forms of toothpaste or health care products, but it does not engage in *selling* its technology. Licensing, which was discussed in Chapter 7, is the most common method of gaining royalties from technologies. Technology is typically considered a public good or common resource that should be used for improving the quality of life for all. Dangerous military technologies, such as nuclear missiles and biological and chemical weapons, are an exception. Problems in transfer can result from differences in legal and economic systems of countries in which the subsidiaries of the global organizations are located or when two diverse corporations are involved. Among the factors influencing technology transfer are:[6]

- *Similar language:* Transfer of technology from an English-speaking country, such as the United States, to another English-speaking country, such as the United Kingdom, is relatively easy.

- *Common ancestry and shared history:* Common elements in ancestry and historical background facilitate technology transfer. For example, Japanese are traditionally successful in transferring technology they create in their cultural context to countries such as South Korea, Taiwan, and Singapore.

- *Physical proximity:* The physical proximity between the United States and Latin America, as well as between Germany and east European countries, facilitates technology transfers. U.S. companies have typically succeeded in transferring technology from the U.S. headquarters to Canadian subsidiaries, such as Ford Motor Company's transfer from Detroit headquarters to its manufacturing subsidiary in Ontario, Canada.

- *Technical competence of the workforce:* This is particularly germane to new, high-tech industries. For example, Microsoft is able to transfer its advanced software technology to various high-tech ventures in India, because of the technical competence of Indian software engineers and developers.

- *Complexity of the technology at the time of transfer:* Transfer of complex technology is not likely to be successful when companies have very different levels of expertise. For example, transfer of nuclear power plant technology from the United States to Peru would be difficult because Peru lacks a trained workforce to understand and implement the complex technology. It would be easier to transfer such technologies to France or Japan, which already have basic nuclear technology.

- *Number of successful prior transfers:* Two companies succeed more easily if attempts to transfer similar forms of technology have been successful in the past. Microsoft and General Motors have been successful in technology transfer and establishing research centers of strategic importance in India because past attempts have been successful.[7]

The Role of Strategy and Cultural Issues

When examining the history of technology transfer, one factor stands out immediately: In the past, such transfers took place primarily among Western nations. However, in today's globalized world, transfers from the United States to various countries in Southeast Asia, Africa, South America, and central and southern Europe are becoming as frequent as transfers between the United States and western Europe.

Technology transfers among developed nations rely on the strategic orientations of the transacting organizations. However, transfers to developing countries in those parts of the world that are culturally dissimilar are likely to be difficult. Transferring technology from the headquarters to various subsidiaries of a multinational company can be a mixed blessing. Some subsidiaries are eager to absorb the technology and realize the need for such technologies for improving market share, efficiency, and innovativeness. Other subsidiaries might resist the absorption because of differences in strategic orientation or because of repeated failures in past transfers. However, such difficulties seem to be relatively minor in global companies because of the centralized method that these companies use for innovation and technology diffusion.

Difficulties in technology transfer across various subsidiaries of a multinational or global corporation or between two organizations located in dissimilar economies and cultures often arise from the following concerns:

1. *Differences in strategic thinking:* When senior managers in companies involved have differing views on the strategic significance of the technology involved in the transfer, the transfer of technology is rarely smooth. Microsoft, as the leading creator of software technology, might not feel inclined to share such technologies with Fijitsu of Japan because both of these companies are competing for global market share.

2. *Characteristics of the technology involved:* We have seen that some technologies are easier to transfer than others. Product-embodied technologies are easier to transfer than process- and person-embodied technologies. In transferring product-embodied technology, the supplying organization or the creator of the technology in the multinational network is simply physically transporting the technology to its needed location. The sophistication of the technical personnel at the recipient organization or other factors that might inhibit its effective absorption and diffusion offer little cause for concern. However, in the case of process- and person-embodied technologies, transferring and diffusing the technology may entail major problems. If the recipient organization does not have well-trained technical personnel who understand the complexities of the technology, or if the infrastructure for diffusing the technology is poor, then product- and person-embodied technologies cannot be transferred easily.

3. *Differences in organizational and corporate cultures:* An organization's receptivity to absorbing new technology often reflects the dominant values of the organizational and corporate cultures. Some organizations value what has been termed "process orientation" in their cultures.[8] As a rule, process orientations facilitate

EXHIBIT 11.1
Rate of Innovation and New Technology Creation

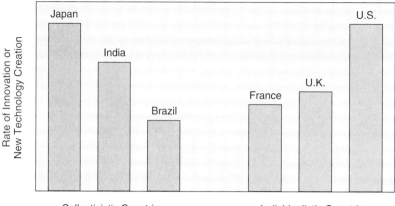

absorption of new technology that comes from another organization. In addition, organizations that are more professional than parochial are better able to absorb technology that is imported from dissimilar national or cultural settings.[9] In professional organizations, the identity of the individuals working for the company comes more from the job than from the organization. In parochial organizations, the social and family backgrounds are more important in defining individuals' identity. Professional organizations are generally better prepared to understand the complexity of technologies that are being imported for diffusion in the organization.

4. *Differences in societal cultures:* Just like organizational cultures, the nature of the societal culture in which the organizations are located greatly influences the success of technology transfer. Consider two organizations that are located in two societies, say, the United States and Greece. One of the hallmarks of Greek culture is its high uncertainty avoidance, as discussed in Chapter 5. On the one hand, managers of Greek work organizations are less likely to be willing to import technologies from other countries because of their need to avoid uncertainty. On the other hand, managers in the United States would be more willing to import technologies from other countries, because their need to avoid uncertainty is not as high as that of Greek managers. The difference between individualist tendencies that managers in different countries exhibit is also important. Managers who are highly individualistic are more effective in their willingness to create, absorb, and diffuse new forms of technology. Naturally, companies located in these cultures are more creative in the way they come up with new technologies and in the way they absorb imported technologies.

Exhibit 11.1 shows that the rate of creation of new technologies is very high in the United States, the United Kingdom, and Germany—countries that are significantly higher than other countries in terms of the value they put on individualism. With the exception of Japan, which is a collectivistic country, the rate at which technology is created and transferred is higher in western European nations and in the United States. Along with an emphasis on individualism, the per capita expenditure on research and development in Germany and Japan was higher than that of the United States during the 1990s.[10] While the level of education and professional orientation of managers make significant differences, the value put on individualism is clearly much more important. Moreover, the number of R&D scientists in Japan alone is higher than the combined number of R&D scientists in Spain, the United Kingdom, and France combined.

EXHIBIT 11.2
A Conceptual Model for Understanding Cultural Constraints on Technology Transfer

Source: B. Kedia and R. S. Bhagat, "Cultural Constraints of Transfer of Technology across Nations: Implications for Research in International and Comparative Management," *Academy of Management Review* 13, no. 4 (1988), p. 561.

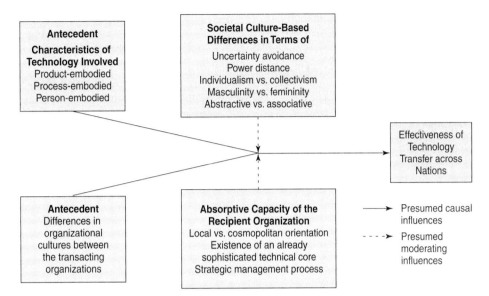

A framework developed by Kedia and Bhagat which summarizes the various differences is seen in Exhibit 11.2.[11] This figure shows the relevance of differences of technology, company cultures, societal cultures, and the capacity of the organization to absorb the technology as some of the major factors that influence or inhibit the process. The major factors that directly influence the effectiveness of technology transfer between companies in different countries are the nature of technology—whether it is product-, process-, or person-embodied—and the differences between cultures of the transacting companies. Product-embodied technologies are relatively easy to transfer. Transfer of process-embodied technologies is slightly more difficult, and may involve barriers of language or culture. Person-embodied technologies are the most difficult to transfer when the societal or organizational cultures of transacting companies are substantially different and when the senior managers have conflicting strategic objectives. These technologies are easier to transfer among subsidiaries of the vertically integrated firm (see Chapter 9).

As discussed in Chapter 9 and shown in Figure 9.2, the five points of the figure (strategy, structure, people and skills, systems, and organizational culture) are important considerations in transferring technology in subsidiaries of a global corporation, but they are more significant for two unrelated companies located in dissimilar cultural contexts which have not successfully transferred technology previously.

Knowledge in Organizations

Like technology, knowledge is an important commodity for multinational and global organizations. In fact, it has become so important that organizations competing globally cannot be effective without understanding the significance of knowledge and processes surrounding the management of knowledge.[12] In this section, we discuss the **strategic significance of knowledge** created by organizations for making their processes effective and their products or services competitive in the global marketplace. Knowledge is embedded in the context of the organization, and managers must make every effort to harness its creation and diffusion for accomplishing the kinds of activities that they need to improve.

Knowledge has been defined in many different ways, and most people have an intuitive sense that knowledge is broader, deeper, and richer than either data or information.[13] Davenport and Prusak have done extensive work on the topic of knowledge management in a large number of global corporations and define knowledge as a "fluid mix of experience, values, contextual information, and expert insight that provides a framework for evaluating and incorporating new experiences and information."[14] Knowledge is typically generated in the minds of "knowers" and is made sense of by others in the organization through a process of continuous interactions with the knowers. This interaction results in the creation of working documents or repositories and archives that organizations use for guiding them in the present and in the future. In addition, interaction with knowers creates organizational routines, processes, practices, and norms that are important for enhancing organizational productivity and performance. Knowledge has certain features, summarized by Nonaka and Takeuchi:

> First, knowledge, unlike information, is about *beliefs* and *commitment*. Knowledge is a function of a particular stance, perspective, or intention. Second, knowledge, unlike information, is about *action*. It is always knowledge "to some end." And third, knowledge, like information, is about *meaning*. It is context-specific and relational.[15]

The *intellectual capital* of a global corporation is the sum total of its stock of knowledge, which is described in procedures and manuals as well as systematically embedded in the organization's unique culture and its individuals. For example, knowledge held in the mental and organizational processes of American Express, a U.S.-based global corporation, would be referred to as its intellectual capital.

Data, which is related to the concept of knowledge, reflects discrete, objective facts about events.[16] Think of a gas station keeping count of how many customers fill up their tanks. Without any other details, these transactions, by themselves, constitute what we might call "raw data." When we know how many are filling up with regular gasoline versus premium gasoline, we have **information.** Information is meant to change a receiver because she perceives something; that is, it typically makes an impact on the judgment and behavior of the decision maker. In the example we just gave, if the gas station owner would like to have more of his customers buy premium gasoline, then he must provide some incentives to the customers to convince more of them to buy premium gasoline. The word "inform" means to give shape to, and important information created in organizational contexts makes some difference in the outlook or insight of the receiver. Strictly speaking, then, it is not the sender but the receiver who typically decides whether the message he or she receives is information or not.

Global organizations keep numerical and quantitative measures of information, such as the degree of connectivity with customers in different parts of the world and the kinds of transactions customers are engaging in. However, having a great deal of information technology does not necessarily enhance the state of information in an organization.

Information can lead to knowledge, the next important concept that we alluded to earlier. Knowledge is typically composed of information that has been transformed through the following processes:

- *Comparison:* How does a given piece of information about an organizational event, such as a sales transaction in a global subsidiary, differ from other information that the company might have had before? If the senior managers feel that the new piece of information is more indicative of a trend that is taking place in the global marketplace, then this new information becomes knowledge of some significance. Consider the case of cell phone use. The number of cell phones sold in the United States is estimated to be increasing exponentially every day. Comparison of sales data of various companies, such as AT&T Wireless, Cingular, and Verizon Communications, on an ongoing basis can inform managers of these companies how successful they are or will be in capturing an increased market share.

- *Consequences:* If a piece of information spells out a significant course of action that managers must undertake, then that information is clearly knowledge. Reliable information about a possible tornado hitting an important manufacturing facility of a global corporation quickly becomes knowledge because it tells the plant managers what they should do in the event the tornado does strike the facility.

- *Connections:* When a piece of information is related to other bits of information that the company already has, then it becomes knowledge. Information that sales figures for a product are low and, moreover, that sales figures for other products are high can be combined to allow managers to decide which products should make up their bundle of offerings. Such information is typically used as reliable knowledge by global companies such as Procter & Gamble of Cincinnati in tracing the growth of their overall offerings in the area of consumer products, health care products, and pharmaceutical products.

- *Conversation:* Related and unrelated pieces of information have the potential to become knowledge when managers begin to talk about such information and to make sense of it to arrive at meaningful and clear decisions. FBI professionals in the United States use this process in detecting criminals. Seemingly unrelated pieces of information eventually may lead to significant amounts of knowledge about the motives of a criminal and his or her whereabouts. In the case of global corporations, various unrelated acts taking place in a developing country when a new product is introduced may, upon reflection by a group of senior marketing managers, yield significant knowledge about what the company should do to enhance the quality of the product or change the product to suit the market.

The Process of Knowledge Management

Increasingly, knowledge work is replacing manual labor.[17] In many places, automation is taking the place of assembly line work, and documents are often delivered by e-mail instead of by messengers. In areas where physical labor is still employed, computers are used to enhance workers' efficiency. To understand how knowledge is managed in the global corporation, we must first understand how knowledge is created in organizations. Then we must focus on the art and science of transmission and diffusion of knowledge.

Knowledge is an intangible asset in an organization, composed of the skills and knowledge of key individuals within the organization, patents, databases, and networks, as well as information regarding relationships with customers, suppliers, and regulatory agencies such as the government. General Electric has been successful in converting knowledge assets by creating a department of learning, and many companies have chief knowledge officers (CKOs).[18]

Knowledge in organizations is accumulated and held collectively in the working memories of individuals in the context of their work role, and unique experience in their specialized positions is developed over time.[19] To convert the personal knowledge and expertise of these individuals, organizations, whether they are global or not, must find appropriate ways of managing (i.e., creating and transferring) knowledge for new-product and process development.[20] Such processes cannot always be spelled out ahead of time.

Two distinct types of knowledge—tacit and explicit—are important to an understanding of knowledge transfer across cultures. **Tacit knowledge** is knowledge that is highly personal, difficult to communicate, and highly specialized. Processing and transferring it is difficult because it is a part of the historical and cultural context in which the organization exists.[21] Tacit knowledge is a process of continual knowing. It consists of specific information and know-how that is obtained through the experience of having "lived" in the environment or having performed a particular task many times over—like walking. Tacit knowledge is transferred, for example, when teaching a child how to walk—although we know how to walk, the knowledge cannot be transferred except by showing the child how to walk and letting the child try to follow. On the other hand, **explicit knowledge** is knowledge that can be written and transmitted.[22] It is discrete or digital, stored in repositories such as libraries and databases. Generally, explicit knowledge can be accessed quickly with little distortion. Blueprints of a building printed in a book allow the transfer of explicit knowledge from the author to the reader.

Tacit knowledge is becoming increasingly recognized as an essential part of organizational knowledge.[23] Sometimes managers have to use their own experience in learning to convert knowledge that is held in a tacit form into more explicit knowledge. For example, professional skills and know-how, a significant part of tacit knowledge, are often so deeply ingrained that they are taken for granted.

Transferring tacit knowledge is much more difficult than the process of transferring explicit knowledge. One cannot say in advance that tacit knowledge is either more or less significant than explicit knowledge in enhancing the quality of product or services that the global organization might offer in the marketplace. It all depends on the nature of the task or technology to be improved.

Tacit knowledge was not recognized as a valued form of knowledge in organizations before the publication of Nonaka and Takeuchi's *The Knowledge-Creating Company* in 1995.[24] They used the example of how Matsushita Electric Company (parent company of Panasonic brand products) was able to develop bread-making machines by encouraging its software engineers to watch the process used by the master baker of the Osaka International Hotel in Osaka, Japan. The process of making bread is something that cannot be taught by spelling out in writing all of the steps that are involved in kneading a loaf of bread. The software engineers observed the minute details that the master baker used in the process of kneading dough, which was a major problem in bread-making machine technology up to that time. The computer simulation they created, by converting the tacit knowledge that the head baker processed into various steps that a machine must go through in order to knead a lump of dough, is a good example of how global companies create explicit knowledge from tacit knowledge.

Creation of new knowledge always begins with an individual. A brilliant R&D researcher may have an insight that can lead to the development of a significant patent for a successful product. An experienced marketing manager's sense of market trends, even without a lot of data, may become an inspiration for a product concept. Sony's chairman, Akio Morita, proposed the idea of the Walkman in the 1980s, when most of his senior managers thought it was not a good product idea for the Western market. Morita, however, knew that most Western consumers tend to be individualistic and might like the idea of a stereo system designed for individual listeners.[25]

Nonaka and Takeuchi explain the process of the creation of new knowledge and its transmission, in other words, how knowledge moves from tacit to explicit.[26] They visualize the process of transferring tacit to explicit knowledge, as well as explicit to tacit knowledge, as a spiral (Exhibit 11.3). When explicit knowledge is converted into usable explicit knowledge, this process is called *combination*. The process of converting explicit knowledge into tacit knowledge is *internalization*. Becoming an effective

EXHIBIT 11.3
Spiral of Knowledge Creation

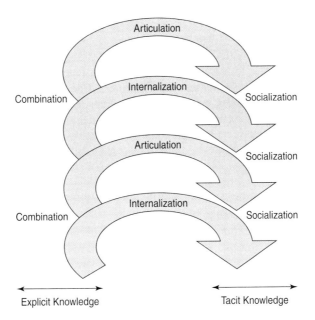

leader after going through a series of seminars on leadership is an example of internalization. The process of converting tacit knowledge into explicit knowledge is called *externalization*. The development of the bread machine, discussed previously, is an excellent example of externalization. The process of converting tacit knowledge into tacit knowledge is *socialization*. Learning about product development from an effective mentor is an example of socialization. Such processes cannot be explicitly described.

Countries that are collectivistic are better in their ability to convert tacit knowledge into explicit knowledge.[27] Tacit knowledge tends to be a favored mode of knowledge creation and retention on the part of individuals in collectivistic societies. In their extensive analysis of knowledge transfer across national boundaries, Bhagat and his colleagues found that explicit knowledge tends to be favored more in individualistic societies—societies where individuals are encouraged to think independently from their childhood, and socialization processes are geared toward developing an abstractive mode of thinking.

Transfer of knowledge from a collectivistic culture to another collectivistic culture is likely to be easier when the knowledge transferred is of the tacit variety.[28] Tacit knowledge is better absorbed in cultures where there is a focus on "give and take" and consensual decision making. Consensual decision making is facilitated when individuals in a society consider themselves to be very similar to others. In general, members of a collectivistic society have similar thought patterns because of the trust they have in each other and the continual communication with the same individuals over time.[29]

Transferring tacit knowledge from a company located in a collectivistic society to a company located in an individualistic society is generally difficult.[30] Individualists are predisposed to use their own perspectives in understanding knowledge and are more accustomed to doing things by absorbing explicit knowledge from company manuals, policy and procedure manuals, and similar material. The transfer becomes even more difficult if the countries involved are horizontal (collectivists) and vertical (individualists) in their orientation. The vertical–horizontal dimension increases the difficulty of transferring knowledge because in vertical societies individuals in organizations like to stand out from each other, whereas the opposite pattern is found in horizontal societies.[31]

Managing the Knowledge Life Cycle

Most executives today realize that knowledge is strategically significant and their companies must be able to manage it effectively. Just how one goes about developing that ability is a challenge. As in other areas of international management, there is no shortage of useful frameworks, models, and checklists that one can choose from. However, some of these solutions are only Band-Aids, conceived as being applicable in any and all situations. Many international managers are left to make their own mistakes as they choose one failing framework after another. A knowledge management model that has potential for significant gain in one context, such as electronic groupware or communities of practice, may have limited use in others.

It seems useful for us to think about knowledge management as a process of evolution through the **knowledge life cycle,** shown in Exhibit 11.4. In the *creation* stage, very few managers understand the idea of the emerging body of knowledge, including those who are creating it. The process of creation is messy, and it does not always respond to rigid time lines. An effective method for working with early stage knowledge is to solidify an idea to the point where its commercial viability can be tested. To encourage knowledge creation at this stage, companies need to create an environment allowing ongoing experimentation and creativity within some structure and discipline. Individuals need to be allowed to make mistakes, as discussed in Practical Insight 11.2.

In the *mobilization* stage, knowledge in organizations continues to be defined and redefined as its use becomes more apparent. Companies that have developed the idea tend to extract value from it. Mobilization is the process of circulating the significance of newly emergent knowledge in the internal organization. It also includes hiding the knowledge from outsiders and keeping it proprietary. Acquisition of patent protection is a good example of this stage.

In *diffusing* the knowledge, the company no longer tries to keep the knowledge or new technology under its continuous vigil. In fact, senior managers accept the idea that leakage and imitation are bound to occur. They also invite other companies to join the bandwagon, actively selling the knowledge to a broad base of customers and marketing the concept through various media. Many knowledge-based service companies, such as McKinsey and Company and Booz, Allen, and Hamilton, appear to gain significantly by moving their ideas rapidly into the diffusion stage. In the case of computer software, diffusing the product has the effect of building a client base, creating a network of users, and preempting competitors.

EXHIBIT 11.4
The Knowledge Life Cycle

Source: Reprinted from "Managing the Knowledge Life Cycle," by J. Birkinshaw and T. Sheehan, *MIT Sloan Management Review,* Fall 2002, pp. 75-83, by permission of publisher. Copyright © 2002 by Massachusetts Institute of Technology. All rights reserved.

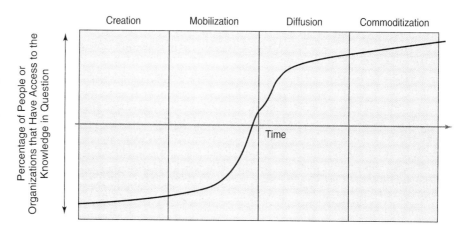

PRACTICAL INSIGHT 11.2

FEAR OF MISTAKES STIFLES INFORMATION TECHNOLOGY INNOVATION IN GOVERNMENTS

An institutionalized fear of making mistakes in a rigidly departmentalized environment that doesn't reward innovation has kept governments from adopting technology at a more rapid pace, according to Robert Reich, former U.S. Secretary of Labor and currently a professor at Brandeis University in Waltham, Massachusetts.

"Government is organized in a way to avoid errors," Reich said today in a speech at the Lotus Global Government Forum here. "One of the reasons that technological innovation is so difficult is that there is a great penalty attached to error in government" while there is little reward for innovation.

To combat the stifling of innovation, Reich recommended that government officials delegate as much responsibility as possible, giving employees clear goals with explicit deadlines. Success and failure should be monitored and widely reported, as governments learn to build on their IT successes and avoid repeated mistakes, he said.

"Improvements (in government) do not make news, errors do," Reich said. "This is an environment that is not conducive to taking appropriate risks."

Much government work is focused simply on preserving control and power, particularly in partisan atmospheres where both parties are on the watch for mistakes from the opposing party, the economist said.

"Command and control is something of a religion in the public sector," Reich said. "As cabinet secretary, given the option to delegate to a team of people, the first thing that would go through my head was 'What happens if they make a mistake? I have to be answerable to Congress.' This is why the public sector is so different from the private sector. The public sector is publicly accountable to legislatures, voters . . . Encouraging people to make their own decisions is a little bit frightening."

But increasingly, governments need to use technology to save money as administrations are often expected to be more efficient with smaller budgets and fewer resources, Reich advised government officials gathered here from 30 countries.

"Governments are being called on to do more with less," Reich said, "All of the pressures in the U.S. and Europe are on fiscal restraints, getting government debts down. It is incumbent on government to use new technologies to show the public that we are using public money as effectively as possible."

By way of example of how to use IT effectively within governments, Reich mentioned the U.S. Federal Drug Administration, which has the one-to-five year approval process for new drugs down to a half year.

"Companies had to put truckloads of evidence on the public record," Reich said. "Now the FDA has reduced the time of filing the application and getting a new drug to market to six months. It is done through e-mail, through the Internet—Viagra took six months."

But things can't stop there, Reich cautioned. "This is just beginning. We are seeing the beginnings of a revolution in the government in being able to rapidly respond to business applications." Many government activities for monitoring businesses and employee claims can be done online, he suggested.

"Government inspectors don't have to go to every work place" to process worker injury claims, for example, if they use IT tools to examine the data and find the regions where injuries are happening, Reich said. "Instead of waiting for a complaint or inspection, we can act almost pre-emptively," he added.

Government should also use technology to help knock down departmental barriers, Reich said. As the U.S. Secretary of Labor, for example, Reich found that his labor department initially didn't work at all with the Department of Education.

"You can imagine how important it is for personnel from the two departments to work together, to be able to innovate together, to suggest ways the programs can be coordinated," Reich said, adding that until recently the two departments worked separately "to avoid mistakes."

Source: Reprinted from J. Brozo, "Fear of Mistakes Stifles IT Innovation in Government," May 26, 1999 issue of *BusinessWeek* by special permission. Copyright © 1999 by The McGraw-Hill Companies, Inc.

The last stage, *commoditization,* is about how to manage knowledge that has gone through the three previous stages and is already well known. Some companies take the view that once knowledge is widely understood, nothing more can be done with it. They tend to move on to other interesting ideas. However, we should remember that international managers have a lot to gain from exploiting opportunities and extracting value from knowledge that has reached the status of a commodity. A good example is baking soda. For many years, it was only a product used in baking. It has since been rejuvenated as a toothpaste additive, a refrigerator freshener, a sink cleaner, and now a trash can deodorizer. Commoditized knowledge will not last forever. Consider an engineering firm that specializes in the construction of skyscrapers. While the knowledge required to build the skyscrapers has been known for a long time, the events of September 11, 2001, may mean that the old principles of structural engineering, which have been considered to be a commodity, will have to be revised.

Managing the knowledge life cycle is important for companies that function in the domestic context of any country. However, it becomes more important for multinational and global companies because the centers of knowledge creation are not necessarily located in a single geographic place. Continuous interchange is necessary among country managers to determine how knowledge is to be created, diffused, transferred, and commoditized.

Integration of Strategic Processes with Knowledge Management

Consider the case of Buckman Laboratories, located in Memphis, Tennessee. When Bob Buckman inherited Buckman Labs, a specialty chemical producer, in the 1960s, it was a top-heavy company with management layers and bureaucratic regulations and it was slow to respond to environmental changes. Knowledge management was not an issue in those days.

Today, Buckman Labs is a model of the knowledge-era company. Its 1,600 staff members are not just "grunt" workers; they are knowledge workers. Buckman, in his efforts to create a knowledge-managed and knowledge management company, asked himself, "How do I close the gap between my workforce and my customers?" He perceived the importance of his workers and created mechanisms for reinventing, not necessarily reengineering, Buckman Labs around people who can create knowledge.[32]

Many other companies link knowledge management with strategic intent. Canon, Ricoh, Matsushita (parent company of Panasonic), and Microsoft are a few of the leading high-technology-based companies that routinely engage in knowledge management. Senior managers in charge of knowledge management operations must recognize that effective management of knowledge is a product of three systems:

- *Strategic considerations:* The strategic intent of management emphasizes knowledge creation through innovation and tangible administrative support for innovation.
- *Technical systems:* Management stresses research and development systems, the sophistication of management information systems, quality, and competence of technical and administrative staff.
- *Administrative heritage:* The firm has a historical emphasis on knowledge creation, the values and practices of founders and senior managers (leadership legacy and organizational culture), the nature of organizational communication, and the quality of professional interactions.

A comprehensive view of these three systems indicates that they are influenced by the distinctive cultural context of the society in which the organization is located. When the organization is viewed as a *knowledge-production system* that directly impacts the effectiveness of management systems, the sophistication of electronic data interchanges (EDIs) and related computer-mediated communication is important, but so is the interaction among the various technical systems, strategic management processes, and administrative heritage of the organization, as illustrated in Exhibit 11.5.

Creators of organizational knowledge do not necessarily use knowledge in an instrumental fashion. Often, they draw from their personal sources as well as collective sources of knowledge.[33] In other words, managers in global and multinational organizations should have the capability to create new knowledge at least within the con-

EXHIBIT 11.5
Knowledge Management Effectiveness as a Product of Strategic Considerations, Technical Systems, and Administrative Heritage

Source: Reprinted from *Research in Personnel and Human Resources Management,* Vol. 21, R. S. Bhagat, D. L. Ford, Jr., C. A. Jones and R. R. Taylor, "Knowledge Management in Global Organizations: Implications for International Human Resource Management," pp. 243-274. Copyright © 2002, with permission from Elsevier.

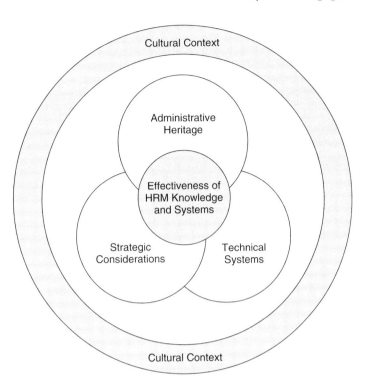

straints and demands of the foregoing three systems. Exhibit 11.5 depicts the strategic considerations, administrative heritage, and technical systems of an organization as influenced by the immediate cultural context. The effectiveness of management knowledge and systems is also dependent on the dominant values of the cultural context in which the organization operates. In the case of global organizations, the process of managing knowledge is dependent on these three systems in the particular cultural contexts of the various subsidiaries.

Denning notes that a company must engage in the following seven steps in order to continuously link strategic management processes with the process of managing technological innovation and knowledge creation:[34]

1. *Assembling a large knowledge base:* A company may have a knowledge management system composed of high-quality staff with appropriate knowledge, but the knowledge within the company needs continuous upgrading and monitoring.

2. *Going beyond the "Help Desk":* Having dedicated staff that can answer questions is not enough. A company must also think of going beyond the Help Desk, developing a mechanism for linking the operational activities of the organization with various features of the environment. In Chapter 1, we discussed the various features that the global organization must monitor.

3. *Establishing a directory of experts:* A director of "who knows what" is useful to have. Another tricky but essential tool to establish is a directory of experts who are developing useful knowledge.

4. *Maintaining developmental data:* Developmental data is information about current knowledge development. Each figure in development data is a judgment about the situation in the country. This differs from pure data, in the sense of stock market data, for example.

5. *Encouraging information:* When organizationally created knowledge has made a major impact, it must be acknowledged. In addition, the parties responsible for its development should be acknowledged by the company's reward system and other mechanisms.

6. *Creating a dialog space:* The ability to ask questions around the organization and get the answers through dialog is tremendously important. This concept is still in the development stage, but it has the potential to be the most powerful aspect of knowledge management systems.

7. *Offering external access:* This is the process of making organizationally created knowledge available in immediately usable form by clients of the organization. McKinsey and Company has been very successful in its management consulting practice by engaging in this technique.

The Learning Organization

The concept of the **learning organization** is very important for senior managers. A learning organization is one that is capable and skilled at creating, acquiring, transferring, and defusing knowledge and, at the same time, modifying the behavior and expectations of its participants to reflect new knowledge.[35] An organization must be effective in:

- Gathering and creating relevant knowledge.
- Storing it for future use.
- Diffusing it though the entire organization.
- Engaging everyone in unlearning ineffective knowledge.
- Evaluating the significance and timeliness of accumulated knowledge.
- Implementing and encouraging appropriate changes based on the knowledge.

Learning organizations are more than organizations with a desire to learn. They reflect an organizational culture that values the desire to learn. Some of the techniques for continually creating and using knowledge are listed in Exhibit 11.6.

EXHIBIT 11.6
Techniques for Enhancing the Creation and Use of Organizational Knowledge

Source: From P. R. Ferguson and G. J. Ferguson, *Organisations: A Strategic Perspective.* Copyright © 2002 P. R. Ferguson and G. J. Ferguson. Reprinted with permission of Palgrave Macmillan.

- Incorporate learning on an individual and team basis as an important part of corporate culture.
- Encourage systematic collection and recording of knowledge in blueprints and manuals.
- Evaluate the contribution of existing knowledge to the value chain.
- Appoint "knowledge brokers" to foster and disseminate knowledge in various subsidiaries.
- Nominate senior managers who can act as "boundary spanners" to sense and monitor the development of new knowledge from the external environment.
- Encourage the formation of multifunctional project groups and quality circles.
- Create networks of professionals who can share information within the organization as well as with relevant parties outside.
- Develop appropriate organizational structures and information systems.
- Encourage professional competence and team development.
- Provide rewards for creating and sharing knowledge.
- Develop routines and rules for sharing knowledge continuously.
- Encourage experimentation with knowledge creation and accept occasional failures as part of the process.
- Provide valued resources, including uninterrupted time, for learning.
- Encourage job rotation leading to a breadth and depth of knowledge and experience.
- Provide opportunities for learning by doing.
- Follow examples of leading organizations in the global marketplace.
- Encourage learning as a primary objective during joint ventures and strategic alliances.
- Make effective use of consultants.

Summary

Management of technology and knowledge has become the most important source of competitive advantage in multinational and global corporations. The Internet has revolutionized the way that international business is conducted. As a tool for managing knowledge, its implications for international management are significant. One must understand the difference between data, information, and knowledge. This chapter presented the concepts of technology and knowledge and discussed their crucial role in enhancing the competitiveness of multinational and global organizations.

Management of knowledge is rapidly becoming the most important topic in the field of international management, and global managers are being entrusted with the responsibility of creating learning organizations that facilitate the process of creating, diffusing, transferring, and commoditizing important types of organizational knowledge. Two types of knowledge—tacit and explicit—present different difficulties for firms transferring them within and across national and cultural boundaries, as do the various methods of knowledge creation. Some cultures are better able to create and diffuse tacit forms of knowledge than others. International managers should recognize strategic and cultural differences before undertaking technology and knowledge transfer.

The knowledge management cycle is essential in understanding the utility of knowledge within the organization over time. The importance of this topic will continue to grow, particularly in countries where knowledge management is the key to international competitiveness. The quest for global dominance will be realized for companies that are able to manage and master this process.[36]

Key Terms and Concepts

data, *334*
explicit knowledge, *336*
information, *334*
knowledge, *334*

knowledge life cycle, *338*
learning organization, *342*
strategic significance of knowledge, *333*

tacit knowledge, *336*
technology, *327*
technology transfer, *327*

Discussion Questions

1. Define technology. What are the three different types of technology that are considered for cross-border transfers? Define each, and give examples. Why is person-embodied technology the most difficult to transfer across cultural boundaries?
2. List the various factors that influence the success of technology transfer and give examples of each.
3. Define knowledge. Distinguish it from the concepts of data and information. Give examples of each from your personal experience and from other sources.
4. Explain the difference between tacit and explicit knowledge. Discuss why explicit knowledge is easier to transfer between individualist countries. Explain why tacit knowledge is difficult to transfer from collectivistic countries to individualistic countries.
5. How do strategic management and administrative heritage influence the process of knowledge management in global organizations? Give some examples.

Minicase

He Loves to Win. At I.B.M., He Did

The revival of I.B.M. over the last nine years is most tellingly measured not in numbers but by its return to pre-eminence as the industry leader. Once again, I.B.M. is the model others follow.

Consider the strategic debate behind the fevered proxy fight at Hewlett-Packard. Its planned purchase of Compaq Computer makes sense, Hewlett-Packard says, because the merger will make it more like I.B.M. A dangerous delusion, reply the deal's opponents. Who, they ask, could possibly compete broadly with I.B.M.?

Even the main question these days about I.B.M.'s future lends perspective. Sure, the skeptics say, I.B.M. is back with a vengeance, a powerhouse in the marketplace with strong profits. But, they ask, how much growth can be expected from a corporate giant with sales last year of $86 billion?

In 1993, when Louis V. Gerstner Jr. became chairman and chief executive, the question asked about I.B.M. was whether it would survive. And in choosing him, the I.B.M. board had taken a historic gamble on a professional manager with no experience in the computer industry.

Last Monday was Mr. Gerstner's first day at I.B.M. bearing just one title—chairman. He will keep it until year-end, then depart. On March 1, he was succeeded as chief executive by Samuel J. Palmisano, a 29-year I.B.M. veteran who built up the vital services business, which now represents about half of I.B.M.'s revenue and profits.

The rearview mirror holds little interest for Mr. Gerstner, who is 60. Yet in a lengthy interview last Monday at the company's headquarters in Armonk, N.Y., he reflected on his worries in taking the job, the challenges he faced and the reasoning behind his crucial strategic, organizational and technical decisions there. He spoke of where he thought I.B.M. had been smart and when luck had helped a lot.

He spoke of matters beyond I.B.M. as well. He explained why he believes there is no new economy, a statement that prompted boos from the dot-com world when he first made it in 1998. He answered the criticism he received in the industry in 1993, when he said, "The last thing I.B.M. needs now is a vision," and explained why he was right. And, ever the outsider in the computer business, he discussed what he thought was special about the industry, what was ordinary and what still irritates, even amuses, him about it.

Mr. Gerstner also offered a bit of personal reflection. After leading three large corporations and achieving vast personal wealth, he said that the enduring thrill of being a chief executive—and the part he would miss—was really quite simple. "I love winning," he said, pausing briefly before answering the question emphatically, "I love the process of leading an institution and being part of an institution that succeeds, that wins. I get excited by our success. I get very frustrated by our failures, too, but I enjoy the game."

At I.B.M., the Gerstner record is mainly a success story. "Lou Gerstner re-established the company's belief in itself," observed Andrew S. Grove, the chairman of Intel, who has known I.B.M. as a partner and competitor for more than two decades. "It's hard to describe how beaten down that company was."

When he took the job, Mr. Gerstner, a former McKinsey consultant who went on to become president of American Express and then chief executive of RJR Nabisco Holdings, was far from the obvious choice for guiding Big Blue, the fallen icon of American technology, back from the brink. Among I.B.M. directors, there had been a sharp debate over whether to hire a technologist or a professional manager. In the end, the board bet that I.B.M. needed a leader, a strategist and a manager—Mr. Gerstner's portfolio of skills—not an executive with a deep understanding of computer technology.

He also had qualms. "If the board had been wrong, and that was my big concern—that underlying it all there was a technical problem in I.B.M.—then it would have been a very short tenure for me," he said, smiling and shrugging.

Those misgivings are a distant memory. Even last week, it was clear that he does not plan to slow down until he leaves. Monday was his first day at the headquarters in two weeks. He had been on the road, going to Philadelphia, Boca Raton and Salt Lake City, and abroad in Stuttgart, Munich, London and Edinburgh, mostly meeting with I.B.M. customers.

The day was the equivalent of a corporate pit stop; he was headed out again on Tuesday, adding to the more than 1.1 million air miles he has logged since 1993. His travel regimen reflects his management philosophy: getting out of the office to deal with customers and dwell in the marketplace is an antidote to the corporate insularity that was nearly I.B.M.'s downfall.

He began traveling to meet customers and to visit I.B.M. outposts as soon as he took over, and what he heard guided his action. He also read. As a former McKinsey consultant, he asked first for the I.B.M. strategic plans, current and recent. There were plans aplenty, he found strategic blueprints for each division, even down to the product level. By the end of his first month, Mr. Gerstner, who always carries two briefcases of reading material when he travels, had read thousands of pages of strategic documents.

The reading left him enlightened—and appalled. I.B.M., he said, was filled with smart people who had recognized the industry's major technological and economic shifts. Yet I.B.M. had repeatedly failed to respond. "Part of the culture was a tendency to debate and argue and raise every issue to the highest level of abstraction," Mr. Gerstner said. "The process almost became one of the elegance of the definition of the problem rather than the actual execution of an action plan."

So, a few months after arriving at I.B.M., when he said the last thing it needed was a vision, he was declaring a break with the old culture of introspection and foot-dragging. Had he spoken of vision at I.B.M., he said, he knew it would have started "a yearlong debate."

"And we didn't need the vision," he added. "We needed to save the company economically."

Instead, he gave marching orders to the I.B.M. troops. "We were going to build this company from the customer back, not the from the company out," he said. "That was the big message from my first six months in the company, that the company was going to be driven from the marketplace."

As one symbolic step, he abolished the ritual of the I.B.M. organization chart. These fold-out charts were minor masterpieces of draftsmanship and printing, an intricate latticework of lines, color-coded boxes and asterisks. Lovely to behold, they recalled the engineering drawings of Leonardo da Vinci, according to one executive. Producing them was a cottage industry within I.B.M., and thousands of them were pinned on the office walls of its workers.

When asked about how to revise the organization chart under his management, Mr. Gerstner declared there would be no more organization charts, that anyone asking for one was focusing on the wrong thing.

Early on, he also changed incentives to put I.B.M. and its people more in step with the marketplace. When he came to the company, only 300 employees received stock options. Today, more than 60,000 do. He told his top 100 executives soon after he arrived that he expected them to own I.B.M. stock equal to one to four times their yearly compensation.

Mr. Gerstner argues that strategy and corporate culture are intimately linked. " You can't talk a culture into changing," he said. "You can't just exhort people to be different. You've got to point to fundamental strategic changes you're going to implement in a company and then drive the execution of that strategy. And it is in the execution of the strategy that the culture begins to change."

The first major decision Mr. Gerstner made was to decide to keep the company together, not split it up into 13 loosely linked "Baby Blues." Under that plan, put forward by his predecessor, John F. Akers, in December 1992, some would be spun off as separate companies with their own names, like AdStar, for the disk storage unit.

This so-called federation plan was moving ahead briskly when Mr. Gerstner arrived. "It was an extraordinary Balkanization of the company under way when I walked in," he said. "There were investment bankers sticking their flag on every piece of I.B.M. they could."

Auditors had been hired, costing millions of dollars, to create stand-alone financial statements for the spinoff candidates. "Every unit had run for the hills," Mr. Gerstner recalled, "creating their own human resources policies, their own communications policies."

In theory, the federation plan addressed I.B.M.'s fundamental trouble—that as an integrated company it was not quick and nimble. It would be better off aping the personal computer industry, where fast-moving technology specialists like Microsoft and Intel prevailed.

"That was the industry model that I.B.M. was responding to," Mr. Gerstner said. "And I looked at that and I said, 'Wait a minute, as a customer of I.B.M.'s, I'm not terribly drawn to that as a model for I.B.M.' "

Mr. Gerstner, an I.B.M. customer at American Express and RJR, liked the concept of "integrated solutions"—that I.B.M. could distill the complexity of computing to solve business problems for companies. In his early travels for I.B.M., he heard similar sentiments from customers.

Aside from its breadth, in Mr. Gerstner's view, I.B.M. had another unique feature: its research prowess. "Now, I walk in and they're atomizing the company," he said. "I see both of I.B.M.'s distinctive competencies being destroyed."

Within 90 days of his arrival, Mr. Gerstner irrevocably decided to keep the company together. "I knew it was a big risk, but I never doubted that it was the right thing to do at I.B.M.," he said.

"What scared me," he added, was the need to do three things at once: change I.B.M.'s economic model, its strategy and its culture.

First, though, Mr. Gerstner had to cut costs. Work force cutbacks and plant closings were already under way, but he went deeper. In July 1993, he announced the company would eliminate an additional 35,000 jobs, bringing the declared total for the year to 50,000 and bringing the charge against earnings to $8.9 billion. As a result, I.B.M. reported a record loss of $8.1 billion in 1993, and the next year, its worldwide employment fell to a low point of 220,000, from 302,000 in December 1992.

Looking back, Mr. Gerstner pointed to three strategic decisions that were "the fundamental underpinnings of building an integrated company." First, he created a broad computer services unit that sold bundles of hardware, software, consulting and maintenance to manage business processes like manufacturing, purchasing or marketing.

I.B.M. had a services arm before, but it merely kept the company's machines up and running for customers. To be a real computer services company, Mr. Gerstner noted, "I had to be product agnostic."

"The customer would not accept a services company if all it did was flog I.B.M. products," he said.

His decision to move into services set off "an incredible bomb in the company," Mr. Gerstner recalled, adding, "Here was a part of I.B.M. that was going to work closely with Oracle, Sun Microsystems and, God forbid, Microsoft." Yet IBM Global Services became the company's biggest business, the corporate vehicle that would, as Mr. Gerstner observed, "look at technology through the eyes of the customer."

His second crucial decision struck at another I.B.M. heritage, that of relying almost exclusively on its own homegrown technology. Before, when the company had gone outside—when it plunged into the personal computer business in 1981 using Intel's microprocessor and Microsoft's operating system—the move had been regarded as a grave mistake.

But by early 1994, Mr. Gerstner had decided that I.B.M. would move to "open systems." In other words, Mr. Gerstner said, "All of I.B.M.'s software would run on major competitive hardware, and all of I.B.M.'s hardware would support competitive software." To do that, the company would have to adopt standard software protocols that allowed different hardware and software products to talk to each other.

To Mr. Gerstner, the move toward openness was a technical manifestation of his broader strategy. "There's no way that you can get a company built around proprietary control to accept the open model unless they start with the customer and realize this is what the customer wants," he explained.

His third decision, made in 1995, was to fully embrace the Internet and what I.B.M. calls the "networked world" model of computing. Moving to open systems made it easier for the company to adapt to the Internet early. But the networked model of computing suited I.B.M.'s strengths—big data-serving computers are the equivalent of power plants on the network, and the Internet shift moved the center of computing away from the personal computer.

As the Internet moved into the mainstream in the mid-1990's, it brought an explosion of computing complexity, as all kinds of hardware and software had to be able to connect to the global network. I.B.M.'s breadth and its services group were big advantages in this new environment.

"Here was a chance for I.B.M. to lead again," Mr. Gerstner declared. "We were able to articulate a role for I.B.M. in the networked world that spoke of the value of all we did."

I.B.M. welcomed the sudden spread of Internet-style computing as a gift, Mr. Gerstner admitted. "The company was extraordinarily lucky that the networked model of computing arrived in the mid-90's," he said. "And let me tell you, having worked in industries where the cycle of change is measured in decades, if not centuries, one of the things that is extraordinary about this industry is that if you miss a turn of the wheel you have a chance to get back in the game" every 10 years or so.

Still, it was his earlier decisions that put I.B.M. in a position to ride the Internet wave. Given the company's size, that strategy evolved quite rapidly. In late 1995, it formed an Internet division, which was not a product group, but more a corporate SWAT team to make sure the entire company was marching toward the Internet. Then, it carved out its niche, trumpeted in a massive advertising and marketing campaign, beginning in 1997, to push "e-business."

Competitors scoffed and advertising experts scratched their heads, but the message resonated with corporate customers.

The message—helping companies do "e-business," documented in ads by examples—remained consistent, as did the strategy. Amid the dot-com mania in 1999, Mr. Gerstner told Wall Street analysts that he regarded the hot Internet start-ups as "fireflies before the storm," suggesting that the big impact of e-business would be in the old economy. At the time, that was hardly conventional wisdom.

At the conclusion of Mr. Gerstner's tenure, his three strategic pillars have come together in what could be mistaken for the very word he avoided, a vision. And that strategy shift actually executed, insured a real change in the corporate culture.

The company's sheer number of recent hires is a clear sign of that—and the buildup of the services business is a big reason IBM Global Services employs 150,000 people, up from 7,600 in 1992. All told more than half of I.B.M.'s employees have worked for the company for five years or less. In 1992, the figure was 14 percent.

Having succeeded in an industry skeptical of outsiders, Mr. Gerstner feels free to assess it. The computer industry tends to go astray, he said, when it "tends to reach to promise value in utopian schemes"—the paperless office, the cashless society, the notion that shopping Web sites would bring the demise of bricks-and-mortar stores.

"The payoff from information technology is going to be in making transactions and processes more effective and efficient," he asserted. "So it's not about creating a new economy, it's not about creating new models of behavior or new models of industry. It's about taking a tool, a powerful tool, and saying. 'How can I make my supply chain more effective and efficient, how can I make any purchasing process more efficient, how can I make my internal employee communications more effective and efficient, how can I as a government deliver services to constituents more efficiently and more effectively?' "

"So the computer," he continued, "is in a sense like the electric motor 120 years earlier. It's an invention that in and of itself is kind of interesting, but doesn't have a lot of value unless you like hitting the alt, control, and delete keys, and all the other things you can do on a keyboard. Its value is in the application to other processes."

His reference to alt, control, delete—the keys users strike to try to reanimate a personal computer, running Windows, that has crashed—was a slap at Microsoft. Like many people, Mr. Gerstner, who travels everywhere with an I.B.M. Thinkpad notebook computer, finds PC's too hard to use. He believes the problem reflects the technical parochialism of the industry.

"There's an absence of concern about ease of use and almost a pride in technical complexity," he said. "What other industry would give you a product that, to turn it off, you first have to press a button labeled start? And you tell me one other industry where somebody could sell a product that you have to reboot on average five or six times a day to get it to work?"

Yet, unlike so many in the software business, Mr. Gerstner did not let his critique of Microsoft drive his business decisions.

In 1996, he decided that I.B.M.'s OS/2 operating system could not compete with Microsoft's Windows. "Most of the big technical decisions we made were half as much business as they were technical," Mr. Gerstner explained. "I mean, the decision to basically stop fighting Microsoft with OS/2 was hardly a technical decision. It was a decision on my part that it looked like we had lost, so why don't we get on with doing something else?"

That kind of unsentimental pragmatism has served I.B.M. pretty well for the last nine years.

Source: From S. Lohr, "He Loves to Win. At IBM, He Did," March 10, 2002. Copyright © 2002 The New York Times Co. Reprinted with permission.

DISCUSSION QUESTIONS

1. How did IBM, under the leadership of Louis Gerstner, improve its technological leadership in the global marketplace?
2. What role did the Internet play in improving the strategic competitiveness of IBM?
3. How did Mr. Gerstner combine the various processes of structure, technology, and people to make IBM a more competitive global company?
4. What lessons have you learned from this case that are useful for analyzing the situation of a similar company, like Apple Computers?

Notes

1. Christine Tierney and Kathleen Kerwin, "Ford: Europe Has a Better Idea: Can Detroit Replicate the European Turnaround at Home? *BusinessWeek,* April 15, 2002.
2. Emily Thornton, "At China's Gates: Microsoft Boss Conquers a Key Asian Market," *Far Eastern Economic Review* 159, no. 1 (1996), pp. 54–55.
3. K. Marton, *Multinational, Technology, and Industrialization* (Lexington, MA: Heath, 1986); K. Marton and R. K. Singh, "Technology Transfer." In I. Walter and T. Murray, eds., *Handbook of International Management* (New York: Wiley, 1988), pp. 17.3–17.26.

4. G. Hall and R. Johnson, "Transfer of United States Aerospace Technology to Japan." In R. Vernon, ed., *The Technology Factor in International Trade* (New York: Columbia University Press, 1970), pp. 305–358.

5. Marton, *Multinational, Technology, and Industrialization.*

6. B. Kedia and R. S. Bhagat, "Cultural Constraints on Transfer of Technology across Nations: Implications for Research in International and Comparative Management," *Academy of Management Review* 13, no. 4 (1988), pp. 559–571.

7. V. Govindarajan and A. K. Gupta, *The Quest for Global Dominance: Transforming Global Presence into Global Competitive Advantage* (San Francisco: Jossey-Bass, 2001).

8. G. Hofstede, B. Neuijen, D. D. Ohayv, and G. Sanders, "Measuring Organizational Cultures: A Qualitative and Quantitative Study across Twenty Cases," *Administrative Science Quarterly* 35 (1990), pp. 286–316.

9. Ibid.

10. P. W. Beamish, A. J. Morrison, P. M. Rosenzweig, and A. C. Inkpen, *International Management: Text and Cases,* 5th ed. (Boston: McGraw-Hill/Irwin 2002).

11. Kedia and Bhagat, "Cultural Constraints on Transfer of Technology across Nations."

12. Govindarajan and Gupta, *The Quest for Global Dominance;* T. H. Davenport and L. Prusak, *Working Knowledge: How Organizations Manage What They Know* (Boston: Harvard Business School Press, 1998); T. A. Stewart, *The Wealth of Knowledge: Intellectual Capital and the Twenty-First Century Organization* (New York: Doubleday, 2001).

13. Davenport and Prusak, *Working Knowledge.*

14. Ibid., p. 5.

15. I. Nonaka and H. Takeuchi, *The Knowledge-Creating Company: How Japanese Companies Create the Dynamics of Innovation* (New York: Oxford University Press, 1995), p. 58.

16. Davenport and Prusak, *Working Knowledge.*

17. M. H. Best, *The New Competitive Advantage: The Renewal of American Industry* (New York: Oxford University Press, 2001).

18. Ibid.

19. S. F. Matusik and C. W. L. Hill, "The Utilization of Contingent Work, Knowledge Creation, and Competitive Advantage," *Academy of Management Review* 23, no. 4 (1998), pp. 680–697; U. Zander and B. Kogut, "Knowledge and Speed of the Transfer and Imitation of Organizational Capabilities: An Empirical Test," *Organization Science* 6, no. 1 (1995), pp. 76–92.

20. D. Leonard-Barton, *Wellsprings of Knowledge: Building and Sustaining the Source of Innovation* (Boston: Harvard Business School Press, 1995); I. Nonaka, "The Knowledge-Creating Company," *Harvard Business Review* 69, no. 6 (1991), pp. 96–104; Nonaka and Takeuchi, *The Knowledge-Creating Company.*

21. R. Reed and R. DeFillippi, "Casual Ambiguity, Barriers to Imitation, and Sustainable Competitive Advantage," *Academy of Management Review* 15 (1990), pp. 80–102.

22. Nonaka and Takeuchi, *The Knowledge-Creating Company.*

23. D. Lei, M. Hitt, and J. Goldhar, "Advanced Manufacturing Technology: Organizational Design and Strategic Flexibility," *Organization Studies* 17, no. 3 (1996), pp. 501–523.

24. Nonaka and Takeuchi, *The Knowledge-Creating Company.*

25. G. Nathan, *Sony* (New York: Norton, 1998).

26. Nonaka and Takeuchi, *The Knowledge-Creating Company.*

27. R. S. Bhagat, B. L. Kedia, P. Harveston, and H. C. Triandis, "Cultural Variations in the Cross-Border Transfer of Organizational Knowledge: An Integrative Framework," *Academy of Management Review* 27, no. 2 (2002), pp. 204–221.

28. Ibid.

29. I. Nonaka, "A Dynamic Theory of Organizational Knowledge Creation," *Organization Science* 5, no. 1 (1994), pp. 14–37.

30. Bhagat, Kedia, Harveston, and Triandis, "Cultural Variations in the Cross-Border Transfer of Organizational Knowledge."

31. Ibid.

32. R. Ruggles and D. Holtshouse, *The Knowledge Advantage* (Dover, NH: Capstone, 1999), p. 46.

33. J. C. Spender, "Making Knowledge the Basis of a Dynamic Theory of the Firm," *Strategic Management Journal* 17 (1996), pp. 45–62.

34. S. Denning, "The Knowledge Perspective: A New Strategic Vision. In R. Ruggles and D. Holtshouse, eds., *The Knowledge Advantage* (Dover, NH: Capstone, 1999), pp. 143–162.

35. D. A. Garvin, "Building a Learning Organization." In *Harvard Business Review, On Knowledge Management* (Boston: Harvard Business School Press, 1998), p. 422.

36. Govindarajan and Gupta, *The Quest for Global Dominance.*

Case II

The Global Branding of Stella Artois

In April 2000, Paul Cooke, chief marketing officer of Interbrew, the world's fourth largest brewer, contemplated the further development of their premium product, Stella Artois, as the company's flagship brand in key markets around the world. Although the long-range plan for 2000–2002 had been approved, there still remained some important strategic issues to resolve.

A BRIEF HISTORY OF INTERBREW

Interbrew traced its origins back to 1366 to a brewery called Den Hoorn, located in Leuven, a town just outside of Brussels. In 1717, when it was purchased by its master brewer, Sebastiaan Artois, the brewery changed its name to Artois.

The firm's expansion began when Artois acquired a major interest in the Leffe Brewery in Belgium in 1954, the Dommelsch Brewery in the Netherlands in 1968, and the Brassiere du Nord in France in 1970. In 1987, when Artois and another Belgian brewery called Piedboeuf came together, the merged company was named Interbrew. The new company soon acquired other Belgian specialty beer brewers, building up the Interbrew brand portfolio with the purchase of the Hoegaarden brewery in 1989 and the Belle-Vue Brewery in 1990.

Interbrew then entered into a phase of rapid growth. The company acquired breweries in Hungary in 1991, in Croatia and Romania in 1994, and in three plants in Bulgaria in 1995. Again in 1995, Interbrew completed an unexpected major acquisition by purchasing Labatt, a large Canadian brewer also with international interests. Labatt had operations in the United States, for example, with the Latrobe brewery, home of the Rolling Rock brand. Labatt also held a substantial minority stake in the second largest Mexican brewer, Femsa Cervesa, which produced Dos Equis, Sol, and Tecate brands. Following this major acquisition, Interbrew went on, in 1996, to buy a brewery in the Ukraine and engaged in a joint venture in the Dominican Republic. Subsequently, breweries were added in China in 1997, Montenegro and Russia in 1998, and another brewery in Bulgaria and one in Korea in 1999.

Thus, through acquisition expenditures of US$2.5 billion in the previous four years, Interbrew had transformed itself from a simple Belgian brewery into one of the largest beer companies in the world. By 1999, the company had become a brewer on a truly global scale that now derived more that 90 per cent of its volume from markets outside Belgium. It remained a privately held company, headquartered in Belgium, with subsidiaries and joint ventures in 23 countries across four continents.

THE INTERNATIONAL MARKET FOR BEER

In the 1990s, the world beer market was growing at an annual rate of one to two per cent. In 1998, beer consumption reached a total of 1.3 billion hectolitres (hls). There were, however, great regional differences in both market size and growth rates. Most industry analysts split the world market for beer between growth and mature markets. The mature markets were generally considered to be North America, Western Europe and Australasia. The growth markets included Latin America, Asia, Central and Eastern Europe including Russia. Although some felt that Africa had considerable potential, despite its low per capita beer consumption, the continent was not considered a viable market by many brewers because of its political and economic instability (see Exhibit 1).

MATURE MARKETS

The North American beer market was virtually stagnant, although annual beer consumption per person was already at a sizeable 83 litres per capita (lpc). The Western European market had also reached maturity with consumption of 79 lpc. Some analysts believed that this consumption level was under considerable pressure, forecasting a decline to near 75 lpc over the medium term. Australia and New Zealand were also considered mature markets, with consumption at 93 lpc and 84 lpc, respectively. In fact, volumes in both markets, New Zealand in particular, had declined through the 1990s following tight social policies on alcohol consumption and the emergence of a wine culture.

GROWTH MARKETS

Given that average consumption in Eastern Europe was only 29 lpc, the region appeared to offer great potential. This consumption figure, however, was heavily influenced by Russia's very low level, and the future for the large Russian market was unclear. Further, some markets, such as the Czech Republic that consumed the most beer per person in the world at 163 lpc, appeared to have already reached maturity. Central and South America, on the other hand, were showing healthy growth and, with consumption at an average of 43 lpc, there was believed to be considerable upside. The most exciting growth rates, however, were in Asia. Despite the fact that the market in this region had grown by more than 30 per cent since 1995, consumption levels were still comparatively low. In China, the region's largest market, consumption was only 16 lpc and 20 to 25 lpc in Hong Kong and Taiwan. Although the 1997 Asian financial crisis did not immediately affect beer consumption (although company profits from the region were hit by currency translation), demand in some key markets, such as

EXHIBIT 1
The World Beer
Market in 1998

Region	% of Global Consumption	Growth Index ('98 Vs 92)	Per Capita Consumption
Americas	35.1%	112.6	57
Europe	32.8%	97.7	54
Asia Pacific	27.2%	146.2	11
Africa	4.6%	107.7	8
Middle East/Central Asia	0.4%	116.0	2

Source: Canadean Ltd.

Indonesia, was reduced and in others growth slowed. The situation, however, was expected to improve upon economic recovery in the medium term.

BEER INDUSTRY STRUCTURE

The world beer industry was relatively fragmented with the top four players accounting for only 22 per cent of global volume—a relatively low figure as compared to 78 per cent in the soft drinks industry, 60 per cent in tobacco and 44 per cent in spirits. This suggested great opportunities for consolidation, a process that had already begun two decades prior. Many analysts, including those at Interbrew, expected that this process would probably accelerate in the future. The driver behind industry rationalization was the need to achieve economies of scale in production, advertising and distribution. It was widely recognized that the best profit margins were attained either by those with a commanding position in the market or those with a niche position. However, there were several factors that mitigated the trend towards rapid concentration of the brewing industry.

One factor that slowed the process of consolidation was that the ratio of fixed versus variable costs of beer production was relatively high. Essentially, this meant that there was a limited cost savings potential that could be achieved by bringing more operations under a common administration. Real cost savings could be generated by purchasing and then rationalizing operations through shifting production to more efficient (usually more modern) facilities. This approach, however, required large initial capital outlays. As a result, in some markets with "unstable" economies, it was desirable to spread out capital expenditures over a longer period of time to ensure appropriate profitability in the early stages. A second factor that may have had a dampening effect on the trend towards industry consolidation was that local tastes differed. In some cases, beer brands had hundreds of years of heritage behind them and had become such an integral part of everyday life that consumers were often fiercely loyal to their local brew. This appeared to be a fact in many markets around the world.

INTERBREW'S GLOBAL POSITION

Through Interbrew's acquisitions in the 1990s, the company had expanded rapidly. During this period, the company's total volumes had increased more than fourfold. These figures translated to total beer production of 57.5 million hls in 1998 (when including the volume of all affiliates), as compared to just 14.7 million hls in 1992. Volume growth had propelled the company into the number four position among the world's brewers.

Faced with a mature and dominant position in the declining Belgian domestic market, the company decided to focus on consolidating and developing key markets, namely Belgium, the Netherlands, France and North America, and expansion through acquisition in Central Europe, Asia and South America. Subsequently, Interbrew reduced its dependence on the Belgian market from 44 per cent in 1992 to less that 10 per cent by 1998 (total volumes including Mexico). Concurrently, a significant milestone for the company was achieved by 1999 when more than 50 per cent of its total volume was produced in growth markets (including Mexico). Interbrew had shifted its volume so that the Americas accounted for 61 per cent of its total volume, Europe added 35 per cent, and Asia Pacific the remaining four per cent.

Taken together, the top 10 markets for beer accounted for 86 per cent of Interbrew's total volume in 1998 (see Exhibit 2). The Mexican beer market alone accounted for 37 per cent of total volume in 1998. Canada, Belgium, the United States and the United Kingdom were the next most important markets. However, smaller, growing markets such as Hungary, Croatia, Bulgaria, and Romania had begun to increase in importance.

Adding to its existing breweries in Belgium, France and the Netherlands, Interbrew's expansion strategy in the 1990s had resulted in acquisitions in Bosnia-Herzegovina, Bulgaria, Canada, China, Croatia, Hungary, Korea, Montenegro, Romania, Russia, the Ukraine, the United States, in a joint venture in South Korea, and in minority equity positions in Mexico and Luxembourg. Through these breweries, in addition to those that were covered by licensing agreements in Australia, Italy, Sweden and the United Kingdom, Interbrew sold its beers in over 80 countries.

EXHIBIT 2
Interbrew's 1998
Share of the World's
Top 10 Markets

Rank	Country	Volume (000 HL)	Market Share
1	USA	3,768	1.6%
2	China	526	0.3%
3	Germany	—	—
4	Brazil	—	—
5	Japan	—	—
6	UK	3,335	5.5%
7	Mexico	21,269	45.0%
8	Spain	—	—
9	South Africa	—	—
10	France	1,915	8.4%
Total		30,813	3.6%

Source: Canadean Ltd.

INTERBREW'S CORPORATE STRUCTURE

Following the acquisition of Labatt in 1995, Interbrew's corporate structure was divided into two geographic zones: the Americas and Europe/Asia/Africa. This structure was in place until September 1999 when Interbrew shifted to a fully integrated structure to consolidate its holdings in the face of industry globalization. Hugo Powell, formerly head of the Americas division, was appointed to the position of chief executive officer (CEO). The former head of the Europe/Africa/Asia division assumed the role of chief operating officer, but subsequently resigned and was not replaced, leaving Interbrew with a more conventional structure, with the five regional heads and the various corporate functional managers reporting directly to the CEO.

RECENT PERFORMANCE

1998 had been a good year for Interbrew in terms of volume in both mature and growth markets. Overall, sales volumes increased by 11.1 per cent as most of the company's international and local brands maintained or gained market share. In terms of the compounded annual growth rate, Interbrew outperformed all of its major competitors by a wide margin. While Interbrew's 1998 net sales were up 29 per cent, the best performing competitor achieved an increase of only 16 per cent. Of Interbrew's increased sales, 67 per cent was related to the new affiliates in China, Montenegro and Korea. The balance was the result of organic growth. Considerable volume increases were achieved also in Romania (72 per cent), Bulgaria (28 per cent), Croatia (13 per cent), and the United States (14 per cent). While volumes in Western Europe were flat, duty-free sales grew strongly. In the U.S. market, strong progress was made by Interbrew's Canadian and Mexican brands, and Latrobe's Rolling Rock was successfully relaunched. In Canada, performance was strong, fuelled by a two per cent increase in domestic consumption. Labatt's sales of Budweiser (produced under license from Anheuser-Busch) also continued to grow rapidly.

Given that the premium and specialty beer markets were growing quickly, particularly those within the large, mature markets, Interbrew began to shift its product mix to take advantage of this trend and the superior margins it offered. A notable brand success was Stella Artois, for which total global sales volumes were up by 19.7 per cent. That growth came from sales generated by Whitbread in the United Kingdom, from exports, and from sales in Central Europe where Stella Artois volumes took off. The strong growth of Stella Artois was also notable in that it was sold in the premium lager segment. In Europe, Asia Pacific and Africa, Interbrew's premium and specialty beers, which generated a bigger margin, increased as a proportion of total sales from 31 per cent in 1997 to 33 per cent in 1998. This product mix shift was particularly important since intense competition in most markets inhibited real price increases.

Success was also achieved in the United States specialty beer segment where total volume had been growing at nine per cent annually in the 1990s. In 1998, Interbrew's share of this growing market segment had risen even faster as Labatt USA realized increased sales of 16 per cent. The other continuing development was the growth of the light beer segment, which had become over 40 per cent of the total sales. Sales of Labatt's Blue Light, for example, had increased and Labatt Blue had become the number three imported beer in the United States, with volumes up 18 per cent. Latrobe's Rolling Rock brand grew by four per cent, the first increase in four years. Interbrew's Mexican brands, Dos Equis, Tecate and Sol, were also up by 19 per cent.

Following solid volume growth in profitable market segments, good global results were realized in key financial areas. Net profit, having grown for each of the previous six consecutive years, was 7.7 billion Belgian francs (BEF) in 1998, up 43.7 per cent from the previous year. Operating profit also rose 7.9 per cent over 1997, from 14.3 to 15.4 BEF; in both the Europe/Asia/Africa region and the Americas, operating profit was up by 8.5 per cent and 4.9 per cent respectively. Further, Interbrew's EBIT [earnings before interest and taxes] margin was up 58.1 per cent as compared to the best performing competitor's figure of 17.0 per cent. However, having made several large investments in Korea and Russia, and exercising an option to increase its share of Femsa Cerveza in Mexico from 22 per cent to 30 per cent, Interbrew's debt-equity ratio increased from 1.04 to 1.35. As a result, interest payments rose accordingly.

Interbrew also enjoyed good results in volume sales in many of its markets in 1999. Although Canadian sales remained largely unchanged over 1998, Labatt USA experienced strong growth in 1999, with volumes up by 10 per cent. There was a positive evolution in Western European volumes as well, as overall sales were up by 6.5 per cent overall in Belgium, France and the Netherlands. Central European markets also grew with Hungary showing an increase of 9.6 per cent, Croatia up by 5.5 per cent, Romania by 18.9 per cent, Montenegro by 29 per cent, and Bulgaria with a rise of 3.6 per cent in terms of volume. Sales positions were also satisfactory in the Russian and Ukrainian markets. Further, while South Korean sales volume remained unchanged, volumes in China were 10 per cent higher, although this figure was still short of expectations.

INTERBREW CORPORATE STRATEGY

The three facets of Interbrew's corporate strategy, i.e., brands, markets and operations, were considered the "sides of the Interbrew triangle." Each of these aspects of corporate strategy was considered to be equally important in order to achieve the fundamental objective of increasing shareholder value. With a corporate focus entirely on beer, the underlying objectives of the company were to consolidate its positions in mature markets and improve margins through higher volumes of premium and specialty brands. Further, the company's emphasis on growth was driven by the belief that beer industry rationalization still had some way to go and that the majority of the world's major markets would each end up with just two or three major players.

OPERATIONS STRATEGY

Cross fertilization of best practices between sites was a central component of Interbrew's operations strategy. In the company's two main markets, Belgium and Canada, each brewery monitored its performance on 10 different dimensions against its peers. As a result, the gap between the best and the worst of Interbrew's operations had narrowed decisively since 1995. Employees continuously put forward propositions to improve processes. The program had resulted in significantly lower production costs, suggesting to Interbrew management that most improvements had more to do with employee motivation than with pure technical performance. In addition, capacity utilization and strategic sourcing had been identified as two areas of major opportunity.

CAPACITY UTILIZATION

Given that brewing was a capital-intensive business, capacity utilization had a major influence on profitability. Since declining consumption in mature markets had generated excess capacity, several of Interbrew's old breweries and processing facilities were scheduled to be shut down. In contrast, in several growth markets such as Romania, Bulgaria, Croatia and Montenegro, the opposite problem existed, so facilities in other locations were used more fully until local capacities were increased.

STRATEGIC SOURCING

Interbrew had begun to rationalize its supply base as well. By selecting a smaller number of its best suppliers and working more closely with them, Interbrew believed that innovative changes resulted, saving both parties considerable sums every year. For most of the major commodities, the company had gone to single suppliers and was planning to extend this approach to all operations worldwide.

MARKET STRATEGY

The underlying objectives of Interbrew's market strategy were to increase volume and to lessen its dependence on Belgium and Canada, its two traditional markets. Interbrew dichotomized its market strategy into the mature and growth market segments, although investments were considered wherever opportunities to generate sustainable profits existed. One of the key elements of Interbrew's market strategy was to establish and manage strong market platforms. It was believed that a brand strength was directly related to a competitive and dedicated market platform (i.e., sales and distribution, wholesaler networks, etc.) to support the brand. Further, Interbrew allowed individual country teams to manage their own affairs and many felt that the speed of success in many markets was related to this decentralized approach.

MATURE MARKETS

Interbrew's goals in its mature markets were to continue to build market share and to improve margins through greater efficiencies in production, distribution and marketing. At the same time, the company intended to exploit the growing trend in these markets towards premium and specialty products of which Interbrew already possessed an unrivalled portfolio. The key markets in which this strategy was being actively pursued were the United States, Canada, the United Kingdom, France, the Netherlands and Belgium.

GROWTH MARKETS

Based on the belief that the world's beer markets would undergo further consolidation, Interbrew's market strategy was to build significant positions in markets that had long-term volume growth potential. This goal led to a clear focus on Central and Eastern Europe and Asia, South Korea and China in particular. In China, for example, Interbrew had just completed an acquisition of a second brewery in Nanjing. The Yali brand was thereby added to the corporate portfolio and, together with its Jingling brand, Interbrew became the market leader in Nanjing, a city of six million people.

In Korea, Interbrew entered into a 50:50 joint venture with the Doosan Chaebol to operate the Oriental Brewery, producing the OB Lager and Cafri pilsener brands. With this move, Interbrew took the number two position in the Korean beer market with a 36 per cent share and sales of 5.1 million hls. The venture with Doosan was followed in December 1999 by the purchase of the Jinro Coors brewery. This added 2.5 million hls and increased Interbrew's market share to 50 per cent of total Korean volume. Thus, the Interbrew portfolio in Korea consisted of two mainstream pilsener brands, OB Lager and Cass, the two local premium brands, Cafri and Red Rock, and Budweiser, an international premium brand.

In Russia, Interbrew expanded its presence by taking a majority stake in the Rosar Brewery in Omsk, adding the BAG Bier and Sibirskaya Korona brands. Rosar was the leading brewer in Siberia with a 25 per cent regional market share, and held the number four position in Russia. New initiatives were also undertaken in Central Europe with acquisitions of a brewery in Montenegro and the Pleven brewery in Bulgaria, as well as the introduction of Interbrew products into the Yugoslavian market. Finally, although Interbrew had just increased its already significant investment in Mexico's second largest brewer from 22 per cent to 30 per cent, Latin America remained a region of great interest.

BRAND STRATEGY

A central piece of Interbrew's traditional brand strategy had been to add to its portfolio of brands through acquisition of existing brewers, principally in growth markets. Since its goal was to have the number one or two brand in every market segment in which it operated, Interbrew concentrated on purchasing and developing strong local brands. As it moved into new territories, the company's first priority was to upgrade product quality and to improve the positioning of the acquired local core lager brands. In mature markets, it drew on the strength of the established brands such as Jupiler, Belgium's leading lager brand, Labatt Blue, the famous Canadian brand, and Dommelsch, an important brand in the Netherlands. In growth markets, Interbrew supported brands like Borsodi Sor in Hungary, Kamenitza in Bulgaria, Ozujsko in Croatia, Bergenbier in Romania, Jingling in China, and OB Lager in Korea. In addition, new products were launched such as Taller, a premium brand in the Ukraine, and Boomerang, an alternative malt-based drink in Canada.

A second facet of the company's brand strategy was to identify certain brands, typically specialty products, and to develop them on a regional basis across a group of markets. At the forefront of this strategy were the Abbaye de Leffe and Hoegaarden brands and, to a lesser extent, Belle-Vue. In fact, both Hoegaarden and Leffe achieved a leading position as the number one white beer and abbey beer in France and Holland. The Loburg premium pilsener brand also strengthened its position when it was relaunched in France. Further, in Canada, Interbrew created a dedicated organization for specialty beers called the Oland Specialty Beer Company. In its first year of operation, the brands marketed by Oland increased its volumes by over 40 per cent. More specifically, sales of the Alexander Keith's brand doubled and the negative volume trend of the John Labatt Classic brand was reversed. The underlying message promoted by Oland was the richness, mystique and heritage of beer.

To support the regional growth of specialty beers, Interbrew established a new type of café. The Belgian Beer Café, owned and run by independent operators, created an authentic Belgian atmosphere where customers sampled Interbrew's Belgian specialty beers. By 1999, Belgian Beer Cafés were open in many of Interbrew's key markets, including top selling outlets in New York, Auckland, Zagreb and Budapest, to name a few. The business concept was that these cafés were to serve as an ambassador of the Belgian beer culture in foreign countries. They were intended to serve as vehicles to showcase Interbrew's specialty brands, benefiting from the international appeal of European styles and fashions. Although these cafés represented strong marketing tools for brand positioning, the key factors that led to the success of this concept were tied very closely to the individual establishments and the personnel running them. The bar staff, for example, had to be trained to serve the beer in the right branded glass, at the right temperature, and with a nice foamy head. It was anticipated that the concept of the specialty café would be used to support the brand development efforts of Interbrew's Belgian beers in all of its important markets.

The third facet of Interbrew's brand strategy was to identify a key corporate brand and to develop it as a global product. While the market segment for a global brand was currently relatively small, with the bulk of the beer demand still in local brands, the demand for international brands was expected to grow, as many consumers became increasingly attracted to the sophistication of premium and super-premium beers.

THE EVOLUTION OF INTERBREW'S GLOBAL BRAND STRATEGY

Until 1997, Interbrew's brand development strategy for international markets was largely *laissez faire*. Brands were introduced to new markets through licensing, export and local production when opportunities were uncovered. Stella Artois, Interbrew's most broadly available and oldest brand, received an important new thrust when it was launched through local production in three of the company's subsidiaries in Central Europe in 1997. This approach was consistent with the company's overall goals of building a complete portfolio in high growth potential markets.

By 1998, however, the executive management committee perceived the need to identify a brand from its wide portfolio to systematically develop into the company's global brand. Although the market for global brands was still small, there were some growing successes (e.g., Heineken, Corona, Fosters and Budweiser) and Interbrew believed that there were several basic global trends that would improve the viability of this class of product over the next couple of decades. First, while many consumers were seeking more variety, others were seeking lower prices. It appeared that the number of affluent and poor consumer segments would increase at the expense of the middle income segments. The upshot of this socioeconomic trend was that eventually all markets would likely evolve in such a way that demand for both premium and economy-priced beers would increase, squeezing the mainstream beers in the middle. A second trend was the internationalization of the beer business. As consumers travelled around the world, consuming global media (e.g., CNN, Eurosport, MTV, international magazines, etc.), global media were expected to become more effective for building brands. A global strategy could, therefore, lead to synergies in global advertising and sponsoring. In addition, the needs of consumers in many markets were expected to converge. As a result of these various factors, Interbrew believed that there would be an increasing interest in authentic, international brands in a growing number of countries. Interbrew had a wide portfolio of national brands that it could set on the international stage. The two most obvious candidates were Labatt Blue and Stella Artois.

The Labatt range of brands included Labatt Blue, Labatt Blue Light and Labatt Ice. To date, however, the exposure of these brands outside of North America had been extremely limited and they were not yet budding global brands. Of the total Labatt Blue volume in 1998, 85 per cent was derived from the Canadian domestic and U.S. markets, with the balance sold in the United Kingdom. The Labatt brands had been introduced to both France and Belgium, and production had been licensed in Italy, but these volumes were minimal. The only real export growth market for Labatt Blue appeared to be the United States, where the brand's volume in 1998 was some 23 per cent higher than in 1995, behind only Corona and Heineken in the imported brand segment. The Labatt Ice brand was also sold in a limited number of markets and, after the appeal of this Labatt innovation had peaked, its total volume had declined by more than 25 per cent since 1996. Total Labatt Ice volume worldwide was just 450,000 hls in 1998, of which 43 per cent was sold in Canada, 33 per cent in the United States, and 21 per cent in the United Kingdom.

STELLA ARTOIS AS INTERBREW'S INTERNATIONAL FLAGSHIP BRAND

The other potential brand that Interbrew could develop on a global scale was Stella Artois, a brand that could trace its roots back to 1366. The modern version of Stella Artois was launched in 1920 as a Christmas beer and had become a strong market leader in its home market of Belgium through the 1970s. By the 1990s, however, Stella's market position began to suffer from an image as a somewhat old-fashioned beer, and the brand began to experience persistent volume decline. Problems in the domestic market, however, appeared to be shared by a number of other prominent international brands. In fact, seven of the top 10 international brands had experienced declining sales in their home markets between 1995 and 1999 (see Exhibit 3).

Stella Artois had achieved great success in the United Kingdom through its licensee, Whitbread, where Stella Artois became the leading premium lager beer. Indeed, the United Kingdom was the largest market for Stella Artois, accounting for 49 per cent of total brand volume in 1998. Stella Artois volume in the U.K. market reached 2.8 million hls in 1998, a 7.6 per cent share of the lager market, and came close to 3.5 million hls in 1999, a 25 per cent increase over the previous year. By this time, over 32,000 outlets sold Stella Artois on draught.

Apart from the United Kingdom, the key markets for Stella Artois were France and Belgium, which together accounted for a further 31 per cent of total brand volume (see Exhibit 4). With these three markets accounting for 81 per cent of total Stella Artois volume in 1999, few other areas represented a significant volume base (see Exhibit 5). Beyond the top three markets, the largest market for Stella Artois was Italy, where the brand was produced under license by Heineken. Stella Artois volume in Italy had, however, declined slightly to 166,000 hls in 1998. Licensing agreements were also in place in Sweden and Australia, but volume was small.

Stella Artois was also produced in Interbrew's own breweries in Hungary, Croatia and Romania, with very pleasing 1998 volumes of 84,000 hls, 120,000 hls, and 60,000 hls, respectively. After only three years, the market share of Stella Artois in Croatia, for example, had reached four per cent—a significant result, given that the brand was a premium-priced product. In all Central European markets, Stella Artois was priced at a premium; in Hungary, however, that premium was lower than in

EXHIBIT 3
Domestic Sales History of Major International Brands (million hectolitre)

	1995	1996	1997	1998
Budweiser (incl. Bud Light until '98)	69.48	71.10	72.43	40.00
Bud Light	n/a	n/a	n/a	30.00
Heineken	3.87	3.78	3.85	3.78
Becks	1.68	1.71	1.72	1.78
Carlsberg	1.47	1.39	1.31	1.22
Stella Artois	1.08	1.00	0.96	0.92
Fosters	1.48	1.11	1.40	1.43
Kronenbourg	5.65	5.53	5.35	5.60
Amstel	2.30	2.23	2.21	2.18
Corona	12.89	14.09	14.80	15.18

Croatia and Romania where, on an index comparing Stella's price to that of core lagers, the indices by country were 140, 260 and 175 respectively.

Promising first results were also attained in Australia and New Zealand. Particularly in New Zealand, through a "seeding" approach, Interbrew and their local partner, Lion Nathan, had realized great success in the Belgian Beer Café in Auckland where the brands were showcased. After only two years of support, Stella Artois volume was up to 20,000 hls, and growing at 70 per cent annually, out of a total premium segment of 400,000 hls. Interbrew's market development plan limited distribution to top outlets in key metropolitan centres and priced Stella Artois significantly above competitors (e.g., 10 per cent over Heineken and 20 per cent over Steinlager, the leading domestic premium lager brand).

EXHIBIT 4
1999 World Sales Profile of Stella Artois

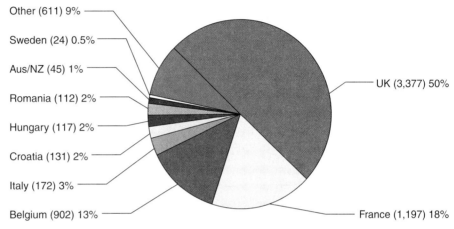

Other (611) 9%
Sweden (24) 0.5%
Aus/NZ (45) 1%
Romania (112) 2%
Hungary (117) 2%
Croatia (131) 2%
Italy (172) 3%
Belgium (902) 13%
UK (3,377) 50%
France (1,197) 18%

Total world volume: 6,691,000 HL

EXHIBIT 5
Stella Artois Sales Volume Summary (000 hectolitre)

	1997	1998	1999
Production:			
Belgium	965	921	902
France	1,028	1,110	1,074
Hungary	59	84	117
Croatia	54	120	133
Romania	17	60	112
Bulgaria	—	—	3
Bosnia-Herzegovina	—	—	2
Montenegro	—	—	0
Total Production	2,123	2,295	2,343
License Brewing:			
Italy	162	166	172
Australia	6	11	22
New Zealand	7	11	22
Sweden	29	27	24
Greece	7	7	10
UK	2,139	2,815	3,377
Total Licensed	2,350	3,037	3,627
Export:			
USA	—	—	7
Canada	—	—	5
Other Countries	92	49	202
Duty Free	245	389	507
Total Export	337	438	721
Overall Total	4,810	5,770	6,691

EXHIBIT 6 **Top 10 Brewers by International Sales**

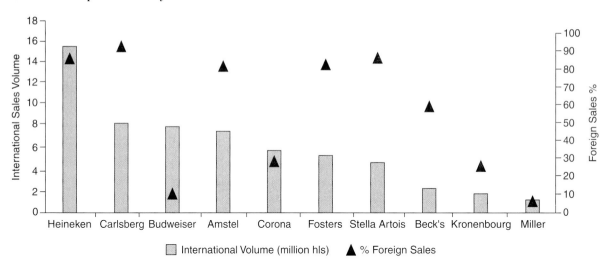

The evolution of the brand looked very positive as world volumes for Stella Artois continued to grow. In fact, Stella Artois volume had increased from 3.4 million hls in 1992 to a total of 6.7 million hls in 1999, a rise of 97 per cent. Ironically, the only market where the brand continued its steady decline was in its home base of Belgium. Analysts suggested a variety of reasons to explain this anomaly, including inconsistent sales and marketing support, particularly as the organization began to favor the rising Jupiler brand.

Overall, given Interbrew's large number of local brands, especially those in Mexico with very high volumes, total Stella Artois volume accounted for only 10 per cent of total Interbrew volume in 1999 (14 per cent if Femsa volumes are excluded). Interbrew's strategy of nurturing a wide portfolio of strong brands was very different as compared to some of its major competitors. For example, Anheuser-Busch, the world's largest brewer, focused its international strategy almost exclusively on the development of the Budweiser brand. Similarly, Heineken sought to centre its international business on the Heineken brand and, to a lesser extent, on Amstel. While the strategies of Anheuser-Busch and Heineken focused primarily on one brand, there were also great differences in the way these two brands were being managed. For example, Budweiser, the world's largest brand by volume, had the overwhelming bulk of its volume in its home U.S. market (see Exhibit 6). Sales of the Heineken brand, on the other hand, were widely distributed across markets around the world (see Exhibit 7). In this sense, Heineken's strategy was much more comparable to that of Interbrew's plans for Stella Artois. Other brands that were directly comparable to Stella Artois, in terms of total volume and importance of the brand to the overall sales of the company, were Carlsberg and Foster's with annual sales volumes in 1998 of 9.4 million hls and 7.1 million hls, respectively. While Foster's was successful in many international markets, there was a heavy focus on sales in the United Kingdom and the United States (see Exhibit 8). Carlsberg sales volume profile was different in that sales were more widely distributed across international markets (see Exhibit 9).

STELLA'S GLOBAL LAUNCH

In 1998, Interbrew's executive management committee settled on Stella Artois, positioned as the premium European lager, as the company's global flagship brand. In fact, the Interbrew management felt that stock analysts would be favorably disposed to Interbrew having an acknowledged global brand with the potential for a higher corporate valuation and price earnings (P/E) multiple.

As the global campaign got under way, it became clear that the organization needed time to adapt to centralized co-ordination and control of Stella Artois brand marketing. This was, perhaps, not unexpected given that Interbrew had until recently operated on a regional basis; the new centralized

EXHIBIT 7
1998 Heineken World Sales Profile

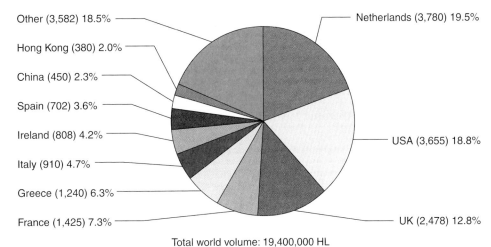

Other (3,582) 18.5%
Hong Kong (380) 2.0%
China (450) 2.3%
Spain (702) 3.6%
Ireland (808) 4.2%
Italy (910) 4.7%
Greece (1,240) 6.3%
France (1,425) 7.3%
Netherlands (3,780) 19.5%
USA (3,655) 18.8%
UK (2,478) 12.8%

Total world volume: 19,400,000 HL

EXHIBIT 8
1998 Foster's World Sales Profile

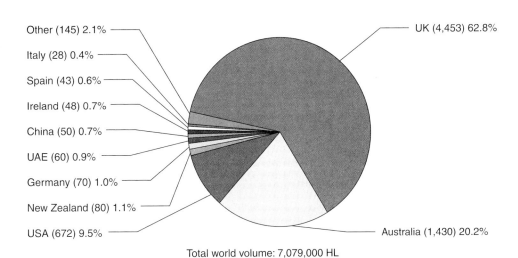

Other (145) 2.1%
Italy (28) 0.4%
Spain (43) 0.6%
Ireland (48) 0.7%
China (50) 0.7%
UAE (60) 0.9%
Germany (70) 1.0%
New Zealand (80) 1.1%
USA (672) 9.5%
UK (4,453) 62.8%
Australia (1,430) 20.2%

Total world volume: 7,079,000 HL

EXHIBIT 9
1998 Carlsberg World Sales Profile

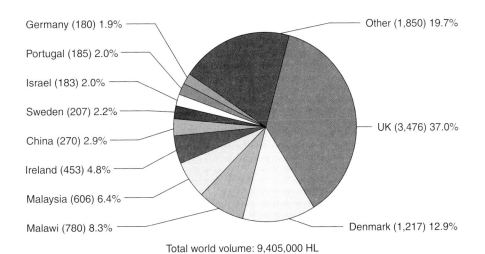

Germany (180) 1.9%
Portugal (185) 2.0%
Israel (183) 2.0%
Sweden (207) 2.2%
China (270) 2.9%
Ireland (453) 4.8%
Malaysia (606) 6.4%
Malawi (780) 8.3%
Other (1,850) 19.7%
UK (3,476) 37.0%
Denmark (1,217) 12.9%

Total world volume: 9,405,000 HL

EXHIBIT 10
Global Positioning
Statement

Brand Positioning

To males, between 21 to 45 years of age, that are premium lager drinkers, Stella Artois is a European premium lager beer, differentially positioned towards the product.

Stella Artois offers a modern, sophisticated, yet accessible drinking experience with an emphasis on the very high quality of the beer supported by the noble tradition of European brewing.

The accent is on the emotional consequence of benefit: a positive feeling of self esteem and sophistication.

Character, Tone of Voice

Sophistication
Authenticity, tradition, yet touch of modernity
Timelessness
Premium quality
Special, yet accessible
Mysticism
European

Stella brand management approach had been in place only since September 1998. In addition, there were often difficulties in convincing all parties to become part of a new global approach, particularly the international advertising campaign that was the backbone of the global plan for Stella Artois. Belgium, for example, continued with a specific local advertising program that positioned Stella as a mainstream lager in its home market, and in the United Kingdom, Whitbread maintained its "reassuringly expensive" advertising slogan that had already proved to be so successful. For other less-established markets, a global advertising framework was created that included a television concept and a series of print and outdoor executions. This base advertising plan was rolled out in 1999 in 15 markets, including the United States, Canada, Italy, Hungary, Croatia, Bulgaria, Romania, New Zealand and France (with a slightly changed format) after research suggested that the campaign had the ability to cross borders. The objective of this campaign was to position Stella Artois as a sophisticated European lager. It was intended that Stella Artois should be perceived as a beer with an important brewing tradition and heritage but, at the same time, also as a contemporary beer (see Exhibit 10).

In 1998, an accelerated plan was devised to introduce Stella Artois to two key markets within the United States, utilizing both local and corporate funding. The U.S. market was believed to be key for the future development of the brand since it was the most developed specialty market in the world (12 per cent specialty market share, growing 10 per cent plus annually through the 1990s), and because of the strong influence on international trends. Thus, Stella Artois was launched in New York City and Boston and was well received by the demanding U.S. consumer and pub owner. Within 1999, over 200 pubs in Manhattan and 80 bars in Boston had begun to sell Stella Artois on tap. To support the heightened efforts to establish Stella Artois in these competitive urban markets, Interbrew's corporate marketing department added several million dollars to Labatt USA's budget for Stella Artois in 2000, with commitments to continue this additional funding in subsequent years.

CURRENT THINKING

Good progress had been made since 1998 when Stella Artois was established as Interbrew's global brand. However, management had revised its expectations for P/E leverage from having a global brand. The reality was that Interbrew would be rewarded only through cash benefits from operational leverage of a global brand. There would be no "free lunch" simply for being perceived as having a global brand. In addition, in an era of tight fiscal management, it was an ongoing challenge to maintain the funding levels required by the ambitious development plans for Stella Artois. As a result, in early 2000 the prevailing view at Interbrew began to shift, converging on a different long-range approach towards global branding. The emerging perspective emphasized a more balanced brand development program, focusing on the highest leverage opportunities.

The experience of other brewers that had established global brands offered an opportunity for Interbrew to learn from their successes and failures. Carlsberg and Heineken, for example, were two comparable global brands that were valued quite differently by the stock market. Both sold over

EXHIBIT 11
A Comparison of Carlsberg and Heineken

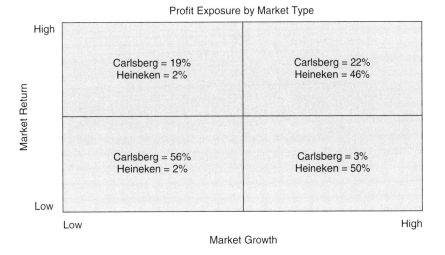

Profit Exposure by Market Type

Market Return

High

Carlsberg = 19%
Heineken = 2%

Carlsberg = 22%
Heineken = 46%

Carlsberg = 56%
Heineken = 2%

Carlsberg = 3%
Heineken = 50%

Low

Low   Market Growth   High

80 per cent of their total volumes outside their domestic market, and yet Heineken stock achieved a P/E ratio of 32.4 in 1999 versus Carlsberg's figure of only 17.1. According to industry analysts, the driving force behind this difference was that Heineken maintained a superior market distribution in terms of growth and margin (see Exhibit 11). The key lesson from examining these global brands appeared to be that great discipline must be applied to focus resources in the right places.

In line with this thinking, a long range marketing plan began to take shape that made use of a series of strategic filters to yield a focused set of attractive opportunities. The first filter that any potential market had to pass through was its long-term volume potential for Stella Artois. This volume had to trace back to a large and/or growing market, the current or potential sizeable premium lager segment (at least five per cent of the total market), and the possibility for Stella Artois to penetrate the top three brands. The second screen was the potential to achieve attractive margins after an initial starting period of approximately three years. The third filter was whether or not a committed local partner was available to provide the right quality of distribution and to co-invest in the brand. The final screen was the determination that success in the chosen focus markets should increase leverage in other local and regional markets. For example, the size and stature of Stella Artois in the United Kingdom was a significant factor in the easy sell-in of Stella Artois into New York in 1999.

Once filtered through these strategic market development screens, the global branding plans for Stella Artois began to take a different shape. Rather than focus on national markets, plans emerged with an emphasis on about 20 cities, some of which Interbrew was already present in (e.g., London, Brussels, New York, etc.). This approach suggested that the next moves should be in such potential markets as Moscow, Los Angeles and Hong Kong. Some existing cities would receive focused efforts only when distribution partner issues had been successfully resolved to solidify the bases for sustained long term growth. The major cities that fit these criteria provided the right concentration of affluent consumers, who would be attracted to Stella's positioning, thus providing scale for marketing and sales, investment leverage, as well as getting the attention and support of motivated wholesalers and initial retail customers. These venues would thereby become highly visible success stories that would be leveragable in the company's ongoing market development plans.

Thus, the evolving global branding development plan required careful planning on a city-by-city basis. Among the demands of this new approach were that marketing efforts and the funding to support them would have to be both centrally stewarded and locally tailored to reflect the unique local environments. A corporate marketing group was, therefore, established and was charged with the responsibility to identify top priority markets, develop core positioning and guidelines for local execution, assemble broadly based marketing programs (e.g., TV, print advertising, global sponsorships, beer.com content, etc.), and allocate resources to achieve the accelerated growth objectives in these targeted cities. To ensure an integrated development effort the company brought all pivotal resources together, under the leadership of a global brand development director. In addition to the brand management team, the group included regional sales managers who were responsible for licensed partner management, a customer services group, a Belgian beer café manager, and cruise business management group. Another significant challenge that faced the corporate marketing group was to ensure that all necessary groups were supportive of the new approach. This was a simpler undertaking among those business units that were wholly owned subsidiaries; it was a more delicate issue in the case of licensees and joint ventures. A key element of managing brands through a global organizational structure was that the head office team had to effectively build partnerships with local managers to ensure their commitment.

Fortunately, much of the initial effort to establish Stella Artois as a global brand had been done on a city-by-city basis and, as such, there was ample opportunity for Interbrew to learn from these experiences as the new global plan evolved. In the late 1990s, for example, Stella Artois was introduced to various Central European cities (e.g., Budapest, Zagreb, Bucharest and Sofia). In each of these cities, Interbrew's marketing efforts were launched when the targeted premium market was at an early stage of development. Further, distribution and promotion was strictly controlled (e.g., product quality, glassware, etc.) and the development initiatives were delivered in a concentrated manner (e.g., a media "blitz" in Budapest). In addition, results indicated that the presence of a Belgian Beer Café accelerated Interbrew's market development plans in these new areas. These early successes suggested that brand success could be derived from the careful and concentrated targeting of young adults living in urban centres, with subsequent pull from outlying areas following key city success.

The key lessons of these efforts in Central Europe proved to be very valuable in guiding the market development plan in New York City. In this key North American city, the rollout of Stella Artois was perceived by the analysts as "one of the most promising introductions in New York over the last 20 years" and had generated great wholesaler support and excitement. Among the tactics used to achieve this early success was selective distribution with targeted point of sale materials support. In addition, a selective media campaign was undertaken that included only prestigious outdoor advertising (e.g., a Times Square poster run through the Millennium celebrations). Similarly, the sponsoring strategy focused only on high-end celebrity events, Belgian food events, exclusive parties, fashion shows, etc. Finally, the price of Stella Artois was targeted at levels above Heineken, to reinforce its gold standard positioning. This concerted and consistent market push created an impact that resulted in the "easiest new brand sell" in years, according to wholesalers. The success of this launch also built brand and corporate credibility, paving the way to introductions in other U.S. cities as well as "opening the eyes" of other customers and distribution partners around the world.

To pursue this new global development plan over the next three years, a revised marketing budget was required. Given that the corporate marketing department was responsible for both the development of core programs as well as the selective support of local markets, the budget had to cover both of these key elements. To achieve these ends, total spending was expected to more than double over the next three years.

While great progress had been made on the global branding of Stella Artois, Cooke still ruminated on a variety of important interrelated issues. Among these issues was the situation of Stella Artois in Belgium—would it be possible to win in the "global game" without renewed growth in the home market? What specific aspirations should Interbrew set for Belgium over the next three years? Further, what expectations should Interbrew have of its global brand market development (e.g., volumes, profit levels, number of markets and cities, etc.)? How should global success be measured? With respect to Interbrew's promotional efforts, how likely would it be that a single global ad campaign could be successful for Stella Artois? Was there a particular sponsorship or promotion idea that could be singled out for global leverage? And what role should the Internet play in developing Stella Artois as a true global brand?

Managing People and Processes across Borders and Cultures

CHAPTER TWELVE

Communicating across Borders and Cultures

Chapter Learning Objectives

After completing this chapter, you should be able to:

- Understand the meaning and significance of communication in international companies and the way that culture differences and cultural context influence the process of communication.

- Discuss the significance of various forms of communication, such as verbal and nonverbal.

- Identify the possible barriers to communication across borders and cultures.

- Understand the implications of computer-mediated communication in global companies.

- Discuss the convergence and divergence of communication patterns around the world.

- Apply concepts that improve communication processes across borders and cultures.

Opening Case: Understanding Others

Much of the debate surrounding the Washington–Beijing standoff over a downed U.S. spy plane involved parsing the linguistic differences of the words regret, sorrow, and apology.

But the incident provides a public illustration of the intricacies that often complicate cross-cultural communication—whether in words, body language, or manners. An unsuspecting person can send the wrong message by how close he stands to someone, how loudly he speaks or by patting someone on the back or even smiling. "I think there are probably more stunning (cultural) contrasts in Asia . . . but boy, you can also get in a lot of trouble in any other part of the world," said Gary P. Ferraro, a cultural anthropologist and author of *The Cultural Dimension of International Business.* Language is perhaps the biggest land mine. Even the best translations can fail when trying to interpret phrases and concepts that have no cultural equivalent.

Americans may be particularly at risk of making mistakes because "ours is a society where words don't mean very much," said Seymour Chatman, a linguist and professor emeritus of rhetoric at the University of California at Berkeley.

For many Americans, getting to the point is more important than choosing words carefully.

In some cases, a cultural gaffe might be dismissed as the funny misstep of a foreigner; other times it can infuriate. In the business sector, companies must be careful in choosing the words for advertising and marketing campaigns for other countries—it can make the difference between success and failure.

"It's about making people comfortable . . . and if they find something offensive, they may not buy from the company," said Michele Scott, a senior account executive with Transperfect Translations in

San Francisco. Scott said her company sends clients some particularly egregious examples of mistakes—such as the infamous Chevy Nova campaign that flopped in Latin America because "no va" means "it does not go" in Spanish.

In 1993, the wildly popular "Got Milk?" campaign was revamped for Spanish-speaking markets after advertisers learned that Latinos interpreted the query more intimately, as in: "Are you lactating?" That same year, confectioner Mars Inc. confused Russians with billboards advertising that M&M's "melt in your mouth, not in your hands." It backfired because the cold climate keeps pretty much anything from melting in anyone's hands.

Soda companies Coca-Cola and Pepsi both faced marketing challenges in China. Coca-Cola can mean "bite the wax tadpole" or "female horse stuffed with wax," depending on the dialect. Coke switched its name to a phonetic equivalent that translated to "happiness in the mouth." Pepsi had its own share of trouble with the advertising slogan it "brings you back to life," which when translated literally means "Pepsi brings your ancestors back from the grave."

The film industry frequently provokes laughs when adding subtitles or renaming movies for foreign distribution. The consensus among Hollywood marketing executives is that Asian distributors give more colorful and descriptive titles for their versions of movies than do their American counterparts. For example, *As Good As It Gets* was shown in Chinese theaters as *Mr. Cat Poop*.

Linguistic misunderstandings can be funny, expensive, even embarrassing for advertisers, tourists or business travelers. But when it comes to international incidents—such as an 11-day dispute over a spy plane—the stakes are great. And often such gaffes point up more profound communications problems between countries.

"This (standoff) was not really about the language per se . . . but the deeper cultural differences," said Kaiping Peng, who teaches classes in Chinese psychology at UC Berkeley. Many Chinese were baffled when American legislators decided to air their opinions publicly by speaking out on television. Elected officials in China are considered government mouthpieces, not independent politicians with individual opinions, said Peng, who comes from China and has published numerous studies on the differences between Asian and American perceptions. The rhetoric "really did not go over very well," he said.

Another culturally telling detail was the Chinese government's insistence that the United States make a statement in writing. "What is interesting is that to Americans, a letter is just a letter, but in Chinese culture, giving a letter symbolizes a show of respect that translates as a letter of apology, even if the words don't exactly say that," Peng said.

There are also major differences in the way Americans and Chinese perceive "group responsibility." Peng said his research has shown that Americans are far more individualistic and reject the notion that an entire country can or should be held responsible for a military action. "One of the good things that will come out of this (standoff) is that people will see that we need to understand people in different cultures better," he said. "Not just the Americans understanding the Chinese perspective, but the Chinese having a greater appreciation of Americans also. Here, we're a superpower, so we tend to take everything for granted and in other places they pay much more attention to the details," Peng said. "And we need to be aware of that."

Source: From *San Francisco Chronicle* "The Nuances of Language," by Anastasia Hendrix, April 15, 2001. Copyright © 2001 by *San Francisco Chronicle*. Reproduced with permission of *San Francisco Chronicle* via Copyright Clearance Center.

Discussion Questions

1. In this case what are the effects of language use on effective communication?
2. What are the effects of ineffective communication on companies such as Coke and Pepsi?
3. In communicating with people from different cultures, did you have any difficulties? Refer to this case as you discuss the unique difficulties you had.

What Is Communication?

The social and cultural environment influences the process that managers use to accomplish tasks in various countries. The variation in beliefs, values, expectations, and the amount of information available influences the process of managing communication. Maintaining effective channels of communication is central in the functioning of multinational and global organizations. Organizations, whether domestic or global, are essentially communication systems, and without an adequate understanding of how communication processes work, managers cannot function effectively.

Communication is the process of conveying data, information, ideas, and thoughts from one person to another. Communicating in the form of writing, talking, listening, or over the Internet is essential to a manager's role and consumes a great deal of time. Previous studies on managerial behavior demonstrate the importance of face-to-face communication. Managers spend 50 to 90 percent of their time communicating orally.[1]

Interpersonal communication is the key to managing the process of motivation, leadership, group interaction, team building, negotiation, and decision making, not only in the home country, but also in subsidiaries around the world. Whether intended or not, cultural values are both explicitly and subtly conveyed in the process of communicating, regardless of the type of communication used. As corporations become global, the success of international business transactions will depend on the ability of managers to communicate effectively across national and cultural boundaries. In culturally diverse countries, such as the United States, United Kingdom, and India, the process of managing heterogeneous work groups and building teams requires an understanding of the role of culture in the communication process.

The Cross-Cultural Communication Process

The person who initiates the communication process is called the *sender,* and the person receiving the communication is the *receiver.* A message is transmitted to the receiver through a *medium,* which can be a face-to-face meeting, a telephone call, an e-mail, or a videoconference, for example. The message is received and interpreted by the receiver and understood. Feedback uses the same processes, with the receiver changing roles to the sender. *Communication effectiveness* is the extent to which the receiver understands the sender's message. *Noise* is distortion or interruption of the message. It can be caused by changes in the message, due to technical problems like phone distortion or by people talking nearby. It can also be caused by selective perception, filtering, language difficulties, information overload, and cultural differences. Exhibit 12.1 outlines the communication process.

Effective communication is accomplished through the use of appropriate language. For example, the variety of English leads to the question: Which English? English spoken in countries where English is the primary business language (such as Britain, Ireland, Scotland, the United States, Australia, New Zealand, India, Nigeria, and South Africa) sounds very different in each country. In some countries, a wrench is a spanner, granulated sugar is caster sugar, and an auto repair shop is a body shop or a panelbeater. In Singapore, Singlish is used, a combination of English, Malay, and a Chinese dialect.

> When I first went to New Zealand, I expected the language to be the same as in the US. After all, I spoke English. My rude awakening came with a television show, a favorite of my husband, who had lived in New Zealand for 30 years. The show was based in Manchester, England, and I could not understand the heavy English dialect at all. In tears, I begged my husband to turn it off. Instead, he explained the words to me. At the beginning, he had to

EXHIBIT 12.1
National and Cultural Influences on the Communication Process

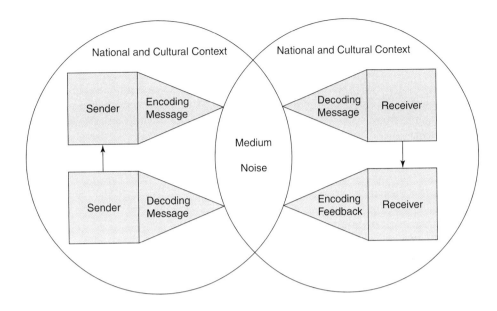

repeat almost every sentence, and luckily the program was rather slow moving. Before we returned to the US, I could "listen with an accent" and understood almost all of the programs on New Zealand television, most of which originated in England or Australia.[2]

Language is closely aligned with environment.[3] Alaskan natives have a myriad of words for different types of snow, depending on the shape, how much is falling, how wet it is, and so on. However, those living at the equator have only the word "snow" to describe the phenomenon. Those living in deserts at the equator have numerous words for different types of dust storms. Whether we are discussing the language use of Alaskan natives or of those living around the equator, different terms for snow and dust have evolved to help them adapt quickly to changing patterns in their environment.

Some cultures have terms for modern technology, but others do not. Maoris (native New Zealanders) have no word for automobile or car, so they use the English words. When the Navaho were enlisted as technicians in World War II, their language was used as code, because it is unique and spoken by only a small group of American natives. However, their language did not have all of the words necessary for military communication, so they created new ones.

People in some cultures object to the encroachments of other languages that might "dilute" their own. The French, for example, have resisted the use of English words for various expressions, and a group of people watch for the infiltration of English language into native French. This group is called the *Académie Française.* The use of words like "sandwich," "weekend," and "jogging," for example, are common in French society, but their use is frowned on by the Académie Française.[4] In modern business, the frequent use of jargon is designed to provide explicit information using only a few words. *Jargon* is technical terminology used in business, science, or art that is specific to the environment in which it evolves. For example, in countries such as Alaska and Siberia, where the climate is generally cold and air-conditioning is not needed, jargon for the technology of air-conditioning has not developed.

Cultural values influence the development of vocabulary. The language of the Navaho, like many other native languages, has few words for the different uses of time.[5] This happens because, in these environments, the flow of time is regulated by seasonal activities and is not based on the movements of an objective clock, as is the

PRACTICAL INSIGHT 12.1

THE CASE OF THE BELGIAN FRENCH FRIES: FOUR PARADIGMS OF INTERNATIONAL COMMUNICATION

You're a U.S. business person who's just begun negotiations in Antwerp. Your Belgian counterparts have taken you to lunch at an outdoor café. When the food comes, one of them turns to you and says, "Have some of these french fries; they're so much better than the terrible fries you have in America!"

How do you respond?

If you're an isolationist, you ignore the challenge and say nothing. Perhaps you change the subject. Conflict is avoided, but communication doesn't happen. The result is lose/lose.

If you're an ugly tourist, you rise to the bait. "Are you kidding? You call these french fries? In America, we wouldn't feed these to a pig." In the right relationship, built over time, a good laugh may follow. But in most cases, the result will be win/lose. You've satisfied your offended honor, but lost a chance to build a relationship.

If you've gone native, you roll over and play dead. "You're absolutely right," you say. "These are much better than we have in the States." You may have ingratiated yourself to your hosts, but you've probably diminished yourself in their eyes. The "lose/win" result has no long-term payoff.

But if you're a global communicator, you say something like, "Ah, I'm sorry that you haven't found good french fries in the United States. Next time you're there, I hope you'll let me take you where you can get some very good ones. Or better yet, I hope you'll let me treat you to some more typically American food. But meanwhile, I certainly enjoy these fries; they're very good indeed!"

The result is win/win. You've shown the courage of your own convictions and a consideration for your hosts' culture. Even more important, you've opened a door to furthering your relationship.

Source: From http://www.komei.com. This article appeared, in a revised form, in the October 1997 issue of *Global Workforce* magazine. It is based, in part, on a model in Stephen R. Covey, Seven Habits of Highly Effective People. Reprinted with permission of the authors.

case in modern cultures. Because of this, Navaho workers, in the past, might have been late for work because the concept of being in a particular place at a specific time was not part of their culture. The concept of "clock time" was not translatable.

Similarly, privacy is not a Chinese cultural value, so there is no word for this concept in the Chinese language.[6] Understanding these differences is important, because if the concept does not exist in the language, then substitutions must be made—but there is no guarantee that such substitutions will be understood correctly. In translations of the word "privacy" from English to Chinese, the Chinese word "reclusiveness" is often used. In the U.S. context, a recluse is considered strange, but in China the word has a much more negative connotation. Therefore, discussing concepts such as "privacy" with Chinese people can lead to noise in communication. Practical Insight 12.1 gives an example of some of these difficulties.

Cultural influences on the use of language cannot be ignored.[7] The choice of words and the form of the message that we send to each other is based on cultural preferences, norms, and values. For example, sending greetings of a personal nature by e-mail is not acceptable in many cultures, particularly in East Asia and Latin America. If the birth of a child or wedding announcement of a daughter were conveyed to a colleague or supervisor by e-mail, many in these countries would find it insulting.

An understanding of the importance of the underlying cultural values is essential when we communicate, particularly across national boundaries. For example, when we say "How are you?" in the United States, most of us do not take it as a question about health, but as an alternative to saying "Hello." In other countries, the other person is likely to interpret the phrase literally and reply in terms of how he or she might be feeling.

Communicating across cultures is more difficult than communicating in one's own culture, because people with different cultural backgrounds have less common information about how to communicate effectively. In Exhibit 12.1, "national and cultural context" refers to culturally based elements of a person's background, such as:

- Beliefs about what is correct to communicate.
- The status of the sender and the receiver.
- Attitude toward the content of the message.
- Stereotypes of the other culture.
- Cultural preferences regarding the medium used.
- Educational level and professional competence of the sender and the receiver.

Exhibit 12.1 shows that the communication process involves the sender of the message, who, through a specific medium, communicates a message to the receiver. All of these elements are influenced by the national and cultural context of the sender and the receiver. The effectiveness of the communication is dependent on a lack of noise, which can occur at any stage, that is in the process of encoding or decoding the message.

The symbols that are used to express an idea can exert a powerful effect on the message content. Symbols are generally highly culture-specific and may introduce noise easily when used excessively. Just as symbols have to be appropriate and communicated with skill, the sender and receiver both must be skilled in adopting appropriate media to convey the message.

The Medium of Communication

A very important part of learning how to communicate in one's own culture, as well as across cultures, is learning how use appropriate media to convey a message. There are two types of media: verbal and nonverbal. **Verbal communication** consists of any oral or written means of transmitting a message through words. **Nonverbal communication** is the art and science of communicating without using words, either in written or spoken form.

Verbal Communication

Different types of verbal communication are used in conducting different types of business transactions. Face-to-face interaction is the preferred method for transmitting emotions or subtle messages and for persuading the receiver to act in a certain way, because nonverbal cues, such as tone of voice, use of silence, and body language, are important. Furthermore, in face-to-face interactions, the sender receives immediate feedback that is rich with both informational and emotional content and has the opportunity to act appropriately.

Telephone communication is the next richer form of communication. It has the potential to transmit some nonverbal cues, such as tone of voice and use of silence, but it is not as effective as face-to-face communication in communicating the content of the total message.

Written communication conveys a great deal of data and information in explicit form and is used widely in all organizations in different parts of the world. Explicit knowledge useful for organizational innovation is best communicated in written form. However, the problem with written communication is that some of the subtleties are not likely to be conveyed effectively, because they can be communicated only by non-verbal means. For example, while the decision to move a manager to a different part of the world can be transmitted in writing, it would be more effectively conveyed face-to-face. We must remember that written communication is the primary method of communicating across subsidiaries of multinational and global communication, and its use is increasing.

Computer-Mediated Communication

Communication through the use of electronic mail (e-mail)—**computer-mediated communication**—has revolutionized communication processes in organizational settings. It is particularly prevalent in global organizations where effective management information systems are the key to maintaining and improving coordination of activities, as discussed in Section 2. In 1970, transmitting the *Encyclopedia Britannica* as an electronic data file from coast to coast within the United States would have cost $187. Today the entire Library of Congress could be transmitted across America for just $40.[8] As the technology of bandwidth expands, costs will fall further, causing even more dramatic improvements in the way managers of multinational and global organizations send and receive information and implement decisions.

E-mail messages are quickly formed, edited, and stored, and they can be transmitted to many people with a simple click of a mouse. There is no need to coordinate a communication session. E-mail allows random access to information, no matter which part of the globe a manager is located in. One can access any message in any order and then move on to others, depending on their usefulness for accomplishing a task or coordinating an activity across geographical boundaries.

E-mail has reduced the need for face-to-face and telephone communication, and it has altered the flow of organizational information. While reducing the need for other types of communication, it has increased the movement of communication across all parts of organizations. Organization- and culture-specific differences in power and status between the sender and receiver are less important in e-mail use than in face-to-face and telephone communication.

However, one problem with e-mail that often causes difficulties is the increased frequency of "flaming"—the act of sending emotional messages without considering the implications. In this respect, e-mails can cause more problems than traditional forms of written communication, which allow more time for reflection before transmission.

Instant messaging is the next step in computer-mediated communication. Instant messaging software connects two or more people located in different parts of the globe, enabling them to communicate with each other instantaneously. For example, if a manager in the United States sends an instant message to a colleague in another part of the world, such as in Brazil, the message will instantly appear not only on the monitor of the Brazilian colleague, but on other monitors connected in the network. Coordinating tasks of multinational and global organizations is becoming easier to accomplish through the technology of instant messaging and networking. Their use is predicted to increase dramatically—from 5.5 million in 2000 to more than 180 million in 2004 and beyond.[9]

Nonverbal Communication

E-mail and other types of computer-mediated communication are changing the way managers of global corporations communicate. But they cannot replace the role of nonverbal communication, which includes facial expressions, tone of voice, physical distance, and the use of silence. For example, Japanese negotiators allow long periods of silence in order to communicate their messages in a manner seldom understood by Western counterparts.[10]

Nonverbal communication is also important in tasks that involve a great deal of emotional labor—the effort, planning, and control needed to express organizationally valued emotions. Individuals in all countries make extensive use of nonverbal cues to transmit necessary feelings to co-workers, customers, and supervisors in the conduct of their duties.

Nonverbal communication differs from verbal communication in many ways. While verbal communication is typically a conscious process, nonverbal communication tends to be somewhat unconscious and culture-specific. For example, Australians tend to be less verbal than Americans in communicating their messages.[11] In many Scandinavian countries, listeners' silence is interpreted as encouragement for the communicator.[12]

The term **kinesic behavior** refers to body movements—physical posture, gestures, facial expressions, and eye contact. While such body movements are universal in nature, their meaning depends on the cultural context, and they cannot be generalized across cultures. Most people worldwide can recognize displays of basic emotions, such as joy, contempt, anger, disgust, fear, and sadness, but the interpretation of special facial expressions that are unique to a cultural context entails significant differences. International managers and visitors who are unaware of the meaning of different facial expressions in different cultures may react incorrectly because they do not have adequate knowledge of the meaning of such expressions. For example, most Westerners would not correctly understand many of the facial expressions of East Asian cultures—sticking out the tongue expresses surprise, scratching the ears and cheeks indicates happiness, and widening of the eyes displays anger.[13]

Proxemics is the study of the role of physical distance between persons and the use of personal space and office layout in the process of communication. Private office space for each manager is common in U.S. organizations. As the manager achieves higher status, the office generally becomes larger and more private. In contrast, in much of Asia as well as in Latin America, an open office layout is more common. Whereas a corner office on the top floor of the building tends to communicate power in the United States and Germany, an office in the middle of the floor reflects power in the United Kingdom and India. The French, on the other hand, like to occupy an office in the middle of subordinates, signifying that they have a central role in the information network, since they like to be in control.[14]

Hall and Hall noted that cultural differences influence how close we allow another person when communicating face-to-face.[15] Americans generally feel uncomfortable and start moving slowly backward when someone is too close. This is because they feel that the person is invading their "space." Proper use of physical distance in maintaining personal space is very important, and unfamiliar approaches that violate our sense of personal space are not appreciated. Some of these distances in the U.S. culture are illustrated in Exhibit 12.2.

EXHIBIT 12.2
A Typology of Physical Distances

Intimate distance	Contact–18 inches—a distance reserved for comforting, protecting, and lovemaking
Personal distance	18 inches–4 feet—a bubble of personal space the size of which depends on the relationship to the other person
Social distance	4–12 feet—used by acquaintances and strangers in more formal settings
Public distance	12–25 feet—distance at which the recognition of others is not required

Source: E. T. Hall and M. R. Hall, *Understanding Cultural Differences* (Yarmouth, ME: Intercultural Press, 1990).

Some cultures encourage people to use their senses—stay close to each other and touch each other in the process of communicating—as part of the communication process. These cultures are called **high-contact cultures,** and they are found among countries around the Mediterranean, the Middle East, Latin America, and southern and eastern Europe. In contrast, cultures of North America, East Asia, and western and northern Europe encourage much less sensory involvement in the communication process. In these **low-contact cultures,** the preference is to stand apart and not touch each other while communicating. We find low-contact cultures in cooler climates of the world, whereas high-contact cultures are found mostly around the equator. For example, Americans stand roughly 18 inches apart when they communicate, and standing closer will result in the person backing away from the contact.

Environmental Context of Communication

Hall and Hall discuss the significance of context in determining the amount of communication that can be accomplished without a great deal of communication noise.[16] Communication takes place in a context, and the specific meaning and interpretation that are provided by individuals in the context is a part of the message.

Cultures of Asia, the Middle East, Latin America, the Mediterranean, and parts of Africa are called **high-context cultures.** In these cultures, members do not convey feeling and thoughts very explicitly and must develop an ability to detect subtle meanings and nonverbal messages that are present in the physical context of the communication. Information and knowledge of relationships are important, such as whether one is communicating with the members of the ingroup or outgroup, the nature of historical relationships that existed among the parties, and the various patterns of obligations and norms.

In **low-context cultures,** which are found in Canada and the United States, as well as countries of western and northern Europe, such attention to the context is not needed. Communication in these cultures does not need the detailed information demanded for communication in high-context cultures. Explicit forms of communication, especially written communication, are preferred. The Swiss culture is least concerned with context in communication, as depicted in Exhibit 12.3.[17]

When people from low-context cultures communicate with those in high-context cultures, the potential for distortion and misunderstanding is significant, as illustrated

EXHIBIT 12.3
Contrasting Patterns of Communication in Low- versus High-Context Cultures

Source: Based on information drawn from Edward T. Hall and M. R. Hall, *Understanding Cultural Differences* (Yarmouth, ME: Intercultural Press, 1990); and Martin Rosch. "Communications: Focal Point of Culture," *Management International Review* 27, no. 4 (1987), p. 60.

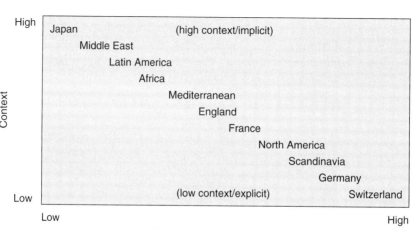

PRACTICAL INSIGHT 12.2

THE RELATIVE IMPORTANCE OF ENCODING MESSAGES IN WORDS

In a training session to orient mainland Chinese to North American work practices, one of the authors delivered a half-day session about putting "messages into words." The theme was that in North American business environments, if you have a problem, you should articulate it to someone rather than struggle along trying to cope in silence.

At mid-day, the trainer and trainees sat together around their conference table to eat lunches they had brought. The room had a kettle along with a box of Chinese tea so the trainees could enjoy a cup of tea with their lunch and throughout the day. The trainees were not accustomed to having trainers eat lunch with them, but nevertheless they graciously asked her if she would like some tea. She said yes, thank you very much, she would like tea.

A few minutes later, she was politely presented with a cup of boiled water. Where was the tea? She asked. All gone, she was told. When? A few days ago. Why, she asked, didn't anyone say anything sooner?

After some exploratory discussion, several reasons emerged. One trainee volunteered that they weren't sure the trainer, a teacher who automatically had high status in their eyes, was the right person to ask about something like tea. They didn't want to insult her. Another trainee said they didn't want to mention the exhausted tea supply to the trainer in case

that made her feel obliged to buy tea, paying out of her own pocket. They weren't certain the program had funds for additional tea for her to be reimbursed if she did buy them tea. They also felt perhaps they should have replaced the tea themselves, but hadn't worked out an equitable mechanism yet for doing so. In any case, that meant the risk of an expenditure that might turn out to be unnecessary.

No doubt the unannounced presence of a trainer at their lunch table raised another uneasy question in their minds: Were they supposed to have reserved some tea in case a trainer decided to have some? Finally, a young man daringly offered the opinion that in China, the person who identified a problem was then identified with the problem and in his words, "became the problem." It was better not to draw attention to a problem, he said, and the others agreed that this could be true.

This episode says a number of things about expectations by the trainer and different expectations by the trainees about communication. The Chinese were conscious of the social impact of their words, and therefore chose to communicate in actions rather than risk a consequence that was difficult for them to calculate accurately. The act of offering a cup of boiled water in a context where tea was expected was as eloquent as any specifically worded message.

Source: From K. Beamer and I. Varner, *Intercultural Communication in the Global Workplace*, 2nd Edition, 2001, p. 144. Copyright © 2001 The McGraw-Hill Companies, Inc. Reprinted with permission.

in Practical Insight 12.2. Those in high-context cultures would like individuals from low-context cultures to understand the importance of things that are not clearly stated. Proxemics, subtle gestures, and various cues that are present in the physical context are important in communicating with members of high-context cultures. Similarly, managers from low-context cultures get the impression that those in high-context cultures are not open in their communication of views and opinions. For example, East Asians tend to like people who are not talkative, whereas Americans dislike silence and will talk to fill silent spaces.[18]

In Germany and the United States, dominance frequently is expressed through talking, but the manner of speaking of the one wishing to dominate the conversation differs between the two countries. Americans who dominate the conversation speak loudly with a greater use of expressive movements, whereas dominant Germans show a lesser range of expressive movements but high degree of verbal fluency.

Barriers to Effective Communication

Barriers that cause difficulties when communicating across borders and cultures include selective perception and stereotypes, saving face, self-disclosure, etiquette, humor, truthfulness, elaborate versus succinct discourse, and silence.

Selective Perception and Stereotypes

Perception is the process of receiving information from the external world around us. We decide what kind of information we should notice carefully, how to categorize the information, and how to incorporate it into our existing knowledge framework. **Stereotyping** is the process of attributing traits to people on the basis of their group membership. Stereotypes tend to define people by their demographic, ethnic, organizational, and national memberships. For example, some stereotypes about cultural groups are reflected in the beliefs that Germans are methodical, Italians are emotional, British are domineering, and Japanese are highly work-oriented.

In Chapter 5, we discussed the role of cultural differences in influencing the way people perceive and stereotype individuals from other countries and cultures. Because of the cultural context in which they function, individuals develop tendencies to pay more attention to certain informational cues from the environment and to ignore others. For example, if a German manager asks German subordinates for some ideas about improving work processes, the subordinates will likely understand that the questions are truly seeking their opinions and perceive them positively. However, these questions asked by a German manager to a group of Greek subordinates create the perception that the German manager is not knowledgeable about the work.

Another example of mistaken perceptions concerns the way colleagues and superiors are addressed in the workplace. Whereas informality is emphasized in the United States, surnames with the appropriate title are more frequently used in India. For example, someone named Rajen Singh would be called "Mr. Singh" as opposed to "Rajen" or "Raj." A U.S. manager who uses the American practice of calling a person by the first name might be introducing some barriers to communication.

Stereotyping acts as a major barrier to effective intercultural communication, because it creates certain expectations that may not be true. For example, if an American manager has preconceived notions that Mexican employees do not work hard, then he or she might not be willing to emphasize the rewards associated with hard work. This can lead to potential misunderstandings in communication and conflict, especially because this stereotype is inaccurate when generalized to Mexican workers. Research has shown that managers who are most effective internationally are able to change their stereotypes quickly as they come into contact with people of different cultures. Managers who are least effective internationally are unable to change their stereotypes, even after working with people who acted differently from the established cultural stereotypes.[19]

Importance of Saving Face

Saving face is the process of preserving one's reputation and connectedness in a social context. In a sense, it is related to the concept of politeness, and it has both verbal and nonverbal connotations. Ting-Toomey[20] suggested that people from all cultures like to save face, but "saving face" is especially important in the collectivistic cultures of East Asia and the Middle East. In individualistic cultures, the concept of face is primarily focused on highlighting the person's positive qualities and deemphasizing the negative qualities. Since smooth maintenance of social connectedness is of secondary importance in individualistic cultures, there is less of an emphasis on saving face.

Despite our best intentions, sometimes we might find ourselves in situations where we lose face. For example, when a manager is told in public that his or her analysis of the marketing strategy is wrong, he or she loses face. Criticizing someone in public, in the East Asian context, is particularly forbidden. Managers wishing to achieve successful communication networks in East Asia and the Middle East should pay particular attention to the concept of saving face.

Importance of Self-Disclosure

Self-disclosure is the process of revealing personal information about oneself to others.[21] Self-disclosure is important in maintaining improved communication ties in Western (individualistic) cultures. But excessive self-disclosure regarding social and personal situations in collectivistic cultures may lead to difficulties unless the person communicates with members of an already established ingroup. Barnlund's study of private and public self in Japan and the United States illustrates the importance of self-disclosure in the communication process.[22] Japanese prefer a communication style where relatively little about oneself is made available to others in everyday interaction. A majority of information that one knows about oneself is kept strictly private—the private self is relatively large. In contrast, the preferred style of communication in the United States is one in which an apparently large amount of information about oneself is given to others—the public self is relatively large—while little information about oneself is hidden from public exposure—the private self is considered to be relatively small. This is shown in Exhibit 12.4. The French consider Americans easy to make

EXHIBIT 12.4
Self-Disclosure and Intercultural Communication

Source: Reprinted with permission from *Business Horizons,* March–April 1989. Copyright © 1989 by the Trustees at Indiana University, Kelley School of Business.

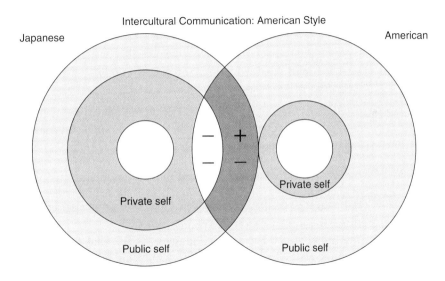

Intercultural Communication: American Style

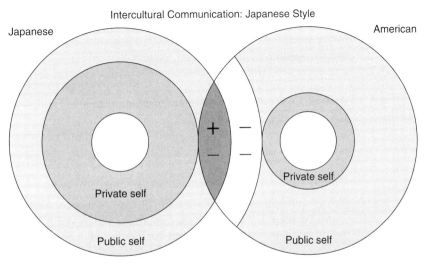

Intercultural Communication: Japanese Style

friends with in the work context, but difficult to develop deep and meaningful relationships with. The difficulties of getting to know an American manager at the personal level has been found by Greeks, Egyptians, Chinese, and other cultures as well.

Etiquette in Communication

Cultures differ in what they consider to be polite communication, and **etiquette** is concerned with the way requests can be conveyed, approved, or refused.[23] For example, social interactions in Filipino and Japanese cultures are based on smooth interpersonal relationships and, as discussed earlier, saving face is important. Americans assigned to the Philippines as Peace Corps volunteers were instructed to be frank and direct in requesting information or supplies from the local community leaders. This turned out to be a big mistake—the American directness was considered impolite and inconsiderate, that is, lacking knowledge of the etiquette of the local culture.[24] Note these other examples:

- The Chinese are known to use ambiguous terms in communication, to a much greater extent than is the case in western Europe and the United States, mainly because of their greater emphasis on face saving.[25]
- In work group discussions, Japanese take shorter turns in which everyone is given an equal time. Americans take longer turns, distributed unevenly, and the initiator of the topic is given more time to express his or her point of view.[26]
- The use of the word "no" is infrequent in many Asian countries, so that a "yes" can mean "no" or "maybe."

Rules about extending and accepting invitations are also related to the communication etiquette of the culture. A Westerner may invite an Asian and receive what would be considered an affirmative reply, only to be surprised when the visitor does not arrive. The Asian's response is not affirmative to *coming to the American's home,* but simply indicates that he received the invitation and was pleased.[27] Triandis tells the story of an American visitor asking his Greek acquaintance what time to arrive for dinner. The Greek villager replied "Anytime."[28] In the United States, the expression "anytime" is a noninvitation that people give to appear polite, and it is not necessarily a serious invitation. The Greek, however, meant that the American would be welcome anytime at all, because in his culture, it would be rude to give a guest a definite time of arrival. In some cultures, "thank you" is expressed in written form, but in other cultures "thank you" can be conveyed by appropriate polite gestures.[29]

The intensity of speaking also varies around the world. Arabs and those from countries around the Mediterranean tend to speak loudly, and northern Europeans interpret this as shouting or disagreement. Americans and French speak louder than the English, who sometime find this overly assertive.

Japanese differ from Americans with respect to situations that might require an apology, and the manner that an acceptable apology is phrased and communicated.[30] In Japan, a remark that might cause a co-worker to lose face in public would be considered a situation requiring immediate remedy and verbal apology. In the United States, the remedy and apology may come later and may be in writing.

Humor in Communication

Not all cultures appreciate the significance of **humor.** Although smiling is associated with happiness in all cultures, a smiling face may not be appreciated as communicating direct and honest information in all cultures.[31] The Chinese associate smiling with a lack of self-control and tranquillity—two culturally significant and valued outcomes

PRACTICAL INSIGHT 12.3

AD CITING KASHMIR STIRS FURY IN INDIA

An advertisement run last week by Cadbury India, the local unit of the multinational candy and soft drink maker Cadbury Schweppes, has stirred up a national political controversy and obliged the company to issue a public apology.

The ad, promoting the company's Temptations brand of chocolates, appeared in copies of *The Times of India* distributed in and around Bombay on Aug. 15, the 55th anniversary of Indian independence. It included a map of India highlighting the state of Jammu and Kashmir—all of it, including the portion that has been controlled for years by Pakistan, which also claims the whole state.

"I'm good," read the text of the ad. "I'm tempting. I'm too good to share. What am I? Cadbury's Temptations or Kashmir?"

Politicians and activists of the Hindu nationalist Bharatiya Janata Party reacted with fury, saying the ad trivialized the conflict over Kashmir, the only predominantly Muslim state to remain part of India when Pakistan was formed. The Kashmir dispute has led to two of the three wars fought by the two countries since 1947, and they appeared on the brink of another war over it earlier this year. Political violence in the state has claimed tens of thousands of lives; India has accused Pakistan of backing extremist groups and infiltrating provocateurs into the state to foment trouble.

After the B.J.P. staged protest rallies outside Cadbury India's offices in Bombay and newspaper editorials lambasted the company for insensitivity, Cadbury India issued a statement on Tuesday retracting the ad.

Source: From "Ad Citing Kashmir Stirs Fury in India," August 23, 2003. Copyright © 2003 The New York Times Co. Reprinted with permission.

in Chinese societies. Research has also shown that Americans tend to associate smiling with intelligence, but Japanese do not make such associations. Americans are offended if they are told that they lack a sense of humor in communication, but this is not the case in East Asia and other collectivistic cultures, where such associations are rare. An instance where humor backfired is illustrated in Practical Insight 12.3.

Truthfulness in Communication

An important aspect of communicating across culture that can be tricky is the concept of what is considered **truthfulness.** In cultures that emphasize universalistic values (see Chapter 5), truth is thought of as an absolute, just as laws of the society are applicable to all citizens, regardless of rank or status. However, in particularistic and collectivistic cultures, social sensitivity and tact might override the importance of blunt truthfulness.[32] "White lies"—vague or ambiguous and untrue statements that are said to preserve harmony in a closely knit group—are widely forgiven in particularistic cultures. Here again, the notion of saving face by saying things that may not be absolutely true is of paramount importance. These tendencies are also present in universalistic cultures, but they are less frequent.

Elaborate versus Succinct Communication

Another barrier to communication is the extent to which members of a given nation or culture prefer elaborate versus succinct ways of communicating. **Elaborate communication** uses a large quantity of words to convey a message, and it often includes exaggeration, metaphors, analogies, and proverbs to make a point. On the other hand, **succinct communication** uses the fewest words necessary to convey a message.

The practice of *mubalaqha,* translated as exaggeration, is common in the Middle East. Arabs are expected to make inflated statements to those who are not members of their ingroup or culture, such as Westerners. If they do not, they are considered to be ineffective at managing the process of communication.[33] An example concerns the manner in which then U.S. Secretary of State James Baker told the Iraqi leader in 1991 that the invasion of Kuwait would lead to massive retaliation. Analysis by commentators suggested that the reason why such threats were not taken seriously was because Baker did not deliver his threats with sufficient exaggeration. Because of this, Iraqi Foreign Minister Tariq Aziz did not think the threats were credible.

Silence

As we discussed earlier, use of **silence** is regarded as effective strategy for communicating in some parts of the world. For example, Americans describe talking as pleasant and important for maintaining smooth communication, whereas Chinese perceive silence and quiet as a way of responding to communication.[34] Expatriate managers from the West working in countries where silence is a valued tool in the communication process must recognize its importance and respect its use.

In Practical Insight 12.4, some ways to avoid problems in cross-cultural communication are highlighted.

The Role of Information Technology in Communication across Borders and Cultures

The use of sophisticated information technology and management information systems—that is, computer-mediated communication systems—allows managers and employees of global corporations to communicate with each other easily and frequently. It has been suggested that the increased use of e-mail, facsimile, Internet and intranets, and other related advances in technology have resulted in a convergence of communication styles. The extensive use of the Internet in multinational and global corporations is making transmission of data, information, and knowledge easier. Mobile phones are not only digital, but also high-speed digital with Internet access available. We are increasingly seeing the merging of various forms of communication technologies, such as e-mail, Internet, mobile phone, PCs, and personal organizers.

These changes, along with the widespread use of English in international communications, will lead to strong tendencies to develop similar communication patterns in dissimilar countries and cultures. However, English may not always be the dominant language of the Internet. Since the use of language and culture are intertwined, whether these technological developments will lead to a universal style of communication is not clear. About 4,000 to 5,000 different languages are spoken in over 140 countries around the world. While the largest group of people in the world, about 1.1 billion, speak Mandarin Chinese, English is the second most commonly used language.[35] Chinese and other East Asian languages use characters for entire words, rather than using an alphabet, so that developing a keyboard for use in computer-mediated communications is a difficult endeavor. This means that global corporations using English as the primary business language must make changes in their patterns of communication with their Chinese subsidiaries. An increase of more than 70 percent in non-English Internet sites and users has been estimated.[36]

Computer-mediated communication increases the amount of information that is available to users on a global scale. However, it does not guarantee that the information will be absorbed correctly or change the preexisting value systems of the receivers. Members of multinational work teams retain their culture-specific ways of communicating, problem solving, and decision making.[37] This is true for virtual teams of global corporations, composed of members of different cultures.[38] E-mail communication is not as personal as face-to-face communication, which is preferred in many parts of the world. Some factors that lead to divergence of communication patterns cannot be

PRACTICAL INSIGHT 12.4

POTENTIAL HOT SPOTS IN CROSS CULTURAL COMMUNICATION

This is not meant to be an exhaustive list, but when working with other people, or traveling abroad for work or pleasure, it may pay to ask some experts about the following communication styles of the area you plan to visit. A little research at the outset can stave off a host of misunderstandings:

1. *Opening and Closing Conversations:* Different cultures may have different customs around who addresses whom when and how, and who has the right, or even the duty, to speak first, and what is the proper way to conclude a conversation. Think about it: no matter where you are, some ways of commencing a conversation or concluding one will be considered as rude, even disrespectful. These are artificial customs, to a certain degree, and there is probably no universally right or wrong way to go about these things, short of behaviors that all cultures would likely consider to be vulgar or abusive. This topic includes modes of address, salutations, levels of deference to age or social position, acceptable ways to conclude gracefully and so on. Obviously, and to the dismay of many of us in the West, this will also cover gender differences.

2. *Taking Turns During Conversations:* In some cultures, it is more appropriate to take turns in an interactive way, and in others, it is more important to listen thoroughly and without comment, without immediate response, lest a response be taken as a challenge or a humiliation, particularly depending on the context of the conversation, the audience, and the levels of personal knowledge/relationship between the two people interacting. For example, a Western couple or pair of executives may feel perfectly comfortable interacting in a give and take way in a public market, but if that public market is in a part of the world where such a public display of give and take is considered to be in bad taste, then they may be giving offense without ever realizing it.

3. *Interrupting:* The same issues arise over the issue of interrupting. In some cultures, interruption, vocal, emotional expression, etc. are considered to be the default conversational style, particularly among those considered to be equals, or among men. Many people of Northern European or American extract might mistake this kind of conversation for argument and hostility, but that would not be the case.

4. *Use of Silence:* In some forms of communication, silence is to be expected before a response, as a sign of thoughtfulness and deference to the original speaker, yet at other times, silence may be experienced as a sign of hostility. In the West, twenty seconds of silence during a meeting is an extraordinarily long time, and people will feel uncomfortable with that. Someone invariably will break in to end the uncomfortable silence. But the same customs around silence are not universal.

5. *Appropriate Topics of Conversation:* In some places, it is considered vulgar to speak openly about money, for example, let alone about the kinds of intimate family issues that commonly form the basis of afternoon television "talk" shows in the West. Travelers or business people should learn the customs that surround the making of deals, the transaction of commerce, and the degree to which details are specified in advance and enumerated in writing across cultures (not all places are as prone to hire lawyers and create detailed contracts as we are in the West).

6. *Use of Humor:* In the West, we often try to build immediate rapport through humor, but of course, this is not universally seen to be appropriate in all contexts. The use of laughter can be experienced as a sign of disrespect by some, and so it is important to understand that this is another area where misunderstandings can be very likely to occur.

7. *Knowing How Much to Say:* In some places, less is definitely more, whereas in other places, it is more valued to wrap a rather small point up in a longer preamble, followed by an extended wrap-up. For Westerners, this can be maddening, as we tend to value speaking directly and to the point. Then again, there are clearly circumstances where Westerners say too much and lose their ability to communicate well, depending on the context. Of course, patterns around presumed areas of deference based on age and social standing can influence how much is appropriate to say, depending on the culture.

8. *Sequencing Elements During Conversation:* At what point during a conversation—or an extended conversation or negotiation—is it appropriate to touch upon more sensitive issues? Or how soon in a conversation is it appropriate simply to ask for directions? Since all cultures develop customs through which sensitive issues can be addressed in a way that connotes respect to all involved, and since those systems all can differ, it is important to understand the influence that sequence has on effectiveness. For us in the West, think about the process of asking, or being asked out on a date (a very Western process and one whose customs can be very fluid indeed). The right question, asked in the right way, but asked too soon or too late, according to custom, can connote very different things to the listener, and highly influence subsequent behavior. Sequencing and timing do matter.

Source: Copyright © 2003 A. J. Schuler. Dr. A. J. Schuler is a speaker, consultant and leadership coach. To find out more about his programs and services, visit www.AJSchuler.com or call (703)370-6545.

PRACTICAL INSIGHT 12.5

THE WAY TO REACH AN ITALIAN? NOT E-MAIL
Italians are famous for their mobile-phone addiction: More than 80% of them own at least one. But an aversion to e-mail may be just as profound, much to the chagrin of Lucio Stanca, the former head of IBM's European operations. As Italy's new technology minister, Stanca must automate as many government procedures as possible. Yet he's having trouble just getting his colleagues to log on. His first report recommends the government adopt across-the-board Internet communication by the end of 2003. But it was sent to government offices only by snail mail because Stanca says that, from what he can tell, "no one opens their e-mail" in Italy.

Maybe Stanca could learn a few tricks from Telecom Italia chief executive Marco Tronchetti Provera, who was looking to gather his telecom managers for a March 6 meeting. Rather than bother with e-mail, Provera sent 2,000 short text messages to their cell phones. The result: record turnout. Perhaps Stanca should learn to make his reports shorter.

Source: Reprinted from Kate Carlisle, "National Aversions: The Way to Reach an Italian? Not E-mail," April 15, 2002 issue of *BusinessWeek* by special permission. Copyright © 2002 by The McGraw-Hill Companies, Inc.

reduced simply by using the same language and the same type of technology. However, if Internet communication can reflect subtleties and nuances of language and business practices, it will foster more effective communication. International managers should be concerned with managing both convergence and divergence of communication patterns. Some of these are illustrated in Practical Insight 12.5.

Guidelines for Managing across Borders and Cultures

The role of communication in successfully coordinating activities of multinational and global corporations is increasing every day. Over 80 percent of a manager's day is spent communicating.[39] As globalization spreads to different parts of the world, and cultural diversity increases in multinational and global corporations, successful communication is critical. Managers should have appropriate communication abilities and skills to carry out their activities and operations—to negotiate and make decisions, to motivate employees, and to exercise leadership. As discussed in this chapter, there are significant problems in encoding and decoding messages that are sent across borders and cultures. A tendency to rely heavily on computer-mediated communication, such as the Internet or e-mail, might lead to the belief that people around the world are beginning to form common patterns of communication. However, this is not necessarily true. National and cultural differences in customs, beliefs, values, attitudes, and intentions regarding how one should communicate to co-workers, supervisors, and customers can make significant differences. These differences have implications for productivity in multinational and global companies.

The following guidelines will be helpful in effective communication across borders and cultures:

- *Learn the language of the country.* It is important to have fluency in the language of the country where one is posted. Even if there is not fluency, some knowledge of the language is a significant plus in communicating effectively with colleagues, customers, workers, and government officials. Some companies offer language training programs to improve language skills. General Electric and ExxonMobil conduct language training for the families of expatriate managers.

- *Develop cultural sensitivity in communication.* Traveling around the globe and encountering different cultures is the best way to develop cultural sensitivity, but such travel is not always possible for young expatriates or managers of global corporations. Therefore, it is important that companies train expatriates and managers who will be dealing with those from different cultures. General Electric and Exxon-Mobil, beyond language training, also offer programs for expatriate managers and families to address diverse cultural issues, such as customs and cultural mores, relevant to communication and other functions. It is important to learn the language of the country in which one is going to be located, but it is not enough. Developing cultural sensitivity in communication requires understanding the bits and pieces of the customs, practices, and manners of the country.

- *Learn to properly encode and decode messages.* Communication, as we discussed earlier, involves clear encoding by senders and distortion-free decoding by the receiver. Managers need to choose the medium with enough richness to be effective in the cultural context.

- *Develop appropriate feedback mechanisms.* Communication effectiveness is improved when individuals and global organizations develop and implement appropriate mechanisms to receive feedback. For example, a company introducing new technology affecting work processes should develop culturally appropriate ways to announce the changes and to allow employees to give feedback.

- *Develop empathy.* Active listening involves trying to understand the other person's point of view and considering that it might be the correct one for that person—given his or her national and cultural background. It is important to develop empathy, which is putting oneself in the speaker's shoes. When this occurs, some of the listener's beliefs might be challenged; however, to be effective, keeping an open mind and listening sensitively are essential.

Summary

Multinational and global corporations cannot be successful without effective use of communication. Success or failure of communication is determined by whether the receiver understands the sender's message. A number of national and cultural factors influence the effectiveness of communication across national borders. Noise in communication due to the type of medium used, status and power differences, and differences in verbal and nonverbal expression can exercise powerful effects.

Other barriers to effective communication are related to selective attention to certain types of informational cues and also to the context of the communication. For example, high-context cultures emphasize nonverbal aspects of communication more than do low-context cultures. Therefore, e-mail may not be as acceptable in high-context cultures (like Japan) as it is in low-context cultures (like the United States or United Kingdom). Extensive use of computer-mediated communication may improve speed and accuracy of data, information, and knowledge transmission; however, there is no guarantee that people in different parts of the world will develop similar styles of communication.

Key Terms and Concepts

communication, *366*	humor, *376*	saving face, *374*
computer-mediated communication, *370*	kinesic behavior, *371*	self-disclosure, *375*
	low-contact cultures, *372*	silence, *378*
elaborate communication, *377*	low-context cultures, *372*	stereotyping, *374*
etiquette, *376*	nonverbal communication, *369*	succinct communication, *377*
high-contact cultures, *372*	perception, *374*	truthfulness, *377*
high-context cultures, *372*	proxemics, *371*	verbal communication, *369*

Discussion Questions

1. What is communication and why is it important in managing multinational and global corporations?
2. Think of the communication model shown in Exhibit 12.1. How do your own experiences in communicating with people from other cultures illustrate some of the processes shown? What were the difficulties? What would you do to overcome these difficulties in the future?
3. What are the various forms of communication that are used in international corporations? Give examples of each type.
4. How do stereotypes and selective perception act as obstacles to effective communication? How important are these factors in communication across cultures?
5. Managers of many global corporations believe that the Internet and e-mail are making communication much easier. Is this necessarily true? Explain why or why not.

Minicase

Johannes van den Bosch Sends an Email

Joseph J. DiStefano

After having had several email exchanges with his Mexican counterpart over several weeks without getting the expected actions and results, Johannes van den Bosch was getting a tongue-lashing from his British MNC client, who was furious at the lack of progress. Van den Bosch, in the Rotterdam office of BigFiveFirm, and his colleague in the Mexico City office, Pablo Menendez, were both seasoned veterans, and van den Bosch couldn't understand the lack of responsiveness.

A week earlier, the client, Malcolm Smythe-Jones, had visited his office to express his mounting frustration. But this morning he had called with a stream of verbal abuse. His patience was exhausted.

Feeling angry himself, van den Bosch composed a strongly worded message to Menendez, and then decided to cool off. A half hour later, he edited it to "stick to the facts" while still communicating the appropriate level of urgency. As he clicked to send the message, he hoped that it would finally provoke some action to assuage his client with the reports he had been waiting for.

He reread the email, and as he saved it to the mounting record in Smythe-Jones's file, he thought, "I'm going to be happy when this project is over for another year!"

Message for Pablo Menendez

> *Subject: IAS 1998 Financial statements*

> *Author: Johannes van den Bosch (Rotterdam)*

> *Date: 10/72/99 1:51 P.M.*

Dear Pablo,

This morning I had a conversation with Mr. Smythe-Jones (CFO) and Mr. Parker (Controller) re the finalization of certain 1998 financial statements. Mr. Smythe-Jones was not in a very good mood.

He told me that he was very unpleased by the fact that the 1998 IAS financial statements of the Mexican subsidiary still has not been finalized. At the moment he holds us responsible for this process. Al-

Author's Note: The author prepared this mini-case as a basis for class discussion rather than to illustrate either effective or ineffective handling of a business situation. The mini-case reports events as they occurred. The email exchanges in both cases are reported verbatim, except for the names, which have been changed. Professor DiStefano acknowledges with thanks the cooperation of Johannes van den Bosch in providing this information and his generous permission to use the material for executive development.

though he recognizes that local management is responsible for such financial statements, he blames us for not being responsive on this matter and inform him about the process adequately. I believe he also recognizes that we have been instructed by Mr. Whyte (CEO) not to do any handholding, but that should not keep us from monitoring the process and inform him about the progress.

He asked me to provide him tomorrow with an update on the status of the IAS report and other reports pending.

Therefore I would like to get the following information from you today:

- *What has to be done to finalize the Mexican subsidiary's IAS financials;*

- *Who has to do it (local management, B&FF Mexico, client headquarters; B&FF Rotterdam);*

- *A timetable when things have to be done in order to finalize within a couple of weeks or sooner;*

- *A brief overview why it takes so long to prepare and audit the IAS f/s; and*

- *Are there any other reports for 1998 pending (local gaap, tax), if so the above is also applicable for those reports.*

As of today I would like to receive an update of the status every week. If any major problems arise during the finalization process I would like to be informed immediately. The next status update is due January 12, 2000.

Mr. Smythe-Jones also indicated that in the future all reports (US GAAP, local GAAP and IAS) should be normally finalized within 60 days after the balance sheet date. He will hold local auditors responsible for monitoring this process.

Best regards and best wishes for 2000.

Johannes

JOHANNES VAN DEN BOSCH RECEIVES A REPLY

A little more than an hour later, with his own patience again wearing thin, Johannes van den Bosch watched with relief as Pablo Menendez's name popped into his Inbox messages. His smile quickly turned to disbelief, and then horror, as he read the response from Mexico City. Not only was the client's need still unmet, but now he had another problem! Stung by the apparent anger from Menendez, and totally puzzled as to the cause, he reread the email to make sure he had not misunderstood the message.

——Original Message——

From:	*Menendez, Pablo (Mexico City)*
Sent:	*Wednesday December 10, 23:11*
To:	*van den Bosch, Johannes (Rotterdam)*
Subject:	*RE: IAS 1998 financial statements*
Importance:	*High*

Dear Johannes,

I am not surprised of the outcome of your meeting with Mr. Smythe-Jones (CFO). However, I cannot answer your request until I heard from local management. As it was agreed on the last meeting, we were precluded from doing any work without first getting approval from management at the headquarters and we were instructed by local management from not doing anything until they finalized what was required from us. It appears to me to be a Catch 22 game! I believe we (your Firm and ours) should not fall in the game of passing the ball to someone else before getting a clear understanding of what is going on. We have had several meetings with local management where the issue has been raised and were responded that other priorities were established by the headquarters (on my end I thought they tell you everything they have been instructed of locally, unfortunately it does not seem to be the case). In my opinion it looks very easy that you accept from management at the headquarters to hold us accountable from something we are not responsible of, and this does not mean I do not understand the pressure you are receiving from your end. However, we are not the enemy. I am not sending copy of this message to our client because I believe that internal issues have to be primarily dealt of internally without involving our clients in the internal politics. The last is what myself truly believe.

Could you tell me how can you accept a deadline from our Firm without first having involved local management? Don't you think they are the first to be involved local management? Don't you think they are the first to be involved on this? I may be wrong but if we are in an international Firm I think we should understand the other side and not just blame someone else of our client's problems.

I really do not want to be rude, but you do not let me any option.

Despite the differences we have had, it has been a pleasure working with you.

Best regards and seasons greeting.

Pablo Menendez

Worried that he had somehow offended Menendez, van den Bosch printed off a copy of the email which he had sent the day before, and asked the two partners on either side of his office for their reaction to the message. The audit and tax specialists, one Dutch and the other Belgian, had nearly identical replies. "It seems to me that you got the point across clearly, Johannes," they said. "You laid out the facts and proposed actions to solve the problem. Why do you ask?" they queried. When he showed them the letter, they too were puzzled. "Smythe-Jones will no doubt be the next person to send me a message!" he thought. As a frown reflected his increasingly grim mood, van den Bosch wondered what he should do now.

DISCUSSION QUESTIONS

1. Why is Mr. Smyth-Jones upset with the situation? Is his upset reasonable? Should he hold the Rotterdam company responsible for the process?

2. Is Mr. van den Bosch correct in assuming that the e-mail from Mr. Menendez reflects anger? Is there anything in Mr. van den Bosch's e-mail that would have upset Mr. Menendez? If so, why?

3. Would you have done anything differently? Why or why not?

4. What should Mr. van den Bosch do to continue with his assignment and monitor the financial statements?

Notes

1. H. Mintzberg, *The Nature of Managerial Work* (New York: Harper & Row, 1973).

2. From an anonymous student at the University of Memphis, 2003.

3. R. Mead, *Cross-Cultural Management Communication* (New York: John Wiley & Sons, 1990).

4. L. Beamer and I. Varner, *Intercultural Communication in the Global Workplace,* 2nd ed. (Boston: McGraw-Hill/Irwin, 2001).

5. E. T. Hall, *The Silent Language* (New York: Doubleday, 1959).

6. Beamer and Varner, *Intercultural Communication.*

7. Ibid.

8. "The 21st Century Corporation," *Business Week,* November 6, 2000.

9. M. McCance, "IM: Rapid, Risky," *Richmond (VA) Times-Dispatch,* July 19, 2001, p. A1; C. Hempel, "Instant-Message Gratification Is What People Want," *Ventura County (CA) Star,* April 9, 2001.

10. J. L. Graham, "The Influence of Culture on the Process of Business Negotiations: An Exploratory Study," *Journal of International Business Studies* 16 (1985), pp. 81–96; H. Morsbach, "Aspects of Non-verbal Communication in Japan." In L. A. Samovar and R. E. Porter, eds., *Intercultural Communication: A Reader.* (Belmont, CA: Wadsworth, 1982), pp. 300–316.

11. R. A. Barraclough, D. M. Christophel, and J. C. McCroskey, "Willingness to Communicate: A Cross-Cultural Investigation," *Communication Research Reports* (1988), pp. 187–192.

12. J. Wiemann, V. Chen, and H. Giles, *Beliefs about Talk and Silence in a Cultural Context.* Paper presented to the Speech Communication Association, Chicago, Illinois, 1986.

13. O. Klineberg, "Emotional Expression in Chinese Literature," *Journal of Abnormal and Social Psychology* (1983), pp. 517–530.

14. E. T. Hall and M. R. Hall, *Understanding Cultural Differences* (Yarmouth, ME: Intercultural Press, 1990).

15. Ibid.

16. Ibid.

17. Ibid.; M. Rosch, "Communications: Focal Point of Culture," *Management International Review* 27, no. 4 (1987), p. 60.

18. Hall and Hall, *Understanding Cultural Differences.*

19. I. Ratiu, "Thinking Internationally: A Comparison of How International Executives Learn," *International Studies of Management and Organization* 13 (1983), pp. 139–150.

20. S. Ting-Toomey, "A Face-Negotiation Theory." In Y. Kim and W. B. Gudykuns, eds., *Theory in Intercultural Communication* (Newbury Park, CA: Sage, 1988).

21. M. Won-Doornink, "Self-Disclosure and Reciprocity in Conversation: A Cross-National Study," *Social Psychology Quarterly* 48 (1985), pp. 97–107.

22. D. Barnlund, *Public and Private Self in Japan and the United States* (Tokyo: Simul Press, 1975).

23. J. P. Dillard, S. R. Wilson, K. J. Tusing, and T. A. Kinney, "Politeness Judgments in Personal Relationships," *Journal of Language and Social Psychology* 16 (1997), pp. 297–325.

24. G. M. Guthrie, "Cultural Preparation for the Philippines," In R. B. Textor ed., *Cultural Frontiers of the Peace Corps* (Cambridge, MA: MIT Press, 1966), pp. 15–34.

25. Z. Lin, "Ambiguity with a Purpose: The Shadow of Power in Communication." In P. C. Earley and M. Erez, eds., *New Perspectives on International Industrial/Organizational Psychology* (San Francisco: New Lexington Press, 1997), pp. 363–376; G. Gao, "Don't Take My Word for It"—Understanding Chinese Speaking Practices," *International Journal of Intercultural Relations* 22 (1998), pp. 163–186; P. C. Earley and A. Randel, "Self and Other: Face and Work Group Dynamics." In C. Granrose and S. Oskamp, eds., *Claremont Symposium on Applied International Psychology* (Thousand Oaks, CA: Sage, 1997).

26. W. B. Gundykunst, "Individualistic and Collectivistic Perspectives on Communication: An Introduction," *International Journal of Intercultural Relations* 22 (1998), pp. 107–134.

27. M. Brein and K. H. David, "Intercultural Communications and the Adjustment of the Sojourner," *Psychological Bulletin* 76 (1971), pp. 215–230.

28. H. C. Triandis, "Culture, Training, Cognitive Complexity, and Interpersonal Attitudes." In R. W. Brislin, S. Bochner, and W. J. Lonner, eds., *Cross-Cultural Perspectives on Learning* (New York: Wiley, 1975), pp. 39–77.

29. C. Ward and A. Rana-Deuba, "Home and Host Culture Influences on Sojourner Adjustment," *International Journal of Intercultural Relations* 24 (2001), pp. 291–306.

30. N. Sugimoto, "Norms of Apology Depicted in U.S. American and Japanese Literature on Manners and Etiquette," *International Journal of Intercultural Relations* 21 (1998), pp. 175–193.

31. P. B. Smith and M. H. Bond, *Social Psychology across Cultures,* 2nd ed. (Boston: Allyn & Bacon, 1999).

32. Ibid.

33. A. Almaney and A. Ahwan, *Communicating with the Arabs* (Prospect Heights, IL: Waveland, 1982).

34. H. Giles, N. Coupland, and J. M. Weimann, "Talk Is Cheap . . . but My Word Is My Bond: Beliefs about Talk." In K. Bolton and H. Kwok, eds., *Sociolinguistics Today: Eastern and Western Perspectives* (London: Routledge, 1992).

35. W. Bright, ed.-in-chief, *International Encyclopedia of Linguistics* (New York: Oxford University Press, 1992).

36. Thomas Dwyer, "Web globalization: Write once, deploy worldwide." Aberdeen Group Insight Report #108. (www.aberdeen.com). Reported in *Lois Enos,* 2001. "English-only a mistake for US sites." *E-Commerce Times,* May 17, 2001. www.EcommerceTimes.com.

37. P. C. Earley and C. B. Gibson, *Multinational Work Teams: A New Perspective* (Mahwah, NJ: Lawrence Erlbaum Associates, 2002), pp. 40–43.

38. C. Simmers, *The Internet in the Classroom: Case Analysis across the Network: Across the Globe.* Paper presented at the 10th Annual Mid-Atlantic Regional Organizational Behavior Teaching Conference, Philadelphia, March 9, 1996.

39. J. Greenberg, *Managing Behavior in Organizations* (Upper Saddle River, NJ: Prentice Hall, 1996).

CHAPTER THIRTEEN

Negotiation and Decision Making across Borders and Cultures

Chapter Learning Objectives

After completing this chapter, you should be able to:

- Understand the processes of negotiation and decision making and their significance for multinational and global corporations.
- Explain the environmental context of international business negotiations and the concept of multinational negotiating strength.
- Identify the various patterns of negotiation and conflict resolution in different national and cultural contexts.
- Understand the influence of national and cultural variations in decision making.
- Discuss the importance of computer-mediated communication in negotiation and decision making.

Opening Case: Blockage in Basel

New Rules for International Banks' Capital Have Hit an Obstacle

By now Basel 2, a new set of rules on international banks' capital, should be almost complete. In essence, the idea is to improve banks' stability by tying their capital more closely to the riskiness of their assets. The committee drawing up the regulations has been working for five years, and should finish by the end of this year if Basel 2 is to be implemented as planned at the end of 2006. Yet the chances of this look slim. The proposals as they stand have many critics. Banks say they are too complicated. Standard & Poor's, a rating agency, says that it might downgrade banks whose capital it deems inadequate, even if the banks comply with Basel 2. China and India have opted out entirely. More troubling, American banks and their regulators are also unhappy.

A committee meeting scheduled for October 10th is likely to confirm that delay, not a deal, is in the offing. The stumbling block is American banks' dissatisfaction on several technical but important questions. "The greatest threat to an accord is from those who want to paper over major problems," says John Hawke, head of the Office of the Comptroller of the Currency (OCC), a regulator of American banks.

The Americans are disgruntled by the definition of capital under the new rules—and therefore by the amount of capital Basel 2 implies that banks should set aside. In particular, they are concerned about capital charges for losses on bad loans. Existing practice requires banks to make capital charges for unexpected losses. Expected losses are dealt with differently, through provisions (a charge against profits every quarter) and pricing (the riskier the borrower, the higher the interest rate). Two years ago, the Basel committee agreed that there should be capital charges for expected losses too.

Partly as a result of a recent "impact study" of Basel 2's likely effects, the magnitude of this new charge has become clear. American banks, which do nicely from credit-card and small-business loans, on which expected losses are high, now want to unpick the proposal. Their regulators want another impact study and more time to sort out the rules.

Europeans are furious that such basic questions are being debated anew this late in the day. A German regulator spoke this week of "Pandora's box" being re-opened. European lawmakers have a timetable to pass legislation on bank capital in parallel with the introduction of Basel 2. They still plan to make the new rules binding for all European Union banks and investment firms even if Basel 2 is delayed indefinitely.

On one reading, the whole Basel 2 process is in jeopardy. America already plans to apply it to only 12 banks, with another dozen expected to comply voluntarily. Developing countries might follow China's and India's lead. Yet an obituary may be premature. Basel 2 is meant to apply to "internationally active" banks. America's two dozen banks comprise 99% of that country's banks' foreign exposure. Few developing-country banks qualify. Moreover, most banks and regulators (including Americans) agree that the existing rules, known as Basel 1, should be updated.

At some point, therefore, some sort of deal will probably be thrashed out. The question is whether this will take weeks or years: the answer depends on whether the Americans are willing to seek a quick compromise. The Americans themselves disagree about this. The Federal Reserve is keener on a deal than the OCC.

Even if the wrangle about expected losses is sorted out, regulators have other important issues to deal with. More work is needed on co-ordinating national supervisors, who are given wide discretion to tweak the rules. This can lead to inconsistency and even outright favouritism. Closer links with emerging international accounting standards, which will also apply across the European Union, would also help.

Critics also say that the committee should think harder about the unintended consequences of Basel 2. The new rules, say some, might exacerbate economic downturns by forcing banks to cut lending and raise capital when the cycle is weakest. Others worry that the regime will discourage banks from well-calculated risk-taking. And then, somehow, the complicated new system will have to be enforced. A delay may be the least of the new accord's problems.

Discussion Questions

1. Why are differences in negotiation styles important?
2. How is the negotiation technique used by the Americans different from that of the Europeans?
3. How might the importance of the negotiation affect the way negotiations are carried out?

What Is Negotiation?

Negotiations between and among multinational and global corporations occur daily. As businesses expand globally, international negotiation has become a routine activity for many global organizations rather than an occasional event. Global managers must negotiate with parties in other countries to develop specific strategies for exporting, setting up joint ventures, and managing subsidiaries. The art of effective negotiation is difficult at best, and it can be challenging for even the most experienced global managers. Effective negotiation requires attention to important aspects of the process before, during, and after the negotiation session itself.

Negotiation is a basic form of interchange between two or more individuals, groups, or organizations—a process that is used in labor–management relations, business deals, such as sales agreements and mergers, and international relations. In simple terms, negotiation is a process in which an individual or a group or an organization tries to change the beliefs, preferences, and behaviors of another individual, group, or organization. It can be defined as the process of verbal and nonverbal exchanges between two or more parties with the goal of reaching a mutually satisfactory agreement. However, mutually satisfactory agreements are not always possible in real-life situations, as we will discuss later.

In everyday life, the concepts of bargaining and negotiation are used interchangeably, but they have different meanings. **Bargaining** is the process of arguing and haggling over prices and other details involved in transactions of goods and services, and it is seen in flea markets, bazaars, and fairs all over the world. Negotiation is a more formal process reflecting genuine concerns by the parties to reach an acceptable solution when interests conflict.[1]

Negotiations take place in order to reach peaceful solutions to conflicts between nations or to end a labor dispute. The process is not necessarily only for professionals, because we encounter the need for negotiating with people we work and live with daily. Individuals tend to negotiate about different things in many different situations, and knowledge about what and how to negotiate is essential for people who need to work with others to accomplish objectives. Sometimes people fail to negotiate because they do not have relevant information, time, and/or power to be effective.

Discussions between the United States, Canada, and Mexico to create the North American Free Trade Agreement (NAFTA), the ongoing diplomatic communications between the United States and Japan aimed at improving the free flow of goods and services between these countries, and the establishment of strategic alliances between Xerox and Fuji-Xerox are examples of **international negotiation.**

Situations in which negotiators may find themselves vary widely according to national contexts. Smart negotiators recognize the impact of situational cues on the bargaining process from their own as well as from their opponent's cultural backgrounds. In preparing for effective negotiations across borders, it is important to imagine how the proposal might look to the other negotiating parties. What are their distinct needs, compared to ours? What kind of outcome is at stake? What is their time frame—long term or short term? Do they prefer a sequential or a holistic approach? Some of the specific situational characteristics that influence the process of cross-border negotiation are:

- *Context of the negotiation:* Is it taking place at their office or yours or at a neutral location? When negotiations take place in comfortable locations, such as a yacht or a resort, the party that provides such surroundings generally tends to achieve desired outcomes. A division of Caterpillar Company in California succeeded in controlling negotiations with its international clients by having them on a luxurious yacht.[2]

- *Physical arrangements:* Paying attention to the seating arrangements of both parties is not trivial. In traditional American negotiations, the two parties face each other across a large table. Negotiators from East Asian countries, however, may view this process as more confrontational and open than their usual format. The Japanese like both parties to sit on the same side of the table, indicating that they are facing the

PRACTICAL INSIGHT 13.1

CULTURE SHOCK: IF YOU DON'T LEARN TO BRIDGE THE GAP, YOU MAY RISK ALIENATING POTENTIAL BUSINESS PARTNERS

Did you know that in Japanese, there are 19 different ways to say "no"? In a world increasingly dominated by international, multinational and transnational corporations, culture plays an important role in negotiation. The literature on this subject is large, fascinating and goes far beyond curious questions of international etiquette.

For example, the Japanese eschew direct confrontation, preferring an exchange of information. Russians love combat; their very word for "compromise" is borrowed from another language. Spanish negotiators are individualistic; Koreans are team players. Nigerians prefer the spoken word, Indians the written one. Asian languages are high in context, so you must pay attention to inflections, body language and what is *not* said. Latin American cultures are physically demonstrative. And we Americans alienate everyone with our impatience and obsession with getting things done . . . fast, fast, fast!

Sensitive negotiators allow for these sorts of differences. Take a tip from Stephen Covey, the author of *The Seven Habits of Highly Successful People* (Simon & Schuster): "Seek first to understand, then to be understood." For one thing, your opponent may not be speaking to you in his mother tongue. The subtleties of negotiating may be lost in translation. Make sure you are really connecting, and be especially clear, lest you talk past each other.

Moreover, those who negotiate outside their culture regularly should study the etiquette, ethics and attitudes of their opponents. It's just part of learning more about how the other side actually negotiates. If you know what to expect when you sit down to bargain, you will dramatically enhance your ability to get what you want. Let General George S. Patton lead you to the negotiating table: "I have studied the enemy all my life. I have read the memoirs of his generals and his leaders. I have even read his philosophers and listened to his music. I have studied in detail the account of every one of his battles. I know exactly how he will react under any given set of circumstances. So when the time comes, I'm going to whip the hell out of him."

Of course, you may not want to be quite so combative. In any case, all sorts of expertise is available on a country-by-country basis, from scholarly treatises to seasoned consultants, to learn about cultural idiosyncrasies. Consider adding a guide to your team, whether it's a professional, a friend who knows how "they" think, or simply a translator. Just be careful whom you choose. A line in one of Jimmy Carter's 1977 speeches in Poland was mistranslated: "I desire the Poles carnally."

Source: Reprinted with permission from *Entrepreneur* magazine, "Culture Shock," July 2003, www.entrepreneur.com.

---

problem rather than confronting each other. Holistic approaches to arranging the physical layout are particularly important in South and East Asian as well as Arabic countries.

- *Time limits:* The duration of negotiation is remarkably important. American negotiators are given a limited time to bring about a successful negotiation. They often communicate with their bosses through e-mail and faxes and respond to sequential processes emphasized in their headquarters. Negotiators from collectivistic cultures realize that Americans are particularly impatient and expect to spend a minimal amount of time. It is not unusual for the Russians and Chinese negotiators to delay the final stage of negotiations until immediately before the Americans are ready to leave for home. Herb Cohen's book *You Can Negotiate Anything* provides a number of interesting examples of how open-minded Americans lost negotiations with Russian counterparts because of the Americans' impatience.[3] And one Brazilian tour guide reported to the second author that he succeeded in making good sales of Brazilian jewelry just before Americans departed for home. He found that Americans were not interested in negotiating just before departure.

- *Status differences:* Americans, in particular among the Westerners, favor an egalitarian, informal approach to life, and negotiations tend to deemphasize status differences. However, negotiators from the United Kingdom, Germany, and France are noted for using status as an informal mechanism for attempting to achieve gains in cross-border negotiations. Managers from most countries respect hierarchy and formality more than Americans and feel more comfortable in situations explicitly recognizing their status. Chinese and Japanese negotiators present their business cards to the Western managers with both hands and expect them to read the card immediately and recognize their status from the titles given. Americans tend to focus on the content and the openness of the negotiation and less on the status of the members of the negotiation party in his or her company.

The Negotiation Process

The process of negotiation consists of four fundamental elements:

1. Two or more parties involved in real or perceived conflict over important goals.
2. Shared interest in reaching an agreeable solution.
3. Background preparations leading to the process of negotiation.
4. A goal, but not a certainty, of reaching mutual agreement.[4]

Negotiation involves continuous communication, as discussed in Chapter 12. In the past, negotiations involved face-to-face meetings, but now negotiations can occur through postal mail, telephone, videoconferencing, e-mail, and the Internet.

The negotiation process entails five stages: (1) preparation, (2) relationship building, (3) information exchange, (4) persuasion, and (5) making concessions and reaching agreement, as illustrated in Exhibit 13.1. The importance and duration of each stage varies across cultures.[5] Cultural, national, and organizational influences are also seen in the exhibit. All of these influences are discussed later, but you must remember that they exert significant pressures on negotiators of all parties.

Preparation

In this stage, negotiators focus on gathering information, planning their strategies, and learning as much as possible about the other party or parties. The headquarters of multinational and global corporations are the appropriate settings for this step. Managers who were involved in previous negotiations of the same kind play the role of coaches, teaching the negotiation team about the other party's objectives, needs, preferences, and so on.

Relationship Building

In this stage, parties meet to discuss their mutual interests in the negotiation and get to know each other. This stage involves both formal and informal meetings at mutually agreeable and neutral locations. Exchange of business cards, many days of conversation, dinners, and other forms of entertainment often accompany this stage. The emphasis on building relationships and the need to know about the other group depends on national and cultural factors. For example, although U.S. negotiators do not like to spend much time in this stage, in much of the rest of the world, moving rapidly to the task of negotiating is not only inappropriate but may violate certain established protocols of behavior. French negotiators do not like to talk about business during dinner. They would rather enjoy fine wines and get to know their counterparts during evening hours. Similarly, Mexican negotiators often schedule sightseeing tours to important cultural sites and expect foreigners to pay some attention to their heritage and culture.

EXHIBIT 13.1   **Stages of Negotiation in International Management**

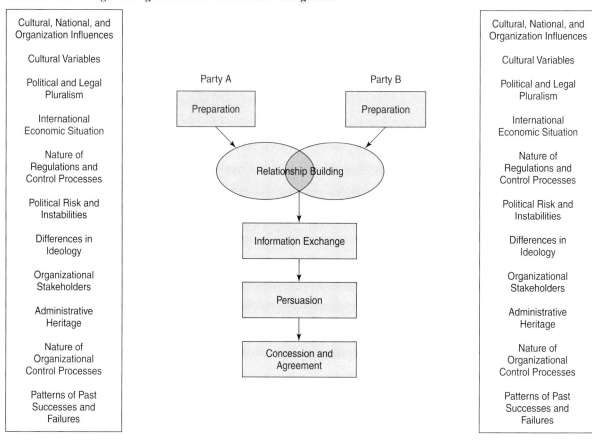

Information Exchange

During this stage, each party formally presents an initial position, and discussion of the issues involved follows. The other party has the opportunity to ask questions and clarify important points. American managers consider this to be the start of the real negotiating process and expect the other party to present relevant information in a succinct, logical, and comprehensive fashion. However, negotiators from other parts of the world may not follow this protocol and may even be skeptical of presenting a great deal of information up front.[6] In fact, in most countries, particularly those with a strong norm of collectivism, the emphasis on relationship building is regarded as the real beginning of the negotiation process.

Persuasion

During this stage, each party is concerned with changing the beliefs, preference structures, attitudes, and interests of the other parties. Attempts are made to work toward a mutually satisfactory agreement that can succeed in both the short and long term. The role of cultural variables is particularly important in this stage. International studies of negotiation have revealed the use of certain tactics and strategies that are culture-specific.[7] Differences in the use of threats, promises, recommendations, self-disclosure, appeals, and rewards are common. Exhibit 13.2 shows some of the differences in three countries, Japan, the United States, and Brazil, which are culturally disparate.

EXHIBIT 13.2
Differences in Negotiator Strategies and Tactics in Three Countries.

Source: From J. L. Graham, "The Influences of Culture on the Process of Business Negotiations: An Exploratory Study," *Journal of International Business Studies.* Vol. 16, 1985. Reproduced with permission of Palgrave Macmillan.

	Individual Tactics as a Percentage of Total Tactics		
	Japanese *N* = 6	**American *N* = 6**	**Brazilian *N* = 6**
Promise	7	8	3
Threat	4	4	2
Recommendation	7	4	5
Warning	2	1	1
Reward	1	2	2
Punishment	1	3	3
Positive normative appeal	1	1	0
Negative normative appeal	3	1	1
Commitment	15	13	8
Self-disclosure	34	36	39
Question	20	20	22
Command	8	6	14
	Occurrences in a 30-minute Bargaining Session		
Number of times word "no" used	5.7	9.0	83.4
Silent periods of 10 seconds or more	5.5	3.5	0
Conversational overlaps (interruptions)	12.6	10.3	28.6
Gazing (minutes per random 10 min period)	1.3 min	3.3 min	5.2 min
Touching	0	0	4.7

Making Concessions and Reaching Agreement

This final stage of negotiation is the stage where parties make appropriate concessions and reach agreement. The agreements could be for the short term or the long term. Skilled negotiators generally decide on the number of final concessions they can make (the bottom line) during the preparation stage. Concessions and agreements may be reached without revealing total strategies that could be of value in future negotiations. Cultural differences play a significant role in the way concessions and agreements are made. U.S. negotiators negotiate sequentially (one issue at a time) and conclude the process with a legal contract, binding on all parties. Many East Asian negotiators do not like the idea of negotiating one issue at a time and find legal contracts to be less honorable than agreements based on mutual trust and respect.[8] Similarly, Russians attach less meaning to contracts and prefer to reach agreements based on a thorough discussion of the whole, rather than one issue at a time.

Environmental Context of International Negotiations

As shown in Exhibit 13.3, cultural, national, and organizational variables significantly impact each stage of negotiation.

Cultural Variables

The cultural value of individualism influences the way American, Australian, and British managers approach the process. They are expected to make decisions by themselves, defend their points of view, and stand firm on issues that are important to them. On the other hand, the value of collectivism influences the way Chinese and other East Asian managers approach negotiations. They emphasize decisions arrived at by consensus, defend group interests over individual interests, and often take a long-term view of the process.[9]

EXHIBIT 13.3   **Comparison of Cultural Approaches to Negotiation**

Source: Adapted from P. Casse and S. Deol, *Managing Intercultural Negotiations: Guidelines for Trainers and Negotiators* (Washington, DC: International Society for Intercultural Education, Training, and Research, 1985), pp. 148–52.

American Negotiator	Indian Negotiator	Arab Negotiator	Swedish Negotiator	Italian Negotiator
Accepts compromise when deadlock occurs	Relies on truth	Protects "face" of all parties	Gets straight to the point of the discussion	Dramatic
Has firm initial and final stands	Trusts instincts	Avoids confrontation	Avoids confrontation	Emotional
Sets up principals but lets subordinates do detail work	Seeks compromises	Uses a referent person to try to change others, e.g., "Do it for your father"	Time conscious	Able to read context well
Has a maximum of options	Is ready to alter position at any point	Seeks creative alternatives to satisfy all parties	Overly cautious	Suspicious
Respects other parties	Trusts opponent	Mediates through conferences	Informal	Intrigues
Is fully briefed	Respects other parties	Can keep secrets	Flexible	Uses flattery
Keeps position hidden as long as possible	Learns from opponent		Reacts slowly to new propositions	Concerned about creating a good impression
	Avoids use of secrets		Quiet and thoughtful	Indefinite

The definition of negotiation and what should occur during the process are also influenced by cultural differences, such as the amount of power distance (real or imagined) between the parties.[10] Selection of negotiators and the use of protocol and formality in the process also differ according to the cultural context of uncertainty avoidance and masculinity versus femininity.[11] Cultural values also have a significant effect on the choice of long- versus short-term goals and objectives.[12] In the United States, where "time is money" and "faster is better" is a general belief, there is an emphasis on achieving short-term goals, even at the expense of long-term goals. The Japanese, French, and others are more inclined to focus on long-term goals and objectives and may choose to ignore short-term objectives. This can cause surprise and confusion. The amount of time that may be spent in formal settings of negotiation also varies from country to country. Americans are seen as always being in a hurry and impatient. They spend less time in negotiating the details, unlike most other countries, which leads to Americans accepting hurried agreements that they regret later.[13]

National Variables

Political Systems

The world consists of more than 100 countries and each has its own distinct political system. International negotiators often get caught in the conflicting values they find between foreign policies of two or more countries. For example, because of the Soviet invasion of Afghanistan, the Carter administration stopped the construction of a trans-Siberian pipeline in the former Soviet Union in the 1980s. Since American foreign policy was hostile toward the Soviet Union at the time, the U.S. government demanded that American companies (e.g., Dresser Industries) stop supplying equipment such as transformers and generators and related items to the construction. Current U.S. policy bans the sale of any technology, products, or services to organizations located in countries that support construction of nuclear weapons or warheads and those that support terrorism.

In the past, political upheaval has often resulted in nationalization of foreign-owned companies. These issues are covered in Chapter 3, but they are mentioned again here because they can affect the negotiation process in numerous ways.

Legal Systems

Each country has its own legislation which influences negotiations in areas such as export and import quotas, antitrust regulations, labor–management relations, patent and trademark protection, product liability and marketing, maintenance of minimum wage, and taxation. For example, a German company transferring technology to a Japanese collaborator must ensure that the transaction is legal in both Germany and Japan. Each country has laws that put limits on certain types of transactions. Certain sectors of the economy, such as the telecommunications and automobile industries, are often protected from wholly owned foreign investments. General Motors, Ford, Volkswagen, Toyota, and other automobile companies have set up manufacturing plants in India and China by establishing joint ventures with Indian companies to meet legal restrictions. The joint venture agreement has an impact on how two parties might negotiate over important issues such as quality control, global marketing rights, the significance and rights to technology, transfer to the joint venture, profit sharing, and royalty payments. Negotiators should be aware of the legal traps that might transform a good-faith agreement into a nightmare. Furthermore, it is essential that negotiators understand issues of political risk and be careful to avoid illegal activities, such as bribing or encouraging corruption.

International Economic Situation

Unlike purely domestic transactions, international business transactions occur with multiple currencies that fluctuate daily. Fluctuations in exchange rates, as reflected in the various currency crises around the world during the mid- to late 1990s, can affect negotiations in many ways. The currency crises in Mexico, Indonesia, and Russia caused significant problems for international firms that negotiated business transactions before the devaluation of currencies in these countries. A business deal that is not appropriately structured to compensate and protect against fluctuations in currency exchanges can lead either to disastrous consequences or to a windfall. Other international economic issues might concern regulation by the International Monetary Fund (IMF), the World Bank, and the United Nations.

Differences in Ideology

Negotiators from Western countries share a common ideology of capitalism and free enterprise, a strong belief in individual rights, protection of human rights, and the importance of making a profit. Negotiators from other countries, particularly from the socialistic or communist traditions (Russia, China, Cuba, eastern European countries) do not necessarily share this ideology. Group rights, as opposed to individual rights, are emphasized more in these countries, often leading to significant clashes during the negotiation process. Countries driven by strong values of idealism versus pragmatism are often unwilling to engage in win–win situations, making negotiation tricky and troublesome. Communication challenges in these types of cross-border negotiations exist because the parties strongly disagree on some of the fundamental issues of what is being negotiated and how long the outcomes of such negotiations are binding.[14]

These differences in ideology also reflect whether the parties follow distributive or integrative approaches to negotiation. Negotiators adopting a *distributive approach* view the negotiation process as a zero-sum game with fixed outcomes. The ideology of a distributive negotiation is such that the goals of one party stand in sharp contrast to those of the other party. In this approach, parties compete to maximize their outcomes, and if one party wins, the other loses. Negotiations between consumer groups and corporations, as well as labor–management negotiations, often reflect this approach.

On the other hand, negotiators using an *integrative approach* accommodate the other parties' interests and are willing to examine the range of possible outcomes that could result. The emphasis is on creating win–win scenarios in which both parties leave the negotiation with a sense of satisfaction. In integrative negotiations, each party is willing to spend time working toward satisfying the goals of the other party as much as possible, according to the circumstances.

The process of integrative negotiation is fundamentally different from that of distributive negotiation. The negotiators must be willing to explore the true mindset of the other party to understand everyone's needs, which are often a product of the national cultural values and political/legal requirements. Negotiations between two successful multinational corporations that result in setting up of a joint venture to produce a good or service that benefits both parties is an example of an integrative approach to negotiation.

Some of the significant differences in negotiating abroad are highlighted in Practical Insights 13.2 and 13.3.

Organizational Variables

Organizational Stakeholders

Stakeholders of multinational and global organizations are those persons and institutions with an interest or stake in the final outcome of negotiations. Examples include competitors, employees, labor unions, consumers, organized business groups (such as the Chamber of Commerce and other industry associations), and the company's shareholders and board of directors. All of these groups are capable of exerting pressure by lobbying for or against a proposed business arrangement, such as a joint venture or strategic alliance.

Competitors may launch a hard-nosed campaign to lobby against a proposed business agreement, especially if they feel that such agreements are detrimental to their own business. For example, agricultural companies in France and Spain did not favor the European Union entering into agricultural transactions with U.S. companies. Their fear was rooted in the fact that the U.S. agricultural sector was so industrialized that they could not effectively compete.

Employees and labor unions also affect the outcome of negotiations by getting involved. Collective bargaining agreements and labor contracts prevent companies, such as Caterpillar,[15] United Airlines, and American Airlines, from competing with firms that do not have such agreements.

Consumer groups that are likely to be affected, either positively or negatively, by the outcome of negotiations between two international firms may also become involved. U.S. consumers do not support business negotiations that might increase the price of popular Japanese products, such as consumer electronics and autos.

Organized business groups, such as the Chamber of Commerce and various industry groups, can also affect the process of international business negotiations. The positive attitude of a country's Chamber of Commerce, such the U.S. Chamber of Commerce in Washington, D.C., or the U.K. Chamber of Commerce in London, can provide impetus for sustaining a negotiation, even when parties have difficulty reaching agreements. Visits of senior executives organized by the U.S. Chamber of Commerce were a major factor in setting up joint ventures and strategic alliances of American companies with their counterparts in China, India, Russia, and eastern Europe, as these countries liberalized their markets.

Organizational Processes

Differences in decision-making processes and control mechanisms of global and multinational corporations play a crucial role in the way two or more corporations reach satisfactory agreements. Japanese multinationals are particularly noted for their group decision making, which affects the power of Japanese negotiators.[16] As discussed in Chapter 10, control mechanisms of Indian public bureaucracies are well known for their rigid and slow approach to negotiation, leading to significant difficulties for Western multinationals. While there have been important changes in streamlining the bureaucratic processes to allow international companies to invest in India after 1991, problems continue.

Companies that have been repeatedly successful in negotiating internationally are those with administrative heritages that allow occasional failures. They succeed in situations that are complex or uncertain, require considerable advance preparation, and consume a great deal of time. It is essential that the organizational culture be designed to tolerate failures in negotiating in East and South Asian, Arabic, and Latin American countries. Long-term objectives in bringing about negotiations should be emphasized, as opposed to coming to a quick agreement, which is the usual practice in Western-style negotiations.

Consider negotiations between members of monochronic cultures and members of polychronic cultures.[17] Monochronic cultures tend to allocate time with a higher emphasis on tasks, while polychronic cultures tend to allocate time with a higher emphasis on relationships.[18] Monochronic cultures tend to have bureaucracies, which are governed by rules and policies and tend to be task-oriented, because the society in which they exist are both. Polychronic cultures, on the other hand, are characterized by flatter organizational charts with fewer levels, which are sprawling and unstructured.[19] Hall suggests that polychronic organizations tend to be flatter because managers deal with many matters and people simultaneously.

Managers from Western MNCs complain about sluggish bureaucracies in their own countries, but their burden tends to be lighter compared to those in polychronic cultures. Without well-established hierarchies for handling negotiations, each bureaucrat in a polychronic culture insists on signing off on pending negotiations. The sheer volume of procedures gets multiplied, as a result. A study of one joint venture in pharmaceuticals revealed that the U.S. government required 26 documents to be filed along with 9 administrative details, the Japanese government required 325 documents in 46 administrative procedures, and the South Korean government required 312 documents in 62 administrative procedures.[20] The interesting point to be noted is that the joint venture was undertaken in South Korea, and the paperwork took two years and nine months.

Monochronic bureaucracies tend to be massive, and the procedures are routinely implemented and are self-perpetuating. If an employee in a corporation in Memphis, Tennessee, wants to be transferred to another location, he or she will consult the company policy and file a request. An employee in a public bureaucracy in Colombia or India is more likely to ask a boss about the transfer, or to call a senior colleague who may have influence in affecting a transfer. In polychronic bureaucracies, negotiations are routed through working with friends, family members, or other network connections. Monochronic organizations give equal treatment to employees of a given rank, and fairness is the organizing principle in these societies. Negotiating with representatives from polychronic bureaucracies will be slow, frustrating, and cumbersome. One may wish to conclude the negotiations out of sheer frustration. However, a satisfactory outcome

PRACTICAL INSIGHT 13.2

HOW TO AVOID BEING THE "UGLY AMERICAN" WHEN DOING BUSINESS ABROAD

You know the stereotype: They're bold, brash, and all business. They've got lots of money but little culture. They're immune to self-doubt and oblivious to cultural nuance.

They're the Ugly Americans.

The 1958 book and 1963 film adaptation gave the stereotype its name. How closely does the stereotype fit the reality of Americans doing business abroad today? How "ugly" are American businesspeople as they work with foreign partners in this our globalized world?

"Americans have a much greater willingness to adapt to other cultures than they did when that book was written," says Prabhu Guptara, director of the Executive Development Centre for UBS bank in Wolfsberg, Switzerland. "But Americans often still need to improve self-consciousness to understand that the qualities that make you win in the U.S. could as easily make you fail in Europe or Asia."

American execs need to be especially sensitive about three aspects of communications when they go abroad:

1. The rhythm of negotiations. Speed and directness are not necessarily qualities that foreigners appreciate, even though Americans like them.
2. The dynamics of personal relationships. Business in most of the developed world is people-based, not deal-based, so don't parachute in with the "lawyers and the dollars."
3. The depth of presentation. Slick speeches and PowerPoint slide shows may not get you far in cultures that value depth. You'd better have all the numbers and know what they mean.

Why these areas in particular? "Because Americans tend to value fast and agile dealmaking, and intense and skilled marketing, while not putting much value on personal relationships in business," explains Ann McDonagh Bengtsson, a France-based international consultant specializing in change management, especially where a number of different cultures are involved. "Whereas, most Europeans and many Asians want to develop a solid personal relationship before even considering a deal, and then expect very detailed and painstaking research to have gone into the preparation of any accord," Bengtsson says.

Says Japanese intercultural expert Shinobu Kitayama: "American culture emphasizes the core cultural idea of independence by valuing attending to oneself and discovering and expressing individual qualities while neither assuming nor valuing overt connectedness. These values are reflected in educational and legal systems, employment and caretaking practices, and individual cognition, emotion, and motivation."

In contrast, Bengtsson and Kitayama argue that Asian and European cultures tend to emphasize interdependence by valuing the self and individuality within a social context, connections among persons, and attending to and harmoniously coordinating with others. When Kitayama asked 65 middle-class American and 90 Japanese students attending the same Oregon university to list situations in which they felt that they were winning or losing, the American students focused more on ways in which they won individually, while the Japanese students won when the group with which they were associated enjoyed a success.

American execs abroad have to take these differences into account. So, when abroad:

Slow Down

The rhythm of negotiations and all business discussion is much slower outside the United States, as executives from the New York–based Bankers Trust had to learn when it merged with the Frankfurt-based Deutsche Bank two years ago.

Deutsche Bank was a very large, "universal" bank, as the Germans call such an entity. The bank was active in all sectors of banking, but the area where it needed the most reinforcement was investment banking. Hence the plan to merge with investment house Bankers Trust, a dedicated merchant bank with an American, "deals-based" culture.

The American executives quickly found that they could not fathom their German partners, reports international management professor Terry Garrison of the Henley Management College (Henley-on-Thames, England). "Accustomed to making split-second decisions, and managing on a project basis in which planning rarely extended beyond a given deal, the Bankers Trust 'hot-shots' found themselves working with 'universal' bankers who planned several years at a time, for whom a given 'deal' was something they felt they could take or leave, and who operated within a corporate governance framework that looked and felt completely alien to the Americans."

Garrison ran a seminar in which he helped the American execs get in tune with Continental banking culture. "It was a matter of teaching the Americans to slow down and think in different terms," Garrison says. "Those Germans who had spent a lifetime in a credit-management culture saw themselves as needing not just a crash course in merchant banking but a whole new vocabulary rooted in American capitalism."

Deutsche Bank executive Siegfried Guterman admits that "there were a lot of unmeasurable factors that were difficult to take into account before we accomplished the merger."

It is not that Asians and European cultures do not value efficiency. Rather, business for them is more conceptual and long-term. A given transaction is only interesting if it is part of the accomplishment of a much more stable, greater objective. "Attempts to hurry your foreign interlocutors along may just make them withdraw from the discussions altogether," Bengtsson points out.

Don't Arrive with "the Lawyers and the Dollars"

Personal and business relationships are more intertwined in Europe and in Asia that they are in the United States.

"Achieving trust with European and Asian partners is a key factor in success outside the U.S.," Guptara says. "Americans may not like each other, but if there is a 'deal' on the table, they do business. Most Asians and Europeans—even the British—want to get to know you first. They want to assure themselves that you are reliable, that you will not only go the distance for them this time, but that you will be there to do it again when they call upon you."

So, take the time to go for lunch with your prospective business partners abroad. Don't talk business right away—ask them about what things are like in their country. Find something that you have in common with them. Maybe you both like a certain sport? Perhaps you share an interest in Italian wine?

During this time, you can observe your interlocutor's reactions. What makes him laugh? Does he react with hostility to certain kinds of expressions? "When you get around to dessert, bring up the subject of the business at hand in a very casual way. Get some indications from his reaction about how to proceed. But let your interlocutor lead you through it all," says Guptara.

Negotiating experts agree that forcing a conclusion with a foreign partner can only cause problems. "Don't be afraid to drop the matter and to talk about the weather," says Garrison. "Don't be too serious, especially at the outset. Show your interlocutor that you are in no hurry to conclude, and he will assume that you are serious. Insist on a conclusion, and he will assume that you are desperate."

Establishing trust is a factor that an American businessperson abroad must take into account not only in negotiations, but also in working with Europeans or Asians on a day-to-day basis.

Disney had to endure an expensive lesson of this type when it opened EuroDisney outside Paris. The management expected the French employees to conform to American expectations in their work, and did little to build up trust. A long and agonizing conflict with French labor unions was the only result of this policy. Finally, Disney gave up and hired French managers. Labor difficulties were smoothed out when managers and workers began to trust each other.

Get the Details Right

Although the British may accept a slick PR demo while negotiating, most of the cultures on the Continent and many in Asia do not.

"There is a real academic side to business in Europe and in parts of Asia," Guptara says. "A business presentation to such interlocutors is like defending a Ph.D. thesis. They expect you to have real depth, all the numbers, and to be able to answer every question. Fail at this and they will never trust you. The word that Europeans apply to a businessman who can't answer key questions is *liar*."

It may seem useless pedantry on the part of your prospective business partners to insist on great detail, "but their view is that the details are the easy part," says Bengtsson. "And a thoroughness in knowledge of your subject means—especially to Europeans, rightly or wrongly—that the risks are being adequately managed."

One American manufacturer recently hit all the wrong buttons in discussions with a French acquisition. Arriving in Paris, the American company promptly invited the board of the French company to lunch. The French board was of the most traditional sort—all graduates of the *grandes écoles,* they perceived themselves to be fashionable, witty, and cultivated.

When the French businessmen arrived at the lunch, they were astonished to find their American colleagues wearing baseball hats and T-shirts with the name of the acquiring company on them. There was also a pile of such hats and shirts on the table, and they were bidden to put them on.

This suggestion did not go over well. But even worse was the period at lunch when the French—after what they thought was a decent delay—began asking strategic questions. It became obvious that the American executives knew little or nothing about the company they were acquiring apart from its balance sheet.

After that, the massive departure of the French businessmen from the company should not have taken the Americans by surprise.

Play by the Rules—Their Rules

When an American executive goes abroad, it's very easy for cultural assumptions to slip into her suitcase. "When negotiations are prolonged, or frustrating, these cultural assumptions tend to jump out of the suitcase, onto the negotiating table," Bengtsson points out. The point to remember at times like this is that you are in someone else's culture and, for the time being, you need to play by their rules.

Because of tighter budgets, companies are sending fewer executives abroad these days, so the executive who is sent to a foreign country has mission-critical work to do. Thus it's essential that the executive adapt to a different culture's rules: for communication, interaction, and negotiation. If he doesn't, if he acts the proverbial "Ugly American," his chances for success are small.

Source: Reprinted by permission of *Harvard Management Communication Letter.* Excerpt from "How to Avoid Being the Ugly American When Doing Business Abroad," by Andrew Rosenbaum, December 2002. Copyright © 2002 by the Harvard Business School Publishing Corporation; all rights reserved.

PRACTICAL INSIGHT 13.3

THROUGH A GLASS NERVOUSLY

How best to approach a cross-cultural negotiation? Be prepared. And keep one eye behind the scenes

Exclusive interview with Jim Sebenius.

Business etiquette in other cultures can be daunting. An Asian manager might be genuinely frightened of dealing with his Western counterparts; an American executive might commit gaffes in France or Russia. But while good manners may help a business transaction, bad manners may not derail it—if the parties involved understand the subtler cultural influences on the negotiation.

In "The Hidden Challenge of Cross-Cultural Negotiations," published last month in the *Harvard Business Review,* Jim Sebenius, a professor at Harvard Business School, discusses these "webs of influence": groups not necessarily formally associated with the participating companies, that can nevertheless exert power over the negotiations. Such "webs" can prove perplexing even when apparent. Anyone approaching a negotiation with a Chinese company, for example, should know it will need to work with the government at some point. But the areas of the deal likely to be affected can vary widely, from the extent to which the approval of a leading official is needed to approve the deal to the local labour laws that might have to be obeyed. A Russian group dealing with a British company might not consider the latter's need to placate shareholders and local environmental activists; the British representatives, on the other side of the table, might not think to look out for the Russian mafia lurking in the shadows.

To be sure, culture can play a role without the influence of behind-the-scenes forces. Jeanne Brett, director of the Dispute Resolution Research Center at Kellogg School of Management, Northwestern University, and the author of "Negotiating Globally," points to the many ways culture influences negotiation: in the sharing of information, for example. Japanese and Chinese negotiators may be much more reluctant to put information on the table than their Western counterparts. They also use preliminary proposals much earlier in the negotiating process, and more frequently, than do Westerners, who then lack the cultural cues necessary to decipher the proposal's implicit information. "We tend to look at other parties through the lens of our own culture, and then we make mistakes," she says.

In theory the number of mistakes should decrease as global business contacts rise. This should be especially true in an academic environment: today's classmate in an MBA or executive programme could be the person approached for a deal tomorrow. Managers can head off some cross-cultural misunderstandings by doing research on the culture in question, or having people on hand familiar with the culture. More than one firm doing business in China has found its path much easier after hiring a Chinese law firm. But knowing that an Asian manager will rarely say "no directly" may be of limited use. Hidden influences can spring not just from a supposedly eternal "culture" but from specific political situations, either inside or outside the company.

Mr. Sebenius, drawing on practical negotiating experience (along with David Lax, a fellow professor, he runs a negotiating consultancy called Lax Sebenius) and a background in economics and mathematics, advocates what he calls a "3-D" approach to negotiations. He runs a week-long course on this approach at Harvard Business School, designed for high-level executives already familiar with the basics of negotiation. He argues that, once the negotiators sit down at the table, half the battle is already won or lost. The table bargaining is only one of three dimensions of making a deal. The second is knowing what agreement will create value on a sustainable basis. The third is setting up the situation so that your negotiator is at an advantage before even beginning to talk.

Some aspects of cross-cultural negotiating are really no different from any other deal making. There is still the potential for social relationships to form, and for partnerships to work across cultures. But again, behind-the-scenes forces can play their part: as alliances proliferate, a deal-making company must take into account not only its partner's needs but those of its partner's partners. Mr. Sebenius likes to point to the partnership that started in 1979 between Honda, a Japanese car maker, and Rover, a car maker then owned by the British government. Rover, which was losing market share, thought Honda's technology would be useful, and Honda wanted a foothold in the European market.

The alliance started as a simple licensing agreement; by 1988, when the British government sold Rover to British Aerospace, the relationship had evolved to exchanging stock and board members. But neither British Aerospace nor BMW, Rover's next owner, was as fond of the arrangement as was Honda, whose executives had taken to calling it a "marriage." When British Aerospace sold Rover to BMW without telling Honda, divorce followed swiftly.

Ms. Brett cheerfully declares that "the global business environment is here to stay." Mr. Sebenius agrees. His next project is to bring Harvard University's Program on Negotiation, where he is a member of the executive committee, into a joint project with the Kennedy School of Government to study negotiations of large projects, and especially those with several behind-the-scenes players such as governments and nongovernmental organisations. It seems that cross-cultural negotiation is such a varied topic that the only way to tackle it is through teamwork.

may be reached if there is a guarantee that the boss will (1) be tolerant of occasional failures in dealing with these bureaucracies and (2) provide more time than would be the case in dealing with monochronic organizations.

Negotiating with the Chinese

In preparing for a business trip to Mainland China, most Western managers are given a book of etiquette "how-tos," including such things as carrying a stack of business cards, having one's own interpreter, speaking softly and in short sentences, and wearing conservative clothing. These strategies are easy to implement and may win meager gains; however, according to Graham and Lam, these precautions will not sustain long-term negotiating relationships.[21] Four significant issues in Chinese culture, bound together for 5,000 years, influence Chinese business negotiations, according to these authors.

The first is *agrarianism.* In contrast to the United States and western Europe, where a majority of the population is urban, most Chinese people still live in rural agricultural areas engaged in rice or wheat cultivation. Group cooperation and harmony result from the communal, not individualistic nature of peasant farming. Many of China's modern entrepreneurs are from agricultural areas, and these agrarian values influence their negotiation approaches. Americans generally believe in openness and (what they believe to be) universally valid approaches to negotiation, whereas Chinese are more interested in outcomes that result in communal and harmonious relationships over the long term.

The second issue relates to morality, based on Confucian writings, which proposed that a society organized under a benevolent moral code would be stable, prosperous, and relatively immune from external aggression. Morality is also based on Taoism, which proposes that the key to life is compromise—a balance between the *yin* (dark, passive forces) and the *yang* (light, active forces). Chinese negotiators are more concerned with how the process occurs than with the outcomes, so negotiations involve long, drawn-out haggling to work through difficulties.

Pictographic language is the third issue, because Chinese is written in pictographs, that is, thousands of pictures rather than different combinations of 26 letters. As children learn through memorization of these pictures, their thinking becomes more holistic. Researchers have found that Chinese children are good at seeing a cohesive picture, whereas American children focus on details.[22]

Wariness of foreigners is the fourth and final issue. Because of the historical background of China, a violent history of wars with both external and internal aggressors, Chinese distrust rules. Most Chinese are confident only of those in their own in-groups. Exhibit 13.4 shows the resulting differences in negotiation processes.

Using the Internet to Manage Negotiations

The use of the Internet in managing negotiations is also increasing.[23] Global organizations with sophisticated computer-mediated communication systems are evolving strategies of managing negotiations through the Internet. Decision support systems can provide support for the negotiation process by:

- Reducing the amount of time that is necessary for feedback from headquarters in order to carry out effective negotiations.
- Providing a large amount of data and information on alternative scenarios that may result from the negotiation process.
- Increasing the likelihood that important data and information are available when needed.

EXHIBIT 13.4
Differences between American and Chinese Culture and Approaches to the Negotiation Process

Source: Adapted from J. L. Graham and N. M. Lam, "The Chinese Negotiation," *Harvard Business Review,* October 2003, p. 85.

Contrast of Basic Cultural Values	
American	**Chinese**
Task- and Information-oriented	Relationship-oriented
Egalitarian	Hierarchical
Analytical	Holistic
Sequential, monochronic	Circular, polychronic
Seeks the complete truth	Seeks the harmonious way
Individualist	Collectivist
Confrontative, argumentative	Haggling, bargaining

Approach to the Negotiation Process

Nontask Sounding

Quick meetings	Long courting process
Informal	Formal
Make cold calls	Draw on intermediaries

Information Exchange

Full authority	Limited authority
Direct	Indirect
Proposals first	Explanations first

Means of Persuasion

Aggressive	Questioning
Impatient	Patient

Terms of Agreement

A "good deal"	A long-term relationship

However, just because information can be sent by electronic media before, during, and after the course of a negotiation, it should not be assumed that negotiations can proceed without hurdles. Significant national and cultural blinders may prevent correct interpretation of information.[24] In other words, the message may not be accurately perceived because of selective filters and cultural biases, as discussed in Chapter 12.

Managing Negotiation and Conflict

Negotiations can become extremely complex in developing joint ventures, strategic alliances, and foreign direct investments (as discussed in Chapter 8) and in dealing with foreign governments. Conflicts can arise in any negotiation, but they are especially frequent in international and cross-border negotiations. Since conflicts can be costly and lead to dysfunctional outcomes, they need to be properly managed. The process of managing conflict for multinational and global organizations becomes tricky because a great many factors must be considered. Differences in cultural, national, and organizational variables, as discussed above, create the potential for conflict to arise.[25]

As we have already discussed, much of the negotiation process involves both explicit and implicit conflict between the parties. **Conflict** can be understood as a state of disagreement or opposition between two parties, where the accomplishment of one party's objectives neutralizes the other party's ability to achieve its desired outcomes. Conflicts present before, during, and after negotiation can cause significant disruptions, such as creating a showdown, a lose–lose situation. The presence of conflict may indicate that the parties will not engage in future negotiations and will not consider alternative scenarios.

EXHIBIT 13.5
Nature of Conflict between Members of Low- and High-Context Cultures

Source: W. Gudykunst, L. Steward, and S. Ting-Toomey, *Communication, Culture, and Organizational Processes* (New York: Sage, 1985).

Key Questions	Low-Context Conflict	High-Context Conflict
Why	Analytic, linear logic; instrumental; oriented; dichotomy between conflict and conflict parties	Synthetic, spiral logic; expressive-oriented; integration of conflict and conflict parties
When	Individualistic-oriented; low collective normative expectations; violations of individual expectations create conflict potentials	Group-oriented; high collective normative expectations; violations of collective expectations create conflict potentials
What	Revealment; direct, confrontational attitude; action and solution oriented	Concealment; indirect nonconfrontational attitude; "face-" and relationship-oriented
How	Explicit communication codes: line-logic style: rational-factual rhetoric; open, direct strategies	Implicit communication codes; point-logic style; intuitive-effective rhetoric; ambiguous, indirect strategies

National and cultural factors, as presented in Exhibit 13.3, are often responsible for creating severe conflicts, leading to breakdown in communication and negotiation. Negotiators from low-context cultures, as discussed in Chapter 12, tend to approach conflict directly through confrontation. A distinction is also made between the people involved and the conflict itself. On the other hand, negotiators from high-context cultures tend to approach conflict indirectly and subtly, through references to history of previous conflicts between the parties. Rarely is a distinction made between the person engaged in the conflict and the conflict itself. The differences between members of low-context and high-context cultures in the handling of conflict are illustrated in Exhibit 13.5.

For example, Western businessmen report that while Chinese put great emphasis on building relationships based on friendship and mutual respect, Americans are interested in getting to the point and are willing to reveal their objectives in the initial stages. The implicit communication styles used by Chinese and other East Asian negotiators also conflict with the explicit styles of communication used by Western negotiators. Even with the emergence of China as a global economic power in the 1990s, most negotiations are still accomplished within the framework of budget allocations, mandated by the government for the project, as opposed to the potential profitability of the project. In addition, the negotiation tends to be understood in the context of culturally ingrained values of politeness and emotional restraint.

The overlapping of work/family and other social obligations enters the context of negotiation in ways that Western negotiators do not understand. The concept of *saving face* in any negotiation is of critical importance in the East Asian cultures. Westerners often do not understand how powerful this concept is and how it affects the entire process of negotiation. If the negotiation leads to unsatisfactory outcomes for the East Asian parties, appropriate concessions must be made to allow them to save face. Future negotiations are likely to be problematic, if not impossible, if the outcomes do not result in saving face for the East Asian negotiators.

In managing effective international negotiations, it is useful to focus on:

- Dealing with people, especially building relationships with members of cultures for whom this is important.
- Allowing time for relationship building, thinking through various unexpected issues, and using interruptions to think through the issues in sufficient detail.
- Assessing possible barriers to communication, such as language and style differences, tendencies to stereotype, explicit versus implicit forms of communication, and the use of interpreters with resulting translation difficulties (see Chapter 12).

PRACTICAL INSIGHT 13.4

CULTURE QUIZ

What Do You Do When . . . ?

1. The Chinese have stalled and stalled and stalled. Now, you have only one more day in Beijing before your flight home. Suddenly, during the final day of the negotiations, they appear to soften some of their demands—but of course, they expect you to give up some of yours as well. How could you have handled this better from the start?
2. You are introduced to Mr. Zhang Minwen at a banquet. You address him as Mr. Minwen, and become aware of his unfavorable reaction. You guess that you've said something wrong. But what?
3. You admire a beautiful Ming vase at your Chinese associate's home. Suddenly, before you leave, he thrusts a paper bag into your hands. You peek inside and see the vase. What do you do?
4. You've finally closed the deal, after exhausting both your patience and your company's travel budget. Now, two weeks later, the Chinese are asking for special considerations that change the terms of the agreement. How can they do this? Why are they doing it? And most important, what do you do?

5. On a business trip to Shanghai, you are invited to a banquet. Should you ask if your spouse may accompany you?

Culturally Sensitive Behavior Would Be . . .

1. This is a typical Chinese negotiating tactic. One way around this is to tell them you're leaving Friday—and actually leave the following Wednesday.
2. His name is Mr. Zhang. Chinese put their family name first.
3. You take it—because you admired it. You also reciprocate as soon as possible with an equally valuable gift.
4. The contract, for most Americans, represents the end of the negotiation. For the Chinese, however, it's just the beginning. Once a deal is made, the Chinese view their counterparts as trustworthy partners who can be relied upon for special favors . . . such as new terms in the contract.
5. Spouses (wives or husbands) aren't welcome at business social functions.

Source: From "In Keeping Up on Chinese Culture," by Valerie Frazee, *Personnel Journal,* October 1996, Vol. 75, No. 10. Reprinted with permission. Copyright Crain Communications, Inc.

- Clarifying agreements, so that a signed, legally enforceable agreement is finalized. This can be an issue for some countries where a handshake is regarded as signifying a contract. Emphasis on too much formality might signal a lack of trust.
- Exercising power, bearing in mind mutual dependences and differences in power between the parties. Too much difference in power might lead to negotiations that might not be honored in the long-term.

Some of these issues are discussed in Practical Insight 13.4.

Ethics in International Negotiations

Accepting bribes, encouraging corrupt practices, and lying about one's true motives and capabilities in honoring the terms of the contract are all unethical. The U.S. Foreign Corrupt Practices Act of 1977, revised in 1998, is an example of a country-specific approach to maintaining *universalism*—ethical standards and values applicable worldwide. This legislation was designed to prevent American companies from accepting or giving bribes and other illegal actions that take place outside the United States and its territories with international companies, foreign governments, and others.

Another view of ethics is *relativism*—a belief that values, rules, and regulations are local and cannot be applied in cross-border and international negotiations. In fact, it is precisely because of this view of ethics held by traditional Asian, Latin American, and African cultures that the U.S. Foreign Corrupt Practices Act was developed. Modifying the terms of a contract after the deal is signed is not uncommon in these cultures, reflecting the notion that what matters is what works. These issues are discussed in detail in Chapter 17.

What Is Decision Making?

The nature of decisions that the parties make during the negotiation process determines the success of the outcomes. Decisions made before, during, and after negotiations should be carefully thought out for their implications and consequences. Effective decision making is crucial in today's highly competitive and global business environment. Managers are faced daily with a variety of decisions that have important cross-border implications for expanding their operations, as well as protecting their businesses. Correct choices can affect the success of global corporations, and the careers of individual managers are often linked to correct decisions, particularly in the West.

One of the first things to understand about decision making is that individualistic and collectivistic cultures promote different styles of information gathering. In individualistic cultures, people often consider their own information and that of experts in the area. In collectivistic cultures, people live in a sea of information embedded in the in-group context.[26] For example, they use an open office design to promote information flow between individuals. Decisions in collectivistic cultures are more often made on a group basis rather than on an individual basis.

The Decision-Making Process

Decision making is the conscious process of moving toward objectives after considering various alternatives.[27] It is concerned with making an appropriate choice among a multitude of possible scenarios. Effective decision making has been called one of the most important management tasks.[28]

Decision making is studied primarily by the descriptive approach and the prescriptive approach. The *descriptive approach* focuses on the various steps that are involved in the way managers carry out the task of decision making. When you describe the various steps that managers take in cross-border transactions, then you are using the descriptive approach. It may involve consideration of such issues as the amount of information they need, the kind of approvals that are required, the chain of command that they must respect, and the amount of time they have to make the decision. Decisions involving implementation of a joint venture agreement or launching a new product in the global marketplace can be described using this approach.

The *prescriptive approach* is concerned with understanding the rational processes that managers use to reach an optimal outcome. The importance of *rationality*—the use of reason and logic—in making a decision is the key to the prescriptive approach. The prescriptive approach highlights the importance of both subjective and objective factors that must be considered in the art and science of making a decision. When you describe how managers arrive at the decision to undertake a joint venture, you are using the prescriptive approach. This approach takes into account the role of situational factors such as time and market pressures, as well as concessions that are needed for an optimal decision. Therefore, international managers must understand the role of culture and other variables, such as the national and organizational contexts, on the decision-making process.

The decision-making process is not just the province of managers. People make decisions on a daily basis when confronted with problems and opportunities. Some problems are routine, and managers can implement standard operating procedures or explicit rules. These are **programmed decisions.** On the other hand, some problems are new or complex, requiring consideration of many alternatives—they are **nonprogrammed decisions** and follow the following seven basic steps seen in Exhibit 13.6:

1. Defining the problem is the first step in decision making, and is probably the most important. A problem represents a state of affairs different from normal and desired functioning. If the problem is not well defined, or if it is defined incorrectly, then the solution will not solve the problem. For example, if the problem in an international negotiation is due to differences in political ideologies but the parties focus only on cultural preferences, the problem will worsen.

EXHIBIT 13.6
Steps in the Decision-Making Process

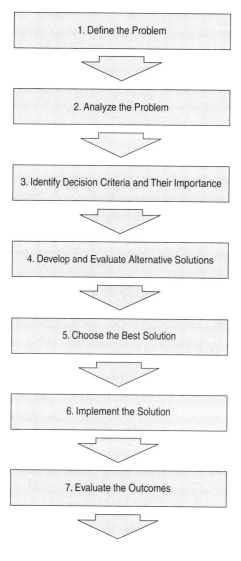

2. Analyzing the problem focuses on finding the key factors responsible for the problem. These factors could be present in the task, the people, or the nature of the situation. In launching a new product, if the key factor is lack of global market demand but the manager identifies product quality as the key factor, then he or she is analyzing the wrong factor to reach a decision.

3. Identifying decision criteria and their importance helps narrow the goals or objectives. For example, in selecting a new site for manufacturing, the manager may want to maximize the benefit of having a qualified workforce and minimize the importance of local taxes and tariffs. If the criteria for making decision are inappropriate, chances are high that the outcome will be poor.

4. Developing and evaluating alternative solutions enables the manager to consider different ways to solve the problem or take advantage of opportunities. The more alternatives considered, the more likely that an optimum solution will be found.

5. Choosing the best solution is not as easy as it may sound. A manager may come up with a set of solutions that look equally attractive, but the one that will maximize the outcome is not always clear. Such dilemmas are routine in international transactions. When confronted with political risk in China, some companies pull out completely without recognizing the long-term benefits of continuing to work with the political system.

6. Implementing the solution involves putting the decision into practice. The manager must consider factors such as the amount of time needed, nature of preferences of those implementing the plan, and the amount of resources needed to implement the decision correctly.

7. Evaluating outcomes is particularly important and often missed. In this step, managers consider whether the outcome actually solved the problem they defined in the first step. If it does not, then they need to assess whether the problem was defined correctly, whether all possible viable alternatives were identified, or whether important criteria were considered when choosing the solution. International managers should pay special attention to this step because there are many conflicting factors that must be carefully considered in decision making in the global context.

Internal and External Factors

External factors identified in the section on negotiation earlier in this chapter are relevant here. The importance of political factors in some countries, such as Brazil, India, and Egypt, requires managers to focus on the political preferences of the key parties involved rather than profitability alone. Economic factors, including volatility of exchange rates and the nature of foreign direct investment, are also factors for consideration. Decisions involving organizational factors include a consideration of whether the decision is made in the headquarters, subsidiaries, or with an alliance partner.

Internal factors important in decision making relate to differences in thought and reasoning processes found in different parts of the world. In most Asian cultures, managers are unwilling to make rapid decisions. This is also true for managers in France and in Middle Eastern, Latin American, and Mediterranean countries. They focus on different aspects of the issues, like to negotiate for a long time, and have a tendency to engage in a great deal of relationship building. This process delays the speed at which decisions are made. There is also an emphasis on associative thinking,

EXHIBIT 13.7
Deductive versus Inductive Styles of Decision Making

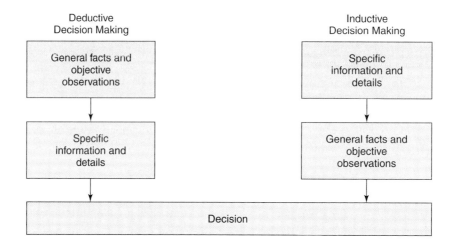

leading to associations among factors that are not necessarily logically linked in most Western countries.[29]

Some differences in reasoning are based on cultural preferences for inductive or deductive reasoning. Societies emphasizing **inductive reasoning** encourage managers to consider all of the specific facts and objective observations and slowly move toward generalizations and then a decision. Societies emphasizing **deductive reasoning** encourage managers to start with broad generalizations or categories and then evaluate the details to arrive at a decision. The difference between the two is illustrated in Exhibit 13.7.

Decisions arrived at through deductive reasoning appear poorly thought out and rapidly executed by people from inductive cultures. "Jumping to a conclusion" is the way many Japanese managers describe U.S. decision making.[30] The speed with which people think and the manner they use to approach the task affect decision making. The use of Internet and computer-mediated technology is making speed an even more important factor in cross-border negotiations and decision making. However, as we have discussed, national differences inherent in the process of decision making are not likely to disappear just because the countries are connected through the Internet.[31]

Implications for Managers

Styles of negotiation, conflict resolution, and decision making may become similar as our knowledge and understanding of other nations and cultures increase. The importance of being explicit about how much each party knows about the other's background cannot be overstated.[32] Increased familiarity with country-specific factors, such as tax and tariff laws, labor relations, and political structure, on the part of expatriates is also leading toward satisfactory outcomes in cross-border business relationships.[33] Awareness of business protocols, such as dress, greeting,[34] and meeting, and taking more time to conduct negotiations are also helping the process. When managers make a conscious attempt to understand the nuances and subtleties of another culture, it becomes easier to develop appropriate approaches to negotiation, conflict resolution, and decision making. Prior knowledge of factors such as whether the other party is likely to take a distributive or an integrative approach to negotiation or is likely to use a inductive or deductive reasoning are useful considerations. Some of these are illustrated in Practical Insight 13.5.

PRACTICAL INSIGHT 13.5

A CULTURAL DILEMMA

Maria and her family hold closely to their Greek roots. Nine siblings and cousins, including Maria, are working in the family's importing business, and their connection to one another is strong.

While Olympia Imports is now in its second generation, leadership is still in the hands of the first-generation patriarch, Nick, who is 73. He and his brother, An, 65, who is Maria's father, founded the company more than 40 years ago.

Given the current international economic scene, the $12 million business is performing fairly well. However, Maria, 35, and a few of her cousins and siblings want to effect some change. Maria heads up sales and sees new product opportunities.

"Times are changing, but my uncle and my father refuse to recognize that as being so," she says. "They come from a culture where leadership is exclusively male. Uncle Nick has no intention of retiring. When he dies, it will be my father's turn to run the business, and when he dies, the next-oldest male will take over."

Maria has a college degree, and so do most of her cousins and siblings, but the values of the males among them are still very rooted in their traditional culture.

"Succession planning really isn't an option for this family," says Maria. "The rules are prescribed in advance. The younger generation, and especially the women, want to be heard. I'd like to know how we can have a voice in decision-making. What happens to consensus? What happens to team-building? And how can we create a forum or structure to encourage the generation of ideas?"

Response 1: Raise the Bar*

Maria needs to realize this is not a Greek tragedy—not yet, anyway.

In a culture where leadership is traditionally male and where birth order dictates organizational hierarchy in a family business Maria's situation is typical if no less frustrating.

As such, Maria's challenges are more "generational" than "gender-based"—pitting her skills, goals, and objectives against the cultural ideologies of her father's generation.

This situation is something she cannot change today or first thing tomorrow.

The best way Maria can constructively bring about change in the business is by accepting this reality and focusing on raising the company's success bar, not by dwelling on the dramatics of "having her voice heard."

Let's look at this from another perspective. Maria already directs sales—a critical role in any business and one that her mother or aunts likely never could have achieved.

In her father's mind, Maria may have already reached rare heights for a female, and she is perceived as a "modern woman and as living proof that an evolution is taking place."

To move forward, Maria must focus on effectively communicating her ideas and goals both for herself and for the business.

If Maria can succeed in delivering on an aggressive sales objective or in carving out a new sales or product initiative, then she will best position herself to have the professional respect and the "ears" that she will need for her ideas.

Response 2: Build Your Own Team†

If we accept Maria's statement that "succession planning really isn't an option," then we must look for other ways to meet the needs of the younger family members.

They must clearly separate issues of participation in and contribution to the company from the issue of who will be the leader. Given the traditional values of the younger males, can this generation present a reasonably congruent view of the future, especially across gender lines?

Can they agree on the direction in which to move the business, on the changes to make, on a timetable for such changes, and on the roles they will play? As these questions suggest, they must begin team-building among themselves.

Would it be possible to assemble the entire family, look 10 years into the future, and talk about the goals and dreams of each family member, for both the family and the business?

If the whole family cannot be brought together, perhaps the younger generation can gather on its own.

Maria, her siblings, and her cousins may find it easier to get their fathers to accept change if the ideas come from their fathers' peers. It might be useful to look outside the company for men their fathers know and respect, men who are not so wedded to tradition and who can act as champions for the younger generation and help begin the process of introducing change.

Maria must decide if her needs can be met at Olympia Imports under any circumstances. Going to another company may be her only means of making a contribution. And if things at the family firm improve, she could rejoin it with more experience.

*By Olga Staios, executive director of the Family Enterprise Institute in Cincinnati.

†By Paul L. Sessions, director of the Center for Family Business at the University of New Haven in West Haven, Conn.

Source: From "A Cultural Dilemma," *Nation's Business,* March 1999. Reprinted with permission of U.S. Chamber of Commerce.

COPYRIGHT 1999 U.S. Chamber of Commerce

Summary

In this chapter, we described the basic processes of negotiation, conflict resolution, and decision making. Multinational and global corporations must be aware of the significance of these issues and how they affect their interest worldwide. Different environments result in different styles of negotiation, conflict resolution, and decision making.

Cross-border negotiations are vital for competition in the global marketplace. Negotiations between corporations occur each day. In order to effectively negotiate across cultures and borders, each step in the negotiation process must be performed with cultural context in mind. Success in negotiation depends on understanding the other party's needs and goals and the situation of the negotiation itself. Cultural, national, and organizational differences can affect success. For example, behaviors and concepts that we take for granted are not considered acceptable negotiating tactics in all cultures.

Much negotiation deals with conflict between two parties, and conflict can also result from breakdowns in communication. Some of these breakdowns are due to cultural and national factors, which can be overcome through understanding and education of the negotiators. Some conflict is also created because cultures promote different types of decision making. Understanding the process of decision making can alleviate some of the problems encountered in negotiating across cultures and borders.

Key Terms and Concepts

bargaining, *389*
conflict, *402*
decision making, *405*

deductive reasoning, *408*
inductive reasoning, *408*
international negotiation, *389*

negotiation, *389*
nonprogrammed decisions, *406*
programmed decisions, *406*

Discussion Questions

1. Define negotiation. Discuss the significance of negotiation involving cross-border and cross-cultural transactions. Give examples.

2. What are the stages of negotiation in international management? Give examples of each of the stages from your own experience in negotiations or from other sources.

3. Why are negotiations difficult to conduct in international transactions? List as many factors as you can think of from cultural, national, and organizational influences that affect the outcome of negotiations.

4. How do conflicts arise between low- and high-context cultures? How would you advise managers of low-context cultures to be more effective in handling conflicts with managers from high-context cultures?

5. Discuss the different types of decision making. How would inductive reasoning affect the way decisions are made? Give an example of how inductive reasoning might conflict with the process of deductive reasoning in negotiations.

Minicase

Conflict Resolution for Contrasting Cultures

An American sales manager of a large Japanese manufacturing firm in the United States sold a multi-million-dollar order to an American customer. The order was to be filled by headquarters in Tokyo. The customer requested some changes to the product's standard specifications and a specified deadline for delivery.

Because the firm had never made a sale to this American customer before, the sales manager was eager to provide good service and on-time delivery. To ensure a coordinated response, she organized a strategic planning session of the key division managers that would be involved in processing the order. She sent a copy of the meeting agenda to each participant. In attendance were the sales manager, four other Americans, three Japanese managers, the Japanese heads of finance and customer support, and the Japanese liaison to Tokyo headquarters. The three Japanese managers had been in the United States for less than two years.

The hour meeting included a brainstorming session to discuss strategies for dealing with the customer's requests, a discussion of possible timelines, and the next steps each manager would take. The American managers dominated, participating actively in the brainstorming session and discussion. They proposed a timeline and an action plan. In contrast, the Japanese managers said little, except to talk among themselves in Japanese. When the sales manager asked for their opinion about the Americans' proposed plan, two of the Japanese managers said they needed more time to think about it. The other one looked down, sucked air through his teeth, and said, "It may be difficult in Japan."

Concerned about the lack of participation from the Japanese but eager to process the customer's order, the sales manager sent all meeting participants an e-mail with the American managers' proposal and a request for feedback. She said frankly that she felt some of the managers hadn't participated much in the meeting, and she was clear about the need for timely action. She said that if she didn't hear from them within a week, she'd assume consensus and follow the recommended actions of the Americans.

A week passed without any input from the Japanese managers. Satisfied that she had consensus, she proceeded. She faxed the specifications and deadline to headquarters in Tokyo and requested that the order be given priority attention. After a week without any response, she sent another fax asking headquarters to confirm that it could fill the order. The reply came the next day: "Thank you for the proposal. We are currently considering your request."

Time passed, while the customer asked repeatedly about the order's status. The only response she could give was that there wasn't any information yet. Concerned, she sent another fax to Tokyo in which she outlined the specifications and timeline as requested by the customer. She reminded the headquarters liaison of the order's size and said the deal might fall through if she didn't receive confirmation immediately. In addition, she asked the liaison to see whether he could determine what was causing the delay. Three days later, he told her that there was some resistance to the proposal and that it would be difficult to meet the deadline.

When informed, the customer gave the sales manager a one-week extension but said that another supplier was being considered. Frantic, she again asked the Japanese liaison to intercede. Her bonus and division's profit margin rested on the success of this sale. As before, the reply from Tokyo was that it would be "difficult" to meet the customer's demands so quickly and that the sales manager should please ask the customer to be patient.

They lost the contract. Infuriated, the sales manager went to the subsidiary's Japanese president, explained what happened, and complained about the lack of commitment from headquarters and Japanese colleagues in the United States. The president said he shared her disappointment but that there were things she didn't understand about the subsidiary's relationship with headquarters. The liaison had informed the president that headquarters refused her order because it had committed most of its output for the next few months to a customer in Japan.

Enraged, the sales manager asked the president how she was supposed to attract customers when the Americans in the subsidiary were getting no support from the Japanese and were being treated like second-class citizens by headquarters. Why, she asked, wasn't she told that Tokyo was committed to other customers?

She said: "The Japanese are too slow in making decisions. By the time they get everyone on board in Japan, the U.S. customer has gone elsewhere. This whole mess started because the Japanese don't participate in meetings. We invite them and they just sit and talk to each other in Japanese. Are they hiding something? I never know what they're thinking, and it drives me crazy when they say things like 'It is difficult' or when they suck air through their teeth.

"It doesn't help that they never respond to my written messages. Don't these guys ever read their e-mail? I sent that e-mail out immediately after the meeting so they would have plenty of time to react. I wonder whether they are really committed to our sales mission or putting me off. They seem more concerned about how we interact than about actually solving the problem. There's clearly some sort of Japanese information network that I'm not part of. I feel as if I work in a vacuum, and it makes me look foolish to customers. The Japanese are too confident in the superiority of their product over the competition and too conservative to react swiftly to the needs of the market. I know that head-quarters reacts more quickly to similar requests from their big customers in Japan, so it makes me and our customers feel as if we aren't an important market."

Said the U.S.-based Japanese: "The American salespeople are impatient. They treat everything as though it is an emergency and never plan ahead. They call meetings at the last minute and expect peo-ple to come ready to solve a problem about which they know nothing in advance. It seems the Amer-icans don't want our feedback; they talk so fast and use too much slang.

"By the time we understood what they were talking about in the meeting, they were off on a dif-ferent subject. So, we gave up trying to participate. The meeting leader said something about time-lines, but we weren't sure what she wanted. So, we just agreed so as not to hold up the meeting. How can they expect us to be serious about participating in their brainstorming session? It is nothing more than guessing in public; it is irresponsible.

"The Americans also rely too much on written communication. They send us too many memos and too much e-mail. They seem content to sit in their offices creating a lot of paperwork without knowing how people will react. They are so cut-and-dried about business and do not care what others think. They talk a lot about making fast decisions, but they do not seem to be concerned if it is the right decision. That is not responsible, nor does it show consideration for the whole group.

"They have the same inconsiderate attitude toward headquarters. They send faxes demanding swift action, without knowing the obstacles headquarters has to overcome, such as requests from many cus-tomers around the world that have to be analyzed. The real problem is that there is no loyalty from our U.S. customers. They leave one supplier for another based solely on price and turnaround time. Why should we commit to them if they aren't ready to commit to us? Also, we are concerned that the sales-force has not worked hard enough to make customers understand our commitment to them."

Source: From C. C. Clarke and G. D. Lipp, "Conflict Resolution for Contrasting Cultures," *Training & Development,* 1998. Copyright © 1998, *T&D Magazine* (formerly *Training & Development*), American Society for Training & Development. Reprinted with permission. All rights reserved.

DISCUSSION QUESTIONS

1. How are the managers of the Japanese manufacturing firm different from the American managers in the way they approach conflict resolution and decision making?
2. Why do the Japanese consider the Americans managers impatient?
3. What would you do to increase the amount of cooperation between the two parties?
4. Why did the Japanese not respond to the e-mails and written messages from the Americans?

Notes

1. R. J. Lewicki, J. A. Litterer, J. W. Minton, and D. M. Saunders, *Negotiation,* 2nd ed. (Burr Ridge, IL: Irwin, 1994).
2. N. J. Adler, *International Dimensions of Organizational Behavior,* 4th ed. (Cincinnati: South-Western, 2002).
3. H. Cohen, *You Can Negotiate Anything* (New York: Bantam Books, 1989); H. Cohen, *Negotiate This! By Caring, but Not THAT Much* (New York: Warner Books, 2003).
4. S. E. Weiss and W. Stripp, "Negotiating with Foreign Business Persons: An Introduction for Americans with Propositions on Six Cultures," New York: New York University Graduate School of Business Administration, Working Paper 85–6 (1985); I. W. Zartman, ed., *The 50% Solution* (Garden City, NY: Anchor Books, 1976).
5. J. L. Graham, "A Theory of Interorganizational Negotiations," *Research in Marketing* 9 (1987), pp. 163–183.
6. Lewicki, Litterer, Minton, and Saunders, *Negotiation.*
7. J. L. Graham, "Brazilian, Japanese, and American Business Negotiations," *Journal of Interna-tional Business Studies,* Spring/Summer 1983, pp. 47–61; J. L. Graham, "The Influence of Cul-ture on the Process of Business Negotiations: An Exploratory Study," *Journal of International Business Studies,* 16 (1985), pp. 81–96; J. L. Graham, D. K. Kim, C. Y. Lin, and M. Robinson, "Buyer–Seller Negotiations around the Pacific Rim: Differences in Fundamental Exchange

Processes," *Journal of Consumer Research* 15 (1988), pp. 48–54; J. L. Graham, A. T. Mintu, and W. Rodgers, "Explorations of Negotiation Behaviors in Ten Foreign Cultures Using a Model Developed in the United States," *Management Science* 40, no. 1 (1994), pp. 72–95.

8. G. Fisher, *International Negotiation: A Cross-Cultural Perspective* (Chicago: Intercultural Press, 1980).

9. R. J. Janosik, "Rethinking the Culture–Negotiation Link," *Negotiation Journal* 3 (1987), pp. 385–395; L. W. Pye, *Chinese Negotiating Style* (New York: Quorum Books, 1992); G. Hofstede, *Culture's Consequences: International Differences in Work-Related Values,* 2nd ed. (Thousand Oaks, CA: Sage, 2001).

10. D. A. Foster, *Bargaining across Borders: How to Negotiate Business Successfully Anywhere in the World* (New York; McGraw-Hill, 1992).

11. Weiss and Stripp, "Negotiating with Foreign Business Persons"; Foster, *Bargaining across Borders.*

12. Hofstede, *Culture's Consequences.*

13. J. L. Graham, "A Comparison of Japanese and American Business Negotiations," *International Journal of Research in Marketing* 1 (1984), pp. 50–68; J. L. Graham, "The Japanese Negotiation Style: Characteristics of a Distinct Approach," *Negotiation Journal* 9 (1993), pp. 123–140.

14. J. W. Salacuse, "Making Deals in Strange Places: A Beginners Guide to International Business Negotiations," *Negotiation Journal* 4 (1988), pp. 5–13.

15. U. S. Rangan and C. A. Bartlett, "Caterpillar Tractor Company Case." In C. A. Bartlett and S. Ghoshal, *International Management, Text, Cases, and Readings in Cross-Border Management,* 3rd ed. (New York: McGraw-Hill/ Irwin, 2000) pp. 259–279; Harvard Business School Case 385-276, 1985.

16. J. L. Graham and Y. Sano, *Smart Bargaining* (New York: Harper Business, 1989).

17. J. Hooker, *Working across Cultures* (Stanford: Stanford University Press, 2003).

18. E. T. Hall, *The Silent Language* (Garden City, NY: Anchor Books/Doubleday, 1959).

19. E. T. Hall, *Beyond Culture* (Garden City, NY: Anchor Press/Doubleday, 1976).

20. B. L. DeMente, *Korean Etiquette and Ethics in Business* (Lincolnwood, IL: NTC Publishing Group, 1994).

21. J. L. Graham and N. M. Lam, "The Chinese Negotiation," *Harvard Business Review,* October 2003, pp. 82–91.

22. M. Bond, *The Psychology of the Chinese People* (Hong Kong: Oxford University Press, 1986).

23. T. J. Mullaney and R. Grover, "The Web Mogul," *Business Week,* October 13, 2003, pp. 62–70.

24. R. S. Bhagat, B. L. Kedia, P. Harveston, and H. C. Triandis, "Cultural Variations in the Cross-Border Transfer of Organizational Knowledge: An Integrative Framework," *Academy of Management Review* 27, no. 2 (2002), pp. 204–221; R. S. Bhagat, B. L. Kedia, P. Harveston, and B. Srivastava, "Creation, Transformation, and Flow of Knowledge across the Individualism–Collectivism Divide: Implications for MNCs." In *European International Business Academy Proceedings* (Copenhagen: Copenhagen School of Business, 2004).

25. Hooker, *Working across Cultures;* Graham and Lam, "The Chinese Negotiation."

26. Hall, *Beyond Culture;* Bhagat, Kedia, Harveston, and Triandis, "Cultural Variations in the Cross-Border Transfer of Organizational Knowledge."

27. F. A. Shull, Jr., A. L. Delbecq, and L. L. Cummings, *Organizational Decision Making* (New York: McGraw-Hill, 1970).

28. H. J. Mintzberg, *Mintzberg on Management: Inside Our Strange World of Organizations* (New York: Free Press, 1998); P. Evans, V. Pucik, and J-L. Barsoux, *The Global Challenge* (New York: McGraw-Hill, 2002).

29. E. Glenn and P. Glenn, *Man and Mankind: Conflicts and Communication between Cultures* (Norwood, NJ: Ablex, 1981).

30. L. Copeland and L. Griggs, *Going International* (New York: Random House, 1985).

31. F. Cairncross, *The Death of Distance: How the Communications Revolution Is Changing Our Lives* (Boston: Harvard Business School Press, 2001).

32. S. E. Weiss, "Negotiating with 'Romans'—Part 1," *Sloan Management Review,* Winter 1994, pp. 51–61; S. E. Weiss, "Negotiating with 'Romans'—Part 2," *Sloan Management Review,* Spring 1994, pp. 85–99.

33. J. S. Black, H. B. Gregersen, M. E. Mendenhall, and L. K. Stroh, *Globalizing People through International Assignments* (Reading, MA: Addison-Wesley, 1999).

34. R. R. Gesteland, *Cross-Cultural Business Behavior: Marketing, Negotiating, and Managing across Cultures* (Copenhagen: Copenhagen Business School Press, 2001).

CHAPTER FOURTEEN

Work Motivation across Cultures and Borders

Chapter Learning Objectives

After completing this chapter, you should be able to:

- Explain how people's conceptions of work and working differ in different national environments.
- Discuss the significance of models of work motivation from a U.S. perspective and the extent to which they might be applied in non-U.S. cultures.
- Understand how various cultural dimensions support different patterns of motivation and related work outcomes in different environments.
- Distinguish among the different patterns of motivation, job involvement, job satisfaction, and organizational commitment.
- Understand the significance of organizational rewards and various monetary and nonmonetary aspects of compensation in motivating different types of people in different parts of the world.

Opening Case: Avon and Mary Kay Create Opportunities for Women

There are more than 15,000 Avon ladies in Russia, and not one of them rings the doorbell.

Bowing both to security fears and old-time Soviet etiquette, Russian representatives of the world's largest direct-sales cosmetics company do not go door to door. They do not even make house calls to established customers. Instead, they sell lipsticks, wrinkle creams and facial toners in factories, airports, beauty parlors, laboratories and, sometimes, from a park bench.

"Russians are afraid to open their door to strangers," explained Mariya Gerasyova, 31, the company's national sales director. "And even if they know you, they don't want you to see how their apartments look, the lack of repair, the dirt."

But Russian women have swept aside almost every other cultural inhibition to embrace the latest capitalist profit notion sweeping the Russian economy—direct-sales marketing. Avon Products Inc. of New York and its main rival, Mary Kay Cosmetics, a unit of the Mary Kay Corporation of Dallas, have invaded the Russian market the last two years and recruited an all-female army to sell tens of millions of dollars worth of beauty products each year.

And Russia—with its swelling rolls of unemployed or underemployed professionals—is a recruiter's dream. Thousands of women trained as engineers, physicists and teachers are grabbing an entrepreneurial opportunity that even five years ago was both illegal and socially taboo.

"The professional qualifications of these women are unbelievable," declared Susan Kropf, president for new and emerging markets at Avon, on her first visit to Russia last month. "When the first Russian coordinator I met told me she was a surgeon, I fell out of my chair." Mrs. Gerasyova, similarly, is a trained linguist and a reserve lieutenant in the Russian Army.

As a result of their new-found wealth and independence, the lives of many of these newly minted entrepreneurs have undergone a more radical make-over than had taken place during the collapse of the Soviet Union five years ago. "When I started, my husband was always furious," said Svetlana Morosova, 29, an area manager for Avon. She sat at a table in the Avon sales office in Moscow with a dozen other managers and sales coordinators. All of them were elegantly turned out in muted pastel business suits. And all of them nodded knowingly.

"He couldn't stand the fact that I was making more money than him, that I had changed, become more self-assured and independent," she said. Her husband, a policeman, earns less than $200 a month.

Two years ago, Mrs. Morosova, who has advanced degrees in mathematics and economics, was sitting at home with her twins, a boy and a girl who are now 4 years old, struggling to find part-time accounting work when a friend introduced her to Avon. She made her first sale to other young mothers at a children's playground.

She is now a manager, a job that pays close to $2,000 a month in a country where the average salary is $120. She drives a company car, a beige Russian-made Zhiguli. Her mother baby-sits for her children, and unlike many Russian marriages that have been torn apart by the wife's sudden financial success, hers has survived. Her husband "has even learned to cook," she said to the laughter of her colleagues.

If many Russian women view the American cosmetics industry as an economic godsend, the industry is embracing Russia—with a population of about 150 million hungry for Western-style goods—as a marketing paradise.

For Avon, which is already active throughout Europe, Russia is one of several hot emerging markets, which also include China, South Africa and Latin America.

It started off gingerly in 1993, having been burned in an ill-fated bid to enter the Soviet market in the early 1980's, and at first it sold its products through stores. But last year, Avon began full-scale direct sales. It has already signed up 16,000 sales representatives in Moscow, St. Petersburg and the Siberian town of Perm and expects $30 million in revenue this year, up from $9 million in 1995. John Law, Avon's general manager in Moscow, says its long-term plan is to "sell a lot of lipstick." Ms. Kropf, the marketing executive, calls the country "Avon heaven."

For Mary Kay, which has less experience in emerging markets, the former Soviet Union is the focus of its overseas growth. It began its operations here in September 1993 and now has 25,000 representatives in Russia and the other former Soviet republics. The company had sales of $25 million in the region last year and expects to triple that figure in 1996.

The American companies' penetration of Russia is all the more impressive given the country's 70 years of Communist indoctrination against private enterprise, which some people still refer to as "speculation." "For the older generation, selling is still viewed as shameful," Mrs. Gerasyova, Avon's national sales director, said. But another Soviet tradition played against that constraint: when shortages were acute, many women lined up for hours, bought in bulk and privately bartered cosmetics for meat, perfume for diapers. "We took it easy at first, contacting friends and relatives, the way it was always done," Mrs. Gerasyova explained.

Avon, which had overall sales last year of $4.5 billion, and Mary Kay, which had revenue of $950 million in 1995, are following slightly different pricing and marketing approaches in Russia. Avon representatives buy Avon products on credit, then resell them to friends, acquaintances and co-workers at a recommended retail price, pocketing a difference that averages 20 percent. They do not have to pay any cash up front. Prices of Avon cosmetics are lower than many popular European brands found in Russian stores. A lipstick costs $5.16, a moisturizing cleanser, $5.79.

Mary Kay representatives, who call themselves "skin care consultants," have to buy start-up demonstration product kits for $85. Their selling efforts focus on a free makeup and skin-care lesson, and they earn commissions of 20 to 40 percent on prices that range from $12 for a cleanser to $18.75 for a moisturizer.

A single purchase can take a big cut out of an average Russian woman's income, but many customers say they do not care. Natasha Matyonina, 28, a mother of one who earns less than $500 a month as a baby sitter, said she considers the Avon products she buys as necessities. "I can go without a lot of things, but I can't imagine not having makeup," she said.

The entrepreneurs who sell Avon and Mary Kay products enjoy advantages that the owners of larger, more visible businesses lack. For one thing, their tiny, home-based ventures can easily escape the notice of tax collectors (though both companies say they instruct their representatives to register with the tax authorities). Better yet, they are unlikely to be detected by the mobsters and racketeers who demand protection money from cash businesses.

At Avon's sales center in Moscow, training new representatives can seem a little like a pink-tinted Parris Island, the Marine training base in South Carolina. The novices huddle in pained shyness, their shabby clothes, florid makeup and awkward body language clashing with the sleek corporate look of company veterans. Within weeks, though, they emerge radiating the trademark poise of professional Avon ladies. "They come to us like mice, and we turn them into firebirds," Mrs. Gerasyova said brightly.

While not a single saleswoman said she considered herself a "feminist"—a word with a sharply negative connotation in Russia—all spoke enthusiastically of the self-reliance they had won and of the opportunity they had gained to commingle with like-minded women. "This kind of independence has changed the way we live; it changes our relationship with men," said Tatyana Navrodskaya, a Mary Kay consultant. "But it's not feminism. You can still remain feminine."

Mrs. Navrodskaya, a high school drama teacher, was teaching an entirely different kind of class to three women in a spare room her Mary Kay team leader rented from a home for the blind in suburban Moscow. Dingy walls were plastered with glossy pastel company posters and pictures of the company founder, Mary Kay Ash, improbably blond and dewy for a woman who is believed to be in her 70's (though she will not reveal her age). "You don't think she's had a face lift?" whispered one customer, as she studied the gauzy portrait. "Come off it," her friend retorted cynically. "Have you seen my grandmother? Of course she's had a face lift."

Mrs. Navrodskaya expertly shepherded all three women back to the subject—the proper application of a walnut mask. An hour later, the women were giddily inspecting their buffed, polished and delicately painted faces. All three bought lipsticks, eyeshadow and cleansers.

"We had good cosmetics in Soviet times, brands like Lancome and Yves Saint Laurent," one of the customers said, "but you could never be sure to find it, there would be lines, shortages, and always unpleasant sales people."

There are no longer lines or shortages of fancy cosmetics in big cities like Moscow and St. Petersburg, but the prices are often too high for average women, and the service mostly remains as before—icily indifferent. "The idea that you can ask for advice or information about the product, and actually get it, that's amazing," one of the other customers said.

Mrs. Navrodskaya, who has three children, said the $300 to $400 she earns a month selling Mary Kay products in her spare time dwarfs her teacher's salary of $150, to say nothing of the $54 a month that her husband earns as a theater director. "It has changed my life," she said simply. "We simply could not survive were it not for this."

Source: From Alessandra Stanley, "Avon and Mary Kay Create Opportunities for Women," August 15, 1996. Copyright © 1996 The New York Times Co. Reprinted with permission.

Discussion Questions

1. Would American women sell cosmetics from a park bench? Why or why not?
2. What motivators of individuals in Russia do not motivate people in the United States? How could a manager encourage motivation in Russia?
3. Based on this case, discuss why it is important for managers to understand motivational differences across national borders and cultures.

What Is Motivation?

Managers talk about motivation constantly, and they work to improve the motivation of their subordinates in order to increase productivity and morale in the workplace. One theme runs through the previous chapters: Because people and societies differ in various ways, international managers must understand the significance of unusual circumstances and become culturally sensitive to differences in varied work environments.

Managers of global corporations have firsthand knowledge and some instinctively feel that cultural differences found in different parts of the world have important influences on how people feel when they work, what energizes them, and what makes them remain committed to their jobs and careers and companies. The motives for working differ widely, according to the important national and cultural values of each society.[1] However, before we can discuss the significance of cultural influences on motivation, we should define motivation.

About 2,000 years ago, Confucius noted that all people are basically the same, but they are motivated to do different things at different points in their lives. Recently, Honda Motor Company cofounder Takeo Fujisawa observed that while Japanese and American managers are 95 percent the same, they differ in the most important aspects. Philosophers from Germany, France, India, Greece, the United States, and other countries have all observed that differences in cultural upbringing makes a difference in how we think and how we behave in work organizations.

Motivation is the amount of effort that an employee is willing to put into work to accomplish an organizationally valued task. Motivation is a cognitive process, that is, it lies in the mind of the worker. It explains how workers get started on a task, how they maintain performance, why they keep working, and why they might quit working. Motivated workers have pleasant internal reactions while performing a task. They come to work earlier, put in longer hours, and do not mind "walking the extra mile" to get the job done. Another way of looking at motivation is to view it as the willingness to exert high levels of effort to accomplish organizational goals, to the extent that these efforts are rewarded.[2]

Managers cannot see motivation by observing employees, unless definite yardsticks measure the output of employees. An employee who produces 10 units an hour is probably twice as motivated as another employee who produces 5 units an hour, if other circumstances which affect productivity are identical in both situations.

Motivation is not the only factor that affects productivity. Managers must take note of appropriate job descriptions that improve the employee's perceptions of the work role of the job, as well as job-relevant ability and other constraints on performance. New employees are unlikely to have a clear-cut perception of what is needed on the job in order to accomplish flawless performance. It takes some time for them to understand the job and to play an active role in removing various constraints that might hinder performance in one way or another. *Ability* is clearly the most important factor in performing a job. Ability reflects the cumulative influence of a multitude of work-related experiences that can be applied to a job to improve performance to a maximum level.[3] A new salesperson selling used cars, who has never sold used cars before in his or her life, cannot perform as well as a person who has some basic abilities developed from years of experience as well as some native inclination to perform sales tasks.

Companies can also create work environments that facilitate productivity on the job. Global companies like Apple Computers, Microsoft Corporation, and Hewlett-Packard have created work environments where one can report to work whenever one feels the impulse to contribute in a meaningful manner to a creative task. In the early 1980s, in particular, Apple Computers created work environments where programmers and hardware engineers could arrive almost any time at the centers and design computers such as Apple I and Apple II. Such environments facilitate work performance and motivate workers to continue working for a long time without experiencing mental or physical fatigue.

Theories of Work Motivation

We begin the discussion by raising a fundamental question: Why do we need theories of work motivation? People in all cultures, whether advanced industrialized countries or emergent economies or traditional cultures, have implicit theories to explain why people come to work, what they might want from work, and why they continue to work. However, the difficulty with these implicit theories is that they are not systematically developed and can be understood only as insightful "hunches" which, while helpful in some circumstances, are often at a loss to describe more than one situation.

Theories of motivation began to evolve in the United States and in some parts of western Europe. You already know some of these theories, but a quick overview is helpful. We begin with the needs theories, outlined in Exhibit 14.1. These theories provide some important foundations for understanding patterns of motivation, not only in the United States, but in dissimilar cultures as well.

EXHIBIT 14.1 Comparing Needs Theories of Motivation

Source: Adapted and expanded from S. L. McShane and M. A. Von Glinow, *Organizational Behavior,* 2nd ed. (New York: McGraw-Hill/Irwin, 2003), p. 135.

Rewards from the Job	Maslow's Needs Hierarchy Theory	Alderfer's ERG Theory	Herzberg's Motivator-Hygiene Theory	McClelland's Achievement Motivation Theory	
Opportunities for advancement Meaningful work Use of valued skills and abilities Opportunities for ongoing learning	Self-actualization	Growth	Motivators: Advancement Growth Achievement	Need for achievement	Generally referred to as higher order needs and are fulfilled in professional, managerial, and creative positions
Acknowledgement of contributions Influence on work processes Respect and appreciation	Esteem			Need for power	
Supervisory support Co-worker support Social support from work	Affiliation	Relatedness	Hygience factors: Working conditions Job security Salary	Need for affiliation	Generally referred to as middle order needs and are fulfilled in administrative, technical, and clerical positions
Job security Fringe benefits Healthy working conditions	Security	Existence			
Basic pay	Physiological				Lower order needs fulfilled in lower level jobs

PRACTICAL INSIGHT 14.1

EFFECTIVE MANAGERS CAN RECOGNIZE AND ADAPT TO DIFFERENT WORK STYLES AND CULTURES

Getting work done through others requires a free flow of accurate information and open, productive relationships with employees. But that's easier said than done in a diverse workplace where many cultures collide.

Many a manager has been frustrated by the employee who nods in apparent understanding of a direction, then does just the opposite. Or there are the staff members who grow cold and distant after receiving feedback on their work, as well as the team members who clam up at meetings when asked for suggestions.

But culture is behind our behavior on the job. Often without our realization, culture influences how close we stand, how loud we speak, how we deal with conflict—even how we participate in a meeting.

While many cultural norms influence a manager's behavior and subsequent reactions, five particularly important ones are hierarchy and status, groups vs. individual orientation, time consciousness, communication and conflict resolution. By failing to understand how culture impacts individual needs and preferences, managers often misinterpret behaviors.

Nurturing a Safe, Inclusive Climate

When we ask people to describe a desirable work climate, we tend to hear very similar answers—regardless of geography or industry. Responses include words such as "high trust," "collaborative," "accountable," "feeling connected," "effective problem solving" and "feeling valued." But trying to create a climate in which complex work groups feel the same way about these matters is not easy.

Consider the norm of hierarchy and status. If you want all people to feel valued and to participate in problem solving or decision-making, differences in this norm could be inhibiting. An employee who has been taught deference to age, gender or title, might—out of respect—shy away from being honest or offering ideas because offering suggestions to an elder or a boss might appear to be challenging authority.

The manager also may need to structure a climate that balances preferences for group and individual work. The employee who can't or won't subordinate individual needs or desires for the good of the group may perform better working alone.

A culturally competent manager will create opportunities for individuals to take some risks and explore projects that don't require coordinating with others. Doing so can encourage employees with a strong individualist bent to draw attention to important matters, such as policies or procedures that don't work.

On the other hand, when managers place too high a premium on avoiding workplace discord, even individualistic employees may be discouraged from providing potentially constructive feedback.

Time-conscious managers may see people whose cultures take a more relaxed view toward deadlines as being less committed to team goals, as well as less dependable, accountable and reliable. Or, consider the employee who nods "yes" but doesn't mean it. Both individuals are not only operating according to their own rules of communication, but they also are interpreting each other's behavior through that lens.

If you are a direct communicator, you probably expect a "tell it like it is" response from the employee. But the employee may be an indirect communicator who expects you to read the contextual clues to understand his response. His cultural background might require you to pick up on nonverbal cues to understand that his nodding and affirmative response is a polite, face-saving gesture, not an indication of agreement or understanding.

What happens with the team that clams up? Your egalitarian approach and individualistic orientation expects teamwork between manager and employees; you expect people to think and speak for themselves. But for staff members with a more hierarchical and group orientation, taking the initiative to make suggestions to an authority figure would be awkward for all involved. They may expect you as the manager to demonstrate your leadership by making decisions and giving directions.

Recognizing the Role of Culture

So what can you do? First, recognize the role culture plays in interactions and try to identify the critical elements of the cultures involved. What are your preferences and expectations, and what are the norms and preferences of your employee?

Needs Theories

Maslow's Motivation Theory

Psychologist Abraham Maslow suggested in the early 1950s that human beings are motivated by five basic needs, and that these needs form a hierarchical structure.[4] According to this U.S.-based theory, the higher order needs for self-esteem and self-actualization become activated and motivate behavior only after lower order needs have

Second, don't interpret their behavior through your cultural background. Most employees don't intend to be deceptive, difficult or unproductive; they are simply adhering to their cultural programming.

However, to get the information and effective communication you need, you have to find alternative approaches that are more in line with the employee's culture. Here are some suggestions:

- Avoid yes/no questions such as "Is that clear?" or "Do you understand?" Give the employee options from which to choose. Ask for specific information, such as "Which step will you do first with this new procedure?"

- If time allows, perform the task along with the employee or watch to see how well he understands your directions.

- Try using passive language that focuses on the situation or behavior, rather than the individual. For example, "Calls must be answered by the third ring" or "All requests need accurate charge codes in order to be processed."

- Give employees enough lead time to collect their thoughts before a meeting so they can feel prepared to bring input.

- Have employees work in small groups, generating ideas through discussion and presenting input as a group.

Developing Employees

One of the most important functions of a manager is developing and grooming employees for promotion. Cross-cultural norms have a huge impact on this job because of the underlying assumptions a manager might make about an employee's potential.

To determine promotion potential, managers consider such questions as: How is initiative demonstrated? What behaviors show commitment? How much is high potential determined by accomplishing the task and how much is determined by good interpersonal skills? How do employees get to use and showcase their unique talents?

In answering these questions, a manager aware of the influence of hierarchy, time consciousness, communication and group orientation 'will make fewer assumptions about' the motivations and drive of certain employees.

Initiative won't necessarily be defined as acting without waiting for directions but seen perhaps through the lens of a good team member who kept the group moving, made some contribution and helped preserve harmony in the face of expected differences.

Commitment may not be defined in terms of meeting deadlines but also as encouraging further exploration of an issue, and thus more creative or flexible in striving to get a best outcome. Perhaps an employee will never openly challenge ideas at a meeting but instead will offer back-door suggestions that can influence the direction of a project.

A manager who is aware of different cultural norms is less likely to incorrectly interpret behaviors and prescribe ineffective courses of action when developing people. Toward this end, here are some suggestions for managers to consider:

- Teach employees to interpret the culture of the organization by pointing out factors such as how people dress, recreational patterns and the formality or informality of communication. Employees can make effective choices when they clearly understand the informal rules of the organizational culture.

- Help employees understand the difference between deadlines that are non-negotiable and those that are more elastic. Get an accurate sense of the person's planning and organizational skills. Then, set clear expectations that help the employee perform better and build in follow-up sessions.

- Coach employees who are uncomfortable acknowledging their own individual work to talk about accomplishments through work group performance. As employees try to move up, the need to sell oneself in an unassuming way as part of a work group is a comfortable way to show one's part in a group's accomplishment.

- Focus on relationship building. An employee can learn that giving a manager feedback is an act of loyalty and help. But this is a paradigm shift that requires rapport, safety and trust.

been satisfied. For example, workers cannot feel motivated to perform on a job that requires complex learning skills if they are frightened about safety at work or do not get enough nutrition to sustain their bodily functions.

It is likely that two or three of the steps in Maslow's hierarchy are universal. However, the physical and economic environment in some countries might activate lower level needs, thus making it difficult for the emergence of higher order needs. In many countries, pressures of daily living preoccupy the minds of workers to such an extent that they are not able to move forward in the hierarchy of needs as proposed by Maslow. We can see differences in environmental effects in countries such as Mexico, Nigeria, and central Asian republics of the former Soviet Union, where global organizations have difficulty in finding highly trained workers.[5]

However, some of the general predictions of Maslow's theory do not apply across cultural and national borders. Numerous studies in Argentina, Canada, Chile, India, Japan, Liberia, Libya, Russia, South Africa, Thailand, Turkey, Venezuela, and the former Yugoslavia have shown that the theory of hierarchy of needs does not apply in some of these cultures, despite some similarities. Some findings involving this theory of motivation, which has been useful in U.S. organizations, are conflicting.

In countries where uncertainty avoidance is high, such as Greece and Japan, the need for security has been found to be more important for improving work motivation than the need for satisfying self-actualizing needs. The need for security in these countries dominates the thoughts of the workers and they rarely get beyond this stage of the hierarchy. On the other hand, in countries that are low in uncertainty avoidance, such as the United States, the United Kingdom, and New Zealand, individuals are more inclined to seek opportunities for satisfying their own self-actualizing needs because their needs for security are much lower and more easily met.

Contrasting with the U.S. pattern, satisfaction of interpersonal needs become more important in countries such as Denmark, Norway, and Sweden, which stress quality of life and social interrelatedness, qualities that are feminine in terms of cultural values.[6] In collectivistic countries such as Japan, Venezuela, Mexico, and Egypt, the need to satisfy group goals, which are often social in nature, is more important than in individualistic countries such as the United States, the United Kingdom, and Australia.[7] In less developed countries, such as Nigeria and other eastern Africa nations, which depict high uncertainty avoidance, low individualism, high power distance, and relatively low emphasis on career success, community values dominate any individualistic tendencies, and condemnation of self-seeking individualism is common.[8] In fact, in some communities, self-seeking tendencies are considered to reflect mental abnormalities.

While definitive conclusions are difficult to draw, one thing is certain: Maslow's theory cannot be applied universally to explain motivation patterns of workers or managers in countries that are different from the United States in cultural values. One cannot say with certainty that the order of needs is the same in all societies.

Alderfer's ERG Theory

Organizational psychologist Clayton Alderfer developed the ERG (existence, relatedness, and growth) theory to provide a more simplified hierarchy of needs with the following three levels,[9] as shown in Exhibit 14.1:

- *Growth needs*—similar to Maslow's needs for self-actualization and self-esteem.
- *Relatedness needs*—similar to Maslow's need for affiliation; these needs are fulfilled through meaningful and effective support from the work group.
- *Existence needs*—lower order needs for security, safety, and survival.

Motivator–Hygiene/Intrinsic–Extrinsic Need Theory

The intrinsic–extrinsic dichotomy is a useful way to understand workforce motivation, regardless of the cultural context of the country involved. These theories were developed by psychologist Frederick Herzberg (motivator–hygiene theory).[10] **Intrinsic factors** are concerned with opportunity for personal growth, development, and advancement, and they deal with the quality of work being performed. Intrinsic factors include complex learning and skill acquisition, as well as autonomy in decision making. Intrinsic factors tend to be more important in countries that are individualistic and low in uncertainty avoidance, such as the United States and the United Kingdom.

Extrinsic factors are concerned with the context of the workplace, such as level of pay, working conditions, and fringe benefits. Extrinsic factors are found to be more important in collectivistic and high uncertainty avoidance cultures, such as Zambia.[11] One's pay and fringe benefits can benefit the family and other important people in the in-group. Since the well-being of the in-group is of primary importance in collectivistic cultures, it makes sense for individuals in countries high in collectivism to be more concerned with extrinsic rewards from the workplace. Similarly, uncertainty avoidance can be dealt with more effectively if the worker gets appropriate extrinsic rewards from the workplace. Pay and medical benefits and other forms of financial compensation can lower the amount of uncertainty that a worker may face in life. Job dissatisfaction tends to increase when companies do *not* provide for these factors.[12] Adequate pay, medical insurance, and safety procedures in the workplace are examples of these extrinsic factors. The extrinsic and potentially demotivating factors largely correspond to the lower order (physiological and safety) needs of Maslow.

Classifying needs to explain motivation and job satisfaction has been questioned in the U.S. context.[13] This process is more complicated in countries whose cultural values are different from the United States. For example, **organizational commitment** differs across cultures. Organizational commitment is the worker's involvement in identification with the work organization. Individuals in some cultures have been found to remain motivated on a particular job because of its value in sustaining commitments made in public, even though such commitments may be contrary to their self-interest.[14] For example, in India, if a manager has committed to work without pay on a government project for the benefit of the community, the manager will continue to work because of the public commitment. The job itself may be boring in terms of its intrinsic properties, but the manager will continue working on the project nevertheless.[15]

The highly individualistic, productivity-oriented U.S. culture focuses on restructuring of individual jobs to enhance intrinsic properties of such jobs with the hope of improving employee motivation.[16] Cultures that are more interested in quality of life, such as Sweden and Norway, and those that are more collectivistic, such as Egypt, Mexico, and India, focus on developing systems, work methods, and restructuring of employees into work groups to achieve increased work motivation and productivity.[17] Managers entering a new country to manage a venture should keenly observe to determine which factors appear important in creating motivation and not assume that their prior experience in the United States or other contexts is easily transferable.

Achievement Motivation Theory

The achievement motivation theory developed by Harvard psychologist David C. McClelland during the 1960s has been highly influential in the United States.[18] According to this theory, needs are learned through the variety of experiences which one undergoes in life. The research revealed that humans have three distinct patterns of needs: need for achievement (nAch), need for affiliation (nAff), and need for power (nPow).

The **need for achievement** reflects a desire to take on tasks and accomplish them satisfactorily. Individuals high in need for achievement enjoy challenges and thrive on stimulating environments. They prefer responsibility and autonomy to pursue goals that they value, and they appreciate constructive feedback. Achievement motivation is high in the personality profiles of entrepreneurs and reflects the willingness to take risks. Employees with high need for achievement tend to get more raises and promotions than those who are higher in their need for power or affiliation. Research also reveals that achievers are not always the best managers because they have difficulties working within hierarchies of organizations.

The **need for affiliation** reflects the desire of individuals to belong to a social group and to participate with others and create friendships. Individuals high in need for affiliation seek to enhance their sense of social esteem. They prefer harmony to individual achievements, seeking work environments that do not produce conflicts. These individuals do not like to get involved in difficult decisions that might result in unpleasant reactions from subordinates. They prefer to work in egalitarian organizations where the hierarchy is less restricting.

Individuals with a high **need for power** are comfortable in executive positions where they can make decisions in highly competitive situations. They place a high value on status and advancement. High power orientation may also reflect a strong tendency to lead and a willingness to accept responsibility for managing others, an attribute which reflects Hofstede's cultural dimension of masculinity. Unlike the need for achievement, the need for power is not necessarily associated with entrepreneurship, yet some with high need for power have begun successful new ventures.

This theory has generally found support in the U.S. context, using data collected by McClelland's projective tests. The assumptions of this theory of motivation that anyone can learn one set of values are central to McClelland's model. McClelland and his colleagues conducted training experiments in India and among groups of less educated individuals in Africa to observe their willingness to enhance the need for achievement. By following the careers of these participants for several years, McClelland and his team determined that achievement training made a significant difference in outcomes.[19]

Countries that are inclined to foster higher needs for achievements in individuals, such as the United States, experience higher rates of economic growth. However, research conducted by Ronen and Shenkar and Flynn showed that emphasis on individual achievement can be considered an undesirable tendency and may even be perceived as antisocial in countries such as China, Indonesia, Malaysia, and perhaps in Africa and Latin America.[20] In paternalistic societies, such as India, achievement may not be valued if it is not part of the immediate family or close referent group, because of the close ties to group goals at the expense of personal goals. In hierarchical cultures, such as Mexico, the need for achievement is considered to be destructive, because conformity to the existing social order and one's duty to the community are valued more.

Individuals with a high need for power are more valued for leadership positions, and managers with high need for affiliation are regarded more favorably by their subordinates. This tendency has been observed in Mexico and several Latin American societies and especially among the Islamic cultures in Southeast Asia.[21] In Nordic countries, as well as in some Latin nations, motivation for both managers and subordinates reflects social esteem, human interaction, and friendship bonds more strongly than in other countries which are lower on the dimension of femininity, another dimension of Hofstede.[22]

While there have been a number of criticisms of this well-known theory, it is generally assumed to have utility. It makes important contributions to improving managerial practices in different countries, because it provides managers with some basic understanding of the variation in motives among employees. Research generally supports McClelland's claims that many motivating characteristics can be learned through experience.

Applicability of Needs Theories across Borders and Cultures

The applicability of these needs theories across cultures is somewhat limited by the fact that most researchers have focused on higher order needs (need for achievement, need for self-actualization, and growth needs) and frequently ignore the lower order needs.[23] The world's working population largely remains focused on trying to fulfill lower order needs of job security, safety, and good pay for maintaining their families, especially in developing and emerging nations (e.g., Mexico, India, China, and Brazil) as well as former Eastern bloc countries (e.g., Romania, Bulgaria, and Poland). Studies show that Kenyan and Malawi managers emphasize security needs and not higher order needs.[24] Russian managers have been found to emphasize needs for security and social needs as opposed to higher order needs.[25]

In fact, research shows that the hierarchy of needs proposed by Maslow is generally valid with middle-class, white, Anglo-Saxon Americans and western Europeans, but it does not represent the hierarchy found in other parts of the world.[26] Economic factors, ecological conditions, and traditions and customs, along with dominant cultural values (discussed in Chapter 5), significantly influence the hierarchy of needs. McClelland's work has been tested widely in different parts of the world by his students and has been used to improve achievement motivation and entrepreneurship when India was a developing country in the 1960s.[27] However, some studies have shown that the relationship between achievement motivation and entrepreneurship is more complex than proposed by McClelland and his associates. Japan's economic growth far exceeded Britain's in the 1970s and 1980s, although achievement motivation is lower than affiliation motivation in Japanese society.[28]

McClelland's work is no longer considered to be widely applicable; in fact, it has been noted that achievement motivation will "arise in different cultural contexts in different forms, stimulated by different situational cues and may be channeled toward accomplishing different types of goals."[29] Immigrants from countries such as India and China often achieve more success outside their countries, where such success is not as highly valued.[30] In these countries, which are generally collectivistic, successful personal relationships with in-group members are valued more highly than economic success or success in attaining need for achievement goals.[31] In collectivistic contexts of eastern Asia (Korea, People's Republic of China, and Japan), achievement motivation is best understood on a group basis as a driving force, as opposed to individually based achievement motivation. In many environments, Japan in particular, individual achievement is neither valued highly nor rewarded. The individual desire to excel in the job at the expense of others may be strongly sanctioned.[32] A study of managers from five countries showed that achievement motivation is more quickly aroused in individualistic countries (United States and Holland) than in more collectivistic countries (Japan, Israel, and Hungary).[33] Therefore, managers of international and global corporations should pay special attention to the selective influences of cultural context before implementing U.S.-based theories of motivation.

Process Theories

In contrast to the needs theories, which explain why people have different needs in their lives and careers, process theories are designed to explain how these needs deficiencies are translated into motivation that energizes performance. Three of the widely known process theories of motivation are expectancy theory, equity theory, and goal-setting theory. We briefly discuss them because they have been useful in explaining different patterns of motivation in different parts of the world. Managers of multinational corporations should be aware of the basic mechanisms as illustrated in these theories.

Expectancy Theory

Expectancy theory proposes that individuals are driven by the expectations that their acts will produce certain anticipated results and rewards.[34] Expectancy theory helps us identify the significance of an individual's perception of the link between effort and performance, as well as of the manager's ability to identify and provide desired rewards. Expectancy theory has advanced our knowledge of motivational processes in the U.S. context, but application of this theory is subject to some cross-cultural variations. According to expectancy theory, motivation is the result of:[35]

- The expectancy that an effort will result in desired level of performance.
- The likelihood that the performance will be linked with important intrinsic and extrinsic outcomes (first- and second-level outcomes).
- The value or attractiveness of the outcome or reward to the individual.

First-level outcomes are those that derive directly from performing the work itself, such as monetary rewards and job satisfaction. Second-level outcomes are those that are derived from the first-level outcomes, such as buying a car or house with the money earned, improvement of personal self-esteem, and improved quality of life.

Performance can be understood as a function of motivation, ability, role perception, and organizational factors that facilitate work. In other words:

$$\text{Work performance} = f(\text{Motivation} \times \text{Job ability} \times \text{Role perception} \times \text{Situational contraints})$$

In some countries, workers who are motivated and have appropriate cumulative experiences to do well on the job do not get to perform at a high level because they lack the kind of support they need from the workplace and often lack the technology that would assist them.

Motivation, in its turn, is a function of two kinds of beliefs and the importance or the attractiveness of the rewards. In other words, motivation is

$$\text{Motivation} = f(\text{Effort} \rightarrow \text{Performance}) \times (\text{Performance} \rightarrow \text{Rewards}) \times \text{Value of rewards}$$

This formulation, which has been tested in the United States and western Europe, has generally been found to accurately portray the degree of work motivation or arousal that employees experience when they believe (1) that there is a clear link between their effort and accomplishment of adequate performance on the job (i.e., expectancy) and (2) that performance leads to valuable rewards (i.e., instrumentality).[36] This is illustrated in Exhibits 14.2 and 14.3.

As these exhibits show, perceptions of how the effort expended would lead to performance are subject to distinct influences. Employee self-esteem is important, but co-workers are influenced significantly in what they tell each other. In countries where working conditions are poor, the actual situation will act as a deterrent for creating efficient beliefs in the effort–performance link. The instrumentality or the belief that the company will appropriately recognize performance is also a very important factor, as shown in Exhibit 14.3. While personality and personal predispositions, including similar experiences in other companies or other work situations, may play an important role, the difficulties inherent in the actual working conditions and the kind of messages the worker receives from his or her co-workers and supervisors also play a critical role.

Motivation is very much related to the features of one's work and nonwork life. Both of these contexts are greatly influenced by cultural variables, which affect emotional predispositions and behaviors of individuals and groups on the job. The frameworks presented in Chapter 5 are helpful and should be kept in mind as we try to understand the scope of applicability of these theories in non-U.S. contexts.

As shown in Exhibit 14.4, expectancy theory explains motivation as several steps. The first is the worker's expectation that he or she can successfully perform the job with the effort expected. The next step is the expectation of receiving the outcome promised, if the performance is successful. First level outcomes are important, but

EXHIBIT 14.2
Determinants of Effort (*E*) to Performance (*P*) Expectancies

Source: From Edward E. Lawler III, *Motivation in Work Organizations,* 1973, Wadsworth Publishing Company. Reprinted with permission of the author.

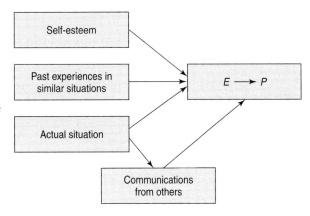

Determinants of $E \longrightarrow P$ expectancies.

EXHIBIT 14.3
Determinants of Performance (*P*) to Outcome (*O*) Expectancies

Source: From Edward E. Lawler III, *Motivation in Work Organizations,* 1973, Wadsworth Publishing Company. Reprinted with permission of the author.

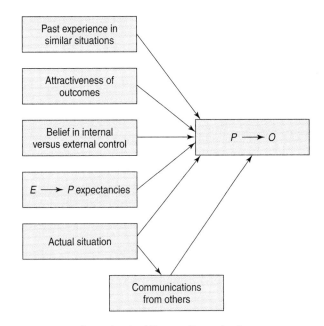

Determinants of $P \longrightarrow O$ expectancies.

some are only important because they lead to others. For some workers, pay is valuable as a first level outcome because of its purchasing value; for others, it has a secondary outcome, such as being a way to keep score with others ("I make more than_____"). Each outcome (at both the first level and second level) has a *valence,* that is, a value to the worker. Values are different for each worker and for each outcome. For example, some workers value praise more than others. Extrinsic outcomes are physical outcomes, e.g., money. Intrinsic outcomes are higher level outcomes, e.g., self-esteem.

In countries that are individualistic, employees see their relationship with the organization from a more calculated and rational perspective, which implies that if the link between their performance and outcomes are unclear or lacking, they feel demotivated

EXHIBIT 14.4 **The Expectancy Model of Motivation**

Source: From J. R. Hackman, E. E. Lawler and L. W. Porter (eds.), *Perspectives on Behavior in Organization,* 1977, p. 34. Copyright © 1994 The McGraw-Hill Companies, Inc. Reprinted with permission.

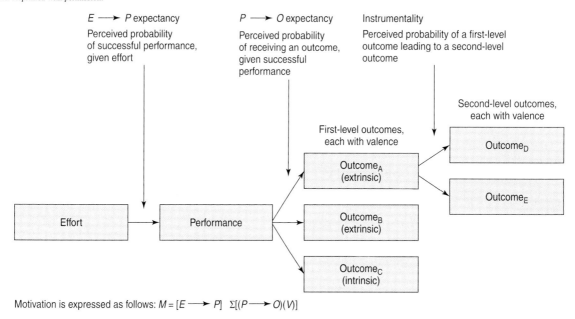

Motivation is expressed as follows: $M = [E \longrightarrow P] \ \Sigma[(P \longrightarrow O)(V)]$

and begin to look for opportunities elsewhere. In collectivistic countries, the ties between the individual and the organization have a moral component.[37] Individuals using a moral component in their commitment are likely to be more tolerant, even if they do not see a strong link between their performance and outcomes. Personal ties with managers, owners, and co-workers are much more important in collectivistic contexts, where they act as guides for enhancing motivation. Therefore, application of expectancy theory in all contexts is not possible.

In many collectivistic countries, employees expect their firms to take care of their personal needs, whereas in the United States and other individualistic countries, employees have no such expectations. In Latin America, especially Brazil, where personal and work lives are highly integrated, major companies frequently assist their employees with personal financial problems such as financial difficulties that might arise from family illness.

Equity Theory

The equity theory of motivation was developed in the United States by J. Stacy Adams, a social psychologist.[38] The basic premise of this theory is that people try to balance their inputs and outputs in relation to others. Inputs include an employee's level of education, work experience, personal characteristics, and loyalty to the company. Outcomes are derived in the context of working, such as pay, benefits, working conditions, co-worker relationships, and opportunities for growth. Each person has his or her own perception regarding the value of the inputs and outcomes. Motivation results when an employee compares inputs with the outcomes received. Each individual compares his or her outcomes with those of another person, called a "comparison other." When the ratio of the individual to the comparison other is about equal, little motivation is likely.

Motivation results when the two outcomes are unequal, resulting in a tension or discomfort that encourages the employee to equalize the ratio. This is seen in the following equation:

$$\frac{\text{Outcomes}_{\text{self}}}{\text{Inputs}_{\text{self}}} = \frac{\text{Outcomes}_{\text{other}}}{\text{Inputs}_{\text{other}}}$$

An important point to consider is that the norms regarding what is equitable differ from country to country. Among the more important norms that compete with the **norm of equity,** which is strongly emphasized in individualistic cultures of the West, are the **norm of need** and the **norm of equality.**[39] The **norm of need** emphasizes distribution of rewards according to the needs of employees. The **norm of equality** is concerned with distribution of equal rewards to everyone performing the same work, usually in a group context. When a person is severely deprived, the only norm that may make sense is the norm of need. In informal situations, the equality norm is more important in the distribution of rewards. For example, at a party it is assumed that resources such as food are shared equally, rather than according to the contributions each makes to the party. This equality norm is also more prevalent in work contexts characterized by strong loyalty to the in-group, which is emphasized in collectivistic cultures.

Goal-Setting Theory

Many companies set goals for employees to motivate them and clarify role perceptions.[40] However, goal setting involves much more than simply telling employees to do their best. It is a process of various steps to maximize effort toward achieving goals.[41] When applied properly, goal-setting techniques require adequate participation from both the employee and the supervisor in specifying and developing the goals while ensuring that the goals are challenging and achievable. It also requires feedback from both the employee and the supervisor regarding any problems that might arise in the process of achieving goals. This process should be separated from the pay process to maximize goal achievement and minimize less than optimal goal setting. Often companies use management by objective (MBO) processes to formalize this theory application.[42] Use of MBO intensifies the effort of the employees to practice specific behaviors that should enable them to achieve their goals.[43]

Application of Process Theories across Borders and Cultures

In 1981, Hulin and Triandis emphasized that in designing reward systems of global organizations, managers should take a close look at how cultural, subcultural, demographic, and personal factors influence motivational and job satisfaction outcomes.[44] For example, motivations of workers in collectivistic countries include:

- Adjustment of personal needs relative to the needs of the in-group.
- Preference for group goal setting and easier acceptance of assigned goals.
- Preference for group-based incentives and rewards.

In contrast, individualists are less sensitive to the needs of others with whom they work. Also, they prefer goals that are individually negotiated and do not easily tolerate group-based incentives.[45]

Research in cross-border utility of process theories shows that countries which are horizontal collectivistic (see Chapter 5) in orientation use group goals, whereas vertical collectivistic countries accept assigned goals without a lot of discussion.[46] To compete with the Japanese, many U.S. companies implemented quality circles and teamwork to improve motivation and performance of groups. However, these attempts have been mostly unsuccessful because of a lack of mutual commitment of members of work groups as well as commitment between work groups and the organization.[47]

Exchanges in individualistic cultures are based on *equity,* which means that individuals are rewarded on the basis of contributions measured by annual or semiannual performance appraisals. The more horizontal the culture is, the more likely that the principle of equality will guide the distribution of rewards. Collectivists apply the principle of equality when exchanging rewards with members of in-groups, but they pay more attention to equity when dealing with out-groups.[48] Equality is associated with harmony, solidarity, and good feelings for members of in-groups. On the other hand, equity leads to enhancement of individual-level productivity, competition with members of the work group, and continuous attention to individual career goals. All other research using concepts from process theories has shown that the psychological significance of rewards works differently in collectivistic and feminine societies compared to individualistic and masculine societies.

One country stands apart from this, however. Japan, the world's second largest economy, built its solid economic growth on collectivistic norms of cooperation, harmony, and lifetime commitment. This is the only country that stands as a success despite being a masculine country with a strong collectivistic foundation. In Japan, rewards based on equity were uncommon during the 1950s through the 1990s. It is only recently that global competition and knowledge of compensation of other executives of non-Japanese global corporations has impacted the reward system to a small extent. The CEO of Nissan, the second largest automotive manufacturer in Japan, earns about 10 times more than the lowest paid worker. On the other hand, the CEO of Ford, the second largest automotive manufacturer in the United States, earns over 540 times more than the lowest paid worker.[49]

Schwartz's framework is of value in understanding the nature of relations among important societal values and their effects on motivation (see Exhibit 5.15). People who work in countries which value stimulation, self-direction, universalism, and achievement are likely to be easily motivated if the linkages between effort and performance and performance and rewards are clear (equity theory). On the other hand, motivation cannot be easily incited on the individual level in countries where security, benevolence, tradition, conformity, and power are emphasized (e.g., countries in eastern and southern Asia, much of Latin America, and southern Europe). Managers of international and global corporations who manage subsidiaries in culturally dissimilar countries should be cognizant of these issues. Some understanding of the limited applicability of these U.S.-based theories, no matter how scientifically valid in Western cultures, will go a long way.

The Meaning of Working across Nations and Cultures

The concern that U.S.-based studies may not be applicable in all cultural contexts was addressed in the **Meaning of Working study,** conducted by George England and the Meaning of Working (MOW) International Research Team.[50] This study examined what working means to people in Japan, Yugoslavia, Israel, the United States, Belgium, the Netherlands, Britain, and Germany. The researchers assessed the meaning using three key concepts:

- *Work centrality:* The degree of general importance and value attributed to the working role in an individual's life.

- *Societal norms about working:* The degree of normative beliefs and expectations regarding entitlement (specific rights) and obligations (duties) attached to working. The entitlement norm represents the underlying work rights of individuals and work-related responsibilities of organizations and society toward individuals. "This norm reflects notions that all members of society are entitled to meaningful and interesting work, proper training to obtain and continue in such work, and the right to participate in work/method decisions."[51] The obligation norm reflects the duties and responsibilities that individuals have in their work roles. "This norm includes the notions that everyone has a duty to contribute to society by working, a duty to save for their own future, and the duty to value one's work, whatever its nature."[52]

- *Work goals:* Work-related outcomes preferred by individuals in the entire span of working life. The 11 goals studied included such things as interesting work, good pay, good job security, opportunity to learn, and a good match between the worker and the job.[53]

The clear implication of the MOW research study was that the higher the mean work centrality score, the more motivated and committed the workers are in that society. Of obvious importance to managers is that the score provides specific reasons for valuing work and the pattern of needs that working satisfies in different societies. Exhibit 14.5 shows that the mean centrality score was highest in Japan (7.78) and lowest in Britain (6.36).

As shown in Exhibit 14.6, in terms of societal norm scores (T-scores), Israel and Yugoslavia have the highest levels of agreement with the entitlement and obligation norms associated with working. The United States and Netherlands show an imbalance. In the United States, the obligation norm is higher than the entitlement norm, and the opposite is true for the Netherlands. Other countries fall in different areas of the grid.

The relative importance of work goals is illustrated in Exhibit 14.7. In four countries, interesting work is ranked highest out of 11 possible work goals. The importance

EXHIBIT 14.5

Work Centrality Scores

Source: Reprinted from *The Meaning of Work: An International Perspective,* MOW International Research Team. Copyright © 1987, with permission from Elsevier.

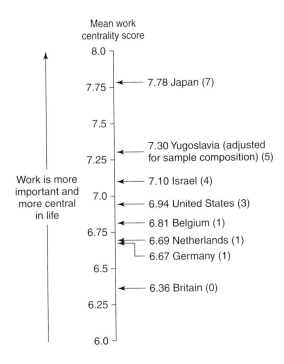

Mean work centrality score

Work is more important and more central in life

- 7.78 Japan (7)
- 7.30 Yugoslavia (adjusted for sample composition) (5)
- 7.10 Israel (4)
- 6.94 United States (3)
- 6.81 Belgium (1)
- 6.69 Netherlands (1)
- 6.67 Germany (1)
- 6.36 Britain (0)

EXHIBIT 14.6

Comparison of Entitlement and Obligation Scores of Eight Countries

Source: Reprinted from *The Meaning of Work: An International Perspective,* MOW International Research Team. Copyright © 1987, with permission from Elsevier.

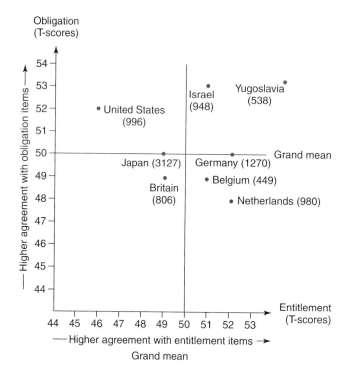

of pay was highest in Britain (ranked 2 of 11) and in Germany (ranked 1 of 11). The importance of achieving a good match between the worker and the job is highest in Japan and lowest in Belgium. The MOW study also found that importance of work remained fairly constant in the United States from immediately after World War II until the early 1980s, even though this observation was more anecdotal than supported by data. In Britain, the centrality of work declined from after World War II to the early 1980s, attributed to the strong influence of unions.

While the results might be different today, due to increased pressures to achieve uniform management practices in multinational and global corporations (as discussed in Chapters 1, 2, and 3), the MOW study highlights an important fact: Individuals differ in their emphasis on the meaning of working, and such differences are rooted in national and cultural differences.

When a manager of a subsidiary located in a culture which is dissimilar to his or her home country culture disregards the importance of these cultural differences, the result is likely to be demotivating and frustrating for employees. In Thailand, for example, the introduction of an individual merit bonus plan for merit pay raises for individuals, which ran contrary to the societal norm of group-based cooperation and incentive in the workplace, failed to improve productivity and resulted in a decline of morale.[54] Managers must recognize the importance of needs, goals, values, and expectations of culturally dissimilar employees. People in every society are driven to achieve goals and fulfill needs according to their cultural preferences and values, but what those goals and needs are may not always be clear.

As discussed in Chapter 5, people in different cultures possess different degrees of control over their environment. In countries where a sense of mastery over nature is a

EXHIBIT 14.7   The Importance of Work Goals

Source: Reprinted from *The Meaning of Work: An International Perspective,* MOW International Research Team. Copyright © 1987, with permission from Elsevier.

Work Goals	Belgium (N = 446)		Germany (N = 1248)		Israel (N = 772)		Japan (N = 2897)		Netherlands (N = 967)		United States (N = 988)		Yugoslavia (N = 512)*		Britain (N = 742)	
Interesting work	8.25	1	7.26	3	6.75	1	7.38	2	7.59	2	7.41	1	7.47	2	8.02	1
Good pay	7.13	2	7.73	1	6.60	3	6.56	5	6.27	5	6.82	2	6.73	3	7.80	2
Good interpersonal relations	6.34	5	6.43	4	6.67	2	6.39	6	7.19	3	6.08	7	7.52	1	6.33	4
Good job security	6.80	3	7.57	2	5.22	10	6.71	4	5.68	7	6.30	3	5.21	9	7.12	3
A good match between you and your job	5.77	8	6.09	5	5.61	6	7.83	1	6.17	6	6.19	4	6.49	5	5.63	6
A lot of autonomy	6.56	4	5.66	8	6.00	4	6.89	3	7.61	1	5.79	8	5.42	8	4.69	10
Opportunity to learn	5.80	7	4.97	9	5.83	5	6.26	7	5.38	9	6.16	5	6.61	4	5.55	8
A lot of variety	5.96	6	5.71	6	4.89	11	5.05	9	6.86	4	6.10	6	5.62	7	5.62	7
Convenient work hours	4.71	9	5.71	6	5.53	7	5.46	8	5.59	8	5.25	9	5.01	10	6.11	5
Good physical working conditions	4.19	11	4.39	11	5.28	9	4.18	10	5.03	10	4.84	11	5.94	6	4.87	9
Good opportunity for upgrading or promotion	4.49	10	4.48	10	5.29	8	3.33	11	3.31	11	5.08	10	4.00	11	4.27	11

Note: Mean ranks. The rank of each work goal within a given country. Rank 1 is the *most* important work goal for a country while rank 11 is the *least* important work goal for a country.
*Combined target group data were used for Yugoslavia.

dominant cultural norm, managers and workers believe that they can control relevant aspects of their work environment. Individuals also tend to be high in **internal locus of control,** that is, they believe that the work-related outcome is mostly the result of their own personal effort[55] and seek appropriate guidance and feedback regarding performance improvement on an ongoing basis.

In contrast, managers and workers in some countries believe that things happen only when God wills them to happen. These individuals are high in **external locus of control,** that is, they believe that they have little or no control over work-related outcomes, regardless of the level of effort.[56] Many Islamic countries, as well as some countries in Asia and Africa, tend to foster this norm of external locus of control. For example, in mainland China and Hong Kong, managers tend to believe that an element of *joss,* or luck, is involved in all transactions. Effective problem solving and hard work would be less important in countries where there is a strong perception that sustained efforts do not necessarily lead to valued outcomes.

Expectancy theory seems to work better in explaining patterns of motivation, job satisfaction, and organizational commitment in those countries where individuals

- Are high in need for achievement.
- Believe in the equity norm.
- Are likely to value intrinsic and extrinsic rewards.
- Possess strong internal locus of control.

Applying Cultural Frameworks

Before we can attempt to understand the influences of cultural factors, ecological factors, and the level of economic development on the process of generating work motivation, we need to examine the World Values Survey.[57] This survey summarizes the attitudes of people toward work and life in 50 countries inhabited by more than three-fourths of the world's population. As shown in Exhibit 14.8, the relative importance of work characteristics varies in nine countries located in different continents. This shows that in some societies work is central and absorbs much of a person's life. People in these societies are willing to work very hard and have a strong commitment to success at work.

Juliet Schorr, in her popular book *The Overworked American,* shows that Americans work the longest number of hours in a year, followed by the Japanese and other countries.[58] In fact, as globalization encompasses more aspects of American life, the distinction between doing work at home and at the office has almost disappeared. In a study conducted in 2002, Bhagat and Moustafa found that immigrants (legal residents born outside the United States) perceived Americans to be excessively concerned with performing activities in their work life which enhance their feelings of self-worth.[59] Work, for Americans, expands into the family arena, and when strong conflicts arise because of the simultaneous pursuit of work and personal life goals, work goals take precedence over family life. Taking this issue further, Richard Florida analyzed the development of a new class of workers, which he called "the creative class," who are professionals somewhat akin to white-collar workers—but their every waking hour is packed with work activities, most of which they truly enjoy.[60] These professionals process symbols and tend to be attracted to companies which allow creative expression at work, regardless of other concerns.

The Role of Cultural Variations in Work Motivation and Job Satisfaction

The amount of motivation or excitement that individuals experience is very much a product of the demands and joys of work and personal life. The context of work and personal life is highly influenced by ecological factors, societal culture, and the level of economic development of the country where one works. Political frameworks, as discussed in Chapter 3, also provide important influences. For example, workers from East Germany who worked for over half a century under the Soviet communist system developed patterns of motivation very different from those of West German workers.[61]

EXHIBIT 14.8 **Ranking of Top Four Work Characteristics in Nine Countries**

Source: Adapted from R. Inglehart, et al., *World Values Surveys and European Values Surveys, 1981-1984, 1990-1993, and 1993-1997,* Institute for Social Research, 2000. Reprinted with permission.

Countries									
Work Values	United States	Germany	Turkey	Russia	Japan	Peru	Nigeria	India	China
Generous holidays	1	1	1	3		1	1	1	1
Job respected	2	2			1		4		
Good hours	3	3	4	4	4	3	2	4	
Use initiative	4			2	2		3	2	3
Responsibility		4	3	1					2
Interesting job			2			2		3	4
Achieve something					3	4			

Before we describe a comprehensive framework for understanding how environmental and cultural factors interplay in inciting an individual to experience motivation and perform according to demands of the task, we can make some generalized statements based on cultural frameworks covered in Chapter 5.

To make meaningful and practical conclusions about the role of motivation in the international context, it is useful to apply Hofstede's research on the cultural dimensions of individualism–collectivism, uncertainty avoidance, power distance, masculinity–femininity, and long-term versus short-term orientation.[62] Exhibit 14.9 shows the role of cultural variations in the meaning of work and work motivation, and these are discussed below.

Individualism–Collectivism

Countries that are high in individualism are likely to have more people who are motivated by opportunities for individual achievement and increased autonomy on the job than do countries that are high in collectivism, which are likely to have more people

EXHIBIT 14.9 The Role of Cultural Variations in the Meaning of Work and Work Motivation

Source: Adapted and expanded from R. M. Steers and C. J. Sanchez-Runde, "Culture, Motivation, and Work Behavior." In M. J. Gannon and K. L. Newman, eds., *Blackwell Handbook of Cross-Cultural Management* (Oxford, UK: Blackwell Business, 2003), p. 194.

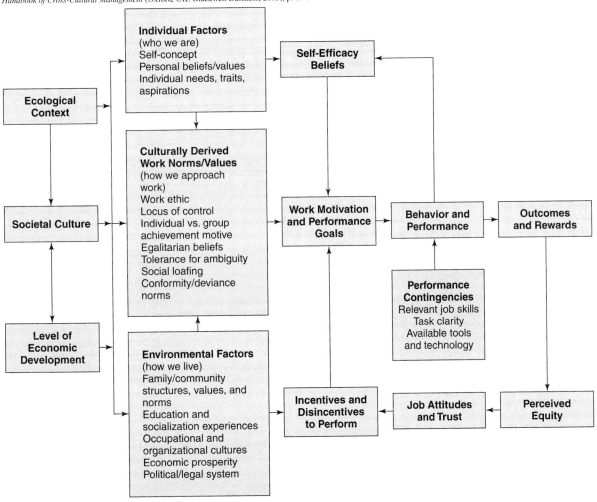

who are motivated by work designed to sustain group goals and community-based activities and rewards. Research by Christopher Earley shows that performance by individualists who were working in groups was lower than the performance of individualists working alone.[63] In contrast, collectivists performed better while working in groups than they did when working alone.

Power Distance

The decision structures within the organization influence the relationship between power distance and process of work motivation. High power distance countries have many layers of management and a large proportion of supervisory personnel. Subordinates rely on formal rules and regulations in performing tasks and are not likely to be consulted by their supervisors in designing work and reward systems. In contrast, in low power distance countries, hierarchy is deemphasized, and when it does exist, it is for convenience and only temporary. Subordinates expect flexibility in performing tasks and expect to be consulted in the design of work and reward systems. Intrinsic motivation is easily fostered in low power distance countries, and creative tendencies are strongly encouraged by supervisors who do not explicitly supervise the day-to-day performance of subordinates. Research by Peterson and his colleagues found that unclear expectations about how to perform the job, called **role ambiguity,** and excessive work, called **role overload,** are generally higher in cultures with high power distance.[64] These two characteristics, often called *work-related stressors,* can reduce work motivation, especially creativity and innovation. In two studies, Bhagat and his colleagues showed that ability to influence work conditions improved reactions to strains experienced at work.[65]

Uncertainty Avoidance

Individuals in high uncertainty avoidance countries generally have a high need for job security and are unwilling to take risks and make independent decisions. In these countries, subordinates expect managers to make decisions and then give explicit instructions, which reduces the potential for creativity and innovation. A preference for tasks with calculated risks and continuous problem solving characterize low uncertainty avoidance countries. In fact, even the themes of traditional stories reflect higher levels of achievement motivation in low uncertainty avoidance countries in contrast to those in high uncertainty avoidance countries, which reflect strong security motivations.[66] The differences between the two preferences have clear implications for work motivation, job satisfaction, and organizational commitment.[67] In countries where individuals are able to engage in appropriate problem-solving strategies in the workplace, they experienced lower levels of strain.[68] In general, when people are strongly motivated both in an intrinsic and extrinsic sense, they are likely to do better in their careers and to progress toward further growth. Progress is usually more rapid in low uncertainty avoidance countries.

Masculinity–Femininity

High degrees of masculinity suggest that most people will be comfortable with traditional divisions of work and nonwork roles. *Work roles* consist of duties and responsibilities in the work organization, such as the role of nurse, mechanic, or manager. *Nonwork roles* are roles that individuals play outside the context of the work organization, such as the role of father, mother, husband, wife, sister, and friend. Work and nonwork roles tend to be distinct in masculine societies. In feminine cultures, the boundaries between work and nonwork roles are more flexible. Because of this, people feel motivated by having accommodating work schedules, such as flextime, part-time, and shift work, and they prefer jobs that nurture quality of work life. Competition, as a societal norm for sustaining motivation, is higher in masculine than feminine countries.[69] While the significance of this cultural dimension has not been widely examined, Hofstede maintains that it has important implications for understanding variations of the quality of work life around the globe. For example, Sweden, Denmark, and Norway are feminine countries where the quality of work life and the sociotechnical method of improving work processes are emphasized. In contrast, in masculine countries, such as the United States and Germany, job design processes are geared toward sustaining performance rather than quality of work life.[70]

Long-Term versus Short-Term Orientation

Countries emphasizing short-term orientation foster short-term results, that is, the immediate or intermediate bottom line, as opposed to those emphasizing long-term orientation. Short-term virtues and norms about workplace values are emphasized, resulting in employees valuing work outcomes that satisfy immediate needs.[71] Compensation schemes and reward systems should reflect these differences in orientation in order to enhance motivation, job satisfaction, and organizational commitment.

The idea of encouraging good work habits is a constant across cultures, as shown in Practical Insight 14.2.

International Differences in Job Satisfaction, Job Involvement, and Organizational Commitment

Just as patterns of motivation differ across countries and cultures, individuals in different parts of the world have different feelings toward their job, their involvement with their job, and the amount of commitment they feel toward their job. Research findings in this area indicate that:[72]

- In countries where the majority of the workers belong to various types of worker unions, job satisfaction tends to be lower compared to countries where the majority of workers are not unionized, regardless of the cultural orientation of the country. This trend is strong in the United States. **Job satisfaction** is an individual's positive attitudes about his or her job, specifically happiness and satisfaction with the job.

- In countries where collectivism is the dominant norm, job satisfaction tends to be highly related to the social context of the job and is less susceptible to changes due to monetary and extrinsic rewards. The role of monetary and extrinsic rewards in determining job satisfaction tends to be of paramount importance in individualistic cultures.

- Job involvement is a different phenomenon. There is a high degree of involvement in Japan, even though the collective context may foster collective achievement on the job rather than individual achievement. However, workers and managers experience involvement with their job and a sustained commitment to their work organization because they have a sense of emotional dependence on their work organization. Hofstede's study has shown that in countries where emotional dependence on the organization is high, workers do not react to variations in job rewards on an individual basis, but rather they wait to see how others in their position react to the reward.

- Career management tends to be a major source of satisfaction among workers in individualistic countries. In collectivistic countries, however, careers are often managed on a group or cohort basis, and commitment to the organization is often a function of how much one feels included within group activities.

PRACTICAL INSIGHT 14.2

INCULCATING A WORK CULTURE

It is a truth of nature that every living being takes care to teach its young one the basic things of sustenance, like how to find food and protect itself from danger, before it is left to fend for itself. We, humans, bestowed with rational thinking, want to do much more for our offspring. But it is disheartening to see our educated youth who are unable to face the challenges in life and stand on their own. Is it not mainly because of the fact that we are failing to inculcate a work culture in them?

The school and the educators' responsibilities do not end in getting their students a high score in their study. It is also their duty to enable them to look at life with a sense of purpose and achievement. In other words, the very aim of education should be to prepare the learner for his life.

But many of today's children, especially those of the upper middle class, who are brought up with all the comforts and luxuries, are growing up as a work-shy lot. They lack motivation to work and the feeling of having-everything-need-nothing is deep-rooted in them. If so, how can their life become meaningful without anything to contribute to society?

Though we are looking towards the West, we have not yet learnt to copy their way when it comes to their approach towards work, which has enabled them to stand far ahead of us. They do not despise work because the habit of working is instilled in them at an early stage in life. Even the Indian students who go abroad for higher studies find a part time job which in turn can act as a supplement in meeting their financial requirement.

As work too is habit-forming and is a healthy one at that, we should spare no effort to inculcate it in our children. Our exam-oriented teaching–learning process has done away with the place of S.U.P.W. [Socially Useful Productive Work] in most of the schools. There is no place for creative work. This is not a welcome change. There should be a period or two allotted for this purpose in every school time-table and should be used fruitfully. The pupils are happy to do group work. If we highlight their work and allow them to come out with novel ideas, we can gauge their creative bent of mind. . . . If they start loving work at a tender age, it can pay them for their lifetime. Also, they get a change from the monotonous routine and offer their mind relaxation for a while. . . .

It would be worthwhile if parents and teachers (first and second teachers) join hands to create a sensitivity towards work. Children should be taught to respect work of any sort. The overall development of a child's personality is dependent on the kind of education one receives. So it is the duty of these educators to develop an urge for achievement in the child's mind. It will act as a driving force throughout his life.

Today corporate companies and industries prefer dynamic and talented youth, with a right attitude to work and join their work force. So, if one is able to capture a work sense at a young age, he can carve a niche for himself by the time he reaches his twenties while others look at him with awe.

It is time we understood that no government can offer jobs for all as they complete university education. Skill and ability are touchstones to success and one who is mentally alert can pick the right job.

Every one is unique with a special talent embedded in each child. If properly channeled, these infinite riches can benefit the whole society. There will neither be any dearth of human resources nor job opportunities for the young, as science and technology are revolutionising the world.

The parents too should be aware of the fact that diverting a certain amount of time for work does not interfere with their ward's studies. In such a case they too will encourage the youngsters taking up part-time jobs to earn while they learn. In this age of the Internet and web-sites, it will not be difficult to find a job which can serve as a base to build up one's career.

Through this sort of work, they can learn many valuable lessons of life too. It develops a sense of responsibility. They learn to be independent, tolerant and patient and to get on with demanding employers and tension at workplace. It can meet their ever-increasing demand for pocket money. They learn to use their leisure time effectively and there is no place for any kind of wanton habits yielding to peer pressure. . . .

Life cannot be meaningful or rewarding without a pleasurable job. The work place has enormous thrills and adventures to offer, if only we have the sense to enjoy it.

Our approach and attitude towards work must change. We should always be motivational and encouraging by narrating the life stories of people who have risen to great heights through sheer hard work. Parents have to realise the prudence behind giving a fish for hunger or teaching fishing to satisfy hunger.

Finally the desire to come up and contribute something to society should be the guiding spirit of every human being. Every piece of work can give creative satisfaction if done perfectly. So it is our duty to safeguard the young without being carried away.

Source: From Leela Msdhusudan, "Inculcating a Work Culture," *The Hindu,* March 27, 2001. Reprinted with permission of *The Hindu,* www.thehindu.com.

- It is safe to say that commitment patterns fluctuate on an individual basis in countries such as the United States, the United Kingdom, Australia, and other individualistic countries. However, commitment patterns are more determined on a group level in countries such as Japan, South Korea, and Spain, which are more collectivistic.

Job design has been applied successfully to improve job satisfaction and quality of work performance in the United States and western Europe,[73] but it does not apply very well in other countries. Sociotechnical approaches to work design and quality circles are more popular in northern European and East Asian countries.[74] In countries where saving face is important, group-based work designs are more effective.

Motivation in International and Global Corporations

International and global companies are culturally diverse organizations (see Chapter 1), which require extensive coordination of practices from a variety of perspectives. Subsidiaries located in different parts of the world provide interesting insights as well as challenges in the way motivation in these companies should be understood and managed. Even within a country context, if the country is culturally diverse, such as the United States, or is in the process of becoming diverse, such as the United Kingdom, France, and Germany, management of conflicting values, norms, and attitudes becomes important. Therefore, the framework for managing a globally diverse workforce to enhance motivation is not significantly different from that of addressing issues on a domestic scale, but the range of issues is more complicated in some contexts.

Exhibit 14.10 shows matching of incentive systems and cultural environments, as adapted from the work of Huo and Steers. National characteristics and cultural characteristics interact in the design of effective incentive systems. For example, countries that are isolated geographically and have the cultural value of social needs tend to design rewards that enhance social interaction as an incentive for motivation.[75] Managers of global corporations need to pay attention to the combination of national and cultural characteristics before designing incentive systems and jobs. In some cultures, rewards may be given in the form of individual bonuses based on performance compensation systems, whereas in other cultures bonuses and performance incentive systems are not highly valued by workers. In the Netherlands and Sweden, for example, bonuses are not regarded as highly as is time off from work, enabling the worker to deal with nonwork obligations.

EXHIBIT 14.10
Match between Cultural Environment and Incentive Systems

Source: Adapted from Y. P. Huo and R. M. Steers, "Cultural Influences on the Design of Incentives Systems: The Case of East Asia," *Asia Pacific Journal of Management* 10, no. 1 (1993), p. 81.

National Characteristics	Cultural Characteristics	Effective Incentive Systems
Frequent disruptions of political stability	High team spirit	Group-based incentives
Long-established socialist system	Strong preference for egalitarianism	Equal distribution of awards
Isolated geographic location	Emphasis on social needs	Rewards that enhance social interaction
Highly equivocal language	High tolerance for ambiguity	Nonspecific rewards tied to overall performance

Sirota and Greenwood studied the work goals of 19,000 employees in a large multi-national electrical equipment manufacturing company, operating in 46 countries.[76] This study reported results for Argentina, Australia, Austria, Belgium, Brazil, Canada, Chile, Colombia, Denmark, Finland, France, Germany, India, Israel, Japan, Mexico, New Zealand, Norway, Peru, South Africa, Sweden, Switzerland, the United Kingdom, the United States, and Venezuela. In every country, the four most important goals were:

- Achievement, especially individual achievement.
- Quality of the immediate work environment.
- General features of the organization.
- Employment conditions, such as pay and work hours.

However, there were some major differences among the countries:

- English-speaking countries ranked higher on their emphasis for individual achievement and lower on their need for security.
- French-speaking countries gave greater emphasis to security and less to challenging work.
- Northern European countries put more emphasis on job accomplishment and less on getting ahead. There was also greater concern for people and less for the organization itself—it was important to separate personal lives from the influence of work lives.
- In Latin American and southern European countries, individual achievement as an organizational reward was less important than job security, and fringe benefits are important in both of these groups.
- Getting ahead was important in Germany, along with an emphasis on security and fringe benefits.
- Interestingly, Japan was low on individual achievement but ranked job-related challenges high. The need for job autonomy was lowest in Japan, but there was a strong emphasis on good working conditions and a friendly work environment.

Summary

People seek various rewards from work organizations, depending on their cultural values, norms, and attitudes. This chapter analyzed the nature of situations where U.S.-based theories of motivation are easily applicable and where they are not. Security is extremely important for some people, whereas others seek status and success over everything else. Some people look for satisfying and fulfilling work, while still others want agreeable relationships.

Human needs exhibit similarities around the globe, but cultural and environmental contexts determine the order of importance of these needs. Expectancy theory of motivation is applicable in many countries, if managers specify the type of rewards that are likely to motivate a given group of workers based on their cultural background. This means that managers must know the type of motivational rewards that are important in the culture in which they operate.

As global companies expand into different countries, they face variations in patterns of motives. Even if the country culture suppresses achievement motives, the experience of working for a multinational subsidiary may create new expectations and therefore make people more achievement-oriented than they were before they started working for the company.

Key Terms and Concepts

external locus of control, *433*
extrinsic factor, *423*
internal locus of control, *433*
intrinsic factor, *422*
job satisfaction, *437*
Meaning of Working study, *430*

motivation, *418*
need for achievement, *423*
need for affiliation, *424*
need for power, *424*
norm of equality, *429*

norm of equity, *429*
norm of need, *429*
organizational commitment, *423*
role ambiguity, *436*
role overload, *436*

Discussion Questions

1. Explain the importance of understanding work motivation in managing multinational and global organizations.
2. Discuss why individuals in different parts of the world prefer different types of work outcomes. Provide reasons for linking work outcomes with the Meaning of Working study.
3. Explain how global managers could design culturally appropriate reward systems.
4. What are the implications of Hofstede's cultural dimensions on work motivation?
5. Develop a cultural profile of workers in a collectivistic country, such as Mexico, and discuss the steps needed to motivate them.

Minicase

Breaking with Tradition in a Foreign Land

When I arrived at Nissan at the close of the 1990s, established business practices were wreaking huge damage on the company. Nissan was strapped for cash, which prevented it from making badly needed investments in its aging product line. Its Japanese and European entry-level car, the March (or the Micra in Europe), for example, was nearly nine years old. The competition, by contrast, debuted new products every five years; Toyota's entry-level car at the time was less than two years old. The March had had a few facelifts over the years, but essentially we were competing for 25% of the Japanese market and a similar chunk of the European market with an old—some would say out-of-date—product. Similar problems plagued the rest of our car lines.

The reason Nissan had cut back on product development was quite simple: to save money. Faced with persistent operating losses and a growing debt burden, the company was in a permanent cash crunch. But it didn't have to be that way. Nissan actually had plenty of capital—the problem was it was locked up in noncore financial and real-estate investments, particularly in keiretsu partnerships. The keiretsu system is one of the enduring features of the Japanese business landscape. Under the system, manufacturing companies maintain equity stakes in partner companies. This, it's believed, promotes loyalty and cooperation. When the company is large, the portfolio can run to billions of dollars. When I arrived at Nissan, I found that the company had more than $4 billion invested in hundreds of different companies.

The problem was that the majority of these shareholdings were far too small for Nissan to have any managerial leverage on the companies, even though the sums involved were often quite large. For instance, one of Nissan's investments was a $216 million stake in Fuji Heavy Industries, a company that, as the manufacturer of Subaru cars and trucks, competes with Nissan. What sense did it make for Nissan to tie up such a large sum of money in just 4% of a competitor when it could not afford to update its own products?

That was why, soon after I arrived, we started dismantling our keiretsu investments. Despite widespread fears that the sell-offs would damage our relationships with suppliers, those relationships are stronger than ever. It turns out that our partners make a clear distinction between Nissan as customer and Nissan as shareholder. They don't care what we do with the shares as long as we're still a customer. In fact, they seem to have benefited from our divestments. They have not only delivered the price reductions that Nissan has demanded but also have improved their profitability. Indeed, all Nissan's suppliers posted increased profits in 2000. Although breaking up the Nissan keiretsu seemed a radical move at the time, many other Japanese companies are now following our lead.

Nissan's problems weren't just financial, however. Far from it. Our most fundamental challenge was cultural. Like other Japanese companies, Nissan paid and promoted its employees based on their tenure and age. The longer employees stuck around, the more power and money they received, regardless of their actual performance. Inevitably, that practice bred a certain degree of complacency, which undermined Nissan's competitiveness. What car buyers want, after all, is performance, performance, performance. They want well-designed, high-quality products at attractive prices, delivered on time. They don't care how the company does that or who in the company does it. It's only logical, then, to build a company's reward and incentive systems around performance, irrespective of age, gender, or nationality.

So we decided to ditch the seniority rule. Of course, that didn't mean we systematically started selecting the youngest candidates for promotion. In fact, the senior vice presidents that I've nominated over the past two years all have had long records of service, though they were usually not the most senior candidates. We looked at people's performance records, and if the highest performer was also the most senior, fine. But if the second or third or even the fifth most senior had the best track record, we did not hesitate to pass over those with longer service. As expected when changing long-standing practices, we've had some problems. When you nominate a younger person to a job in Japan, for example, he sometimes suffers for being younger—in some cases, older people may not be willing to cooperate with him as fully as they might. Of course, it's also true that an experience like that can be a good test of the quality of leadership a manager brings to the job.

We also revamped our compensation system to put the focus on performance. In the traditional Japanese compensation system, managers receive no share options, and hardly any incentives are built into the manager's pay packet. If a company's average pay raise is, say, 4%, then good performers can expect a 5% or 6% raise, and poor performers get 2% or 2.5%. The system extends to the upper reaches of management, which means that the people whose decisions have the greatest impact on the company have little incentive to get them right. We changed all that. High performers today can expect cash incentives that amount to more than a third of their annual pay packages, on top of which employees receive company stock options. Here, too, other Japanese companies are making similar changes.

Another deep-seated cultural problem we had to address was the organization's inability to accept responsibility. We had a culture of blame. If the company did poorly, it was always someone else's fault. Sales blamed product planning, product planning blamed engineering, and engineering blamed finance. Tokyo blamed Europe, and Europe blamed Tokyo. One of the root causes of this problem was the fact that managers usually did not have well-defined areas of responsibility.

Indeed, a whole cadre of senior managers, the Japanese "advisers" or "coordinators," had no operating responsibilities at all. The adviser, a familiar figure in foreign subsidiaries of Japanese companies, originally served as a consultant helping in the application of innovative Japanese management practices. That role, however, became redundant as familiarity with Japanese practices spread. Yet the advisers remained, doing little except undermining the authority of line managers. So at Nissan, we eliminated the position and put all our advisers into positions with direct operational responsibilities. I also redefined the roles of the other Nissan managers, as well as those of the Renault people I had brought with me. All of them now have line responsibilities, and everyone can see exactly what their contributions to Nissan are. When something goes wrong, people now take responsibility for fixing it.

DISCUSSION QUESTIONS

1. Why did Carlos Ghosn conclude that Nissan's problems were not financial but cultural?
2. What were the various steps that Ghosn and the managers took to remove some of the culture-specific barriers to performance to make Nissan a stronger company?
3. What was the specific impact of the compensation system on the managers' motivation to take responsibility?
4. How did Ghosn begin to eliminate unproductive positions and replace them with individuals with direct line and operational responsibilities?

Notes

1. C. L. Hulin and H. C. Triandis, "Meaning of Work in Different Organizational Environments." In P. C. Nystrome and W. H. Starbuck, eds., *Handbook of Organizational Design* (New York: Oxford University Press, 1981), pp. 336–357; H. C. Triandis, "Motivation to Work in Cross-Cultural Perspective." In J. M. Brett and F. Drasgow, eds., *The Psychology of Work: Theoretically Based Empirical Research* (Mahwah, NJ: Lawrence Erlbaum Associates, 2002), pp. 101–117.

2. S. P. Robins, *Organizational Behavior: Concepts, Controversies, and Applications,* 7th ed. (Upper Saddle River, NJ: Prentice Hall, 1996), p. 212.

3. M. D. Dunnette, "Aptitudes, Abilities, and Skills." In M. D. Dunnette, ed., *Handbook of Industrial and Organizational Psychology* (Chicago: Rand McNally College Publishing, 1976), (pp. 473–520).

4. A. Maslow, *Motivation and Personality* (New York: Harper and Row, 1954).

5. S. Suterwalla, "Immigration and Reality," *Newsweek.* January 28, 2001.

6. G. Hofstede, *Cultures' Consequences,* 2nd ed. (Thousand Oaks, CA: Sage, 2001).

7. Ibid.

8. G. K. Stephens, and C. R. Greer, "Doing Business in Mexico: Understanding Cultural Differences," *Organizational Dynamics,* Summer 1995, pp. 39–55.

9. C. P. Alderfer, R. E. Robert, and K. Ken, "The Effect of Variations in Relatedness Need Satisfaction on Relatedness Desires," *Administrative Science Quarterly* 19 (1974), pp. 507–553; C. P. Alderfer, *Existence, Relatedness, and Growth: Human Needs in Organizational Settings* (New York: Free Press, 1972).

10. F. Herzberg, "One More Time: How Do You Motivate Employees?" *Harvard Business Review* 87, no. 5 (1987), pp. 109–117.

11. P. D. Machungwa and N. Schmitt, "Work Motivation in a Developing Country," *Journal of Applied Psychology,* February 1983, pp. 31–42.

12. F. Herzberg, "One More Time: How Do You Motivate Employees?" *Harvard Business Review,* 87, no. 5 (1987), pp. 109–117.

13. E. Locke, "The Nature and Causes of Job Satisfaction." In M. D. Dunnette, ed., *Handbook of Industrial and Organizational Psychology* (Chicago: Rand McNally, 1976), pp. 1297–1350.

14. J. B. P. Sinha, "Culture Embeddedness and the Developmental Role of Industrial Organizations in India." In H. C. Triandis, M. D. Dunnette, and L. M. Hough, eds., *Handbook of Industrial and Organizational Psychology,* 2nd ed., Vol. 4. (Palo Alto, CA: Consulting Psychologists Press, 1994), pp. 727–764.

15. R. House et al., "Cultural Influences on Leadership and Organizations: Project GLOBE." In W. H. Mobley, M. J. Gessner, and V. Arnold, eds., *Advances in Global Leadership,* Vol. 1 (Stamford, CT: JAI Press, 1999).

16. M. Erez, "A Culture-Based Model of Work Motivation." In P. C. Earley and M. Erez, eds., *New Perspectives on International Industrial/Organizational Psychology* (San Francisco: New Lexington Press, 1997), pp. 193–242.

17. R. N. Kanungo, "Work Alienation: A Pancultural Perspective," *International Studies in Management and Organization* 13 (1983), pp. 119–138. See also O. Shenkar and S. Ronen, "Culture, Ideology, or Economy: A Comparative Exploration of Work Goal Importance among Managers in Chinese Societies," *Managing in a Global Economy III: Proceedings of the Third International Conference* (Amherst, MA: Eastern Academy of Management, 1989), pp. 162–167.

18. D. C. McClelland, "Toward a Theory of Motive Acquisition," *American Psychologist* 20, no. 5 (1965), pp. 321–333.

19. Ibid.

20. S. Ronen and O. Shenkar, "Clustering Countries on Attitudinal Dimensions: A Review and Synthesis," *Academy of Management Review* 10 (1985), pp. 435–454; G. Flynn, "HR in Mexico: What You Should Know," *Personnel Journal* 73, no. 8 (1994), pp. 34–44.

21. Flynn, "HR in Mexico."

22. P. T. Poulsen, "The Attuned Corporation: Experience from 18 Scandinavian Pioneering Corporations," *European Management Journal* 16, no. 3 (1988), pp. 229–235.

23. R. M. Steers and C. J. Sanchez-Runde, "Culture, Motivation, and Work Behavior." In M. J. Gannon and K. L. Newman, eds., *Blackwell Handbook of Cross-Cultural Management* (Oxford, UK: Blackwell Business, 2002), pp. 190–216.

24. P. Blunt and M. L. Jones, *Managing African Organizations* (Berlin: Walter de Gruyter, 1992).

25. D. S. Elenkov, "Russian Aerospace MNCs in Global Competition," *Columbia Journal of World Business* 30 (1995), pp. 66–78.

26. R. S. Bhagat and S. J. McQuaid, "Role of Subjective Culture in Organizations: A Review and Directions for Future Research," *Journal of Applied Psychology Monograph* 67, no. 5 (1982), pp. 653–685; R. S. Bhagat, B. L. Kedia, S. E. Crawford, and M. R. Kaplan, "Cross-Cultural Issues in Organizational Psychology: Emergent Trends and Directions for Research in the 1990's." In C. L. Cooper and Ivan T. Robertson, eds., *International Review of Industrial and Organizational Psychology,* Vol. 5 (New York: John Wiley and Sons, 1990), pp. 59–99; Steers and Sanchez-Runde, "Culture, Motivation, and Work Behavior."

27. D. C. McClelland and D. G. Winter, *Motivating Economic Achievement* (New York: Free Press, 1969).

28. S. Iwawaki and R. Lynn, "Measuring Achievement Motivation in Japan and Great Britain," *Journal of Cross-Cultural Psychology* 3 (1972), pp. 219–220.

29. Bhagat and McQuaid, "Role of Subjective Culture in Organizations."

30. G. A. DeVos, "Achievement and Innovation in Culture and Personality." In E. Norbeck, D. Price-Williams, and W. M. McCords, eds., *The Study of Personality: An Interdisciplinary Approach* (New York: Holt, Rinehart & Winston, 1968).

31. M. L. Maehr, "Socio-cultural Origins of Achievement Motivation," *International Journal of Intercultural Relations* 1 (1977), pp. 81–104; M. L. Maehr, and J. G. Nichols, "Culture and Achievement Motivation: A Second Look." In N. Warren, ed., *Studies in Cross-Cultural Psychology,* Vol. 3 (New York: Academic Press, 1980), (pp. 221–267).

32. J. C. Abegglen and G. Stalk, *Kaisha: The Japanese Corporation* (New York: Basic Books, 1985); R. M. Steers, Y. Shin, and G. Ungson, *The Chaebol: Korea's New Industrial Might* (New York: Harper Business, Ballinger Division, 1989); Steers and Sanchez-Runde, "Culture, Motivation, and Work Behavior."

33. A. Sagie, D. Elizur, and H. Yamauchi, "The Structure and Strength of Achievement Motivation: A Cross-Cultural Comparison," *Journal of Organizational Behavior* 17 (1996), pp. 431–444.

34. V. H. Vroom, *Work and Motivation* (New York: John Wiley & Sons, 1964). See also V. H. Vroom and A. G. Jago, *The New Leadership: Managing Participation in Organizations* (Englewood Cliffs, NJ: Prentice Hall, 1988).

35. D. A. Nadler and E. E. Lawler, "Motivation: A Diagnostic Approach." In J. R. Hackman, E. E. Lawler, and L. W. Porter, eds., *Perspectives on Behavior in Organizations* (New York: McGraw-Hill, 1977), p. 34.

36. E. E. Lawler III, *Motivation in Work Organizations,* 1st classic edition (San Francisco: Jossey-Bass, 1994); L. W. Porter, R. M. Steers, and G. A. Bigley, *Motivation and Work Behavior,* 4th ed. (New York: McGraw-Hill, 2002).

37. R. Nath and W. K. Narayanan, "A Comparative Study of Managerial Support, Trust, Openness, Decision-Making and Job Enrichment," *Academy of Management Proceedings* 40 (1980), pp. 48–52.

38. J. Adams, "Toward an Understanding of Inequity," *Journal of Abnormal and Social Psychology* 67 (1963), p. 97.

39. H. C. Triandis, *Culture and Social Behavior* (New York: McGraw-Hill, 1994), p. 100.

40. L. A. Wilk and W. K. Redmon, "The Effects of Feedback and Goal Setting on the Productivity and Satisfaction of University Admissions Staff," *Journal of Organizational Behavior Management* 18 (1998), pp. 45–68; A. A. Shikdar, and B. Das, "A Field Study of Worker Productivity Improvements," *Applied Ergonomics* 26 (1995), pp. 21–27.

41. E. A. Locke and G. P. Latham, *A Theory of Goal Setting and Task Performance* (Englewood Cliffs, NJ: Prentice Hall, 1990).

42. T. H. Poister and G. Streib, "MBO in Municipal Government: Variations on a Traditional Management Tool," *Public Administration Review* 55 (1995), pp. 48–56.

43. Locke and Latham, *A Theory of Goal Setting and Task Performance.*

44. C. L. Hulin and H. C. Triandis, "Meaning of Work in Different Organizational Environments."

45. H. C. Triandis, "Generic Individualism and Collectivism." In M. J. Gannon and K. L. Newman, eds., *Blackwell Handbook of Cross-Cultural Management* (Oxford, UK: Blackwell Business, 2002), pp. 17–46.

46. M. Erez, "The Congruence of Goal-Setting Strategies with Socio-cultural Values and Its Effects on Performance," *Journal of Management* 12 (1989), pp. 83–90; M. Erez and P. C. Earley, *Culture, Self-Identity, and Work* (New York: Oxford University Press, 1993); Erez, "A Culture-Based Model of Work Motivation."

47. R. E. Cole, *Work, Mobility, and Participation: A Comparative Study of American and Japanese Industry* (Berkeley: University of California Press, 1980); E. E. Lawler III, "Total Quality Management and Employee Involvement: Are They Compatible?" *Academy of Management Executive* 8 (1994), pp. 68–76.

48. K. Leung, "Negotiation and Reward Allocations across Cultures." In P. C. Earley and M. Erez, eds., *New Perspectives on International Industrial and Organizational Psychology* (San Francisco: Lexington Press, 1997), pp. 640–675.

49. Triandis, "Generic Individualism and Collectivism."

50. MOW International Research Team, *The Meaning of Work: An International Perspective* (London: Academic Press, 1987).

51. Ibid., p. 94.

52. Ibid.

53. Ibid., pp. 118–119.

54. E. Rieger and D. Wong-Rieger, "A Configuration Model of National Influence Applied to Southeast Asian Organizations," *Proceedings of the Research Conference on Business in Southeast Asia,* University of Michigan, May 12–13, 1990.

55. J. B. Rotter, "Generalized Expectancies of Internal versus External Control of Reinforcement," *Psychological Monographs: General and Applied* 80, no. 1 (1966), p. 609.

56. Ibid.

57. R. Inglehart et al., *World Values Surveys and European Values Surveys, 1981–1984, 1990–1993, and 1993–1997* (Ann Arbor, MI: Institute for Social Research, 2000).

58. J. B. Schorr, *The Overworked American: The Unexpected Decline of Leisure* (New York: Basic Books, 1993).

59. R. S. Bhagat and K. S. Moustafa, "How Non-Americans View American Use of Time: A Cross-Cultural Perspective." In P. Boski, F. J. R. van de Vijver, and A. M. Chodynicka, eds., *New Directions in Cross-Cultural Psychology: Selected Papers from IAAP Congress in Warsaw, Poland* (Wydawnictwo: Polish Psychological Association, 2002), pp. 183–192.

60. R. Florida, *The Rise of the Creative Class* (New York: Basic Books, 2002).

61. "Togetherness: a Balance Sheet," *The Economist,* September 28, 2000, p. 25–27.

62. G. Hofstede, *Cultures' Consequences,* 2nd ed. (Thousand Oaks, CA: Sage, 2001).

63. P. C. Earley, "East Meets West Meets Mideast: Further Explorations of Collectivistic and Individualistic Work Groups," *Academy of Management Journal* 36 (1993), pp. 319–348.

64. P. Peterson et al., "Role Conflict, Ambiguity, and Overload: A 21-Nation Study," *Academy of Management Journal* 38 (1995), pp. 429–452.

65. R. S. Bhagat, M. P. O'Driscoll, E. Babakus, and L. T. Frey, "Organizational Stress and Coping in Seven National Contexts: A Cross-Cultural Investigation." In G. P. Keita and J. J. Hurrell Jr., eds., *Job Stress in a Changing Workforce* (Washington, DC: American Psychological Association, 1994); Bhagat, Kedia, Crawford, and Kaplan, "Cross-Cultural Issues in Organizational Psychology."

66. Hofstede, *Cultures' Consequences.*

67. Peterson et al., "Role Conflict, Ambiguity, and Overload."

68. R. S. Bhagat, B. Krishnan, R. Renn, D. L. Harnish, and K. S. Moustafa, "Organizational Stress and Psychological Strain in Eight National Contexts: Do Cultural Variations Matter?" (forthcoming, 2004).

69. Hofstede, *Cultures' Consequences.*

70. Ibid.

71. Ibid.

72. Ibid.

73. J. R. Hackman and G. R. Oldham, *Work Redesign* (Reading, MA: Addison-Wesley, 1980).

74. Erez and Earley, *Culture, Self-Identity, and Work.*

75. Y. P. Huo and R. M. Steers, "Cultural Influences on the Design of Incentive Systems: The Case of East Asia," *Asia Pacific Journal of Management* 10, no. 1 (1993), p. 81.

76. D. Sirota and M. J. Greenwood, "Understanding Your Overseas Workforce," *Harvard Business Review* 14 (January–February 1971), pp. 53–60.

CHAPTER FIFTEEN

Leadership across Borders and Cultures

Chapter Learning Objectives

After completing this chapter, you should be able to:

- Explain the significance of leadership in international management.
- Understand why some U.S. theories are applicable outside the United States, and why some are not.
- Identify the factors that affect the quality of leadership in different countries and the significance of non-Western theories of leadership in the global context.
- Understand the role of effective global leadership.
- Explain the significance of reckless and unethical leadership.

Opening Case: Sina.com: Is This Any Way to Dress for an IPO?

The Chinese-language portal welcomed Silicon Valley execs. Now they're out.

Taiwanese entrepreneur Daniel Chiang used to enjoy boasting that Sina.com, the hot Chinese-language portal he helped create, was different from the other Internet companies in Greater China. While most Chinese entrepreneurs are loath to surrender control of their companies to outsiders, Chiang and Chinese co-founder Wang Zhidong in March installed experienced Silicon Valley professionals in most top executive posts. "You have to play by the U.S. rules of the game," Chiang said in July, explaining why he stepped aside as chief executive officer.

That open attitude enabled Sina to line up $25 million from foreign investors, including Goldman, Sachs & Co. and Singapore's Economic Development Board. Boasting 1 million registered users, it also became the odds-on favorite to be the leading Internet content provider for the Chinese-speaking world.

But now it appears Sina wasn't as ready for the U.S. high-tech fast lane as Chiang had hoped. Most of its vaunted American execs have left in the past month, victims of a thorough management purge led by Wang and Chiang, sources say. The outcasts include CEO Jim Sha—a veteran of Netscape Communications and Oracle—as well as Sina's chief financial and chief technical officers. Gone from its board are two respected outside directors: Pehong Chen, CEO of Redwood City (Calif.) e-commerce pioneer BroadVision Inc., and Jerry Colonna, founder of venture-capital firm Flatiron Partners and a director for TheStreet.com. Wang and Chiang have even fired investment banker Goldman Sachs, which was preparing to list Sina on Nasdaq or in Hong Kong by yearend. "This is an absolute and utter meltdown of a company," says a banker familiar with Sina. It's unclear whether all the turmoil is affecting operations. But with Net stocks struggling in the U.S., it could hurt efforts to lure new investors.

New Hitch

Behind the rift, sources say, was a clash in personality and management judgment that shows the difficulty of marrying the business cultures of Silicon Valley and Wall Street with those of China and Taiwan. Sina was formed last year by the merger of Beijing-based software firm Stone Rich Sight Information Technology Service Co., run by Wang, with Sinanet, a portal popular in Taiwan. Sinanet was founded in 1995 and managed by Chiang, 41, a former executive of Taiwanese antivirus software firm Trend Micro Inc. But tense relations between Taipei and Beijing meant the merger wouldn't be easy.

By putting its headquarters in Silicon Valley, Sina aimed to secure a politically neutral base. It also hoped to attract the talent needed to be a hit with investors. "Both Chiang and Wang were convinced that bringing in professional management would be the best thing, and push them toward an IPO," says Bo Feng, a Shanghai-based banker and early Sina investor. So they hired Sha and other Valley veterans. But problems arose quickly. The Asian founders and U.S. managers and advisors soon split into opposing factions. "Their visions and ways of doing things weren't the same," says Feng. Chiang and Wang pushed for a focus on China, where business was growing faster than first expected. The Americans wanted to focus on other markets. Before long, the factions were "constantly disagreeing and fighting," says a source close to the company.

Another major point of dispute was the timing of Sina's plan to go public. Sources say Wang felt a sense of urgency after China.com Corp., the Hong Kong-based portal that was the first to go public in the U.S., successfully listed on Nasdaq in July. That whetted the appetites of many Asian Internet companies—including Sina. The Americans urged Sina to wait until management, a solid business plan, and detailed financial forecasts were all in place.

"Utmost Respect"

The conflict began coming to a head in late August. Sha, 49, was forced out as CEO, and Wang replaced him. CFO Riley Willcox, who had spent 15 years as a financial officer for Valley companies, was demoted. Soon after, sources say, he quit after Wang insisted over his objections on asking the board to go public quickly. When that board meeting was held on Sept. 11 at the Menlo Park (Calif.) offices of Venture Law Group, Sina's counsel, the proposal prompted BroadVision's Chen and Flatiron's Colonna to quit as directors. Wang had enough control of the board to approve his plan. Besides, says the banking source, "Wang decided he wanted control of his company back." Chiang and Wang declined to comment for this story, as did Sha and Willcox.

Sina won't say when it plans to go public. One hitch is that it again has no CFO: Willcox's replacement, Mark Fagan, quit after a few weeks. Morgan Stanley Dean Witter is the new lead underwriter, though Goldman remains a Sina investor. "We have the utmost respect for Sina.com and its vision for the Internet," says Goldman spokesman Peter Rose. Morgan Stanley won't comment.

Sina also won't discuss where the company goes next. If it presses ahead with an IPO, however, investors will want plenty of financial details—and an explanation of what became of its prized U.S. team. As investors turn more skeptical of Net plays in general, it's a lesson in cross-cultural management that other Asian companies should study.

Source: Reprinted from Bruce Einhord with Linda Himelstein, "Sina.com: Is This Any Way to Dress for an IPO?" April 22, 2002 issue of *BusinessWeek* by special permission. Copyright © 2002 by The McGraw-Hill Companies, Inc.

Discussion Questions

1. From this case, discuss ways that leadership affects business practice across cultures and borders.
2. In your opinion, what factors should someone consider before attempting leadership in another culture?
3. What are some of the pressures that U.S. leaders face in dealing with the Chinese?

What Is Leadership?

One of the most challenging tasks that international managers face is the need to work with and lead people of different national and cultural backgrounds. The process of leading others to accomplish tasks effectively is one of the most complex yet least understood areas of management. In this chapter, we examine the concept and theories of leadership as they evolved in Western countries, particularly in the United States, and analyze their suitability in other nations and cultures.

Managers of multinational and global corporations need to understand the factors that enable the manager to be an effective leader, not only in Western countries, but also in non-Western countries. Examples of indigenous and non-Western theories of leadership need to be understood to enhance this process, and we discuss examples of these approaches as well.

Leadership has existed as a concept since the beginning of recorded history, but the word leadership seems to be relatively new. Descriptions of great leaders who have accomplished important goals for their followers and succeeded despite significant hardships exist in culturally diverse books and manuscripts, such as Homer's *Iliad,* the Indian *Gita,* the *Bible* and other religious texts, including the writings of Confucius. Powerful, influential leaders have moved masses and accomplished objectives that ordinary men and women might find impossible. George Washington, Abraham Lincoln, Franklin D. Roosevelt, Eleanor Roosevelt, Winston Churchill, Andrew Carnegie, Mahatma Gandhi, Nelson Mandela, Golda Meir, and Anwar Sadat, for example, come from diverse parts of the world and have been powerful forces in their countries.

Despite 50 years of research on this topic, no generally accepted definition of leadership exists.[1] Generally, **leadership** is defined as the process of influencing people and providing a work environment so that they can accomplish their group or organizational objectives. Effective leaders create appropriate conditions to help groups of people define their goals and find appropriate ways of achieving them.[2] Definitions given by researchers in the West tend to focus on the ability of individuals to influence their followers toward goal accomplishment.[3] Acceptance of this definition seems to be growing in different parts of the world; however, differences rooted in beliefs, attitudes, values, and norms present important challenges in understanding the importance of leadership in different nations and cultures.[4] Terms for leaders include boss, administrator, supervisor, director, manager, coach, head, chief, chair, master. In the United States, distinctions in titles, such as assistant vice president, managing director, division head, senior vice president, and president have a great deal of meaning. Not all countries make such fine distinctions between ranks as is found in U.S. corporations.

The difference between being a leader and assuming other organizational roles is the degree of influence that leaders have over their followers. Effective leaders tend to exercise both substantial and subtle influence over their followers to perform actions that go beyond simple compliance with their job descriptions.[5] Administrators and managers can get routine tasks accomplished without practicing acts of leadership, but tasks that force individuals to go beyond the normal requirements of their jobs demand the act of leadership. Effective leaders achieve effective group and organizational performance by emphasizing creativity and involvement of the followers over the long term. Their vision tends to have significant appeal for a large majority of their followers, and such vision has the potential to transform a collection of individuals into a group that can accomplish tasks with a sense of continued commitment and satisfaction.

No matter how leadership is defined around the world, only about 8 percent of executives in large firms think that their organizations employ a sufficient number of leaders.[6] Programs for enhancing leadership skills of managers and supervisors exist in both large and small corporations. Universities and many consulting organizations have programs to train leaders from both profit and nonprofit organizations. Although individuals may say "Oh, I'm not a leader," when they are able to get tasks accomplished using their influence, they are exercising leadership.

Perspectives on Leadership

Research on the role of leadership in organizations has been conducted mostly in the United States, and it is often understood in terms of five phases, as shown in Exhibit 15.1. Each has its own distinct theoretical approach. We examine trait-based theories, behavioral theories, contingency theories, implicit theories, and transformational theories in this section.

Trait-Based Perspectives

Louis Gerstner Jr., who went to IBM as chairman and chief executive in 1993, with no previous experience in the computer industry, is credited for having turned this computer industry giant into the industry leader. Gerstner is recognized for his drive and his love of winning.[7] Among numerous examples of such leaders is Lee Iococca of Chrysler Corporation, who also turned a failing company into a success in the early 1980s. Lee Iacocca was credited for his vision and his sustained energy.

From these accounts, it appears that these individuals possess several leadership traits or competencies. The **trait-based perspective** of leadership developed from the belief that certain leadership competences or traits were natural to some and not to others. Leadership competencies include natural and learned abilities, values, personality traits such as drive, ability to forecast the future, and other characteristics that lead to the ability to create a credible vision and inspire others to follow.

For the first part of the twentieth century, management scholars used scientific methods to determine personality traits and physical characteristics that distinguished leaders from others. The "great men" theories of the early 1900s, however, failed to identify traits that are both necessary and sufficient for exhibiting leadership. We do not know if certain traits are important in all situations of leadership. Recent research has shown that some individual traits are related to the emergence of leaders and their effectiveness.[8] These traits are described in Exhibit 15.2.

EXHIBIT 15.1
Perspectives of Leadership

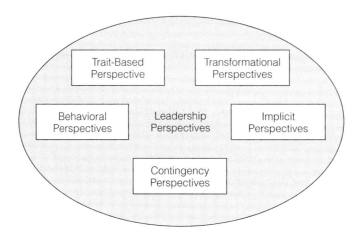

Leaders who are high in need for achievement are driven to succeed. Their inner motivation sustains their vision and encourages others to move forward with them. We can see this drive in Louis Gerstner of IBM. Leadership motivation is concerned with a strong need for power, and this motivation is kept in check by a strong sense of personal and social responsibility.[9] Effective leaders tend to seek power, not necessarily for themselves, but for the benefit of their work group and organization. Integrity, as a leadership trait, refers to the leader's truthfulness and reliability in translating his or her vision into action.

Traits of self-confidence, intelligence, knowledge of the business, and emotional intelligence are all necessary in different combinations for leadership. The last of these traits, emotional intelligence, has only recently been studied and is regarded as crucial for effectiveness.[10] Leaders who are high on this trait are able to monitor their own and other's emotions, discriminate among them, and use the information to guide their thoughts and actions.

Behavioral Perspectives

The **behavioral perspective** of leadership focuses on behaviors that make leaders effective. Studies done at Ohio State University, the University of Michigan, and Harvard University identified two clusters of leadership behaviors with more than 1,800 items.[11] One cluster was called **consideration,** which reflected people-orientated behaviors, such as showing trust, respect, and a concern for others' well-being. Leaders rated high on consideration supported employees' interests and treated employees with respect. The other cluster was called **initiation of structure,** which focused on behaviors that define and structure work roles. Leaders rated high on initiation of structure were concerned with assigning specific tasks, clarifying their duties and procedures, ensuring that they follow company rules, and encouraging them to reach their maximum performance potential.

In general, the findings of these studies suggest that, with some exceptions, leaders high on both consideration and initiation of structure tended to achieve higher subordinate performance. However, only the University of Michigan studies showed that higher group productivity and satisfaction were found in groups with a more considerate leader.

EXHIBIT 15.2
Leadership Traits

Sources: Most elements of this list were derived from S. A. Kirkpatrick and E. A. Locke, "Leadership: Do Traits Matter?" *Academy of Management Executive* 5 (May 1991), pp. 48–60. Several of these ideas are also discussed in H. B. Gregersen, A. J. Morrison, and J. S. Black, "Developing Leaders for the Global Frontier," *Sloan Management* 40 (Fall 1998), pp. 21–32; R. J. House and R. N. Aditya, "The Social Scientific Study of Leadership: Quo Vadis?" *Journal of Management* 23 (1997), pp. 409–473.

Leadership Trait	Description
Drive	The leader's inner motivation to pursue goals
Leadership motivation	The leader's need for socialized power to accomplish team or organizational goals
Integrity	The leader's truthfulness and tendency to translate words into deeds
Self-confidence	The leader's belief in his or her own leadership skills and ability to achieve objectives
Intelligence	The leader's above-average cognitive ability to process enormous amounts of information
Knowledge of the business	The leader's understanding of the company's environment to make more intuitive decisions
Emotional intelligence	The leader's ability to monitor his or her own and others' emotions, discriminate among them, and use the information to guide his or her thoughts and actions

A number of cross-cultural studies have shown the importance of these two dimensions.[12] The findings show that considerate, or relationship-oriented, leaders are generally able to improve subordinates' satisfaction. The influence of initiation of structure, or task orientation, is more complex, and it is not clearly understood. Some researchers have suggested that a culture-specific interpretation of what task orientation means is important. The responses of subordinates to relationship-oriented leadership is consistently positive across cultures; however, the responses to task-oriented leadership depends on the nature of the culture in which the leader functions. Leaders must adapt their behavior to the situation and understand the needs of the followers in a clearer fashion in cross-cultural situations.

Contingency Perspectives

The **contingency perspective** framework was developed in the United States to account for leadership effectiveness that did not follow the predictions of behavioral theories. The contingency model, developed by Fiedler, presented the idea that the nature of the situation moderates the relationship between the leader's style and group effectiveness.[13] A leader's style is assessed by the Least Preferred Co-Workers (LPC) scale, and it reflects the leader's ability to work with the least preferred co-workers in his or her work group. The nature of the situation is determined by the leader's position power, quality of leader–member relations, and the amount of structure in the task itself. This theory predicts that a leader with stronger position power tends to improve group performance in highly structured task situations. On the other hand, leaders who are more relationship-oriented get the best out of groups in situations where the task is somewhat unstructured and where the nature of power that they have is less defined.

A number of cross-cultural studies have been conducted using this approach.[14] Filipino managers who are more task-oriented were better at creating high-performing groups but Chinese managers, who were more relationship-oriented, were more effective in achieving goals. Research on this theory in Japan has not succeeded in finding support for this, and support in Mexico, where self-monitoring (being sensitive to one's behavior and the reactions of others) was used as another leader characteristic, is mixed.

The *path–goal theory,* developed by House and his colleagues, identified four leader behaviors and a number of situational and follower characteristics which influence the relationship between leader style and follower satisfaction and performance.[15] While there is good support for this theory in the United States, it has not been adequately tested in other countries. Cultural differences may be a key situational characteristic that, as we have seen, have many different dimensions.

Substitutes for leadership theory is another approach to highlighting the role of contingency.[16] The characteristics of subordinates, such as their degree of interest in the task, skill level, and professionalism, may substitute for leadership behavior, such as being directive or showing consideration. Contradictory results have been found, but the cross-cultural and international applicability of the substitutes for leadership theory has not been fully tested.

Implicit Perspectives

These theories, developed in the United States, focus on the way subordinates perceive a leader.[17] Followers develop prototypes or mental representations of leaders through their life experiences and interactions with others, according to this theory. Specific leader behaviors do not necessarily make a person a leader unless the followers perceive him or her as a leader.

The idea that different cultures have different prototypes for leader behavior has found support in international studies. Leaders who meet the expectations of their followers gain their trust and are effective in some cultures.[18] Results from this and other international studies suggest that some characteristics of leaders are universally accepted and preferred.

Transformational Perspective

The **transformational leadership** theories focus on the process of a leader using his or her charisma to inspire followers to go beyond their immediate self-interests for the good of the work group and the organization.[19] **Charisma** is a special quality of interpersonal influence that some leaders possess and that enables their followers to develop respect and trust for the leader.

As noted early in the chapter, examples of these charismatic leaders are found in almost all nations and cultures. Roosevelt, Churchill, Gandhi, Carnegie, and Mandela have had great influence on their followers that led to admiration, respect, trust, ongoing commitment, and loyalty for these leaders. Charismatic leaders are self-confident, have an ideal vision, and are deeply committed to their goals. They are seen as being unconventional and radical thinkers who can bring about important changes.

U.S. researchers argue that charismatic leaders are more effective than noncharismatic leaders regardless of national and cultural differences. This notion is supported across cultures.[20] Research on the effectiveness of this transformational perspective in countries like the Netherlands, Singapore, and the Dominican Republic has shown that, while the charismatic leader is perceived as being effective, the processes leaders use to influence subordinates toward accomplishing goals vary a great deal from country to country. However, in Japan this perspective of leadership does not have a great deal of validity.[21] Charismatic leadership has been found to have more effect on U.S. employees than on Mexican employees.[22]

This perspective has the best potential for being applicable in different countries and cultures, but more research needs to be done to fully understand how charisma and cultural differences act together to produce effective leaders.

Leadership across Cultures and Borders

The emergence of leadership, especially the way a leader influences followers, is often a product of cultural factors. Deeply ingrained values regarding the rights and duties of employees differ from country to country and present different worldviews. These values, reflected in laws, constitutions, and various social customs, provide prescriptions for leader behavior. Like other aspects of culture, discussed in Chapter 5, these are taken for granted by the members of a society, whether others see them as correct or not. If a leader violates core values, for example, by engaging in immoral or illegal activities or if the leader behaves in a more individualistic manner in a country that is more collectivistic, he or she can lose authority over subordinates and would be less effective. In some cases, the leader may immediately lose the positions of leadership.

The act of leadership is often a product of socially and culturally constructed legal, moral, ethical, and work obligations. For example, in Western countries, such as the United States, United Kingdom, Sweden, and Norway, women are becoming organizational leaders, and the concept of equalizing pay between men and women has received considerable attention. Although some social barriers conflict with the cultural ideals of equality, most Westerners clearly anticipate that women have the potential for leadership. In contrast, in high power distance countries, such as Mexico, China, Saudi Arabia, and

Japan, women do not have much opportunity to advance their careers or to become leaders in their organizations. A study of Arab executives and foreign expatriates in the United Arab Emirates reported that a consultative or participative style was preferred by both groups.[23] However, other studies have found that in Jordan and other Middle Eastern countries, an authoritative management style was preferred.[24] Autocratic styles of leadership have also been found in Indian managers.[25]

The political values of a country also influence the type of leader that will emerge and how leaders function. Political culture reflects idealized values about effective leadership and can exercise strong influences on how leaders should act in the workplace. Countries with democratic traditions, such the United States, United Kingdom, Sweden, and Germany, have well-defined processes that encourage participative leadership, whereas countries with autocratic political philosophies, such as most Middle Eastern, Latin American, and Asian countries, tend to favor no participation by followers.

The culture of the organization affects the type of leaders that will emerge and how they function. One view proposes that the leaders' major contribution is the effective management of organizational culture.[26] Leaders create, maintain, and play a major role in changing organizational culture, but we should note that they are also influenced by the constraints and values of their company. For example, a leader who favors equal participation of men and women in senior management ranks might find difficulty in sustaining this in a company where the past tradition did not favor equal treatment of women. Another example is where the leader has a preference for decentralized decision making but does not find support for the change in an organization that has traditionally had centralized decision making.

Jürgen Schrempp, the CEO of DaimlerChrysler, initiated changes in the corporation that reflect the influence of organizational culture on leadership. Schrempp and the previous CEO, Edzard Reuter, rid the company of businesses that were not profitable and discouraged old-fashioned thinking in order to make the company more global in its focus. The changes were felt throughout the corporation, and it presented a new view of Chrysler in the minds of managers and employers—a view of the company moving away from its solely German management style and becoming global. It imposed an unfamiliar view of what Daimler-Benz, a former German company, represented. These changes were needed to reorient the company as a more global company.

Functions of Leadership across Borders and Cultures

As we discussed earlier, Western theories focus on traits, behaviors, interaction patterns, leader–member relationships, perception of followers, and influence as determinants of leadership. Research examining the role of societal culture is important, especially because it helps us draw implications for what international managers can do to provide effective leadership in different parts of the world.

Some functions of leadership are similar across borders and cultures; however, the definition of an effective leader varies greatly across cultures. The generally accepted images of leaders in different countries are important to understand. Industry leaders in Mexico, India, Italy, and France are highly regarded for their social status and access to political power. In many countries in Latin America, such as Brazil, Argentina, and Chile, organizational leaders are expected to present a holistic view of themselves, be prominent in society, and have a strong appreciation for the arts. Decisiveness and knowledge of the industry are respected in leaders in Germany, Poland, and Russia, where they receive a great deal of formal organizational prestige.[27]

Research on leadership from the U.S. perspective is mostly concerned with managerial behaviors and tends to describe leaders as autocratic versus democratic, participative versus directive, task- versus relationship-oriented, high on initiation of structure or consideration.[28] These styles of leadership reflect opinions of mostly U.S. workers and subordinates in terms of what they consider to be effective. For example, the democratic, participative, and consultative style of leadership has generally been found to be beneficial in maintaining effectiveness of leaders in the United States. Managers of multinational and global corporations should remember that considerable changes may be needed in their leadership styles when they go abroad to manage a subsidiary or when they manage a culturally diverse workforce in their home countries.

Research on leadership clearly tells us that no style of leadership works well in all cultures and nations. A significant amount of research supports the idea that culture acts as a contingency factor in exercising leadership. This means that culture-based norms, beliefs, roles, and values about what is expected of leaders, the influence they have over their subordinates, and the amount of organizational status or prestige that they are given vary across nations.

When Is Leadership Needed?

Concern about the significance of leadership in managing organizations extends beyond the desire for improved profitability and higher levels of performance in the stock market. The concern has been exacerbated in the last few years, due to unethical and illegal behaviors on the part of leaders of companies such as Enron, WorldCom, and Tyco. The business press is replete with examples of reckless leaders in the United States who are responsible for causing great emotional injuries and pain to their employees.[29] We discuss the significance of ethical behavior of leaders in Chapter 17.

Leaders are not always needed to enhance performance of work groups. Research has clearly shown that in some task environments a work team may be entirely self-managing.[30] In fact, attempts to change the directions of the work group can be counterproductive in these cases. There is a saying in the leadership literature that leaders should not reward person A while hoping that person B's performance will improve.[31]

A leader in an individualistic culture is best seen as an individual who provides the task or relationship functions lacking in a group at a given point in time, especially when leaders are able to accurately perceive the need for these functions and provide them competently and in a timely manner. However, many situations in high-tech and symbol processing organizations (such as investment banks, universities, and research laboratories) are of such a nature that leaders' knowledge could be lower than the subordinates'.[32] These situations exemplify the substitutes for leadership theory mentioned earlier.

In contrast, it is difficult, if not impossible, to find a well-managed team without a leader in a collectivistic culture with high power distance. Since the principle of seniority and respect for organizational superiors is embedded in these contexts, an effective leader is one who has all of the necessary attributes of task and group maintenance functions. Such leaders are often not clearly differentiated in terms of calling the person a manager or supervisor or other title more prevalent in the individualist societies. However, we should not assume that the presence of a culturally appropriate seniority system means that these groups are autocratic in the same sense as understood in the West.[33]

The way group leaders and followers relate to each other is largely determined by the patterns of communication and motivation (including reward systems), as well as organizationally specific culture and control systems. The leader may be given due respect, but in one culture, such as Sweden, it may be conveyed by giving the leader suggestions for improving work processes. However, in another culture, such as Mexico, respect is conveyed by waiting for the leader to say what to do next.[34] Managers of global corporations with responsibilities for managing work groups in different parts of the world should recognize the distinct cultural influences on how respect may be conveyed, especially when they find themselves in collectivistic contexts. As discussed in Chapter 5, some 70 percent of the world's population lives in cultures characterized by moderate to high levels of collectivism and power distance.

A number of studies show that group decision making reflected in the well-known Japanese techniques of *quality circles* (a group of workers who discuss ideas about improving work processes when difficulties arise) is highly effective in East Asian cultures. Surprisingly, this technique has failed miserably, not only in the United States, but also in India, Egypt, and Latin America, despite multiple attempts by many companies to benefit from it.[35] Quality circles are effective in Japan because of the low level of influence that leaders exercise in improving work processes. Although Japan is a hierarchical culture, the influences of these hierarchical processes benefit Japanese organizations where leaders do not need to exercise forceful, autocratic styles, which might be prevalent in Latin America, India, the Middle East, and parts of Africa. The method for improving quality in Japan is based on a procedure called *ringi* (consulting all concerned),[36] where group members show respect for the leader through making suggestions and actively participating.

Leadership in Guilt versus Shame Cultures

Most of us have a commonsense understanding of guilt versus shame. *Guilt* results from violating established social and moral principles and standards. Embezzling company resources and using company credit cards for personal benefits are acts that should result in feelings of guilt. On the other hand, *shame* results from acts that lead to public embarrassment. In other words, you can feel guilty about something you do, but shame does not occur unless the act becomes known to the relevant social group. One feels ashamed when one assumes that the female president of a company is a secretary and asks her during a boardroom meeting to make coffee for everyone. However, one may not feel guilty for this.[37]

A relationship-based culture regulates interactions among co-workers with whom one already has established relationships through the mechanism of shame. Shame results when an individual is admonished or punished by superiors, as well as when one loses face or suffers humiliation in a work context. The fact that people can feel ashamed of their behavior is of supreme importance in sustaining moral leadership in many parts of East Asia, but it is particularly important in Japan.[38]

For example, Shohei Nozawa, president of Yamaichi Securities, stood before world TV cameras and profusely apologized, weeping, for announcing his firm's inability to pay stockholders. He showed shame, as appropriate in Japanese culture. This was the largest bankruptcy in post–World War II Japan. Many non-Japanese viewers, particularly Westerners, were shocked and disgusted by the display of tears.[39] Contrast this with the public display of confidence by Martha Stewart, CEO of Martha Stewart Living Omnimedia, Inc., who, despite being convicted of obstruction of justice refused to show any shame.

Western scholars implicitly believe that leaders should feel guilty and show shame when they engage in inappropriate behaviors, such as wrongful treatment of subordinates, downsizing, sexual harassment, and presiding over corporate failures due to excessive greed. However, public displays of shame are rare in the United States and Western European countries. For example, the CEO of Enron, Kenneth Lay, and the CEO of WorldCom, Bernie Ebbers, refused to express any shame for having engaged in some of the largest bankruptcies in the history of global business. However, such mechanisms of social control in the form of shame are of critical importance in the behavior of public officials as well as businesspersons in many East Asian countries.

We do not advocate shame versus guilt as a mechanism for controlling wrongful and unethical impulses on the part of leaders. The point is that leaders managing across borders and cultures should carefully scrutinize the nature of the culture in which they are managing subsidiaries and work groups. One method that has been found particularly effective is to pay keen attention to a confidante and listen to the suggestions about how to be sensitive to using the appropriate mechanism. Also, a careful reading of the important literary works of the country and observation of the social practices and rituals will provide insights.

The GLOBE Project on Leadership

The largest study on leadership effectiveness is the Global Leadership and Organizational Effectiveness (GLOBE) research program, led by Robert House of the Wharton School of the University of Pennsylvania.[40] A global network of more than 170 management scholars and social scientists from 62 countries collaborated for the purpose of understanding cultural influences on leadership in organizations, using both quantitative and qualitative methods to collect data from over 18,000 managers, representing a majority of the world's population.

The goal of the GLOBE project is to understand patterns of leadership that are universally accepted and those that are subject to the unique influences of the cultural context in which they operate. Findings show that specific leader behaviors—being trustworthy, encouraging, an effective communicator, a good bargainer, and a team builder, for example—are accepted almost everywhere. Negative behaviors that are universal include being uncooperative, egocentric, ruthless, and dictatorial. Behaviors that are dependent on the cultural context include group orientation, self-protectiveness, participative skills, humaneness, autonomy, and charisma. The major concepts investigated in the GLOBE research project are nine aspects of culture that were measured by administering questionnaires. These are reproduced in Exhibit 15.3.

Some of the findings of the GLOBE project show that being a participative leader is regarded as more important in Canada, Brazil, and Austria than in Egypt, Hong Kong, Mexico, and Indonesia. In Brazil, a leader who is charismatic, group-oriented, participative, and humane, but does not function autonomously, is more effective. In the United States, the leaders should stand out through their individual achievements, inspire others through their optimism, stand up for their beliefs, have a clear focus for their efforts, seek continuous improvements, and strive for excellence.[41] The charismatic leader, according to the GLOBE project, is one who is a visionary, acts as an inspiration to subordinates, and is high on performance orientation. The participative leader is one who is willing to delegate responsibility to subordinates and is comfortable in sharing decision-making responsibilities. An autonomous leader is an individualist and does not score as high as a leader in countries where participation in decision making is highly regarded.

Some of the other findings from the GLOBE project are:

- Americans like two kinds of leaders, those who provide workers with empowerment, autonomy, and authority and those who are bold, forceful, confident, risk takers.
- Malaysians expect their leaders to be humble, modest, dignified, and group-oriented.
- Arabs treat their leaders as heroes and worship them as long as they remain in power.
- Iranians expect their leaders to exhibit power and strength.
- The French expect their leaders to appreciate the finer aspects of French culture and arts and to have a good knowledge of mathematics.

EXHIBIT 15.3 Definitions of Various Aspects of the Concept of Culture and Sample Questionnaire Items from the GLOBE Project

Source: Reprinted from *Advances in Global Leadership,* Vol. 1, W.H. Mobley, M.J. Gessner and V. Arnold, "Cultural Influences on Leadership and Organizations: Project Globe," pp. 171-234. Copyright © 1991, with permission from Elsevier.

Culture Construct Definitions	Specific Questionnaire Item
Power distance: The degree to which members of a collective expect power to be distributed equally.	Followers are (should be) expected to obey their leaders without question.
Uncertainty avoidance: The extent to which a society, organization, or group relies on social norms, rules, and procedures to alleviate unpredictability of future events.	Most people lead (should lead) highly structured lives with few unexpected events.
Humane orientation: The degree to which a collective encourages and rewards individuals for being fair, altruistic, generous, caring, and kind to others.	People are generally (should be generally) very tolerant of mistakes.
Collectivism I: The degree to which organizational and societal institutional practices encourage and reward collective distribution of resources and collective action	Leaders encourage (should encourage) group loyalty even if individual goals suffer.
Collectivism II: The degree to which individuals express pride, loyalty, and cohesiveness in their organizations or families.	Employees feel (should feel) great loyalty toward this organization.
Assertiveness: The degree to which individuals are assertive, confrontational, and aggressive in their relationships with others.	People are (should be) generally dominant in their relationships with each other.
Gender egalitarianism: The degree to which a collective minimizes gender inequality.	Boys are encouraged (should be encouraged) more than girls to attain a higher education. (Scored inversely.)
Future orientation: The extent to which individuals engage in future-oriented behaviors such as delaying gratification, planning, and investing in the future.	More people live (should live) for the present rather than for the future. (Scored inversely.)
Performance orientation: The degree to which a collective encourages and rewards group members for performance improvement and excellence.	Students are encouraged (should be encouraged) to strive for continuously improved performance.

- The Dutch place high value on equality and are not so sure about the importance of leadership. Terms like "leader" and "manager" often carry a social stigma. Children don't like to tell their schoolmates that a parent is employed as a manager.

Research on this project is ongoing. The findings of this project are useful for managers of multinational and global companies, providing them with important culture-specific information about what kind of leaders are effective in each country studied in this large international project.

Other research that provides us with important insights about the relative level of preference for autocratic versus participative leaders is based on the work of Hofstede, discussed in Chapter 5. Hofstede noted that participative management approaches that are recommended by U.S. researchers to improve satisfaction and productivity of work groups may not work in high power distance and masculine countries.[42] We can say with confidence that employees in high power distance countries, such as Mexico, the Philippines, and Malaysia, are likely to prefer an autocratic leader who also exhibits some degree of paternalism toward subordinates. Employees in low power distance countries are more likely to prefer a consultative, participative leadership style, and they expect their superiors not to deviate from this style.

As we discussed in implicit perspectives of leadership, to understand the significance of leadership in different countries, we must focus on the perceptions and attitudes that followers have about their leaders. *Subordinateship* (attitude toward leaders) is a strong factor in determining the types of leaders that are likely to be effective in

EXHIBIT 15.4   Subordinateship for Three Levels of Power Distance

Source: Reprinted from *Organizational Dynamics,* Vol. 1, Geert Hofstede, "Motivation, Leadership, and Organization: Do American Theories Apply Abroad?" Copyright © 1980, with permission from Elsevier.

Low Power Distance	Medium Power Distance (United States)	High Power Distance
Subordinates have weak dependence needs.	Subordinates have medium dependence needs.	Subordinates have strong dependence needs.
Superiors have weak dependence needs toward their superiors.	Superiors have medium dependence needs toward their superiors.	Superiors have strong dependence needs toward their superiors.
Subordinates expect superiors to consult them and may rebel or strike if superiors are not seen as staying within their legitimate role.	Subordinates expect superiors to consult them but will accept autocratic behavior as well.	Subordinates expect superiors to act autocratically.
Ideal superior to most is a loyal democrat.	Ideal superior to most is a resourceful democrat.	Ideal superior to most is a benevolent autocrat or paternalist.
Laws and rules apply to all, and privileges for superiors are not considered acceptable.	Laws and rules apply to all, but a certain level of privilege for superiors is considered normal.	Everybody expects superiors to enjoy privileges; laws and rules differ for superiors and subordinates.
Status symbols are frowned upon and will easily come under attack from subordinates.	Status symbols for superiors contribute moderately to their authority and will be accepted by subordinates.	State symbols are very important and contribute strongly to the superior's authority with the subordinates.

each situation. This attitude is strongly conditioned by the beliefs, norms, and values of not only the society in which the leader functions, but also by the political, organizational, and industry cultures. In high power distance cultures, regardless of the educational level of the subordinate, the ideal boss is a benevolent autocrat, or a good father, and less powerful people take it for granted that they will be dependent on the more powerful. In practice, Hofstede notes that less powerful people are at one extreme or the other:[43] Those who have strong emotional dependence on their leaders and those who do not have any emotional dependence on their leaders. Exhibit 15.4 shows the kind of subordinate behaviors found in three countries characterized in terms of three levels of power distance.

Expectations about managerial authority versus participation were studied by Andre Laurent, a French researcher.[44] Americans and Germans prefer more participation than Italians and Japanese. Indonesians are comfortable with an autocratic style of decision making, but managers in Sweden, Denmark, and Great Britain believe that subordinates should participate in decision making and problem solving. Results of this study seem to conflict with the common knowledge about Japan's participative style of decision making. However, the research by Hampden-Turner and Trompenaars found that although Swedish managers are the most willing to delegate authority, Japanese managers rate second in terms of their willingness to delegate to their subordinates.[45] As shown in Exhibit 15.5, participative leadership does not necessarily signal the manager's lack of willingness to take initiative or responsibility.

In a study conducted in the mid-1960s, Haire, Ghiselli, and Porter, using information collected from over 3,000 managers in 14 countries, found that managers consistently preferred the act of delegation and participation, yet they also had a lower sense of comfort in the capacity and the willingness of subordinates to engage in the process of management.[46]

Another study found that Turks prefer authoritarian styles of leadership, as do Thais.[47] In the Middle East, there is little delegation, and managers who are powerful and have the right connections are regarded as strong leaders. A comparison of the Middle Eastern stereotype with the Western stereotype is presented in Exhibit 15.6.

EXHIBIT 15.5

A Comparison of Willingness to Delegate Authority and Managerial Initiative by Leaders

Source: C. Hampden-Turner and A. Trompenaars, *The Seven Cultures of Capitalism* (New York: Doubleday, 1993).

Managerial Initiative, Managers' Sense of Drive and Responsibility (0 = low; 100 = high)		Extent to Which Leaders Delegate Authority (0 = low; 100 = high)	
United States	73.67	Sweden	75.51
Sweden	72.29	Japan	69.27
Japan	72.20	Norway	68.50
Finland	69.58	United States of America	66.23
Korea	67.86	Singapore	65.37
Netherlands	67.11	Denmark	64.65
Singapore	66.34	Canada	64.38
Switzerland	65.71	Finland	62.92
Belgium/Luxembourg	65.47	Switzerland	62.20
Ireland	64.76	Netherlands	61.33
France	64.64	Australia	61.22
Austria	62.56	Germany	60.85
Denmark	62.79	New Zealand	60.54
Italy	62.40	Ireland	59.53
Australia	62.04	United Kingdom	58.95
Canada	61.56	Belgium/Luxembourg	54.55
Spain	61.55	Austria	54.29
New Zealand	59.46	France	53.62
Greece	58.50	Italy	46.80
United Kingdom	58.25	Spain	44.31
Norway	54.50	Portugal	42.56
Portugal	49.74	Greece	37.95

EXHIBIT 15.6 **A Comparison of Middle Eastern and Western Management Functions**

Source: Adapted from M. K. Badawy, "Styles of Mid-Eastern Managers," *California Management Review,* Spring 1980, p. 57.

Management Functions	Middle Eastern Style	Western Style
Leadership	Authoritarian in scope. Strict instructions. Too many management initiatives.	Less emphasis on the personality of the leader, more on leader style and performance.
Communication	The tone depends on who communicates and to whom. Social position, power, and family influences are always present. The chain of command is rigidly followed, and people relate to each other by showing proper respect for rank in a highly formal manner.	Communication emphasizes equality between parties and minimizes differences. People relate to each other less formally and in general terms. Friendships are not as intense and binding.
Patterns of decision making	Emphasis on ad hoc planning. Decisions are made at the highest level of management. Managers don't like to make risky decisions.	Rational planning techniques and modern tools of decision making are used. Elaborate management information systems are used.
Performance evaluation and control	Informal control mechanisms. Routine checks on performance. Lack of standard and sophisticated performance evaluation system.	Advanced control systems focusing on cost reduction and organizational effectiveness. Performance evaluation is formal and sophisticated.
Manpower policies	Heavy reliance on personal contacts and recruiting individuals from the right family and social origins to fill important positions.	Sound personnel management policies. Candidate qualifications are the primary criteria for selecting individuals.
Organizational structures	Bureaucratic, highly centralized, with power and authority in the hands of top managers. Vague relationships. Unclear and unpredictable organizational environments.	Less bureaucratic, less centralized, more delegation of power and authority.
Management methods	Generally traditional and outdated by Western values and standards.	Generally high emphasis on implementing modern and more scientific methods of management.

EXHIBIT 15.7   **An Integrative Model of Leadership Effectiveness Across Nations and Cultures**

Environmental Factors	→	Content Factors	→	Leader–Follower Interaction	→	First-Level Outcomes	→	Second-Level Outcomes

External in Origin:
Political
Economic
Technological
Social
Cultural

Level of
Convergence
and Divergence

Internal in Origin:
Organizational
structure,
culture, and climate
Availability of
resources
Management systems

Arrows indicate
possible causal
influence

Specific to Leaders:
Ability
Experience
Personality
Image
Position power
Style
Motives
Cultural awareness

Specific to Followers:
Beliefs
Attitudes
Motives and
motivation
Locus of control
Experience

Specific to Work
Groups:
Values
Norms
Work roles
Patterns of decision
making
Substitutes for
leadership

Acts of Leadership:
Autocratic versus
participative
Task versus people
orientation
Transactional versus
Transformational

Follower Behavior:
Desire for achievement
versus affiliation
Value of rewards
Sensitivity and response
to leadership

Amount of effort
Group performance
(quality and quantity)
Satisfaction of
followers
Feeling of well-being
Absenteeism
Turnover

Accomplishment of
individual group and
organizational goals
Organizational
effectiveness
High morale
Creativity and
innovation

The differences between Middle Eastern and Western leadership styles were clear during the Gulf War of 1991 and the recent war with Iraq in 2003. President George W. Bush in 1991 and President George Herbert Walker Bush in 2003 both depicted a Western style of leadership in contrast to the Iraqi leader, Saddam Hussein. Differences in the emphasis of religions and ideas about truth, freedom, honor, trust, family, and other values played a major role in the leaders' beliefs in these two vastly different cultures. Arabs tend to use the past as the basis for their reference and decision making; Americans and the English look forward to the future.[48] Significant differences in leadership styles also exist between Western leaders and President Kim Jung II of North Korea. Western leaders emphasize the idea of team building, consulting others widely, and building consensus around the action that they believe is necessary. On the other hand, autocratic leaders do not believe in building teams or in consulting others; they make their decisions unilaterally.

In Exhibit 15.7, we provide a model of leadership effectiveness that incorporates the role of cultural differences. This model shows factors external to the organization interact with those internal in origin and determine the content of the leadership process. The outcome of this interaction is reflected in the level of convergence and divergence between external factors and internal factors that are present in the work context. This level of convergence and divergence affects the way leaders interact with followers and work groups and exhibit acts of leadership. Follower behaviors are important in the process, as shown in Exhibit 15.7. Leader–follower interaction determines the first-level outcomes of group performance, satisfaction of the followers, feelings of well-being, and so on. These first-level outcomes lead to second-level outcomes such as organizational effectiveness, high morale, and creativity and innovation. The feedback arrow shows that second-level outcomes potentially change the nature of content factors specific to what the leaders and followers bring to the work. International and global managers can use this model to examine the role of both company culture and societal culture in determining the type of leadership that is likely to be valued.

We emphasize that outcomes of leadership are embedded in a complex web of societal, cultural, and organizational factors. The type of leaders that emerge and their effectiveness are determined by the interaction of these factors.

Non-Western Styles of Leadership

Leadership in Japan

Descriptions of Japanese management have existed for a long time; however, a careful evaluation of leader behavior in this culture, which is highly group oriented, is rare.[49] Misumi's performance-maintenance (PM) theory identifies leaders based on two basic dimensions, performance and maintenance. The *performance dimension* comprises behaviors that lead a group toward goal accomplishment, including those that put pressure on followers and emphasize planning. Misumi defines pressure as supervisory behavior that puts strong emphasis on regulations and production, whereas planning concerns the scheduling and processing of work. The *maintenance dimension* is concerned with keeping harmony in the group and preserving the importance of the group in the organization. The effectiveness of PM leadership has been found in the Japanese context,[50] but its applicability in other countries depends on the specific leader behaviors that followers perceive to be effective in their unique cultural context. Recent research indicates that the performance- or task-oriented dimension is affected more strongly by cultural values of the subordinates than is the maintenance dimensions.[51] Managers should be aware of this framework in understanding the nature of the leadership process in Japan.

Leadership in India

India is an emerging economic giant. The findings from the GLOBE research program confirm the complexity and diversity of Indian society and culture, resulting in the need for special types of leadership. Indian culture has functioned by referring to the past, but it is currently undergoing a rapid transition to a modern society. Values of individualism tend to characterize a large portion of Indians in urban areas. Although management in India was based on autocratic processes, formal authority, and charisma, a move toward emphasizing democratic processes in the workplace is under way. Family values tend to influence a significant number of leaders in their decisions and **nurturant leadership** (taking a personal interest in the well-being of each subordinate) is still expected from managers, but changes, particularly in high-technology firms, are apparent.

Companies such as Gillette, Rank-Xerox, Texas Instruments, and Microsoft are encountering these issues and are developing programs that integrate Indian values into the work context. Failure to include an Indian partner who understood the styles of Indian management and leadership led to problems between former energy giant Enron and the Indian government, and Enron decided not to build plants in India in 2001.[52]

Leadership in the Arab World

Leadership behavior in Arab countries is strongly influenced by the belief systems of the Islamic religion and past traditions, as well as by some Western values.[53] Along with these influences, the rigidity of a bureaucratic mentality introduced by the Ottoman Empire (from the thirteenth century until the end of World War I) and Europeans complicate matters even further. The patriarchal approach found in these cultures is called **sheikocracy**.[54] This style reflects an emphasis on hierarchical authority, personal connections, human relations, and conformity to rules and regulations based on the personality and power of those who made the rules. Efficiency and effectiveness are not as important. The combination of this leadership style with influences from Western management practices has produced a duality in managers in the Arab world, who aspire to become more sophisticated and modern in their leadership styles yet remain tied to traditional values. The Arab world is an important and growing part of the global marketplace, and international and global managers should be aware of this duality.

Leading in an Increasingly Interconnected World

The meaning of leadership will change in a world where companies are flexible and fluid, and the pace of change is rapid. Leading in e-business and virtual organizations (discussed in Chapter 11) is different from leading in traditional organizations. The differences between leadership in traditional organizations and e-businesses are the speed at which decisions must be made, the importance of flexibility, and the need to create an ongoing vision of the future. While data may be available to make rapid decisions, the knowledge that results from the data may be hard to obtain. Maintaining flexibility is easier said than done. Leaders must move with the flow of businesses and should be able to redirect their group or organization when they find that something that worked in the past does not work any longer.

Continuous focus on the vision is difficult. In a cyber world, people expect more from their leaders. The rules, policies, and regulations that are used in traditional companies reduce uncertainty for both leaders and followers, but this is not the case in a cyber world. Since formal guidelines have short life spans in digital organizations, it becomes the leader's responsibility to provide continuous direction as to where the company is headed. Getting employees to accept the vision may require more radical actions—actions that might not have been necessary in the past. Regardless of whether the digital company exists in an individualist or collectivistic culture, there is a convergence of what leaders of e-businesses are expected to be. Thus cultural and national differences may not matter as much as differences rooted in the company culture.

Implications for the Practice of Global Leadership

Leadership entails continuous interaction with others, and we have discussed the role of various societal and cultural influences on this critical management function. Of the Fortune 500 firms surveyed in a recent study, 85 percent think they do not have an adequate number of effective global leaders, and 65 percent believe that their existing leaders need to acquire additional skills and knowledge before they can meet or exceed needed capabilities in the global marketplace.[55]

PRACTICAL INSIGHT 15.1

BUILT ON TRUST: STRENGTHENING LEADERSHIP CULTURE

The purposes are for members of a leadership team to establish a firm business trust base with each other and to begin to establish that working base throughout the organization.

The process begins with extensive up front assessment, always including one-on-one interviews with leadership and members of representative sections of the organization further down, and sometimes including written surveys.

Key Objectives

1. To establish increased coordination, closure and accountability within the leadership team.
2. To establish trust.
3. To establish understanding of the performance objectives throughout the organization.
4. To establish the basis for increased performance and accountability organizationwide.
5. To establish buy-in plans for implementation further down the organization.
6. To deliver specific, actionable plans for the management team's most critical current objectives.
7. To follow and adjust those plans to successful completion.

Source: From "Built on Trust, Strengthening Leadership Culture," http://www.learningcenter.net/training/trust.shtml. Reprinted with permission.

Characteristics of **global leadership** are an inquiring mind, integrity, the ability to manage uncertainty and tensions, and emotional connections with people throughout the company's worldwide operation. Leaders should also possess an acute sense of their business to recognize worldwide market opportunities quickly and organizational savvy to manage the unique capabilities of their companies to capture new market opportunities.[56]

A global leader should have the skills and abilities to interact and manage people from diverse cultural backgrounds who work in the multinational or global corporation in different parts of the world. Some of these traits are:[57]

- A combination of the skills of a strategist with those of a builder of organizational architectures and coordinating the architecture seamlessly.[58]
- A strong cosmopolitan orientation encompassing the ability to operate flexibly and with a sensitive eye toward distinctive demands of different cultures where the corporation operates.
- Intercultural communication skills and cultural sensitivity. The role of effective communication cannot be overemphasized. It is critical for a leader to develop appropriate skills to communicate face-to-face as well as through such things as videoconferencing, e-mails, and other computer-mediated methods.
- The ability to acculturate rapidly without being judgmental and to be highly selective in perceiving culturally dissimilar cues and processes.
- Eagerness to continue learning about economic, institutional, political, and cultural influences relating to how organizations function and about the significance of the meaning of working in different parts of the world.

Building on trust is important for strengthening leadership culture, as shown in Practical Insight 15.1, as is being able to understand cultural differences and their effect on business, as shown in Practical Insight 15.2.

PRACTICAL INSIGHT 15.2

A GUIDE FOR THE GLOBALLY CLUELESS

McDonald's took 13 months to realize that Hindus in India don't eat beef. When the company finally caught on and started making hamburgers out of lamb, sales sizzled. The unappetizing Chinese translation of Kentucky Fried Chicken's "Finger-lickin' good" slogan used to be "Eat your fingers off," until someone at the company got a clue. "Fresca" means "lesbian" in Mexican slang—odd name for a soda pop.

Blunders like these are hilarious only if you aren't the one summoned upstairs to explain why sales in your part of the world have fallen off a cliff. Partly to forestall recurrences, Robert Rosen (and his three co-authors, Patricia Digh, Marshall Singer, and Carl Phillips) wrote *Global Literacies: Lessons on Business Leadership and National Cultures* (Simon & Schuster). But Rosen, the head of consulting firm Healthy Companies International and, intriguingly, a psychiatrist on the faculty of George Washington University School of Medicine—wants to do more than just spare hapless marketing people from embarrassment. His ambitious goal here: to set forth a new style of management, aimed at preparing U.S. business for an avalanche of global competition. He bases his musings on an exhaustive survey of more than 1,000 executives around the world, including detailed interviews with 75 CEOs who have mastered the art of thinking globally. A few of them are American. Most are not.

Why is that? Simple. American CEOs don't fret much about overseas markets, even the ones they're already in. The survey shows that just 28% of U.S. executives think multicultural knowledge is important. (Only Canadian and Australian CEOs care less.) How to fix that? Not so simple. Rosen takes 376 pages to propose some steps toward true citizenship in the global village. What makes them surprisingly readable are short, vivid portraits of the 75 CEOs. When Shelly Lazarus, head of Ogilvy & Mather Worldwide, tells her employees to get a life outside the office, she means it. That's because she sees outside interests and commitments as a sine qua non of O&M's chief asset: creativity. Lazarus once skipped a board meeting in Paris to go on a ski trip with her family. "People were horrified . . . [but] you must keep your perspective," she says. "It's only business."

Summary

The process of leading others is one of the most complex yet least understood areas of management. Managers must consider non-Western views of leadership as globalization spreads economic activities through the world. The perception of what a good leader is, in terms of both traits and behaviors, varies a great deal from society to society, and the act of leadership itself is a product of culture. Although no generally accepted definition of leadership exists, it can be defined as the process of influencing others to achieve goals.

Although trait leadership theories were popular in the United States in the early 1900s, no traits both necessary and sufficient for exhibiting leadership have been found. Behavioral theories of leadership have been found useful, but responses to task-oriented leadership vary across cultures. Contingency theory is applicable to cross-cultural leadership situations because a vast number of variables can affect the emergence and exercise of leadership. The notion of charismatic leadership is also supported across cultures, but influence processes differ across cultures.

Like other aspects of culture, leadership and leadership behaviors are taken for granted by society members, and they may not be transferable across cultures. For example, leadership in an individualistic culture may differ markedly from one in a collectivistic culture. Outcomes of leadership are embedded in a complex web of societal, cultural, and organizational factors which determine the emergence and effectiveness of leadership.

Key Terms and Concepts

behavioral perspective, *451*
charisma, *453*
consideration, *451*
contingency perspective, *452*
global leadership, *464*

implicit perspective, *452*
initiation of structure, *451*
leadership, *449*
nurturant leadership, *462*

sheikocracy, *463*
trait-based perspective, *450*
transformational leadership, *453*

Discussion Questions

1. Discuss the concept of leadership and its importance in achieving organizational goals.
2. What are the various approaches for understanding the process of leadership that were developed by U.S. researchers?
3. What are the factors that affect the quality of leadership as found in the GLOBE project? Define the concept of autocratic versus democratic styles of leadership.
4. How can we use cultural dimensions of Hofstede to gain insights into leader–follower relationships around the world? Give specific examples and explain.
5. Discuss how you would develop a profile of an effective leader from the research findings of the GLOBE project. Give an example.
6. How will the exercise of leadership in a digital organization differ from that in traditional organizations?

Minicase

All Eyes On the Corner Office

After more than a decade at the head of Siemens, the icon of German industry, Chief Executive Heinrich von Pierer is something of an icon himself.

In 2003, his name was floated briefly as a candidate for the German presidency. After years of investor criticism that he moved too slowly to transform the $93 billion electronics conglomerate into a global competitor, von Pierer is getting the last laugh. While competitors such as Netherlands-based Philips Group suffered losses during the recent economic downturn, Siemens remained profitable. The share price has doubled over the past year, to almost $87 on the New York Stock Exchange. "He has done good work," allows shareholder advocate Daniela Bergdolt, a Munich lawyer who once told von Pierer at a stockholders' meeting that he should leave the company.

Now Bergdolt is worried about what will happen when von Pierer does just that. The 63-year-old executive's contract expires in September. He is widely expected to accept a two-year extension, but the question of who will succeed one of Germany's most important executives is fast becoming a hot topic in Germany—and elsewhere in Europe, where a new generation of CEOs is fast taking over. The race to succeed von Pierer, in fact, has already started in earnest. Von Pierer and Siemens supervisory board members are now closely watching a handful of candidates. Front-runners include former U.S. division chief Klaus Kleinfeld and Thomas Ganswindt, who runs the fixed-line telecom equipment business.

The oddsmakers currently favor 46-year-old Kleinfeld. Last November, he was promoted to the seven-member central committee of the management board in recognition for his work as CEO of Siemens' $20 billion U.S. operations from January, 2002, until December, a post seen as good training for the top slot. Like Siemens worldwide, the U.S. operations are a collection of fiefdoms that often need to be strong-armed into cooperating. But there are other credible candidates, including 47-year-old Johannes Feldmayer, another central committee member.

Whoever prevails, a new generation of managers is already moving into Siemens' top echelons. In just a year, the average age of top management has fallen from 58 to 53, J.P. Morgan Chase & Co. calculates. While rising fortysomethings won't foment revolution at consensus-driven Siemens, they are likely to speed the company's shift away from its conservative German roots. The new managers will focus more intensely on profit, move faster to unload underperforming units, and shift more production to cheaper locations abroad. "Obviously, von Pierer will be a tough act to follow," says Henning Gebhardt, head of German equities at DWS, the fund management arm of Deutsche Bank. "But after

10 years, sometimes a change at the top is good." Von Pierer wrought mighty changes, even if his slow-but-steady pace didn't always satisfy investors. When he took over in 1992, Siemens relied heavily on government contracts, rarely disciplined managers who delivered poor results, and employed 61% of its workforce in high-wage Germany. Transparency? The company published no profit figures for its divisions, and often even employees didn't know if their units were making money.

POLITICIAN'S TOUCH. Now Siemens gives detailed company and divisional results quarterly and has sacked numerous underperforming managers. Net return on sales has risen from 2.4% in 1993, the year after von Pierer took charge, to 4% in the latest quarter. Von Pierer responded to criticism that Siemens, which makes everything from locomotives to X-ray machines, had too many moving parts. He spun off dozens of units, including chipmaker Infineon Technologies and the electronic-components unit known as Epcos. Now, 60% of employees work outside Germany and the domestic workforce has been cut by a third, to 167,000. Von Pierer, an engineer with a politician's touch, managed that without provoking extensive labor unrest—no small feat in a land where layoffs are deemed unpatriotic.

The new generation of managers, though, is likely to be more willing to bust heads. Consider the way Ganswindt turned around the company's $8.9 billion Information & Communication Networks division. He cut the workforce by nearly 40%, or 20,000 workers, to reduce costs by $4.4 billion. He shifted production to Brazil and China. From a loss of nearly $865 million in the fiscal year that ended Sept. 30, 2002, ICN returned to a profit of $64 million in the last quarter.

Despite the improvements, Siemens still gets heat for mediocre margins. Ganswindt and the other young managers are sensitive to the criticism. "You can't innovate if you don't have money to invest," he says.

Rising managers will also continue pushing the engineer-dominated company to focus more on customers' needs. They will maintain Siemens' steady drive to globalize—not only by investing in Asia and the Americas but also by importing non-German ways of doing business back to Munich.

There is no question, however, of Siemens transforming itself into something other than a German company. "A new CEO will mean change, but I don't expect a radical departure from the existing philosophy and strategy," says analyst Roland Pitz of HVB Group in Munich. The fear is that some company directors will try to keep things too German. The supervisory board could name a lower-profile candidate such as Kurt-Ludwig Gutberlet, head of BSH Bosch & Siemens Household Appliances, a profitable joint venture with Stuttgart-based Robert Bosch. "It could be someone who is not the strongest but has the strongest consensus among the gray heads," says a source who works closely with Siemens. Still, it's clear that at Siemens, gray heads are becoming ever more scarce.

Source: Jack Ewing, *BusinessWeek Online,* March 1, 2004, http://www.businessweek.com/magazine/content/04_09/b3872073_mz054.htm.

DISCUSSION QUESTIONS

1. What leadership skills have contributed to the success of the incumbent CEO, Heinrich von Pierer? Describe his leadership style.
2. Siemens faces challenges in the global marketplace. The company will likely require a different leadership style than von Pierer's to face these challenges. What style would you recommend to Siemens?
3. Why would the age of the leader be an important consideration in a global company? Would it be important in your consideration of the candidates for CEO of Siemens? Why?

Notes

1. P. W. Dorfman, "International and Cross-Cultural Leadership." In J. Punnett and O. Shenkar, eds., *Handbook for International Management Research* (Cambridge, MA: Blackwell, 1996), pp. 276–349.
2. D. Miller, M. F. R. Ket de Vries, and J. M. Toulouse, "Top Executive Locus of Control and Its Relationship to Strategy-Making, Structure, and Environment," *Academy of Management Journal* 25 (1982), pp. 237–253.
3. G. Yukl, *Leadership in Organizations,* 3rd ed. (Upper Saddle River, NJ: Prentice Hall, 1994).

4. R. J. House, N. S. Wright, and R. N. Aditya, "Cross-Cultural Research on Organizational Leadership: A Critical Analysis and a Proposed Theory." In P. C. Earley and M. Erez, eds., *New Perspectives on International Industrial/Organizational Psychology* (San Francisco: New Lexington Press, 1997), pp. 535–625.

5. D. Katz and R. Kahn, *The Social Psychology of Organizations,* 2nd ed. (New York: John Wiley & Sons, 1978).

6. M. Groves, "Cream Rises to the Top, but from a Small Crop," *Los Angeles Times,* June 8, 1998.

7. S. Lohr, "He Loves to Win. At I.B.M., He Did," *New York Times,* March 10, 2002, Section 3, p. 1.

8. Dorfman, "International and Cross-Cultural Leadership."

9. R. J. House and R. N. Aditya, "The Social Scientific Study of Leadership: *Quo vadis?" Journal of Management* 23 (1997), pp. 409–473.

10. D. Goleman, "What Makes a Leader?" *Harvard Business Review* 76 (November–December 1998), pp. 92–102.

11. Yukl, *Leadership in Organizations.*

12. L. M. Ah Chong and D. C. Thomas, "Leadership Perceptions in Cross-Cultural Context: Pacific Islanders and Pakeha in New Zealand," *Leadership Quarterly* 8, no. 3 (1997), pp. 275–293.

13. F. E. Fiedler, *A Theory of Leadership Effectiveness* (New York: McGraw-Hill, 1967).

14. M. Bennett, 1977. "Testing Management Theories Cross-Culturally," *Journal of Applied Psychology* 62, no. 5 (1977), pp. 578–581; J. Misumi, *The Behavioral Science of Leadership: An Interdisciplinary Japanese Research Program* (Ann Arbor: University of Michigan Press, 1985); J. Misumi, and M. F. Peterson, "Supervision and Leadership." In B. M. Bass, P. J. D. Drenth, and P. Weissenberg, eds., *Advances in Organizational Psychology: An International Review* (Newbury Park, CA: Sage, 1987), pp. 220–231.

15. J. House, "A Path-Goal Theory of Leader Effectiveness," *Administrative Science Quarterly* 16 (1971), pp. 556–571; R. J. House, and T. R. Mitchell, "Path–goal Theory of Leadership," *Contemporary Business* 3 (1974), pp. 81–98.

16. Dorfman, "International and Cross-Cultural Leadership."

17. R. G. Lord and K. J. Maher, *Leadership and Information Processing: Linking Perceptions and Performance* (Boston: Unwin-Everyman, 1991); R. G. Lord, R. J. Foti, and C. L. DeVader, "A Test of Leadership Categorization Theory: Internal Structure, Information Processing, and Leadership Perceptions," *Organizational Behavior and Human Performance* 34 (1984), pp. 343–378.

18. D. C. Thomas and E. C. Ravlin, "Responses of Employees to Cultural Adaptation by a Foreign Manager, *Journal of Applied Psychology* 80 (1995), pp. 133–146.

19. B. M. Bass, *Leadership and Performance beyond Expectation* (New York: Free Press, 1985); T. Burns, *Leadership* (New York: Harper & Row, 1978); J. A. Conger and R. Kanungo, "Toward a Behavioral Theory of Charismatic Leadership in Organizational Settings," *Academy of Management Review* 12 (1987), pp. 637–647; R. J. House, "A 1976 Theory of Charismatic Leadership." In J. G. Hunt and L. L. Larson, eds., *Leadership: The Cutting Edge* (Carbondale: Southern Illinois University Press, 1977), pp. 189–207.

20. Dorfman, "International and Cross-Cultural Leadership."

21. Bass, *Leadership and Performance beyond Expectations;* G. Howell, "Culture Tails: A Narrative Approach to Thinking, Cross-Cultural Psychology, and Psychotherapy," *American Psychologist* 46 (1994), pp. 187–197.

22. J. P. Howell and P. W. Dorfman, "A Comparative Study of Leadership and Its Substitutes in Mixed Cultural Work Settings." Paper presented at the Western Academy of Management Meeting, Big Sky, Montana, April 1988.

23. A. J. Ali, A. A. Axim, and K. S. Krishnan, "Expatriates and Host Country Nationals: Managerial Values and Decision Styles," *Leadership & Organization Development Journal* 16, no. 6 (1995), pp. 27–34.

24. O. Dahhan, "Jordanian Top Managers: Characteristics, Activities, and Decision-Making Style," *Abhath Al-Yarmouk, Humanities and Social Sciences* 4, no. 1 (1988), pp. 37–55; M. K. Badawy, "Styles of Mid-Eastern Managers," *California Management Review* 22, no. 2 (1980), pp. 51–58.

25. R. Kaur, "Managerial Styles in the Public Sector, *Indian Journal of Industrial Relations* 28, no. 4 (1993), pp. 363–369.

26. E. H. Schein, *Organizational Culture and Leadership,* 2nd ed. (San Francisco: Jossey-Bass, 1992).

27. L. Copeland and L. Griggs, *Going International* (New York: Random House, 1985).

28. F. E. Fiedler, "Engineering the Job to Fit the Manager," *Harvard Business Review* 43, no. 5 (1965), pp. 115–122.

29. R. M. Kramer, "The Harder They Fall," *Harvard Business Review,* October 2003, pp. 58–66; P. Dwyer, "Nowhere to Run, Nowhere to Hide," *BusinessWeek,* October 14, 2002, pp. 44–45.

30. S. Kerr and J. M. Jermier, "Substitutes for Leadership: Their Meaning and Measurement," *Organizational Behavior and Human Performance* 22 (1978), pp. 375–403; C. C. Manz, *The Art of Self-Leadership* (Englewood Cliffs, NJ: Prentice Hall, 1983).

31. S. Kerr, "On the Folly of Rewarding A, while Hoping for B." In L. L. Thompson, ed., *The Social Psychology of Organizational Behavior* (New York: Psychology Press, 2003).

32. Kerr and Jermier, "Substitutes for Leadership."

33. P. B. Smith and M. H. Bond, *Social Psychology across Cultures* (Boston: Allyn & Bacon, 1999).

34. Ibid.

35. R. Hackman, *Why Groups Fail* (San Francisco: Jossey-Bass, 1986); A. J. Marrow, "Risks and Uncertainties in Action Research," *Journal of Social Issues* 20, no. 3 (1964), pp. 5–20; R. S. Juralewicz, "An Experiment in Participation in a Latin American Factor," *Human Relations* 27 (1974), pp. 627–637.

36. P. B. Smith and J. Misumi, "Japanese Management: A Sun Rising in the West?" In C. L. Cooper and I. T. Robertson, eds., *International Review of Industrial and Organizational Psychology,* Vol. 4 (Chichester, UK: Wiley, 1989).

37. H. Markus and S. Kitayama, "Culture and the Self: Implications for Cognition, Emotion, and Motivation," *Psychological Review* 98 (1991), pp. 224–253; H. Markus and S. Kitayama, "A Collective Fear of the Collective: Implications for Selves and Theories of Selves," *Personality and Social Psychology Bulletin* 20 (1994), pp. 568–579.

38. J. Hooker, *Working across Cultures* (Palo Alto: Stanford University Press, 2003).

39. Ibid.

40. R. J. House, P. J. Hanges, S. A. Ruiz-Quintanilla, P. W. Dorfman, M. Javidan, M. Dickson, V. Gupta, and GLOBE Country Co-Investigators, "Cultural Influences on Leadership and Organizations: Project GLOBE." In W. H. Mobley, M. J. Gessner, and V. Arnold, eds., *Advances in Global Leadership,* Vol. 1 (Stamford, CT: JAI Press, 1999), pp. 171–234.

41. M. Hoppe and R. S. Bhagat, "Leadership in the United States of America: The Leader as Cultural Hero." In R. House, ed., *Anthology of Leadership around the World* (Thousand Oaks, CA: Sage, 2004).

42. G. Hofstede, *Culture's Consequences: International Differences in Work-Related Values,* 2nd ed. (Thousand Oaks, CA: Sage, 2001).

43. G. Hofstede, *Cultures and Organizations: Software of the Mind* (New York: McGraw-Hill, 1991).

44. A. Laurent, "The Cultural Diversity of Western Conceptions of Management," *International Studies of Management and Organization* 13, no. 1–2 (1983), pp. 75–96.

45. C. Hampden-Turner and A. Trompenaars, *The Seven Cultures of Capitalism* (New York: Doubleday, 1993).

46. M. Haire, E. E. Ghiselli, and L. W. Porter, *Managerial Thinking: An International Study* (New York: John Wiley & Sons, 1966).

47. I. Kenis, "A Cross-Cultural Study of Personality and Leadership," *Group and Organization Studies* 2 (1977), pp. 49–60; F. C. Deyo "The Cultural Patterning of Organizational Development: A Comparative Case Study of Thailand and Chinese Industrial Enterprises," *Human Organization* 37 (1978), pp. 68–72.

48. M. K. Badawy, "Styles of Mid-Eastern Managers," *California Management Review,* Spring 1980.

49. Misumi, *The Behavioral Science of Leadership.*

50. Ibid.; M. F. Peterson, "PM Theory in Japan and China: What's in It for the United States?" *Organizational Dynamics* 16 (1988), pp. 22–38; Dorfman, "International and Cross-Cultural Leadership."

51. Ah Chong and Thomas, "Leadership Perceptions in Cross-Cultural Context"; M. F. Peterson, P. B. Smith, and M. H. J. Tayeb, "Development and Use of English Version of Japanese PM Leadership Measures in Electronics Plants," *Journal of Organizational Behavior* 14 (1993), pp. 251–267.

52. "Enron switches signals in India," *Business Week,* January 8, 2001; "Enron Calls on Guarantees by India to Collect Debts," *Wall Street Journal,* February 9, 2001.

53. A. J. Ali, "Management Theory in a Transitional Society: The Arab's Experience," *International Studies of Management and Organization* 20 (1990), pp. 7–35.

54. A. Al-Kubaisy, "A Model in the Administrative Development of Arab Gulf Countries," *Arab Gulf* 17, no. 2 (1985), pp. 29–48.

55. S. P. Robbins and M. Coulter, *Management,* 7th ed. (Upper Saddle River, NJ: Prentice Hall, 2001).

56. H. B. Gregersen, A. J. Morrison, and J. S. Black, "Developing Leaders for the Global Frontier," *Sloan Management Review,* Fall 1998, pp. 21–32.

57. R. Rosen, P. Digh, M. Singer, and C. Phillips, *Global Literacies: Lessons on Business Leadership and National Cultures* (New York: Simon & Schuster, 2000); A. Morrison, "Global Leadership." In P. W. Beamish, A. J. Morrison, A. C. Inkpen, and P. M. Rosenzweig, *International Management: Text and Cases* (New York: McGraw-Hill/Irwin, 2003).

58. C. A. Bartlett and S. Ghoshal, "What Is a Global Manager?" *Harvard Business Review,* September–October 1992, pp. 124–132.

CHAPTER SIXTEEN

International Human Resources Management

Chapter Learning Objectives

After completing this chapter, you should be able to:

- Understand the various approaches that multinational and global organizations undertake for managing and staffing subsidiaries in various parts of the world.
- Distinguish between various functions of international human resources management.
- Identify the various strategies for selecting staff for foreign assignments.
- Explain how training programs prepare managers for overseas assignments.
- Understand the various schemes for compensation and benefits used by multinational and global organizations.
- Identify the issues inherent in repatriation and discuss the reasons that multinational and global companies need to address issues concerning managers returning from overseas assignments.
- Understand that labor relations practices differ in each country and outline how these differences affect multinational and global companies.

Opening Case: How to Avoid Culture Shock

The biggest hurdles to overcome when doing business internationally often have less to do with technology than with culture. "When we first went to Europe, we were shocked by the number of things that were different from the way we thought they were going to be," says Larry Schwartz, president of Hill Arts & Entertainment Systems Inc., a software VAR in Guilford, Conn. "The way they do business is just very different."

And each country has its own idiosyncrasies. For example, Schwartz had a difficult time cracking the German market because his company had first established a presence in England. "They saw us as English," he says, "which is even worse than being American."

When Schwartz finally did win German customers, he learned that the colors Americans find pleasing on a graphical user interface seemed ugly to the Germans.

"The Germans said, 'What are these?' They wanted garish colors, the brighter and bolder the better," he says. Schwartz realized why it's difficult for Americans to program for European customers. The English have one color preference, the Germans have another and the Italians look at color another way. "If you don't know the customs," Schwartz says, "you're just sunk."

Schwartz also made a gaffe during his first day of meetings in Munich by calling people by their first names, American style. "I was with one of my European people and I asked her why the Germans kept referring to each other by their last names, Herr This and Herr That, and she said that's what is expected in Germany." He adds that as an American, if you go in using first names at a meeting, from day one you've started alienating people.

Schwartz says the best thing to do is realize that business etiquette changes from country to country, and find local guides who can help you.

Don't Be an Ugly American

Don Howren, director of strategic alliances at Platinum Software Corp., Irvine, Calif., says his company has stepped on plenty of land mines while trying to expand into foreign markets. "We've done all the ugly American things you can come up with," he says. "But having good partnerships can help you dodge any issues that could hold you back."

Platinum tries to form partnerships with VARs and consultants in each new market. "There are a lot of things outside of the technical sphere that you have to deal with," Howren says. "Those are the greatest challenges for companies moving into those markets." For example, in the burgeoning Latin American market, Platinum is dealing constantly with a whole set of issues that are unique to those markets, such as hyperinflation and political situations.

American companies should also be aware that in some countries there is a cultural bias working against them before they even show up.

"I have found that the most difficult markets to break into are Germany and Japan," says Jennifer Meighan, an international business development consultant in San Francisco. "Both cultures are very tightly knit, very uniform and wary of American companies."

Business, American-Style

Some aspects of American business culture do have appeal in Europe, says Denise Sangster, president of Global Touch Inc., a channels consulting company in Berkeley, Calif.

"Europeans like nothing better than American-style service," Sangster says. "With some software companies in France, if you call during lunchtime with a question or a problem, they'll tell you to call back after lunch. So if you can provide them immediate support and service, they love you."

Also, European customers aren't accustomed to the "solution selling" approach that American software VARs espouse, but they appreciate it, Sangster says.

"If you can bring over that style of business, that approach of 'Let me help you solve your business problem,' which is not the normal way of doing things there, you'll have a tremendous opportunity," Sangster says. "You can win some very loyal and dedicated customers."

It can be tricky, though, to convince your European business partners, including VARs and distributors, to adopt your "solution sell" approach. "A lot of it has to do with your presentation," Sangster says. "There's a fine line between saying, 'Hey, look, we do things better, we're the best,' and saying, 'Let us show you a different way of looking at the same situation.'"

This kind of finesse is even more crucial in Asia, according to Bob Hoover, general manager of Asia/Pacific for Speedware Corp. in Toronto.

For example, forget about cold calling or making deals on the phone. Business is done in person, and introductions from mutual acquaintances or business contacts are often necessary, Hoover says. And it's important to build strong relationships before a deal is done, which means that compared to the West, business in Asia can seem to take forever.

"It took me 18 to 24 months to build ties there, work that would have taken about three months in the States," Hoover says.

The biggest mistake that U.S. companies make is to see Asia as a single entity. "Each country has a unique business culture," Hoover says. For example, in Japan and Korea, decisions are made by groups, so sales cycles are long—as much as three times longer than in the States. And Korean and Japanese companies tend to think strategically, with a long-term view.

In Taiwan, however, the business culture is built around small, family-owned companies. "Decisions are made very quickly. They tend to think tactically rather than strategically," Hoover says. "With Taiwanese customers you're always talking about new things, trying to keep them excited."

Hoover has a list of dos and don'ts that he gives to his sales reps when they move to Asia. Perhaps the biggest "don't" has to do with emotion. "You must never show emotion or lose your temper," Hoover says. "It's a sign of weakness. Customers will become very concerned about doing business with your company."

Americans should also avoid behaving in a way that is seen as stereotypically American: loud, fast-talking, slapping people on the back.

Rather than trying to crack into Asian markets on your own, Hoover suggests hiring a well-connected consultant who can help you make connections. "This really can help you shorten the start-up period."

Source: "How to Avoid Culture Shock," by Daniel Lyons, *VarBusiness*, June 15, 1995, Vol 11, No. 10. Copyright © 1995 by CMP Media LLC, 600 Community Drive, Manhasset, NY 11030, USA. Reprinted from *VarBusiness* with permission.

Discussion Questions

1. Discuss gaffes made when dealing with different cultures and their effects on management of companies.
2. What do you think are some effects from the failure to understand cultural differences on managing human resources?
3. What other insights can be gained from this case?

What Is International Human Resources Management?

International human resources management (IHRM) comprises the development of human resource capabilities to meet the diverse needs of various subsidiaries of multinational and global corporations. Management of human resources in multinational and global organizations differs greatly from management in domestic companies. Each multinational and global organization has a different approach for managing employees. In most cases, how firms find employees, pay, train, develop, and promote them varies in each subsidiary. These issues are complex, because they have to continuously link corporate strategy to human resources management. National and cultural differences play important roles in the selection, compensation, training, development, placement, and promotion of employees.[1]

In this chapter, we discuss the three major functions of international human resources management:

1. Managing human resources in global corporations, including issues of expatriation and repatriation.
2. Implementing corporate global strategy by adapting appropriate human resources management practices in different national, economic, and cultural environments.
3. Adopting labor relation practices in each subsidiary that matches local requirements.

International human resources management is increasingly being recognized as a major determinant of success in the global environment. In the highly competitive global economy, where factors of production—capital, technology, raw material, and information—can be easily duplicated, the quality of human resources in the organization will be the sole source of competitive advantage.[2] Multinational and global corporations need to pay careful attention to this most critical resource, which, in its turn, can provide appropriate access to other resources needed for effective implementation of global strategy.

More than 37,000 multinational corporations are engaged in business worldwide, and they control over 200,000 foreign affiliates and have over 73 million employees. Foreign multinationals operating in the United States employ over 3 million Americans, more than 10 percent of the U.S. manufacturing work force. About 80 percent of middle to large U.S. multinationals have managers working in subsidiaries in other countries, and their numbers are increasing.[3] According to a recent estimate by the National Foreign Trade Council, more than 300,000 U.S. expatriates work in different countries.

Managing and Staffing Subsidiaries

Multinational and global organizations take different approaches to managing and staffing subsidiaries. These approaches are linked with the overall strategy, and they reflect its human resources policies and practices. The four major approaches are as follows:[4]

1. **Ethnocentric staffing approach:** The company uses the approach developed in the home country, and the values, attitudes, practices, and priorities of headquarters determine the human resources policies and practices. Managers from the home country are preferred for leadership and other major positions in the subsidiary. Foreign staffing decisions are made in the headquarters.

2. **Polycentric staffing approach:** The company considers the needs of the local subsidiary when formulating human resources policies and practices. Individuals from host countries are selected for managerial positions; however, promotion of a manager from foreign subsidiaries to headquarters is rare. Human resources decisions, policies, and practices are developed at the local level.

3. **Regiocentric staffing approach:** The company considers the needs of an entire region when developing human resources policies and practices. Managers from the host country are often selected for managerial positions in their own countries, and some may be promoted to regional positions. Subsidiaries in a given region, such as Latin America, may develop a common set of human resource management policies that are uniquely applicable in the particular regional context.

4. **Geocentric or global staffing approach:** The company's priority is the optimal use of all resources, including human resources, and local or regional concerns are not considered important for the success of the corporate strategy. Managers are selected and promoted on a global basis without regard to their country of origin or cultural background. HRM policies are developed at headquarters, and these policies are generally consistent across all subsidiaries.

Companies with ethnocentric or geocentric approaches generally have human resource policies and practices that are consistent globally. Those taking a polycentric or regiocentric approach vary their policies and practices depending on the local or regional culture and practices.

While international corporate strategy determines the choice of one of the four approaches, the following important factors must be considered in the ultimate selection of a IHRM approach:[5]

- *National concerns:* Subsidiaries have to function within the legal framework of the host country. For example, some countries require that an employee who is laid off must be given compensation at a certain percentage of his or her basic pay. Some countries restrict the number of employees the subsidiary may bring from outside the country. In these countries, the head and a few senior managers of the subsidiary may be from the headquarters or another country, but the majority of the managers and employees must be local. Laws governing occupational safety also vary a great deal from country to country and have to be incorporated in the formulation of international human resource management practices. In addition, political volatility inherent in some countries requires that global corporations provide appropriate measures for the physical well-being and safety of not only their expatriate managers but the local workforce as well.

- *Economic concerns:* The cost of living, such as housing, food, and other expenses, varies widely from country to country. This often poses significant economic concerns that must be addressed when the corporation formulates its international human resources management policies and practices.

- *Technological concerns:* The availability of skilled employees, especially for global service corporations such as Citicorp and McKinsey & Company, is a growing concern. As the use of highly sophisticated manufacturing technology and the need to produce high-quality products on a global scale increase, IHRM managers need to ensure that skilled employees are selected and developed in all of the subsidiaries. When the basic product must be modified to appeal to local or regional markets, a polycentric or regiocentric approach is most appropriate.

- *Organizational concerns:* The stage of the internationalization of the company and the product life cycle are important determinants of the IHRM approach. For example, when a company first ventures into international business, it often adopts an ethnocentric approach, but as subsidiaries are added and managed by locals, a polycentric approach makes more sense. Later, growth, increased productivity, and cost control may cause the firm to adopt a regiocentric or geocentric approach. As operations become strictly global in nature, a complete geocentric IHRM policy is the best approach.

- *Cultural concerns:* The differences between corporate and societal cultures of the headquarters and subsidiaries also influence the IHRM approach. If the corporate cultures are different, as is often the case for European multinationals, it becomes necessary to adopt a polycentric or regiocentric approach. If the societal cultures are different, a polycentric or regiocentric approach may be more appropriate. For example, the need for extended bereavement leave in many cultures, such as East Asian and Polynesian cultures, makes most U.S. or European HRM policies pertaining to such leave difficult to enforce. In some countries, the societal culture encourages the adoption of an ethnocentric HRM approach, as is the case with most Japanese multinationals.[6] For example, most Japanese multinationals hire only Japanese as senior managers, which is acceptable and expected in their culture. Furthermore, if the number and degree of cultural differences among the subsidiaries are of paramount significance, the adoption of a geocentric HRM policy will be difficult, regardless of its usefulness in implementing the overall corporate strategy.

The choice of an approach to IHRM is difficult at best. A multinational or global corporation whose overall corporate strategy is reflected in its HRM practices will be more competitive in launching new products and services. We should, however, note that of all corporate functions, IHRM tends to be more reflective of local norms, customs, traditions, values, and practices.[7] Whereas U.S. researchers emphasize the need for consistency between corporate-level strategy and adoption of IHRM policies of subsidiaries, European managers are less inclined to emphasize consistency in practice. European HRM managers are likely to closely follow guidelines from top management,

PRACTICAL INSIGHT 16.1

AN ABC APPROACH TO HANDLING A STRIKE

A strike triggered by religious holidays and summer breaks nearly brought ABC Consumer Electronics' flagship *maquiladora* plant at Juarez to its knees. But it ultimately forced revisions in labor laws which improved the workers' lot across the consumer electronics industry in Mexico.

The dispute over consolidating religious holidays into a "Holy Week" soon escalated into a strike at the end of January 1995, with workers and administrative staff leaving before being blockaded inside the works. A further grievance was the decision to keep the factory running throughout July rather than shutting down for its usual two-week break. But there were deeper underlying causes, and fanning the flames was *maquiladora* itself, as a case study by Dowlatshahi reveals.

A Strategy to Reduce Costs

Maquiladora is a business strategy whereby a company imports raw materials to Mexico, assembles the goods using low-cost labor and then exports the finished products: production and admin staff are usually Mexican, while senior managers are predominantly Anglo expatriates. The strategy is good for Mexico, earning the country much needed foreign exchange. It is also good for the companies: under Mexican legislation, before the strike the most highly-paid ABC worker could earn as much as NP$103.21—or US$14.96—for a 45-hour week, compared with a US average weekly wage of $472 plus benefits for 41 hours.

Dowlatshahi outlines how, in January 1995, a number of factors came together to create the right atmosphere for industrial action. The devaluation of the peso a month earlier was the key factor, slashing workers' purchasing power by half in a single day, and more in the border regions than other parts of the country. This was followed by a minimum wage increase of 10 percent—but gas prices rose 30 percent and food 20 percent: the more highly-paid admin workers then received a 12 percent pay rise after threatening to strike, further adding to the production workers' woes. In addition, workers felt like second-class citizens and that they were being mistreated by ABC, for example by poor canteen conditions, their union status and a lack of corporate support for workers' concerns. Two managers—both Mexican—were also the focus of workers' grievances. The last straw was the cancellation of the July shutdown, which upset all company staff. A previous shutdown dispute had been resolved when ABC paid employees off, and managers wanted to get round this—hence the changed work pattern.

Demands and Concessions—On All Sides

Once the strike bit, it bit hard with all the issues brought sharply into focus. Dowlatshahi recounts how workers demanded a host of concessions including a better canteen and food, reinstatement of the shutdown week, the removal of the two managers, more vacation time and a 30 percent wage increase. However, the union did not escape either, as workers wanted more say in the way strikes were called and an accounting of how union funds were used.

A locked-door summit was called, with representatives from the unions, the company (one of the controversial man-

---

which gives them less control and strategic autonomy in running the HRM operations of subsidiaries compared to their American counterparts. For example, causes of strikes can differ across borders and cultures, as shown in Practical Insight 16.1.

Major IHRM Functions

International human resources managers have the responsibility for the six functional human resource areas: recruitment and selection, classifying employees, performance evaluation, compensation and benefits, training and development, and labor relations. Management of expatriate workers is an additional function of IHRM. Exhibit 16.1 illustrates the way that aspects of strategy influence IHRM.

Recruitment and Selection

Recruitment and selection are key processes through which a multinational or global corporation brings new employees into its network. *Recruitment* is the process of attracting a pool of qualified applicants for available positions. *Selection* is the process

agers who headed HR) and the company's legal advisers. And while the strike only lasted a week, it was apparent that because of the lack of communication between company and workforce things could have been worse. A deal was brokered that involved concessions on all three sides—workers, company and unions. The company raised wages 13 percent, with 2 percent linked to bonuses, which gave the best paid worker NP$113.84 (US$16.03), plus food coupons worth NP$50.40 to be redeemed at grocery stores. In addition, a commission looked at the canteen issue and subsequently sub-contracted it out to a catering company. The July shutdown was reintroduced in a backstairs move designed to save corporate face; this isn't guaranteed by law, but the company has "acceded" to a request from the workers. There were also improvements in shift patterns, days off and promotion opportunities. However, the demand for the replacement of the managers was not acceded to: one has since left the company, but the more senior remains in post.

Strong Unions . . . Too Strong?

On the union front, the election of new union representatives was sanctioned—the newly elected reps then negotiated this deal for their members. In addition, there was to be accounting of union dues and how the monies were spent; but although the union agreed to this, at the time of writing nothing has been done; nor has the request for voting before the union makes any decisions on workers' behalf. This reflects the strong union role in Mexico.

There was a further corporate cost for ABC. The company lost money during the strike, and had to work overtime to catch up; Mexican law required the workers to be paid double time for the first nine hours of overtime, then triple time for the rest. Other companies saw the writing on the wall, and hiked wages 10–15 percent voluntarily to avoid being forced to do so later.

The workers' victory was hardly bloodless. Some 100 team leaders and workers were sacked after the strike, because they "disobeyed direct orders."

The Aftermath

The picture has improved for workers subsequently though, as laws passed in 1997 gave the most highly paid production workers a weekly income of NP$186.412 or US$23.45 a week, compared with $532 for a US worker.

In addition, ABC provides benefits for its workers in the form of mandatory and voluntary savings plans, soft loans, free transportation to and from work, life insurance and educational scholarships (though work patterns meant the last were not often taken up). However, the company imposed some restrictions on its workers: workers had to be aged 16–35, and there is a preference for females who are said to be more precise then men. However pregnant women are generally not allowed to work. Most of these benefits and work requirements did not exist or were banned in the USA, and were designed to retain workers with experience, and attract good replacements.

Source: From "An ABC Approach to Handling a Strike," *Human Resource Management International Digest,* Vol. 10, No. 1, 2002. Permission granted by Emerald Group Publishing Limited, www.emeraldinsight.com.

of choosing qualified applicants from the available candidates and ensuring that the skills, knowledge, and abilities of the selected employees match the requirements of the positions.

Classifying Employees

Employees of multinational and global organizations are typically classified in one of the following categories:

1. *Parent-country national (PCN):* The nationality of the employee is the same as that of the headquarters of the global organization. For example, a U.S. citizen working in Italy for a U.S. company, such as Microsoft, is an PCN.

2. *Host-country national (HCN):* The employee's nationality is the same as that of the subsidiary. For example, an Italian citizen working in Rome for a U.S. company, such as Microsoft, is an HCN.

3. *Third-country national (TCN):* The employee's national is neither that of the headquarters nor that of the local subsidiary. For example, an Italian citizen working in Brazil for a U.S. company, such as Microsoft, is a TCN.

EXHIBIT 16.1   **Strategic Approach, Organizational Concerns, and IHRM Approach**

Source: From *Multinational Organization Development* by D. A. Heenan and H. V. Perlmutter. Copyright © 1979. Used with permission of Pearson Education, Inc., Upper Saddle River, NJ 07458.

Aspects of the Enterprise	Orientation			
	Ethnocentric	**Polycentric**	**Regiocentric**	**Global**
Primary strategic orientation/stage	International	Multidomestic	Regional	Transnational
Perpetuation (recruiting, staffing, development)	People of home country developed for key positions everywhere in the world	People of local nationality developed for key positions in their own country	Regional people developed for key positions anywhere in the region	Best people everywhere in the world developed for key positions everywhere in the world
Complexity of organization	Complex in home country, simple in subsidiaries	Varied and independent	Highly interdependent on a regional basis	"Global web"; complex, independent, worldwide alliances/network
Authority; decision making	High in headquarters	Relatively low in headquarters	High regional headquarters and/or high collaboration among subsidiaries	Collaboration of headquarters and subsidiaries around the world
Evaluation and control	Home standards applied to people and performance	Determined locally	Determined regionally	Globally integrated
Rewards	High in headquarters; low in subsidiaries	Wide variation; can be high or low rewards for subsidiary performance	Rewards for contribution to regional objectives	Rewards to international and local executives for reaching local and worldwide objectives based on global company goals
Communication; information flow	High volume of orders, commands, advice to subsidiaries	Little to and from headquarters; little among subsidiaries	Little to and from corporate headquarters, but may be high to and from regional headquarters and among countries	Horizontal; network relations
Geographic identification	Nationality of owner	Nationality of host country	Regional company	Truly global company, but identifying with national interests ("glocal")

The classification of employees is important because it determines which IHRM approach is adopted. However, the classification scheme does not cover all possibilities. In many countries, classifications are related to seniority, compensation, and stage of career.

In multinational and global corporations, the staffing policy strongly affects the type of employee the company prefers. Companies with an ethnocentric orientation usually staff important positions with PCNs. Those adopting a polycentric orientation usually select HCNs for subsidiaries while PCNs manage headquarters. Those with regiocentric orientations staff positions with PCNs or with HCNs and TCNs from the region—the needs of the company and the product strategy determine the staffing. Those adopting a geocentric approach are likely to favor the selection of the most suitable person for the job, regardless of type.

It is important to consider the prevalent practices of the headquarters, as well as practices and legal requirements of the countries where the subsidiaries are located, as discussed earlier. In many countries, for example, Mexico, it is common practice to recruit family members to work in the same subsidiary[8]—a practice which is strongly discouraged in the United States, the United Kingdom, and western Europe. In some eastern European countries, such as Hungary, the need to reduce unemployment means that multinationals must obtain permission from the Ministry of Labor before hiring an expatriate.[9]

It is important that a balance be struck between internal corporate consistency and sensitivity to local needs and practices. Different cultures emphasize different attributes in the selection process. Some cultures emphasize the need for universal criteria—it doesn't matter who the person is, but what the person can do for the organization. Other cultures emphasize ascriptive criteria—who the person is, and his or her family background and connections, is more important than what he or she can do for the organization. The selection process in achievement-oriented countries, such as the United States, the United Kingdom, Australia, and Western European countries, highlights skills, knowledge, and abilities. Although family or social connections might help, the emphasis is on hiring those who are best able to perform the job. In an ascriptive culture, age, sex, family background, and social connections are important, and the selection of someone whose personal characteristics fit the job is emphasized. For example, in Japan and parts of Latin America, advertisements in newspapers might explicitly state that the company is looking for a young male within a specific age range for a job, although these specifications may be external to the job requirements. Such advertisements would violate the Fair Employment Practices Act in the United States. Many countries place few restrictions on recruitment, selection, or hiring, and an employer can ask any question or actively recruit candidates who fit certain personal characteristics.

Companies using a geocentric approach to IHRM have considerable difficulties in integrating practices of various subsidiaries because they often vary from being heavily regulated by governments (as is the case in the Netherlands) to having little regulation (as is the case in Mexico). One approach emphasizes the need for selecting applicants not only on the basis of ability and motivation, but also on fit between the person and the organization, modifying selection to suit cultural requirements.[10] This is important, for example, in some East Asian cultures such as Korea and Japan, where answering a question immediately is not seen as a positive attribute. The geocentric approach also highlights the development of a global system, based on achievement motivation, which may not be suitable in every country. Japanese managers feel that too much attention to qualifications and not enough on personal characteristics leads to selecting the wrong person for the company. The tendency in Japan is to recruit by emphasizing the fit with the entire company rather than with a specific job.

Performance Evaluation

Performance evaluation is the process of appraising employees' job performance. It is a systematic process and, in Western multinational organizations, performance appraisals are usually done on a routine basis. Supervisors are required to discuss the results of the appraisal with the particular employee.

Performance evaluation is often challenging, because it has two explicit purposes that often conflict. The first is evaluative, while the second is developmental. Evaluative aspects of performance appraisal provide information for organizational decisions relating to compensation and advancement. Development aspects focus on feedback to help employees develop and improve their performance.

For international and global corporations, the complexity of performance evaluation increases because such organizations have the responsibility of developing systematic processes for the evaluation of employees from different countries who work in different locales. The need to develop consistent performance evaluations often conflicts with the need to consider cultural factors. For example, in China, saving face is very important, and public criticism of an employee is counterproductive and may lead to turnover. This is also true in Mexico, where public criticism as a part of performance appraisal is avoided.[11] Developing a balanced performance review system for the Mexican situation requires an appreciation of Mexican culture, where tact and courtesy are key factors.

The organization's overall HRM strategy is the major determinant of the effectiveness of its performance evaluation system. A company with an ethnocentric approach designs appraisal systems that use the same techniques developed in headquarters, regardless of the desirability of incorporating some unique characteristics of each local subsidiary, such as national culture or legal issues. Some of these companies translate their appraisal form into local languages. Multinational companies with polycentric or regiocentric approaches tend to be more sensitive to local conditions within each country or region. Those with a geocentric orientation use the same system of evaluating employees in various subsidiaries, but unlike ethnocentric organizations, the company develops universally applicable performance appraisal systems. Developing a global system of performance appraisal is time-consuming and requires a comprehensive consideration of many factors, as discussed earlier.

Compensation and Benefits

The compensation and benefit function of HRM is designed to develop uniform salary systems and other forms of remuneration, such as health insurance, pension funds, vacation, and sick pay. An international system of compensation is more difficult to develop, in that it must be concerned with comparability across various subsidiaries located in various economic environments. The system must also be competitive, in order to attract and retain qualified employees. The salary structure of employees in different locations should reflect appropriate compensation schemes, taking into account local market conditions as well as consistency throughout the organization. Another concern is the overall cost of compensation to the multinational or global organization.[12]

Regardless of the approach to IHRM, compensation and benefits schemes reflect local market conditions. The availability of qualified local people to fill positions, the prevailing local wage rates, the use of expatriates, and various labor laws influence the level of compensation and benefits. If the supply of qualified applicants is limited, the wage rates typically rise. To lower such expenses, international HR managers may consider bringing in home-country or third-country nationals.

Typically, a global company attempts to develop a policy and apply it uniformly, offering salaries and benefits representing a specific market level. When the company emphasizes the quality of its products and employees, it often has a global policy to pay high wages everywhere to improve retention of quality employees. Another method is to pay high salaries in those countries where the company has its R&D operations, but pay average wages elsewhere.

Training and Development

The training and development function involves planning for effective learning processes, organizational development, and career development. In the United States, *human resource development (HRD)* is a recognized field of HR. In global organizations, human resource development professionals are responsible for training and development of employees located in subsidiaries around the world. They specialize in training employees for assignments abroad and in developing managers with a global mindset—that is, managers who understand the complexities of managing in different countries.

The delivery of international training programs is either very centralized or decentralized.[13] A centralized approach originates at the headquarters, and corporate trainers travel to subsidiaries and adapt the program to local situations. This is an ethnocentric approach to training. In contrast, a geocentric approach allows the development of programs using inputs from both headquarters and subsidiary staff. Trainers are sent from headquarters or subsidiaries to any location where they are needed. In more polycentric approaches, the cultural backgrounds of the trainers and trainees tend to be similar. Subsidiary HR managers develop training materials and techniques for use in their own countries.

The learning process is an important aspect of implementing effective training programs. Cultural differences in learning processes must be taken into account in developing training programs. An effective training program should focus on the specific needs of a subsidiary in a specific country and the cultural background of the trainees. In individualistic countries, learning mechanisms on an individual level are emphasized, whereas in collectivistic countries, learning as a group is more effective. Similarly, where power distance is small, the relationship between the trainer and trainee tends toward equality, and challenging the trainer is acceptable. On the other hand, in countries where power distance is large, a trainer receives great respect, and challenging the trainer in any way is unacceptable. Exhibit 16.2 shows the impact of culture on

EXHIBIT 16.2 **Impact of Culture on Training and Development Practices**

Source: Adapted from M. Marquardt and D. W. Engel, *Global Human Resource Development,* Prentice-Hall, 1993, pp. 25-32.

	United States/ Canada	East Asia	Middle East/ North Africa	Latin America
HRD roles	Trainer and trainee as equals; trainees can and do challenge trainer, trainer can be informed and casual.	Trainees have great respect for trainer, who should behave, dress, and relate in a highly professional, formal manner.	Trainer highly respected, trainees want respect and friendly relationship, formality is important.	Preference for a decisive, clear, charismatic leader as trainer; trainees like to be identified with and loyal to a successful leader.
Analysis and design	Trainer determines objectives with input from trainees and their managers, trainees openly state needs and want to achieve success through learning.	Trainer should know what trainees need, admitting needs might represent loss of face to trainees.	Difficult to identify needs because it is improper to speak of other's faults; design must include time for socializing, relationship building, and prayers.	Difficult to get trainees to expose weaknesses and faults; design should include time for socializing.
Development and delivery	Programs should be practical and relevant, using a variety of methodologies with lecturing time limited.	Materials should be orderly, well organized and unambiguous; trainees most accustomed to lecture, note taking, and limited questioning.	Need adequate opportunity for trainer and trainees to interact, rely on verbal rather than written demonstrations of knowledge acquired, avoid paper exercises and role playing.	Educational system relies on lecture and has more theoretical emphasis; training should be delivered in local language.
Administration and environment	Hold training in comfortable, economical location; trainee selection based on perceived needs of organization and individual.	Quality of program may be judged on the basis of quality of location and training materials, ceremonies with dignitaries, certificates, plaques, and speeches taken as signs of value of program.	The learning process should be permeated with flourishes and ceremonies; program should not be scheduled during Ramadan, the month of fasting.	Value and importance judged by location, which dignitaries invited for the ceremonies, and academic affiliation of trainer; time is flexible: beginning or ending at a certain time not important.

training and development practices in four different parts of the world: the United States and Canada, East Asia, the Middle East/North Africa, and Latin America. It also identifies the main differences among the regions, although the specifics of training practices may differ somewhat from country to country within each region.

Labor Relations

The labor relations function is designed to assist managers and workers determine their relationships within the workplace.[14] The concept and practice of labor relations vary greatly in different parts of the world. In the United States, labor relations practices are generally formal, confrontational, and governed by union contracts. In Japan, the relationship between management and unions is cooperative, and union leaders are selected by managers. In many countries, the government regulates labor relations. Therefore, a polycentric approach is generally more effective in managing this aspect of the HRM function. Even though labor relations are best addressed at the local or regional level, some research suggests that the organization should coordinate and develop labor relations policies uniformly across various subsidiaries.[15]

Although some unions are termed "international," most unions are organized at the local, company, regional (within country), or national level. No union organizes activities across national boundaries. However, some unions are in the process of developing regional (groups of nations) offices in various countries. These offices focus on issues that arise as a result of multiple country trading blocks, such as the European Union, ASEAN bloc (Association of Southeast Asian Nations), or NAFTA. In Europe, 50 industrywide unions exist across the continent, but multinational and global companies have not yet begun to negotiate with them. Membership in unions varies greatly around the world, as seen in Exhibit 16.3.

The relative power of unions is not necessarily reflected by the number of members. Although only about 12 to 15 percent of Italian and French workers are union members, union agreements affect 85 percent or more of the workers in these countries.[16]

EXHIBIT 16.3
Union Membership in Selected Countries

Source: U.S. Department of Labor, Bureau of International Labor Affairs, Foreign Labor Trends and Bureau of Labor Statistics. Dates as indicated in table.

Country	Percentage of Union Membership	Year
Argentina	28%	1993
Brazil	13–30 (est.)	1993
Canada	29.5	1993
Chile	12.3	1993
China	92	1993
Costa Rica	15	1993
Egypt	50	1992
France	8–10	1993
Germany	39.5	1992
Greece	30	1993
Italy	15	1992
Japan	24.2	1993
Malaysia	9.1	1992
Mexico	25–30	1991
New Zealand	34.3	1993
Spain	11	1992
United States	15.8	1992
Zimbabwe	17	1993

Selecting Expatriates

Most research indicates that technical competence is the primary decision criteria used by global firms in selecting employees for overseas assignments.[17] Persons living in a foreign land are known as **expatriates.** Companies continue to endorse this practice, and other criteria that can have substantial effects on expatriates' adjustment and performance are not given enough attention.[18] This overemphasis on technical and job-related competence has guided the selection process because these factors are relatively easy to measure. Host-country organizations also prefer technically competent expatriates. However, as we discussed in Chapter 5, cultural and national differences make expatriate adjustment difficult, and the ability to adapt to unfamiliar conditions is crucial.[19] Language skills and knowledge of the local area are straightforward criteria that could be incorporated, but what is not understood very well is that the factors that can ease adjustment to the new environment are generally less concrete.

Culture Shock

Culture shock—a state of anxiety and disorientation caused by exposure to a new culture—can be a significant barrier in adjustment and performance of the expatriate. Differences in daily styles of interaction, including such things as whether to shake hands, when to present a gift, when and how to pay compliments, present difficulties in adjusting to the new environment. Coupled with this is the loss of familiar signs and ways of doing things, such as street signs, driving rules, and use of telephone and e-mail, which creates further problems for the expatriate.

The effects of culture shock on adjustment can be visualized as a U-shaped curve, as seen in Exhibit 16.4. Individuals who visit a country for a short time, such as tourists and others on short-term missions, do not go through the various degrees of adjustment. However, people who go to work or live abroad for a long period of time go

EXHIBIT 16.4
Effects of Culture Shock on Adjustment

Source: From D. C. Thomas, *Essentials of International Management: A Cross-Cultural Perspective.* Copyright © 2002 by Sage Publications, Inc. Reprinted by permission of Sage Publications, Inc.

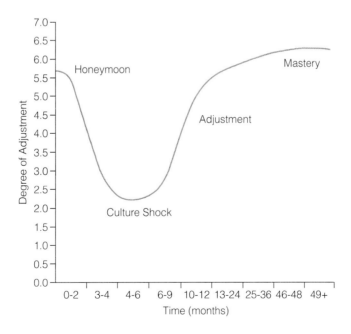

through the phases of adjustment shown in the exhibit. The first phase, the *honeymoon,* begins with the initial contact with another culture, and a sense of optimism and euphoria are common. They live in pleasant surroundings and are welcomed by colleagues and other host-country nationals, who may arrange special welcome events and make them feel comfortable.

In the second stage, *culture shock,* difficulties in language, inadequate schooling for the children, lack of adequate housing, crowded buses and subways, differences in shopping habits, and other problems can create stress, unhappiness, and a dislike for the country. During this period, expatriates often seek others from their home country with whom they can compare experiences about their difficulties. They may try to escape through drinking and socializing, as they experience as sense of powerlessness and alienation. Over time, these feeling may intensify in some expatriates and lead to depression and physical health problems. Some of the problems are illustrated in Practical Insight 16.2. Especially after the September 11, 2001 terrorist attack on the Pentagon and the World Trade Center, the incidences of terrorism are affecting placement of expatriates. While there are no guarantees that the guidelines provided are foolproof, they will help.

In the third stage, *adjustment,* expatriates begin to develop new sets of skills that enable them to cope with their new environment. Anxiety and depression become less frequent, and expatriates begin to feel more positive about their new surroundings.

In the fourth and last stage, *mastery,* expatriates know how to deal with the demands of their local environment and have learned enough about local customs and culture to feel "at home."

Managing Expatriates

Multinational and global organizations that make use of parent-country and third-country nationals must develop a process of handling the complexities of moving people outside of their home countries. Employing expatriates may be linked with the global strategy, but it tends to be an expensive process most of the time. We should note that careful use of expatriate HRM is extremely important.

Cost of Failure

The cost of failure of the overseas assignments is much more than simply the cost of the executive's salary and transfer. Because of additional compensation, an expatriate stationed in an expensive city such as Tokyo, London, or Paris could cost a company up to $350,000 in the first year.[20] It is more cost-efficient to prevent a bad transfer than to have an expatriate return home because of difficulties in adjusting to foreign assignments.

Some managers fail because they are unhappy in their assignment. This is often due to the poor organizational support that promotes the feeling within the company that overseas assignments are not high profile and may not lead to advancement.[21] The lack of family adjustment to the new culture also may lead to failure.

Compensation Issues

Sending home-country nationals abroad is expensive, perhaps costing one to two times more than keeping managers at home. Moreover, transferring a home-country national to a subsidiary has been estimated to cost 10 times more than hiring a host-country national.[22] Until there is a global salary system, companies are generally forced to resort to one of two types of compensation system, a headquarters salary system or a citizenship salary system.

PRACTICAL INSIGHT 16.2

STAYING SAFE ON FOREIGN ASSIGNMENTS

Overseas travel has become an increasingly important part of conducting business in the era of globalization. This article outlines some of the precautions which human-resource specialists can take to help to protect their company employees who travel abroad.

Business Travelers Make Easy Targets

Increasing crime directed at business travelers abroad makes it more important than ever that human-resource specialists have a strategy for protecting company employees who travel overseas for the firm.

While companies see foreign trade as an exciting opportunity in the era of globalization, so too do some of the world's criminals.

Says Alan Stokes, of insurer CIGNA International: "Business travelers make easy targets. They often travel in unfamiliar territory, wear formal clothes, carry expensive laptop computers in readily-identifiable bags, use mobile telephones and wear watches which can cost more than a year's salary in less-privileged countries. All these factors combine to make them highly visible."

"Improved travel has made so many destinations accessible that business travelers can almost forget they are on foreign territory. The security of corporate-credit-card bookings, executive-club lounges and international hotel chains can cocoon them into a false sense of security. But believing they can go anywhere in the world and behave exactly as they do at home can make business travelers an easy target for anything from mugging to armed-car theft and even kidnap."

"The challenge for human-resource professionals is not only to ensure the personal safety of the individual, but also to ensure that their organization is not exposed to the business implications of losing the services of a key employee, of disruption to customer relationships or the loss of a contract, by preparing corporate travelers in advance."

Assets to Be Protected

"Companies generally send key personnel to conduct business overseas, so they should be seen as an asset to be protected."

Mr Stokes offers the following advice to human-resource specialists:

1. *Prepare the ground.* Make use of free pre-travel advice from the travel agent or insurance company. Do some homework on the destination. Check well in advance about inoculation and visa requirements. Find out about any dress codes and ask which taxi company to use on arrival at the destination. Make sure there is a contact number for the embassy and know if there are any areas of town which should be avoided.

2. *Check the insurance.* Make sure your company insurance covers the basics such as medical expenses, repatriation, personal injury and sickness for the area the executive is traveling to. Insurance bought with a travel ticket may be geared towards the needs of the holidaymaker. Business travelers need different support, such as cover for business equipment. Encourage the executive to carry the helpline number listed in the insurance documents, so that help is always at hand.

3. *Do not stand out from the crowd.* Avoid business luggage tickets. If the executive has a laptop computer, make sure he or she carries it in an ordinary holdall or briefcase. To the average thief, computer bags scream: "I have $2,000 of equipment on my shoulder."

If possible, the executive should travel in casual clothes. Expensive business clothes mark him or her as someone likely to be carrying valuable possessions and part of a larger, wealthy organization. Thieves target airports in the knowledge that business travelers will be carrying cash and credit cards. Keep credit cards on one's person and in separate places.

Thieves know which hotels are used by comparatively wealthy business travelers. If the executive feels like taking fresh air or sightseeing, he or she should ask the hotel staff where is safe to walk alone and which areas to avoid. Leave valuables such as jewellery and passport in the hotel safe, or keep them with money in a concealed money belt.

Take care when showing a gold or platinum credit card. Something which is taken for granted at home can also be a status symbol which clearly marks a person out as a target.

If the executive is to be met at an airport, ask the driver to use a code by which he or she can be recognized. Name and company on a card advertises the executive as a target to follow.

Such simple precautions can help to prevent a dream trip to an exotic foreign location from becoming a nightmare.

Source: From "Staying Safe on Foreign Assignments," *Human Resource Management International Digest,* May/June 1999. Permission granted by Emerald Group Publishing Limited, www.emeraldinsight.com.

The *headquarters salary system* is based on the headquarters pay scale plus differentials. The salary for the same job at headquarters determines the base salary of the home-country national. The differential can be a positive addition to an expatriate's salary, or it can be a negative allowance to account for the extra benefits that might be associated with the particular overseas placement. When an expatriate is provided free housing and transportation and an equivalent sum is subtracted from his basic pay, he has received a negative allowance. Under the headquarters salary system, host-country nationals are entitled to neither the base salary nor to the differentials of home-country nationals. Their salaries are based on local salary standards. Third-country nationals pose a unique compensation challenge. The company may treat them either as home- or host-country nationals, so inequities arise. The headquarters salary system is the more ethnocentric of the two compensation systems.

The *citizenship salary system* solves the problem of what to do about the third-country national. The manager's salary is based on the standard for the country of his or her citizenship or native residence. An appropriate differential is then added, based on comparative factors between the two countries. This system works well as long as expatriates with similar positions do not come from countries with different salary scales. It is difficult to avoid this problem, and inequities arising from either compensation program are noticed by the managers.

Benefits In the United States, approximately 27 percent of compensation for home-country employees is benefits. Issues surrounding expatriate benefits are different from those that affect host-country employees. Expatriates need vacations to return home for extended visits. Multinational companies often pay airfare for home visits, emergency leave, illnesses, and when there is a death in the expatriate's family. However, other questions must be dealt with on a country and case-by-case basis. For example, some benefits are taxable overseas but tax deductible at home. Another example is when subsidiaries are located in countries that have government-sponsored social benefits, such as universal health care. The company must reach an agreement with either the government or the home-country manager about coverage for these necessities.

Allowances Multinational and global companies often pay allowances for cost of living, relocation expenses, cars, and club memberships in the host country, as well as housing. In addition, education allowances for children are often expected, either to allow the children to attend private school in the host country or to allow them to be educated in the home country. Hardship allowances are often required to attract qualified individuals to less desirable locations, such as the Middle East or other less developed areas.

Incentives Only 20 percent of companies pay higher compensation to expatriates than to home-country managers. Instead, most offer a one-time lump-sum premium. The company benefits as follows by offering this one-time payment:[23]

- Expatriates realize that they will get it only once when they move to the overseas assignment.
- Cost to the company is less than percentage compensation, since it is a one-time incentive.
- The expatriate receives readily available money for spending or saving, and thus sees a noticeable incentive.

Incentives are beginning to be phased out, because the manager sees the assignment is its own reward or as a step toward globalization.[24]

Taxes   Often multinational and global companies pay any extra tax burden. Taxes can be an extremely complex area in compensating expatriates. In some countries, expatriates' salary is taxable only when paid locally. In most countries, local authorities do not tax compensation based on a worldwide scheme. American companies prefer a tax equalization plan that allows the company to withhold the expatriate's U.S. tax liability and pay his or her local taxes. British companies, on the other hand, change their policy depending on the country in which the subsidiary is located. The tax equalization plan may create a situation where the company pays taxes in multiple countries because taxes paid on behalf of an expatriate by the headquarters are also taxable locally. International compensation experts have suggested that companies with operations in many countries should adopt a policy of tax equalization. The company would gain in some countries, and lose in some others. However, if the scale of international operations is limited, it is best to leave the payment of local taxes to the expatriate and adjust other allowances in accordance with local standards.[25]

Managing Dual-Career Expatriates

The number of dual-career couples has been rapidly growing in the United States, from 52 percent of all couples to 59 percent in the early 1990s, and the trend is on the rise. Over 50 percent of the expatriates being transferred abroad have spouses who worked before relocating.[26] Thus the dual-career expatriate couple has become a major concern of global companies, especially in those companies where overseas experience can significantly advance one's career. An interesting phenomenon where couples sustain their marriages by using the Internet and e-mail is becoming common, as married men and women with careers take assignments in different parts of the world. Global companies must have sound policies to lessen the chances that a talented male or female manager terminates employment because of the difficulties associated with separation from his or her spouse. Some of the suggestions for policies are:

- Frequent visitation trips of the family or the expatriate to prevent the pain of separation from becoming too intense. One trip every two months is not unreasonable.
- Generous allowance for long-distance telephone calls and other costs of communication. A phone conversation can ease the tension and loneliness of the expatriate and the family.
- Offering employment to the spouse within the company or job-search assistance in the local area if the spouse is willing to quit his or her job in the home country to be with the married partner. The U.S. State Department has the practice of finding local jobs for spouses of employees sent abroad.
- Making connections with other global companies for employment of spouses. For example, the Hong Kong subsidiary of an international company, such as Procter & Gamble, might be in a position to hire the spouse of an IBM expatriate manager working in Hong Kong.

Repatriation

Most overseas assignments last for five years. **Repatriation** is the term given to the return of the home-country manager. Managers return for a number of reasons.[27]

- The time of the overseas assignment is up.
- Children's education.
- Unhappiness with the assignment.
- Family unhappiness.
- Failure.

PRACTICAL INSIGHT 16.3

YOUR CAREER MATTERS: DAIMLERCHRYSLER'S TRANSFER WOES—WORKERS RESIST MOVES ABROAD—AND HERE

In a windowless conference room 15 stories below the executive suite, seven German and American employees of DaimlerChrysler AG were in debate over the newly merged automaker's future. The question: Should the pamphlet encouraging employees to volunteer for overseas postings be round—like a globe—or rectangular. At the heart of the dispute was a nontrivial problem: Months after the former Daimler-Benz AG and Chrysler Corp. joined to form DaimlerChrysler, the new corporation remained essentially two separate companies, one German and one American.

If DaimlerChrysler was to become a global trailblazer, one thing it must do is convince employees at all levels that picking up and moving around the world will pay. Dozens of groups are now shuttling between the company's dual headquarters in Stuttgart, Germany, and here in Auburn Hills for marathon meetings to hammer out the minutiae of the merger. But most important to the company's future as a global giant may be the group drafting a new expatriate policy for employees.

Getting employees to move abroad has been a tough sell. By 2000, the company wanted to exchange 60 employees between Germany and the U.S. on merger-related stints lasting between two and five years. Persuading Americans to move to Germany was particularly difficult, company officials say, and so DaimlerChrysler now encourages shorter stints abroad.

Part of the problem with Americans has been personal concerns: Most don't speak German and don't want to leave their spacious U.S. homes for apartments or smaller houses in Stuttgart, where real estate is far more expensive than in the Midwestern U.S.

But the Americans' reticence to work abroad also reflects a fundamental difference between the former Daimler and Chrysler. Chrysler was a much less global company than Daimler, so it put less value on international assignments as stepping stones for its rising executives. While the Chrysler side has only about 300 employees living outside the U.S., the Daimler side has about 1,500 living outside Germany.

Even chairman Jürgen Schrempp spent a few years living in Cleveland, Ohio, as chairman of a former Daimler commercial-truck unit. It's "not so much embedded in the American culture as it is in the European culture to go abroad," says Christoph Seyfarth, a leader of the German contingent on the expat working group.

One of the most contentious issues has been how generously DaimlerChrysler expats will be paid. At one meeting here, American Raymond Wilhelm ticks off the goodies Chrysler provided its expats: a lump sum worth three months' salary to cover miscellaneous expenses for setting up house overseas; moving expenses, including hotel and meals; and a salary bonus if the cost of living in the new country was higher than in the U.S.

The litany of payments shocks Anja C. Vahldiek, a Daimler lawyer in the group. Daimler offered a cost-of-living adjust-

---

Readjustment problems occur when individuals arrive back after their overseas assignments. Tung found that the longer the assignment, the more problems with reabsorption.[28] Transition strategies are needed to retain these individuals and the experience they have acquired. One study showed:

- Three-fourths of expatriates felt they returned to a demotion.
- 60 percent felt they were unable to use they overseas experience because it was devalued by the organization.
- 60 percent believed that the company lacked any commitment to them on their return.[29]

The study also found that 25 percent of the expatriates had left the organization within a year after their return.

Other readjustment problems are more personal, such as adjusting to lower pay and benefits after the overseas assignments. Some find difficulty in the return to the housing market after they sold their house to go overseas. Children of expatriates may find that returning to public school is difficult after the smaller classes in private school. The change in the cultural lifestyle can affect those who transfer from cultural centers such as Paris or London or New York to less cosmopolitan areas in the home country.

ment, but it gave only a small lump-sum relocation payment, and it paid only for a hotel room—not for meals—for a relocating expat. Chrysler expats are "getting quite a lot of lump sums at the beginning," she says. "Wow. In other areas, it's the Chrysler officials who want to pinch pennies. Take the debate over the expat brochure. Mr. Wilhelm questions the need for an elaborate brochure, suggesting that much of the information be posted on the company's intranet. The Germans object. The union representing German workers "would tell us that not everybody has access to the intranet, and we have to provide something on paper," says Mr. Seyfarth.

Mr. Wilhelm shakes his head. "I'm just amazed," he mutters.

The group's German and American contingents have historically approached each other warily. The Americans saw Germans as "running around in steel helmets and always saying, 'Yes, General,' " Mr. Seyfarth says. The Germans, says Mr. Wilhelm, who grew up in Brooklyn, N.Y., thought of Americans as "cowboys—shoot from the hip."

Tactical gestures helped. One evening, Mr. Seyfarth, Mr. Wilhelm and others met for dinner at a steak house near Auburn Hills. Mr. Seyfarth, who had lived from 1993 to 1996 in New Jersey as a finance official in the U.S. headquarters of Daimler's Mercedes-Benz unit, doctored his steak with Heinz 57 sauce. Mr. Wilhelm noticed, and on his way home stopped by a 24-hour warehouse store to buy Mr. Seyfarth a bottle of the brew. The next morning, when Mr. Wilhelm presented the gift to Mr. Seyfarth, "he was just amazed," Mr. Wilhelm recalls. "Where can you get steak sauce at 1 o'clock in the morning?"

the German asked. Says Mr. Wilhelm: "We broke the ice immediately."

Over the next few months, the group's members spent virtually every third week together. The Germans would fly to Auburn Hills for a week, return home for about two weeks, and then host the Americans in Stuttgart the following week—and on and on. Each time, travel between the two cities took between 10 and 14 hours. "I don't think we ever got used to the jet lag," Mr. Wilhelm says.

Typically, the group would meet all day and then head out to dinner together. In Stuttgart they usually ended up at the Dopo, an Italian eatery with a good wine list. "We were the group that sat the longest and drank the most wine and laughed the loudest," Mr. Seyfarth recalls. But the meetings were less buoyant than the meals. Early on, the Germans and Americans bogged down in comparisons of their respective company's former expat policies. The rambling discussions "led to nothing," says Mr. Seyfarth. "We said, 'Let's start from scratch.' "

Over the past several months the group racked up hundreds of additional hours in intricate talks—some of them by conference call or video camera, in an effort to cut down on grueling travel schedules. Ultimately, the group reached compromises. They decided, for example, to give DaimlerChrysler expats a lump sum of one month's salary to cover expenses. As for the pamphlet, the group opted for the fancier globe-shaped version favored by the Germans.

Source: Adapted from J. Ball, *Wall Street Journal* (eastern edition), August 24, 1999, p. 31.

Companies can prevent some of these problems by using transition strategies, such as repatriation agreements. These agreements define the company's responsibilities to the expatriate upon return, providing the security often sought by managers on overseas assignments. Some companies have set up separate departments to deal with expatriates' special needs.[30] Another strategy used by some companies is the purchase of the manager's home until the foreign assignment is complete. This allows the expatriate to keep up with the generally increasing housing market while overseas. Some companies assign senior managers to be sponsors of expatriate managers.[31] These mentor programs maintain the individual's communication lines with headquarters, of crucial importance to expatriates on their return. Assigning expatriates to projects that are centered at the home office also enhances communication with headquarters.

International Human Resource Management and Competitive Advantage

In an era of globalization, when technology and capital flow freely across national and cultural boundaries, human resources take on new importance as critical strategic assets or factor of production that are not easily mobile. People resist permanent moves across cultures and boundaries, even if it means that they refuse better compensation

PRACTICAL INSIGHT 16.4

CULTURE SHOCK IN AMERICA?

Imagine you're embarking on your first foreign assignment. You had an outstanding academic career and are now in great demand in your field. After only a few years on the job, you're an undisputed star at your company. You've become so stellar, in fact, that with your ability to speak the international language of business—English—you're the obvious choice to be sent abroad. It's a developmental assignment, shall we say: five, maybe 10, years overseas. Then you'll return home with a skill set bulging with international savvy and your own personal spotlight on the world stage of business.

With confidence, you accept that exotic assignment abroad. Destination: the United States of America. But you soon discover that the Land of Opportunity is really the Land of "What's Your Social Security Number?" Without that nine-digit track record of your material viability, it doesn't matter where you came from or where you're going. You find yourself struggling to open accounts; to get an apartment, a phone, and electricity; and to figure out the bus route while you're waiting for a car loan to come through. You have somehow dropped into the Dead Zone; you're stuck in Culture Shock Purgatory.

It's ironic that this would be the case in a country with one of the world's most-traveled populations. Still, being sent to the United States on foreign assignment is not just a stressful business—it's a lonely one. From New Delhi to Cape Town to Minas Gerais, the observation is the same: Americans are friendly but hard to make friends with. We gregarious Americans don't truly bring international assignees into our lives, because we don't bring them into our homes after work.

What about corporate support? With rare exception, Corporate America is still focused more on making Americans' adventures abroad successful than on providing the same levels of support to those coming here on corporate assignments. This perspective will eventually come at great cost to any U.S. corporation with international ambitions, says Willa Hallowell,

a partner with Brooklyn, N.Y.-based Cornelius Grove and Associates, a consultancy emphasizing cross-cultural support. You have to regard this person coming in as a business investment, and you therefore must guard that investment in every possible way. "If you don't, the mess you will have to clean up will be an even greater expense," Hallowell says. The costs associated with the mess include loss of productivity, the diminishment of the employee's self-confidence, the potential destruction of the employee's home life, and the corrosion of the company's reputation abroad.

"If things aren't going well, the returning employee will spread the seeds of discontent," Hallowell says. "Then, the next round of employees brought here will be prepared for problems, or they might choose to come here to look for another job."

The good news is that companies are moving toward seeking support services for their expatriates from all nations. "More and more companies are bringing expats to us," says Franchette Richards, until recently manager of Arthur Andersen's International Employment Solutions group. "We're helping them deal with visas and other immigration issues—financial obstacles, cultural differences. It's important for companies to realize that they must be consistent in the support of their expats, whether the employees are coming here or going outbound. An expat is an expat is an expat."

And no matter where they come from, expats share a critical concern: how well their spouses adjust to their new life. "It is the main reason why employees go home early," says Cornelius Grove, partner at Grove & Associates and an expert on the physiological effects of the stress of culture shock.

Most damaging to a spouse's accommodation: Under U.S. immigration laws, most spouses are not allowed to find jobs while they are "in country," so they are without the automatic social network that the office provides the employee.

Source: From Martha I. Finney, "Culture Shock in America?" *Across the Board,* May 2000. Reprinted with permission of the author.

and adequate living facilities. While political barriers to intercountry mobility have largely been removed, thus allowing free movement of labor, as in the case of integrated European Union countries, the number of talented people moving across national boundaries remains small. The main barriers are rooted in language differences, cultural preferences, and natural propensities to stay and work in the country of birth.

Intercountry competition in a global economy is likely to result in successes and failures of many large to medium-sized organizations. One of the major ways failures can be averted and sustained competitive advantage maintained is by recruiting from a global workforce talented personnel who are able to manage technology and knowledge, motivate people in various worldwide subsidiaries, and exercise proper leadership and negotiating skills.

Increasing the recruitment of women is one way to ensure continued success in the global work force. Women are joining men as examples of successful global leaders and effective expatriates. Despite such successes, many multinationals, particularly from collectivistic and developing economies, remain reluctant to employ women as senior-level managers in leadership roles. In addition, corporations avoid placement of women in cultures where they feel women are not accorded proper respect. While some of these assumptions might be true, research conducted in the human resource field shows that women are more effective than men as expatriate managers in parts of the world where relationship-oriented managers do much better.

Summary

International human resources management is the process of managing human resources globally. An organization's corporate strategy drives the approach it takes to IHRM. The approach can influence implementation of the major functions, such as recruitment and selection, performance evaluation, compensation and benefits, training and development, and labor relations.

Multinational companies adopting a purely ethnocentric approach attempt to impose their home-country methods on their subsidiaries. Polycentric and regiocentric approaches tend to follow local practices more consistently. The geocentric or global approach develops practices for uniform worldwide use.

Management of expatriates is one of the major concerns of IHRM. Because expatriates function in dissimilar economic, political, and cultural environments and also need to function effectively in foreign work and living situations, they need special attention. It is important to motivate them in their assignments and upgrade their compensation and benefits to make foreign assignments attractive.

Approaches to IHRM are both converging and diverging worldwide, and there is evidence that both exist. Large global corporations, such as Microsoft, IBM, Sony, Toyota, and Unilever, prefer uniform practices, whereas smaller companies prefer IHRM practices tailored to the local needs. International managers have the important responsibility for managing human resources in various countries, and they should upgrade their knowledge continuously in order to effectively implement corporate strategies.

Key Terms and Concepts

culture shock, *483*
ethnocentric staffing approach, *474*
expatriate, *483*
geocentric (or global) staffing approach, *474*

international human resources management (IHRM), *473*
performance evaluation, *479*

polycentric staffing approach, *474*
regiocentric staffing approach, *474*
repatriation, *487*

Discussion Questions

1. What is international human resources management? Why is it difficult to manage human resources on a worldwide basis?
2. What are the various functions of international human resources management? How does the process of recruitment and selection differ in international corporations compared to domestic corporations?
3. How does the process of performance appraisal differ in organizations that adopt a geocentric approach compared to those that adopt an ethnocentric approach?
4. When should an international corporation use universal compensation policies and practices? When should it use policies and practices tailored to local needs?
5. Explain the concept of culture shock. What is the role of the spouse of an expatriate in adjusting to foreign countries?

Minicase

Reuters' Offshore "Experiment"

Now you can add journalist to the growing list of white-collar jobs—along with radiologist, animator, and Wall Street analyst—that can be outsourced overseas. Reuters, the British news agency that employs some 2,400 journalists and photographers around the globe, said last month that it would hire six journalists in Bangalore, India, to cover news on small- and mid-cap U.S. companies.

Technically, it isn't outsourcing, which involves handing off work to another company, says David Schlesinger, Reuters' global managing editor, who's based in New York. The Bangalore scribes will be Reuters employees with Reuters training. Even so, under what the company is calling a pilot program, they'll be doing something unusual in a news organization: Covering U.S. companies from a distant shore. Mainly, it will be grunt work—writing routine financial news stories from corporate press releases.

It may seem a bit odd that a profession that's already known for modest pay—trust me, the multi-million-dollar contracts of TV news personalities such as Barbara Walters are the exception—is the latest to be shipped to a low-wage country. But thanks to union agreements, Reuters journalists in the U.S. make a decent living. An entry-level reporter in New York can earn about $58,000 a year, says Peter Szekely, chairman of the Reuters unit of the Newspaper Guild of New York.

"A LOT OF ANXIETY." With Reuters striving to trim $1.6 billion in costs by 2006 vs. what it spent in 2000, there's no doubt that it likes the idea of paying Indian-size wages. Archrival Bloomberg has overtaken Reuters in the highly profitable business of selling financial-data terminals used by traders and other financial professionals. And as part of its cost-cutting, Reuters is already moving technical jobs to Bangalore and software positions to Bangkok.

Talk that Reuters could some day expand its Bangalore news operation has made its reporting ranks nervous about job security, Szekely says. "There's a lot of anxiety as a result of this," he adds. Reuters responds by saying it'll always need plenty of journalists on the ground in the U.S. and elsewhere around the world to gather news that can't be obtained from a press release.

Although Reuters isn't a U.S. company, it's now likely to be drawn into the debate on overseas outsourcing, which is shaping up as a Presidential campaign issue. The wire agency's initiative could even end up influencing coverage of the subject, as its employees worry that their jobs could one day be at risk.

Recently, Wahlgren, who worked at Reuters before joining BusinessWeek Online, chatted with Global Managing Editor Schlesinger about the plans for Bangalore. Edited excerpts of their conversation follow:

Q: So you plan to outsource six journalists overseas?

A: First of all, outsourcing is the wrong word. Basically, what we're doing is offshoring. We're simply experimenting with doing reporting from a different location. It's no different from what we've always done. If you think about your time at Reuters, we had [the] New York [bureau] cover California companies, or [the] Chicago [bureau] cover companies throughout the Midwest.

All we're doing here is having some journalists in Bangalore cover the basic earnings announcements of U.S. companies. So it's certainly not outsourcing, which is giving work to another company. This will be a Reuters office, [with] Reuters journalists, Reuters training, Reuters standards. It's simply moving the work.

Q: What will the reporters be doing exactly?

A: Well, this is a pilot program. They will be monitoring the PR wire and the business wire [both transmit corporate and other press releases] for announcements of small- and mid-cap companies that we're currently not even covering on a regular basis. And then they'll be doing the basic earnings *pro formas* off of that.

Q: Is there interest from Reuters clients [which include investment banks, other media organizations, and Web sites] in more coverage of these companies?

A: Yes, there seems to be. But more important than that, I want to prove the concept.

Q: These journalists aren't going to be replacing Reuters journalists in other parts of the world? They're going to be hired on top of the existing editorial staff, right?

A: These six, that's right.

Q: If the experiment proves to be successful, what's next? Are you going to hire more people to do this coverage in India, or are you going to replace journalists in other parts of Reuters?

A: The key thing is to prove the concept. I have to see that we get the right people, that we can train them well, that the communications work, that the work is of sufficiently high quality, that it comes up to Reuters standards. After that, we will see where it takes us. Since we can get the standardized wires anywhere in the world, I would like to be able to expand the operation.

The six journalists in the pilot project are going to be part of a much larger Reuters data operation there, so we can get some synergies between the people who are entering company results into databases and people who are reporting them for the wire. So I think it's quite exciting to be able to take advantage of what we can do in India.

Q: This is the first time that Reuters is doing this with editorial jobs, right?

A: I don't think that's accurate. During down times in New York, sometimes we send stories to London for [editing]. Is that offshoring? We have operations around the world. Equities stories are covered everywhere in the world. [Editing] is done, copy editing is done everywhere in the world. Reuters has a long tradition of being a global organization, doing work where it can be done best.

Q: Where do you see expansion of this program going?

A: It really depends on how well it goes. I want to do work where it's best done. So in the New Yorks, Londons, Singapores, Tokyos, I want reporters breaking news, doing interviews, doing real value-added reporting. In Bangalore, I would want people monitoring standardized wires and trying to get the synergies with the data operations.

Q: Could coverage of large-cap companies that Reuters typically does out of New York and London or other financial centers be done out of Bangalore?

A: Sure, but only the part of the coverage that can be done off a PR wire or a results wire. You always need to have the specialist reporters back in the home country doing the breaking news, doing the interviews, going to the analyst meetings, visiting the company itself.

So I think it really splits the reporting into two: The monitoring of the standardized wire is one thing, and that can be done in Bangalore. But then you free up the reporters to do the value-added reporting in New York or London.

Q: To what extent does that value-added reporting need to be done where the news is breaking? Can it be done anywhere in the world?

A: I think value-added reporting you want to do where the news is breaking. I think the wire monitoring you can do anywhere. But for value-added reporting, you need to be able to go to the meetings, visit the company, have the relationship with the analyst and the company officials.

We had more than 70 people in the [Iraq] theater, and some of our competitors had nobody. Reuters has always had a tradition of having people on the spot for doing the real value-added reporting.

Q: What would a typical Bangalore reporter be paid, vs. an entry-level reporter in New York or elsewhere in the Reuters organization?

A: We're just in the process of hiring people, so it's difficult to say. There will be a significant difference. But at the moment, we haven't hired the people yet, so it's hard to give any firm numbers.

Q: Will what you're looking for in a new hire be different in Bangalore then in New York?

A: Absolutely not. We will be giving writing tests. We will be looking for people who are numerate and who have an appreciation of business news. And certainly, one of the appealing things about India is that there's a good tradition of a vibrant press. There's a good standard of written English and a very good education level in terms of being able to read company accounts.

I think it's an exciting way to add content to our wires and that it's really being done with the needs of our clients in mind—so we can add coverage and free up reporters here to do more value-added coverage.

Q: What have you found to be the response within Reuters?

A: I think a huge range of response. There are some people who are very excited by it. There are some people who are a touch apprehensive about it. But that's to be expected any time you do something new.

Source: *BusinessWeek Online,* March 4, 2004, http://www.businessweek.com/bwdaily/dnflash/mar2004/ nf2004034_9957_db053.htm.

DISCUSSION QUESTIONS

1. What benefits will Reuters gain in hiring Indian journalists?
2. What problems might be encountered in this "experiment," other than the compensation mentioned in the article?
3. What form of payment would you suggest for the Indian journalists, if you were in the human resource department of Reuters? What would be the benefits of your suggestion? What possible problems could result from your suggestion?

Notes

1. P. J. Dowling, R. S. Schuler, and D. E. Welch, *International Dimensions of Human Resource Management,* 2nd ed. (Belmont, CA: Wadsworth, 1994).
2. J. L. Laabs, "HR Pioneers Explore the Road Less Traveled," *Personnel Journal,* February 1996, pp. 70–72, 74, 77–78.
3. J. S. Black and H. B. Gregersen, "The Right Way to Manage Expats," *Harvard Business Review,* March/April 1999, pp. 52–62.
4. B. S. Chakravarthy and H. V. Perlmuter, "Strategic Planning for a Global Business," *Columbia Journal of World Business* 20, no. 2 (1985), pp. 3–10; P. J. Dowling, R. S. Schuler, and D. E. Welch, *International Dimensions of Human Resource Management.*
5. C. D. Fisher, L. F. Schoenfeldt, and J. B. Shaw, *Human Resource Management,* 2nd ed. (Boston: Houghton Mifflin, 1993).
6. R. Tung, *The New Expatriates: Managing Human Resources Abroad* (Cambridge, MA: Ballinger, 1988).
7. P. M. Rosenweig and N. Nohria, "Influences on Human Resource Management Practices in Multinational Corporations," *Journal of International Business Studies* 25 (1994), pp. 229–251.
8. M. B. Teagarden, M. A. Von Glinow, M. C. Butler, and E. Drost, "The Best Practices Learning Curve: Human Resource Management in Mexico's Maquiladora Industry." In O. Shenkar, ed., *Global Perspectives of Human Resource Management* (Upper Saddle River, NJ: Prentice Hall, 1995).
9. D. C. Bangert and J. Poor, "Human Resource Management in Foreign Affiliates in Hungary." In O. Shenkar, ed., *Global Perspectives of Human Resource Management.* (Upper Saddle River, NJ: Prentice Hall, 1995).

10. J. Artise, "Selection, Coaching, and Evaluation of Employees in International Subsidiaries." In O. Shenkar, ed., *Global Perspectives of Human Resource Management* (Upper Saddle River, NJ: Prentice Hall, 1995).

11. M. E. de Forest, "Thinking of a Plant in Mexico?" *Academy of Management Executive* 8 (1994), pp. 33–40.

12. Dowling, Schuler, and Welch, *International Dimensions of Human Resource Management.*

13. M. Marquardt and D. W. Engel, *Global Human Resource Development* (Upper Saddle River, NJ: Prentice Hall, 1993).

14. R. M. Hodgetts and F. Luthans, *International Management,* 2nd ed. (New York: McGraw-Hill, 1994).

15. Dowling, Schuler, and Welch, *International Dimensions of Human Resource Management.*

16. D. R. Briscoe, *International Human Resource Management* (Upper Saddle River, NJ: Prentice Hall, 1995).

17. E. L. Miller, "The Job Satisfaction of Expatriate American Managers: A Function of Regional Location and Previous Work Experience," *Journal of International Business Studies* 6, no. 2 (1975), pp. 65–73; R. L. Tung, "Selection and Training of Personnel for Overseas Assignments," *Columbia Journal of World Business* 16 (1981), pp. 68–78.

18. A. Haselberger and L. K. Stroh, "Development and Selection of Multinational Expatriates," *Human Resource Development Quarterly* 3 (1992), pp. 287–293.

19. R. J. Stone, "Expatriate Selection and Failure," *Human Resource Planning* 29, no. 1 (1991), pp. 9–17; R. L. Tung, "American Expatriates Abroad: From Neophytes to Cosmopolitans," *Journal of World Business* 33, no. 2 (1998), pp. 125–144.

20. Briscoe, *International Human Resource Management.*

21. M. L. Kraimer, S. J. Wayne, and R. A. Jaworski, "Sources of Support and Expatriate Performance: The Mediating Role of Expatriate Adjustment," *Personnel Psychology* 54 (2001), pp. 71–99.

22. C. Reynolds, "Expatriate Compensations in Historical Perspective," *Journal of World Business* 32, no. 2 (1997), p. 127.

23. R. B. Peterson, N. K. Napier, and W. Shul-Shim, "Expatriate Management: A Comparison of MNCs across Four Parent Countries," *Thunderbird International Business Review,* March–April 2000, p. 155.

24. G. W. Latta, "Expatriate Incentives: Beyond Tradition," *HR Focus,* March 1998, p. 24.

25. D. Young, "Fair Compensation for Expatriates," *Harvard Business Review* 51, no. 4 (1973), p. 119.

26. J. S. Lubin, "Companies Use Cross-Cultural Training to Help Their Employees Adjust Abroad," *Wall Street Journal,* August 4, 1992, p. B1.

27. I. Torbiorn, *Living Abroad* (New York: John Wiley & Sons, 1982), p. 41; M. L. Kraimer, S. J. Wayne, and R. A. Jaworski, "Sources of Support and Expatriate Performance: The Mediating Role of Expatriate Adjustment," *Personnel Psychology* 54 (2001), pp. 71–99; Y. Zeira and M. Banai, "Attitudes of Host-Country Organization toward MNCs' Staffing Policies: A Cross-Country and Cross-Industry Analysis," *Management International Review* 21, no. 2 (1981), p. 34.

28. R. L. Tung, "Career Issues in International Assignments," *Academy of Management Executive,* August 1988, p. 242.

29. J. E. Abueva, "Return of the Native Executive," *New York Times,* May 17, 2000, p. C1.

30. Tung, "Career Issues in International Assignments," p. 243.

31. Ibid.

Case III

Ellen Moore (A): Living and Working in Korea

Ellen Moore, a Systems Consulting Group (SCG) consultant, was increasingly concerned as she heard Andrew's voice grow louder through the paper-thin walls of the office next to her. Andrew Kilpatrick, the senior consultant on a joint North American and Korean consulting project for a government agency in Seoul, South Korea, was meeting with Mr. Song, the senior Korean project director, to discuss several issues including the abilities of the Korean consultants. After four months on this Korean project, Ellen's evaluation of the assigned consultants suggested that they did not have the experience, background, or knowledge to complete the project within the allocated time. Additional resources would be required:

> I remember thinking, "I can't believe they are shouting at each other." I was trying to understand how their meeting had reached such a state. Andrew raised his voice and I could hear him saying, "I don't think you understand at all." Then, he shouted, "Ellen is not the problem!

WSI IN KOREA

In 1990, Joint Venture Inc. (JVI) was formed as a joint venture between a Korean company, Korean Conglomerate Inc. (KCI), and a North American company, Western Systems Inc. (WSI) (Exhibit 1). WSI, a significant information technology company with offices world wide employing over 50,000 employees, included the Systems Consulting Group (SCG). KCI, one of the largest Korean *chaebols* (industrial groups), consisted of over 40 companies, with sales in excess of US$3.5 billion. The joint venture, in its eighth year, was managed by two Regional Directors—Mr. Cho, a Korean from KCI, and Robert Brown, an American from WSI.

The team working on Ellen's project was led by Mr. Park and consisted of approximately 40 Korean consultants further divided into teams working on different areas of the project. The Systems Implementation (SI) team consisted of five Korean consultants, one translator, and three North American SCG consultants: Andrew Kilpatrick, Ellen Moore, and Scott Adams (see Exhibit 2).

This consulting project was estimated to be one of the largest undertaken in South Korea to date. Implementation of the recommended systems into over 100 local offices was expected to take seven to ten years. The SCG consultants would be involved for the first seven months, to assist the Korean consultants with the system design and in creating recommendations for system implementation, an area in which the Korean consultants admitted they had limited expertise.

Andrew Kilpatrick became involved because of his experience with a similar systems implementation project in North America. Andrew had been a management consultant for nearly 13 years. He had a broad and successful background in organizational development, information technology, and productivity improvement, and he was an early and successful practitioner of business process reengineering. Although Andrew had little international consulting experience, he was adept at change management and was viewed by both peers and clients as a flexible and effective consultant.

The degree of SCG's involvement had not been anticipated. Initially, Andrew had been asked by SCG's parent company, WSI, to assist JVI with the proposal development. Andrew and his SCG man-

Richard Ivey School of Business
The University of Western Ontario

Chantell Nicholls and Gail Ellement prepared this case under the supervision of Professor Harry Lane solely to provide material for class discussion. The authors do not intend to illustrate either effective or ineffective handling of a managerial situation. The authors may have disguised certain names and other identifying information to protect confidentiality. Ivey Management Services prohibits any form of reproduction, storage or transmittal without its written permission. This material is not covered under authorization from CanCopy or any reproduction rights organization. To order copies or request permission to reproduce materials, contact Ivey Publishing, Ivey Management Services c/o Richard Ivey School of Business, The University of Western Ontario, London, Ontario, Canada, N6A 3K7; phone (519) 661-3208; fax (519) 661-3882; e-mail cases@ivey.uwo.ca.

Copyright © 1997, Ivey Management Services. Version: (A) 2000-01-10. One time permission to reproduce granted by Ivey Management Services on February 2, 2004.

EXHIBIT 1   **Organizational Structure—Functional View**

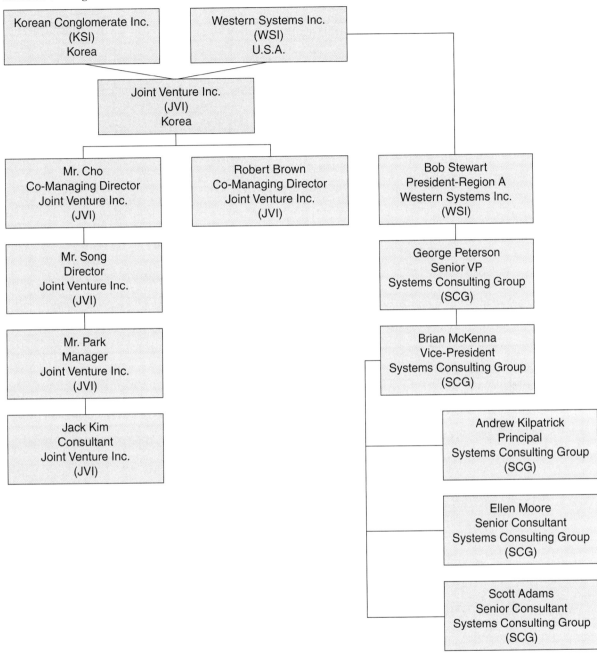

agers viewed his assistance as a favor to WSI since SCG did not have plans to develop business in Korea. Andrew's work on the proposal in North America led to a request for his involvement in Korea to gather additional information for the proposal:

When I arrived in Korea, I requested interviews with members of the prospective client's management team to obtain more information about their business environment. The Korean team at JVI was very reluctant to set up these meetings. However, I generally meet with client management prior to preparing a proposal. I also knew it would be difficult to obtain a good understanding of their business environment from a translated document. The material provided

EXHIBIT 2 **Organizational Structure—SI Project Team**

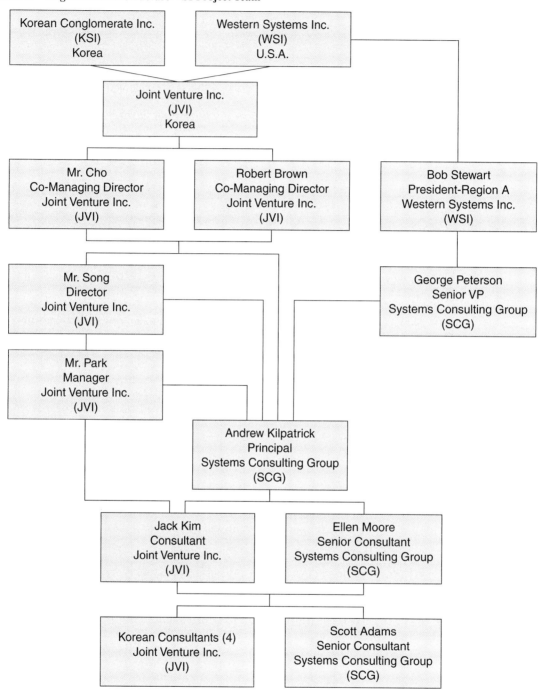

to me had been translated into English and was difficult to understand. The Korean and English languages are so different that conveying abstract concepts is very difficult.

I convinced the Koreans at JVI that these meetings would help demonstrate our expertise. The meetings did not turn out exactly as planned. We met with the same management team at three different locations where we asked the same set of questions three times and got the same answers three times. We did not obtain the information normally provided at these fact-gathering meetings. However, they were tremendously impressed by our line of questioning because it reflected a deep interest and understanding of their business. They also were very impressed with my background. As a result, we were successful in convincing the government agency that we had a deep understanding of the nature and complexity of the agency's work and strong capabilities in systems development and implementation—key cornerstones of their project. The client wanted us to handle the project and wanted me to lead it.

JVI had not expected to get the contract, because its competitor for this work was a long-time supplier to the client. As a result, winning the government contract had important competitive and strategic implications for JVI. Essentially, JVI had dislodged an incumbent supplier to the client, one who had lobbied very heavily for this prominent contract. By winning the bid, JVI became the largest system implementer in Korea and received tremendous coverage in the public press.

The project was to begin in June 1995. However, the Korean project team convened in early May in order to prepare the team members. Although JVI requested Andrew to join the project on a full-time basis, he already had significant commitments to projects in North America. There was a great deal of discussion back and forth between WSI in North America, and JVI and the client in Korea. Eventually it was agreed that Andrew would manage the SI work on a part-time basis from North America, and he would send a qualified project management representative on a full-time basis. That person was Ellen Moore.

At that time, Andrew received immediate feedback from the American consultants with WSI in Korea that it would be impossible to send a woman to work in Korea. Andrew insisted that the Korean consultants be asked if they would accept a woman in the position. They responded that a woman would be acceptable if she were qualified. Andrew also requested that the client be consulted on this issue. He was again told that a woman would be acceptable if she were qualified. Andrew knew that Ellen had the skills required to manage the project:

> I chose Ellen because I was very impressed with her capability, creativity, and project management skills, and I knew she had worked successfully in Bahrain, a culture where one would have to be attuned to very different cultural rules from those prevalent in North America. Ellen lacked experience with government agencies, but I felt that I could provide the required expertise in this area.

ELLEN MOORE

After graduating as the top female student from her high school, Ellen worked in the banking industry, achieving the position of corporate accounts officer responsible for over 20 major accounts and earning a Fellowship in the Institute of Bankers. Ellen went on to work for a former corporate client in banking and insurance, where she became the first female and youngest person to manage their financial reporting department. During this time, Ellen took university courses towards a Bachelor Degree at night. In 1983, she decided to stop working for two years, and completed her degree on a full-time basis. She graduated with a major in accounting and minors in marketing and management and decided to continue her studies for an MBA.

Two years later, armed with an MBA from a leading business school, Ellen Moore joined her husband in Manama, Bahrain, where she accepted a position as an expatriate manager for a large American financial institution.[1] Starting as a Special Projects Coordinator, within one year Ellen was

---

[1]For an account of Ellen's experience in Bahrain, see Ellen Moore (A): Living and Working in Bahrain, 9A90C019, and Ellen Moore (B), 9A90C020; Ivey Publishing, Ivey Management Services, c/o Richard Ivey School of Business, University of Western Ontario, London, Ontario, Canada, N6A 3K7.

promoted to Manager of Business Planning and Development, a challenging position that she was able to design herself. In this role, she managed the Quality Assurance department, coordinated a product launch, developed a senior management information system, and participated actively in all senior management decisions. Ellen's position required her to interact daily with managers and staff from a wide range of cultures, including Arab nationals.

In March 1995, Ellen joined WSI working for SCG. After the highly successful completion of two projects with SCG in North America, Ellen was approached for the Korea project:

> I had never worked in Korea or East Asia before. My only experience in Asia had been a one-week trip to Hong Kong for job interviews. I had limited knowledge of Korea and received no formal training from my company. I was provided a 20-page document on Korea. However, the information was quite basic and not entirely accurate.

After arriving in Korea, Ellen immediately began to familiarize herself with the language and proper business etiquette. She found that English was rarely spoken other than in some hotels and restaurants which catered to Western clientele. As a result, Ellen took advantage of every opportunity to teach herself the language basics:

> When Andrew and I were in the car on the way back to our hotel in the evening, we would be stuck in traffic for hours. I would use the time to learn how to read the Korean store signs. I had copied the Hangul symbols which form the Korean language onto a small piece of paper, and I kept this with me at all times. So, while sitting back in the car, exhausted at the end of each day, I would go over the symbols and read the signs.

The third SCG consultant on the project, Scott Adams, arrived as planned three months after Ellen's start date. Upon graduation, Scott had begun his consulting career working on several international engagements (including Mexico, Puerto Rico, and Venezuela), and he enjoyed the challenges of working with different cultures. He felt that with international consulting projects the technical aspects of consulting came easy. What he really enjoyed was the challenge of communicating in a different language and determining how to modify Western management techniques to fit into the local business culture. Scott first met Ellen at a systems consulting seminar, unaware at the time that their paths would cross again. A few months later, he was asked to consider the Korea assignment. Scott had never traveled or worked in Asia, but he believed that the assignment would present a challenging opportunity which would advance his career.

Scott was scheduled to start work on the project in August 1995. Prior to arriving in Seoul, Scott prepared himself by frequently discussing the work being conducted with Ellen. Ellen also provided him with information on the culture and business etiquette aspects of the work:

> It was very fortunate for me that Ellen had arrived first in Korea. Ellen tried to learn as much as she could about the Korean language, the culture, mannerisms, and the business etiquette. She was able to interpret many of the subtleties and to prepare me for both business and social situations, right down to how to exchange a business card appropriately with a Korean, how to read behavior, and what to wear.

ABOUT KOREA[2]

Korea is a 600-mile-long peninsula stretching southward into the waters of the western Pacific, away from Manchuria and Siberia to the north on the Asian mainland. Facing eastward across the Sea of Japan, known to Koreans as the East Sea, Korea lies 120 miles from Japan. The Republic of Korea, or South Korea, consists of approximately 38,000 square miles, comparable in size to Virginia or Portugal. According to the 1990 census, the South Korean population is about 43 million, with almost 10 million residing in the capital city, Seoul.

Korea has an ancient heritage spanning 5,000 years. The most recent great historical era, the Yi Dynasty or Choson Dynasty, enlisted tremendous changes in which progress in science, technology,

[2]Some of the information in the "About Korea" and "Women in Korea" sections was obtained from *Fodor's Korea*, 1993, Fodor's Travel Publications, Inc.: NY; and Chris Taylor, *Seoul—city guide*, 1993, Lonely Planet Publications: Colorcraft Ltd., Hong Kong.

and the arts were achieved. Although Confucianism had been influential for centuries in Korea, it was during this time that Confucian principles permeated the culture as a code of morals and as a guide for ethical behavior. Confucian thought was designated as the state religion in 1392 and came to underpin education, civil administration, and daily conduct. During this time, Korean rulers began to avoid foreign contact and the monarchy was referred to as the "Hermit Kingdom" by outsiders. Lasting over 500 years and including 27 rulers, the Yi Dynasty came to a close at the end of the 19th century. Today, in Korea's modern era, the nation is quickly modernizing and traditional Confucian values mix with Western lifestyle habits and business methods.

Although many Korean people, particularly in Seoul, have become quite Westernized, they often follow traditional customs. Confucianism dictates strict rules of social behavior and etiquette. The basic values of the Confucian culture are: (1) complete loyalty to a hierarchical structure of authority, whether based in the family, the company, or the nation; (2) duty to parents, expressed through loyalty, love, and gratitude; and (3) strict rules of conduct, involving complete obedience and respectful behavior within superiors–subordinate relationships, such as parents–children, old–young, male–female, and teacher–student. These values affect both social and work environments substantially.

MANAGING IN KOREA

Business etiquette in Korea was extremely important. Ellen found that everyday activities, such as exchanging business cards or replenishing a colleague's drink at dinner, involved formal rituals. For example, Ellen learned it was important to provide and to receive business cards in an appropriate manner, which included carefully examining a business card when received and commenting on it. If one just accepted the card without reading it, this behavior would be considered very rude. In addition, Ellen also found it important to know how to address a Korean by name. If a Korean's name was Y. H. Kim, non-Koreans would generally address him as either Y. H. or as Mr. Kim. Koreans would likely call him by his full name or by his title and name, such as Manager Kim. A limited number of Koreans, generally those who had lived overseas, took on Western names, such as Jack Kim.

WORK TEAMS

Teams were an integral part of the work environment in Korea. Ellen noted that the Korean consultants organized some special team building activities to bring together the Korean and North American team members:

> On one occasion, the Korean consulting team invited the Western consultants to a baseball game on a Saturday afternoon followed by a trip to the Olympic Park for a tour after the game, and dinner at a Korean restaurant that evening. An event of this nature is unusual and was very special. On another occasion, the Korean consultants gave up a day off with their families and spent it with the Western consultants. We toured a Korean palace and the palace grounds, and we were then invited to Park's home for dinner. It was very unusual that we, as Western folks, were invited to his home, and it was a very gracious event.

Ellen also found team-building activities took place on a regular basis, and that these events were normally conducted outside of the work environment. For example, lunch with the team was an important daily team event which everyone was expected to attend:

> You just couldn't work at your desk every day for lunch. It was important for everyone to attend lunch together in order to share in this social activity, as one of the means for team bonding.

Additionally, the male team members would go out together for food, drink, and song after work. Scott found these drinking activities to be an important part of his interaction with both the team and the client:

> Unless you had a medical reason, you would be expected to drink with the team members, sometimes to excess. A popular drink, soju, which is similar to vodka, would be poured into a small glass. Our glasses were never empty, as someone would always ensure that an empty glass was quickly filled. For example, if my glass was empty, I learned that I should pass it to

the person on my right and fill it for him as a gesture of friendship. He would quickly drink the contents of the glass, pass the glass back to me, and fill it for me to quickly drink. You simply had to do it. I recall one night when I really did not want to drink as I had a headache. We were sitting at dinner, and Mr. Song handed me his glass and filled it. I said to him "I really can't drink tonight. I have a terrible headache." He looked at me and said "Mr. Scott, I have Aspirin in my briefcase." I had about three or four small drinks that night.

Ellen found she was included in many of the team-building dinners, and soon after she arrived in Seoul, she was invited to a team dinner, which included client team members. Ellen was informed that although women were not normally invited to these social events, an exception was made since she was a senior team member.

During the dinner, there were many toasts and drinking challenges. During one such challenge, the senior client representative prepared a drink that consisted of one highball glass filled with beer and one shot glass filled to the top with whiskey. He dropped the whiskey glass into the beer glass and passed the drink to the man on his left. This team member quickly drank the cocktail in one swoop, and held the glass over his head, clicking the glasses to show both were empty. Everyone cheered and applauded. This man then mixed the same drink, and passed the glass to the man on his left, who also drank the cocktail in one swallow. It was clear this challenge was going around the table and would eventually get to me.

I don't generally drink beer and never drink whiskey. But it was clear, even without my translator present to assist my understanding, that this activity was an integral part of the team building for the project. As the man on my right mixed the drink for me, he whispered that he would help me. He poured the beer to the halfway point in the highball glass, filled the shot glass to the top with whiskey, and dropped the shotglass in the beer. Unfortunately, I could see that the beer didn't cover the top of the shot glass, which would likely move too quickly if not covered. I announced "One moment, please, we are having technical difficulties." And to the amazement of all in attendance, I asked the man on my right to pour more beer in the glass. When I drank the concoction in one swallow, everyone cheered, and the senior client representative stood up and shouted, "You are now Korean. You are now Korean."

The norms for team management were also considerably different from the North American style of management. Ellen was quite surprised to find that the concept of saving face did not mean avoiding negative feedback or sharing failures:

It is important in Korea to ensure that team members do not lose face. However, when leading a team, it appeared just as important for a manager to demonstrate leadership. If a team member provided work that did not meet the stated requirements, a leader was expected to express disappointment in the individual's efforts in front of all team members. A strong leader was considered to be someone who engaged in this type of public demonstration when required.

In North America, a team leader often compliments and rewards team members for work done well. In Korea, leaders expressed disappointment in substandard work, or said nothing for work completed in a satisfactory manner. A leader was considered weak if he or she continuously provided compliments for work completed as required.

HIERARCHY

The Koreans' respect for position and status was another element of the Korean culture that both Ellen and Scott found to have a significant influence over how the project was structured and how people behaved. The emphasis placed on hierarchy had an important impact upon the relationship between consultant and client that was quite different from their experience in North America. As a result, the North Americans' understanding of the role of a consultant differed vastly from their Korean counterparts.

Specifically, the North American consultants were familiar with "managing client expectations." This activity involved informing the client of the best means to achieve their goals and included frequent communication with the client. Generally, the client's customer was also interviewed in order to understand how the client's system could better integrate with their customer's requirements. Ellen recalled, however, that the procedures were necessarily different in Korea:

> The client team members did not permit our team members to go to their offices unannounced. We had to book appointments ahead of time to obtain permission to see them. In part, this situation was a result of the formalities we needed to observe due to their rank in society, but I believe it was also because they wanted to be prepared for the topics we wanted to discuss.

The Korean consultants refused to interview the customers, because they did not want to disturb them. Furthermore, the client team members frequently came into the project office and asked the Korean consultants to work on activities not scheduled for that week or which were beyond the project scope. The Korean consultants accepted the work without question. Ellen and Scott found themselves powerless to stop this activity.

Shortly after arriving, Scott had a very confrontational meeting with one of the Korean consultants concerning this issue:

> I had been in Korea for about a week, and I was still suffering from jet lag. I was alone with one of the Korean consultants, and we were talking about how organizational processes should be flowcharted. He was saying the client understands the process in a particular manner, so we should show it in that way. I responded that, from a technical standpoint, it was not correct. I explained that as a consultant, we couldn't simply do what the client requests if it is incorrect. We must provide value by showing why a different method may be taken by educating the client of the options and the reasons for selecting a specific method. There are times when you have to tell the client something different than he believes. That's what we're paid for. He said, "No, no, you don't understand. They're paying our fee." At that point I raised my voice: "You don't know what you are talking about. I have much more experience than you." Afterwards, I realized that it was wrong to shout at him. I pulled him aside and apologized. He said, "Well, I know you were tired." I replied that it was no excuse, and I should not have shouted. After that, we managed to get along just fine.

The behavior of subordinates and superiors also reflected the Koreans' respect for status and position. Scott observed that it was very unusual for a subordinate to leave the office for the day unless his superior had already left:

> I remember one day, a Saturday, when one of the young Korean consultants who had been ill for some time, was still at his desk. I made a comment: "Why don't you go home, Mr. Choi?" Although he was not working for me, I knew his work on the other team was done. He said, "I can't go home because several other team members have taken the day off. I have to stay." I repeated my observation that his work was done. He replied: "If I do not stay, I will be fired. My boss is still here, I have to stay." He would stay and work until his boss left, until late in the evening if necessary.

Furthermore, Scott found that the Korean consultants tended not to ask questions. Even when Scott asked the Korean consultants if they understood his instructions or explanation, they generally responded affirmatively which made it difficult to confirm their understanding. He was advised that responding in a positive manner demonstrated respect for teachers or superiors. Asking a question would be viewed as inferring that the teacher or superior had not done a good job of explaining the material. As a result, achieving a coaching role was difficult for the North American consultants even though passing on their knowledge of SI to the Korean consultants was considered an important part of their function on this project.

WOMEN IN KOREA

Historically, Confucian values have dictated a strict code of behavior between men and women and husband and wife in Korea. Traditionally, there has been a clear delineation in the respective responsibilities of men and women. The male preserve can be defined as that which is public, whereas women are expected to cater to the private, personal world of the home. These values have lingered into the 1990s, with Korean public life very much dominated by men.

Nevertheless, compared to the Yi dynasty era, the position of women in society has changed considerably. There is now virtual equality in access to education for men and women, and a few women have embarked on political careers. As in many other areas of the world, the business world has until recently been accessible only to men. However, this is changing as Korean women are beginning to seek equality in the workplace. Young Korean men and women now often participate together in social activities such as evenings out and hikes, something that was extremely rare even 10 years ago.

Dual income families are becoming more common in South Korea, particularly in Seoul, although women generally hold lower-paid, more menial positions. Furthermore, working women often retain their traditional household responsibilities, while men are expected to join their male colleagues for late night drinking and eating events which exclude women. When guests visit a Korean home, the men traditionally sit and eat together separately from the women, who are expected to eat together while preparing the food.

Although the younger generation are breaking from such traditions, Scott felt that the gender differences were quite apparent in the work place. He commented:

> The business population was primarily male. Generally, the only women we saw were young women who were clerks, wearing uniforms. I suspected that these women were in the workforce for only a few years, until they were married and left to have a family. We did have a few professional Korean women working with us. However, because we are a professional services firm, I believe it may have been more progressive than the typical Korean company.

THE SYSTEMS IMPLEMENTATION TEAM

Upon her arrival in Korea, Ellen dove into her work confident that the Korean consultants she would be working with had the skills necessary to complete the job in the time frame allocated. The project work was divided up among several work groups, each having distinct deliverables and due dates. The deliverables for the SI team were required as a major input to the other work groups on the project (see Exhibit 3). As a result, delays with deliverables would impact the effectiveness of the entire project:

> JVI told us they had assigned experienced management consultants to work on the project. Given their stated skill level, Andrew's resource plan had him making periodic visits to Korea; I would be on the project on a full time basis starting in May, and Scott would join the team about three to four months after the project start. We were informed that five Korean consultants were assigned. We believed that we had the resources needed to complete the project by December.

JACK KIM

J. T. Kim, whose Western name was Jack, was the lead Korean consultant reporting to Mr. Park. Jack had recently achieved a Ph.D. in computer systems from a reputable American university and he spoke English fluently. When Andrew initially discussed the organizational structure of the SI team with Mr. Park and Jack, it was agreed that Jack and Ellen would be co-managers of the SI project.

Three weeks after her arrival, Jack informed Ellen, much to her surprise, that he had never worked on a systems implementation project. Additionally, Ellen soon learned that Jack had never worked on a consulting project:

> Apparently, Jack had been made the lead consultant of SI upon completing his Ph.D. in the United States. I believe Jack was told he was going to be the sole project manager for SI on a daily basis. However, I was informed I was going to be the co-project manager with Jack. It was confusing, particularly for Jack, when I took on coaching and leading the team. We had a lot of controversy—not in the form of fights or heated discussions, but we had definite issues during the first few weeks because we were clearly stepping upon each other's territory.

Given Jack's position as the lead Korean consultant, it was quite difficult for Ellen to redirect team members' activities. The Korean team members always followed Jack's instructions. Scott recalled:

EXHIBIT 3

Project Time Frame

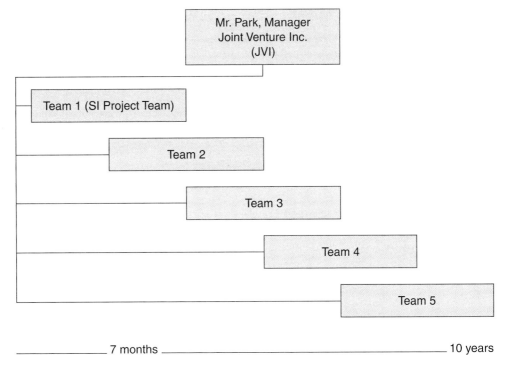

There were frequent meetings with the team to discuss the work to be completed. Often, following these meetings the Korean consultants would meet alone with Jack, and it appeared that he would instruct them to carry out different work. On one occasion, when both Andrew and Ellen were traveling away from the office, Andrew prepared specific instructions for the team to follow outlined in a memo.

Andrew sent the memo to me so I could hand the memo to Jack directly, thereby ensuring he did receive these instructions. Upon his return, Andrew found the team had not followed his instructions. We were provided with the following line of reasoning: you told us to do A, B and C, but you did not mention D. And, we did D. They had followed Jack's instructions. We had a very difficult time convincing them to carry out work as we requested, even though we had been brought onto the project to provide our expertise.

In July, a trip was planned for the Korean client team and some of the Korean consulting team to visit other project sites in North America. The trip would permit the Koreans to find out more about the capabilities of WSI and to discuss issues with other clients involved with similar projects. Jack was sent on the trip, leaving Ellen in charge of the SI project team in Korea. While Jack was away on the North American trip, Ellen had her first opportunity to work with and to lead the Korean consultants on a daily basis. She was very pleased that she was able to coach them directly, without interference, and advise them on how to best carry out the required work. Ellen felt that everyone worked together in a very positive manner, in complete alignment. When Jack returned, he saw that Ellen was leading the team and that they were accepting Ellen's directions. Ellen recalled the tensions that arose as a result:

On the first day he returned, Jack instructed someone to do some work for him, and the person responded, "I cannot because I am doing something for Ellen." Jack did not say anything, but he looked very angry. He could not understand why anyone on the team would refuse his orders.

506 Section Three *Managing People and Processes across Borders and Cultures*

THE MARKETING RESEARCH PROJECT

A few days after Jack returned from the North American trip, the project team realized they did not have sufficient information about their client's customer. Jack decided a market research study should be conducted to determine the market requirements. However, this type of study, which is generally a large undertaking on a project, was not within the scope of the contracted work. Ellen found out about the proposed market research project at a meeting held on a Saturday, which involved everyone from the entire project—about 40 people. The only person not at the meeting was Mr. Park. Jack was presenting the current work plans for SI, and he continued to describe a market research study:

> I thought to myself, "What market research study is he talking about?" I asked him to put aside his presentation of the proposed study until he and I had an opportunity to discuss the plans. I did not want to interrupt his presentation or disagree with him publicly, but I felt I had no choice.

DINNER WITH JACK

Two hours following the presentation, Ellen's translator, Susan Lim, informed her that there was a dinner planned for that evening and Jack wanted everyone on the SI team to attend. Ellen was surprised that Jack would want her present at the dinner. However, Susan insisted that Jack specifically said Ellen must be there. They went to a small Korean restaurant, where everyone talked about a variety of subjects in English and Korean, with Susan translating for Ellen as needed. After about one hour, Jack began a speech to the team, speaking solely in Korean. Ellen thought it was unusual for him to speak Korean when she was present, as everyone at the dinner also spoke English:

> Through the limited translations I received, I understood he was humbling himself to the team, saying, "I am very disappointed in my performance. I have clearly not been the project leader needed for this team." The team members were responding "No, no, don't say that." While Jack was talking to the team, he was consuming large quantities of beer. The pitchers were coming and coming. He was quite clearly becoming intoxicated. All at once, Susan stopped translating. I asked her what was wrong. She whispered that she would tell me later. Five minutes went by and I turned to her and spoke emphatically, "Susan, what is going on? I want to know now." She realized I was getting angry. She told me, "Jack asked me to stop translating. Please don't say anything, I will lose my job."
>
> I waited a couple of minutes before speaking, then I interrupted Jack's speech. I said, "Susan is having difficulty hearing you and isn't able to translate for me. I guess it is too noisy in this restaurant. Would it be possible for you to speak in English?" Jack did not say anything for about 30 seconds and then he started speaking in English. His first words were, "Ellen, I would like to apologize. I didn't realize you couldn't understand what I was saying."

Another thirty minutes of his speech and drinking continued. The Korean team members appeared to be consoling Jack, by saying: "Jack, we do respect you and the work you have done for our team. You have done your best." While they were talking, Jack leaned back, and appeared to pass out. Ellen turned to Susan and asked if they should help him to a taxi. Susan insisted it would not be appropriate. During the next hour, Jack appeared to be passed out or sleeping. Finally, one of the team members left to go home. Ellen asked Susan, "Is it important for me to stay, or is it important for me to go?" She said Ellen should go.

When Ellen returned to her hotel, it was approximately 11 P.M. on Saturday night. She felt the situation had reached a point where it was necessary to request assistance from senior management in North America. Andrew was on a wilderness camping vacation in the United States with his family, and could not be reached. Ellen decided to call the North American project sponsor, the Senior Vice President, George Peterson:

> I called George that Saturday night at his house and said: "We have a problem. They're trying to change the scope of the project. We don't have the available time, and we don't have the resources. It is impossible to do a market research study in conjunction with all the contracted

work to be completed with the same limited resources. The proposed plan is to use our project team to handle this additional work. Our team is already falling behind the schedule, but due to their inexperience they don't realize it yet." George said he would find Andrew and send him to Korea to further assess the situation.

THE MEETING WITH THE DIRECTOR

When Andrew arrived in August, he conducted a very quick assessment of the situation. The project was a month behind schedule. It appeared to Andrew that the SI team had made limited progress since his previous visit:

> It was clear to me that the Korean team members weren't taking direction from Ellen. Ellen was a seasoned consultant and knew what to do. However, Jack was giving direction to the team which was leading them down different paths. Jack was requesting that the team work on tasks which were not required for the project deliverables, and he was not appropriately managing the client's expectations.

Andrew held several discussions with Mr. Park concerning these issues. Mr. Park insisted the problem was Ellen. He argued that Ellen was not effective, she did not assign work properly, and she did not give credible instructions to the team. However, Andrew believed the Korean consultants' lack of experience was the main problem.

> Initially, we were told the Korean team consisted of experienced consultants, although they had not completed any SI projects. I felt we could work around it. I had previously taught consultants to do SI. We were also told that one of the Korean consultants had taught SI. This consultant was actually the most junior person on the team. She had researched SI by reading some texts and had given a presentation on her understanding of SI to a group of consultants.

Meanwhile, Andrew solicited advice from the WSI Co-Managing Director, Robert Brown, who had over ten years experience working in Korea. Robert suggested that Andrew approach Mr. Park's superior, Mr. Song, directly. He further directed Andrew to present his case to the Joint Venture committee if an agreement was not reached with Mr. Song. Andrew had discussed the issues with George Peterson and Robert Brown, and they agreed that there was no reason for Ellen to leave the project:

> However, Robert's message to me was that I had been too compliant with the Koreans. It was very important for the project to be completed on time, and that I would be the one held accountable for any delays. Addressing issues before the Joint Venture committee was the accepted dispute resolution process at JVI when an internal conflict could not be resolved. However, in most cases, the last thing a manager wants is to be defending his position before the Joint Venture committee. Mr. Song was in line to move into senior executive management. Taking the problem to the Joint Venture committee would be a way to force the issue with him.

Andrew attempted to come to a resolution with Mr. Park once again, but he refused to compromise. Andrew then tried to contact Mr. Song and was told he was out of the office. Coincidentally, Mr. Song visited the project site to see Mr. Park just as Ellen and Andrew were completing a meeting. Ellen recalls Mr. Song's arrival:

> Mr. Song walked into the project office expecting to find Mr. Park. However, Mr. Park was out visiting another project that morning. Mr. Song looked around the project office for a senior manager, and he saw Andrew. Mr. Song approached Andrew and asked if Mr. Park was in the office. Andrew responded that he was not. Mr. Song proceeded to comment that he understood there were some concerns about the project work, and suggested that perhaps, sometime, they could talk about it. Andrew replied that they needed to talk about it immediately.

Andrew met with Mr. Song in Mr. Park's office, a makeshift set of thin walls that enclosed a small office area in one corner of the large open project office. Ellen was working in an area just outside the office when she heard Andrew's voice rise. She heard him shout, "Well, I don't think you're listening to what I am saying." Ellen was surprised to hear Andrew shouting. She knew Andrew was very sensitive to what should and should not be done in the Korean environment:

> Andrew's behavior seemed so confrontational. I believed this behavior was unacceptable in Korea. For a while, I heard a lot of murmuring, after which I heard Andrew speak adamantly, "No, I'm very serious. It doesn't matter what has been agreed and what has not been agreed because most of our agreements were based on inaccurate information. We can start from scratch." Mr. Song insisted that I was the problem.

The Richard Ivey School of Business gratefully acknowledges the generous support of The Richard and Jean Ivey Fund in the development of this case as part of the Richard and Jean Ivey Fund Asian Case Series.

Ethical Dilemmas in International Management

CHAPTER SEVENTEEN

Ethics and Social Responsibility for International Firms

Chapter Learning Objectives

After completing this chapter, you should be able to:

- Explain moral philosophies of relevance to business ethics.
- Define business ethics and describe the relationships among host-country laws, ethics, and cultural relativism.
- Identify several international accords that address business ethics and ethical codes of conduct for international companies and list five prominent issues on which they provide guidance.
- Discuss the issues of bribery and corruption and their role in the international business arena.
- Explain how a company can effectively inculcate ethics and business conduct in its managers and employees.

Opening Case: Scandals and Corruption— A Historical Perspective

The accounting scandals involving Enron, Arthur Andersen, WorldCom, Qwest Communications, Tyco and other once highly regarded companies have caused a crisis of confidence among many Americans. Some ask whether the problems are so severe as to represent an irreparable fault in the economic system.

From an historical perspective, the answer is that economies are capable of recovering and making progress, even after near devastation—not only from war, as in the case of Germany and Japan after World War II, but also from economic chicanery, which is scarcely new. After bubbles collapse and interfere with economic growth, the resulting loss of income stimulates efforts to maintain and increase income, both honestly and in corrupt ways.

Starting in 1600 with the establishment of the British East India Company, followed by its Dutch counterpart two years later, Europeans learned how to extract great wealth from the Far East. Warren Hastings, the first governor-general of India, and Robert Clive, a civil servant with the East India Company who became known as "the conqueror of India," were perhaps the earliest private malefactors of great wealth. Hastings accumulated £200,000 in India and transferred it to England in the 18th century; in the same period Clive transferred £280,000.

Edmund Burke, the 18th-century statesman, argued that Clive ought to be removed. At the same time Lord North, who served as Britain's prime minister from 1770 to 1782, contended that Hastings's

£200,000 was not excessive. A few hundred lesser employees of the company also did well. On nominal salaries, clerks (known then as writers), cadets, assistant surgeons, ship captains and ship husbands, who handled charters, all found opportunities to acquire wealth.

Human nature has not changed. Andrew S. Fastow—who, while serving as Enron's chief financial officer, was also running partnerships, particularly LJM2 [private equity fund], set up by Enron to keep debt off the books—has been indicted on 78 counts of fraud, money laundering, conspiracy and obstruction of justice. The East India employees smuggled goods to Europe and dealt in opium with China. The role of ship commander was bought and sold, typically for £2,000 to £5,000, but sometimes for up to £10,000 and once for double that.

So egregious were their activities that British historians were not the only ones to single out Hastings and Clive. A German economic historian, Jacob van Klaveren, writing in the 1950's on the origins of corruption between the state and private business, asserted that corruption in business had begun with the East India Companies.

By the 19th century, business corruption was so much a fact of life that it became a prominent theme for European novelists. Among them were Honoré de Balzac in *The Human Comedy;* Charles Dickens, *Little Dorrit;* William Makepeace Thackeray, *The Newcomes;* Anthony Trollope, *The Way We Live Now;* Gustav Freytag, *Soll und Haben;* Alexandre Dumas, *Black Tulip;* and Emile Zola, *L'Argent.*

And like many European fashions, swindling found its place in America by the 19th century, where Mark Twain and Theodore Dreiser included it in the plots of their books, while Boston produced Charles Ponzi, a swindler so prominent that his name became synonymous with one type of chicanery. He borrowed money for 45 days at 50 percent interest and paid early investors with cash from later suckers whose money he kept.

The writers had abundant examples to inspire them, including Eugene Bontoux, founder and director of Union Générale, a French bank that collapsed in 1882, and in the United States, Daniel Drew, James Fisk Jr. and Jay Gould, who manipulated the stock of the Erie Railroad.

Financial scandals abounded on both sides of the Atlantic in the 20th century, as well. Among the perpetrators were the cabinet members involved in the Teapot Dome scandal during the administration of President Warren G. Harding; Ivar Kreuger, the Swedish Match King, who put together an empire of companies and became a private lender to governments before the empire collapsed, fraudulent accounting was exposed and he committed suicide in Paris in 1932; Robert L. Vesco, who looted Investors Overseas Services, the Swiss-based mutual fund empire founded by Bernard Cornfeld; Michele Sindona, the financier behind the Franklin National Bank in New York and Banca Ambrosia in Milan; and Nicholas Leeson, the rogue trader who brought down Barings Bank.

Two famous 18th-century swindlers—Sir John Blunt, chairman of the South Sea Trading Company, and John Law, a Scot, who persuaded the French government in 1716 to let him open a bank that could issue paper currency in Louisiana, which France owned—might be said to have a modern counterpart. Sir John's stock manipulation led to what became known as the South Sea bubble and produced the crash of the London stock exchange. Law's issuance of paper money, which was used to drive up shares that then plunged, became known as the Mississippi bubble.

Before the bubbles burst, each took vast earnings and invested in real estate. Sir John had six contracts to buy estates when the South Sea bubble burst in 1720; Law owned one-sixth of the Place Vendôme in Paris, plus a dozen estates in the French countryside, when the Banque Royale and the Compagnie d'Occident failed that same year.

Some figures in current scandals have also shown an eye for real estate. One of them is Kenneth L. Lay, the former chief executive of Enron. He acquired a multimillion-dollar penthouse in Houston, his home city, plus three large houses in Aspen, Colo., worth more than $5 million each, along with a building site valued at more than $1 million.

Investors have good reason to worry that next year may produce new disclosures of illegal insider trading, overstated profits and other dubious accounting practices. But the year could also bring new rules for corporate accounting, as the Securities and Exchange Commission, the new Public

Accounting Oversight Board, federal and state governments, the courts and securities exchanges take up the issues raised by the scandals. It is still too early to say whether they will succeed in overhauling the rules and restoring investor confidence.

Source: From Charles Kindleberger, "Corruption, Crime, Chicanery: Business Through the Ages," December 16, 2002. Copyright © 2002 The New York Times Co. Reprinted with permission.

Discussion Questions

1. As shown in this story, corruption and unethical behavior have been prevalent in history. Is it in human nature to be dishonest and corrupt? Can we legislate honesty and transparency in one's dealings with others?
2. Discuss the impacts of corrupt and unethical behavior on the well-being of society that is affected by it.
3. Is giving a holiday gift to your postman or local Police Athletic League any different from (a) bribing a customs officer to clear parcels through customs, (b) payoffs to a politician to secure a business deal?

Business Ethics and Corporate Social Responsibility Defined

Most people would agree that a set of moral principles or values should govern the actions of executives, and most executives would agree that their decisions should be made in accordance with accepted principles of right or wrong. **Ethics** has been defined as "inquiry into the nature and grounds of morality where the term morality is taken to mean moral judgments, standards and rules of conduct."[1] It is a system of principles, a guide to human behavior that helps to distinguish between good and bad, or between right and wrong. Business ethics "is the moral thinking and analysis by corporate decision-makers and other members regarding the motives and consequences of their decisions and actions."[2]

International managers are confronted with a variety of decisions that create ethical dilemmas for the decision makers. The following situations illustrate some real-life ethical dilemmas faced by companies.

Situation 1   Should a company continue to market in a foreign country, where it is legal, a product that is banned in the home country because it is harmful? Companies in industrialized countries are continuing to sell products in foreign countries that are illegal at home but legal abroad. For instance, several pesticides such as Velsicol, Phosvel, and 2,4-D (which contains dioxin) are being sold directly or indirectly in other countries even though they have been banned in the United States. A strong link has been found between the chemicals in the pesticides and cancer. The manufacturers of these pesticides argue that the benefits of using the pesticides to increase crop yields in poor countries with severe food shortages far outweigh the health risk associated with their use. The profit motive is also involved in this issue. For example, American Vanguard Corporation, which was banned from selling the pesticide DBCP directly to American companies, continues to export it to other nations. American Vanguard claimed that it would have gone bankrupt had it not sold the DBCP in other countries.[3]

Situation 2   Cigarette smoking has been generally accepted as harmful to human health in most advanced countries. Scientific studies have proven that cigarette smoke causes cancer and that it is associated with the onset of heart disease. Laws in the United States require that product labeling on cigarette packets warn customers of the harmful side-effects of smoking. Cigarette smoking has been banned in offices and restaurants in the State of New York. Almost all companies and government offices have a ban on smoking in the workplace. Still, smoking is big business in other countries, and especially in eastern Europe and Asia, where little has been done to make the public aware that smoking is harmful to health. Cigarette company giants like Philip Morris, RJR Nabisco, American Brands, and Rothmans International have targeted these world regions as the growth markets for cigarette sales to compensate for the mature home markets. The sales volume abroad of some companies like Philip Morris is larger than at home. The ethical issue here is whether tobacco companies should target young men and women in other countries as potential long-term customers of a product, when cigarette smoking is generally accepted to be addictive and harmful.

Situation 3   The search for enhanced efficiencies and lower costs has induced international companies to transfer labor-intensive operations to countries that offer cheap labor. Companies have also resorted to buying products made by contract manufacturers in foreign countries. International human rights groups have documented that in many cases the foreign contract manufacturers use child labor to make the goods. Chinese companies have used prison labor. The ethical question that arises in such cases is: Is it ethical for companies to sell products made by children or forced prison labor?

Situation 4   A foreign government official informs the vice president for marketing of a French aerospace company that the minister of defense will approve the purchase of aircraft from the aerospace company, worth several hundred million francs, if the selling price is hiked by 15 percent. He is also told to deposit the 15 percent increase in a numbered Swiss bank account. Failing to comply with this request, he is told, would cause the purchase order to be canceled and possibly given to a competing firm from another country. French law prohibits bribery in France but does not prohibit bribery of foreign officials abroad. If he refuses to give the bribe, the company would not get the order for the aircraft, and several hundred jobs at home would be lost. What should the vice president for marketing do?

The four situations presented above are illustrative of the innumerable ethical dilemmas faced by international managers almost daily. Unquestionably managers could use frameworks that could serve as benchmarks in identifying ethical problems and for arriving at ethically sound solutions. To that end, we must define corporate social responsibility and subsequently draw upon the field of philosophy to offer moral philosophies to better understand the basis of ethical dilemmas faced by managers.

Corporate social responsibility may be defined as the integration of business operations and values whereby the interests of all stakeholders, including customers, employees, investors, and the environment, are reflected in an organization's policies and actions. Consumers in many countries expect firms to meet high health and safety, worker, human rights, consumer protection, and environmental standards regardless of where their operations are located. Furthermore, investors and stakeholders are increasingly asking their suppliers to exhibit their respective corporate social responsibility programs.[4]

What are the drivers of corporate social responsibility? The following three specific motivations, as described by Maignan and Ralstan, have emerged:[5]

1. From a utilitarian perspective, corporate social responsibility is an instrument useful to help achieve a firm's performance objectives defined in terms of profitability, return on investment, or sales volume.

2. The **positive duty approach** suggests that businesses may be self-motivated to have a positive impact regardless of social pressures calling for social initiatives. When this

positive duty is prevalent, corporate social responsibility principles are a component of the firm's true identity, expressing values considered by organizational members as central, enduring, and distinctive values to the firm.[6]

3. From a **negative duty approach,** businesses are compelled to adopt social responsibility initiatives in order to conform to stakeholder norms defining appropriate behavior. When negative duty is prevalent, self-motivation is replaced by corporate social responsibility initiatives that are a reaction to what is expected from stakeholders.[7]

Moral Philosophies of Relevance to Business Ethics

A moral philosophy is "the set of principles or rules that people use to decide what is right or wrong."[8] Moral philosophies help explain why a person believes that a certain choice among alternatives is ethically right or wrong. Managers fall back on their personal principles, values, and belief systems to evaluate the "good" or "bad," and "right" or "wrong" aspects that are at the core of each alternative course of action available in decision making.

Managers and businesspersons are guided by moral philosophies when confronted with ethical and moral dilemmas as they formulate their strategies and action plans, but they do not all use the same moral philosophy. Some managers, for example, may view the producing of a product at the lowest cost to be of foremost importance and may therefore choose to locate the production plant in a country that offers the cheapest labor, even though the minimum health and safety standards that must be legally observed in production plants in that country would be considered below acceptable standards, and therefore illegal, in the home country. Other managers may believe that making profits at the expense of the health and safety of workers, although legal in the host country, is actually unethical and immoral and hence may decide to provide working conditions that are both healthy and safe for the workers, even at the expense of higher production costs and lower profits for the company. Some managers may believe that giving bribes to obtain business is unethical, whereas other managers may think that it is not wrong to obtain business through bribes to politicians if it helps preserve jobs in the company.

Several moral philosophies appear in the literature on the subject. Studying each one is beyond the scope of this book. Therefore, we limit our discussion to those that are most relevant to the study of business ethics. The four moral philosophies which have evolved during the twentieth century and which serve as the principal foundations for the field of normative ethics are teleology, deontology, theory of justice, and cultural relativism.[9]

Teleology

According to the moral philosophy called **teleology,** an action or behavior is acceptable or right if it is responsible for producing the desired outcomes, for example, a promotion at work, a bigger market share for a product or service, realization of self-interest, or utility. Teleological philosophies are often referred to as *consequentialism* by moral philosophers because of the emphasis placed by such philosophies on evaluating the morality of an action mainly by examining its consequences. The two key teleological precepts that serve as guides for managerial decision making are egoism and utilitarianism.

Egoism evaluates how right or acceptable a behavior is depending upon its consequences on the person. The egoists profess that self-interest should be the primary determinant of a person's behavior. Self-interest may be different for different individuals. It may mean the acquisition of wealth, fame, or power; a good family life; leisure; or prestige. When faced with the prospect of having to choose among a set of alternatives, an egoist will probably choose one that maximizes her personal self-interest. A more calculating form of egoism does indeed consider the interests of others if in so doing the egoist's own self-interests are advanced. For example, a manager may promote community development projects not because of some deep-seated altruistic motive, but because projects that benefit the community surrounding the company ultimately bring the manager personal prestige and elevate her standing within the company.

Utilitarianism, like egoism, holds that actions should be judged by their consequences; however, unlike egoists, utilitarians claim that behaviors that are moral produce the greatest good for the greatest number of people.[10] Utilitarians believe that a moral decision is one that creates the greatest total *utility*—that is, the greatest benefit for each and every person affected by a decision. A utilitarian would be inclined to make an analysis of the costs versus the benefits of each alternative course of action to those affected by the decision, and to choose the one alternative that results in the greatest utility.

Selecting a decision that not only considers the interests, but also maximizes the utility, of all individuals and groups that are affected by the decision can be very difficult and perhaps impossible. A utilitarian can take a shortcut and reduce the complexity of utilitarian decision making by simply obeying the rules of behavior prescribed by a preferred ideological system. Some utilitarian philosophers, called "rule utilitarians," have argued that general rules should be followed to decide which action is best.[11] They believe that certain principles or rules, when observed in ones's behavior, would result in the greatest utility. Decision making that is based on the foundation of rules or principles reduces the complexity of utilitarian decision making and erases the need to examine each particular situation. For example, some religious ideologies prescribe behavioral norms which, if followed, are supposed to improve the human condition; for example, the Holy Koran preaches that craving excess profit is immoral. Guided by this principle, a Moslem utilitarian businessperson will make business decisions that do not, in his eyes, exploit workers, suppliers, or customers.

There are those who believe that bribery is bad for everyone. They theorize that bribery distorts the efficient allocation of resources by market forces and therefore everyone suffers because of the misallocation of resources. For example, a company whose product is far superior to those of its competitors may not get the business if a government official is bribed to buy from someone else. In this instance, the taxpayers are the losers, as their taxes have been misused to buy an inferior product. A rule utilitarian would refuse to bribe an official, even if that meant the loss of workers' jobs, but would firmly stick to the rule: "No bribes!"

Other utilitarian philosophers, called "act utilitarians," profess that whether an individual action is right or wrong should be evaluated on the basis of its ability to create the greatest utility for the greatest number of people and that rules such as "bribery is bad" should serve only as guidelines in decision making. Act utilitarians would agree that bribery is wrong, not because bribery is inherently wrong, but because the total utility decreases when bribery places self-interest ahead of societal interests. Act utilitarians would argue that offering a bribe to obtain business would be quite acceptable if the alternative is to lose hundreds of jobs in the factory, which in turn would adversely affect the welfare of the surrounding community.

Deontology: The Theory of Rights

Deontology (from the Greek word *deontos,* which means binding, necessity) is "an ethical theory holding that acting from a sense of duty rather than concern for consequences is the basis for establishing our moral obligation."[12] Unlike utilitarians, deontologists would argue that certain acts or behaviors must never be permitted, even though they might maximize utility. The German philosopher Immanuel Kant (1724–1804) was the main proponent of deontology. He believed that "some acts are right, and some acts are wrong, quite independent of their consequences. He professed that it is irrelevant in determining our moral obligation whether an action makes us happy, or whether it contributes to human pleasure. We do that which is right because it is the right thing to do. No other consideration is relevant to our moral deliberation."[13]

Deontology also refers to "moral philosophies that focus on the rights of individuals and on the intentions associated with a particular behavior, rather than on its consequences."[14] Deontologists believe that "human beings have certain fundamental rights that should be respected in all decisions."[15] The following are the fundamental rights, several of which have been incorporated into the U.S. Bill of Rights, that deontologists say should never be violated:

- *The right of free consent:* Every human being in an organization has the right to be treated only as he or she freely consents to be treated.
- *The right to free speech:* Every person has the right to truthfully criticize the behavior and actions of others so long as the criticism does not violate the rights of other persons.
- *The right to privacy:* Individuals have the right to keep from public scrutiny information about their private lives which they are not legally obliged to make public.
- *The right to freedom of conscience:* No one should be forced to carry out any order or to engage in any act that violates his or her moral or religious norms.
- *The right to due process:* Every human being has the right to a fair and impartial hearing when he or she believes that his or her rights are being violated.

Basing decisions on deontological principles is much easier than basing them on the utilitarian theory. One need only "do the right thing" and not interfere with the rights of others who might be affected by one's decisions. Consider a product that a manager cannot sell in her home country because of its cancer-causing properties. It is, however, not illegal to sell it in a poor, developing country. The manager still might choose not to sell it because her conscience tells her that to do otherwise would be wrong.

The Theory of Justice

There are three fundamental guidelines that the **theory of justice** provides to managers in their decision making: be equitable, be fair, and be impartial. The behavioral prescriptions of the justice theory are captured in the following principles:

1. Do not treat individuals differently based on arbitrary characteristics. Those who are similar in relevant attributes should be treated similarly, and those who are different in the relevant attributes should be treated differently in proportion to the differences between them.
2. Attributes and positions of individuals that are the basis for differential treatment must be justifiably connected to the goals and tasks at hand.

3. Rules must be clearly stated and promulgated, administered fairly, and consistently and fairly enforced. Those who do not obey the rules because of ignorance, or those who are forced to break them under duress, should not be punished.

4. Do not hold individuals responsible for matters over which they have no control.[16]

Although not as difficult to apply as the utilitarian theory, justice theory demands that justifiable attributes be determined upon which differential treatment of people may be based. Furthermore, this theory also requires the determination of facts to ensure the fair administration of rules as well as individuals' accountability.

Cultural Relativism

Cultural relativism asserts that "words such as 'right,' 'wrong,' 'justice,' and 'injustice,' derive their meaning and value from the attitudes of a given culture."[17] Thus, to the cultural relativist, ethical standards are culture-specific, and one should not be surprised to find that an act that is considered ethical in one culture might be looked upon with disdain in another. For instance, the Koran forbids usury because it is considered unethical and immoral, and therefore Muslims must refrain from collecting interest on loans. Usury is therefore illegal in Saudi Arabia and in countries that have Islamic banking (discussed in Chapter 4). Christians and Jews do not share this belief. Relativists would argue that businesspersons in fundamentalist Islamic countries like Saudi Arabia and Iran ought to conform to the ethical and moral norms of those cultures when conducting business in those countries. Any other strategy might prove disastrous.

The Hindu religion considers the consumption of beef to be both unethical and immoral, but not illegal. To succeed in India companies in the food industry must respect this precept and not mix beef with nonbeef ingredients and attempt to pass off the products as nonbeef—even if they have foolproof ways to conceal the true identity of the ingredients. McDonald's in India does not sell any dishes that contain meat of any sort.

Figure 17.1 illustrates the effect of cultural relativism on the varying legal and ethical perceptions of six activities in the United States, China, and Saudi Arabia. For instance, where alcohol consumption, usury, and women drivers are legal, ethical, and commonplace in both China and the United States, these three activities are considered both legal and unethical in Saudi Arabia. Thus path A in the figure links the similar perspectives of these three activities between the United States and China. Path B, in contrast, links the diametrically opposing perspectives between the United States and Saudi Arabia.

As you can see, other activities are viewed differently in the three countries. For instance, child labor is ethically frowned on in the United States, which has many laws banning child labor. Thus there are ethically consistent home boycotts of U.S. companies that legally employ children overseas at low wages. In China and Saudi Arabia, child labor is more acceptable, both from the ethical and legal perspectives. Taking time to pray in the workplace setting is understood in Islamic cultures. However, even though many people in the United States believe that to pray is ethical, it still is illegal in the workplace under the U.S. Constitution. And under the current political regime in China, stopping work to pray is viewed as both unethical and illegal. Later in this chapter, we discuss the implications of bribery in different countries. Foreshadowing that discussion, Figure 17.1 illustrates that bribery, or facilitating payments, is also viewed differently between the United States and the other two countries depicted.

FIGURE 17.1 **Ethical and Legal Distinctions in International Management**

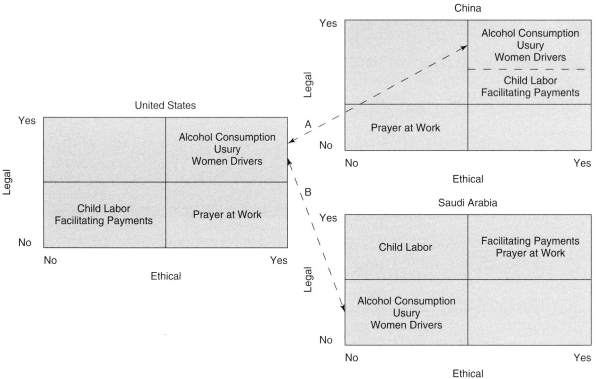

The motto of the cultural relativists might be summed up as: "When in Rome, do as the Romans do, ethically." Still, many firms that followed the laws of the host countries in which they, or a licensee of theirs, did business have had problems at home. For instance, many U.S. firms have been accused of promoting sweatshops in Asia and have subsequently faced a backlash of protests in America. Nike is one example of a firm whose licensees in Asia do not break any host-country laws by employing children workers for long weekly hours at low wages. Still, protestors argue that Nike and other firms in these positions should be doing more for the host society, regardless of laws. Thus, in this age of globalization, home-country ethics now cause firms to rethink host-country practices.

Philosophers urge us to resort to ethical reasoning to ensure that managers make moral decisions. Nevertheless, as interpolated from Figure 17.1, different philosophies of ethical reasoning may lead to different behaviors in similar circumstances. Moreover, because of cultural differences, what is considered "right" and "good" in one culture may be actually taken as "wrong" and "bad" in another culture. Therefore, managers in two different cultures, adhering to the same ethical philosophy, may choose behavioral patterns that are at the opposite ends of a spectrum. For example, managers in India and the United States may interpret differently the following principle:

Principle: *Attributes and positions of individuals that are the basis for differential treatment must be justifiably connected to the goals and tasks at hand.*

Indian manager: "I must hire persons who belong to my caste because it is the right thing to do. The cohesiveness and morale of the group is the key for the success of my company."

American manager: "I must hire the best person for the job regardless of her class, race, religion, or national origin."

In this illustration, both managers are right in their judgment. In India, persons from the same caste are generally, if not always, given preference in hiring, whereas such a practice would not only be considered ethically unacceptable but is illegal in America. What this means is that moral philosophies provide the *criteria* for making ethical decisions; however, it is the manager who must reach into his system of *values and beliefs* and make the judgment call as to what makes an action ethical or unethical. But as Clarence C. Walton points out, the potential problem with this reality is that one rationale may be used as a foil against another, thus permitting the decision maker to employ whichever best suits his or her purposes at the time.[18]

The Basic Moral Norms

Multinationals may claim that because their foreign affiliates are citizens of each of the countries in which they operate, the pattern of behavior reflecting "good citizenship" may vary from country to country. Richard T. De George, a noted authority in the field of international business ethics, challenges this view:

> There is an important difference between customs, mores, and law on the one hand and ethics on the other. Customs, mores, and law do vary from country to country, and a business that wishes to succeed must consider these differences and on the whole respect them. Yet despite the claims of some simplistic critics, basic morality does not vary from country to country, even though certain practices may be ethical in one country and not in another because of differing circumstances. Getting this subtle difference straight is the crux of the matter.[19]

De George identified basic **moral norms,** which apply to any business operating anywhere. Application of these norms is essential for the effective functioning of a society or for business transactions to occur. "They are widely held, and everyone is expected to live by them and up to them; they are obvious, commonsensical, and available to all. If they were arcane or difficult or available only to an intellectual elite, they could not serve as basic norms governing all human interaction."[20] The following six moral norms are universally applicable.[21]

1. *No arbitrary killing of other members of the community to which one belongs.* A society must guarantee the safety of others who visit it, or enter into alliances with it. Civil war that does not ensure safety of individuals would inhibit international trade and commerce. Criminal acts like kidnapping or killings of expatriate managers, as has happened in Russia and Colombia, would place a damper on international investments and trade.

2. *Telling the truth and not lying.* Interpersonal and interorganizational relationships are built on communications, that is, the transfer of knowledge and information between and among those involved in the transaction. Trust and faith between the communicators is built on the fundamental premise that the parties to the interaction are telling the truth. For a business firm this may mean truthfulness in advertising, business negotiations, or in any interactions in which there is a transfer of information from the firm to its stakeholders like the employees, customers, stockholders, suppliers, governmental agencies, and the public at large.

3. *Respecting others' property.* All societies have the concept of property, although rules governing ownership, sale, and use of property may differ from society to society. Seizure of private property without reason or just compensation to the property owner for property seized should be deplored. Instances of expropriation without just compensation of property owned by foreign companies under the guise of nationalization have occurred mostly in developing countries of Africa, Asia, and Latin America.

Such actions caused a severe fall in foreign investments in these countries, and the resultant loss of valuable technology transfer from abroad, jobs, and international trade.

4. *Honoring contracts and exercising fairness in transactions.* A signed contract should be honored with the utmost integrity. The nuances of the contract language should not disguise hidden traps for either side in the agreement.

5. *Exercising fairness in business dealings.* Business dealings should be fair to all sides. The *Merriam-Webster Dictionary* defines fairness as "marked by impartiality and honesty, free from self-interest, prejudice, or favoritism."

6. *Functioning in a fair market.* A fair market is one in which every person has an equal chance to succeed in a transaction. For example, equal access to relevant information must be available to all investors in the stock market. This means that some investors should not have privileged access to such information.

The noted ethicist Thomas Donaldson believes that both multinational and domestic corporations are bound to respect the following 10 rights.[22]

1. The right to freedom of physical movement.
2. The right to ownership of property.
3. The right to freedom from torture.
4. The right to a fair trial.
5. The right to nondiscriminatory treatment.
6. The right to physical security.
7. The right to freedom of speech and association.
8. The right to minimal education.
9. The right to political participation.
10. The right to subsistence.

All 10 rights should be the responsibility of peoples and governments in all societies regardless of their political ideology. Although the list may appear general and noncontroversial, it demands specific responsibilities and duties for corporations. The first four rights apply to societal obligations; the last six rights are directly aimed at the social responsibilities of companies worldwide. For example, the right to nondiscriminatory treatment requires that companies do not discriminate in their employment policies against women, certain racial groups, or religious groups. The right to physical security demands that companies provide safe working conditions to workers. The right to form workers' union is reflected in the right to freedom of speech and association. Employing children in sweatshops means that they are in the factory and not in school. Nike, the athletic shoes company, has the policy of not employing children. Nike provides schooling to children who are subsequently hired when they reach the age of 16 years. The right to participate in the political process and to support the political party of one's choosing is inherent in the right to political participation. The right to a minimum wage is reflected in the tenth right, the right to subsistence.

Incorporating Corporate Social Responsibility and Ethics into International Business Decisions

Of the moral philosophies discussed thus far, none can by itself take care of issues of concern in the other philosophies. Utilitarianism, for instance, seeks decisions that produce the greatest good for the greatest number of people; however, a decision that brings forth this outcome may very well result in the abridgement of the rights of some

FIGURE 17.2

A Decision Tree Incorporating Ethics in International Business Decision Making

Source: Adapted from Gerald F. Cavanagh, Dennis J. Moberg, and Manuel Velasquez, "The Ethics of Organizational Politics," *Academy of Management Review* 6, no. 3 (1981), p. 368.

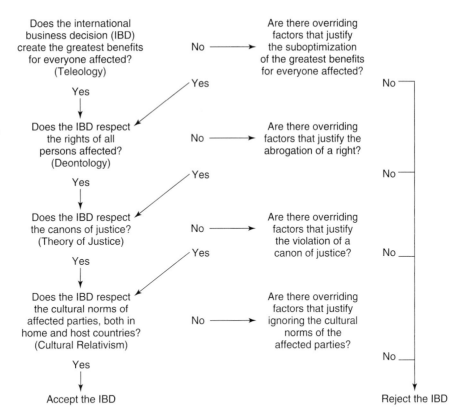

people. By the same token, a decision that respects the rights of all persons affected may at the same time prove to be ineffective in optimizing the benefits for the people involved. And decisions that may appear to be equitable, fair, and impartial in one culture may have the opposite appearance in another culture. Approaches in business ethics based on such classical theories as teleology, deontology, justice, and cultural relativism have come under criticism for being too abstract and general to provide adequate guidance to managers.[23]

One way to resolve such problems resulting from a focus on one particular philosophy is to combine all four philosophical approaches into one unifying eclectic decision-making framework. With this is mind, we have incorporated all four moral philosophies in a decision tree, presented in Figure 17.2. Practical Insight 17.1 illustrates an example of a firm in China that has prospered due to corporate social responsibility initiatives.

International Ethical Codes of Conduct for International Companies

The fact that cultural differences in various countries make it difficult to determine ethical conduct has not deterred countries and international organizations from promulgating codes of ethical conduct for international companies. Since 1948, we have seen a proliferation of intergovernmental treaties, conventions, agreements, accords, compacts, and declarations that have been intended to prescribe principles governing the activities of governments, groups, international companies, and individuals. The six most prominent accords of relevance to the activities of international companies are listed in Table 17.1.

PRACTICAL INSIGHT 17.1

MEANINGFUL ACTION WITHIN A DEFINED STRATEGY

Corporate social responsibility [CSR] is all very well in theory, but organizations have found it increasingly difficult to turn such a concept into a meaningful business reality. There is no doubt that donating a one-off sum to a local charity is an ethical and morally sound thing to do, but to promote it in the same way you would a new product or service turns a worthy action into a meaningless gesture. A common problem is that CSR is not incorporated into an organizational strategy and so simply becomes a nice-to-have entity that creates a feel-good factor for board members but can be dispensed with when times get tough. Efforts like these can even have adverse effects:

- employees feel that they are working for an insincere, uncaring organization;
- the public sees token action more to do with publicity than community;
- the organization does not see much benefit of social initiatives and sees no need to develop the concept.

All this paints something of a grim picture for the future of ethical business. However, there is hope in the form of the more forward thinking organizations which see corporate social responsibility as a meaningful part of their business strategy and something that can bring certain benefits to the company. This approach has been described as "enlightened self-interest" and stems from the realization that human resources can make a serious strategic contribution through this channel.

How? In a world where money is increasingly playing second fiddle to job satisfaction, people are looking to the nonfinancial aspects of an organization when it comes to choosing an employer. As one employee of a medium-sized enterprise noted, "there's more to life than money. I want my kids to grow up in a nice neighborhood and if I see my company working to make this community better, I'm going to work harder for them." This sort of sentiment is echoed across the globe and the innovative human resource specialists are beginning to capitalize on such feelings. After all, who would not want to be employer of choice? Of course, there is still a great deal of cynicism to overcome. People have heard too many empty promises to believe that organizations will change overnight, and there is always one question at the back of everyone's mind: Can an organization really make money by being nice? It is one thing to concentrate on corporate social responsibility once you have made billions of dollars profit, but to make money initially is another thing altogether.

But it is not impossible, as the Weizhi Group has shown. This Chinese clothing manufacturer and wholesaler was founded in 1987 by Xiang Bing-Wei and is a truly virtuous corporation. Wei's tale is very much one of rags to riches. He was supporting his family from the age of 16 and suffered many hardships as a child. After working as a tailor he took out a small loan and set up his own business. Wei founded his company on four basic principles: (1) kindness; (2) sincerity; (3) wisdom; and (4) diligence.

These beliefs are his own and permeate the Weizhi culture. The organization has many moral maxims based on the value of kindness and honesty and although management by rules and regulations exists, it is coupled with management by values and feelings. But most importantly, this is more than just rhetoric. For example:

1. The Weizhi Group was the first company in China to introduce a no quibbles refund policy. In a country flooded with shoddy quality and imitation goods, this strategy immediately boosted consumer trust and loyalty.
2. It has a department of corporate culture in a bid to promote company values on a continuous and evolutionary basis.
3. The CEO, Wei, is an inspirational leader who practices what he preaches. Because the four key principles of the organization are the very beliefs he lives by, a strong positive cultural message cascades through the organization.
4. When recruiting staff, the Weizhi Group sees morality as more important than competence.

These values have been cultivated over time. Wei was aware that such a moral culture would take a long time to fully establish itself and so took gradual, lasting steps (that began by institutionalizing ideas into procedures). This left employees in no doubt that becoming a virtuous organization was more than just a fad. To the surprise of many critics, Wei's organization is thriving in a highly competitive market. For the past five years it has consistently been listed in the top 100 enterprises in the garment industry, with annual sales values of over $72 million.

In addition, employees appear genuinely motivated by working for a valuebased organization. When questioned, 100 percent of respondents said they knew their corporate mission, 95 percent agreed that a business should have ethics, and over 95 percent agreed that honesty and trustworthiness are paramount in business. The Weizhi Group has proved that, contrary to popular belief, principles and profit can live side by side. All you need is time, commitment and, of course, morals.

Source: Adapted from "McDonald's Jumps on the CSR Bandwagon," *Strategic Direction* 18, no. 9 (September 2002), pp. 8–12.

TABLE 17.1
Prominent International Accords

Accord		Year
United Nations Universal Declaration of Human Rights	UDHR	1948
European Convention on Human Rights	ECHR	1950
Helsinki Accords (final act of the Conference on Security and Cooperation)	Helsinki	1975
Organization for Economic Cooperation and Development Guidelines for Multinational Enterprises	OECD	1976
International Labor Office Tripartite Declaration of Principles of Multinational Enterprises and Social Policy	ILO	1977
United Nations Code of Conduct on Transnational Corporations	TNC Code	1988

TABLE 17.2
Employment Practices and Policies

Policy	Organization(s)
MNCs should not contravene the manpower policies of host nations.	ILO
MNCs should respect the right of employees to join trade unions and to bargain collectively.	ILO; OECD; UDHR
MNCs should develop nondiscriminatory employment policies and promote equal job opportunities.	ILO; OECD; UDHR
MNCs should provide equal pay for equal work.	ILO; UDHR
MNCs should give advance notice of changes in operations, especially plant closings, and mitigate the adverse effects of these changes.	ILO; OECD
MNCs should provide favorable work conditions, limited working hours, holidays with pay, and protection against unemployment.	UDHR
MNCs should promote job stability and job security, avoiding arbitrary dismissals and providing severance pay for those unemployed.	ILO; UDHR
MNCs should respect local host-country job standards and upgrade the local labor force through training.	ILO; OECD
MNCs should adopt adequate health and safety standards for employees and grant them the right to know about job-related health hazards.	ILO
MNCs should, minimally, pay basic living wages to employees.	ILO; UDHR
MNCs' operations should benefit lower income groups of the host nation.	ILO
MNCs should balance job opportunities, work conditions, job training, and living conditions among migrant workers and host-country nationals.	Helsinki

TABLE 17.3
Consumer Protection

Policy	Organization(s)
MNCs should respect host-country laws and policies regarding the protection of consumers.	OECD; TNC Code
MNCs should safeguard the health and safety of consumers by various disclosures, safe packaging, proper labeling, and accurate advertising.	TNC Code

The fact that several countries would agree on international codes of conduct signifies the need to recognize that, in spite of cultural differences in the world's community of nations, the nation-states find much "common ground." Codes of conduct are particularly relevant in a discussion of ethics in business, for they are seen as an alternative means to constitute an international *moral* authority by agreements among governments and to provide guidelines for multinational business activities.[24]

Tables 17.2 through 17.6 present an inventory of code-of-conduct principles in the form of explicitly normative guidelines for the policies, decisions, and operations of international firms. The principles serve as normative anchors for the conduct of business operations, as well as fundamental obligations and responsibilities regarding basic human rights.[25]

TABLE 17.4
Environmental Protection

Policy	Organization(s)
MNCs should respect host-country laws, goals, and priorities concerning protection of the environment.	Helsinki; OECD; TNC Code
MNCs should preserve ecological balance, protect the environment, adopt preventive measures to avoid environmental harm, and rehabilitate environments damaged by operations.	Helsinki; OECD; TNC Code
MNCs should disclose likely environmental harms and minimize risks of accidents that could cause environmental damage.	OECD; TNC Code
MNCs should promote the development of international environmental standards.	Helsinki; TNC Code
MNCs should control specific operations that contribute to pollution of air, water, and soils.	Helsinki
MNCs should develop and use technology that can monitor, protect, and enhance the environment.	Helsinki; OECD

TABLE 17.5
Political Payments and Involvement

Policy	Organization(s)
MNCs should not pay bribes or make improper payments to public officials.	OECD; TNC Code
MNCs should avoid improper or illegal involvement or interference in the internal politics of host countries.	OECD; TNC Code
MNCs should not interfere in intergovernmental relations.	TNC Code

TABLE 17.6
Basic Human Rights and Fundamental Freedoms

Policy	Organization(s)
MNCs should respect the rights of all persons to life, liberty, security of person, and privacy.	ECHR; Helsinki; ILO; TNC Code; UDHR
MNCs should respect the rights of all persons to equal protection of the law, work, choice of job, just and favorable work conditions, and protection against unemployment and discrimination.	Helsinki; ILO; TNC Code; UDHR
MNCs should respect all persons' freedom of thought, conscience, religion, opinion and expression, communication, peaceful assembly and association, and movement and residence within each state.	ECHR; Helsinki; ILO; TNC Code; UDHR
MNCs should promote a standard of living to support the health and well-being of workers and their families.	Helsinki; ILO; TNC Code; UDHR
MNCs should promote special care and assistance to motherhood and childhood.	Helsinki; ILO; TNC Code; UDHR

The guidelines outlined should be viewed as a collective whole since they do not all exist in each of the six conventions. The international bodies that formulated the codes of conduct clearly intended that they be taken seriously and that they be enforced in the policies and operations of international companies.

The Issues of Bribery and Corruption

Of all the issues of ethics confronting international managers, bribery and corruption have been the most troublesome and pervasive. In Chapter 4, we reviewed bribery from the legal perspective of the Foreign Corrupt Practices Act. Here, we focus on the ethical and social responsibility perspectives of bribery and corruption. *Bribery* may be defined as the payment voluntarily offered for the purpose of inducing a public official to do or to omit to do something in violation of his or her lawful duty, or to exercise his official discretion in favor of the payer's request for a contract, concession, or privilege on some basis other than merit. The greed of politicians and political parties has created systems of corruption and graft that one encounters to some degree in almost every country of the world. The phenomenon of bribery exists in rich industrialized countries as well as poor and underdeveloped countries, in democracies as well as dictatorships, in capitalist and socialist economies. Business firms are required, and sometimes forced, to bribe government officials merely to perform what to an objective observer would look like ordinary business activities. The following example from Italy is illustrative of the nature and problem of bribery in many countries throughout the world:

> Virtually every major Italian political party and many of the country's most prestigious companies have been tarred by a bottomless, tangled-as-spaghetti scandal that swallowed trillions of taxpayer lire—billions of dollars.
>
> For decades, the (political) parties were routinely and generously financed by illegal kickbacks for public contracts and boosted by jobs-for-votes deals. In some regions of Sicily, there is no end to forest rangers on public payrolls, but hardly any trees.
>
> Payoffs, called *targenti,* were standard operating procedure at virtually every level in virtually every city.[26]

Corruption scandals have affected the highest levels of government in Japan, South Korea, France, and several countries in Africa. Practical Insight 17.2 illustrates the problem of corruption in Mexico, a partner of the United States in the NAFTA accord.

Transparency International* is an organization based in Berlin, Germany, that has served as a watchdog of corruption worldwide. It rates the extent of corruption in countries on a scale of 10 to 1, with 10 being the best—the least corrupt country—and 1 being the worst—the most corrupt country. Thus the higher the country score, the less is the level of corruption in the country. In its latest survey for the year 2000, it rated 102 countries on the degree of corruption as seen by businesspeople, academics, and risk analysts. Exhibit 17.1 shows that Finland tops the list of the five least corrupt countries globally. It is interesting that three of the five least corrupt countries are in northern Europe. Exhibits 17.2 through 17.5 illustrate the degree of corruption in various geographic parts of the world.

Transparency International also rates countries that pay the most bribes to senior foreign officials in foreign countries. Its latest survey for the year 2000 was conducted by Gallup International Organization. Gallup conducted surveys in 15 emerging market countries that are among the largest such countries involved in trade and investment with multinational firms: Argentina, Brazil, Colombia, Hungary, India, Indonesia, Mexico, Morocco, Nigeria, the Philippines, Poland, Russia, South Africa, South Korea, and Thailand. The survey asked questions related to the propensity of companies from 21 leading exporting countries to pay bribes to senior public officials in the countries surveyed. Exhibit 17.6 displays the five worst bribe-payer countries in the world.

International business managers will face the problem of bribery and corruption in most places in this world. The bribe goes by different names in different countries. It is called *la mordida* in Mexico, *dash* in South Africa, *baksheesh* for a tip or gratuity in India, Pakistan, and in the Middle East, *schimengeld* for grease money in Germany, and the Italians call it *bustarella,* a little envelope.

Many businesspeople believe that bribes are a necessary cost of doing business in certain countries. A unit of Teledyne Inc. has admitted to paying $3.2 million in illicit commissions between 1986 and 1990 to sell aerospace equipment to the

---

*Transparency International Web page: www.transparency.org.

PRACTICAL INSIGHT 17.2

THE CHALLENGE OF ERADICATION OF CORRUPTION IN MEXICO

When Vicente Fox was sworn in as president of Mexico on Dec. 1, 2000, he carried with him a huge burden: the public's expectation that he would liberate from corruption a country that had become symbolic of the scourge. Fox was the first Mexican president from an opposition party after 71 years of autocratic control by the Institutional Revolutionary Party, or PRI, which maintained its grip on Mexico principally through corruption.

Mexico's hopes for Fox were extraordinary, but new presidents nearly everywhere assume their nations' leadership with the expectation that they will clean up graft of some kind—usually because they have promised it.

Yet just as sure as a new leader's pledge to clean up the corruption of his predecessor is the certainty that his successor will, in a few years, be doing the same. Presidents who come to office promising to fight graft almost always fail—occasionally leaving office several million dollars richer themselves.

Arrests are made—but often only of political rivals. Anti-corruption campaigns come and go—and still it requires a 30-per-cent payoff to build a highway, buildings fall down because inspectors are bribed and drivers prepare for an assault on their wallets when they see a cop.

Today, the costs of corruption are widely discussed, and they are stunning. Francisco Barrio, until April Mexico's anti-corruption czar, estimates that graft costs his country 9.5 per cent of its GDP—twice the education budget—and Mexico ranks only in the middle of the corruption charts.

Corruption also distorts spending. There is evidence that when levels of graft are high, governments spend less on education and health and more on public works—projects chosen not for their value to the nation but for their kickback potential. Corruption greatly discourages foreign investment.

And with globalization, its effects have become borderless: when the Bank of Credit and Commerce International went down in 1991, 40,000 depositors in Bangladesh lost their life savings.

In the last couple of decades, anti-corruption campaigns have met with sporadic success in isolated countries. But now, for the first time, the struggle against corruption has gone global.

A non-governmental group founded in 1993, Transparency International, today has chapters in 90 countries. It is best known for its annual ranking of the perception of corruption—that is, the general sense among people doing business in a given country that officials are demanding bribes. But Trans-

parency, based in Berlin, also mobilizes people to fight corruption and provides information on how best to do so.

International organizations are taking new steps against money laundering and bank secrecy. And since 1996, the World Bank and the International Monetary Fund have also been tackling the corruption issue. Before then, World Bank higher-ups ignored corruption, labeling it a political problem and claiming that it was thus outside the bank's economic mandate.

Under Fox, Mexico (where I have been living for more than a year) has become an ideal laboratory in which to observe and understand this new global focus on corruption. Mexico shows how easy it is to fight corruption once a government really wants to—and how hard it is to reach that point, despite what presidents say in their inaugural addresses.

In July 1989, Francisco Gil Diaz, an assistant secretary of the Mexican treasury, took control of the country's customs system. Customs services have historically fed the pockets of high government officials. When Pompilio Cardenas, who was hired to run customs at Mexico City's international airport, walked into the warehouse on his first day, his instinct was to go home.

"The disorder was deliberate," Cardenas tells me as he shows me photos of the old warehouse. "There was effectively no registry of what came in. If you don't know what comes in on 100 flights a day from all over the world, you can imagine the magnitude of the corruption."

There was outright theft—especially at night, when anyone could come in and cart away valuables. People could even go into the planes. A mafia ran the customs house, with the eager participation of airline personnel, government officials, customs agents, truck drivers and police officers.

Another problem was the thicket of requirements necessary for getting goods through customs. There were 16 steps, hence 16 opportunities for officials to solicit bribes.

Gil Diaz got Mexico's congress to convert customs to the system now in use in most of the world. Major shipments now had to be handled by licensed customs brokers, who would inventory the merchandise and calculate the correct duty. After the duty was paid, the merchandise would pass through a random customs "stoplight." Ten per cent of the merchandise got a red light and was inspected, and there were steep penalties for lying, including the possibility of prison.

The 16 steps became three. A process that had taken as long as a month was cut down to 10 minutes. From one month to the next, officially collected duties jumped by 30 per cent.

In addition to raising revenue and greasing the movement of goods, that reform also curtailed corruption. The stoplight reduced the ability of inspectors to choose targets and took away a major source of bribes. Gil Diaz changed the behavior of customs workers by removing opportunities for theft and bribery and increasing the probability of their being caught. In short, he made illegal acts difficult.

In his book *Controlling Corruption,* Robert Klitgaard, now dean of the RAND Graduate School in Santa Monica, Calif., shows how in some of the most unlikely places corruption has been fought using such simple administrative reforms. His most spectacular example is the cleanup of the Philippine Bureau of Internal Revenue under that renowned graft-buster Ferdinand Marcos.

It is amusing to recall that Marcos declared martial law in 1972 in part to combat corruption. Three years later, he installed Efren Plana, a respected judge, as the commissioner of internal revenue. Plana fired about a hundred of the most corrupt officials. He set higher professional standards and banned the hiring of officials' relatives.

Previously, tax assessors won promotion by bribing their superiors. Plana developed incentives that gave promotions and cash prizes to the most effective and fairest assessors. He brought in outside auditors and instituted frequent audits and spot checks. He recommended changes to simplify the tax laws, so that an individual agent's discretion was reduced. In short, he used strategies any first-year business student could have designed.

All those inaugural speeches declaring all-out war on graft? Lies. It's actually easy to clean up corruption, absurdly easy, when you want to. What is difficult is really wanting to. Gil Diaz was able to break the customs mafia because he had one crucial weapon: NAFTA. The Mexican government and powerful businessmen needed to clean up customs in order to get a trade deal they were panting for.

Two years ago, the Mexican chapter of Transparency International surveyed households in all 31 states and the Federal District of Mexico City, asking people how often they paid bribes for government services. Corruption was found to be spectacularly concentrated in Mexico City. People in the capital stopped by a transit cop reported paying a bribe 69 per cent of the time.

I hate corruption enough to write an article about it, but during my first year in Mexico City, when my family lived in a house in the Condesa neighborhood, I bribed my garbage man every Friday, as did all my neighbors. With two kids in diapers, I didn't even want to contemplate the consequences of having our trash left on the stoop.

What people really need, of course, is a system that doesn't require bribery to get things done. But this is so far from people's experience in places like Mexico City that they do not punish officials for failing to produce it. Nor do many people here believe in their own ability to influence a process of change.

In theory, of course, citizens can now throw out corrupt officials. But I don't think it has ever happened in Mexico City. Officials here ignore corruption because they can—it doesn't cost them at election time.

Most voters have more urgent needs than clean government, like jobs, security and food. And if voters don't really believe that corruption will ever disappear, then they figure they would be chumps not to get their own little piece.

In Mexico, democracy has not brought immediate gains. But slowly, I believe, it is helping the nation create a system of political pressure for the long run. Even before Fox became president, Mexico's political opening-up was unleashing independent forces against corruption.

Perhaps the single most important victory over corruption in Mexico is the electoral process itself. Mexico's PRI victories were the stuff of global infamy for decades. Today, Mexico's electoral institute advises other nations on how to organize clean balloting. On the basics, like registration, voting and counting ballots, Mexico probably does better than the United States.

Still, I have yet to meet a Mexican who says that Fox is doing much of anything to fight corruption, except those who work for him. The year after Fox took office, more people actually thought corruption was rising rather than going down.

But Fox has actually made important investments in the future of clean government. He is bringing the anti-corruption agency up to global standards. And at his urging, this year Congress created a federal civil service. It will professionalize government and cut down on patronage, nepotism and jobs allocated by the applicant's willingness to pay kickbacks to his superior.

Also, in June, Fox's new access-to-information law went into effect. The law recognizes that government information is the property of citizens and establishes a mechanism to allow them to request it.

To call Mexico, where civil society is barely breathing after years on the PRI payroll, a successful example of corruption-fighting is an overstatement at this point. But it might not be in a few years.

EXHIBIT 17.1
Least Corrupt Countries Worldwide

Source: Transparency International, www.transparency.org. Reprinted with permission.

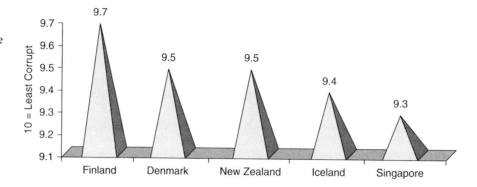

EXHIBIT 17.2
Corruption in Western and Eastern Europe

Source: Transparency International, www.transparency.org. Reprinted with permission.

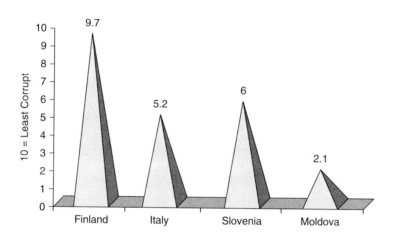

EXHIBIT 17.3   **Corruption in North, Central, and South America**

Source: Transparency International, www.transparency.org. Reprinted with permission.

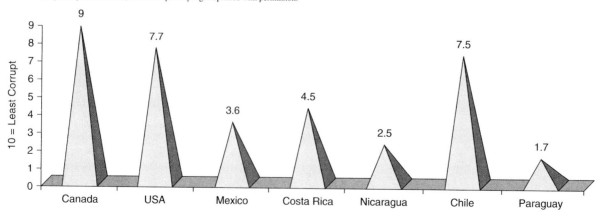

EXHIBIT 17.4

Corruption in Middle East and Asia

Source: Transparency International, www.transparency.org. Reprinted with permission.

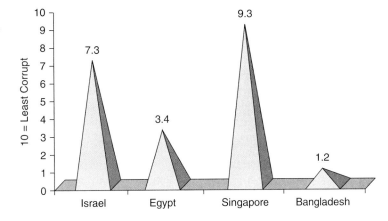

EXHIBIT 17.5

Corruption in Northern and Southern Africa

Source: Transparency International, www.transparency.org. Reprinted with permission.

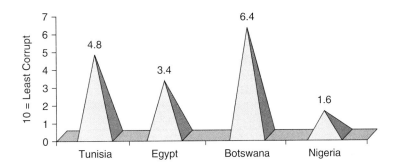

EXHIBIT 17.6

Worst Bribe-Payer Countries

Source: Transparency International, www.transparency.org. Reprinted with permission.

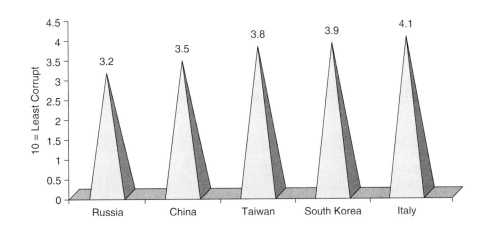

Taiwanese military. Litton industries is also accused by the U.S. government of surreptitiously funneling millions of dollars to a middleman for obtaining business abroad. And General Electric is being accused by an engineer in the company who discovered that the company had paid hundreds of thousands of dollars to win a $124.7 million contract with the Egyptian government for a sophisticated radar system.[27] Practical Insight 17.3 illustrates the use of middlemen by oil companies to obtain contracts in Kazakhstan.

PRACTICAL INSIGHT 17.3

UNLAWFUL PAYMENTS TO FOREIGN OFFICIALS

A former senior executive of Mobil Corp. was indicted Wednesday on conspiracy and tax-evasion charges stemming from the U.S. government's probe into alleged bribing of Kazakhstan officials. J. Bryan Williams, who was responsible for Mobil's trading operations in the former Soviet Union, allegedly received a $2 million kickback for negotiating Mobil's $1.05 billion purchase in 1996 of a 25% stake in Tengiz, one of Kazakhstan's largest oil fields. The money came from a $51 million consulting fee paid by Mobil to Mercator Corp., a small merchant bank in New York run by James H. Giffen, a consultant to Kazakh officials, according to an indictment announced Wednesday by Manhattan U.S. Attorney Jim Comey.

Mr. Giffen was arrested Sunday in New York on charges of making millions in unlawful payments to Kazakh officials in order to retain his longtime job as an influential adviser. Tom Cirigliano, a spokesman for Exxon Mobil Corp., confirmed that Mr. Williams no longer works for the oil giant and was employed before Mobil's merger with Exxon. "We plan to investigate this matter," he said.

The U.S. government announced a separate 62-count indictment expanding its case against Mr. Giffen, charging him with routing $78 million in payments from U.S. oil companies to senior Kazakh officials. Besides Mobil, the companies include Amoco,

Texaco and Phillips Petroleum, prosecutors said. Mr. Giffen's attorney, William Schwartz, couldn't be reached for comment. He said earlier this week that Mr. Giffen would be exonerated. Mr. Williams' attorney, David Schertler, said he hadn't yet reviewed the indictment and couldn't comment.

Mr. Williams is charged with one count each of conspiracy and failing to pay taxes on the $2 million payment. He faces up to five years in prison on each count, plus three years in prison on each of five counts of filing false tax returns. Mr. Giffen is accused of diverting money from oil deals and using it to buy luxury items for Kazakh officials, including snowmobiles, an $80,000 Donzi speedboat and fur coats worth $30,000 for an official's wife and daughter.

The officials, who weren't identified in court papers, also used funds provided by Mr. Giffen to pay for more than $180,000 in jewelry, a stay at a Swiss spa, $45,000 in tuition for an exclusive Swiss high school attended by an official's daughter and other expenses. Mr. Giffen faces up to 20 years in prison, plus fines, if convicted on the most serious count of money laundering.

By no means are American companies the only ones involved in making questionable payments. There is enough evidence to suggest that Japanese, German, and French companies are heavily involved in the bribery of foreign officials to obtain business worth millions and sometimes billions of dollars.

Why Payoffs?

Why do companies feel obliged to pay huge sums of money to generate business abroad, and why do people in host countries accept such payments? The reasons that induce international companies to offer questionable payments abroad and the host-country factors that elicit bribes are presented in Table 17.7.

Types of Payoff

Bribery takes different forms and bribes are made in a variety of ways in different parts of the world. Table 17.8 depicts four categories of bribe used by international companies to obtain business in foreign countries, while Practical Insight 17.4 discusses bribes paid by Halliburton to Nigerian tax officials.

The Social Costs of Bribery and Corruption

Bribery, when used as the primary weapon to obtain business, has several dysfunctional consequences. First, a company that has the best product or service, or the best value at a given price, may not get the business. The business may go to that company which has given the biggest bribe to the government official who has the discretionary authority to

TABLE 17.7
Factors Responsible for Bribes

Home-Country Factors	Host-Country Factors
Competitors are giving bribes to obtain business.	Host government has control over business activity permits and licenses. Government officials are required to conduct normal business functions. Government officials are poorly paid and use bribes to supplement salary.
There is constant pressure for higher levels of performance by top management and shareholders.	
Bribery is an accepted practice in the host country. Cannot expect to get any business without conforming.	Bureaucratic delays can be costly for business (e.g., clear products through customs on time to meet delivery schedules).
Tax laws of the country encourage bribery (e.g., some bribes can be written off as a business expense in Germany but not in the U.S.).	Political pressure exists to make contributions to political parties or favorite political organizations or causes.

TABLE 17.8
Major Types of Bribe

Source: From Subash C. Jain, "What Happened to the Marketing Man When His International Promotion Pay-Offs Became Bribes?" In Peter J. LaPlaca, (ed.) *The New Role of the Marketing Professional*, American Marketing Association, 1977 Business Proceedings, Series No. 40. Reprinted with permission.

Facilitating payments: Disbursement of small amounts of cash or kind as tips or gifts to minor government officials to expedite clearance of shipments, documents or other routine transactions. Example: "In India not a single tile can move if the clerk's palm is not greased. Distribution of *bustarella* (an envelope containing a small amount of money) in Italy to make things move in an inefficient and chaotic social system."

Middlemen commissions: Appointment of intermediaries (agents and consultants) to facilitate sales in a nonroutine manner and payment to them of excessive allowances and commissions, which are not commensurate with the normal commercial services they perform. Often, the middlemen may request that part or all of their commission be deposited in a U.S. bank or a bank in a third country. Example: Northrup Corporation's payment of $30 million in fees to overseas agents and consultants, some of which was used for payoffs to government officials to secure favorable decisions on government procurement of aircraft and military hardware.

Political contributions: Contributions which can take the form of extortion since they are in violation of local law and custom. Also payments which, while not illegal, are specifically made with the intent of winning favors directly or indirectly. Example: Gulf Oil Corporation's payment of $3 million in 1971 to South Korea's Democratic Republican Party under intimidation and threat.

Cash disbursements: Cash payments made to important people through slush funds or in some other way, usually in a third country (i.e., deposit in a Swiss bank) for different reasons such as to obtain a tax break or sales contract or to get preferential treatment over a competitor. Example: Payment of $2.5 million, via Swiss bank accounts, to Honduran officials by United Brands Company for the reduction of the export tax on bananas.

decide which company may sell its products in the local market. In such a situation, the consumers are the real losers because their money does not fetch the best products or services that could have been available absent the bribes. Second, if bribes are used to sell capital equipment like a factory or military hardware to the government, the taxpayer's money is being misallocated if government officials choose an inferior piece of equipment over one which may clearly be the better choice. Third, the incentive to compete on the basis of quality, price, and service is destroyed when these factors are rendered irrelevant by decisions influenced by factors such as bribery and corruption.

Thus, bribery can cause the misallocation of a country's resources because the intervention of bribes causes officials to direct resources away from where they can be best put to use based on a purely objective set of criteria like price, quality, and service. The economic costs of corruption can be quite significant. For instance, underreporting of income taxes in exchange for a bribe to the tax collector could reduce income tax revenues collected by the government by up to 50 percent. Also, the overinvoicing by government officials for public works projects or for imported capital goods could raise the prices of goods and services by as much as 100 percent. Ultimately it is the country's consumers who bear the burden of these increased costs due to corruption.

PRACTICAL INSIGHT 17.4

HALLIBURTON DISCLOSES BRIBES IN NIGERIA

A subsidiary of Halliburton Co. paid a Nigerian tax official $2.4 million in bribes to get favorable tax treatment, the company disclosed in a federal filing. In a filing made Thursday with the Securities and Exchange Commission, the company said its KBR subsidiary "made improper payments of approximately $2.4 million to an entity owned by a Nigerian national who held himself out as a tax consultant when in fact he was an employee of a local tax authority."

The filing stated that the payments were found during a routine audit, and that several employees were fired as a result. Halliburton said it was cooperating with the SEC in its review, and added that none of the Houston company's senior officers were involved. A company spokeswoman told the *Houston Chronicle* for its Friday editions that the bribes were paid between 2001 and 2002.

Company officials are trying to determine how much it owes Nigeria in back taxes. It could be as much as $5 million, the filing said. Vice President Dick Cheney led the company until August 2000. Wednesday, the Bush administration denied there was any connection between Cheney's former role in running the company and a $76.7 million no-bid contract with the government to extinguish Iraqi oil well fires and help restart Iraq's oil industry. In Nigeria, the engineering, construction and oil-field services company is constructing a liquefied natural gas plant and developing an offshore oil and gas facility.

Source: From "Halliburton SEC Filing Discloses Bribery," The Associated Press, May 9, 2003. Reprinted with permission of The Associated Press.

Child Labor and Sweatshops

Child labor and its abuses in sweat shops are of great concern to most people of conscience. The following item, which appeared in the *Philadelphia Inquirer*, illustrates the cruelties of child labor in developing countries:

> Demanding an end to child labor, thousands of children and other protesters marched through Lahore yesterday to commemorate the killing this month of young activist Iqbal Masih.
>
> About one-third of the 3,000 marchers were children, many of them workers in carpet-weaving factories and other industries that routinely employ child laborers for as low as one rupee, or about 3 cents a day. The march, which led to the governor's office in Punjab Province, was organized by the Bonded Labor Liberation Front, a private group trying to end the widespread practice of child labor in Pakistan.
>
> The group two years ago rescued Iqbal, who was then 10 and had already spent six years working in carpet-weaving factories. Iqbal, who achieved international recognition for his activism, was gunned down April 17 in his village of Muridke, 22 miles northwest of Lahore. Eshan Ullah Khan, head of the Bonded Labor Liberation Front, alleges that people in the carpet industry who were angry at his campaign against child labor killed Iqbal.[28]

Few companies have taken steps to eliminate the abuses of child labor. Most argue that competition forces the company to use child labor. Others claim that the company itself does not employ child labor, but its contractors do, and the company can do little to control the employment of workers who it does not hire directly. A fine example is provided by Levi Strauss & Company of how a company indeed can prohibit the use of child labor by manufacturing contractors linked with the company.

Levi Strauss has operations in many countries and diverse cultures. Robert D. Haas, chairman and CEO of the company, says: "We must take special care in selecting our contractors and those countries where our goods are produced in order to ensure that our products are made in a manner that is consistent with our values and reputation. In early 1992, we developed a set of global sourcing guidelines that established standards our contractors must meet to ensure that their practices are compatible with our values. For instance, our guidelines ban the use of child labor and prison labor."[29] The company rules stipulate that working hours cannot exceed 60 hours a week, with at least one day off in seven, and wages must, at a minimum, comply with local law and prevailing local practice. The company accepts the fact that at times there are issues that are beyond the control of the local contractor, and therefore the company has a list of country-selection criteria. For instance, Levi Strauss refuses to source in countries where conditions such as human rights violations run counter to the values of the company and would adversely affect the company's global brand image.

Levi Strauss's phased withdrawal from China reflected its concern for human rights violations in that country. Another example of the application of this principle is in the way the company handled the problem of two of its manufacturing contractors in Bangladesh and one in Turkey who employed underage workers. This was a clear violation of Levi Strauss's guidelines against the use of child labor. The company could have (1) instructed the contractors to fire the children, knowing that this action would have caused severe hardships on the children's families, many of whom depended on the earnings of the children as their only source of income; or (2) continued to employ the children, ignoring the company's position against the use of child labor. Neither of these options was acceptable to Levi Strauss, and therefore a third, win–win solution was found and implemented. The company worked out an arrangement with the contractors that called for the contractors to pay the children their salaries and benefits while they went to school on the factory site (the children did not work during this time), and Levi Strauss paid for books, tuition, and uniforms. The children would be offered full-time jobs in the plant when they reached working age. At times the contractors passed on to Levi Strauss in the form of higher unit price the costs of adhering to these company standards. In other cases the company has forgone cheaper sources of production due to unsatisfactory working conditions or concerns about the country of origin.[30] We end this section with these words of Robert D. Haas:

> There is a growing body of research evidence from respected groups that shows a positive correlation between citizenship and financial performance. These studies underscore that companies driven by values and a sense of purpose that extends beyond just making money outperform those that focus only on short-term profits. The former have higher sales, sustain higher profits, and have stocks that outperform the market. These findings mirror our experiences. Our values-driven approach has helped us:
>
> - identify contractors who really want to work for Levi Strauss;
> - gain customer and consumer loyalty because they feel good about having us as a business partner or about purchasing our products;
> - attract and retain the best employees;
> - improve the morale and trust of employees because the company's values closely mirror their own personal values;
> - initiate business in established and emerging markets because government and community leaders have a better sense of what we stand for and what to expect from us; and
> - maintain credibility during times of unplanned events or crisis.
>
> The conclusion is clear: There are important commercial benefits to be gained from managing your business in a responsible way that best serves the enterprise's long-term interests. The opposite is also clear: There are dangers of not doing so.[31]

So, what can companies do to ensure that employees do not engage in unethical behavior to obtain business abroad? Most companies have addressed this issue, in conjunction with a host of other ethical and moral dilemmas that employees face all over the world, in so-called company ethics programs. We consider this topic next.

What Companies Can Do to Integrate Ethics and Business Conduct

The issue of business ethics has attracted the attention of companies worldwide and several companies have incorporated ethics training as part of the general orientation of all employees. The following are recommendations to integrate ethics into business conduct.

1. The Top Management Must Be Committed to the Company's Ethics Program Top management involvement is essential. At Chemical Bank, for example, some 250 vice presidents took part in a two-day seminar on corporate values that began with an appearance by the bank's chairman.

2. A Written Company Code that Clearly Communicates Management's Expectations Must Be Developed The code must be explicit in stating management's intent, for example, "The law is the floor. Ethical business conduct should normally exist at a level well above the minimum required law" (from *A Code of Worldwide Business Conduct,* Caterpillar Tractor Company). Extensive interviews with managers at different levels of the organization, in various subsidiaries at home and abroad, may be conducted before and after the ethics code is drafted to ensure that the code is comprehensive in its coverage of the variety of ethical dilemmas that managers are most likely to encounter. For example, to develop the company's ethical guidelines, Levi Strauss formed a working group of 15 employees from a broad section of the company. The working group spent nine months in developing the guidelines, during which time it researched the views of various key stakeholder groups—vendors, contractors, plant managers, merchandisers, sewing-machine operators, contract production staff, shareholders, and others.[32] The Code of Business Conduct of Rohm and Haas, specialty materials company as it pertains to gifts and entertainment and the Foreign Corrupt Practices Act, is presented in Table 17.9.

3. Provide an Organizational Identity to the Ethics Program Most companies would agree that there should be strong organizational support for a company's ethics program. The best way to ensure that ethics is not downplayed is to establish a high-level ethics committee at the board of directors' level and an ethics committee at different organizational levels. For example, McDonnell Douglas has a Board of Directors Ethics Committee, an internal corporate committee led by a senior executive, and a committee at each division (component company) level reporting the highest level. Further down the line, an ombudsman, who is a senior manager, is available to counsel employees who wish to have private and confidential advice.

In a similar vein, international companies could establish ethics committees at different organizational levels, starting with the top management levels of the parent company, and within the various divisions and subsidiaries of the company at home and abroad. The Boeing Company, a leading aircraft manufacturer, has "ethics advisers" in subsidiaries and a corporate office for employees to report infractions.[33]

4. A Formal Program Must Be in Place to Implement the Ethics Code Every employee must be made to go through a formal training program that teaches employees and indoctrinates them with the ethical code of the company. Case studies and role playing that highlights ethical dilemmas faced by international managers most frequently have proved to be very useful in encouraging participants to look at the operating principles in the company code for guidance. For instance, Levi Strauss held

TABLE 17.9
Rohm and Haas Company: Political Payments, and Gifts and Entertainment

Source: Rohm and Haas, *Code of Business Conduct,* January 1994, pp. 1, 3.

The company

Rohm and Haas Company is an ethical company which complies with applicable laws. This Code of Business Conduct applies to all directors, officers and employees of the Company, its subsidiaries and controlled affiliates.

Political payments

(a) We encourage participation in the political process, and we recognize that participation is primarily a matter for individual involvement.

(b) Any payment of corporate funds to any political party, candidate, or campaign may be made only if permitted under applicable law and approved in advance by the General Counsel. U.S. laws generally prohibit payments of corporate funds to any U.S. political party, candidate, or campaign.

Gifts and entertainment

(a) Gifts of cash or property may not be offered or made to any officer or employee of a customer or supplier or any government official or employee unless the gift is (1) nominal in value, (2) approved in advance by the appropriate regional director, business group executive, or corporate staff division manager, and (3) legal. In most countries it is illegal for corporations to make gifts to government officials or employees; any gift to a government official or employee must be approved in advance by the general counsel as well as the appropriate regional director, business group executive, or corporate staff division manager.

(b) Employees of the company should decline or turn over to the company gifts of more than nominal value or cash from persons or companies that do (or may expect to do) business with Rohm and Haas.

(c) Business entertainment (whether we do the entertaining or are entertained) must have a legitimate business purpose, may not be excessive, and must be legal. Business entertainment of government officials or employees is illegal or regulated in most countries; therefore, the propriety of such entertaining should be reviewed in advance with the general counsel or his delegates.

Translation

Translations of the code will be prepared in French, German, Italian, Portuguese, Spanish, and Japanese. Other translations will be prepared if necessary to ensure that recipients of the code are able to understand it fully. The general or resident manager in each country will be responsible for translations.

Dissemination

(a) A copy of the code in the appropriate language will be given to all employees of the company (including employees of domestic and foreign subsidiaries and controlled affiliates). New employees will be given a copy of the code at the time of their employment.

(b) The regional or staff division personnel directors are responsible for dissemination of the code.

Compliance

(a) All salaried employees of the company (its subsidiaries and controlled affiliates) will be asked to certify annually in writing their compliance with the code substantially as follows (with such exceptions as may be noted therein):

"I have reviewed and understand the Code of Business Conduct. I hereby confirm that (1) I have complied with the code during the preceding year, and (2) each recipient of the code who reports to me has certified in writing his or her compliance with the code."

(b) The regional and business directors will be responsible for obtaining certifications not later than February 1 with respect to the preceding year.

---

training sessions for 100 in-country managers who would have to enforce the company's ethical global sourcing guidelines in the plants of the company's 700 contract manufacturers worldwide. The training included case studies and exercises in decision making. Following this training, the managers made presentations on the guidelines to the contractors, performed on-site audits, and worked with the contractors to make the necessary improvements.[34] Companies often require employees to sign a statement that they have read, understood, and agree to comply with the company's ethics code.

5. The Line Managers, not Consultants, Train Employees in Ethics   The line manager is the "role model" of ethical behavior for his or her subordinates. Each line manager must be cognizant of his or her own responsibilities in creating a culture of ethical norms that would be strictly adhered to. A line manager who deviates from the

PRACTICAL INSIGHT 17.5

U.S. COMPANIES BACK OUT OF BURMA, CITING HUMAN-RIGHTS CONCERNS, GRAFT

A number of U.S. companies are backing out from their recent forays into Burma, partly because of pressure from human-rights groups and partly because doing business in the corrupt, junta-run country just isn't worth the trouble. Macy's said it would stop making clothing in Burma within 90 days because of a "lack of infrastructure" as well as corruption in the country.

The retailer, a unit of Federated Department Stores Inc., is the latest U.S. multinational to withdraw from the Southeast Asian nation, where the ruling military regime has been accused of widespread human-rights violations since it overturned a democratic election in 1990 that would have handed political power to civilians. Burma, which was renamed Myanmar by its military rulers in 1989, is "fast becoming the South Africa of the '90s," said Simon Billenness, an analyst at Franklin Research & Development Corp.

Only in the past few years has the long-isolated nation with a population of about 43.5 million, even tried to woo foreign business. And it was beginning to have some success, albeit limited, mainly because of its low wages. However, in recent years, Liz Claiborne Inc. and Spiegel Inc.'s Eddie Bauer have pledged to stop importing apparel from Burma. Earlier this month, Starbucks Corp., the specialty-coffee company, asked that a new cold coffee drink it is creating not be bottled or distributed in Burma by PepsiCo Inc., which does business in Burma and is Starbuck's partner in the coffee-drink effort.

In withdrawing from Burma, the companies have acknowledged the human-rights concerns. "The consumer pressure is beginning to have an effect," says Thomas Lansner, a member of the Free Burma Action Group in New York. "Even if there's good business to be done in Burma, it has become an embarrassment for them to make money there." For its part, Macy's wasn't embarrassed—just disappointed because it was "impossible to make money there," a spokeswoman said. The company added that Burma's corruption "makes normal operations impossible."

Macy's had been contracting out private-label men's clothing in Burma for about 15 months. It thought the three factories it was using were private, but they turned out to be partly owned by the military government. Not all multinationals find Burma inhospitable. Unocal Corp., which has paid the Burmese government at least $10 million so far for rights to develop offshore gas fields, said it is "absolutely committed to this project." A spokesman added that Unocal thinks its involvement in Burma "will bring sustainable long-term benefits to (the) people of Myanmar."

Critics argue that such investment only nourishes the military junta. Burma's elected government-in-exile has called for economic sanctions against the country. But some investment advocates think private corporations actually may have more sway over such regimes than international bodies or other governments. "These companies can really press for change . . . because the country needs them and their investment," says Deborah Leipziger, director of international programs for the Council on Economic Priorities.

Source: From *The Wall Street Journal, Eastern Edition* by G. Pascal Zachary. Copyright © 1995 by Dow Jones & Co. Inc. Reproduced with permission of Dow Jones & Co. Inc. via Copyright Clearance Center.

ethics code at crunch time will send the signal to subordinates that "the code is just a bunch of words that don't matter." The company's chief executive is the supreme line manager, and therefore ethical guidelines, of what is acceptable, what isn't, and why, are established by the messages sent by his or her own behaviors and actions over time.

6. *Strict Enforcement of Codes is Essential* Those who violate the company code ought to be punished. Chemical Bank has fired employees for violation of the company's code of ethics even when there are no violations of the law. Xerox Corporation has dismissed employees not only for taking bribes but also for minor manipulation of records and petty cheating on expense accounts.[35]

7. *Actions Speak Louder than Words* It is not what a company code or what a company's top management and line managers say, but what they actually do in their decisions and actions on behalf of the company that counts. Companies like Federated Department Stores, Liz Claiborne, and Spiegel have pledged to stop their business activities in Burma because of human rights concerns in that country, whereas Unocal and others have decided to continue their involvement in Burma, giving as justification for their continued involvement the influence that they and other like-minded companies would have on changing the policies of the government of Burma. This is illustrated in Practical Insight 17.5.

Multinational companies play a dominant role in determining the well-being of people worldwide. Their behavior can have both beneficial and harmful consequences on the quality of life and living standards in various countries in which they conduct trade and commerce. This issue was covered in various chapters in this book. However, one should always be cognizant that decisions in companies are made by the people who manage them, so national or international companies can be no more ethical than the persons who run them. Companies that act with integrity are largely a function of individuals within firms who act with integrity. Executives in a firm's organizational hierarchy take their directions from their top management executives. As such, the board of directors and the chief executive officer are the crucial players in ensuring that the moral and ethical codes governing the behavior of the firm are communicated to all managers throughout the length and breadth of the global enterprise.

Summary

Business ethics and corporate social responsibility infuse the consideration of moral issues in corporate decision making and actions. Corporate social responsibility is specifically defined as the integration of business operations and values whereby the interests of all stakeholders—customers, employees, investors, and the environment—are reflected in the organization's policies and actions. It is motivated through a combination of utilitarian, positive duty, and negative duty approaches.

International managers may be confronted with a variety of ethical dilemmas, usually due to differences among different markets or nations in what constitutes legal or acceptable practice. Beyond the practical motivations to institute corporate social responsibility initiatives, there are moral underpinnings as well. These include teleology, deontology (the theory of rights), the theory of justice, and cultural relativism. Regarding the latter theory, a host country's legal and ethical perspectives of an international firm's activities and products must be understood and related to the cultural relativism of the country.

Several prominent international accords address ethical behavior by international companies. One or more of these provide specific guidance with respect to employment practices and policies, consumer and environmental protection issues, political payments and involvement, and basic human rights and fundamental freedoms. Although the accords are not legally binding with force of law, they display the clear intent of the international community to foster ethical conduct.

Bribery and corruption are the most troublesome and pervasive ethical issues confronting international managers, common to industrialized and developing countries alike. The line between proper and improper behavior is not always clearly drawn, and in many cases, making a payoff may appear obligatory if the international company wishes to continue to do business. Laws and practices differ widely in different countries.

A growing number of international companies have adopted comprehensive ethics programs involving ethics training and, often, a published code of conduct for all company personnel. An effective integration of the company's ethics program and the business behavior of the company's people depends on top management, and the entire organization, demonstrating that they are serious about the program on an ongoing basis. Training, enforcement, and leadership by example are essential to success.

Key Terms and Concepts

corporate social responsibility, *513*
cultural relativism, *517*
deontology, *516*
egoism, *515*

ethics, *512*
moral norms, *519*
negative duty approach, *514*
positive duty approach, *513*

social costs of bribery, *530*
teleology, *514*
theory of justice, *516*
utilitarianism, *515*

Discussion Questions

1. Should "ethics" be a subject that must be taught in all business schools? Doesn't the axiom "Do the Right Thing" really say it all?

2. Think of an issue that poses an ethical dilemma and apply Figure 17.2 to arrive at a decision on this issue.

3. In the text, we discussed five areas of interest to international companies that are covered by specific guidelines for ethical behavior from international accords. Find an article in the current business press that reports negatively on a company's behavior with respect to one of these five areas. What repercussions does the company face as a result of its actions? In your opinion, is the company justified? Why do you suppose the company's decision makers acted as they did? Are "right" and "wrong" clearly defined in this situation? Discuss.

4. Different companies exhibit differing degrees of formality in their corporate ethical policies and programs, but all incorporate the seven recommendations contained in the chapter to some extent. Which of the seven is most critical to the success of a company's program, in your opinion? Why? Would your answer be the same for all firms in all industries? If not, what factors might determine the most essential recommendation for a given firm?

Minicase

Hondurans in Sweatshops See Opportunity

Each morning, the workers spill off the buses and past the guards at the front gates of the industrial parks here, rushing to punch the clock before the 7:30 start of their workday. Outside, anxious onlookers are always waiting, hoping for a chance at least to fill out a job application that will allow them to become part of that throng.

With wages that start at less than 40 cents an hour, the apparel plants here offer little by American standards. But many of the people who work in them, having come from jobs that pay even less and offer no benefits or security, see employment here as the surest road to a better life. "In the countryside, a peon is a peon for all of his life," said Yensy Melendez, 29, a father of two and former farm worker who migrated seven years ago to this bustling city of 350,000 near Honduras's Caribbean coast and now has a factory job. "Here, it's not perfect, but at least you have a chance to improve your situation."

What residents of a rich country like the United States see as exploitation can seem a rare opportunity to residents of a poor country like Honduras, where the per capita income is $600 a year and unemployment is 40 percent. Such conflicts of standards and perceptions have become increasingly common as the global economy grows more intertwined, and have set off a heated debate about international norms of conduct and responsibility.

The recent controversy involving the television personality Kathie Lee Gifford and a line of clothing made here that bears her name provides a widely publicized case in point.

To critics in the United States, the apparel assembly plants here, known in Spanish as maquiladoras, are merely "monstrous sweatshops of the New World Order," to use the phrase of the National Labor Committee, the New York-based group that originally accused Mrs. Gifford of turning a blind eye to Hondurans working for "slave wages."

The National Labor Committee, a nonprofit group, is largely financed by foundations but also receives money from labor unions in the United States.

After the attacks on her, Mrs. Gifford has now endorsed efforts to monitor and improve conditions in apparel plants around the world. But the debate over what constitutes adequate wages, what minimum working conditions should be required and at what age it becomes permissible for minors to work continues here and in other developing countries that have eagerly welcomed assembly plants as a source of employment for their poor.

Whether workers think they are better off in the assembly plants than elsewhere is not the real issue, argues Charles Kernaghan, executive director of the National Labor Committee. Employers, he said, have a moral obligation to pay not merely what the market will bear, but a wage they know to be just.

LOW WAGE RATES DRAW CRITICISM

"The salaries being paid in a place like Honduras amount to less than 1 percent of the price of the garment in the United States," he said. "That's a crime." Companies could easily double their employees' wages, he added, and "it would be nothing."

But many of the people who work here and are most familiar with conditions in the plants argue that the situation in Honduras, at least, where about one-fifth of the clothing workers are unionized, is far more complicated than portrayed in the American debate over "sweatshops."

To make any kind of sweeping generalization is dangerous and misleading, many said during interviews here with more than 75 apparel workers and union leaders and visits to half a dozen plants, including the one that made clothes for the Gifford line.

Many here say critics from the north are more interested in protecting jobs in the United States than in improving the lot of Honduran workers.

Yes, workers and employers here say, some companies verbally abuse their workers on a regular basis, insist on compulsory overtime, impose unreachable production quotas or dismiss employees who become pregnant in order not to have to pay maternity benefits.

But other plants supply a subsidized lunch and free medical care to employees, are modern and air-conditioned, have agreed to union shops and generally respect workers' rights.

"You will find varying conditions and outlooks here," said Israel Salinas, president of the Federation of Independent Workers of Honduras, one of three rival labor groups seeking to organize the approximately 75,000 employees who work in the estimated 160 assembly plants in this country. "It all depends on whom you talk to and where you go."

A WORKER'S ESCAPE FROM RURAL POVERTY

The story told by one apparel worker, Eber Orellana Vasquez, is not unusual. He is one of some 450 employees at the King Star Garment assembly plant just south of here, a Taiwanese-owned company that produces beach shirts, shorts and other sportswear for the United States market.

At 26 he is a veteran of three years as an apparel worker and a strong supporter of the union that represents the employees in their dealings with the company.

"This has been an enormous advance for me," Mr. Orellana said, "and I give thanks to the maquila for it. My monthly income is seven times what I made in the countryside, and I've gained 30 pounds since I started working here."

Before he became an apparel worker here, Mr. Orellana explained, he worked for a decade on a dairy ranch, milking and herding cows and living in a rented shack. "My only possession there was a bicycle," he said, so small was his salary.

Now, thanks to his job as a quality control checker, he owns a house of his own, "made of brick with a zinc roof," he noted proudly, in contrast to the flimsy wood and thatch roof dwellings that are the norm in the countryside, and has access to electricity and water.

He has been able to bring his wife and a younger brother, now 17, from the ranch and find them jobs in the plant.

"Every time I go to visit the ranch, everyone wants to come back with me," Mr. Orellana said. "The work there is very hard, exhausting. You get up at 1 o'clock in the morning to start your chores, and the bosses are always mean. If you drink too much milk, they will fire you."

COMPANY ACCUSED OF RIGHTS ABUSES

The clothes for the Kathie Lee Gifford line were produced by the Global Fashion plant at the South Korean-run Galaxy Industrial Park just north of town, which has been singled out by human rights advocates here and abroad as being especially harsh and abusive to workers.

In recent testimony to Congress, a former employee at the factory, Wendy Diaz, 15, said she had been forced to work up to 74 hours a week by supervisors who regularly screamed at, hit and sexually harassed employees.

"We knew that factory wasn't the greatest," Mr. Kernaghan said in a telephone interview from New York. "We knew that conditions were pretty rough there, that people were being fired for trying to organize, that it was not a good place, not near to being among the better factories in Honduras."

Wal-Mart, which markets Mrs. Gifford's line of clothes, has no production contracts at the moment with Global Fashion. But it continues to have clothing made under contract at numerous other apparel plants in Honduras, and is being pressed by the National Labor Committee to consent to an independent monitoring program.

In an interview at the plant, Paul Kim, president of Global Fashion, acknowledged that his company required compulsory overtime of its employees, had a high employee turnover rate and might demand more effort of workers than some other companies here.

But he denied Miss Diaz's charge of systematic abuse, and described the regimen here as a form of tough love that works for the good of all concerned.

"Korea used to be a poor country, like Honduras," Mr. Kim said, speaking in Korean through a Spanish-language interpreter, "but we have had a lot of development because we worked very hard. The more you work, the more you earn. That's what Central America needs if it is going to become prosperous."

AN INDUSTRIAL BOOM BRINGS LABOR SHORTAGE

A decade ago, Honduras had virtually no assembly plants, and poor people had few options. Now, the factories have absorbed so many workers that they are creating labor shortages that have helped drive up wages for workers in other sectors, including agriculture, forestry, mining, fishing and even domestic work, traditionally the worst paid and most abusive.

"It used to be easy to get a nanny or a maid, but not now," said Jesus Canahuati, whose family owns an industrial park and several assembly plants here. "Everybody wants to work in the maquilas, because they represent an opportunity for a better life."

Within the apparel assembly industry itself, workers and employers agree, explosive growth has also encouraged the labor force to be on the move, always looking for the best offer. When workers do not like conditions where they are, both sides say, they often move to other jobs offering production incentives and increased benefits that in some cases double their base wage.

"If you don't pay more than the legal minimum, you don't get any employees," said Perry Keene, acting manager of Certified Apparel Services of Honduras, a plant here that makes infants' wear for department stores in the United States. "They will all go to other people, because it's a competitive labor market."

Another sharp difference of perspective surrounds the issue of teen-agers working in the assembly plants. The National Labor Committee and other critics in the United States contend that the practice, widespread here, is "destroying a whole generation of young women" and have called for American apparel concerns to stop doing business with all suppliers who hire children.

HONDURAN UNIONS DEFEND CHILD LABOR

But all three of the leading labor federations here, including unions that have worked closely with the National Labor Committee in denouncing abuses of workers, disagree with that position. Instead, acting in accordance with the demands of members whose own children are already working, they want the Honduran Government to enforce regulations that are already on the books. Under Honduran law, adolescents between the ages of 14 and 16 can be employed for up to six hours a day. To do so, they must first obtain the permission of their parents, which is usually readily granted, and of the Labor

Ministry, also easily obtained in a country in which education for the majority of the population ends at sixth grade.

"This country is not the United States," said Evangelina Argueta, a labor organizer in Choloma, a suburb just north of here with a large concentration of industrial parks. "Very few Honduran mothers can afford the luxury of feeding children until they are 18 years old without putting them to work."

Nevertheless, responding to complaints from the United States and to the fears of blacklisting that have arisen as a result, the Honduran Maquiladora Association says its members have now stopped hiring any workers under 16. Union leaders and workers say factory owners have also been reviewing their personnel records and dismissing all employees who are minors.

But that does not mean the dismissed youngsters are returning to school. On the contrary, management and labor agree that most of the children have instead sought new jobs outside the assembly sector that are lower paying and more physically demanding or are buying fake documents in an effort to sneak their way back into the apparel plants.

CAMPAIGN BRINGS UNINTENDED RESULT

Mr. Kernaghan acknowledged that his group's effort to end child labor had produced unanticipated consequences. "Obviously this is not what we wanted to happen," he said.

He added that his group had discussed with Honduran factory owners an arrangement that would permit the 14- to 16-year-olds already employed to keep their jobs but shift future hiring toward adults.

"It's a tragic situation that needs to be resolved," he added. When asked how that should be done, he replied, "I may not be the right person to answer that kind of question, since I'm not an economist."

Many older workers who themselves began working at a young age assert that the American campaign may actually be hurting the very people it is intended to help.

Rene Javier Robertson, for example, left school at 13 to work as a fare collector on a bus "because with four kids besides me, my family needed me to work" and opportunities for teen-agers were limited.

"In 11 years on that job, I worked 14 hours a day, seven days a week, never got a day's vacation, didn't get paid when I was sick, and had to content myself with whatever wage the bus driver felt like paying me at the end of the day," said Mr. Robertson, who got a job on the assembly line three years ago and is now 27. "I was a slave, with no rights."

Teen-agers working at assembly plants "are a million times better off in here than out there on the street, because the maquila represents progress," Mr. Robertson added. "The work here isn't heavy, there are many benefits, and they have to respect your rights. I wish the maquila had existed when I started to work, because I could have avoided a lot of suffering."

Source: From Larry Rohter, "Hondurans in Sweatshops See Opportunity," July 18, 1996. Copyright © 1996 The New York Times Co. Reprinted with permission.

DISCUSSION QUESTIONS

1. Many employees in sweatshops, having come from jobs that pay even less and offer no benefits or security, see employment in a sweatshop as a means to a better life. What rights do human rights advocates from developed countries have to oppose the use of sweatshops by foreign firms?

2. Are organizations like the National Labor Committee acting in good faith on behalf of the workers in sweatshops? Or is their ulterior motive to save jobs of American workers which are exported to sweatshops abroad?

3. A decade ago, Honduras had virtually no assembly plants, and poor people had few options. Now, the factories have absorbed so many workers that they are creating labor shortages that have helped drive up wages of workers in other sectors, including agriculture, forestry, mining, fishing, and even domestic work, traditionally the worst paid and most rife with abuse. Is this not an argument in favor of sweatshops?

4. Does free trade stimulate the growth of the number of sweatshops worldwide?

5. What would be the impacts on the global competitiveness of international companies if all nations do not adopt uniform policies that would eliminate sweatshops?

Notes

1. Paul W. Taylor, *Principles of Ethics: An Introduction to Ethics,* 2nd. ed. (Encino, CA: Dickenson, 1975), p. 1.

2. Sita C. Amba-Rao, "Multinational Corporate Social Responsibility, Ethics, Interactions, and Third World Governments: An Agenda for the 1990s," *Journal of Business Ethics* 12 (1993), p. 553.

3. Davis Weir and Mark Schapiro, *Circle of Poison* (San Francisco: Institute for Food and Development Policy, 1981), p. 22.

4. Kennedy Smith, "ISO Considers Corporate Social Responsibility Standards," *Journal for Quality and Participation* 25, no. 3 (2002), p. 42.

5. Isabelle Maignan and David A. Ralston, "Corporate Social Responsibility in Europe and the U.S.: Insights from Businesses' Self-Presentations," *Journal of International Business Studies* 33, no. 3 (2002), pp. 497–515.

6. R. Hooghiemstra, "Corporate Communication and Impression Management—New Perspectives: Why Companies Engage in Corporate Social Reporting," *Journal of Business Ethics* 27 (2000), pp. 55–68.

7. J. Handelman and S. Arnold, "The Role of Marketing Actions with a Social Dimension: Appeals to the Institutional Environment," *Journal of Marketing* 63 (1999), pp. 33–48.

8. O. C. Ferrell and John Fraedrich, *Business Ethics: Ethical Decision Making and Cases,* 2nd ed. (Boston: Houghton Mifflin, 1994), p. 60.

9. Tom L. Beauchamp and Norma E. Bowie, eds., *Ethical Theory and Business* (Englewood Cliffs, NJ: Prentice Hall, 1979).

10. J. S. Mill, *Utilitarianism* (Indianapolis:Bobbs-Merrill, 1957). First published 1863.

11. Richard Brandt, *Ethical Theory* (Englewood Cliffs, NJ: Prentice Hall, 1959), pp. 253–254.

12. Donald M. Borchert and David Stewart, *Exploring Ethics* (New York: Macmillan, 1986), p. 199.

13. Ibid.

14. Ferrell and Fraedrich, *Business Ethics,* p. 57.

15. Gerald F. Cavanagh, Dennis J. Moberg, and Manuel Velasquez, "The Ethics of Organizational Politics," *Academy of Management Review* 6, no.3 (1981), p. 366.

16. Adapted from Cavanagh, Moberg, and Velasquez, "The Ethics of Organizational Politics," p. 366.

17. Thomas Donaldson, *The Ethics of International Business* (New York: Oxford University Press, 1989), p. 14.

18. Clarence C. Walton, *The Moral Manager* (Cambridge, MA: Ballinger, 1988), p. 110.

19. Richard T. De George, *Competing with Integrity in International Business* (New York, Oxford University Press, 1993), p. 11

20. Ibid., p. 19.

21. Ibid., pp. 19–21

22. Thomas Donaldson, "Can Multinationals Stage a Universal Morality Play?" *Business and Society Review,* 2001, pp. 51–55

23. Thomas W. Dunfee, N. Vraig Smith, and William T. Ross Jr., "Social Contracts and Marketing Ethics," *Journal of Marketing,* July 1999, pp. 14–32; Andrew Stark, "What Is the Matter with Business Ethics?" *Harvard Business Review* 71 (May–June 1993), pp. 38–48.

24. Kathleen A. Getz, "International Codes of Conduct: An Analysis of Ethical Reasoning," *Journal of Business Ethics* 9, no. 7 (1990), pp. 567–578.

25. The following material on codes of conduct for MNCs is quoted from William C. Frederick, "The Moral Authority of Transnational Corporate Codes," *Journal of Business Ethics* 10 (1992), pp. 166–167.

26. William D. Montalbano, "A Challenge to Italy's Status Quo," *Philadelphia Inquirer,* March 21, 1993, pp. E1, E4.

27. Andy Pasztor and Bruce Ingersoll, "Buying Business: Some Weapons Makers Are Said to Continue Illicit Foreign Outlays," *Wall Street Journal,* November 5, 1993, pp. A1, A5; Douglas Pasternak, "Selling Hardware Overseas," *U.S. News and World Report,* November 15, 1993, p. 64.

28. "Thousands in Pakistan Call for End to Child Labor," *Philadelphia Inquirer,* April 26, 1995, p. A8.

29. Robert D. Haas, "Ethics in the Trenches," *Across the Board,* May 1994, pp. 12–13.

30. Ibid.

31. Ibid.

32. Ibid.

33. John Byrne, "Businesses Are Signing Up for Ethics 101," *BusinessWeek,* February 15, 1988, p. 5.

34. Haas, "Ethics in the Trenches," pp. 12–13.

35. Byrne, "Businesses Are Signing Up for Ethics 101," pp. 56–57.

Case IV

Hitting the Wall: Nike and International Labor Practices

Debora L. Spar

Moore: Twelve year olds working in [Indonesian] factories? That's O.K. with you?
Knight: They're not 12-year-olds working in factories . . . the minimum age is 14.
Moore: How about 14 then? Does that bother you?
Knight: No.
>—Phil Knight, Nike CEO, talking to Director Michael Moore in a scene from documentary film *The Big One,* 1997.

Nike is raising the minimum age of footwear factory workers to 18 . . . Nike has zero tolerance for underage workers.[1]
>—Phil Knight, 1998

In 1997, Nguyen Thi Thu Phuong died while making sneakers. As she was trimming synthetic soles in a Nike contracting factory, a co-worker's machine broke, spraying metal parts across the factory floor and into Phuong's heart. The 23 year-old Vietnamese woman died instantly.[2]

Although it may have been the most dramatic, Phuong's death was hardly the first misfortune to hit Nike's far-flung manufacturing empire. Indeed, in the 1980s and 1990s, the corporation had been plagued by a series of labor incidents and public relations nightmares: underage workers in Indonesian plants, allegations of coerced overtime in China, dangerous working conditions in Vietnam. For a while, the stories had been largely confined to labor circles and activist publications. By the time of Phuong's death, however, labor conditions at Nike had hit the mainstream. Stories of reported abuse at Nike plants had been carried in publications such as *Time* and *BusinessWeek* and students from major universities such as Duke and Brown had organized boycotts of Nike products. Even Doonesbury had joined the fray, with a series of cartoons that linked the company to underage and exploited Asian

[1] "Nike CEO Phil Knight Announces New Labor Initiatives," *PR Newswire,* May 12, 1998.
[2] Tim Larimer, "Sneaker Gulag: Are Asian Workers Really Exploited?" *Time International,* May 11, 1998, p. 30.

workers. Before these attacks, Nike had been widely regarded as one of the world's coolest and most successful companies. Now Nike, the company of Michael Jordan and Tiger Woods; Nike, the sign of the swoosh and athletic prowess, was increasingly becoming known as the company of labor abuse. And its initial response—"We don't make shoes"—was becoming harder and harder to sustain.[3]

NIKE, INC.

Based in Beaverton, Oregon, Nike had been a corporate success story for more than three decades. It was a sneaker company, but one armed with an inimitable attitude, phenomenal growth, and the apparent ability to dictate fashion trends to some of the world's most influential consumers. In the 1970s, Nike had first begun to capture the attention of both trend-setting teenagers and financial observers. Selling a combination of basic footwear and street-smart athleticism, Nike pushed its revenues from a 1972 level of $60,000 to a startling $49 million in just ten years.[4] It went public in 1980 and then astounded Wall Street in the mid-1990s as annual growth stayed resolutely in the double digits and revenues soared to over $9 billion. By 1998, Nike controlled over 40% of the $14.7 billion U.S. athletic footwear market. It was also a growing force in the $64 billion sports apparel market, selling a wide range of sport-inspired gear to consumers around the globe.[5]

What differentiated Nike from its competitors was not so much its shoes as its strategy. Like Reebok and adidas and New Balance, Nike sold a fairly wide range of athletic footwear to a fairly wide range of consumers: men and women, athletes and non-athletes, in markets around the world. Its strategy, though, was path breaking, the product of a relatively simple idea that CEO Phil Knight had first concocted in 1962 while still a student at Stanford Business School. The formula had two main prongs. First, the company would shave costs by outsourcing *all* manufacturing. There would be no in-house production, no dedicated manufacturing lines. Rather all product would be made by independent contracting factories, creating one of the world's first "virtual" corporations—a manufacturing firm with no physical assets. Then, the money saved through outsourcing would be poured into marketing. In particular, Knight focussed from the start on celebrity endorsements, using high-profile athletes to establish an invincible brand identity around the Nike name. While other firms had used celebrity endorsements in the past, Nike took the practice to new heights, emblazoning the Nike logo across athletes such as Michael Jordan and Tiger Woods, and letting their very celebrity represent the Nike image. "To see name athletes wearing Nike shoes," Knight insisted, "was more convincing than anything we could say about them."[6] With the help of the "swoosh," a distinctive and instantly recognizable logo, Nike became by the 1990s one of the world's best known brands, as well as a global symbol of athleticism and urban cool.

But within this success story lay a central irony that would only become apparent in the late 1990s. While the *marketing* of Nike's products was based on selling a high profile fashion item to affluent Americans who only wished they could "Just Do It" as well as Woods or Jordan, the *manufacture* of these sneakers was based on an arms-length and often uneasy relationship with low-paid, non-American workers. For according to Knight's original plan, not only would Nike outsource, but it would outsource specifically to low cost parts of the world.

Nike signed its first contracts with Japanese manufacturers but eventually shifted its supply base to firms in South Korea and Taiwan, where costs were lower and production reliable. In 1982, 86% of Nike sneakers came from one of these two countries and Nike had established a large network of suppliers in both nations. But as South Korea and Taiwan grew richer, costs rose and Nike began to urge its suppliers to move their operations to new, lower cost regions. Eager to remain in the company's good graces, most manufacturers rapidly complied, moving their relatively inexpensive plants to China or Indonesia. By 1990, these countries had largely replaced South Korea and Taiwan as the

---

[3] The quote is from Martha Benson, Nike's regional spokeswoman in Asia. See Larimer, p. 30.

[4] David B. Yoffie, *Nike: A (Condensed)*, HBS Case 391-238 (Boston: HBS Press, 1991), p. 1.

[5] Both figures are for retail sales. *Footwear 1999* (North Palm Beach; Athletic Footwear Association, 1999), introduction; Dana Eisman Cohen and Sabina McBride, *Athletic Footwear Outlook 1999* (New York: Donaldson, Lufkin & Jenrette, 1998), p. 3.

[6] Yoffie, p. 6.

core of Nike's global network. Indonesia, in particular, had become a critical location, with six factories that supplied Nike and a booming, enthusiastic footwear industry.[7]

TAKING CARE OF BUSINESS

At first, Indonesia seemed an ideal location for Nike. Wages were low, the workforce was docile, and an authoritarian government was yearning for foreign direct investment. There were unions in the country and occasional hints of activism, but the Suharlo government clearly was more interested in wooing investors than in acceding to any union demands. So wages stayed low and labor demands were minimal. In 1991, the daily minimum wage in Indonesia's capital city was barely $1, compared to a typical daily wage of $24.40 in South Korea[8] and a U.S. hourly wage in athletic shoe manufacturing of about $8.[9] For firms like Nike, this differential was key: according to a reporter for the *Far Eastern Economic Review,* shoes coming out of China and Indonesia cost roughly 50% less than those sourced from Taiwan and South Korea.[10]

Just as Nike was settling into its Indonesian operations, though, a rare wave of labor unrest swept accross the country. Strikes, which had been virtually nonexistent in the 1980s, began to occur with increasing frequency; according to government figures, there were 112 strikes in 1991,[11] a sharp increase from the 19 reported in 1989.[12] A series of polemical articles about foreign companies' labor abuses also appeared in Indonesian newspapers, triggering unprecedented demands from factory workers and empowering a small but potent band of labor organizers.

The source of these strikes and articles was mysterious. Some claimed that the Indonesian government was itself behind the movement, trying to convince an increasingly suspicious international community of the country's commitment to freedom of speech and labor rights. Others saw the hand of outside organizers, who had come to Indonesia solely to unionize its work force and embarrass its foreign investors. And still others saw the outbursts as random eruptions, cracks in the authoritarian veneer which quickly took on a life of their own. In any case, though, the unrest occurred just around the time of Nike's expansion into Indonesia. In 1991 the Asian-American Free Labor Association (AAFLI, a branch of the AFL-CIO) published a highly critical report on foreign companies in Indonesia. Later that year, a group of Indonesian labor economists at the Institut Teknology Bandung (ITB), issued a similar report, documenting abusive practices in Indonesian factories and tracing them to foreign owners. In the midst of this stream of criticism was a labor organizer with a deep-seated dislike for Nike and a determination to shape its global practices. His name was Jeff Ballinger.

THE ROLE OF JEFF BALLINGER

A labor activist since high school, Ballinger felt passionately that any company had a significant obligation towards even its lowliest workers. He was particularly concerned about the stubborn gap between wage rates in developed and developing worlds, and about the opportunities this gap created for rich Western companies to exploit low-wage, politically repressed labor pools. In 1988, Ballinger was assigned to run the AAFLI office in Indonesia, and was charged with investigating labor conditions in Indonesian plants and studying minimum wage compliance by overseas American companies. In the course of his research Ballinger interviewed workers at hundreds of factories and documented widespread worker dissatisfaction with labor conditions.

Before long, Nike emerged as a key target. Ballinger believed that Nike's policy of competing on the basis of cost fostered and even encouraged contractors to mistreat their workers in pursuit of unrealistic production quotas. Although Indonesia had worker protection legislation in place, widespread corruption made the laws essentially useless. While the government employed 700 labor

---

[7] Philip M. Rosenzweig and Pam Woo, *International Sourcing in Footwear: Nike and Reebok,* HBS Case 394-189 (Boston: HBS Press, 1994), pp. 2–5.

[8] Elliot B. Smith, "K-Swiss in Korea," *California Business,* October 1991, p. 77.

[9] Rosenzweig and Woo, p. 3.

[10] Mark Clifford, "Pain in Pusan," *Far Eastern Economic Review,* November 5, 1992, p. 59.

[11] Suhaini Aznam, "The Toll of Low Wages," *Far Eastern Economic Review,* April 2, 1992, p. 50.

[12] Margot Cohen, "Union of Problems: Government Faces Growing Criticism on Labour Relations," *Far Eastern Economic Review,* August 26, 1993, p. 23.

inspectors, Ballinger found that out of 17,000 violations reported in 1988, only 12 prosecutions were ever made. Bribery took care of the rest.[13] Nike contractors, in particular, he believed, were regularly flouting Indonesian labor laws and paying below-subsistence wages that did not enable workers to meet their daily requirements for food and other necessities. And to top matters off, he found Nike's attitude in the face of these labor practices galling: "It was right around the time that the swoosh started appearing on everything and everyone," Ballinger remembered. "Maybe it was the swagger that did it."[14]

What also "did it," though, was Ballinger's own strategic calculation—a carefully crafted policy of "one country–one company." Ballinger knew that his work would be effective only if it was carefully focused. And if his goal was to draw worldwide attention to the exploitation of third-world factory workers by rich U.S. companies, then Nike made a nearly ideal target. The arithmetic was simple. The same marketing and branding power that drove Nike's bottom line could also be used to drive moral outrage against the exploitation of Asian workers. After the publication of his AAFLI report, Ballinger set out to transform Nike's competitive strength into a strategic vulnerability.

For several years he worked at the fringes of the activist world, operating out of his in-laws' basement and publishing his own newsletter on Nike's practices. For the most part, no one really noticed. But then, in the early 1990s Ballinger's arguments coincided with the strikes that swept across Indonesia and the newfound interest of media groups. Suddenly his stories were big news and both the Indonesian government and U.S. firms had begun to pay attention.

EARLY CHANGES

The first party to respond to criticism from Ballinger and other activists was the government itself. In January 1992 Indonesia raised the official minimum daily wage from 2100 rupiah to 2500 rupiah (US$1.24). According to outside observers, the new wage still was not nearly enough: it only provided 70% of a worker's required minimal physical need (as determined by the Indonesian government) and was further diluted by the way in which many factories distributed wages and benefits.[15] The increased wage also had no impact on "training wages," which were lower than the minimum wage and often paid long after the training period had expired. Many factories, moreover, either ignored the new wage regulations or successfully petitioned the government for exemption. Still, the government's actions at least demonstrated some willingness to respond. The critics took note of this movement and continued their strikes and media attacks.

Despite the criticism, Nike insisted that labor conditions in its contractors' factories were not—could not—be Nike's concern or its responsibility. And even if labor violations did exist in Nike's contracting factories, stated the company's general manager in Jakarta, "I don't know that I need to know."[16] Nike's company line on the issue was clear and stubborn: without an inhouse manufacturing facility, the company simply could not be held responsible for the actions of independent contractors.

Realizing the severity of the labor issue, though, Nike did ask Dusty Kidd, a newly-hired member of its public relations department, to draft a series of regulations for its contractors. In 1992, these regulations were composed into a Code of Conduct and Memorandum of Understanding and attached to the new contracts sent to Nike contractors. In the Memorandum, Nike addressed seven different aspects of working conditions, including safety standards, environmental regulation and worker insurance. It required its suppliers to certify they were following all applicable rules and regulations and outlined general principles of honesty, respect, and non-discrimination.

Meanwhile, other shoe companies had been facing similar problems. Reebok, a chief competitor of Nike, also sourced heavily from Indonesia and South Korea. Like Nike, it too had been the subject of activist pressure and unflattering media. But unlike Nike, Reebok had moved aggressively into the human rights arena. In 1988, it created the Reebok Human Rights Award, bestowed each year on youthful contributors to the cause of human rights, and in 1990 it adopted a formal human rights pol-

---

[13] Interview with casewriter, Cambridge, MA, July 6, 1999.

[14] Ibid.

[15] A factory, for example, could pay a base wage lower than 2500 rupiah, but bring total compensation up to legal levels by the addition of a food allowance and incentive payments (see Aznam, p. 50).

[16] Adam Schwarz, "Running a Business," *Far Eastern Economic Review*, June 20, 1991, p. 16.

icy.[17] When activists accused the company of violating workers' rights in Indonesia, Reebok responded with a far-reaching set of guidelines, one that spoke the explicit language of human rights, set forth specific standards for the company's contractors and promised to audit these contractors to ensure their compliance.[18] It was a big step for an American manufacturer and considerably farther than Nike had been willing to go.

INTO THE SPOTLIGHT

By 1992, criticism of Nike's labor practices had begun to seep outside of Indonesia. In the August issue of *Harper's* magazine, Ballinger published an annotated pay stub from an Indonesian factory, making the soon-to-be famous comparison between workers' wages and Michael Jordan's endorsement contract. He noted that at the wage rates shown on the pay stub, it would take an Indonesian worker 44, 492 years to make the equivalent of Jordan's endorsement contract.[19] Then the Portland *Oregonian,* Nike's hometown newspaper, ran a series of critical articles during the course of the 1992 Barcelona Olympics. Also at the Olympics, a small band of protestors materialized and handed out leaflets that charged Nike with exploitation of factory workers. The first mainstream coverage of the issue came in July 1993, when CBS interviewed Indonesian workers who revealed that they were paid just 19¢ an hour. Women workers could only leave the company barracks on Sunday, and needed a special letter of permission from management to do so. Nike responded somewhat more forcefully to this next round of allegations, hiring accounting firm Ernst & Young to conduct formal audits of its overseas factories. However, because Ernst & Young was paid by Nike to perform these audits, activists questioned their objectivity from the start. Public criticism of Nike's labor practices continued to mount.

Then suddenly, in 1996, the issue of foreign labor abuse acquired a name and a face: it was Kathie Lee Gifford, a popular daytime talk show host. In April human rights activists revealed that a line of clothing endorsed by Gifford had been manufactured by child labor in Honduras. Rather than denying the connection Gifford instantly rallied to the cause. When she appeared on television, crying and apologetic, a wave of media coverage erupted. Or as Ballinger recalls, "That's when my phone really started ringing."[20] Although Nike was not directly involved in the Gifford scandal, it quickly emerged as a symbol of worker exploitation and a high-profile media scapegoat.

Child labor was the first area of concern. In July, *Life* magazine ran a story about child labor in Pakistan, and published a photo of a 12 year old boy stitching a Nike soccer ball.[21] Then Gifford herself publicly called upon fellow celebrities such as Michael Jordan to investigate the conditions under which their endorsed products were made and to take action if need be. Jordan brushed away suggestions that he was personally responsible for conditions in Nike factories, leaving responsibility to the company itself. When Nike refused to let Reverend Jesse Jackson tour one of its Indonesian factories the media jumped all over the story, noting by contrast that Reebok had recently flown an executive to Indonesia just to give Jackson a tour.

At this point, even some pro-business observers began to jump on the bandwagon. As an editorial in *BusinessWeek* cautioned: "Too few executives understand that the clamor for ethical sourcing isn't going to disappear with the wave of a magic press release. They have protested, disingenuously, that conditions at factories run by subcontractors are beyond their control . . . Such attitudes won't wash anymore. As the industry gropes for solutions," the editorial concluded, "Nike will be a key company to watch."[22]

---

[17] Rosenzweig and Woo, p. 7.

[18] Ibid., pp. 16–17.

[19] Jeff Ballinger, "The New Free-Trade Heel," *Harper's Magazine,* August 1992, p. 64.

[20] Casewriter interview.

[21] Nike's vigorous protests stopped the magazine from running the photo on its cover. Nike convincingly argued that the photo was staged, because the ball was inflated so that the Nike "swoosh" was clearly visible. In fact, soccer balls are stitched while deflated. However, the company did admit it had inadvertently relied on child labor during its first months of production in Pakistan.

[22] Mark L. Clifford, "Commentary: Keep the Heat on Sweatshops," *BusinessWeek,* December 23, 1996, p. 90.

THE VIEW FROM WASHINGTON

Before long, the spotlight on the labor issue extended all the way to Washington. Sensing a hot issue, several senators and representatives jumped into the action and began to suggest legislative solutions to the issue of overseas labor abuse. Representative George Miller (D-CA) launched a campaign aimed at retailers that would mandate the use of "No Sweat" labels to guarantee that no exploited or child labor had been employed in the production of a garment. "Parents," he proclaimed, "have a right to know that the toys and clothes they buy for their children are not made by exploited children." To enforce such guarantees, Miller added, "I think Congress is going to have to step in."[23]

On the heels of this public outcry, President Clinton convened a Presidential task force to study the issue, calling on leaders in the apparel and footwear industries to join and help develop acceptable labor standards for foreign factories. Known as the Apparel Industry Partnership (AIP), the coalition, which also included members of the activist, labor, and religious communities, was meant to be a model collaboration between industry and its most outspoken critics, brokered by the U.S. government. Nike was the first company to join.

In order to supplement its hiring of Ernst & Young, in October 1996 Nike also established a Labor Practices Department, headed by former public relations executive Dusty Kidd. In a press release, Knight announced the formation of the new department and praised Nike's recent initiatives regarding fair labor practices, such as participation in Clinton's AIP, membership in the organization Business for Social Responsibility, and an ongoing dialogue with concerned non-governmental organizations (NGOs). "Every year we continue to raise the bar," said Knight. "First by having Ernst & Young audits, and now with a group of Nike employees whose sole focus will be to help make things better for workers who make Nike products. In labor practices as in sport, we at Nike believe 'There is No Finish Line.' "[24] And indeed he was right, for the anti-Nike campaign was just getting started.

THE HOTSEAT

As far as public relations were concerned, 1997 was even worse for Nike than 1996. Much as Ballinger had anticipated, Nike's giant marketing machine was easily turned against itself and in a climate awash with anti-Nike sentiment, any of Nike's attempts at self promotion became easy targets. In 1997 the company began expanding its chain of giant retail stores, only to find that each newly opened Niketown came with an instant protest rally, complete with shouting spectators, sign waving picketers, and police barricades. Knowing a good story when they saw it, reporters eagerly dragged Nike's celebrity endorsers into the fracas. Michael Jordan was pelted with questions about Nike at press conferences intended to celebrate his athletic performance, and football great Jerry Rice was hounded to the point of visible agitation when he arrived at the grand opening of a new Niketown in San Francisco.[25]

Perhaps one of the clearest indicators that Nike was in trouble came in May 1997, when Doonesbury, the popular comic strip, devoted a full week to Nike's labor issues. In 1,500 newspapers, millions of readers watched as Kim, Mike Doonesbury's wife, returned to Vietnam and found a long-lost cousin laboring in dismal conditions at a Nike factory. The strips traced Kim's growing involvement in the activist movement and the corrupt factory manager's attempts to deceive her about true working conditions in Nike contracting factories. In Doonesbury, Nike had reached an unfortunate cultural milestone. As one media critic noted: "It's sort of like getting in Jay Leno's monologue. It means your perceived flaws have reached a critical mass, and everyone feels free to pick on you."[26] The appearance of the Doonesbury strips also marked the movement of anti-Nike sentiment from the fringes of American life to the mainstream. Once the pet cause of leftist activists, Nike bashing had become America's newest spectator sport.

Even some of the company's natural friends took a dim view of its actions. The *Wall Street Journal* ran an opinion piece alleging that "Nike Lets Critics Kick It Around." The writer argued that Nike had been "its own worst enemy" and that its public relations efforts had only made the problem worse.

[23] "Honduran Child Labor Described," *The Boston Globe,* May 30, 1996, p. 13.

[24] "Nike Establishes Labor Practices Department," *PR Newswire,* October 2, 1996.

[25] "Protestors Swipe at the Swoosh, Catch Nike's Jerry Rice Off Guard," *The Portland Oregonian,* Feburary 21, 1997, p. C1.

[26] Jeff Manning, "Doonesbury Could Put Legs on Nike Controversy," *The Portland Oregonian,* May 25, 1997, p. D01.

According to the writer, had Nike acknowledged its wrongdoing early on and then presented economic facts that showed the true situation of the workers, the crisis would have fizzled.[27] Instead it had simply gathered steam. Even more trouble loomed ahead with the anticipated release of *The Big One,* a documentary film by Michael Moore that was widely expected to be highly critical of Nike's labor practices.

DAMAGE CONTROL

Late in 1996 the company decided to turn to outside sources, hiring Andrew Young, the respected civil rights leader and former mayor of Atlanta, to conduct an independent evaluation of its Code of Conduct. In January 1997, Knight granted Young's newly-formed GoodWorks International firm "blanket authority . . . to go anywhere, see anything, and talk with anybody in the Nike family about this issue."[28]

Shortly thereafter Young went to Asia, visited Nike suppliers and returned to issue a formal report. On the day the report was released, Nike took out full-page advertisements in major newspapers that highlighted one of Young's main conclusions: "It is my sincere belief that Nike is doing a good job . . . But Nike can and should do better."[29] Young did not give Nike carte blanche with regard to labor practices. Indeed, he made a number of recommendations, urging Nike to improve their systems for reporting workers' grievances, to publicize their Code more widely and explain it more clearly, and to implement cultural awareness and language training programs for expatriate managers. Young also stated that third party monitoring of factories was necessary, but agreed that it was not appropriate for Nike's NGO critics to fulfill that function.

Rather than calming Nike's critics, though, Young's report had precisely the opposite effect. Critics were outraged by the report's research methodology and conclusions, and unimpressed by Young's participation. They argued that Young had failed to address the issue of factory wages, which was for many observers the crux of the issue, and had spent only 10 days interviewing workers. During these interviews, moreover, Young had relied on translators provided by Nike, a major lapse in accepted human rights research technique. Finally, critics also noted that the report was filled with photos and used a large, showy typeface, an unusual format for a research report.

From the start, Nike executives had argued in vain that they were the target of an uninformed media campaign, pointing out that although Nike was being vigorously monitored by activists and the media, no one was monitoring the monitors. This point was forcefully made by the publication of a five page *New Republic* article in which writer Stephen Glass blasted the Young report for factual inaccuracies and deception, and summed up: "This was a public relations problem, and the world's largest sneaker company did what it does best: it purchased a celebrity endorsement."[30] Glass's claims were echoed by several other media outlets that also decried Nike's disingenuousness and Young's ineptitude. However, within months a major scandal erupted at the *New Republic* when it was discovered that most of Glass's articles were nearly fictional. Apparently, Glass routinely quoted individuals with whom he had never spoken or who did not even exist, and relied upon statistics and information from organizations he invented himself.

THE ISSUE OF WAGES

In the public debate, the question of labor conditions was largely couched in the language of human rights. It was about child labor, or slave labor, or workers who toiled in unsafe or inhumane environments. Buried beneath these already contentious issues, though, was an even more contentious one: wages. According to many labor activists, workers in the developing world were simply being paid too little—too little to compensate for their efforts, too little compared to the final price of the good they produced, too little, even, to live on. To many business economists, though, such arguments were moot at best and veiled protectionism at worst. Wages, they maintained, were simply set by market

---

[27] Greg Rushford, "Nike Lets Critics Kick It Around," *The Wall Street Journal,* May 12, 1997, p. A14.

[28] Andrew Young, *Report: The Nike Code of Conduct* (GoodWorks International, LLC, 1997) p. 27.

[29] Young, p. 59.

[30] Stephen Glass, "The Young and the Feckless," *The New Republic,* September 8, 1997, p. 22.

forces: by definition, wages could not be too low, and there was nothing firms could or should do to affect wage rates. As the debate over labor conditions evolved, the argument over wages had become progressively more heated.

Initially, Nike sought to defuse the wage issue simply by ignoring it, or by reiterating the argument that this piece of the labor situation was too far beyond their control. In the Young Report, therefore, the issue of wages was explicitly set aside. As Young explained in his introduction: "I was not asked by Nike to address compensation and 'cost of living' issues which some in the human rights and NGO community had hoped would be a part of this report." Then he went on: "Are workers in developing countries paid far less than U.S. workers? Of course they are. Are their standards of living painfully low by U.S. standards? Of course they are. This is a blanket criticism that can be leveled at almost every U.S. company that manufactures abroad . . . But it is not reasonable to argue that any one particular U.S. company should be forced to pay U.S. wages abroad while its direct competitors do not."[31] It was a standard argument, and one that found strong support even among many pro-labor economists. In the heat of public debate, however, it registered only as self-serving.

The issue of wages emerged again in the spring of 1997, when Nike arranged for students at Dartmouth's Amos Tuck School of Business to conduct a detailed survey on "the suitability of wages and benefits paid to its Vietnamese and Indonesian contract factory workers."[32] Completed in November 1997, the students' *Survey of Vietnamese and Indonesian Domestic Expenditure Levels* was a 45 page written study with approximately 50 pages of attached data. The authors surveyed both workers and residents of the areas in which the factories were located to determine typical spending patterns and the cost of basic necessities.

In Vietnam, the students found that "The factory workers, after incurring essential expenditures, can generate a significant amount of discretionary income."[33] This discretionary income was often used by workers to purchase special items such as bicycles or wedding gifts for family members. In Indonesia, results varied with worker demographics. While 91% of workers reported being able to support themselves individually, only 49% reported being able to also support their dependents. Regardless of demographic status, 82% of workers surveyed in Indonesia either saved wages or contributed each month to their families.[34]

Additionally, the survey found that most workers were not the primary wage earners in their households. Rather, in Vietnam at least, factory wages were generally earned by young men or women and served "to *augment* aggregate household income, with the primary occupation of the household parents being farming or shopkeeping."[35] The same was often true in Indonesia. For instance, in one Indonesian household the students visited, a family of six had used one daughter's minimum wage from a Nike factory to purchase luxury items such as leather couches and a king sized bed.[36] While workers in both countries managed to save wages for future expenditure, the authors found that Indonesians typically put their wages in a bank, while Vietnamese workers were more likely to hold their savings in the form of rice or cows.

Economically, data such as these supported the view that companies such as Nike were actually furthering progress in the developing countries, providing jobs and wages to people who formerly had neither. In the public view, however, the social comparison was unavoidable. According to the Tuck study, the average worker in a Vietnamese Nike factory made about $1.67 per day. A pair of Penny Hardaway basketball sneakers retailed at $150. The criticism continued to mount.

In November there was even more bad news. A disgruntled Nike employee leaked excerpts of an internal Ernst & Young report that uncovered serious health and safety issues in a factory outside of Ho Chi Minh City. According to the Ernst & Young report, a majority of workers suffered from a respiratory ailment caused by poor ventilation and exposure to toxic chemicals. The plant did not have

[31] Young, pp. 9–11.

[32] Derek Calzini, Shawna Huffman, Jake Odden, Steve Tran, and Jean Tsai, *Nike, Inc: Survey of Vietnamese and Indonesian Domestic Expenditure Levels,* November 3, 1997, Field Study in International Business (Dartmouth, NH: The Amos Tuck School, 1997), p. 5.

[33] Ibid., p. 8.

[34] Ibid., p. 9.

[35] Ibid., p. 31.

[36] Ibid., p. 44.

proper safety equipment and training, and workers were forced to work 15 more hours than allowed by law. But according to spokesman Vada Manager the problems no longer existed: "This shows our system of monitoring works. We have uncovered these issues clearly before anyone else, and we have moved fairly expeditiously to correct them."[37] Once again, the denial only made the criticism worse.

HITTING THE WALL

FISCAL YEAR 1998

Until the spring of 1997, Nike sneakers were still selling like hotcakes. The company's stock price had hit $76 and futures orders reached a record high. Despite the storm of criticism lobbied against it, Nike seemed invincible.

Just a year later, however, the situation was drastically different. As Knight admitted to stockholders, Nike's fiscal year 1998 "produced considerable pain." In the third quarter 1998, the company was beset by weak demand and retail oversupply, triggered in part by the Asian currency crisis. Earnings fell 69%, the company's first loss in 13 years. In response, Knight announced significant restructuring charges and the layoff of 1,600 workers.[38]

Much the same dynamic that drove labor criticism drove the 1998 downturn: Nike became a victim of its own popularity. Remarked one analyst: "When I was growing up, we used to say that rooting for the Yankees is like rooting for U.S. Steel. Today, rooting for Nike is like rooting for Microsoft."[39] The company asserted that criticism of Nike's labor practices had nothing to do with the downturn. But it was clear that Nike was suffering from a serious image problem. For whatever reasons, Americans were sick of the swoosh. Although Nike billed its shoes as high performance athletic gear, it was well known that 80% of its shoes were sold for fashion purposes. And fashion was a notoriously fickle patron. Competing sneaker manufacturers, particularly adidas, were quick to take advantage of the giant's woes. Adidas' three-stripe logo fast replaced Nike's swoosh among the teen trendsetter crowd; rival brands New Balance and Airwalk tripled their advertising budgets and saw sales surge.

To make matters worse, the anti-Nike headlines had trickled down to the nation's campuses, where a newly invigorated activist movement cast Nike as a symbol of corporate greed and exploitation. With its roots deep in the University of Oregon track team (Knight had been a long distance runner for the school), Nike had long treasured its position as supplier to the top athletic universities. Now, just as young consumers were choosing adidas over Nike at the cash register, campus activists rejected Nike's contracts with their schools and demanded all contracts cease until labor practices were rectified. In late 1997, Nike's $7.2 million endorsement deal with the University of North Carolina sparked protests and controversy on campus; in early 1998 an assistant soccer coach at St. John's University, James Keady, publicly quit his job rather than wear the swoosh. "I don't want to be a billboard for a company that would do these things," said Keady.[40]

Before long, the student protests spread to campuses where Nike had no merchandising contracts. Organized and trained by unions such as UNITE! and the AFL-CIO, previously apathetic college students stormed university buildings to protest sweatshop labor and the exploitation of foreign workers. In 1999, activists took over buildings at Duke, Georgetown, the University of Michigan and the University of Wisconsin, and staged sit-ins at countless other colleges and universities. The protests focused mostly on the conditions under which collegiate logo gear was manufactured. Declared Tom Wheatley, a Wisconsin student and national movement leader: "It really is quite sick. Fourteen-year-old girls are working 100-hour weeks and earning poverty-level wages to make my college T-shirts. That's unconscionable."[41] University administrators heeded the student protests, and many began to consider codes of conduct for contract manufacturers.

[37] Tunku Varadarajan, "Nike Audit Uncovers Health Hazards at Factory," *The Times of London,* November 10, 1997, p. 52.

[38] Nike Corporation, *Annual Report 1998* (Nike, Inc.: Beaverton, OR) p. 1, 17–30.

[39] Quoted in Patricia Sellers, "Four Reasons Nike's Not Cool," *Fortune,* March 30, 1998, p. 26.

[40] William McCall, "Nike's Image Under Attack: Sweatshop Charges Begin to Take a Toll on the Brand's Cachet," *The Buffalo News,* October 23, 1998, p. 5E.

[41] Nancy Cleeland, "Students Give Sweatshop Fight the College Try," *Los Angeles Times,* April 22, 1999, p. C1.

SAVING THE SWOOSH

Nike's fiscal woes did what hundreds of harsh articles had failed to do: they took some of the bravado out of Phil Knight. In a May 1998 speech to the National Press Club, a humbled Knight admitted that "the Nike product has become synonymous with slave wages, forced overtime, and arbitrary abuse."[42] Knight announced a series of sweeping reforms, including raising the minimum age of all sneaker workers to 18 and apparel workers to 16; adopting U.S. OSHA clean air standards in all its factories; expanding its monitoring program; expanding educational programs for workers; and making micro loans available to workers. Although Nike had been formally addressing labor issues since 1992, Knight's confession marked a turning point in Nike's stance towards its critics. For the first time, he and his company appeared ready to shed their defensive stance, admit labor violations did occur in Nike factories, and refashion themselves as leaders in the effort to reform third world working conditions.

Nike's second step was to get more involved with Washington-based reform efforts. In the summer of 1998, President Clinton's initial task force on labor, the Apparel Industry Partnership (AIP), lay deadlocked over the ever-delicate issues of factory monitoring and wages. Although the AIP had a tentative proposal, discussion ground to a halt when the task force's union, religious, and corporate members clashed.

While the AIP proclaimed itself as an exemplar of cooperative solution making, it soon became apparent that its members had very different views. One key concept "independent monitoring"—was highly contentious. To Nike, the hiring of a separate and unrelated multinational firm like Ernst & Young fulfilled any call for independent monitoring. But activists and other critics alleged that if an independent monitor, such as an accounting firm, was hired by a corporation, it thereby automatically lost autonomy and independence. According to such critics, independent monitoring could only be done by an organization that was not on a corporate payroll, such as an NGO or a religious group. The corporations, by contrast, insisted that a combination of internal monitoring and audits by accounting firms was sufficient. Upset at what they saw as corporate intransigence, the task force's union and religious membership abruptly exited the coalition.

The remaining corporate members of the AIP were soon able to cobble together a more definitive agreement, complete with an oversight organization known as the Fair Labor Association (FLA). The FLA was to be a private entity controlled evenly by corporate members and human rights or labor representatives (if they chose to rejoin the coalition). It would support a code of conduct that required its members to pay workers the legal minimum wage or the prevailing local standard, whichever was higher. The minimum age of workers was set at 15, and employees could not be required to work more than 60 hours per week. Companies that joined the Association would be required to comply with these guidelines and to establish internal monitoring systems to enforce them; they would then be audited by certified independent inspectors, such as accounting firms. In the first three years after a company joined, auditors would inspect 30% of a company's factories; later they would inspect 10%. All audits would be confidential.

Nike worked tirelessly to bring other manufacturers into the FLA, but the going was tough. As of August 1999, the only other corporate members were adidas, Liz Claiborne, Reebok, Levi's, L. L. Bean, and Phillips Van Heusen. However, Nike's efforts to foster the FLA hit pay dirt with U.S. colleges and universities. The vocal student anti-sweatshop movement had many administrators scrambling to find a solution, and over 100 colleges and universities eventually signed on. Participants ranged from the large state universities that held Nike contracts to the eight Ivy League schools. The FLA was scheduled to be fully operational by the fall of 2000.

Meanwhile, by 1999 Nike was running extensive training programs for its contractors' factory managers. All managers and supervisors were required to learn the native language of their workers, and received training in cultural differences and acceptable management styles. In addition to 25 em-

[42] John H. Cushman Jr., "Nike to Step Forward on Plant Conditions," *The San Diego Union-Tribune,* May 13, 1998, p. A1.

ployees who would focus solely on corporate responsibility, Nike's 1,000 production employees were explicitly required to devote part of their job to maintaining labor standards. In Vietnam, the company partnered with the National University of Vietnam in a program designed to identify and meet worker needs. It also helped found the Global Alliance, a partnership between the International Youth Foundation, the MacArthur Foundation, the World Bank, and Mattel, that was dedicated to improving the lives of workers in the developing world.

Although Nike's various concessions and new programs were welcomed as a victory by several human rights groups, other observers argued that Nike still failed to deal with the biggest problem, namely wages.[43] Wrote *New York Times* columnist Bob Herbert: "Mr. Knight is like a three-card monte player. You have to keep a close eye on him at all times. The biggest problem with Nike is that its overseas workers make wretched, below-subsistence wages. It's not the minimum age that needs raising, it's the minimum wage."[44] Similarly, while some labor leaders accepted the FLA as the best compromise possible, others decried it as sham agreement that simply provided cover for U.S. corporations. A main objection of these critics was that the FLA standards included notification of factories that were to be inspected, a move criticized by some as equivalent to notifying a restaurant when a critic was coming to dine. According to Jeff Ballinger, Nike's original critic, the company's reform record was mixed. Ballinger was confident that Nike had at least removed dangerous chemicals from factories, but otherwise he remained skeptical: "If you present yourself as a fitness company you can't very well go around the globe poisoning people. But on wages, they're still lying through their teeth." [45]

[43] John H. Cushman Jr., "Nike Pledges to End Child Labor and Apply U.S. Rules Abroad," *The New York Times,* May 13, 1998, p. D1.
[44] Bob Herbert, "Nike Blinks," *The New York Times,* May 21, 1998, p. A33.
[45] Casewriter interview.

EXHIBIT 1   Nike Inc. Financial History, 1989–1999 (in millions of dollars)

Source: Nike, Inc., *Annual Report 1999.*

Year Ended May 31	1999	1998	1997	1996	1995	1994	1993	1992	1991	1990	1989
Revenues	$8,776.9	$9,553.1	$9,186.5	$6,470.6	$4,760.8	$3,789.7	$3,931.0	$3,405.2	$3,003.6	$2,235.2	$1,710.8
Gross margin	3,283.4	3,487.6	3,683.5	2,563.9	1,895.6	1,488.2	1,544.0	1,316.1	1,153.1	851.1	636.0
Gross margin %	37.4	36.5	40.1	39.6	39.8	39.3	39.3	38.7	38.4	38.1	37.2
Restructuring charge, net	45.1	129.9	—	—	—	—	—	—	—	—	—
Net income	451.4	399.6	795.8	553.2	399.7	298.8	365.0	329.2	287.0	243.0	167.0
Cash flow from operations	961.0	517.5	323.1	339.7	254.9	576.5	265.3	435.8	11.1	127.1	169.4
Price range of common stock											
High	65.500	64.125	76.375	52.063	20.156	18.688	22.563	19.344	13.625	10.375	4.969
Low	31.750	37.750	47.875	19.531	14.063	10.781	13.750	8.781	6.500	4.750	2.891
Cash and equivalents	$198.1	$108.6	$445.4	$262.1	$216.1	$518.8	$291.3	$260.1	$119.8	$90.4	$85.7
Inventories	1,199.3	1,396.6	1,338.6	931.2	629.7	470.0	593.0	471.2	586.6	309.5	222.9
Working capital	1,818.0	1,828.8	1,964.0	1,259.9	938.4	1,208.4	1,165.2	964.3	662.6	561.6	419.6
Total assets	5,247.7	5,397.4	5,361.2	3,951.6	3,142.7	2,373.8	2,186.3	1,871.7	1,707.2	1,093.4	824.2
Long-term debt	386.1	379.4	296.0	9.6	10.6	12.4	15.0	69.5	30.0	25.9	34.1
Shareholders' equity	3,334.6	3,261.6	3,155.9	2,431.4	1,964.7	1,740.9	1,642.8	1,328.5	1,029.6	781.0	558.6
Year-end stock price	60.938	46.000	57.500	50.188	19.719	14.750	18.125	14.500	9.938	9.813	4.750
Market capitalization	17,202.2	13,201.1	16,633.0	14,416.8	5,635.2	4,318.8	5,499.3	4,379.6	2,993.0	2,942.7	1,417.4
Geographic Revenues:											
United States	$5,042.6	$5,460.0	$5,538.2	$3,964.7	$2,997.9	$2,432.7	$2,528.8	$2,270.9	$2,141.5	$1,755.5	$1,362.2
Europe	2,255.8	2,096.1	1,789.8	1,334.3	980.4	927.3	1,085.7	919.8	664.7	334.3	241.4
Asia/Pacific	844.5	1,253.9	1,241.9	735.1	515.6	283.4	178.2	75.7	56.2	29.3	32.0
Americas (exclusive of U.S.)	634.0	743.1	616.6	436.5	266.9	146.3	138.3	138.8	141.2	116.1	75.2
Total revenues	$8,776.9	$9,553.1	$9,186.5	$6,470.6	$4,760.8	$3,789.7	$3,931.0	$3,405.2	$3,003.6	$2,235.2	$1,710.8

All per common share data has been adjusted to reflect the 2-for-1 stock splits paid October 23, 1996, October 30, 1995 and October 5, 1990. The Company's Class B Common Stock is listed on the New York and Pacific Exchanges and traded under the symbol NKE. At May 31, 1999, there were approximately 170,000 shareholders.

EXHIBIT 2
Estimated Cost Breakdown of an Average Nike Shoe, 1999

Source: Jennifer Lin, "Vietnam Gives Nike a Run for Its Money," *The Philadelphia Enquirer,* March 23, 1998, p. 1.

Labor costs	$3.37
Manufacturer's overhead	$3.41
Materials	$14.60
Profit to factory	$1.12
Factory price to Nike	$22.50
Wholesale price	$45
Retail price	$90

EXHIBIT 3   **Prices of Some Popular Running Shoe Styles in New York City, 1996**

Source: "Feet Don't Fail . . . ," *The New York Times,* November 3, 1996, Section 13, p. 12.

	Nike Air Max		New Balance 999		Saucony Grid Shadow	
	Men's	**Women's**	**Men's**	**Women's**	**Men's**	**Women's**
Foot Locker	$140	$135	$124	$105	$85	$85
Paragon Sports	140	135	135	109	70	70
Sports Authority	140	140	101	101	78	78
Super Runners Shop	140	130	125	110	85	85

EXHIBIT 4   **Summary Revenue and Expense Profile of Minimum Wage Workers by Demographic Type (in Indonesian Rupiah)**

Source: Derek Calzini, Shawna Huffman, Jake Odden, Steve Tran, and Jean Tsai, *Nike, Inc: Survey of Vietnamese and Indonesian Domestic Expenditure Levels,* November 3, 1997, Field Study in International Business (Dartmouth, NH: The Amos Tuck School, 1997), pp. 9–10.

	SH	**SO**	**Dorm**	**MH**	**MO**	**Total (weighted)**
Number of respondents	67	161	33	21	32	314
Base wages	172,812	172,071	172,197	173,905	172,650	172,424
Total wages	**225,378**	**238,656**	**239,071**	**248,794**	**244,458**	**236,893**
Rent	14,677	40,955	12,121[a]	24,775	56,050	32,838
Food	84,774	95,744	90,455	103,421	128,793	103,020
Transportation	48,984	24,189	7,219	17,471	38,200	28,560
Savings	38,369	41,783	70,303	29,412	49,185	44,154
Contribution to home	22,175	37,594	57,644	25,222	25,089	34,441
Total uses	**208,980**	**240,266**	**237,741**	**200,301**	**297,318**	**243,013**

[a]17 of the 33 respondents were provided free housing by the factory. The remaining 16 paid a subsidized monthly rent of Rp 25,000.
Note: Monthly Wages and Total Uses of wages may not match due to averaging.
Key to demographic type:
  SH—Single workers living at home
  SO—Single workers living away from home and paying rent
  Dorm—Single workers living away from home and living in factory subsidized housing
  MH—Married workers living at home
  MO—Married workers living away from home

EXHIBIT 5

Typical "Basket" of Basic Food Expenditures for Indonesian workers (in rupiah)

Source: Derek Calzini, Shawna Huffman, Jake Odden, Steve Tran, and Jean Tsai, *Nike, Inc: Survey of Vietnamese and Indonesian Domestic Expenditure Levels,* November 3, 1997, Field Study in International Business (Dartmouth, NH: The Amos Tuck School, 1997), p. 45.

Rice	800–1,300	per 5 servings
Instant Noodles	300–500	per serving
Eggs	2,800–3,000	per 18 eggs
Tofu	1,500	per 15 servings
Tempe	1,500	per 15 servings
Kancang Pangung	1,500	per 15 servings
Peanuts	2,600	per kilogram
Oil	2,300	per liter
Other "luxury" foods		
Fish	6,000	per kilogram
Chicken	4,500–5,000	per chicken

EXHIBIT 6 Strikes and Lockouts in Indonesia, 1988–1997

Source: International Labour Office, *Yearbook of Labor Statistics 1998* (Geneva: ILO, 1999), p. 1213.

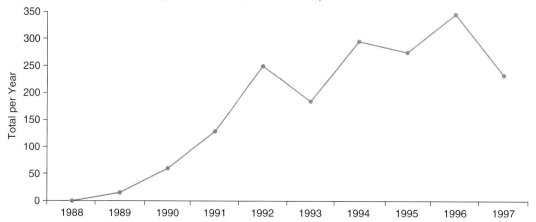

EXHIBIT 7   Wages and Productivity in Industrialized and Developing Nations (figures in $ per year)

Source: World Bank, *World Development Indicators 1999* (Washington, DC: World Bank, 1999), pp. 62–64.

	Average Hours Worked Per Week		Yearly Minimum Wage		Labor Cost Per Worker in Manufacturing		Value Added Per Worker in Manufacturing	
	1980–84	1990–94	1980–84	1990–94	1980–84	1990–94	1980–84	1990–94
North America								
United States	35	34	6,006	8,056[b]	19,103	32,013[b]	47,276	81,353
Canada	32	33	4,974	7,897[b]	17,710	28,346[b]	36,903	60,712
Mexico	—	34	1,002	843	3,772	6,138	17,448	25,991
Europe								
Denmark	—	37	9,170	19,933[b]	16,169	35,615[b]	27,919	49,273
France	39	39	10,815	22,955[b]	16,060	38,900[b]	26,751	61,019[e]
Germany	41	40	—[a]	—[a]	21,846[d]	63,956[b,d]	—	—
Greece	—	41	—	5,246	6,461	15,899[b]	14,561	30,429
Ireland	41[c]	41[c]	—	—	10,190	25,414[b]	26,510	86,036
Netherlands	40	39	9,074	15,170[b]	18,891	39,865[b]	27,491	56,801
Asia								
China (PRC)	—	—	—	—	472	434[d]	3,061	2,885
Hong Kong	48	46	—	—	4,127	13,539[b]	7,886	19,533
India	48	48	—	408	1,035	1,192	2,108	3,118
Indonesia	—	—	—	241	898	1,008	3,807	5,139
Japan	47	46	3,920	8,327[b]	12,306	40,104[b]	34,456	92,582
South Korea	52	48	—	3,903[b]	3,153	15,819[b]	11,617	40,916
Malaysia	—	—	—	—[a]	2,519	3,429	8,454	12,661
Philippines	—	43	—	1,067	1,240	2,459	5,266	9,339
Singapore	—	46	—	—	5,576	21,534[b]	16,442	40,674
Thailand	48	—	—	1,083	2,305	2,705	11,072	19,946

[a]Country has sectoral minimum wage but no minimum wage policy.
[b]Data refer to 1995–1999.
[c]Data refer to hours worked per week in manufacturing.
[d]Data refer to wage per worker in manufacturing.
[e]International Labour Organisation data.

EXHIBIT 8   Indonesia: Wages and Inflation, 1993–97

Source: International Monetary Fund. Economist Intelligence Unit.

	1993		1994		1995		1996		1997	
	Minimum	Maximum	Minimum	Maximum	Minimum	Maximum	Minimum	Maximum	Minimum	Maximum
Monthly wages in manufacturing industry (thousands of rupiah)	196	2,920	207	3,112	238	3,453	241	3,453	439	6,050
Minimum wage regional average[a] (thousands of rupiah)	72		94		112		118		130	
Annual percent change	17.7		30.8		19.5		5.4		10.2	
Consumer price inflation	8.5		9.4		8.0		6.7		57.6	
Exchange rates (average Rp:$)	2,161		2,249		2,342		2,909		10,014	

Figures are based on periodic surveys of primarily urban-based business establishments and include transportation, meal, and attendance allowances.
[a]Calculated from minimum daily figure for 30 days per month. Increased by 9% to Rp122,000 in 1996 and by 10% to Rp135,000 in 1997.

EXHIBIT 9   *Life* Magazine Photo of Pakistani Child Worker

Source: *Life*, June 1996, p. 39.

EXHIBIT 10 **Doonesbury Cartoons about Nike**

EXHIBIT 11 Anti-Nike Activist Materials

Source: Jeff Ballinger; http://www.nikeworkers.org (10/29/99); http://www.corpwatch.org/nike/(10/29/99).

Nike, Inc. in Indonesia I

JUST DO IT!

"You know when you need a break. And you know when it's time to take care of yourself, for yourself. Because you know it's never too late to have a life. " (Nike advertisement)

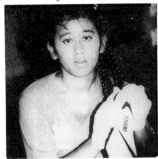

Twelve thousand Indonesian woman work 60 hours a week making Nike shoes. Many earn less than their government's minimum wage of $1.80 a day. Numerous strikes and protests have been broken up by security forces eager to placate foreign capital; labor activists have even been murdered. Factories producing Nike shoes have been cited in the State Department's Human Rights Report to Congress. Asked about local labor practices, Nike VP David Taylor said: "I don't feel bad about it. I don't think we are doing anything wrong."

One percent of Nike's advertising budget would double the wages of the women making the company's shoes and raise them above the poverty line.

Nike, Inc. in Indonesia newsletter: $20 for six months, teachers free
Press for Change, Inc. PO Box 230, Bayonne, New Jersey, 07002-9998

Name Index

Harveston, P., 348, 349, 413
Harzing, A., 300
Haselberger, A., 495
Havrylyshyn, O., 133
Hayashi, Toshio, 212
Hayes, Samuel L., III, 160, 161
Hedlund, G., 300
Held, D., 71
Hempel, C., 385
Hendrix, Anatasia, 365
Henisz, Witold, 105
Herskovits, M. J., 168
Herzberg, Frederick, 419, 422–423, 443
Hickson, D. J., 169
Hill, Charles W. L., 6, 37, 246, 323, 348
Hill, Richard E., 6, 37
Hitt, M., 323, 348
Hodgetts, R. M., 495
Hofstede, Geert, 145–152, 156, 159, 168, 169, 348, 413, 443, 445, 446, 458, 459, 469
Holmes, S., 220
Holtshouse, D., 349
Hooghiemstra, R., 542
Hooker, J., 413, 469
Hoppe, M., 469
Hoskisson, R., 323
Hough, L. M., 443
House, R. J., 443, 451, 452, 457, 458, 468, 469
Hout, T., 217
Howell, G., 468
Howell, J. P., 468
Howell, Jarry J., 250
Howell, Llewellyn D., 96, 97, 106
Hsu, Jamie C., 250
Huber, Hans-Michael, 24, 25
Hulin, C. L., 443, 445
Hunt, J. G., 468
Huo, Y. P., 439, 446
Hurrell, J. J., Jr., 445
Hussein, Saddam, 93, 461
Hwang, Peter, 246
Hymer, S. H., 23, 38

Iacocca, Lee, 450
Ihlwan, M., 303
Imura, Hisako, 142
Ingersoll, Bruce, 543
Inglehart, R., 434, 445
Ingrassia, Paul, 37
Inkpen, A. C., 253, 271, 348, 470
Ireland, R., 323
Ito, Kiyomichi, 24, 25
Iwao, S., 169
Iwawaki, S., 444

Jabr, M. Hisham, 134
Jaeger, A., 323
Jagan, Larry, 119
Jain, Subash C., 531

Janosik, R. J., 413
Javidan, M., 458, 469
Jaworski, R. A., 495
Jenkins, Brian, 94
Jennergren, P., 300
Jermier, J. M., 469
Johansson, J., 217
Johnson, J., 241, 247
Johnson, R., 348
Jones, C. A., 341
Jones, C. I., 105
Jones, M. L., 444
Josephberg, K., 133
Joshi, Mahesh, 189
Joyce, Romy, 292
Joyned, C., 133

Kagitcibasi, C., 155, 169
Kahn, R., 468
Kalemli-Ozcan, S., 133
Kalyani, Baba, 25
Kant, Immanuel, 516
Kanungo, R. N., 443
Kaplan, M. R., 444
Kapur, Arvind, 24, 25
Kapuria, Deep, 25
Kashlak, Roger, 38, 105, 189, 217, 218, 255, 257, 272, 313, 314, 323
Katz, D., 468
Kaufmann, D., 105
Kaur, R., 469
Keating, P., 299
Kedia, B. L., 333, 348, 349, 413, 444
Keita, G. P., 445
Ken, K., 443
Kenis, I., 469
Kerr, C., 168
Kerr, Graeme, 261
Kerr, S., 469
Kerwin, Kathleen, 276, 326, 347
Ket de Vries, M. F. R., 467
Khan, Eshan Ullah, 532
Khomeini, Ayatollah, 94
Kim, Chan W., 246
Kim, D. K., 412
Kim, K., 299
Kim, U., 155, 169
Kim, Y., 385
Kim Jung Il, 461
Kindleberger, Charles, 247, 512
King, Tim, 118
Kinney, T. A., 385
Kirkpatrick, S. A., 451
Kitayama, Shinobu, 398, 469
Klineberg, O., 385
Klitgaard, Robert, 527
Kluckhorn, F., 143–145, 154, 168
Knickerbocker, F. T., 38
Kobrin, S., 86, 105, 106
Kogut, Bruce, 38, 220, 237, 241, 242, 245, 246, 247, 271

Kolde, Endel J., 6, 37
Konigsberg, A. S., 245
Kotabe, M., 272
Koza, M., 271
Kraay, A., 105
Kraimer, M. L., 495
Kramer, R. M., 469
Krishna, Sonali, 181
Krishnan, B., 446
Krishnan, K. S., 468
Kukura, Sergei P., 95
Kumar, Sanjay, 217
Kundu, Sumit K., 232, 235, 245, 246
Kunii, Irene M., 32, 220
Kurtenbach, Elaine, 105
Kwok, H., 386

Laabs, J. L., 494
Lagace, Martha, 161
Lall, Sanjay, 247
Lam, N. M., 401, 402, 413
Landis, D., 168
Lansner, Thomas, 536
LaPlaca, Peter J., 531
La Porta, R., 133
Larson, Andrew, 257
Larson, L. L., 468
Latham, G. P., 444
Latta, G. W., 495
Laurent, Andre, 459, 469
Lawler, Edward E., III, 300, 427, 428, 444, 445
Lax, David, 400
Lay, Kenneth, 456
Lazarus, Shelly, 465
Leach, Peter L., 71
Lee Kwan Yew, 91
Lei, D., 348
Leipziger, Deborah, 536
Leman, Lac, 319
Leonard-Barton, D., 348
Lessard, D., 323
Leung, K., 445
Lewicki, R. J., 412
Lewin, A., 271
Li, Sandy, 118, 245
Lin, C. Y., 412
Lin, Z., 385
Linn, J. J., 133
Lipp, G. D., 412
Litterer, J. A., 412
Locke, E. A., 443, 444, 451
Lohr, S., 347, 468
Lonner, W. J., 139, 168, 386
Lopez-de-Silanes, F., 133
Lopez-Pacheco, Alexandra, 77, 271
Lorange, P., 271, 323
Lord, R. G., 468
Lorenzi, Dena, 217
Losq, E., 106
Lowe, Peter, 118

Subject Index